EDI DEVELOPMENT STUDIES

Labor Markets in an Era of Adjustment

Volume 2

Case Studies

Edited by

Susan Horton
Ravi Kanbur
Dipak Mazumdar

The World Bank
Washington, D. C.

The Economic Development Institute (EDI) was established by the World Bank in 1955 to train officials concerned with development planning, policymaking, investment analysis, and project implementation in member developing countries. At present the substance of the EDI's work emphasizes macroeconomic and sectoral economic policy analysis. Through a variety of courses, seminars, and workshops, most of which are given overseas in cooperation with local institutions, the EDI seeks to sharpen analytical skills used in policy analysis and to broaden understanding of the experience of individual countries with economic development. Although the EDI's publications are designed to support its training activities, many are of interest to a much broader audience. EDI materials, including any findings, interpretations, and conclusions, are entirely those of the authors and should not be attributed in any manner to the World Bank, to its affiliated organizations, or to members of its Board of Executive Directors or the countries they represent.

Because of the informality of this series and to make the publication available with the least possible delay, the manuscript has not been edited as fully as would be the case with a more formal document, and the World Bank accepts no responsibility for errors. Some sources cited in this book may be informal documents that are not readily available.

The material in this publication is copyrighted. Requests for permission to reproduce portions of it should be sent to the Office of the Publisher at the address shown in the copyright notice above. The World Bank encourages dissemination of its work and will normally give permission promptly and, when the reproduction is for noncommercial purposes, without asking a fee. Permission to copy portions for classroom use is granted through the Copyright Clearance Center Inc., Suite 910, Rosewood Drive, Danvers, Massachusetts 01923, U. S. A.

The backlist of publications by the World Bank is shown in the annual *Index of Publications*, which is available from Distribution Unit, Office of the Publisher, The World Bank, 1818 H Street, N.W., Washington, D.C. 20433, U.S.A., or from Publications, Banque mondiale, 66, avenue d'Iéna, 75116 Paris, France.

Susan Horton is an associate professor of economics at the University of Toronto; Ravi Kanbur is the World Bank's resident representative in Ghana; and Dipak Mazumdar is a labor markets specialist in the World Bank's Office of the Chief Economist, Africa.

Library of Congress Cataloging-in-Publication Data

Horton, Susan.
    Labor markets in an era of adjustment / Susan Horton, Ravi Kanbur,
    Dipak Mazumdar.
        p.   cm.—(EDI development studies)
        Includes bibliographical references.
        Contents: v. 1. Issues papers—v. 2. Case studies.
        ISBN 0-8213-2680-5 (v.1).—ISBN 0-8213-2681-3 (v. 2)
        1. Labor market—Developing countries—Congresses. 2. Structural
    adjustment (Economic policy)—Developing countries—Congresses.
    3. Labor market—Developing countries—Case studies—Congresses.
    4. Structural adjustment (Economic policy)—Developing countries—
    Case studies—Congresses. I. Kanbur, S.M. Ravi.   II. Mazumdar,
    Dipak, 1932–   . III. Title. IV. Series.
    HD5852
    331.12'09172'6—dc20   93-34978
                                                                          CIP

CONTENTS

VOLUME 2: CASE STUDIES

iii

VOLUME 1. ISSUES PAPERS

Labor Markets in an Era of Adjustment: An Overview
Susan Horton, Ravi Kanbur, and Dipak Mazumdar

1. Recent Developments in the Developed-Country Literature on Labor Markets and the Implications for Developing Countries
   Jean-Paul Azam

2. Labor Market Distortions and Structural Adjustment in Developing Countries
   Alejandra Cox Edwards and Sebastian Edwards

3. The Poverty Effects of Adjustment with Labor Market Imperfections
   Tony Addison and Lionel Demery

4. Wage Indexation, Adjustment, and Inflation
   Michael B. Devereux

5. The Long-Run Consequences of Short-Run Stabilization Policy
   Edward F. Buffie

6. Gender Aspects of Labor Allocation during Structural Adjustment
   Paul Collier, A. C. Edwards, J. Roberts, and Kalpana Bardhan

7. Organized Labor, Politics, and Labor Market Flexibility in Developing Countries
   Joan M. Nelson

NA

FOREWORD

This two-volume study is the result of a series of five conferences organized by the Economic Development Institute of the World Bank in collaboration with the University of Toronto and Warwick University and supported by the Overseas Development Administration of the United Kingdom and the governments of Canada and Ireland.

It comprises the research papers presented at the conferences and revised in light of comments and suggestions by the participants as well as by other experts in the field. Various chapters have been presented in seminars for World Bank staff and at the annual meetings of the American Economic Association.

Amnon Golan, Director
Economic Development Institute

ACKNOWLEDGMENTS

This book is the result of a large research project that was initiated by Ravi Kanbur and Dipak Mazumdar early in 1988. They were subsequently joined by Susan Horton, who had at that time begun to do work on a similar theme for Bolivia.

The research was facilitated by a series of five conferences: three at Warwick University and two at the University of Toronto. The editors would like to thank the universities for their support and the following organizations for providing funding: the Overseas Development Administration of the United Kingdom and the governments of Canada and of Ireland for their support through trust funds established at the World Bank.

Many people participated in the conferences. Some presented papers, others provided useful comments, and all contributed to the progress of the research. In addition to the authors, these included (with their affiliation at the time): A. Berry, D. Benjamin, M. Faig, and Y. Kotowitz (University of Toronto); P. Brixen, L. Haddad, M. Johnson, J. MacKinnon, A. McKay, S. Nath, G. Pyatt, and J. Round (Warwick University); A. Chhibber, J. Daniel, L. Fox, C. Grootaert, T. King, J. Newman, A. van Adams, and M. Walton (World Bank); A. Atsain (University of Abidjan), C. Bean (London School of Economics), J. Bradley (ESRI, Dublin), G. Fields and E. Thorbecke (Cornell University), N. Gregory (ODA), T. Besley, P. Horsnell, S. Kheng-Kok, J. Knight, C. Yves, and A. Zegeye (Oxford University), S. Morley (Vanderbilt University), N. N'geno (University of Nairobi), A. Plourde (University of Ottawa), B. Renison (USAID), G. Rodgers (ILO), B. Salome and D. Turnham (OECD), J. Svejnaar (University of Pittsburgh), R. van der Hoeven (UNICEF), K. Yao (CIRES, Abidjan), and Z. A. Yusof (Malaysian Institute of Economic Research).

PREFACE

ed.

Our interest in undertaking a project on structural adjustment and labor markets in developing countries arose from our perception of a gap in the existing literature. A good deal of work had been done on structural adjustment and poverty, but without work on the labor market little was known about how the effects of structural adjustment were transmitted to the poor, most of whom depend heavily on labor market earnings. At the same time some policymakers and international institutions seem to believe that labor market rigidities are an obstacle to structural adjustment, and several developing countries have implemented rather draconian policies to regulate their labor markets. However few empirical studies of developing countries exist to justify such policies.

At the start of the project we invited researchers to tell us what the existing theory and studies from developed countries suggested about adjustment and labor markets. We then commissioned a series of theory papers to extend the literature to developing countries, looking at topics such as structural adjustment and poverty, the effects on women, the political economy aspects, the long-run effects of adjustment, and so on. At the same time we began twelve country studies to examine the effects of adjustment on labor markets. The country studies took longer and, as a result, were enriched by insights from the theory papers, which were completed earlier.

In choosing countries to study, we wanted to have as wide a geographic coverage as possible. Data availability proved to be one limitation. We felt that it was essential to have access to household labor-force survey data over time (corresponding to the adjustment period) for the countries concerned. Without these data, the effects on women, on income distribution, on real wages, and on unemployment could not easily be studied. Existing international compilations (primarily the ILO *Yearbook of Labour Statistics*) have somewhat uneven coverage since not all countries report and the data they publish are for a mix of household surveys and establishment surveys. Data constraints were most serious for Africa, where very few countries had repeated labor force surveys at different times. The final sample of countries included five from Latin America, three from Asia, one from North Africa and the Middle East, and three from Sub-Saharan Africa.

At the outset we were not aware of different "patterns" of adjustment. In the course of the research, however, the countries fell into four groups of three. One group (the Republic of Korea, Malaysia, and Thailand) reflected what might be termed an "East Asian" pattern of adjustment, with short, sharp recessions and a resumption of fast growth of GDP (more than 5 percent per year). Another group (Bolivia, Chile, and Ghana) undertook "severe" adjustment. These economies had had more serious problems in the 1970s and 1980s, experiencing either sharp falls in GDP in some years, or prolonged stagnation or decline. Real wages fell more than 50 percent in the course of adjustment, and in the case of Chile there was high unemployment (more than 25 percent at the worst points). A third group of countries (Brazil, Costa Rica, and Kenya) might be described as having undergone "partial" adjustment, where adjustment was less painful than in the Asian case but the resumption of growth was also less strong. The final group (Argentina, Côte d'Ivoire, and Egypt) represent "frustrated" adjustment, in that adjustment was delayed for a number of reasons—for example, stop-go cycles in Argentina, difficulties in devaluing because of membership in the franc zone for Côte d'Ivoire, and the later onset of problems for Egypt, as an oil exporter.

The research suggested that labor markets in developing countries were in fact working quite well to permit structural adjustment. Three important conclusions were reached: real wages were more flexible than generally supposed, which would support adjustment; labor reallocation across sectors has been more or less in the desired direction; and labor market institutions such as unions and minimum wages, often argued to be an impediment to adjustment, have more subtle effects on the workings of labor market—a finding that is worthy of further study.

As occurs in all research projects, we discovered other gaps in the literature and topics that seemed worthy of attention but that did not fit within the scope of the existing effort. Much more could be learned about labor markets in developing countries by constructing time series from regular labor force surveys. In some countries, particularly the richer countries in Asia and Latin America, these series have already been put together, but the same is not true for the poorer countries. Time series for key variables are very important since fluctuations and cycles in the economy render one-year "snapshots" derived from a single survey quite misleading. A great deal of work also remains to be done in such areas as quantifying changes in income distribution over time, analyzing the effect of structural adjustment on women, and exploring the effects of labor market institutions in developing countries.

ABBREVIATIONS AND ACRONYMS

BCEAO	Banque Centrale des Etats de l'Afrique de l'Ouest
CACM	Central American Common Market
CAPMAS	Central Agency for Public Mobilization and Statistics (Egypt)
CBS	Central Bureau of Statistics (Kenya)
COB	Confederación Obrera de Bolivia
CPI	consumer price index
c.i.f.	cost, insurance, freight (term for describing imports)
EPB	Economic Planning Board (Kenya)
f.o.b.	free on board
GDP	gross domestic product
GLSS	Ghana Living Standards Survey
GNP	gross national product
IEERAL	Institute of Economic Studies on Argentina
IMF	International Monetary Fund
INE	Instituto Nacional de Estadistica (National Bureau of Statistics) (Bolivia, Chile)
LSMS	Living Standards Measurement Survey
NBER	National Bureau of Economic Research
NEP	New Economic Policy (Bolivia, Malaysia)
NEER	nominal effective exchange rate
OECD	Organization for Economic Cooperation and Development
RDER	real domestic exchange rate
REER	real effective exchange rate
UMOA	Western Africa Monetary Union
UNICEF	United Nations Children's Fund
USAID	United States Agency for International Development
WPI	wholesale price index

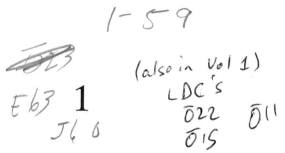

Labor Markets in an Era of Adjustment: An Overview

Susan Horton
Ravi Kanbur
Dipak Mazumdar

Issues and Country Studies

Labor markets play a central role in determining the macroeconomic success of stabilization and adjustment policies and in mediating the impact of these policies on the population's standards of living, in particular the poor. The 7 issues papers and 12 country studies in these volumes examine the different aspects of this interaction between labor markets and adjustment. The object of this chapter is to provide an overview and to draw out general conclusions, policy lessons, and areas for further research.

Issues

To start with, let us define what we mean by adjustment and by labor markets. Under adjustment we include both stabilization and structural adjustment. Following convention, by stabilization we mean the reduction of national expenditure to bring it in line with national income or output, usually following external shocks. By structural adjustment we mean attempts to increase national income or output through more efficient use of resources. Of course, a myriad of macro policy instruments, such as exchange rates, monetary policy, and fiscal policy, are available to achieve these goals, which may sometimes be stated in terms of inflation, balance of payments, and growth targets.

The links between instruments and targets, however, almost always touch on labor markets and their operation.

A labor market is a mechanism for matching the supply and demand of the factor of production labor, through the terms of the contract between buyer and seller. As many different types of labor exist, differentiated by skill, location, gender, and so on, many different labor markets exist, but these markets are linked with each other because the conditions in one can influence the workings of another. The system of interlinked individual labor markets in a country can be called the labor market. The labor market is itself linked to other markets in the economy: it influences their workings and is in turn influenced by them.

The terms of the contract between buyers and sellers in a labor market can vary, from wage payment in markets for unskilled labor to complex packages of remuneration and benefits over time in markets for skilled labor. The markets can vary in structure, from many buyers and many sellers to small groups of buyers and sellers. Some analysts talk of internal labor markets within large firms. National policy and regulation affect the workings of the labor market, and the labor market in turn produces institutions that become important in setting national policy. While any individual labor market may be small, the outcomes in the labor market as a whole can influence macroeconomic conditions in the economy. Since the outcomes determine the payment to labor, they also affect the distribution of income in the economy.

Policymakers are often interested in knowing whether a country's labor market is "working well," and what can be done to "improve" its workings. But what does it mean to say that the labor market is working well? As always, a general characterization is difficult. The most general statement we can make is in the context of a competitive general equilibrium model of the economy. In this stylized setting, we know that if every other market operates in the manner of classical competitive markets, then if the labor market also operates in this manner the economy will achieve a Pareto optimal outcome. Thus, in this framework and under these conditions what is meant by the labor market working well is clear: it is that the labor market is working like a classical competitive market where price adjusts to equate supply and demand. In most practical settings, this is indeed the test that is applied, and discussion of policy and regulation is highly colored by the use of this benchmark. However, the slightest reflection should reveal how fragile this benchmark is, and how severe and unrealistic are the conditions under which it is viable, as in reality there is no guarantee that other markets are themselves working like classical competitive markets, and a Pareto optimal outcome may not satisfy distributional criteria for evaluating the economic system as a whole.

Since the search for any general characterization is likely to prove futile, the best way to approach the analysis is with a more specific notion of what is being asked of the labor market, given the structure of other markets in the economic system and the particular economic policy problem under consideration. The particular policy problems we focus on here are those of stabilization and structural adjustment through the use of macroeconomic policy instruments.

We discuss stabilization first. The role of the labor market here is to ensure that the reduction in national expenditure takes place without inducing a substantial reduction in national output. The basic mechanisms are well known. As national expenditure falls there will be downward pressure on output prices if output markets behave like classical competitive markets. This downward pressure on output prices will lead to cutbacks in production, and hence in the demand for labor. If the price of labor falls in response to this reduced demand, then this reduction in cost will help maintain the level of production. If the price of labor falls sufficiently in relation to the original fall in output prices, under certain conditions there need be no fall in total output at all. To the extent that the real wage does not fall this far, total output will be lower than it otherwise would be and, because of unemployment, the wage bill will be distributed more unequally than it otherwise would be.

In this framework, therefore, the test for whether the labor market was working well would focus on whether the real wage fell sufficiently to maintain employment and output in the face of a reduction in total national expenditures (vol. 1, chapters 1 and 3). Clearly, labor market institutions are relevant here. If the labor market is unionized, and the union cares more about the real wage of employed members than about the number of the unemployed, then bargaining between the union and employers will lead to a real wage that is too high for maintaining employment and output (vol. 1, chapter 7). The extent to which the union can indeed be sanguine about the unemployed will in turn depend on the nature and extent of unemployment benefits. Wage indexation is also relevant. To the extent that automatic wage adjustments, mandated by national law or agreed by employers as part of a long-term contract, stop the real wage from falling, unemployment and output loss will occur (vol. 1, chapter 4). Also important is how much of the labor market is covered by these adjustments.

Although a fall in demand will lead to unemployment in a particular labor market if the real wage in that market does not fall, at the macroeconomic level the real wage is also one of the determinants of aggregate demand. The mechanism (as developed by Taylor 1988, for example) depends on the assumption that the propensity to save is markedly lower for wage earners than for recipients of profits. If falling real wages are accompanied by a fall in the share of wages in national income, the aggregate demand will fall. We may see persistent unemployment despite large falls in real wages. Thus, the conclusion to be drawn from the coexistence of these phenomena is not necessarily that the labor market is not working well, and that if only real wages fell even further unemployment would go down, but that beyond a certain point the macroeconomic consequences of real wage declines may lead to an additional cost of adjustment that relies too heavily on labor markets.

Another case where observed unemployment does not necessarily mean that the labor market is not working well is where output markets do not behave like classical competitive markets. When competition in product markets is imperfect, unemployment may result even if labor markets are competitive with flexible real wages (vol. 1, chapter 1). With persistent unemployment, therefore, the finger of blame can point to at least one of three factors: imperfectly competitive product markets, aggregate demand feedback from real wages, or labor markets not working well. One cannot automatically assume that the root cause is the latter.

Let us turn now to the role of labor markets in the process of structural adjustment. Structural adjustment has many components, but at its heart is a shift in the composition of national output toward the production of exportables and import-competing output (tradables) through the use of relative price instruments such as the exchange rate. Clearly, such a shift in the pattern of production requires a corresponding shift in factors of production toward certain sectors, and it is the labor market through which the sectoral composition of labor use is altered. The general issue to which this gives rise is the nature and extent of reallocations between different labor markets. Essentially, what is required is for labor to flow to the production of tradables, that is, to flow to those labor markets that serve the production of tradables. This may require reallocation across firms in the same area, across the formal/informal or covered/uncovered divide, or across regions.

In principle, this reallocation could take place through a number of mechanisms, but economic analysis focuses on the role of temporary wage differentials in attracting labor to markets where demand is high. Note, however, that the very reallocation to which the differentials give rise will tend to mitigate the differentials. If the wage differentials are constrained between limits because of institutional factors, standard results on the impact of changes on the relative output price in the composition of employment and output will not occur (vol. 1, chapter 2). The same would happen if gender differences led to significant misallocation of labor (vol. 1, chapter 6). Movements in relative wages can therefore be a deceptive test of whether the labor market is working well. Concentrating directly on the nature and extent of reallocation between output sectors is far better. The faster this reallocation, the faster the desired adjustment in national output. However, labor is only one of the factors of production, and one must take care before one pronounces that because labor reallocation has not taken place, the labor market is not working well. If markets for complementary inputs (for example, credit) are not playing their role, the labor market may be hampered in achieving the desired reallocation of labor, and therefore of output.

Whatever the role of the labor market in achieving the macroeconomic objectives of stabilization and structural adjustment, how the labor market responds to macroeconomic instruments will certainly determine the distribution of income in the economy. At the simplest level, if stabilization necessitates a period of high unemployment because of downwardly rigid wages, then inequality will increase, and perhaps poverty will increase more than if real wages had fallen sufficiently to maintain employment. The extent and nature of the reallocation of labor across sectors will also influence the distribution of income. If, for example, in the initial situation the poor are concentrated in sectors producing tradables, then the increase in wages necessary to attract labor to those sectors will reduce poverty on this count in the short to medium run, although what happens in the long run depends on how markets for other factors operate. One can conduct a systematic analysis of the impact of adjustment on poverty in the presence of a variety of labor market structures (vol. 1, chapter 3). To the extent that the labor market is segmented along gender lines, the distribution of income will also be affected (vol. 1, chapter 6).

Economists now realize that stabilization and structural adjustment policies, although designed to achieve macroeconomic balance in the short and medium term, will have long-run consequences through their impact on investment. There is a similar impact on human capital investment. To the extent that investment in human capital is affected by changes in relative wages, short-run policies (via their effects on labor markets) will also have long-run consequences (vol. 1, chapter 5).

Country Studies

The interactions between labor markets and adjustment thus throw up a number of interesting issues and questions. The answers to many of these questions will be context and country specific. The issue papers in this symposium take up specific conceptual matters and develop or review the analysis on areas highlighted in this section. The country studies, however, are at the heart of this symposium, since they insert reality into the conceptual framework. Each country study author was asked first to give a brief account of the adjustment process: the nature of the shock, the policy responses, and the macroeconomic outcomes. The authors were then asked to give an account of the relevant characteristics of the labor market, for example, labor force composition, wage differentials, and wage setting mechanisms. Armed with these two accounts, the studies then assess the labor market's role in the adjustment process, paying due attention to institutional features. With these basics, the authors were also asked to evaluate the impact of adjustment, as mediated by the labor market, on poverty and on women. Finally, they were invited to consider the long-run consequences of labor market adjustment.

This symposium contains 12 country studies: four from Africa (of which three are from Sub-Saharan Africa), five from Latin America, and three from Asia. The countries span a range of different income levels (using the World Bank's classification), ranging from two low-income countries (Ghana and Kenya), seven lower-middle-income countries (Bolivia, Chile, Costa Rica, Côte d'Ivoire, Egypt, Malaysia, and Thailand), and three upper-middle-income countries (Argentina, Brazil, and the Republic of Korea). The countries also span a range of adjustment experience.

Not all the country studies address all the issues, sometimes because particular issues were important in particular countries but not in others, and sometimes due to data limitations. Almost all the Latin countries, many of those in Southeast Asia, and some in North Africa have periodic labor force surveys, although the data from these vary in terms of accessibility and amount of previous analysis. However, few labor force surveys cover the rural sector (exceptions are Kenya, although the survey is infrequent, and Thailand for occasional years). To the authors' knowledge, Sub-Saharan Africa has no regular labor force surveys, and Kenya is the only country with comparable household surveys for a year in the 1970s and a year in the 1980s. The two other Sub-Saharan African studies rely on cross-sectional data for the 1980s from the World Bank Living Standards Surveys. Data from these surveys have the advantage of covering rural areas, and with some ingenuity (for example, using information on length of tenure in current job or length of residence in current location) can be used to shed light on some changes that have occurred in the labor market over time.

In addition to labor force surveys, many countries have other data from employment and earnings surveys, collected usually at the establishment level. These series tend to cover mainly the formal sector and not a representative sample of households, and can sometimes be misleading, especially during a period of substantial sectoral shifts and declines in formal sector employment (see, for example, Lavy and Newman 1989 on the Côte d'Ivoire). The Bolivian case study similarly points out discrepancies between the real wage and the unemployment series from household surveys as compared to establishment surveys.

The 12 country studies pull together a wealth of information. This is particularly useful given the dearth of centralized international reporting of labor data. The International Labour Organisation's (ILO's) regional subdivisions do collate and report information within the respective regions (Latin America, Africa, and Asia). However, the ILO yearbook, for example, the basis for Johnson's 1986 work, is spotty in terms of country coverage and seems to rely on establishment survey results rather than the (arguably) more reliable household survey data. The country studies here contain not only whatever aggregate data are available, but in many cases also contain original econometric analyses (both micro and macro) of the data.

Although the workings of the labor market have been well studied for some countries, there are relatively few comparative studies of the effects of the crisis of the late 1970s and the 1980s. Fallon and Riveros (1988), ILO (1987), and Johnson (1986) compare a range of countries, Ghai (1987) and JASPA (1988) examine African countries, and some work on Latin America is available, for example, by Tokman (1984) and Riveros (1989), and by the Programa Regional del Empleo para America Latina y el Caribe (PREALC). Investigators have also examined the public sector labor force (Lindauer and others 1988). The present set of studies tries to cover a broad range of countries, including some that had not been studied much previously. Although structural adjustment is by no means complete in these countries, enough years of data have been accumulated since the onset of crisis and adjustment, that it may be timely to assess experience so far. As such, the country studies may provide a valuable basis for generalization.

Varieties of Adjustment Experience

Before drawing conclusions on the role of labor markets in adjustment on the basis of our case studies, it is useful to consider the nature of the adjustment that has taken place in these countries. Although quantifying the type or success of adjustment is hard, we suggest that our 12 countries fall into four groups of three. One group consists of the three Asian countries in the sample, which have by and large had short and successful adjustments (based on previously relatively outward-oriented economies). A second group consists of three countries that had previously had strongly inward-oriented economies that undertook severe and painful adjustment (Bolivia, Chile, and Ghana). The remaining countries all undertook less severe adjustments than the second group, but with less immediate success than the Asian group. These six countries form somewhat of a continuum, but three of them (Brazil, Costa Rica, and Kenya) had moderate success in adjusting without requiring major policy reversals, and the last three (Argentina, Côte d'Ivoire, and Egypt) had somewhat less success (in the case of Egypt as an oil exporter, efforts to adjust began only very late in the time period under study).

Tables 1.1 and 1.2 summarize information on two key economic variables: GDP growth rates (the most frequently used indicator of economic performance) and real effective exchange rate (one possible indicator of relative prices key to the adjustment process). As table 1.1 shows, the Asian countries have had occasional less successful years, but in general exhibit growth rates of 5 percent per annum or greater, and no years of negative growth. Of the "severe adjustment" countries, Chile and Ghana exhibit economic problems dating back to the 1970s, with large negative growth of GDP in some years, but since 1983 each country has grown at close to or more than 5 percent in three of the following years. Bolivia (the other country in the group) encountered economic problems later (bolstered by hydrocarbon exports in the 1970s), and experienced the longest span without positive growth of all the sample countries. Economic recovery there remains weak. Brazil, Costa Rica, and Kenya (characterized here as "moderate adjustment" countries) appear to resume reasonable growth rates of GDP after the worst years (around 1980–82), although their year-to-year growth rates following adjustment are more variable than those of the Asian countries.The remaining three cases (Argentina, Côte d'Ivoire, and Egypt, characterized here as "less successful adjustment" countries) exhibit rather heterogeneous

Table 1.1 Growth Rates of GDP, 1970/71–1986/87
(constant prices)

Country	1970-71	1971-72	1972-73	1973-74	1974-75	1975-76	1976-77	1977-78	1978-79	1979-80	1980-81	1981-82	1982-83	1983-84	1984-85	1985-86	1986-87
Argentina	3.4	1.9	3.2	6.3	-0.7	-0.2	6.4	-3.2	7.0	1.5	-6.7	-4.9	3.0	2.6	-4.5	5.5	2.0
Bolivia	4.9	5.8	6.7	5.1	6.6	6.1	4.2	3.4	0.0	-0.6	0.9	-4.9	-6.5	-0.3	-0.2	-2.9	2.2
Brazil	12.3	10.9	13.5	9.7	9.9	9.7	2.9	4.9	6.8	9.3	-4.4	0.6	-3.5	5.1	8.3	7.6	3.6
Chile	9.0	-1.2	-5.6	0.1	-12.9	3.5	9.9	8.3	7.8	5.5	-14.1	-0.1	6.3	2.4	5.7	5.7	n.a.
Costa Rica	6.8	8.2	7.7	5.5	2.1	5.5	8.9	6.3	4.9	0.8	-2.3	-7.3	2.9	8.0	0.7	5.5	5.4
Côte d'Ivoire	n.a.	n.a.	n.a.	n.a.	n.a.	12.0	4.7	9.9	5.2	6.3	1.4	3.0	0.0	-8.9	n.a.	n.a.	n.a.
Egypt	n.a.	n.a.	0.8	2.7	9.1	15.3	13.5	5.9	6.2	10.3	3.8	10.1	7.6	6.2	6.7	2.7	2.5
Ghana	5.6	-2.5	15.3	3.4	-12.9	3.5	2.3	8.5	-3.2	0.0	-1.8	-7.2	0.2	2.6	5.1	5.2	4.8
Rep. of Kenya	6.9	9.5	6.8	1.5	3.4	7.0	9.4	9.0	3.8	5.6	3.7	0.6	2.7	2.0	3.8	5.2	5.8
Korea	9.2	5.9	5.4	14.4	7.9	6.5	13.2	10.9	9.7	7.4	9.8	6.7	7.3	11.8	9.4	6.9	12.4
Malaysia	7.1	9.4	11.7	8.3	0.8	11.6	7.8	6.7	9.3	7.4	6.9	5.9	6.3	7.8	9.9	1.2	5.2
Thailand	n.a.	5.0	4.1	9.8	4.8	9.4	9.9	10.4	5.3	4.8	6.3	4.1	7.3	7.1	3.5	5.0	7.1

n.a. = not available
Sources: Calculated from IMF, *International Financial Statistics* (various years) except Bolivia data from country study.

Table 1.2 Real Effective Exchange Rate, 1976–86
(index, 1980 = 100)

Country	1976	1977	1978	1979	1980	1981	1982	1983	1984	1985	1986
Argentina	n.a.	n.a.	54.5	76.7	100.0	91.1	50.6	42.7	49.7	44.0	44.1
Bolivia	n.a.	n.a.	87.3	91.6	100.0	125.9	136.6	125.4	162.6	279.7	82.2
Brazil	n.a.	n.a.	122.8	112.5	100.0	121.5	128.4	104.2	104.2	100.1	94.4
Chile	93.7	102.1	85.2	86.1	100.0	118.0	106.7	86.8	85.3	68.8	58.2
Costa Rica	91.4	90.0	86.6	90.9	100.0	63.5	72.5	83.4	81.9	80.9	72.7
Côte d'Ivoire	n.a.	n.a.	89.1	98.0	100.0	85.7	78.2	75.2	72.0	72.2	84.5
Egypt	n.a.	n.a.	114.1	92.6	100.0	106.0	118.3	133.7	156.0	164.0	156.4
Ghana	n.a.	n.a.	96.8	76.5	100.0	222.4	278.1	186.9	72.2	52.5	30.2
Kenya	94.2	97.3	104.2	101.0	100.0	96.7	100.3	95.0	101.7	100.3	87.0
Korea, Rep. of	n.a.	n.a.	97.6	107.4	100.0	104.4	106.9	102.7	101.3	95.5	80.6
Malaysia	106.5	105.9	101.4	105.8	100.0	100.4	106.7	111.8	116.1	110.3	92.6
Thailand	n.a.	n.a.	91.2	92.4	100.0	102.8	105.8	108.6	107.2	95.3	85.0

n.a. = not available
Note: Increase implies appreciation.
Sources: Calculated from IMF data.

behavior. Argentina has continual stop-and-go cycles dating back to at least 1974. Côte d'Ivoire encountered problems in the 1980s after successful growth in the 1970s, but its ability to adjust has been limited by its membership in the West African Monetary Union. Finally, Egypt, as an oil exporter only, began to experience a growth slowdown after 1985.

As the time pattern of growth rates in table 1.1 show, the timing of adjustment was somewhat different in the various countries. Figure 1.1 shows the sequence of events described in the country studies. The years 1978 and 1982 were obviously watershed years (corresponding to the second oil price shock and start of the rise in real interest rates in one case, and to the onset of the debt crisis as signaled by inability to pay in Brazil and Mexico in the other). Some of the variation depends on price collapses in different commodity markets (coffee, cocoa, and tin affected different countries in the sample), as well as good or bad harvests and weather, particularly for the African countries. At least three countries had begun adjustment in the mid 1970s (Brazil, Chile, and Kenya), and Argentina had also made some efforts in this direction. (Of course, countries such as Korea and Brazil had made structural adjustments earlier still, changing their trade regimes.) After 1982 all the countries in the sample undertook some form of stabilization and/or structural adjustment.

Quantifying adjustment policy efforts or their success is somewhat difficult. The real effective exchange rate (REER) may provide some useful information, insofar as structural adjustment attempts to change relative prices, and the exchange rate is a key price. However, one encounters some problems in interpreting these data. First, some countries may experience policy outcomes that differ from their intentions (for example, Côte d'Ivoire recently tried to mimic a devaluation, but due to changes in other currencies the value of Côte d'Ivoire's currency actually appreciated). Second, there is no benchmark as to what the equilibrium real exchange rate should be. Some countries therefore appear to have succeeded in deep currency depreciations, but from previously highly distorted rates, whereas others appear to have been less successful, but because the previous rate was less distorted.

Figure 1.1 Timing of Adjustment Efforts

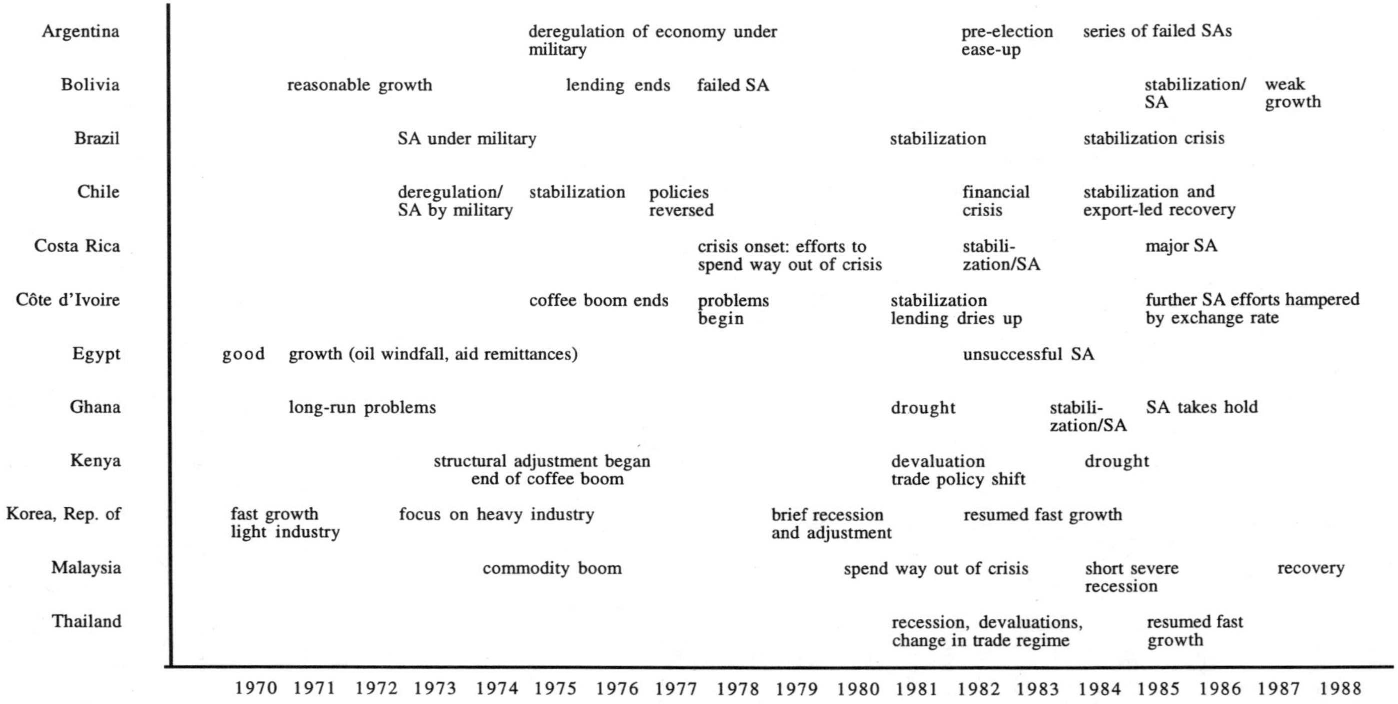

Country	1970	1971	1972	1973	1974	1975	1976	1977	1978	1979	1980	1981	1982	1983	1984	1985	1986	1987	1988
Argentina		reasonable growth					deregulation of economy under military								pre-election ease-up	series of failed SAs			
Bolivia								lending ends	failed SA							stabilization/SA			weak growth
Brazil				SA under military								stabilization				stabilization crisis			
Chile				deregulation/SA by military		stabilization		policies reversed					financial crisis			stabilization and export-led recovery			
Costa Rica										crisis onset: efforts to spend way out of crisis			stabilization/SA			major SA			
Côte d'Ivoire							coffee boom ends		problems begin			stabilization lending dries up					further SA efforts hampered by exchange rate		
Egypt	good	growth (oil windfall, aid remittances)												unsuccessful SA					
Ghana			long-run problems									drought			stabilization/SA		SA takes hold		
Kenya						structural adjustment began end of coffee boom						devaluation trade policy shift			drought				
Korea, Rep. of				focus on heavy industry						brief recession and adjustment					resumed fast growth				
Malaysia					commodity boom						spend way out of crisis					short severe recession			recovery
Thailand	fast growth light industry												recession, devaluations, change in trade regime					resumed fast growth	

Note: SA = structural adjustment
Source: Country studies.

13

Table 1.2 provides some information on REERs. Of the three countries with the least success in adjustment, two also failed to achieve real currency depreciations after 1982 (Egypt's currency appreciated quite sharply), and the third country (Argentina) did not sustain depreciations. Most of the other countries for which data are available achieved some depreciation of their currency: Kenya after the 1981 devaluation and reforms (although the policy may have begun to slip in 1986), Bolivia after the 1985 policy change, Chile after the 1984 stabilization, Costa Rica after the major structural adjustment efforts in 1984, Malaysia after the onset of the 1984 recession, and Ghana after the economic recovery program began in 1983. With this background on the nature of the adjustment experience in the 12 countries, we turn now to labor markets and their role in the adjustment process.

The Role of Labor Markets during Adjustment

The country studies all address the issue of how well labor markets worked during adjustment. The discussion here is organized as follows: first, aggregate real wages and unemployment are examined, then the effect of distributive conflicts and the ensuing macro-tradeoffs are discussed, third, sectoral employment shifts and relative wage are examined, and finally, the role of labor market institutions is dealt with.

Unemployment and Real Wages

Tables 1.3 and 1.4 summarize country experience as regards unemployment and real wage trends for the 12 country studies. Unemployment series are available for nine of the countries studied (they are not available for the three countries in Sub-Saharan Africa). As the definition of unemployment varies across countries, cross-country comparisons require some caution. Most of the countries do show cyclical or trend increases in unemployment related to periods of recession and stabilization (see also figure 1.1). Chile exhibits the most dramatic unemployment, with unemployment levels of over 10 percent in all the years from 1976 (when the series begins) until 1987, reaching a peak of 26 percent in 1982. Understanding how the rate could remain so high for so long in the absence of unemployment benefits is difficult. At the other extreme, Korea's exceptionally low unemployment rate despite the large shocks it encountered as an oil-importing open economy is noteworthy.

Several of the studies discuss the composition of the unemployed and generally confirm the "luxury unemployment" hypothesis, whereby those openly unemployed are more frequently secondary household workers (that is, not household heads) and are often the more educated. Egypt represents an extreme case where a national survey found that 76 percent of the unemployed were new entrants to the labor force, and 74 percent had a high school education or above. Educated female unemployment is a particular problem in Egypt, as few opportunities are available outside the government sector. Of the female unemployed, 97 percent were new entrants to the labor force and 96 percent had a high school education or above. In Thailand, unemployment is highest among those with a vocational education, and unemployment of university graduates rose in the 1980s, when government employment growth slowed dramatically. Likewise in Malaysia, the educated unemployed phenomenon has changed over time, from unemployed high school graduates to unemployed college graduates, and as in Egypt, educated unemployment is concentrated among women. The Costa Rica and Bolivia studies both document another feature of the composition of the unemployed, namely, an increase in the share of heads of households and of job leavers among the unemployed in crisis years.

In most of the countries, weak labor demand did not result only in unemployment. Underemployment increased, although this is hard to measure (Argentina, Bolivia, and Costa Rica studies provide data and show that it has generally moved with the unemployment rate). Participation rates also changed, and informalization increased. Only Bolivia and Chile used formal emergency employment programs, but many of the countries bolstered public employment at least as a temporary measure during the crisis until fiscal stabilization measures dictated cuts in public sector employment.

Changes in participation rates can affect the measurement of unemployment. However, researchers do not agree as to whether the added or the discouraged worker effect will predominate. (The added worker effect is where the income effect of lower earnings during recessions leads to the household supplying additional labor. The

Table 1.3 Unemployment Rates, 1979–89
(percent)

Country	1970	1971	1972	1973	1974	1975	1976	1977	1978	1979	1980	1981	1982	1983	1984	1985	1986	1987	1988	1989
Argentina	n.a.	n.a.	n.a.	n.a.	4.2	3.4	4.8	3.3	3.3	2.5	2.5	4.8	5.3	4.7	4.6	6.1	5.2	5.6	6.1	n.a.
Bolivia	n.a.	n.a.	n.a.	n.a.	n.a	n.a.	n.a.	n.a.	n.a.	n.a.	7.5	6.2	7.5	8.2	6.6	5.7	4.2	5.9	11.5	10.7
Brazil	n.a.	n.a.	n.a.	n.a.	n.a..	n.a.	n.a.	n.a.	-6.8	6.4	6.3	7.9	6.3	6.7	7.1	5.3	3.6	3.8	n.a.	n.a.
Chile	n.a.	n.a.	n.a.	n.a.	n.a.	n.a.	17.4	16.9	17.9	17.0	15.0	25.0	26.2	21.4	19.0	13.6	10.9	7.2	n.a.	n.a.
Costa Rica	n.a.	n.a.	n.a.	n.a.	n.a.	n.a.	6.2	4.6	4.5	4.9	5.9	8.8	9.4	9.0	n.a.	6.9	5.9	5.6	5.5	n.a.
Côte d'Ivoire	n.a.	n.a.	n.a.	n.a.	n.a.	n.a.	n.a.	n.a.	n.a.	n.a.	2.5	n.a.	n.a.	n.a.	n.a.	2.8	2.5	n.a.	n.a.	n.a.
Egypt	2.4	1.8	1.5	4.7	2.3	2.5	n.a.	3.1	3.6	4.6	5.2	5.4	5.7	6.6	6.0	n.a.	n.a.	n.a.	6.8	n.a.
Ghana	n.a.	n.a.	n.a.	n.a.	n.a.	n.a.	n.a.	n.a.	n.a.	n.a.	n.a.	n.a.	n.a.	n.a.	n.a.	n.a.	n.a.	n.a.	n.a.	n.a.
Kenya	n.a.	n.a.	n.a.	n.a.	n.a.	n.a.	n.a.	6.1	n.a.	n.a.	n.a.	n.a.	n.a.	n.a.	n.a.	n.a.	6.9	n.a.	n.a.	n.a.
Korea, Rep. of [a]	4.5	4.5	4.5	4.0	4.1	4.1	3.9	3.8	3.2	3.8	5.2	4.5	4.3	4.1	3.8	4.0	3.8	3.1	2.5	n.a.
Malaysia	7.6	n.a.	n.a.	n.a.	6.7	n.a.	n.a.	n.a.	6.3	5.7	5.7	5.0	4.7	5.5	6.3	7.6	8.5	8.2	n.a.	n.a.
Thailand	n.a.	n.a.	n.a.	n.a.	n.a.	0.4	0.8	0.8	0.7	0.9	0.9	0.9	3.6	1.9	2.3	3.7	3.5	5.8	n.a.	n.a.

n.a. = not available

a. Manufacturing only.

Sources: Argentina, Bolivia, Chile, Costa Rica, Kenya: country studies. Brazil: Riveros (1989). Côte d'Ivoire: 1980 census; Fields (1990). Egypt: population census. Korea: Bank of Korea, *Principal Economic Indicators*. Malaysia: Wong (1985) for the 1970s; Fifth Malaysia Plan 1986–90 for 1980; World Bank economic reports for 1981–89. Thailand: *Statistical Yearbook* (various years).

Table 1.4 Real Wages Indices, 1970–88

(index, 1980 = 100)

Country	1970	1971	1972	1973	1974	1975	1976	1977	1978	1979	1980	1981	1982	1983	1984	1985	1986	1987	1988
Argentina	108	112	105	115	129	124	80	74	77	86	100	91	80	97	106	87	82	72	n.a.
Bolivia	100	114	113	118	94	86	98	107	108	110	100	80	56**	42	36	55	34	42	n.a.
Brazil	79	n.a.	n.a.	n.a.	n.a.	84	85	89	94	95	100	109	122	113	105	113	122	106	n.a.
Chile	110	n.a.	n.a.	n.a.	n.a.	63	72	82	91	100	100	114	133	95	89	76	73	71	n.a.
Costa Rica[a]	n.a.	n.a.	n.a.	n.a.	n.a.	n.a.	80	96	97	105	100	85	63	77	n.a.	92	95	n.a.	n.a.
Costa Rica[b]	n.a.	n.a.	n.a.	n.a.	n.a.	n.a.	n.a.	n.a.	n.a.	n.a.	100	84	65	77	n.a.	93	97	n.a.	n.a.
*Côte d'Ivoire	n.a.	n.a.	n.a.	n.a.	n.a.	n.a.	n.a.	n.a.	n.a.	n.a.	100	n.a.	n.a.	n.a.	n.a.	115	n.a.	n.a.	n.a.
*Egypt[c]	n.a.	n.a.	n.a.	89	92	73	79	92	89	105	100	103	104	108	118	120	103	91	n.a.
*Egypt[d]	n.a.	n.a.	n.a.	93	96	86	88	109	100	103	100	105	108	104	108	101	92	84	n.a.
*Egypt[e]	n.a.	n.a.	n.a.	125	109	104	105	104	103	103	100	108	109	98	96	89	75	69	n.a.
*Ghana	n.a.	n.a.	n.a.	n.a.	n.a.	n.a.	n.a.	n.a.	113	93	100	59	53	41	60	87	141	n.a.	n.a.
*Kenya[f]	n.a.	n.a.	n.a.	88	88	86	89	87	90	91	100	90	81	79	80	78	79	82	84
*Kenya[g]	n.a.	n.a.	n.a.	106	106	103	114	109	110	106	100	96	85	84	81	78	83	80	81
Korea, Rep. of	44	45	46	53	57	58	68	82	96	105	100	99	106	115	122	130	139	150	168
Malaysia	83	83	80	71	76	80	85	87	89	95	100	106	111	118	125	135	133	130	127

n.a. = not available
* Denotes data from employment and earnings surveys or household surveys.
** Denotes possible break in series.

a. Paid workers (employees). c. Private sector. e. Government. g. Public sector.
b. All workers. d. Public enterprises. f. Private sector.

Sources: Argentina, Bolivia, Chile, Costa Rica, Egypt, Ghana, Kenya: country studies. Brazil: Riveros (1989). Côte d'Ivoire: Lavy and Newman (1989). Korea: Bank of Korea, *Principal Economic Indicators*. Malaysia: Department of Statistics, Monthly Industrial Statistics for 1975–87; Department of Statistics, Industrial Surveys for 1968–74.

discouraged worker effect is where the substitution effect of lower wages during recessions decreases household labor supply.) Three of the studies discuss the issue and suggest that the added worker effect predominated in Costa Rica during the crisis and the discouraged worker effect in Bolivia. In Argentina the authors argue that the discouraged worker effect prevailed in the 1970s and the added worker effect in the 1980s, although they do not explain the change. One complication in interpreting the data is that most countries have also observed a trend increase in female labor force participation rates (the Bolivia, Costa Rica, Kenya, Korea, and Malaysia studies all mention this). Thus, separating trends in female labor force participation over time from temporary fluctuations in response to economic crisis is not easy.

A final form of quantity adjustment involved a shift from formal to informal sector employment. As employees lost their jobs, one option in the absence of unemployment compensation was to become self-employed, and likewise output, and thus employment, often shifted from large formal sector firms to smaller informal sector ones. This is again a difficult topic on which to obtain data, and studies often define the informal sector differently. Tokman (1984) and others have studied the phenomenon extensively for Latin America. The Bolivia case study argues that informalization was an important method of labor market adjustment. In Argentina, although the authors state that the informal sector was less important than elsewhere in Latin America, nonwage employment grew faster than wage employment in nontradables in all three periods considered (the 1960s, the 1970s, and the 1980s), and in both manufacturing and agriculture nonwage employment grew faster in two of the three periods. In Brazil the main shift was into the unprotected employee sector (those without signed contracts) rather than into self employment.

Informalization has been less well documented in Africa. The Côte d'Ivoire study, however, does mention a shift between formal and informal establishments in manufacturing, and the authors of the Kenya paper argue that a similar employment shift occurred in Kenya, where employment in the informal sector grew 11 percent in 1988 when wage employment growth slowed. There is also similar evidence for Asia. In Malaysia the trend rise in employees as a proportion of the labor force was reversed during the short recession. In Korea the trend toward an increased employment share in large firms in manufacturing was arrested in the early 1980s, and the proportion of women who were regular employees, as opposed to temporary or casual, likewise reversed its upward trend.

Real wage behavior, perhaps more than unemployment rates, differentiates the country groups discussed earlier (note that the wage data available are for the formal sector except for the Latin countries). The Asian countries show a fairly steady advance in real wages, with brief interruptions during the recession (although the authors stress the importance of these real wage slowdowns in allowing productivity to stay ahead of real wage growth and ensuring declining unit costs). The severe adjustment countries show dramatic wage fluctuations, with wages at their lowest less than 50 percent of the peak, and with real wage declines far greater than the fall in GDP. Real wages in Ghana recovered by 1986, are still not back to peak levels in Chile, and are continuing to fall in Bolivia. The other countries are somewhat intermediate: in two of the three moderate adjustment countries (Brazil and Costa Rica) there are gains between the start and end of the time series, albeit less marked than for the Asian countries, and Kenya has a wage decline in the public sector, but private wages are closer to holding their own. The difference between Kenya and the other countries in this group is probably due to population pressure. Finally, the less successful adjustment countries show a less severe wage decline than the severe adjustment ones, perhaps explaining a little of the political opposition to such severe adjustments. However, one must be somewhat cautious in interpreting the real wage data, particularly in cases where it is not from household survey data, because of the employment composition issue. Earnings functions can be helpful in this regard.

How can we interpret the evidence discussed above, and what can we infer about labor market workings? As discussed earlier, there are three possible explanations as to why unemployment may persist during stabilization. The first is that the labor market is not working well because of real wage rigidity. The evidence presented by the case studies certainly does not favor the view that real wages were rigid, and therefore led to unemployment. Even for Chile, where unemployment was highest and persisted the longest, real wages fell dramatically. Real wages have also been flexible in Brazil and Argentina, despite wage indexation. Devereux (vol. 1, chapter 4) argues that the failure of disinflation plans in these countries is due more to inappropriate and noncredible fiscal policies. The effect of wage indexation is only to magnify and lengthen the inflation response. Some critics might still argue that real wages did not fall fast enough, but a good case for this remains to be made. If the inflexible real wage explanation is inappropriate because of the observed severe falls in real wages, this leaves the other two explanations: aggregate demand feedback from declining real wages and output market imperfections.

The wage level enters the system as a determinant of aggregate demand through its effect on the distribution of private income. The mechanism depends crucially on the assumption (generally valid empirically) that the propensity to save is markedly lower for wage earners than for recipients of profits. If the share of wages in total disposable income falls, for example, savings in the economy increase, and aggregate demand will fall unless there is an offsetting increase in investment or government spending. These ideas are implicit in the works of Keynes and Kalecki, and have recently been discussed in the context of developing countries' stabilization and adjustment problems by Taylor (1988) and others.

Taylor distinguishes between what he calls "exhilarationist" and "stagnationist" economic scenarios. In the former, output is constrained by bottlenecks related to a short supply of capital. Real wage cuts leading to a higher profit share will increase the supply of savings, and may translate into higher investment. In the stagnationist economic scenario, however, the binding constraint on output growth is the low level of consumer demand relative to capacity. A fall in the share of wages in these conditions leads to stagnation. It is possible for an economy to start from an exhilarationist position, but then slip into a stagnationist position as wage share falls steeply.

The existence of a dual labor market, with a distinctly lower wage level in one sector compared to the other, reinforces the conclusions drawn from the model with a homogeneous labor market. Consider the case of a recession with a fall in labor demand in the formal sector. Although the typical scenario as analyzed in the country studies is that a fall in wages occurs, sometimes fairly drastic, this is not always the case. In Malaysia the average earnings of workers in the formal sector actually increased because those most recently hired and at the lower spectrum of wages and skills were laid off first. In all cases, however, the workers displaced from the formal sector as well as those entering the labor force entered the informal sector in growing numbers. The share of total employment at the lower wage levels increased significantly. For the economy as a whole, therefore, average wages fell faster and to a greater extent than in the formal sector.

Does the stagnationist hypothesis still hold if we allow for the possibility of exports? In the traditional model of the small open economy (such as the one reviewed in vol. 1, chapter 3) it will not hold unless wages are rigid downward in both the tradable and the nontradable sectors. As demand contracts, with wage rigidity in the nontradable sector, unemployment will occur in this sector, but if wages are flexible in the tradable sector, costs will fall in tradables. However, the small open economy model assumes unlimited demand for tradables at the going product price, thus the unemployed labor will be absorbed in the more profitable tradable sector. Total demand will be restored to its initial level with a larger share of GDP accounted for by tradables. However, even if there are wage rigidities in both sectors, the profitability of the tradable sector needed to attract resources can still be achieved by a real devaluation that increases the ratio of the prices of tradables to the prices of nontradables (P_T/P_N). This is why in the textbooks devaluation is sometimes called an alternative to wage flexibility.

The Asian and Latin American country studies provide sharp contrasts as concerns the role of wages and devaluation in macro demand contraction. Korea, for example, depended on continuous nominal devaluation of its currency over a long period of time as well as maxi devaluations during periods of severe external shock. As an export-oriented economy, Korea had to increase its competitiveness by reducing its unit labor costs in dollar terms. Due to the rapid growth of labor productivity, the response to external shocks was to hold constant real wages rather than requiring a wage decline. The combination of a maxi devaluation and temporarily preventing wages from rising with productivity led to a very quick recovery of exports.

At the same time, since the slowdown in real wage growth was so short, there was no significant deflationary impact in the domestic market.

Another factor important in recovery was government policies to counter the increase in nonwage costs following devaluation. Because of its important role in the finance of large-scale industry, the government was to some extent able to offset the increase in the cost of borrowed foreign capital caused by devaluation by offering cheap, subsidized credit to businesses. An important feature of the Korean case of adjustment to the shocks was that exports increased rapidly in Korea despite the rise in wages.

The last point touches on a general point about the role of wage flexibility in adjustment. In Southeast Asian economies the share of wages in value added is typically one-third or a little more (according to Riveros 1989, it is closer to 40 percent in Latin America). Thus, changes in capital costs are often as important in determining competitiveness as changes in wage levels. The course of events leading up to the recession in Malaysia in the mid-1980s, and the subsequent adjustments triggering recovery, illustrate the point vividly. Unlike Korea, Malaysia is an oil exporter. In the early 1980s, government spending in Malaysia increased enormously, partly to bolster an attempt to prolong the boom associated with the oil boom. The resultant pressure on external competitiveness came from three sources: (a) wages increased, even after employment growth had slowed down; (b) interest rates increased sharply as demand for private capital funds competed with the public demand; and (c) the currency appreciated in real terms because the capital account was uncontrolled, and there was a massive inflow of capital to finance the budget deficit.

The loss of competitiveness created an external imbalance that could only be corrected through a sharp recession. Malaysia was fortunate, however, in that all the relevant factor markets showed remarkable flexibility. As wages fell from their early 1980s level, the interest rate fell to a level that was nearly a third of its peak, and there was a sharp depreciation of the currency. Clearly the "collapse" of all the factor markets was instrumental in making the recession short-lived. Of course, the improvement in the world economy was a factor triggering the recovery, but it was the gain in competitiveness fed by the downwardly flexible wages, interest rates, and exchange rates that allowed Malaysia to seize the opportunity in the second half of the 1980s.

The Latin American studies illustrate almost the opposite case in terms of the effects of real wages on demand, with Bolivia providing the clearest example. The fall in real wages in the 1980s was twice the size of the fall in real GDP. Even by the end of the decade, real wages and employment showed little sign of any recovery. The fall in the share of wages must have depressed the domestic market considerably. At the same time, despite the real value of the currency falling to less than a third of the 1985 level, there was no sign of export-led recovery. Evidently the market structure for favoring large shifts to export did not exist in Bolivia.

By contrast, another Latin American country, Costa Rica, hints at the existence of a basic structure of links to the world market, and also illustrates the advantages of an institutional mechanism that limits the direction of wage deflation. Real wages fell between 1980–82 as indexation tied to past inflation failed to protect workers as inflation accelerated. In mid-1982, when stabilization was instituted, real wages turned upward again as inflation decelerated. By 1986, real wages had regained their 1980 value. The short period to which the real wage decline was confined might have helped to stabilize the domestic aggregate demand. At the same time, the decline in the dollar price of exportables, helped by the fall in real wages and the devaluation of 1980, was instrumental in improving the export situation. Thus, two factors helped Costa Rica to stage a recovery in the post-1982 period. Market links were important in ensuring that the fall in the real value of the currency and in wage costs had the desirable impact on exports. More surprisingly, indexation was significant in engineering the initial fall in real wages and in limiting the period of wage stagnation.

Another instance of sharp deflation caused by a fall in the share of wages in GDP comes from the case of Chile during the drastic policies of stabilization pushed through by the military *junta* after the fall of the Allende regime. This case illustrates the importance of product markets in the process of adjustment. Although extreme, it is worth discussing because, as Ramos (1980, p. 468) points out: "other countries may simply be experiencing in slow motion (stagflation) what Chile experienced all at once (hyperstagflation)."

In October 1973, the *junta* freed prices that had been controlled under the previous socialist regimes, but unlike Germany after World War II, Chile did not have a monetary reform to put a cap on the freed inflationary prices. Inflation immediately accelerated to 90 percent during the month of October alone. Although prices moderated after October, they continued to increase at rates higher than 300 percent in 1974 and 1975, clearly overshooting by a good deal the expected equilibrium level.

On the labor front, the *junta's* policy was to separate wage readjustments from the freezing of prices to prevent a wage-price spiral. It postponed adjustment of wages by several months. When it did take place, it was consistent with a much lower rate of inflation. Thus, real wages dropped sharply, and by 1975 stood at nearly half their pre-Allende level. Astonishingly, the real wage decline was accompanied not only by high rates of inflation, but also by a rapidly increasing rate of unemployment, which climbed from 3 percent in the first half of 1973 to 10 percent in 1974 and 19 percent in the first half of 1976. The rise in unemployment was, as one would expect, associated with a sharp decline in industrial output, at least until the end of 1975 (the index of industrial output halved between end-1973 and end-1975).

What explains the coexistence of a high inflation rate, falling real wages, and declining output? The crux of the problem would seem to be the inflationary expectations and noncompetitive behavior in the product market. There was clearly no demand pressure because consumer demand fell very early with the fall in real wages, and demand contraction intensified as real wages fell and unemployment increased at a high rate. Nor was there any cost pressure, for "whereas the prices of imported inputs in the last quarter of 1973 rose to 30 times and wages rose 14 times their 1969 levels, product prices rose to 40 times their 1969 levels upon being freed in October 1973" (Ramos 1980, p. 472). Prices seem to have increased in anticipation of much higher demand and cost pressures than actually existed. "Producers seem to have set prices to balance supply and demand not as of the moment, but in three months' time so to speak" (Ramos 1980). The anticipated increase could be on the side of money demand, or in terms of unforeseen wage adjustments, devaluation, and a rise in input costs.

The continuation of inflationary price increases in the face of serious disequilibrium in the product market with producers unable to sell their products is a difficult proposition to explain in terms of textbook economics, and indeed came as a surprise to policymakers. A major factor in the continuation of the process was that price setters were not penalized soon enough for their erroneous expectations because of the massive increase in the share of profits that the fall in real wages entailed.

The inflationary expectation was finally broken when the currency was revalued in 1976, when the balance of payments situation reversed, showing a net surplus, and tariff reductions were undertaken for reasons connected with the economy's long-run development. The downward jolt these measures gave to the prices of both inputs and final goods seems to have fueled the recovery after 1976. Prices finally began growing less than the money supply, with output rising, unemployment falling, and real wages rising much more than total output.

Problems of Distributive Conflicts

The availability of enough evidence to suggest that wages have been flexible in many countries during the periods of adjustment does not imply that distributive conflicts have not been major issues in several countries. The country studies show that in Latin America, in particular, the conflict between maintaining or increasing labor's share of output and achieving external balance has been an important factor in the limited success of stabilization policies. Countries, of course, differ in the importance of distributive conflict in their economic history. Apart from differences in labor market institutions, the economy's structure seems to be critical in some cases.

One factor that seems to be important is whether or not food is an important tradable. The case of Argentina is a good example that shows how the different objectives could be in conflict when basic foods in the workers' consumption budget (cereals, meats, and so on) are tradable goods, and the government does not interfere significantly with the domestic prices of these commodities. In this case there is a close relationship between the exchange rate and the product wage in the economy's nontradable sector. Currency devaluations lead to increases in the domestic price of food, which in turn leads to upward pressure on money wages. Such an increase will not affect product wages in the tradable sector, since product prices of traded goods would also have increased in the domestic market, but other things being equal, the product wage in the nontradable sector will increase. In this case a conflict of interests arises between the producers of nontradables and the workers employed in this sector.

This exchange rate wage tradeoff, taken together with the nontradable sector's more powerful political position because of its urban location, has given rise to the wage cycle documented in the country study. When external markets for Argentina's food exports are strong, the currency tends to slide into overvaluation, which helps increase real wages without hurting profitability in the urban nontradable sector and fiscal balance in the public urban nontradable sector. However, when the external terms of trade weaken, devaluation is imperative to ease the problem of external imbalance, and various forces are set in motion that depress real wages to protect profitability. In Argentina, as in much of Latin America, bursts of inflation have often been the mechanism for reducing real wages.

Note that not all countries have a large proportion of their wage goods or food as tradables as Argentina does. In particular, in many Asian economies (including the two in our sample, Korea and Malaysia) rice, although an internationally traded good, is more like a nontradable because of government price policies. In these countries, the government plays a dual role in the rice market. On the one hand, it buys rice from the farmers at a high procurement price to help support the level of earnings in this sector. On the other hand, it distributes the rice through its retail outlets at a subsidized price for the benefit of, for the most part, urban consumers. The financial deficit caused by the difference between the buying and selling price of rice is covered by the central government's overall budget. Thus, although the government imports rice to supplement the amount procured from local farmers, the domestic price of rice is insulated from the border price. This important wage good is, in effect, a nontradable. The problem analyzed above, which stems from an inverse relationship between the external value of the currency and the price of the wage good, does not exist for such economies (although the fiscal issue does).

The supply of capital may also lead to a tradeoff between wages and the exchange rate. Let us assume that the growth of output is constrained by the supply of capital (savings) rather than by demand (in other words, the economic scenario is an exhilarationist one). The share of wages in value added has a direct effect on total savings, and hence on the growth rate of output. The exchange rate also affects output growth from two angles. First, the higher the value of the currency, the greater the trade deficit that, if it can be sustained, increases foreign savings (borrowing) in the economy. Second, a higher value of the currency reduces the cost of intermediate inputs, and effectively increases the marginal impact of savings on output growth.

An exchange rate/wage tradeoff exists in the sense that a given rate of savings (and growth rate) could be achieved with different pairs of values of the exchange rate and the wage share; the higher the latter, the higher must the degree of overvaluation be. Government policy affects both the exchange rate and the wage share through its determination of the rate of growth of the money supply, and hence the rate of inflation. With indexation rules determining both exchange rate and wage adjustments, lags in the system mean that a higher rate of inflation achieves both a higher rate of overvaluation and a lower share of wages. Thus, an equilibrium relationship exists that connects the rate of inflation, the value of the exchange rate, the wage share, and the real growth rate of the economy.

The case of Brazil illustrates the key problems and constraints in this system. During 1967–83, Brazil followed a policy of stepping up the growth rate by expanding the money supply. This led to a rise in the rate of inflation and a fall in the share of wages. The associated increase in the real exchange rate and the fall in the share of wages both increased real output growth by increasing foreign and domestic savings and reducing the domestic cost of imported inputs. The mechanism for bringing about this change worked as long as changes in the values of the relevant variables were sustainable. The feasibility of a fall in the share of wages depended on the existence of an authoritarian political system. Similarly, the appreciation of the currency meant an increase in the trade deficit that could only be financed by foreign borrowing. The persistent increase in foreign debt was one of the costs of this strategy of boosting the real rate of growth.

The first oil shock of the mid-1970s meant, in effect, a change in the parameters of the Brazilian production function, so that at the old values of the variables, output growth was depressed. At the same time the import bill increased sharply. The government's response to this situation was to undertake a program of import substitution in capital and intermediate goods, financed by stepped up foreign borrowing. The second oil shock and the increase in interest rates finally made this policy unsustainable. The debt burden had reached a level when further foreign borrowing was no longer an option to maintain an overvalued currency. A new element in the situation was the change in the political system. It was no longer easy to reduce the share of wages with a higher rate of inflation. The country study discusses the distributional conflicts in more detail.

Thus, two barriers prevented achievement of a higher real savings rate to counteract the effect of the deterioration of the external terms of trade. The government could not continue to overvalue the currency nor to depress wages. Nor could these be changed with a higher rate of inflation in such a way that a new equilibrium set of values of the relevant variables could be achieved. This was at the heart of the failure of stabilization efforts in the 1980s. One way out would have been if total factor productivity growth could have been increased to a sufficient degree, but evidently the Brazilian economy was unable to achieve this goal. On the contrary, the country study indicates that labor productivity actually fell as labor hoarding in the formal tradable sector increased significantly in response to the deteriorating employment situation. The contrast with Korea's experience is striking. The country study documents the enormous importance of total factor productivity growth in the Korean economy's successful adjustment to the oil price shocks. Because of the increase in total factor productivity, the required decline in the share of wages could be achieved with a negligible decrease in the absolute level of real wages, and the increase in the cost of imported inputs due to devaluation could be largely offset.

Sectoral Employment Shifts and Relative Wages

Sectoral employment shifts are a key part of structural adjustment, and Edwards and Edwards (vol. 1, chapter 2) discuss these in a basic two-sector two-factor dependent economy model in the presence of labor market distortions. They examine four different scenarios plus the basic competitive case. In the basic model, standard results apply and labor would tend to benefit from trade liberalization, which the authors define as tariff cuts: the effects of devaluation, which usually accompanies adjustment, are not considered. Even if economywide wage rigidity is allowed for, the authors argue that trade liberalization will result in unemployment in the short run where capital is immobile. However, in the longer run, if importables are the less labor-intensive sector, starting from an initial condition of unemployment, trade liberalization will increase total employment in the economy.

The authors then take the case where only the importable sector is covered by a minimum wage. In the short run there will be lower employment in importables and higher employment in exportables, but employment in nontradables and total employment is ambiguous. They conclude that: "In the presence of labor market distortions, trade liberalization policies usually considered to be beneficial may generate nontrivial (short run) unemployment problems." This conclusion holds also in the third variant considered, that of capital account liberalization.

The fourth and final case considered is where wage distortions in importables are related to the degree of tariff protection. In the short run, trade liberalization increases unemployment and depresses wages in the economy's other sectors. Although some of this would disappear in the long run, the scenario highlights possible political economy conflicts. Labor, "the factor of production that is supposed to gain from freer trade, is negatively affected in the short run, and the long run gains are hard to perceive when compared to the initially distorted situation of the economy."

The country studies provide information on wages and employment by various sectoral groupings: economic sectors (agriculture, manufacturing, construction, and so on), formal/informal, public/private, tradable/nontradable, and occasionally even finer categories such as importable/exportable/nontradable. They also provide some information on skill groups. How formal/informal or skilled/unskilled categorizations correspond to the tradable/ nontradable distinction that is of key interest is not always clearly specified in the country studies, and varies between countries (the Brazil study provides the most complete breakdown). One important problem in many of the studies is that the agriculture sector is an important component of tradables, but no agricultural wage data over time exist for the Latin American countries, and neither agricultural wage nor employment data over time exist for the African countries.

Let us consider sectoral employment first, and then sectoral relative wages. Table 1.5 provides information on employment shifts by sector of GDP for 8 of the 12 countries in the study (the ILO Yearbook does not have data for the other four countries). The ILO Yearbook reports sectoral employment data by 10 sectoral groups, which are here further grouped into primary, manufacturing, utilities and construction, and tertiary. This classification is used on the assumption that, roughly speaking, primary and manufactured goods are tradable, whereas the output of the construction, utilities, and tertiary sectors are not. Obviously this grouping is rather crude, and the Costa Rica and Argentina studies provide more detailed information on the tradable/nontradable shift, even to the extent of comparing employment in the traditional and nontraditional export sectors (Costa Rica).

The debt crisis years had clear effects on structural transformation in the countries studied, in that the usual changes accompanying development either halted or reversed in all cases. In Brazil, Costa Rica, Korea, Malaysia, and Thailand (the Asian and partial adjustment countries), the manufacturing share declined somewhat during stabilization, but then resumed growth. The recovery is strongest in Korea. The data series for Malaysia and Thailand both end before recovery sets in strongly. In Chile and Bolivia, declines in the manufacturing share were more striking. These were reversed under structural adjustment in Chile, but not as yet in Bolivia. The data series for Egypt stops before economic problems intensified, but a decline in the share of manufacturing employment is already evident.

The ILO Yearbook does not contain data on sectoral employment trends for Sub-Saharan Africa, but the country studies contain some information. The Kenya country study argues that urban employment figures suggest that the manufacturing share stagnated after 1978. Data for the formal sector for the Côte d'Ivoire suggest a large decrease in modern manufacturing employment despite subsidies.

The debt crisis slowed the transition out of agriculture for most countries, and for Bolivia, Côte d'Ivoire, and Ghana shifts back into agriculture are evident. The ILO data for Bolivia show that although the primary share overall declined, the agriculture share increased in the worst years (1982–83) and stagnated thereafter. In the Côte d'Ivoire a shift back into agriculture occurred (based on labor force transition behavior). In Ghana, the capital city, Accra, changed from being the destination of 46.5 percent of migrants prior to 1970 to being the source of 60.0 percent of recent migrants in 1982–87. Even in the higher-income countries, agriculture played an important role in absorbing labor market entrants: one-third of new jobs in Malaysia during the 1986–87 recession were in agriculture, and agricultural employment grew as fast as total employment in Chile in the successful adjustment period after 1985.

The Argentina and Costa Rica studies both examine employment shifts between the tradable and nontradable sectors. Argentina has seen a secular trend toward increased employment in nontradables, and Costa Rica has seen a similar trend out of exportables. As Argentina did not have a sustained adjustment program, this trend continued in the 1980s, but in Costa Rica adjustment arrested, but did not reverse, the trend. However, the study authors find some cause for optimism in the growth of the small, nontraditional export sector.

A useful exercise is to examine sectoral wage data in conjunction with sectoral employment figures. Simple theory suggests that the effect of structural adjustment policies should lead to a relative increase in wages in tradables to encourage labor movement (unless markets are so frictionless that the reallocation does not require price signals). However, employment shifts may also cause changes in

Table 1.5 Employment by Sector, 1971–89

(percentage of total employment)

Country/sector	1971	1972	1973	1974	1975	1976	1977	1978	1979	1980	1981	1982	1983	1984	1985	1986	1987	1988	1989
Bolivia																			
Primary	53.7	53.1	52.6	52.2	51.6	50.5	50.5	50.2	49.4	50.9	51.0	50.9	52.1	51.9	51.5	50.0	49.9	50.0	50.0
Manufacturing	8.8	8.8	8.9	9.0	9.0	9.1	9.2	9.3	9.4	10.3	10.0	9.1	8.9	8.8	8.7	7.0	7.1	7.1	7.1
Utilities and construction	4.3	4.7	5.0	5.5	5.9	6.4	6.4	6.5	6.5	5.9	5.1	3.7	3.7	3.3	3.2	3.1	3.2	3.2	3.2
Tertiary	33.2	33.4	33.5	33.3	33.4	33.6	34.2	34.1	34.7	32.9	33.9	36.3	35.2	36.0	36.5	39.9	39.8	39.8	39.8
Brazil																			
Primary[a]	n.a.	n.a.	38.2	n.a.	n.a.	34.8	33.0	30.4	28.9	27.4	29.3	29.5	27.1	29.8	28.5	25.9*	24.6	n.a.	n.a.
Manufacturing[b]	n.a.	n.a.	12.9	n.a.	n.a.	14.6	15.8	15.2	16.5	16.3	24.7	23.4	14.0	14.2	14.7	16.2	15.7	n.a.	n.a.
Utilities and construction	n.a.	n.a.	6.9	n.a.	n.a.	6.5	6.4	7.4	8.2	7.8	n.a.	n.a.	11.4	7.5	7.4	8.0	8.1	n.a.	n.a.
Tertiary	n.a.	n.a.	42.0	n.a.	n.a.	44.0	44.8	47.0	47.7	48.5	46.1	47.1	47.6	48.4	49.3	50.0	51.6	n.a.	n.a.
Chile																			
Primary	n.a.	n.a.	n.a.	n.a.	24.6	20.6	21.1	20.2	19.3	18.5	17.5*	18.1	17.7	18.0*	22.5	22.8	22.9	22.3	21.7
Manufacturing	n.a.	n.a.	n.a.	n.a.	16.8	16.8	16.7	16.3	16.5	16.1	15.5	12.7	12.6	13.8*	13.3	13.6	15.1	15.7	16.9
Utilities and construction	n.a.	n.a.	n.a.	n.a.	5.3	4.8	4.7	4.8	5.1	5.4	6.0*	3.7	3.6	4.4*	4.6	5.4	5.8	7.1	7.3
Tertiary	n.a.	n.a.	n.a.	n.a.	52.6	57.4	57.2	58.5	58.9	59.8	60.7*	65.4	66.0	63.7*	59.6	58.2	56.0	54.8	54.1
Costa Rica																			
Primary	n.a.	n.a.	n.a.	n.a.	n.a.	n.a.	n.a.	n.a.	n.a.	n.a.	27.6	30.0	28.2	30.0[d]	27.3	26.9*	28.1	28.1	26.2
Manufacturing	n.a.	n.a.	n.a.	n.a.	n.a.	n.a.	n.a.	n.a.	n.a.	n.a.	15.4	15.2	16.6	15.2[d]	15.9	17.1*	17.5	16.7	18.8
Utilities and construction	n.a.	n.a.	n.a.	n.a.	n.a.	n.a.	n.a.	n.a.	n.a.	n.a.	6.7	5.7	5.1	4.9[d]	5.1	5.8*	5.9	5.9	6.2
Tertiary[c]	n.a.	n.a.	n.a.	n.a.	n.a.	n.a.	n.a.	n.a.	n.a.	n.a.	50.3	49.1	50.1	49.9[d]	51.7	50.2*	48.5	49.3	48.8
Egypt																			
Primary	54.2	53.8	51.5	47.6	49.1	n.a.	45.8	42.5	42.1	42.6	40.5	39.3	41.3	40.9	n.a.	n.a.	n.a.	n.a.	n.a.
Manufacturing	12.5	12.8	14.1	15.3	14.3	n.a.	14.7	15.1	16.0	14.7	15.9	15.3	14.7	13.9	n.a.	n.a.	n.a.	n.a.	n.a.
Utilities and construction	2.7	2.8	3.3	3.1	3.2	n.a.	4.2	4.8	5.4	5.2	5.9	6.3	6.2	5.9	n.a.	n.a.	n.a.	n.a.	n.a.
Tertiary	30.6	30.6	31.0	33.5	33.3	n.a.	35.3	37.6	36.5	37.5	37.8	39.1	37.8	39.3	n.a.	n.a.	n.a.	n.a.	n.a.

Korea																			
Primary	49.4	51.1	50.4	48.6	46.4	45.1	42.6	39.2	36.6	34.9	35.1	32.8	30.5	28.1	26.0	24.8	23.0	21.5	20.1
Manufacturing	13.3	13.7	15.9	17.4	18.6	21.3	21.6	22.4	22.9	21.7	20.4	21.1	22.5	23.2	23.4	24.7	27.0	27.7	27.6
Utilities and construction[c]	3.7	4.1	3.6	4.2	4.6	4.5	5.1	6.3	6.5	6.4	6.5	6.0	6.0	6.5	6.4	6.0	5.9	6.4	6.8
Tertiary[c]	33.7	31.0	30.0	29.8	30.4	29.0	30.7	32.1	34.1	37.0	38.0	40.1	41.1	42.2	44.3	44.5	44.1	44.5	45.5
Malaysia																			
Primary	n.a.	n.a.	n.a.	n.a.	n.a.	n.a.	n.a.	n.a.	n.a.	38.2	36.8	32.1	32.9	31.3	31.1	31.3	31.4	n.a.	n.a.
Manufacturing	n.a.	n.a.	n.a.	n.a.	n.a.	n.a.	n.a.	n.a.	n.a.	16.1	16.1	15.5	17.0	15.4	15.0	15.2	15.5	n.a.	n.a.
Utilities and construction	n.a.	n.a.	n.a.	n.a.	n.a.	n.a.	n.a.	n.a.	n.a.	7.1	8.3	7.9	8.9	8.9	8.0	7.0	6.2	n.a.	n.a.
Tertiary	n.a.	n.a.	n.a.	n.a.	n.a.	n.a.	n.a.	n.a.	n.a.	38.7	38.8	44.4	45.2	45.0	45.5	46.5	46.8	n.a.	n.a.
Thailand[d]																			
Primary	79.3	72.9	72.6	65.7	73.1	75.9	73.7	73.8	n.a.	70.9	64.5	61.9*	63.4	64.9	63.9	63.9	n.a.	n.a.	n.a.
Manufacturing	4.0	7.7	7.0	9.9	7.5	6.2	6.5	6.8	n.a.	7.9	9.2	10.2*	9.6	9.2	9.4	9.1	n.a.	n.a.	n.a.
Utilities and construction	1.2	1.7	1.8	2.0	1.4	1.5	1.9	1.7	n.a.	2.2	3.3	3.2*	3.2	3.3	3.2	3.1	n.a.	n.a.	n.a.
Tertiary[c]	15.5	17.7	18.5	22.4	18.0	16.3	17.9	17.7	n.a.	18.9	22.9	24.7*	23.8	22.6	23.5	23.8	n.a.	n.a.	n.a.

n.a. = not available

* Change in sample or methodology. See ILO (1989).

a. Excludes mining.

b. Includes mining.

c. Includes utilities.

d. November not July (usual).

Note: For Thailand, repair and installation services are included in manufacturing, sanitary services are included in utilities. Prior to 1983, unpaid family workers working less than 20 hours were excluded. The primary sector throughout includes agriculture and mining, the tertiary sector includes commerce, transport, banks, services, and other. Figures may not sum exactly to 100 percent due to rounding.

Source: ILO (various years), author's calculations.

relative wages. In practice, structural adjustment has been associated with labor shedding from government and from formal sector activities (either due to reduced tariff protection or the removal of job security legislation). As workers cannot remain unemployed for long in developing countries due to the lack of unemployment benefits, labor has tended to move to sectors with flexible entry, frequently the informal sector or agriculture. The crowding of labor in these sectors may have also depressed relative wages in the short run. Thus, relative wages in nontradable sectors with easy entry (for example, commerce, services) may have been depressed both directly due to exchange rate changes and indirectly due to labor crowding, while wages in tradable sectors with easy entry (for example, agriculture) could go in either direction in the short run due to opposing effects. Furthermore, changes in labor force composition within sectors can obscure trends. Sectors losing labor may experience increases in aggregate wages due to the loss of workers with the lowest levels of human capital and seniority. The latter effect can be dealt with by the use of earnings functions as discussed later.

All the studies (except Côte d'Ivoire and Thailand) provide some information on the changes in relative wages, whether between economic sectors, formal/informal sector, tradable/nontradable, or skill categories. Table 1.6 summarizes the results by broad GDP sectoral categories for seven countries, and table 1.7 shows the results by tradables/nontradables for two countries and for the public/private sectors for five countries. The data in table 1.6 are for agriculture, manufacturing, construction, and service sector wages, where available. As construction is the largest component of the group utilities plus construction, and services are similarly the largest component of the tertiary group, the sectoral wage data in table 1.6 correspond reasonably well to the sectoral employment data of table 1.5. In general, relative wage changes did support structural adjustment objectives, although this is not necessarily true for each country and every sector.

In Ghana relative wages increased in agriculture and mining, sectors featuring heavily in the Economic Recovery Program (see table 1.6 and the Ghana study). In Egypt relative wages increased in agriculture (see table 1.6 and the Egypt study) largely because other

Table 1.6 Real Wage Indices by GNP Sectoral Classification, 1970–89
(index, 1980 = 100)

Country/sector	1970	1971	1972	1973	1974	1975	1976	1977	1978	1979	1980	1981	1982	1983	1984	1985	1986	1987	1988	1989
Bolivia																				
Manufacturing	98	111	112	121	97	96	112	109	109	112	100	*	81[a]	114[a]	136[a]	52[a]	59[a]	n.a.	n.a.	n.a.
Construction	83	98	96	90	80	74	90	95	95	108	100	*	85[a]	47[a]	93[a]	52[a]	74[a]	n.a.	n.a.	n.a.
Services	125	128	125	130	109	88	95	115	111	105	100	*	63[a]	57[a]	104[a]	46[a]	72[a]	n.a.	n.a.	n.a.
Chile																				
Manufacturing	114	135	93	50	54	72	80	85	102	108	100	132	147	112	101	85	79	81	86	n.a.
Total	112	118	104	58	56	63	72	81	91	100	100	114	133	95	89	76	73	71	72	n.a.
Egypt[b]																				
Agriculture	n.a.	n.a.	n.a.	48	53	63	75	84	87	97	100	115	129	139	157	158	140	116	n.a.	n.a.
Manufacturing[c]	n.a.	n.a.	n.a.	74	82	79	85	100	99	100	100	107	113	118	132	124	110	99	n.a.	n.a.
Construction[c]	n.a.	n.a.	n.a.	64	81	95	104	110	108	112	100	97	93	85	85	90	85	74	n.a.	n.a.
Services[c]	n.a.	n.a.	n.a.	80	80	77	82	85	112	107	100	101	101	99	104	126	101	86	n.a.	n.a.
Ghana																				
Manufacturing	n.a.	n.a.	n.a.	n.a.	n.a.	n.a.	n.a.	n.a.	121	85	100	71	64	46	85	92	153	n.a.	n.a.	n.a.
Construction	n.a.	n.a.	n.a.	n.a.	n.a.	n.a.	n.a.	n.a.	115	91	100	65	54	61	67	188	175	n.a.	n.a.	n.a.
Services	n.a.	n.a.	n.a.	n.a.	n.a.	n.a.	n.a.	n.a.	116	92	100	57	49	36	55	70	131	n.a.	n.a.	n.a.
Kenya[b]																				
Manufacturing	n.a.	n.a.	n.a.	119	107	107	106	107	103	97	100	90	85	85	83	81	81	84	87	84
Construction	n.a.	n.a.	n.a.	93	93	93	95	92	97	90	100	92	69	69	68	66	64	71	66	67
Services	n.a.	n.a.	n.a.	99	99	88	96	90	87	93	100	90	79	79	84	83	86	91	88	90
Korea																				
Agriculture	50	61	64	68	73	76	81	89	93	99	100	107	114	120	138	146	n.a.	n.a.	n.a.	n.a.
Manufacturing	45	47	49	53	57	58	68	82	96	105	100	99	106	115	121	130	n.a.	n.a.	n.a.	n.a.
Rubber	80	77	76	82	86	71	86	91	93	97	100	92	93	92	91	91	95	99	n.a.	n.a.
Oil palm	64	61	63	66	73	73	76	80	88	96	100	107	103	101	106	110	111	108	n.a.	n.a.
Manufacturing	83	83	80	71	76	78	84	88	89	96	100	106	111	119	125	135	133	129	n.a.	n.a.
Construction	86	87	89	92	82	90	94	96	97	100	n.a.	112	122	126	126	128	129	124	n.a.	n.a.

n.a. = not available
* Break in series
a. March 1982 = 100.
b. Private sector only (separate series for public sector available).
c. Enterprises of 10 and more workers.
Note: Definitions of sectors may not be identical across countries.
Source: Country studies. Data for Bolivia and Chile are household surveys, the rest are employment and earnings surveys.

Table 1.7 Real Wage Indices by Tradable/Nontradable and Public/Private Sectors, 1970–89

Country/sector	1970	1971	1972	1973	1974	1975	1976	1977	1978	1979	1980	1981	1982	1983	1984	1985	1986	1987	1988	1989
Tradable and nontradable (ratio of average wages)																				
Argentina																				
Tradables/nontradables	0.89	0.91	0.91	0.88	0.93	0.92	0.93	0.94	0.91	0.93	0.89	0.91	0.91	0.95	0.96	0.97	0.96	n.a.	n.a.	n.a.
Potentially traded/nontradables	1.04	1.04	1.03	1.00	1.05	1.02	1.04	1.04	1.01	1.04	0.99	1.03	1.03	1.05	1.10	1.10	1.12	n.a.	n.a.	n.a.
Costa Rica*																				
Export/nontradables	n.a.	n.a.	n.a.	n.a.	n.a.	n.a.	0.92	0.93	0.87	0.68	0.83	0.83	0.91	0.97	n.a.	0.90	n.a.	0.75	0.78	n.a.
Imports/nontradables	n.a.	n.a.	n.a.	n.a.	n.a.	n.a.	0.98	1.01	1.09	1.05	0.96	1.10	0.98	1.05	n.a.	1.03	n.a.	0.96	1.00	n.a.
Public/nontradables	n.a.	n.a.	n.a.	n.a.	n.a.	n.a.	1.20	1.34	1.19	1.15	1.03	1.13	1.15	1.18	n.a.	1.08	n.a.	1.03	1.01	n.a.
Public and private (index, 1980 = 100)																				
Brazil																				
Private**	n.a.	n.a.	n.a.	n.a.	n.a.	n.a.	n.a.	n.a.	n.a.	n.a.	100	107	114	106	99	105	117	108	95	n.a.
Public	n.a.	n.a.	n.a.	n.a.	n.a.	n.a.	n.a.	n.a.	n.a.	n.a.	100	97	103	86	78	99	116	n.a.	n.a.	n.a.
Egypt																				
Private	n.a.	n.a.	n.a.	89	92	73	79	92	89	104	100	103	104	108	118	120	103	91	n.a.	n.a.
Public	n.a.	n.a.	n.a.	125	109	104	105	109	104	103	100	108	109	98	96	89	75	69	n.a.	n.a.
Public entities	n.a.	n.a.	n.a.	93	96	86	88	95	100	103	100	105	108	103	108	101	92	84	n.a.	n.a.
Ghana																				
Private	n.a.	n.a.	n.a.	n.a.	n.a.	n.a.	n.a.	n.a.	116	95	100	53	56	38	69	89	115	n.a.	n.a.	n.a.
Public	n.a.	n.a.	n.a.	n.a.	n.a.	n.a.	n.a.	n.a.	113	92	100	61	52	41	58	86	147	n.a.	n.a.	n.a.
Kenya																				
Private	n.a.	n.a.	n.a.	n.a.	88	86	89	87	90	91	100	90	81	79	80	78	79	82	84	85
Public	n.a.	n.a.	n.a.	n.a.	106	103	114	109	110	106	100	96	85	84	81	78	83	80	81	81
Costa Rica*																				
Private	n.a.	n.a.	n.a.	n.a.	n.a.	n.a.	n.a.	n.a.	n.a.	n.a.	100	82	63	79	n.a.	96	n.a.	108	105	n.a.
Public	n.a.	n.a.	n.a.	n.a.	n.a.	n.a.	n.a.	n.a.	n.a.	n.a.	100	94	71	91	n.a.	101	n.a.	115	106	n.a.

n.a. = not available
* Adjusted for human capital
** São Paulo
Source: Country studies.

sectors were unable to adjust employment. In Bolivia manufacturing wages did relatively badly, which is consistent with falling employment (table 1.5). In Chile manufacturing wages increased relative to average wages (table 1.6), again consistent with an increasing share of employment. In Malaysia manufacturing and construction wages tended to increase during the recession. The Argentina study found that relative wages had tended to increase in nontradables during 1940–62 (vol. II, chapter 1), but that the failed structural adjustment attempts since then had at least managed to arrest the trend. In Costa Rica relative wages in importables and nontradables fell during the 1980–82 recession, but recovered faster during the ensuing adjustment period, thus maintaining their relative position overall during the period (table 1.7).

Government wages (table 1.7) seem to have fallen universally during adjustment due to pressures on government expenditures (although some country study authors suggest that the trends were different in the central government and in the parastatals). This is documented in the Brazil, Costa Rica, Egypt, Ghana, and Kenya studies. The Bolivia study also provides evidence on falling relative wages in government, and the Malaysia study states that government wages rose less rapidly than in other sectors. The government sector generally consists of nontradables. Thus changes in sectoral wages seem to have generally supported structural adjustment aims, and also corroborate the trends in employment.

Six of the country studies also examine trends in the formal/informal wage differential. Here wage trends are likely to reflect not only goods prices, but also the effects of crowding discussed earlier. The country studies suggest that the patterns also depend on institutions in place in individual countries. For example, the formal sector is generally better able to protect itself during anticipated inflation, provided that institutional mechanisms provide full compensation for inflation. The informal sector, however, is less tightly bound by wage freezes, and in periods of unanticipated inflation informal wages are more closely tied to the goods market. In countries where the informal sector thrives because of distortions in the formal economy, Ghana, for example, structural adjustment may remove rents, and therefore benefit the formal sector.

Crowding seems to have been important in the early 1980s recession in Brazil, Chile, and Costa Rica, when the informal sector did relatively worse. In Korea also the formal/informal earnings gap widened during recessions, probably because of a composition effect (the formal sector shed the lower paid workers). However, in the Bolivian hyperinflation and during the Brazilian heterodox stabilization under the Cruzado Plan, where a price freeze was combined with strong demand, informal sector earnings improved relative to formal sector earnings. The Malaysian evidence is somewhat mixed, as men's and women's wages performed oppositely. The wages of self-employed men rose faster than employee wages during the whole period (partly explained by the increase in education of the self-employed). Employed women fared better during the boom, but then their wages fell relative to those of the self-employed during the recession (the Malaysian results are from earnings functions, not aggregate wages, unlike the results for the other countries). The author of the Malaysia study suggests that this indicates the existence of pockets of women employed in the informal sector that did not participate in the boom affecting the rest of the economy.

Finally, a couple of studies mention skill differentials. These narrowed during inflation and the first structural adjustment period in Chile (1970–76) and never recovered. In Egypt white collar/blue collar differentials narrowed throughout the oil boom and continued to narrow through the recession, perhaps due to slower growth in the public sector.

Some further information on earnings can be obtained from analyzing earnings functions (table 1.8). Altogether six of the case studies present earnings functions, of which four have separate functions for years before and after the onset of structural adjustment (Bolivia, Costa Rica, Kenya, and Malaysia). Two other African country studies present earnings functions for a single year (Côte d'Ivoire and Ghana), although the Ghana study divides the sample by length of job tenure, which is an ingenious way to get some information on changes in the labor market. Thus, in five cases (that is, all but the Côte d'Ivoire), one can get additional information on changes in sectoral, male/female, and formal/informal differentials purged of the effect of changes in human capital characteristics within sectors. Such a correction is important during a period of large structural change (see, for example, Lavy and Newman's 1989 work on the Côte d'Ivoire), or when participation rates change greatly.

The two Latin American countries exhibit changes in the earnings functions, both rather similar. The coefficient of determination (R^2) falls in both cases, and the size of the coefficients of characteristics associated with the formal sector declines, particularly in Bolivia (namely, the coefficients on education and experience, and for Bolivia being male, being married, and working in the formal sector). One possible explanation is that labor market institutions, and hence segmentation, were perhaps strongest in Latin America, and have weakened somewhat during adjustment (this was an explicit aim of Bolivia's adjustment program).

Earnings functions for the other countries also show changes consistent with adjustment: in Ghana the returns to urban location, working in the service sector, and being a union member declines, and the mining coefficient increases. Kenya is an exception. The authors argue that Kenyan labor markets did not adjust, and the coefficients on formal sector characteristics (age, being male, working in the formal sector, and working in Nairobi) increase.

For Ghana, earnings functions suggested a relatively well-working labor market, which complemented the findings from the few trend data available. Men's and women's hourly earnings were not too dissimilar (although total earnings differed), first and second jobs had similar hourly earnings (except in agriculture), and there was a premium for seasonal labor.

For the Côte d'Ivoire data were available for two consecutive years, including some repeated data on the same individuals. Participation and employment transition equations were estimated rather than earnings functions. The panel data showed that labor market transitions generally were toward sectors favored by adjustment, particularly agriculture, and that within manufacturing there was a shift toward the informal sector. As regards the probability of leaving employment, this was higher for women, lower for the services, higher for construction, and lower for the more educated. Likewise higher levels of education had a positive effect on the probability of entering

Table 1.8 Changes in Earnings Functions Over Time: Coefficients for Selected Independent Variables, Selected Years

				Independent variable				
Country	Year	Employment characteristic	Schooling	Experience	Experience²	Women (dummy)	Other variables included	R^2
Bolivia	1981		.122	.053	-.000640	-.327	unmarried, informal, 3 cities	.478
	1988		.0951	.0322	-.000308	-.234		.253
Côte d'Ivoire	1985		.207	.053	-.082	-.002	nationality, years technical educational	.585
Costa Rica	1980	paid workers	.1348	.0505	-.00063	.3318	n.a.	.472
		all workers	.1325	.0464	-.00055	-.3217	n.a.	.402
	1988	paid workers	.123	.03911	-.00045	-.1945	n.a.	.356
		all workers	.113	.03911	-.00045	-.1945	n.a.	.251
Ghana	1987–88	tenure > 5	.110[a]	.011	-.0001	-.268	region, sector, formal, urban, others	.278
		tenure < 5	.085[a]	.027	-.0003	.272		.281
Kenya[b]	1977–78		.0073 (.0033S^2)	.0759[c]	-.0008[c]	-.1188	occupation, city, age, education	.413
	1986		-.0222 (.0057S^2)	.0784[c]	-.0008[c]	-.1587		.537
Malaysia[c]	1970	Malay men	.142	.093	-.0012	n.a.	n.a.	.451
		Malay women	.147	.071	-.0011	n.a.	n.a.	.421
		Chinese men	.139	.110	-.001	n.a.	n.a.	.521
		Chinese women	.133	.680	-.0007	n.a.	n.a.	.437
	1987	Malay men	.171	.111	-.0014	n.a.	n.a.	.439
		Malay women	.196	.110	-.0016	n.a.	n.a.	.421
		Chinese men	.153	.098	-.0012	n.a.	n.a.	.437
		Chinese women	.152	.076	-.0009	n.a.	n.a.	.326

n.a. = not available
a. Secondary school dummy.
b. Urban only.
c. Age.
Sources: Country studies, except Côte d'Ivoire source is van der Gaag and Vijverberg (1989).

employment, in contrast to the results for Asia and Latin America, where structural adjustment often adversely affected earnings and unemployment for the educated. Unemployment could be relatively persistent: of those seeking employment in 1985, 81 percent were still unemployed in 1986, although 42 percent of the original group had stopped looking. Finally, the study had some interesting results on the effects of crop price indexes on work behavior in rural areas. Increases in these indexes had a positive effect on work supply both for those who were working and in school in the first of the two survey years, but a negative effect on work supply for those in full-time education in the first year. In other words, crop price increases could increase effort, but not at the expense of interrupting human capital acquisition, an interesting finding.

The use of earnings functions is obviously a useful direction for further work on labor markets and adjustment, and in this respect the technique of dividing the sample (as used in the Ghana study) seems a promising way of teasing out trends from a single cross-section of data, which might be particularly useful for African countries.

Labor Market Institutions

Two issues papers deal with labor market institutions, Devereux's on wage indexation (vol. 1, chapter 4) and Nelson's on political economy issues (vol. 1, chapter 7). The latter paper focuses on the effect of unionism, both private and public, on labor market flexibility. It also discusses economic and political factors that affect how militant or cooperative labor movements are likely to be.

Nelson argues the existence of theoretical reasons that explain why unions in developing countries might be more militant than in developed ones. The relationship between union organization and militancy is an inverted U-shape: weak unions exhibit a low level of militancy, and very strong centralized unions are also less militant as they can no longer consider only sectoral gains. Developing country unions fall in the middle, with some strongly organized sectors, but no strong central union body. Unions in most developing countries do not fit the corporatist model, where wage gains are traded off for better employment security and where labor may take account of the macro impact of sectoral wage demands. Another feature of unions in developing countries is the greater role of public sector unions due to the greater share of public sector employment in total formal employment. A feature of the public sector is the greater difficulty experienced in laying off workers and the large severance payments offered.

Economic factors may affect labor's intransigence: they tend to show more concern for wages during upswings and more concern for employment protection during downswings, although unions foreseeing times getting worse may try to grab what they can early in the downswing. Political factors also matter: authoritarian regimes tend to use coercion more than democratic regimes, with some exceptions on both sides. The stage of the electoral cycle matters, as does labor's role in the political and party process. Labor may be attached to one party in a polarized system, or have access to more than one party in a more open system, or be largely excluded from the political arena. Likewise the regime's degree of stability matters, with new democracies in particular being susceptible to the revolution of rising expectations. Nelson makes the important point that successful adjustment in the long run not only requires investor confidence in the government's long-run ability to fulfill its promises, but also the confidence of the labor movement. The degree of equity in a society may be an important ingredient in sustaining such confidence.

The Latin American country studies dwell at length on labor market institutions: unions, indexation, minimum wages, legislation on benefits and job security, and segmentation. For the African countries these institutions receive less coverage in the country studies, although they do exist. As the Kenya study shows, however, it is one thing for the institutions to exist, and another for them to be effective, and their force tends to be weakened by the highly elastic labor supply to urban areas in Africa. It is also likely that the much lower proportion of urbanization and of formal sector employment makes a difference. The Asian countries have some similar institutions (two-year wage contracts in Malaysia and the same kind of long-term contract/temporary labor division in Korea as in Brazil). However, the role of unions in Asia is clearly very different from their role in Latin America and Africa.

The five Latin American country studies provide an interesting contrast in terms of the alleged effect of labor market institutions in causing rigidities in the labor market. In three of the countries (Argentina, Brazil, and Costa Rica) the institutions remain strong despite the economic crisis, whereas in the other two (Bolivia and Chile) they have been substantially weakened and/or dismantled. Some of the country authors criticize these institutions. For Argentina and Brazil they argue that they impeded adjustment and labor market mobility, and in Chile they receive partial blame for the painful nature of the recession and ensuing high unemployment. At the same time the Bolivian and Costa Rican cases are interesting counterpoints. In Costa Rica labor institutions survived relatively unscathed, for example, over 500 minimum wages are legislated, and are generally enforced, which did not prevent moderate adjustment. In Bolivia much labor legislation was dismantled and large-scale labor shedding occurred without as yet strong recovery. To some extent it seems that labor market institutions are often a symptom of underlying political and economic difficulties, which make adjustment difficult, and the institutions are unfairly blamed for causing problems.

The Brazil study describes labor market institutions in some detail. Unions are very strong (in the form in which they reemerged during the democratization period from the late 1970s onward), and are linked to political parties along the lines of the corporatist state discussed by Nelson. They combine strong plant-level organization with a previously legislated strong centralized structure, which allows them to transmit bargains struck at the best organized plants to national level. Wage indexation is perhaps the most sophisticated in Latin America, with monthly adjustments. Job security legislation used to be an important hindrance to mobility, but the setting up in 1964 of a fund (to which employers contribute) to provide severance pay has eased the problem. Tradables predominantly hire formal sector (that is, signed contract), unionized workers, whereas nontradables hire all types of workers, formal and informal, unionized and nonunionized.

Argentina has many of the same institutions. The author links union strength to inward-oriented economic policy, since the oligopolistic nature of employers demands an equally centralized representation for labor. The author also mentions a compulsory wage policy, whereby bargains struck by the unions are obligatory for all firms, which he argues harmed small firms. One difference from the Brazil case is that the main exportable in Argentina is food, and unionization is therefore concentrated in nontradables or importables. This arguably has been a major hindrance in changing the relative price of tradables and nontradables.

One difference in Costa Rica is that although legislation is equally strong, unions are relatively weak, having been broken in an unsuccessful face-off with Standard Fruit in the 1970s. Wage indexation in Costa Rica, far from being an impediment to desirable relative price changes, is given much of the credit for allowing a real wage decline at a critical point following devaluation. Since indexation was imperfect, real wages fell, but by an apparently impartial mechanism. This tactic, however, can only be used infrequently, and Brazil, for example, is no longer able to make such gains from unanticipated inflation.

Two Latin American countries undertook major labor market reforms. Chile between 1973 and 1975 eliminated unions and job security and removed much of the force from minimum wages, benefits, and wage indexation mechanisms (the government actually cheated on the price index used for wage indexation). However, the author argues that lack of labor legislation during 1973–79 was detrimental to growth because employers feared that the law, once reinstated, would be unduly favorable to labor. Bolivia, the other Latin American severe adjustment case, likewise removed similar institutions, with the exception that wage indexation had never been particularly important and had not survived the hyperinflation as an institution. Job tenure was ended and job security reduced, thus allowing labor shedding. The government stepped out of previously centralized wage bargaining. In both Bolivia and Chile the public sector shed a substantial amount of labor, equal to 25 percent of Bolivia's public sector labor force and 3 percent of Chile's total labor force (the author does not specify as to whether total urban or total urban plus rural is meant).

Comparisons between the Latin American countries in terms of the success of adjustment are instructive. Contrasting, for example, the relatively successful adjustment in Costa Rica and the problematic one in Bolivia, evidently dismantling labor institutions is neither necessary (Costa Rica) nor sufficient (Bolivia) for successful adjustment. Another interesting comparison is between Brazil and Costa Rica. In Brazil large political-economic tensions exist, such that consensus over the division of output is lacking, which causes continual inflationary tendencies (tensions that similarly pushed Bolivia over the brink into hyperinflation). Although wage indexation has sometimes been blamed for perpetuating Brazil's inflation, it is more a symptom of the defensive ability of one of the groups engaged in underlying conflict. In Costa Rica, by contrast, a higher degree of social consensus allowed a union-backed president to undertake some of the painful initial steps toward successful adjustment, in which wage indexation actually helped the process.

The Asian countries also have institutional structures in the labor market. The Korean government has followed a highly interventionist policy with respect to unions. The right to strike was banned in 1971 and only recently reinstated, and unions need government permission to undertake collective bargaining. The author argues that wage and productivity trends and their consequent effect on unit costs has been crucial in Korea's export success. In this respect the government was heavily involved in ensuring that wages did not get ahead of productivity, and at the same time that workers did share in the fruits of higher productivity. Increasing union autonomy and increasing strikes in the late 1980s may herald a change in the so far virtuous productivity and wage nexus in Korea.

In Malaysia union power is similarly limited. The level of unionization is low, less than 25 percent in manufacturing, and unions are banned in some sectors. Paradoxically unions are strongest in the plantation sector, where wages stagnated in the 1980s. Malaysia has relatively long (three-year) wage contracts, which may have hindered adjustment. Unions in Thailand are also weak except in the public sector. In both Malaysia and Korea the importance of bonuses in earnings (around 30 percent of pay in Korea and 15 percent in Malaysia) has been argued to cause flexibility, since earnings and profits are related. Latin American countries also have bonuses, but less related to productivity and profits than to Christmas, seniority, and so on.

Although studies of Latin American countries frequently blame labor market segmentation (formal/informal) as a problem, some kinds of segmentation also exist in the Asian countries. In Korea labor is divided into permanent, temporary, and casual, and much labor market adjustment falls upon the casual and temporary workers, particularly women. Another type of segmentation between large and small firms is also quite marked in Korea, and small firms tend to pick up the slack during recessionary periods. Segmentation also seems to persist over time, although taking the form of a widening gap in the human capital levels of large as compared to small firms, rather than a widening of wage differentials.

Finally public sector employment and adjustment is a topic worthy of separate study in its own right. The growth of public sector employment as an initial response to economic crisis is mentioned in many of the studies (all of the Latin American studies, Egypt, and Malaysia). The eventual need to shed public sector labor was a difficult undertaking. Bolivia, Chile, Costa Rica, and Ghana have bitten the bullet, Argentina has been unable to; and in Egypt, Kenya, and Malaysia adjustment took the form of a substantial slowdown in government hiring. In the latter three countries one consequence discussed was a rise in educated unemployment, particularly of women in Egypt and Malaysia, where educated women have few private sector alternatives. The relative decline in public sector wages observed in almost all the countries reflects the greater difficulty of adjusting labor quantity in the public than the private sector.

Consequences of Labor Market Adjustment

Labor market adjustment has consequences for income distribution and poverty, and on long-run growth. The country study authors were asked to consider these, paying particular attention to the role of women in labor markets.

Income Distribution

As Addison and Demery show (vol. 1, chapter 3), theoretical discussion of the effects of adjustment on poverty yields ambiguous predictions. Their paper begins with the standard Salter-Swan account of expenditure reduction and expenditure switching, and works out wage and employment effects, assuming competitive labor markets. These wage and employment effects are then fed through a poverty index, but yield ambiguous predictions.

The rest of the paper examines how these effects are modified by the introduction of different labor market imperfections. The first case is where there exists an economywide "quantity rationing" framework, that is, unemployment can persist. In this case the discussion of poverty becomes more complicated, since one must consider poverty among those employed in tradables, those employed in nontradables, and those unemployed. In this case although a devaluation may increase poverty because it shifts workers to the tradable sector, where greater poverty is assumed, and because it lowers the real wage, it will decrease poverty because of the unemployment reduction. Thus, ambiguity in predictions persists, but of a different type than before.

The paper then moves on to discuss partial labor market imperfections, dividing the labor market into a formal and an informal sector. The analysis is similar to that by Edwards (1988) and Edwards and Edwards (vol. 1, chapter 2). The authors consider different types of wage inflexibility and trace out the consequences for sectoral employment, wages, and unemployment. These are again fed through a poverty index. Ambiguity is again the order of the day, although the analysis does illuminate the different components.

A third variant is where barriers exist to entry into the formal labor market. Here Addison and Demery (vol. 1, chapter 3) argue that an expenditure switching policy is quite likely to reduce poverty if barriers to entry into nontradables or tradables exist.

The fourth and final case is where labor market imperfections exist in both sectors, and the authors distinguish between unemployment and employment in informal tradables, formal tradables, informal nontradables, and formal nontradables. They follow through the real wage and labor allocation consequences of expenditure switching, and again feed them through the poverty index. They conclude that the effects of switching under these assumptions seem to be the most promising as far as poverty reduction is concerned.

Tracing the effect of adjustment on poverty and income distribution empirically is no easier than doing so theoretically.

Asking the counterfactual question as to what happened during adjustment as compared to what would have happened otherwise is difficult, as many countries were on unsustainable courses. The data available also affect the conclusions that one can reach. It is usually more difficult to obtain information on overall economywide changes in income distribution from nationwide income-expenditure surveys than to obtain results on the urban distribution of earned income from labor force surveys. However, if real wages fall by more than GDP and urban-rural differentials change, then the latter data only tell part of the story.

We focus here on relative earnings distribution. Several studies also document increases in poverty, unsurprising as a consequence of economic crisis. For Africa almost no time series data exist with which to make comparisons. The Kenya study does cite UNICEF's finding that the share of the bottom 10 percent declined. For Egypt no distribution data are available after 1981/82. Changes in urban-rural income differentials are of great interest in the case of Africa and are the focus of studies elsewhere (Jamal and Weeks 1987), but country studies here lacked the data to examine the issue.

In Latin America income distribution is a key issue related to the political economy of the economic growth process, and all the studies provided data. Brazil's income distribution has long been of interest given that inequality increased during the long boom "economic miracle" period between 1967 and 1974, when there was a type of structural adjustment as the economy became more open. Some improvement in income distribution is evident between 1974 and 1981, with a worsening during the recession and stabilization (1981–85), and since then a slight recovery. One interesting finding is that interregional equality increased during structural adjustment, which hit harder at the more affluent urbanized south than the more rural northeast.

For Chile the pattern was somewhat similar, but more exaggerated, with a sharp increase in 1974–76 accompanying the start of adjustment, the Gini remaining constant during 1976–79, increasing again in 1979–84, and since then decreasing slightly, but to a level much higher than at any time during 1960–74. It is not surprising that distribution worsened so much, given the massive cuts in real wages and the very high unemployment levels. The measured changes may be offset somewhat by changes in social expenditures. In Argentina income distribution also worsened during the stop-go cycles (although the only data available are for income earners in Buenos Aires during 1974–88). The top two deciles gained at the expense of all others.

For Bolivia and Costa Rica data are more scanty and knowing exactly what happened is harder. In Costa Rica inequality may have increased between 1971 and 1983 (before adjustment), but after the onset of adjustment different data sources give conflicting trends. For Bolivia the data are also not very good, but suggest a possible improvement between 1982–85, when informal sector wages rose relatively during the hyperinflation, but by 1988 distribution had reverted back to 1982 levels.

In Asia, income distribution may have improved in Malaysia and worsened in both Thailand and Korea. In Malaysia resources were put into agriculture, including food agriculture, whereas in Korea policy focused for at least some of the period on heavy industry, and in Thailand little was done about the problem of urban primacy (concentration in Bangkok).

Women and Labor Market Adjustment

Much of the literature on women and structural adjustment has concentrated on the effects of structural adjustment on women. Collier and others (vol. 1, chapter 6), using evidence from Africa, examine the opposite issue, namely, how women's economic mobility may affect the success of adjustment. They argue that women face constraints not only in the labor market and in access to education, but also in credit markets, which may affect adjustment. In particular, women in Africa are frequently concentrated in food production. The authors present three possible cases relevant to adjustment. Food may be a tradable, in which case its output should expand with adjustment; it may be a nontradable, in which case output should contract; or it might be nontradable in rural areas but tradable in urban areas, in which case food marketing (again frequently a female preserve, at least in West Africa) would need to expand. If food crops are to contract, this requires a reallocation of women's labor into other activities, and if they are to expand, this requires women's access to credit. In either case, constraints on women's flexibility will hinder the success of structural adjustment.

Collier and others therefore urge that government policies should focus on relaxing constraints to women's economic activities. Another reason cited in favor of this strategy is that it also improves household income security if higher women's incomes offset the loss of men's jobs in the formal or government sectors during adjustment, although they do not consider the potential costs involved, such as women's responsibilities for children.

The paper by Collier and others also discusses women in South Asia, again focusing on women as participants in, rather than victims of, structural adjustment. It deals with both rural and urban activities of women, and draws somewhat on the earlier experiences of women in export-oriented industries in East Asia. Bardhan sees structural adjustment as potentially altering the existing U-shaped pattern of female labor force participation with education: in South Asia women tend to participate either with very low education in menial and low-productivity activities, or in high-skilled, high-education activities. The author argues that adjustment may increase the demand for labor-intensive industry output, requiring women workers with medium education, with resulting beneficial effects on reduced fertility and increased incentives for female education. Adjustment may also involve costs for women, such as those where the male family members or the whole family migrate, and the costs imposed particularly on women's time when social infrastructure deteriorates. Like Collier, she sees a role for government in relaxing the constraints on women's activity. Labor market legislation aimed at protecting women has ended up tending to exclude them from the formal sector. Bardhan foresees benefits to women in selective deregulation of some sectors in India, such as electronics.

Another aspect of the paper by Collier and others focuses rather more on the effects of structural adjustment on women. In Latin America, studies on women seem to focus mainly on labor force participation, and little information is available on trends in relative earnings. Women's labor force participation has been increasing, partly due to sectoral shifts, in particular, increased employment in the service sector, but largely due to higher participation within sectors.

The participation increases vary somewhat across countries. The authors undertake econometric analysis for Chile, which suggests that unemployment that accompanies structural adjustment does not have differential effects on discouraging female and male labor force participation. One interesting avenue they suggest for future work is to examine how increased female participation fits in with the trend in much of Latin America toward increased informalization of the labor force.

The country studies concentrate more on the effects of structural adjustment on women. As Collier and others argue, the effects are likely to depend on the preceding sectoral distribution of women workers and on the effect on participation rates. However, the likelihood exists that women workers' more tenuous attachment to the labor force means that they are more likely to lose jobs during periods of labor shedding. The country studies do not give a single story, although there seems to be a lot of evidence of adverse impacts, but the data are not very complete. Even for the United States, where data are available, understanding how male/female wages, for example, had changed over time due to changes in female labor force participation was difficult. For the developing countries female labor force participation has exhibited trend changes plus cyclical responses due to crisis. Tracing the effects on women's welfare is even harder if most women live in households with men. Although the effects on female-headed households are less ambiguous to interpret from the data, this was a topic well beyond the scope of the country studies.

The Ghana study documents that women suffered rather more from structural adjustment than men as they were concentrated in the informal sector, which tended to absorb excess labor. Women are also predominantly in food crop agriculture, whereas resources have gone instead to cash crops. In Côte d'Ivoire, insofar as education had a positive effect on the probability of remaining in employment or of entering employment, and women tend to have less education, they are likely to have faced disadvantages. The Egypt study documents an adverse effect on women due to the lengthening queue for government employment, and the more limited private sector alternatives available to women.

In Bolivia the male/female differential fell between 1981 and 1987 as measured from earnings functions, although aggregate data suggest the opposite (the difference is perhaps explained by changes in participation rates). Although anecdotal evidence suggested that labor shedding from the formal sector was to the detriment of women, who are more costly workers in terms of benefits, this may have been offset by much of the employment loss being focused in mining, a male-dominated sector. In Costa Rica the male/female earnings differential increased during the crisis and decreased thereafter, which the authors attribute to rising female participation during the crisis (added worker effect), where the female entrants were less well qualified. In both Bolivia and Chile the emergency employment schemes explicitly targeted male workers, at least initially, and in Chile public sector hiring in the early part of the crisis also favored men.

In Malaysia some evidence suggests that women lost ground during the recession due to the firing of labor in a weaker position in the labor market; however, a trend increase in female wages is evident over the 1970s and 1980s. The relative earnings of Malay women in particular increased between 1970 and 1984, and the returns to female education and experience rose absolutely and relative to the same returns for men. However, these gains were all reversed in the 1984–87 recession. Nevertheless, Malaysia differs from some of the other countries studied in that women are a higher proportion of wage employment than of self-employment, and are concentrated in some export industries, such as electronics. In Korea women are at a disadvantage, crowded into low paying, white collar sectors, and providing a disproportionately high share of family workers, the most disadvantaged group in the labor force. Female participation rates are also surprisingly low in Korea compared to other East and Southeast Asian countries. Women also tended to lose out in the recession. Whereas male employment shifted continuously toward the permanent category, this proportion declined for women during the recession.

Effects on Long-Run Growth

Most of the issues papers focus on demand side effects of adjustment and the labor market. Buffie's (vol. 1, chapter 5), by contrast, highlights the supply side consequences of fiscal contraction, and hence the impacts on long-run growth. Demand side complications are abstracted from by assuming that the economy is small and open. Two traded goods, agricultural exports and manufactures, are produced using labor and capital. Manufacturing also requires an intermediate input, which is supplied by the public sector. Labor employed in the public sector and in manufacturing is paid a higher than competitive wage, and the rest of the labor is underemployed in agriculture. Buffie assumes a fixed wage differential between the modern and the informal/agricultural sectors. Capital accumulation dynamics are also modeled.

Human capital is modeled by distinguishing between skilled and unskilled labor. Skilled labor growth is determined by human capital investment by the government. If factors are complementary, then the productivity of unskilled labor declines when investment is cut, as does the productivity of capital. Overall, Buffie shows that disinvestment in human capital leads to capital decumulation. The paper suggests two broad policy lessons. First, productive government investments in human capital should be protected, which requires broadening the tax base. Second, a more gradual approach to adjustment is likely to entail fewer adverse impacts on productive investments vital for long-run growth.

To some extent the topic of adjustment and long-run growth is a difficult one to study empirically, since many countries are still grappling with short- and medium-term issues, but some of the studies provide information on investment, in particular, human capital investment, as discussed by Buffie. The Kenya and Côte d'Ivoire studies discuss falling investment, but do not blame labor markets. The Argentina study throws the blame for stop-go cycles onto the labor market's inability to allow prices of tradables to rise relatively in a sustained way, thereby harming long-run growth. Similarly, in Chile a lack of labor legislation and fears of a return to previous laws that favored labor are assigned the blame for lack of investment.

As regards human capital investments, the Costa Rica study documents a sharp drop in school enrollment during the crisis, especially at the secondary and technical levels, with likely adverse effects on growth and distribution. By contrast, no such effect was predicted from cross-section regressions for the Côte d'Ivoire. In Asia where short-run problems of adjustment have been largely solved, the studies had more room to focus on long-run issues. The Malaysia and Korea studies examine changing returns to education, and the Thai study examines potential labor market skill mismatch issues.

Conclusion

This overview has summarized theoretical predictions and country study experience on two important topics related to labor markets and adjustment. First, how well have labor markets functioned, and have they assisted or impeded macro adjustment efforts? Second, what were the effects of some of these adjustments on the labor market?

With respect to the issue of labor market functioning, labor markets have at least three allocative functions: they match workers to employment in such a way that overall unemployment levels and real wages matter; they allocate workers between sectors, and match worker skills to job requirements so that relative wages and employment matter, both for economic sectors and for skill categories; and they provide incentives for intertemporal allocation of resources, specifically for human capital accumulation in education and firm-specific training. Applying these three criteria to the often descriptive country studies to assess how well or how badly labor markets performed is not easy. By and large individual country authors argue that the labor markets performed well, although authors of the studies for the big three Latin American countries, Argentina, Brazil, and Chile, were more critical.

Theory suggests that labor market rigidities are only one of three possible reasons for unemployment. With the exception of Chile, the countries have not had prolonged unemployment despite severe recession, however, cyclical increases have occurred. This fits with the presumption that in developing countries without unemployment insurance schemes, unemployment is not an option for primary household earners unless the household is unusually wealthy. The evidence on real wages casts considerable doubt on theoretical concerns about aggregate real wage rigidity and labor market inflexibility as a hindrance to adjustment. Real wage declines have been dramatic, and often far greater than the fall in GDP. For some countries the real wage declines may have been excessively large and led to a fall in domestic demand, which inhibited recovery.

With regard to the sectoral employment shifts, these have generally been in the desired direction, that is, toward tradables, although this has generally meant that agricultural employment has increased relatively and manufacturing employment declined in all but the most successful countries. Shifts of employment into services and commerce are, however, indicative of weak GDP growth, and hence growth of labor demand. Sectoral wage changes have also been largely in the appropriate direction, although little information is available on agricultural wages. The decline in relative government wages is one factor causing relative wages in nontradables to decline.

Finally, on the intertemporal aspect, the evidence is a little more mixed. In Costa Rica the evidence showed that the recession had induced decreases in school enrollment, whereas in Côte d'Ivoire econometric results suggested that increases in crop prices, which would help adjustment, would not lead to parents pulling their children out of school. Earnings functions for Bolivia, Costa Rica, and Malaysia showed that returns to all formal sector characteristics including education and experience declined during adjustment, and in that government relative wages declined universally, and government tends predominantly to hire the more educated, this would decrease the incentives to acquire schooling. The country studies did not discuss another human capital issue, namely international migration, although for at least three of the countries— Côte d'Ivoire, Egypt, and Ghana—this was important.

The country studies also explicitly discussed labor market institutions, thought to be a source of rigidity. One possible interpretation is that where these institutions lack binding force, whether because of elastic labor supply (Africa) or weak unions (Asia and perhaps Costa Rica), they were not perceived as obstacles to adjustment. Nevertheless, dismantling of the institutions and weakening of the unions as in Bolivia does not seem to be sufficient to ensure recovery, in that country imperfections in the functioning of the capital market seem to bear at least part of the responsibility for poor growth. The authors also argued here that labor market institutions in Latin America often receive the blame, whereas they are only the symptoms of underlying political economy problems detrimental to growth.

Turning now to the second broad topic, the outcomes of labor market adjustment, the authors had some difficulties in separating how far outcomes were due to structural adjustment, how far due to recession, and how far due to pre-existing trends. Severe adjustment, as in the case of Chile with high unemployment and sharp falls in real wages in an economy where urban employment predominates, can be very adverse to income distribution. Perhaps Brazil's worsening during the 1964–79 structural change period has some parallels, as does Korea's heavy industry phase. That is, unless countries make explicit provision for poorer groups, for example, the emphasis on food crop agriculture in Malaysia, structural change can worsen income distribution, although some of the changes, such as improved rural-urban relative income and possible improvement in informal/formal relative income, might militate in the opposite direction. Country-specific factors—success of indexation, wage and price freezes—also affect distribution. The effects on distribution also depend on the level of the GDP. No data are available for Africa to test this hypothesis, but it seems plausible that improving rural-urban terms of trade and abolishing rents from price distortions as part of adjustment programs could improve income distribution nationally.

The effects on women might be somewhat country specific, depending whether women were in tradables or not, but women are likely to face adverse effects of the employment shrinkages in some sectors due to their weaker attachment to the labor market. The country studies generally confirmed this. Finally, the effects on long-term growth were adverse, but not directly attributable to labor market malfunctioning.

Where should one go from here? One issue is that the apparently benign conclusion that labor shifted into tradables masks that in response to structural adjustment, labor has moved in the direction opposite to that usually associated with economic development. Labor has shifted back into agriculture, out of manufacturing, and out of the public sector, although one might argue that this latter sector was too large given the level of development reached. Recession plus adjustment has also resulted in an increase in informalization, increased use of casual labor, decreased worker benefits, and declines in skill and possibly education differentials. These trends are observed even in the most successful adjustment cases in Asia. Developing countries have long resisted being relegated to the role of primary producers in the international economic order, and it is unlikely that structural adjustment entailing further shifts of labor into agriculture would be highly sustainable.

As regards possible further research, country study and some issues paper authors pointed the finger of blame for adjustment problems onto the capital market and possible price rigidities in the output market. Another possibly fruitful topic is that of the role of labor market institutions, unions, and the political economy; something worth examining before launching into a wholesale advocacy of dismantling such institutions. Finally, as in all empirical research, better data are needed. One useful step would be to improve international collation of labor force statistics, clearly separating the results from household surveys from those of establishment surveys. Another would be to encourage further analysis of, and increased accessibility to, labor force surveys, which tend to be more expensive to analyze, but arguably yield more reliable results.

References

Dutt, A. K. 1984. "Stagnation, Income Distribution and Monopoly Power." *Cambridge Journal of Economics* 8(1): 25–40.

Edwards, S. 1988. "Terms of Trade, Tariffs and the Labor Market Adjustment in Developing Countries." *World Bank Economic Review* 2(2): 165–185.

Fallon, P. R., and L. A. Riveros. 1988. "Macroeconomic Adjustment and Labor Market Response: A Review of the Recent Experience in LDCs." Washington, D.C.: World Bank. Draft, processed.

Fields, G. 1990. "Labor Market Policy and Structural Adjustment in Côte d'Ivoire." Ithaca, New York: Cornell University. Draft.

Ghai, D. 1987. *Economic Growth, Structural Change and Labor Absorption in Africa: 1960–85*. Discussion Paper No. 1.

Geneva: United Nations Research Institute for Social Development.

Horton, S., R. Kanbur, and D. Mazumdar. 1988. "Labor Markets in an Era of Adjustment: A Project Proposal." Washington, D.C.: World Bank, Economic Development Institute. Processed.

ILO (International Labour Organisation). 1987. *World Recession and Global Interdependence: Effects on Employment, Poverty and Policy Formation in Developing Countries.* Geneva: ILO World Employment Program.

_____. Various years. *Yearbook of Labour Statistics.* Geneva: ILO.

_____. 1989. *Yearbook of Labour Statistics.* Geneva: ILO.

Jamal, V., and J. Weeks. 1987. *Rural-Urban Income Trends in Sub-Saharan Africa.* World Employment Programme Labor Market Analysis and Employment Planning Working Paper No. 18 (WEP 2–43/WP.18). Geneva: ILO

JASPA (Jobs and Skills Program for Africa). 1988. *Africa Employment Report 1988.* Addis Ababa: ILO.

Johnson, O. E. G. 1986. "Labor Markets, External Developments, and Unemployment in Developing Countries." Washington, D.C.: IMF Staff Studies for the *World Economic Outlook.*

Lavy, V., and J. Newman. 1989. "Wage Rigidity: Micro Evidence on Labor Market Adjustment in the Modern Sector." *World Bank Economic Review* 1(1): 97–117.

Lindauer, D. L., O. A. Meesook, and P. Suebsaeng. 1988. "Government Wage Policy in Africa: Some Findings and Policy Issues." *World Bank Research Observer* 3(1): 1–26.

Ramos, J. R. 1980. "The Economics of Hyperstagflation: Stabilization Policy in Post 1973 Chile." *Journal of Development Economics* 7(4): 467–88.

Riveros, L. 1989. "Recession, Adjustment and the Performance of Urban Labor Markets in Latin America." Washington, D.C.: World Bank. Processed.

Taylor, L. 1988. *Varieties of Stabilization Experiences Towards Sensible Macroeconomics in the Third World.* Oxford, U.K.: Clarendon Press.

Tokman, V. E. 1984. "The Employment Crisis in Latin America." *International Labor Review* 123.

van der Gaag and Vijverberg. 1989. "Wage Determinants in Côte d'Ivoire: Experience, Credentials, and Human Capital." *Economic Development and Cultural Change* 37: 371–381.

Wong, P. K. 1985. "Economic Development and Labor Market Changes in Peninsular Malaysia." Working Paper No. 12. Kuala Lumpur and Canberra. ASEAN-Australia Joint Research Project.

2

ARGENTINA

Luis A. Riveros
Carlos E. Sánchez

Poor growth and macroeconomic imbalances have characterized Argentina's recent history. In combination with long-run stagnation, the country has suffered chronic high inflation and deep cyclical fluctuations compounded by intractable balance of payment crises. Attempts to stabilize the economy and achieve a structural adjustment to restore sustained growth and basic balances have failed due to both a fragile political climate and inconsistent policies. The lack of adjustment has also been partly due to anticipated negative short-run labor market outcomes. In turn, the existence of persistent economic imbalances over the long run has negatively affected wages, employment, and income distribution.

This chapter analyzes the performance of Argentina's labor markets in recent years. It points out both how poor economic performance has affected labor market outcomes and how anticipated short-run costs have hindered reform efforts.

Long-Term Economic Trends and Short-Term Adjustment Policies

Global economic trends in Argentina have produced contradictory quantitative results and forced growing state intervention in the labor market.

The authors gratefully acknowledge comments on earlier drafts by M. Faig, R. Newfarmer, S. Horton, R. Paredes and seminar participants at the World Bank, the University of Chile, and the University of Warwick, as well as the efficient research assistance of O. Giordano.

Macroeconomic Policies, Economic Organization, and Growth

An understanding of the trade and macroeconomic policies Argentina followed after the Great Depression helps explain the country's poor economic performance. During 1860–1929, the government pursued an export-led growth strategy, which included almost free trade and appropriation of the benefits of trade according to the country's comparative advantages. After the Great Depression, the government adopted an import substitution strategy. After 1945, government policies aimed at expanding domestic markets through overvalued exchange rates and high import tariffs, which distorted resource allocation and thwarted exports over the long-run. The economic results of the inward-oriented policies were poorer than those under the export-led strategy (table 2.1).

Macroeconomic policies that affect variables such as the share of government consumption, public debt, and the money stock in total income, as well as commercial (export taxes and import controls) and exchange rate policies, were mostly responsible during the 1950s for the increase in the effective exchange rate for imports relative to that for exports. The resulting price increase of import goods made import substitution activities relatively more attractive for investment decisions, thereby prompting an inefficient specialization of production. Macroeconomic policies also affected the relative prices of productive

Table 2.1 Strategies and Growth
(real growth in per capita GDP)

Strategy	Years	Growth (percent)
Export-led strategy	1900–29	1.5
Inward-oriented strategy	1929–58	0.9
	1958–87	0.7
(Entire period)	1900–87	1.0

Source: IEERAL data base.

factors, resulting in a distorted capital/labor mix in production that affected resource allocation at the sectoral and regional levels (see Cavallo 1986; Cavallo and Cottani 1986; Cavallo and Domenech 1988; Cavallo and Mundlak 1982; Nogues 1981; Sánchez 1987).

The Argentinian economy can be divided into three sectors: a rural sector and two urban sectors (Llach and Sánchez 1984). The rural sector is a net exporter of wage-goods, mainly agricultural. Therefore, real wages are inversely related to the incentives to produce exportable goods for a given exchange rate. The two urban sectors are net importers. They consist of an import substituting sector (which under the prevailing inward-oriented strategy is both a marginal exporter and a net importer of inputs and capital goods), and a sector producing nontradables.

This economic structure led to a tradeoff between the trade balance situation and the prospects for domestic growth. Long-term economic growth requires a stable, high real exchange rate, but a high exchange rate implies higher food prices, and thus lower urban real wages. Since the level of urban real wages have traditionally been a key political variable, the government has tended to hold down incentives to export. Thus, due to a deliberate policy of overvalued exchange rates (that is, a policy mix aimed at yielding high real wages in combination with low real exchange rates), relative prices attained two simultaneous roles: a mechanism for resource allocation and a distributive device. This led to contradictory economic targets in a long-term context: inefficient organization of production or improved well-being of urban workers; a conflict generally resolved in favor of the latter.

A deliberate policy of overvalued exchange rates was the usual mechanism the government used to enlarge domestic markets, and therefore to increase real GDP and real wages in the short run. As soon as the growth in foreign terms of trade began to decline, a balance of payments crisis arose, which made a devaluation and a decline in wages unavoidable. Thus, in the context of a deliberate policy of overvaluation, FTT can be seen as a determinant of the real exchange rate (figure 2.1).[1] As a result of this policy, Argentina's economic

---

1. Cavallo and Domenech (1988) have modeled the behavior of the real exchange rate depending on the foreign terms of trade, taxes on imports and exports, the income level, and macroeconomic policy.

Figure 2.1 Real Exchange Rate, Foreign Terms of Trade, 1962–87 *(index, 1970 = 100)*

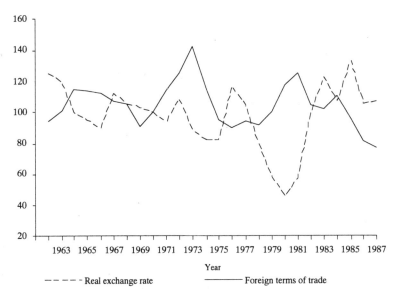

Source: Institute of Economic Studies of Argentina (IEERAL).

history in recent decades can be described as a series of redistributive periods (domestic currency overvaluation as well as increased activity and real wages) followed by periods of stabilization (devaluation and reductions in the levels of activity and real wages).

Political and Economic Developments of the 1970s

Argentina experienced crucial political and economic changes during the second half of the 1970s. The years 1963–73 had seen unusually high growth rates of per capita GDP, which averaged 3.9 percent per annum. However, this growth was not a result of specific domestic policies, but of favorable foreign terms of trade, especially during 1964–66 and 1971–73. Nonetheless, this economic growth allowed for policies aimed at overvaluing the real exchange rate and at increasing both the domestic absorption of goods and real wages (table 2.2, figures 2.2 and 2.3). The new (Peronist) administration that took over in 1973 inherited the combination of a satisfactory economic performance with persistent imbalances associated with the economy's structural organization.

Table 2.2 Economic Indicators, 1963–87
(index, 1970 = 100)

Year	Foreign terms of trade	Real exchange rate	Per capita GDP	Real wages
1962	94	125	78	83
1963	101	120	75	81
1964	115	100	81	92
1965	114	95	87	98
1966	112	90	87	98
1967	107	112	88	96
1968	106	106	90	91
1969	101	103	96	96
1970	100	100	100	100
1971	114	94	103	104
1972	125	109	105	98
1973	142	88	109	107
1974	114	82	114	120
1975	95	82	111	115
1976	90	117	109	74
1977	94	105	114	69
1978	92	80	107	72
1979	100	58	113	80
1980	117	46	113	93
1981	125	57	104	85
1982	105	100	97	74
1983	102	122	98	90
1984	111	107	99	99
1985	95	128	93	81
1986	81	102	96	76
1987	70	105	97	66
1988	82	107	93	63
1989	88	123	87	50

Source: IEERAL data base.

Figure 2.2 Real Wages and Per Capita GDP, 1962–87
(index, 1970 = 100)

Source: IEERAL.

Figure 2.3 Foreign Terms of Trade and Real Wages, 1962–87
(index, 1970 = 100)

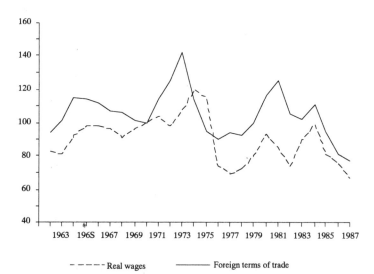

Source: IEERAL.

The foreign terms of trade were still changing favorably in 1973–74, and the Peronist administration continued to use redistributionist policies. Achievement of increasing real per capita GDP and real wages at the cost of deteriorating real exchange rates was still feasible. However, the increase in oil prices and the ensuing global recession revealed the fragility of this policy. Imported inflation and a sharp decline in foreign terms of trade in 1975 made it virtually impossible to maintain an overvalued domestic currency without creating a sharp external deficit. When the military overthrew the Peronist government in 1976, it inherited an acute balance of payments crisis and a huge fiscal deficit of more than 13 percent of GDP.

The military government's objective was to reduce inflation drastically and to initiate a longer-term strategy that would encourage sustained growth and full employment. A central part of that strategy was a two-stage trade reform in 1976–81. During the first stage (1976–78), the government introduced an unannounced tariff cut, eliminated export taxes, and replaced quotas with tariffs for all commodities except steel and aluminum. During the second stage (1979–81), the government implemented a preannounced schedule of quarterly tariff reductions. Even though the program was supposed to have continued until January 1984, trade reforms were reversed in 1981 due to a sharp balance of payments crisis.

Completion of the trade liberalization was jeopardized not only by the excessive gradualism used in the second stage, but also because a uniform tariff was not the final objective. Strikingly, the final result on overall nominal protection—including tariff and nontariff barriers—was contradictory: in 1979–80 the unweighted average nominal tariff rate decreased slightly from 51.9 to 49.2 percent, but its dispersion increased greatly (Cavallo and Cottani 1986).

Another problem with the trade liberalization program was the use of an accompanying inconsistent mix of fiscal/monetary and exchange rate policies. In 1979 and 1980, the government's use of an active crawl reduction scheme based on a preannounced schedule of future devaluations resulted in a severe overvaluation. Although tax collection increased, the fiscal policy produced a large budget deficit because of the increase in both current spending and public investment. Thus, the overall deficit rose from 13 percent of GDP in 1976 to 16 percent in 1981 and 17 percent in 1982. Since a basic aim of the macro policy was to curb inflation, the government reduced the monetary financing of the deficit and began to rely heavily on domestic and external borrowing, thereby pushing up market interest rates and significantly increasing the public external debt. The persistence of a large fiscal imbalance in combination with a severe overvaluation produced disequilibrium in the balance of payments accompanied by high real interest rates and low employment, production, and investment.

The economic policy of the late 1970s did not improve the prevailing domestic imbalances. Although stabilization reduced annual inflation of the consumer price index from a peak of 441 percent in 1976 to 101 percent in 1980, inflation remained high: in 1981 it was still 104 percent per annum. Likewise, the active crawl reduction scheme implemented after 1978 and the external financing of the government's excess demand caused the real exchange rate to appreciate: taking 1976 as a base year, its level was 39 in 1980 and 49 in 1981.

The financial policies used after 1978 also resulted in volatile real interest rates. In January 1979, the government implemented its previously announced nominal devaluations and eliminated most restrictions on capital mobility. During the first eight months of 1979, when the policy still had some credibility, real interest rates were low, but reached negative values at times. Later on, uncertainty increased and risk premiums became high, which raised real interest rates from 2 to 6 percent per month. The increased uncertainty observed in 1980–81 was closely related to both the existing gap between inflation and the rate of devaluation (in 1980 inflation was 17 percent while the rate of devaluation was only 6 percent) and to observed changes in external accounts (table 2.3).

The long-term structural adjustment program was barely implemented, and its final result was a shift in incentives in favor of nontradable activities. The short-term stabilization program failed: in the presence of a persistent budget deficit, financing via capital markets (which replaced simple money creation) produced a crowding out effect and was strongly deflationary (Mann and Sánchez 1984, 1985). Table 2.2 also shows the significant variability in real output between

Table 2.3 Selected External Accounts, 1980–84
(US$ millions)

Account	1980	1981	1982	1983	1984
Exports	8,021	9,143	7,623	7,838	8,100
Imports	10,540	9,430	5,336	4,505	4,600
Trade balance	-2,519	-287	2,286	3,331	3,500
Interest payments	956	2,925	4,400	4,983	5,273
Current account balance	-4,769	-4,714	-2,357	-2,461	-2,492

Source: Cavallo (1986, table 1).

1975 and 1980, before the economy moved into another recession in 1981.

The Crisis of the 1980s

In 1981, new economic authorities had to address the external and internal imbalances that had resulted from overvaluation and the fiscal/monetary mismanagement. The authorities instituted a drastic program of exchange rate devaluations to deal with the most urgent policy problem. From 1981 to 1983, the real exchange rate depreciated by 115 percent. In 1981 and 1982, years of macroeconomic adjustment, the real exchange rate depreciated sharply and both the real per capita GDP and real wages experienced large reductions (table 2.2). The current account deficit in 1982 was substantially smaller than that observed in 1980 and 1981 (table 2.3), thus many policymakers probably believed that further adjustment was not necessary, and opted for a new shift in policies during 1983 and 1984.

During 1983, the last year of the military government, policies were aimed at recovering real wages, thereby reinstating the deliberate policy of overvalued exchange rates. As a result, real wages rose 22 percent in 1983, while the wage/exchange rate ratio increased over 40 percent. The overvaluation was accompanied by active fiscal policies and a resurgence of inflation. Long-term adjustment was abandoned and traditional populist policies returned to guide policymaking.

A civilian administration (the Radical Party) took office in December 1983. This government inherited a very weak economic situation and vast public expectations of improved social welfare resulting from the restoration of democratic institutions. Activity levels and wages continued to grow in 1984 accompanied by a high fiscal deficit, growing inflation, low public utility rates, and exchange rate overvaluation (table 2.2 shows that the real exchange rate declined 13 percent between 1983 and 1984, while real wages increased 10 percent).

At the end of 1984, the government signed an agreement with the International Monetary Fund (IMF) that initiated an external sector adjustment based on demand reduction. During the last quarter of 1984 and the first half of 1985, the economy suffered a drop in real wages and activity levels, a depreciation of the exchange rate, and rising inflation. In June 1985, after sharp increases in public utility rates and a drastic devaluation, the government introduced the Austral Plan, which contained both heterodox and orthodox measures to curb inflation. The former included a wage and price freeze and a deindexation of debt. The latter included long-term measures, such as a high exchange rate and fiscal restraint.

Inflation declined rapidly in 1985 due to price and wage controls. However, since the fiscal problem remained unsolved, monetary policy continued to play an active role. At first, the demand for money increased substantially, but then inflation returned because of perceptions that the program was unsustainable. In August 1986 and February 1987, the government made two other attempts to reduce inflation by means of a tight monetary policy and control on wages and prices. However, inflation remained high because its primary source—lack of fiscal discipline—was not eliminated. In addition, in August 1986 a period of overvaluation began: The real exchange rate averaged 113 (index, December 1976 = 100) during the first seven months of 1986 and then dropped to 106 during August 1986 to August 1987.

A Frustrated Process of Adjustment (1987–88)

During September and October 1987 the government began to implement some new policies that were much more in line with a program of structural adjustment. However, no positive result has been yet observed and no structural adjustment has taken place. The relevant question is why a government politically committed to structural adjustment ended up with quite different results. The period 1987–88 can be divided into two phases. During the first one, from September 1987 to July 1988, the government implemented a devaluation followed by a crawling peg adjustment of the exchange rate. During the second one, after July 1988, the real exchange rate again appreciated significantly.

During the first phase, the wholesale prices of nonagricultural (essentially tradable) goods experienced significant increases with respect to private services and construction (49 and 15 percent, respectively). Cereal and oilseed prices increased 84 percent with respect to private services with the help of the increase in international grain prices. These figures give some idea of the improvement in the relative price of tradables versus nontradables. During this phase, the exchange rate policy provided substantial incentives to the tradable sector (table 2.4). As a result, export activities expanded and a reallocation of resources towards export-oriented activities began. The effects of this policy on the volume of exports and the trade surplus were significant: in 1988, exports increased 43.6 percent and the trade surplus increased 607.0 percent. In the specific case of manufacturing—a potentially exportable sector in Argentina—the change in relative prices (wages, exchange rate, and domestic terms of trade) led to a pattern of increasing profits and remarkable export growth.

Inflation accelerated, mainly due to the failure to reduce the fiscal deficit. After falling from 25 percent per month in October 1987 to 3 percent per month in December, the inflation rate climbed to over 20 percent per month in July 1988. At the time it imposed price and exchange controls, the government announced long-term measures aimed at shifting resources to tradable activities, improving the x-effi-

Table 2.4 Changes in Relative Prices, June 1985–October 1988
(percent)

Ratios	June 1985– Aug. 1987	Aug. 1986– Aug. 1987	Sept. 1987– July 1988	July 1988– Oct. 1988
Versus private services:				
Exchange rate	-40.1	-5.2	25.0	-12.7
Nonagricultural WPI	-44.7	-8.9	49.0	-0.5
Cereals-oilseeds	-37.6	11.0	84.0	-21.8
Versus construction cost:				
Nonagricultural WPI	-7.2	1.0	15.1	-4.2

Note: WPI = wholesale price index.
Source: Institute of Economic Studies on Argentina (IEERAL).

ciency of the public sector, and freeing up rigidities in factor and output markets.

During the second phase—after July 1988—real wages in manufacturing increased and profits began to decline (table 2.5 and figure 2.4). Table 2.4 also indicates that nonagricultural wholesale prices (that is, mainly manufacturing prices) deteriorated compared to private services (-0.5 percent), and construction (-4.2 percent). In other words, the domestic terms of trade turned in favor of nontradables. Since the increase in wages and in the price of nontradables was accompanied by overvaluation and elimination of import restrictions, the manufacturing sector faced falling profit margins and lower domestic market shares. The poor timing and lack of coordination between short-term and long-term economic policies hindered the achievement of structural adjustment.

Table 2.5 Manufacturing Wage, Exchange Rate, and Product Wage, 1987 and 1988
(index, 1988 3rd quarter = 100)

Year	Quarter	Wage/ exchange rate[a]	Product- wage/ gains[b]	Year	Quarter	Wage/ exchange rate[a]	Product- wage/ gains[b]
1987	1	*	*	1989	1	116	115
	2	*	*		2	43	78
	3	121	125		3	47	56
	4	111	116		4	74	86
1988	1	114	125	1990	1	70	81
	2	109	109		2	111	101
	3	100	100		3	177	111
	4	102	116		4	207	133

* not calculated for this study
a. Manufacturing nominal hourly wage divided into the exchange rate at which imports are traded.
b. Ratio of wage cost (ratio between the nominal hourly wage paid in manufacturing and the corresponding wholesale product price) to productivity (output per manhour).
Source: IEERAL data base.

Figure 2.4 Real Wage and Product Wage in Manufacturing
(index, 1988 3rd quarter = 100)

Source: IEERAL.

The Structure and Trends of Labor Markets

The performance of labor markets has reflected overall economic trends, which have produced low wage growth over the long run, as well as reduced employment growth in the private sector.

Observed Trends in Real Wages

Observed labor market results are paramount in analyzing Argentina's import substitution policy. The driving force behind labor markets was a wage setting mechanism based on a deliberate policy of overvalued exchange rates, restricted by the trade balance/domestic growth tradeoff. The basic policy tool was government intervention supported by urban-based unions and political groups. The main observed outcomes were a slight growth in real wages over the long run, significant short-run economic fluctuations, and distorted relative wages among productive sectors.

Between 1940 and 1985, real wages neither rose nor fell for more than three consecutive years. In all but one case (1969–71), periods of growth in real wages were followed by periods of sustained decline. By 1985, real wages were only 61 percent higher than in 1940, implying an average yearly growth rate slightly higher than 1 percent (Riveros 1989; Sánchez 1987). If the shorter period 1962–87 is considered, the evidence more than confirms the wage deterioration over time (see table 2.2 and figure 2.2). After growth during 1962–74, real wages declined much more than real per capita GDP. In addition, the magnitude of short-term fluctuations increased. For instance, in 1962–74 real wages rose at a yearly rate of 3.1 percent, only to drop subsequently at an even higher rate (-4.4 percent). During the whole period 1962–87, real wages fell by an average of 0.8 percent per year.

The observed trend in relative wages between tradable and nontradable sectors is an outcome of the inward-oriented growth strategy. Domestic market-oriented growth required relative prices favorable to urban activities and high purchasing power for wage earners. Most of Argentina's population is concentrated in a few urban centers, while services, construction, and import substituting industries produce and sell most of their output in these markets.

Thus, the evolution of relative wages from the 1940s to the 1980s has clearly favored labor in nontradable activities (Riveros 1989; Sánchez 1987). Moreover, observed wage changes did not reflect changes in labor productivity in nontradable activities (Sánchez 1987), and did so only mildly in manufacturing.

During 1962–87, however, relative wages in tradables and nontradables remained relatively stable (see table 2.6 and figure 2.5). However, this stability probably reflects government intervention more than relatively stable relative labor productivity. To avoid problems of interpretation associated with the peculiar behavior of public sector wages after 1985, namely, sharp wage cuts due to stabilization policies, they are not included in the group of nontradables.

Table 2.6 The Evolution of Relative Wages, 1962–86

Year	Wages in tradable industries/wages in nontradable industries	Wages in potentially tradable industries/ wages in nontradable industries	Year	Wages in tradable industries/wages in nontradable industries	Wages in potentially tradable industries/ wages in nontradable industries
1962	0.83	0.99	1976	0.93	1.04
1963	0.79	0.95	1977	0.94	1.04
1964	0.82	0.96	1978	0.91	1.01
1965	0.88	1.01	1979	0.93	1.04
1966	0.90	1.03	1980	0.89	0.99
1967	0.89	1.05	1981	0.91	1.03
1968	0.88	1.03	1982	0.91	1.03
1969	0.88	1.04	1983	0.95	1.05
1970	0.89	1.04	1984	0.96	1.09
1971	0.91	1.04	1985	0.96	1.08
1972	0.91	1.03	1986	0.95	1.10
1973	0.88	1.00	1987	1.02	1.16
1974	0.93	1.05	1988	1.05	1.21
1975	0.92	1.02	1989	0.94	1.10
			1990	0.95	1.06

Source: IEERAL data base.

Figure 2.5 The Evolution of Relative Wages, 1962–89

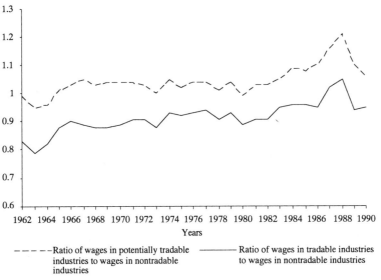

Source: IEERAL.

Regional and Sectoral Labor Allocation

The concentration of population in a few urban centers is a result of trends in public investment and social expenditures, and of distorted relative output prices and prevailing wages in the regions that, in turn, resulted from the centralized nature of the wage setting process. Although population growth has traditionally been low in Argentina, the urban population has grown much more rapidly, while rural population growth rates have been negative for many years (table 2.7).

According to 1980 figures, the urban population represented 83 percent of the total population. In 1988, of the country's 33 million inhabitants, 42 percent lived in Greater Buenos Aires, Córdoba, and Rosario. This pattern of demographic concentration is probably a consequence of the deliberate policy of overvalued exchange rates (and of the accompanying commercial and macroeconomic policies) that affected relative prices and wages and biased labor allocation

Table 2.7 Average Annual Rate of Population Growth
(percent)

Census period	Total	Urban	Rural	Greater Buenos Aires	Córdoba	Rosario
1914–47	2.1	2.5	1.40	n.a.	n.a.	n.a.
1947–60	1.8	2.8	-0.50	6.1	3.6	2.4
1960–70	1.6	2.5	-1.40	3.8	3.0	2.0
1970–80	1.8	2.6	-0.03	2.5	2.2	1.6

n.a. = not available
Source: Sánchez (1986, tables 1 and 2).

against tradables. Any increase in the average wage of urban residents achieved through government mandated increases and/or union demands, increased wages in the nontradable sectors by more than labor productivity. Since nontradables are primarily urban goods while agriculture is an important component of tradables, a policy of favoring nontradables inevitably favored the urban sector. Thus, prices in this sector had to grow at a quicker rate relative to that of tradables to maintain relative wages at their targeted levels. The final outcome was that the change in relative prices necessary to obtain a given increase in the average wage of the urban population increased over time.

In addition to the bias in favor of nontradable sectors derived from aggregate economic policies, government investment in education, health, housing, transport, communications, and culture was also concentrated in urban areas. This allocative pattern was reinforced by social policies that were characterized by subsidies that instead of supplementing the income of the poor regardless of where they lived, provided free public services to people living in the largest cities, regardless of their income (Sánchez 1986, 1987).

Legal regulations on nominal wage setting also contributed to the concentration of resources in urban areas. Nominal wages, whether determined by legal procedures for bargaining or established by the government during periods when union activity was prohibited, were compulsory for all workers and firms. Therefore, differences in the relative availability of labor in different regions did not affect the level of wages. At the same time, this wage policy discriminated against small firms and marginal investors, which also restrained the creation of modern activities in rural areas and produced a one-way flow of migrants from the provinces to urban centers.

This latter result is consistent with economic theory. A disaggregation of labor into two groups, skilled and unskilled, reveals that the provinces have excess demand for the former and excess supply of the latter, while the opposite occurs in the wealthiest urban areas. Wage differentials among provinces should move accordingly and instigate a flow of skilled workers toward the regional markets, and a flow of unskilled workers in the opposite direction. For this to occur, wage differentials would have to be large enough to compensate for the cost of moving in either direction. Thus, labor flows did not occur as expected for two reasons. First, even though wage differentials existed, they were not large enough to compensate fully for the rate of institutional wage intervention in equalizing wages among provinces. Therefore, wage differentials were lower than those that would have prevailed in a decentralized and more competitive wage setting process. Second, welfare policies and related social expenditures increased the cost of moving for the skilled and reduced it for the unskilled. For both groups, any move away from urban areas entailed the loss of cheap or free social services.

The effects of the government interventions discussed above on sectoral labor allocation were as expected. The share of construction, commerce, and services in total employment was almost 50 percent in 1940 and more than 64 percent in 1980 (table 2.8). Likewise, the share of construction tripled during the same period. The nontradable sector accounted for 69 percent of all new employment created between 1947 and 1980 (85 percent in 1960–70 and 87 percent in 1970–80). Finally, the share of the nontradable sector in total employment was 64.1 percent in 1980 compared with 49.6 percent in 1940. By contrast, the share of agriculture in total employment declined by more than half, from 27.1 in 1940 to 12.9 percent in 1980, and the share of manufacturing has declined steadily since 1947.

Labor Market Segmentation and Increasing Informality

As well as the notable expansion of employment in services and construction relative to that in the tradable sectors, economic growth caused a higher increase in nonwage than in wage employment (table 2.8). Following a standard approach to analyzing labor markets in developing countries, urban employment can be classified into the broad categories of formal and informal. This classification depends on the existence or lack of protection of certain sectors with regard to coverage by and enforcement of labor regulations. Thus, formal employment corresponds to the public sector and to relatively large private sector firms, while informal employment corresponds to private sector firms that employ fewer than five persons. Since not all the workers in the second category earn a low income, informal employment may be further classified on the basis of income levels: those earning high incomes due to advanced skills, high capital intensity, or an oligopolistic market environment are classified in the quasi-formal sector, while those earning low incomes are classified in the informal sector (Sánchez and others 1981).

Table 2.8 Employment by Sector, Selected Years
(percent)

| | | | | Average annual employment growth | | | | | |
| | Sectoral distribution | | | Agriculture | | Manufacturing | | Nontradables | |
Year	Agri-culture	Manu-facturing	Rest	Wage employ-ment	Nonwage employ-ment	Wage employ-ment	Nonwage employ-ment	Wage employ-ment	Nonwage employ-ment
1940	27.1	23.3	49.6	n.a.	n.a.	n.a.	n.a.	n.a.	n.a.
1947	26.1	27.2	46.7	0.1	n.a.	7.2	n.a.	3.8	n.a.
1960	20.8	27.1	52.1	-1.6	1.3	1.2	2.2	1.9	3.6
1970	16.2	23.3	60.5	-0.6	-2.1	0.4	-3.6	2.6	2.8
1980	12.9	23.0	64.1	-0.9	-0.6	1.1	2.6	1.7	3.2

n.a. = not available
Notes: Data on sectoral distribution are expressed as a proportion of total employment.
Source: Sánchez (1984, table 8).

The proportion of quasi-formal and informal workers in Argentina—which is equivalent to the concept of the informal sector used elsewhere—is about 30 percent of the urban work force. Therefore, compared to other Latin American countries, where the informal sector accounts for 40 percent or more of the labor force, Argentina's informal sector is less important in urban labor markets. Nonetheless, given that formal wages are protected by labor regulations and government and union intervention, adjustment policies have increased the formal-informal wage gap (Lopez and Riveros 1989). This increase probably has a negative influence on the political sustainability of adjustment programs.

The lack of macroeconomic adjustment has probably been at the root of the relatively high income levels observed in the informal sector, which produces mostly nontradables. For example, statistics for 1984 and 1985 show that self-employed workers with less than eight years of schooling (a reasonable proxy for the unskilled) earned approximately 18 percent more than wage earners with the same level of education. Indeed, the average self-employed income was only 7 or 8 percent less than the national average wage. However, if one uses the concept of total labor costs to account for all incomes received by wage labor in the formal sector, a different conclusion may arise: in 1985, for example, nonwage labor costs (fringe benefits, social security, and regular bonuses) were about 51 percent of total wage costs (Riveros 1989).

Labor Market Institutions

The role of labor market institutions is important in leading to the formal/informal distinction, which is, in turn, a key factor with regard to the labor market response to macro policies. The Argentinian economy is characterized by politically strong oligopolistic firms producing for domestic markets that have created powerful protectionist lobbies. Their counterpart is an equally powerful labor union, organized as a corporation, whose influence on government policies has been paramount. Although some changes in the labor movement's power structure have occurred during the last decade, unions are still extensive, disciplined, and politicized.

The law allows workers to organize unions freely, but to obtain the legal right to bargain with employers, unions must have "trade union representative" credentials. The government usually grants these to the most important union (mainly in terms of membership) in each area of activity, although exceptionally they have been granted to more than one union.

Even though the law protects workers' rights to join or not join a union, the terms of the labor contract agreed to by the representative union and the employer are compulsory for all workers in the activity. In turn, unions may join federations and confederations that, once they have obtained legal representative credentials, can negotiate wages at a very aggregate level. In this manner, wages and working conditions are centrally determined by negotiation between national unions and entrepreneurs; a process also characterized by strong government intervention. During periods when collective bargaining was practiced, wages were centrally determined by government decrees and resolutions.

Job security regulations hinder labor mobility. The law maintains workers' rights to keep their jobs regardless of the circumstances, although it does not guarantee income maintenance. The law also states that in case of dismissal, employees must receive severance payment equal to the highest monthly wage or salary earned in the current job (up to a ceiling of three times the minimum wage), multiplied by the number of years worked.

Mandated minimum wages also exert important effects on labor market outcomes. First, they set a limit for severance payments, thus affecting the normal rate of job turnover. Second, they affect prevailing equilibrium wages due to the effect of minimum wages in shifting the entire wage structure upward (Paldam and Riveros 1988; Sánchez and Giordano 1988). Third, given the positive effect of minimum wage changes on average wage changes, the former are also related to existing inflationary pressures (Paldam and Riveros 1988). Fourth, evidence suggests that relatively high minimum wages affect the formal-informal wage gap positively and the employment level in formal activities negatively (Lopez and Riveros 1989; Sánchez and Giordano 1988).

The Role of Labor Markets in the Adjustment Process

Successive attempts to introduce macroeconomic equilibrium in Argentina have failed, partly due to the absence of accompanying labor market policies. The populist aim of maintaining relatively high real wages has determined the existence of an overvalued exchange rate.

The Performance of Labor Markets in Adjustment

As discussed above, the two most recent attempts to introduce structural adjustments in Argentina failed. Tables 2.2, 2.6, and 2.9 illustrate the interactions among policies and relative prices affecting labor markets. Despite a series of nominal devaluations, the government followed populist policies of overvalued exchange rates between 1962 and 1983, which resulted in wage rigidity and increasing nontradable prices relative to the price of exportables.

As discussed earlier, Argentina has seen a sequence of devaluation-recession periods followed by periods of exchange rate appreciation. During the latter, wage indexation normally hindered the intended adjustment process initiated through an usually severe devaluation. Devaluation, via its effect on food prices in particular, led to union attempts to restore real wages. These were usually attained first in the manufacturing sector (where unions acted as the leaders of the entire urban labor movement), and then spread to services and construction. (Llach 1987 estimated sectoral productivity figures and concluded that urban sector development depends much more on agricultural productivity than its own productivity.)

The strong relationship between the exchange rate policy and relative wages discussed earlier is illustrated by table 2.10, which is derived from tables 2.2 and 2.6. The figures show the important role of an appropriate exchange rate in the success of a stabilization effort. Despite the structural adjustment program announced in 1976, the relatively low real exchange rate that prevailed from 1973 to 1980 held the ratio of wages in tradables and nontradables practically constant. This suggests that the effects of the policy of overvalued rates were more important than those of the trade liberalization and other adjustment measures announced in the mid-1970s. By

Table 2.9 Relative Prices and GDP, 1962–87

Year	P_u/P_t	P_u/P_x	P_n/P_m	W/e	W_h/W_n	GDP
1962	91	98	78	57	0.99	69
1963	89	92	78	58	0.95	67
1964	84	82	73	79	0.96	74
1965	87	92	72	90	1.01	81
1966	97	106	87	98	1.03	82
1967	98	106	90	78	1.05	84
1968	102	109	97	80	1.03	87
1969	103	110	100	90	1.03	95
1970	100	100	100	100	1.04	100
1971	96	89	99	114	1.04	105
1972	87	79	186	97	1.03	108
1973	95	88	99	149	1.00	115
1974	102	104	102	211	1.05	122
1975	108	138	95	219	1.02	121
1976	99	123	83	103	1.04	121
1977	101	111	94	114	1.04	128
1978	110	118	112	166	1.01	122
1979	111	114	116	289	1.04	131
1980	125	134	135	487	0.99	133
1981	127	150	131	391	1.03	125
1982	103	129	89	196	1.03	118
1983	101	127	85	199	1.05	121
1984	106	134	92	254	1.09	124
1985	113	164	95	175	1.08	118
1986	110	138	110	199	1.10	125
1987	112	137	115	174	1.16	127
1988	111	143	100	168	1.21	124
1989	107	147	89	120	1.10	118

P_u = urban price, or price of goods and services produced by the import substitution sector (manufacturing) and the service (including commerce) and construction sectors

P_t = price of tradables, i.e., price of goods produced by the export and import sectors

P_x = price of exportables, i.e., goods produced by the rural sector and by the food and beverage sectors

P_n = price of nontradables, i.e., the price of goods and services produced by the service and construction sectors

P_m = price of importables, i.e., the price of goods produced by the import substitution sector and the price of imported goods

W = wages and salaries

e = nominal exchange rate

W_h = wages and salaries paid in the import substitution or home goods sector

W_n = wages and salaries paid in the nontradable sector

Source: IEERAL.

Table 2.10 Relationship Between Exchange Rate Policy and Wages *(index, 1962–72 = 100)*

Reform period	W_t/W_n	W_h/W_n	Real exchange rate
1973–76	105	101	83
1976–80	106	101	80
1981–83	106	103	92
1984–87	113	111	112

W_t = wages in agriculture and manufacturing
W_n = wages in nontradables
W_h = wages in the import substitution or home goods sector
Source: Authors' calculations.

comparison, the 1987 adjustment program resulted in an immediate increase in relative prices of urban tradables. Policymakers had expected that in response to this change in relative prices, wages in nontradables would have increased relative to wages in manufacturing, thereby creating incentives for labor reallocation. As discussed earlier, this did not occur due to a series of policy reversals.

The outcomes of these two adjustment attempts suggest that labor market variables played a negative role in the effort to achieve structural changes. While the main policy target was a change in relative prices of tradables to nontradables to permit the economy to shift toward production for external markets, a wage indexation mechanism supported by government and union intervention created substantial rigidities. This prevented sufficiently large falls in real wages in response to the devaluation, and the inevitable result was a loss in international competitiveness. In addition, each adjustment attempt worsened inflation, the resource allocation across industries, and poverty.

Level and Composition of Aggregate Employment

Traditionally, Argentina did not have employment problems resulting from an excess labor supply. The situation tended to be one of labor scarcity, especially in the least skilled segment of the labor force

(Llach 1978). Nevertheless, urban labor markets, especially in the largest cities, experienced successive periods of scarcity and of relative abundance of labor due to fluctuations in domestic and foreign immigration to large urban centers and in labor force participation. (Researchers have studied this adjustment problem in urban labor markets extensively since 1979, when Sánchez and others published their first paper on the subject. See, for example, Beccaría 1980; Beccaría and Orsatti 1985; Dieguez and Gerchunoff 1984; Llach 1980; Mann and Sánchez 1984; Riveros 1989; Sánchez 1982, 1987.)

During the second half of the 1970s, the large urban centers experienced a situation of relative labor scarcity. Migratory flows changed after 1970 when the largest urban markets were no longer the recipients of large number of workers in search of better job opportunities. Rural-urban migration continued in the second half of the 1970s, but from rural areas of each province to its capital city (Sánchez 1984, 1986). In addition, a series of institutional and economic developments, particularly the 1976–81 adjustment program, reinforced the falling trend observed in labor force participation: the real wage was probably below the reservation wage of many labor market participants, and a considerable number of women, young adults, and even males aged 20–59 abandoned the labor force.

The period from the early 1970s to the early 1980s witnessed not only declining labor force participation rates and employment (table 2.11), but the sectoral allocation of labor tended to diminish the supply of wage labor to the goods producing sectors. Workers were transferring to construction and service activities and to nonwage occupations, thereby effecting the amount of labor available to the industrial sector (table 2.8). Although relative sectoral wages did not show a well-defined trend (table 2.6), employment creation in manufacturing and agriculture was poor.

Due to these economic trends, open unemployment was not a significant problem in the urban labor markets until the early 1980s, and an open employment problem has now arisen.[2] Although labor force participation rates have moved in the same direction as

---

2. Open unemployment is defined as the ratio of those identified as unemployed in the Permanent Household Survey to the economically active population.

Table 2.11 Indicators for Main Urban Labor Markets, 1980–85 *(percent)*

Year	LFP	L	U	Year	LFP	L	U
1950	46	44	4.3	1970	44	42	5.0
1951	46	44	3.5	1971	43	41	5.9
1952	45	43	4.0	1972	42	40	6.7
1953	45	43	4.8	1973	41	39	5.5
1954	46	43	6.2	1974	40	39	3.9
1955	46	43	5.8	1975	40	39	3.2
1956	46	43	6.8	1976	39	38	4.7
1957	46	43	6.3	1977	39	38	3.2
1958	46	43	7.8	1978	39	38	3.0
1959	44	42	5.5	1979	39	38	2.2
1960	45	42	5.6	1980	39	38	2.5
1961	45	42	7.2	1981	39	37	4.7
1962	45	42	7.3	1982	39	37	4.9
1963	45	41	8.9	1983	38	36	4.4
1964	45	42	6.3	1984	38	37	4.2
1965	45	43	5.3	1985	39	37	5.6
1966	45	42	5.8	1986	39	37	5.2
1967	46	41	6.4	1987	40	38	5.7
1968	44	42	5.3	1988	40	37	6.0
1969	44	42	4.4	1989	41	38	7.5
				1990	40	37	7.2

LFP = labor force participation as a percentage of total population
L   = employment as a percentage of the economically active population
U   = unemployment as a percentage of the labor force
Source: Sánchez (1987). 1950–62 computed from population and census data; employment data from Llach and Sánchez (1984); 1963–85 data from the Permanent Household Survey.

economic activity in the short-term, long-run trends have also had an effect. As table 2.12 and figures 2.6 and 2.7 show, participation rates decreased from 1974 through 1983, while open unemployment and underemployment remained low compared to their historic levels (table 2.11).[3] Labor force participation has increased during the last five years despite high variability in output growth and the recent slowdown in activity levels (table 2.12 and figures 2.6 and 2.7). The reason is that the labor force response to the existing labor market

---

3. The underemployed are those who work less than 35 hours per week and are actively seeking a job.

situation is now different than that which prevailed until the late 1970s. The "discouraged worker" effect was predominant in those years as declines in employment and real wages were accompanied by withdrawal of people from the labor force (including migrants from nearby countries). Currently, however, the dominant effect derives from the loss of family income and shows up in the increase in the net inflow of secondary workers into the labor market. Of course, if the probabilities of finding a job are low in the case of experienced

Table 2.12 Labor Participation and Unemployment, 1974–88 *(percent)*

Year	Labor force participation rate	Open unemployment rate[a]	Under-employment rate[a]	Equivalent rate[a]
1974	40.4	4.2	5.0	6.7
1975	39.9	3.7	5.3	6.4
1976	39.3	4.8	5.3	7.5
1977	38.7	3.3	4.0	5.3
1978	38.9	3.3	4.7	5.7
1979	38.3	2.5	3.8	4.4
1980	38.4	2.5	5.2	5.1
1981	38.4	4.8	5.5	7.6
1982	38.3	5.3	6.6	8.6
1983	37.3	4.7	5.9	7.7
1984	37.9	4.6	5.7	7.4
1985	38.1	6.1	7.3	9.8
1986	38.9	5.6	7.8	9.5
1987	39.2	5.9	8.2	9.9
1988	39.3	6.3	7.9	10.2
1989	40.6	7.6	8.7	12.0
1990	38.9	7.4	9.0	11.9

Notes: The data are from Greater Buenos Aires, 20 provincial capitals, and 5 other cities. An underemployed person is one who is working less than 35 hours a week and is seeking more work. The equivalent unemployment rate is calculated using the convention that two underemployed people are equivalent to one unemployed person, and these "converted" unemployed are added to open unemployment.

a. Given as percentage of the economically active population.

Source: Permanent Household Survey.

Figure 2.6 Labor Force Participation Rate, 1974–90
(percentage of total population)

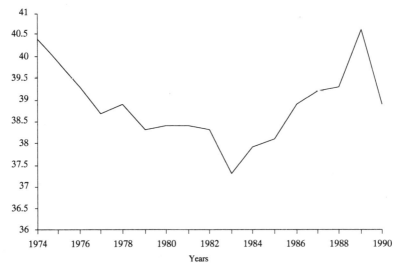

Source: Permanent Household Survey.

Figure 2.7 Equivalent Unemployment Rate, 1974–90
(percentage of economically active population)

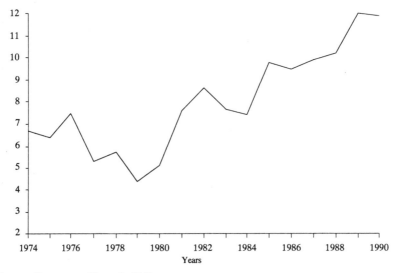

Source: Permanent Household Survey.

workers (for example, males 20–59 years of age), they are even lower in the case of secondary workers. The result has been an increase in open unemployment and underemployment in association with the "added" worker effect.

Unemployment and the Public Sector

The foregoing analysis suggests that construction and services of low productivity are characterized by substantial hidden unemployment. Another sign of hidden unemployment is observed in public sector employment trends: estimates indicate that in 1985, total public sector employment was over two million people, representing as much as 17.5 percent of the labor force and 25.0 percent of all wage earners (table 2.13).

Argentina has exhibited rapid growth of public sector employment in the provinces. Table 2.14 shows that during 1960–87, public employment grew by more than 40 percent. Most of this growth was associated with a huge increase in employment in local governments (more than 200 percent), which took place during the periods of unsuccessful adjustment programs. Thus, at the time that overall adjustment failed, partly as a consequence of labor market intervention policies and the overvalued exchange rate, the resulting low employment growth demanded active job creation in the public sector.

Table 2.13 Public Sector Employment, 1985

| | | Relative share (percent) | | |
| | | Public | | |
Subsector	Total (thousands)	sector employment	Labor force	Wage earners
National administration	605	30.1	5.3	7.5
Public enterprises	398	19.8	3.3	4.9
Local government	1,006	50.1	8.9	12.6
Total	2,009	100.0	17.5	25.0

Source: Sánchez and Giordano (1988).

Table 2.14 Growth in Public Sector Employment, Selected Years
(index, 1960 = 100)

Subsector	1960	1965	1970	1975	1980	1985	1987
National administration	100.0	93.7	100.1	110.3	97.6	106.3	104.5
Public enterprises	100.0	81.1	76.6	101.4	73.9	80.5	79.1
Provincial governments	100.0	105.7	131.7	178.1	205.7	239.0	259.7
City governments	100.0	116.0	134.4	181.6	179.2	202.4	220.0
Total	100.0	94.4	103.2	129.2	122.0	136.9	141.7

Source: Estimated from figures published in *El Cronista Comercial,* April 27, 1988, p. 15.

In addition to the political commitment of keeping open unemployment low, high employment growth in local governments was associated with changing migratory patterns. Domestic migratory flows changed after 1970 as economic incentives to move to the large cities declined. Instead, people moved from rural areas to provincial capitals, where their chances of finding employment were higher. Local governments started active job creation mostly due to the resulting demands for more employment (see Lindenboim 1985; Sánchez 1986).

Another problem with public employment is its internal composition. In 1985, about 20 percent of public employment was in public firms, in many cases with very low levels of labor productivity, as in the case of railroads. By contrast, less than 30 percent of public employment was in services like health and education. Thus, the relative amount of workers in purely bureaucratic activities is high, and a thorough public sector reform program is probably needed.

Women, Labor Markets, and Adjustment

The 1980s saw a sustained increase in the rate of female labor force participation, especially by women aged 35–49. The drop in family income due to the economic crisis and the need to compensate for the associated loss in welfare might explain the higher participation of the secondary labor force. As table 2.15 shows, the main sources of em-

Table 2.15 Sectoral Composition of Female Employment, Selected Years
(percent)

Sector	1960	1970	1980
Tradable	32	25	21
Agriculture	5	4	3
Industry	27	21	18
Nontradable	68	75	79
Total	100	100	100

Source: Estimated from census data.

ployment for the rising female labor supply were nontradable activities, possibly in occupations of low productivity. In 1970, approximately 58 percent of the total female employment was in clerical positions, sales, and other services (mostly domestic services). In 1980 this figure was 63 percent. As expected, the female average wage was approximately 56 percent of the male wage.

Income Distribution and Poverty

The absence of structural adjustment in Argentina has been associated with an increasing deterioration in income distribution. This deterioration derives from poor economic growth, which has, in turn, resulted from the disarray of policies that have produced higher relative prices of nontradables and protective regulations that favor urban workers in the formal sector.

Examination of the distribution of poverty by economic sectors is less satisfactory than analyses based on geographic or functional characteristics or the formal/informal sector distinction. Unfortunately, however, data are not available to study the latter disaggregation. In addition, data are limited to the cities of Córdoba and Buenos Aires.

Finance, a nontradable sector, and industry, a tradable sector, enjoy the highest income levels per worker, the lowest unemployment rates, and the lowest levels of poverty (table 2.16). Commerce, services, and construction, all nontradable, not only have relative incomes lower

Table 2.16 Unemployment, Sectoral Income Distribution, and Poverty

Sector	Relative income		Equivalent unemployment rate (%)		Percentage of poor in total employment	
	Greater Buenos Aires	Córdoba	Greater Buenos Aires	Córdoba	Poor	Indigent
Finance	1.4	1.6	7.1	5.1	9.6	2.7
Industry	1.1	1.1	7.1	5.5	11.7	1.8
Commerce	1.0	1.0	11.7	11.1	13.0	4.3
Services	0.9	0.9	11.2	10.6	15.5	4.5
Construction	0.8	0.8	15.3	14.5	25.2	4.6
Tradables	1.1	1.1	7.1	5.5	11.6	1.6
Nontradables	0.9	0.9	10.2	10.0	15.6	4.3
Total	1.0	1.0	9.4	8.9	14.6	3.3

Notes: Relative income includes wages and the income of the self-employed for Córdoba, and only wages for Buenos Aires. For percentage of poor, data refer only to Córdoba. The poor were identified based on (a) size and composition of household; (b) calorie intake; (c) average per capita income. The poverty line was defined as the income level necessary to buy a basic basket of food (IPA-INDEC 1988) and to cover other basic needs. Household members with per capita incomes below the poverty line were classified as poor, while the indigent were those with incomes below the amount required to buy the basic basket of food only.
Source: Own estimates based on Permanent Household Survey data: October 1986 for Córdoba, and April 1987 for Greater Buenos Aires.

than the other two sectors, but also a significantly higher level of un-employment and underemployment. The result is a large incidence of poverty in the latter sectors. These characteristics—lower than average incomes, high unemployment rates, and an above average incidence of poverty—are typical of the nontradable sectors.

The increase in poverty in Argentina during the last 15 years is mostly a result of failed adjustment. In addition to rigid wages and distorted labor allocation, open unemployment and underemployment have been growing for the last five years. Young males and females in the age group 35–49 are the most significant group of secondary workers swelling the labor supply in the informal sector. Most of this surplus labor probably engages in construction, commerce, and services; activities that have very low productivity rates and higher incidences of unemployment and poverty.

At least in the short and medium term, any adjustment process will inevitably increase poverty due to higher transitional unemployment and the drop in real wages. Adjustment will also imply declining public sector employment and wages and reduced expenditure on social welfare programs. Until now, however, Argentina has been suffering the social cost of not adjusting and trying to maintain an inappropriate productive structure, combined with intervention in the labor market and use of a deliberate policy of overvalued exchange rates.

Political Economy, Labor Markets, and Adjustment

Hyperinflation is now forcing the government to attempt a thorough adjustment program that includes profound changes in the functioning and institutional organization of the labor and goods markets. Deregulation, privatization, reduction in public expenditures, trade liberalization, a shift of factors of production against the nontradable sector, and other similar actions are not without cost. Therefore, a set of labor market policies are required to facilitate efficient change at minimum cost.

The government will face severe difficulties in shifting labor among sectors. Reforms in the labor market should be designed to facilitate this shift at minimum cost, which requires deregulation policies. Therefore, a set of policies should aim at decentralizing collective bargaining and the labor unions. Another set of policies should aim at making labor contracts more flexible to attain higher labor mobility and to implement feasible programs to assist the unemployed. Finally, macroeconomic policies should be applied in combination with a dismantling of labor market intervention, which will probably diminish labor market segmentation and increase the trickle down effect of growth.

The program of economic reforms needs to be sustainable and credible. In Argentina, this implies strong political support and clear commitment on the part of the government. This in turn requires involving the unions in the reform process, or a substantial change in their traditional political attitudes. This is not going to be an easy task, not only because of the enormous lags that may be involved in changing institutions, but also because the unions are aware that structural adjustment will mean a loss of power.

Conclusion

Although implementing and sustaining a program of structural adjustment will involve severe difficulties, change is inevitable in Argentina. The current economic crisis is not only the result of inappropriate domestic policies in response to recent external shocks, it is a result of poor policies applied for years that have damaged the economy. Even if no external shocks had occurred, the country would still have to shift the structure of production in appropriate directions.

Frustrated adjustment experiences provide some lessons that can help policymakers design a sustainable program to achieve price stability and to change the system of incentives as outlined below.

- Policymakers must ensure that macroeconomic and trade policies are consistent. In particular, they must combine trade policy with fiscal reforms, since a reduction in public spending will exert downward pressures on the real exchange rate.

- Policymakers must also emphasize changes in labor relations and labor market institutions. Institutional changes, such as decentralizing wage bargaining and eliminating both wage indexation and government intervention, are necessary to shift resources among sectors and regions.

- A shift in resources among regions and industries requires eliminating labor mobility rigidities and restrictions. Restrictions have resulted from the regional allocation of public investment and social welfare expenditures and regulations concerning public services and subsidized urban utilities. Thus, more mobility will require less pervasive intervention.

- Prospective losers in an adjustment program may have sufficient power to stop its implementation. Thus, incorporating these losers into the program is vital. Public expenditures must be reallocated to reduce the social cost of the transition period. This will require external financing and debt alleviation.

APPENDIX

Table 2.A1 City of Buenos Aires, Income Distribution in Total Population
(income earners only)

October / year	Decile									
	I	*II*	*III*	*IV*	*V*	*VI*	*VII*	*VIII*	*IX*	*X*
1974	4.4	4.4	4.5	6.2	7.5	9.2	10.7	13.6	15.9	23.6
1975	3.1	4.1	5.5	6.6	7.3	9.0	10.9	12.5	16.4	24.6
1976	2.9	4.2	4.8	5.8	6.9	8.2	10.7	14.5	14.5	27.5
1977	2.9	4.3	4.4	6.1	6.3	10.8	10.8	10.8	17.3	26.3
1978	2.7	4.0	5.4	5.6	7.1	9.9	9.9	12.3	18.4	24.7
1979	2.8	4.7	4.7	4.8	7.8	7.8	9.6	13.4	16.6	27.8
1980	3.2	4.6	4.6	5.3	7.7	7.7	9.8	14.0	16.4	26.7
1981	1.9	5.1	5.1	5.1	5.7	8.6	9.4	13.4	17.1	28.6
1982	2.5	3.7	4.4	5.4	6.2	7.6	9.2	11.1	14.8	35.1
1983	2.2	3.7	4.6	5.5	6.7	8.1	9.6	11.9	15.9	31.8
1984	2.4	3.5	4.2	5.4	6.6	7.7	9.5	11.3	14.8	34.6
1985	2.6	3.4	4.0	5.3	6.4	7.7	9.4	11.8	15.9	33.5
1986	2.5	3.3	3.8	5.0	6.2	7.3	9.2	11.5	15.4	35.8
1987	2.0	3.0	4.1	5.0	6.1	7.4	9.0	11.4	16.0	36.0
1988	2.0	3.3	4.0	4.8	5.9	7.2	9.0	11.5	16.4	36.0

	Bottom 40%	Middle 40%	Top 20%
1974	19.5	41.0	39.5
1975	19.3	39.7	41.0
1976	17.7	40.3	42.0
1977	17.7	38.7	43.6
1978	17.7	39.2	43.1
1979	17.0	38.6	44.4
1980	17.7	39.2	43.1
1981	17.2	37.1	45.7
1982	16.0	34.1	49.9
1983	16.0	36.3	47.7
1984	15.5	35.1	49.4
1985	15.3	35.3	49.4
1986	14.6	34.2	51.2
1987	14.1	33.9	52.0
1988	14.1	33.6	52.4

References

Beccaría, L. 1980. "Los Movimientos de Corto Plazo en el Mercado de Trabajo Urbano y la Coyuntura 1975–78 en la Argentina." *Desarrollo Económico* 20:78.

Beccaría, L., and A. Orsatti. 1985. "La Evolución del Empleo y los Salarios en el Corto Plazo. El Caso Argentino 1970–1983." Documento de Trabajo No. 14. Buenos Aires: United Nations, Economic Commission for Latin America.

Cavallo, D. 1986. "Long-Term Growth in the Light of External Balance Policies: The Case of Argentina." Washington, D.C.: World Bank.

Cavallo, D., and J. Cottani. 1986. "The Timing and Sequencing of Trade Liberalization Policies: The Case of Argentina." Washington, D.C.: World Bank.

Cavallo, D., and R. Domenech. 1988. "Políticas Macroeconómicas y Tipo de Cambio Real, Argentina, 1913–84." International Food Policy Research Institute, IEERAL, and International Center for Economic Growth. Unpublished manuscript.

Cavallo, D., and Y. Mundlak. 1982. *Agriculture and Economic Growth in an Open Economy: The Case of Argentina.* Research Report 36. Buenos Aires: International Food Policy Research Institute.

Dieguez, H., and P. Gerchunoff. 1984. "La Dinámica del Mercado Laboral Urbano en la Argentina, 1976–1981." *Desarrollo Económico* 24:93.

IPA-INDEC. 1988. *Canasta Básica de Alimentos, Gran Buenos Aires.* Documento de Trabajo no. 3. Buenos Aires.

Lindenboim, J. 1985. *La Terciarización del Empleo en la Argentina. Una Perspectiva Regional.* Proyecto PNUD/OIT, ARG/84/029, Ministerio de Trabajo y Seguridad Social Secretaría de Planificación. Buenos Aires.

Llach, J. 1978. "Estructura Ocupacional y Dinámica del Empleo en la Argentina. Sus Peculiaridades 1947–1970." *Desarrollo Económico* 17:68.

_____. 1980. "Población Económicamente Activa, Tasas de Desempleo y Demanda Agregada: La Experiencia Argentina Reciente en Busca de una Teoría." *Anales de la Asociación Argentina de Economía Política, XV.* Annual meeting. Mar del Plata, Argentina.

_____. 1987. *Mercados de Trabajo, Términos del Intercambio Externo y Salarios Reales en el Largo Plazo. La Argentina y América Latina, 1940–1985.* Serie Documentos de Trabajo. Buenos Aires: Instituto Torcuato Di Tella.

Llach, J., and C. Sánchez. 1984. "Los Determinantes del Salario en la Argentina. Un Diagnóstico de Largo Plazo y Propuestas de Política." *Estudios* 7:29.

Lopez, R., and L. Riveros. 1989. "Macroeconomic Adjustment and the Labor Market in Four Latin American Countries." PRE Working Paper 335. Washington, D.C.: World Bank.

Mann, A., and C. Sánchez. 1984. "Monetarism, Economic Reform and Socioeconomic Consequences: Argentina 1976–1982." *International Journal of Social Economics* 11:3–4.

_____. 1985. "Labor Market Responses to Southern Cone Stabilization Policies: The Cases of Argentina, Chile, Uruguay." *Inter-American Economic Affairs* 38:4.

Nogues, J. 1981. "Sustitución de Importaciones Versus Promoción de Exportaciones: Impactos Diferenciales sobre el Empleo en el Sector Manufacturero Argentino." *Desarrollo Económico* 22:86.

Paldam, M., and L. Riveros. 1988. "El Rol Causal de los Salarios Mínimos en Seis Mercados Laborales de América Latina." *Estudios* 11:46.

Riveros, L. 1989. "Labor Market Reforms for Structural Adjustment in Argentina." Washington, D.C.: World Bank, Country Economics Department. Processed.

Sánchez, C. 1982. "Salario Real y Oferta de Trabajo en la Argentina." *Estudios* 5:21.

_____. 1984. "Empleo y Crecimiento en la Economía Argentina." *Estudios* 7:31.

_____. 1986. "La Distribución Regional de la Población Argentina y los Efectos Distorsionantes de los Subsidios Sociales e Inversiones en Infraestructura Social." In *Economías Regionales y Crecimiento.* Córdoba, Argentina: IEERAL.

_____. 1987. "Characteristics and Operation of Labor Markets in Argentina." Report No. DRD 272. Washington, D.C.: World Bank, Development Research Department.

Sánchez, C., and O. Giordano. 1988. "El Salario Mínimo en la Argentina: Alcances y Evolución (1964–1988)." Documento de Trabajo/18 Proyecto Gobierno Argentino-PNUD-OIT, ARG/87003. Buenos Aires: PNUD-OIT

Sánchez, C., F. Ferrero, and W. Schulthess. 1979. "Empleo, Desempleo y Tamaño de la Fuerza Laboral en el Mercado de Trabajo Urbano de la Argentina." *Desarrollo Económico* 16:15–24.

Sánchez, C., H. Palmieri, and F. Ferrero. 1981. "The Informal and the Quasi-Formal Sectors in Córdoba." In S. V. Sethuraman, ed., *The Urban Informal Sector in Developing Countries, Employment Poverty and Environment.* Geneva: International Labor Office.

3

BOLIVIA

Susan Horton

Bolivia is a particularly interesting country to study from the viewpoint of structural adjustment. In the late 1970s and 1980s it suffered from a number of dramatic events: the debt crisis, falling world commodity prices, the collapse in the world market for its main export (tin), domestic political instability, hyperinflation, currency reorganization, a stringent stabilization that succeeded in controlling inflation, and a structural adjustment with as yet only very modest effects on long-run growth. As Bolivia is the poorest country in South America (and the second poorest in the Western hemisphere), it is a particularly useful case study for comparison with low-income countries in Sub-Saharan Africa and Asia.

The Origin and Nature of the Adjustment Problem

Like all the developing countries, Bolivia suffered external shocks in the 1970s and 1980s. As a not very diversified, mineral exporting economy, in the 1980s it suffered particularly from the fall in commodity prices and the collapse in the market for tin, its principal export. However, the magnitude of its economic collapse has suggested to observers (such as Morales and Sachs 1988) that both

The author would like to thank the Instituto Nacional de Estadistica (INE) in Bolivia for assistance in obtaining data and for performing some of the cross-tabulations. Thanks also to a large number of people who assisted with providing information and references, including Alejandro Mercado, Marcel Mercado, Miguel Fernandez, and Teresa Reinaga (INE); Rodney Pereira and Arthur Mann, Unidad de Análisis de Políticas Económicas (UDAPE); Juan Antonio Morales, Universidad Católica Boliviana (UCB); Roberto Casanovas, Centro de Estudios para el Desarrollo Laboral y Agrario (CEDLA); John Newman, Peter Miovic, Steen Jorgenson, and Beatriz Balcazar (World Bank); to Luis Riveros and Dipak Mazumdar for helpful comments on an earlier draft; and to Rodney Schmidt for capable computer assistance.

internal and external factors were to blame for its poor performance. Bolivia's macroeconomic performance has been well documented, in part due to the notoriety of the hyperinflation. The discussion here is therefore fairly brief. The events of the 1970s and 1980s draw heavily on Morales and Sachs (1988), Morales (1987), and unpublished World Bank documents. Table 3.1 sets down some of the salient macroeconomic indicators for the 1970s and 1980s.

Table 3.1 Selected Macroeconomic Indicators, 1970–89

Year	(1) Percentage growth in GDP	(2) Inflation (percent)	(3) Debt/ export ratio[a] (percent)	(4) Current balance (US$m)	(5) Trade balance (US$m)	(6) Government deficit (percent of GDP)	(7) Effective exchange rate index[b]	(8) REER index[c]
1970	n.a.	n.a.	231.0	1.8	13.8	n.a.	95.9	n.a.
1971	4.90	n.a.	n.a.	-3.3	16.8	n.a.	95.6	n.a.
1972	5.80	n.a.	n.a.	-3.7	24.9	n.a.	104.7	n.a.
1973	6.68	n.a.	n.a.	-0.1	30.3	n.a.	135.5	n.a.
1974	5.15	n.a.	n.a.	146.1	190.3	n.a.	98.8	n.a.
1975	6.60	n.a.	166.6	-171.5	-130.6	n.a.	100.0	n.a.
1976	6.10	n.a.	n.a.	-70.8	-25.5	n.a.	101.0	n.a.
1977	4.21	n.a.	n.a.	-86.8	15.4	n.a.	98.3	n.a.
1978	3.35	13.5	n.a.	-288.7	-139.9	n.a.	96.0	31.3
1979	-0.02	45.5	n.a.	-345.5	-134.5	n.a.	92.1	32.8
1980	-0.56	23.9	214.5	-54.1	263.8	-9.1	85.7	35.8
1981	0.92	25.1	272.1	-492.0	-63.0	-7.6	72.7	45.1
1982	-4.92	296.5	313.4	-219.1	250.2	-15.9	83.2	48.9
1983	-6.51	328.5	367.0	-204.1	166.0	-17.7	82.3	44.9
1984	-0.30	2,177.2	401.8	-194.5	232.9	-24.0[p]	82.9	58.2
1985	-0.15	8,170.5	478.7	-429.8	-69.4	-9.9[e]	97.9	100.0
1986	-2.93	66.0	596.1	-405.0	-117.5	-4.0[e]	109.9	29.4
1987	2.16	10.7	743.4	-531.2	-234.1	-9.8[e]	n.a.	28.4
1988	2.78	21.5	n.a.	-396.1	-158.8	n.a.	n.a.	26.9
1989	n.a.	n.a.	n.a.	n.a.	n.a.	n.a.	n.a.	25.4

n.a. = not available

Notes: [p] = preliminary, [e] = estimate, minus sign shows a deficit.
a. Includes public and publicly guaranteed debt only.
b. 1975 = 100, less than 100 implies undervalued, more than 100 implies overvalued relative to base year.
c. 1985 = 100, more than 100 implies overvalued, 1989 value is for September.
Sources: Column (1) Muller y Asociados (1988), for 1988 World Bank data; column (2) World Bank data; column (3) World Bank (1988); columns (4), (5), (6) World Bank and Central Bank of Bolivia data; column (7) Cottani (1988); column (8) IMF (various years).

The Bolivian economy suffers from some unusual problems. The country is landlocked and relatively sparsely populated (6.6 million people spread over 1.099 million square kilometers), and there are extreme variations in altitude between the main cities, making transport problematic. The country has three main climatic zones (figure 3.1): the mountains and *altiplano* (high plains), location of mining and traditional agriculture and site of the capital La Paz; the adjacent valleys; and the eastern tropical lowlands, the most promising area for future agricultural expansion and site of the most prosperous lowland city, Santa Cruz. The poorly developed transport infrastructure means that the internal market is fragmented. It also means that the best export potential is in items with high value per unit volume (at present tin, other minerals, and coca).

Bolivia's modern economic growth dates from the 1952 revolution, which set the course of economic policy until 1985. The economy was then and is now highly dependent on the primary sector, particularly agriculture and mining. Two important cornerstones of the 1952 policy changes were agrarian reform (land was transferred from the large landowners to the peasants), and nationalization of the mines. Another important step was the heavy emphasis placed on the state's role in subsequent industrialization. As in many Latin American countries, the industrialization strategy involved import substitution, with high tariffs and an overvalued exchange rate.

The problems that ensued from this strategy in the difficult years of the 1970s and 1980s can be illustrated by some World Bank (1989) figures. In 1965, Bolivia was an average to good performer among the lower-middle-income countries in terms of the structure of production, savings, export performance, and so on. By 1987 it was a poor performer. The share of agriculture in GDP had actually risen to 24 percent of GDP (the primary sector overall contributed 34 percent of GDP by sector of production). Savings performance was dismal, 2 percent of GDP compared to an average of 21 percent for lower-middle-income countries, and so was investment at 9 percent of GDP for Bolivia versus an average of 21 percent for lower-middle-income countries. Exports had sunk to 14 percent of GDP compared to 21 percent in 1965 and to an average of 22 percent for lower-middle-income countries in 1987. Of legal merchandise exports, 93 percent

Figure 3.1 Bolivia

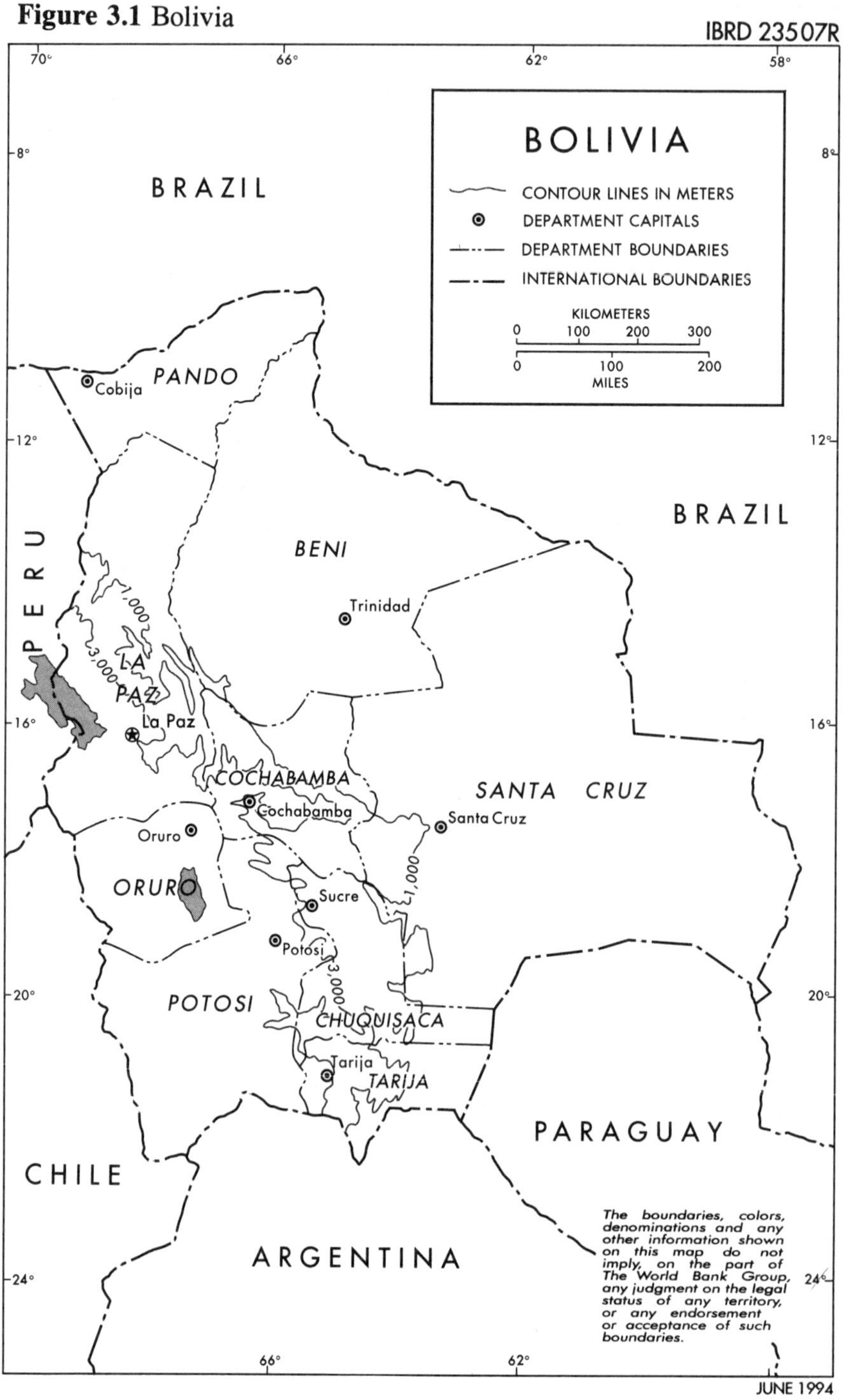
IBRD 23507R
BOLIVIA
CONTOUR LINES IN METERS
DEPARTMENT CAPITALS
DEPARTMENT BOUNDARIES
INTERNATIONAL BOUNDARIES
KILOMETERS
0 100 200 300
0 100 200
MILES
BRAZIL
BRAZIL
PERU
CHILE
ARGENTINA
PARAGUAY
PANDO
Cobija
BENI
Trinidad
LA PAZ
La Paz
COCHABAMBA
Cochabamba
SANTA CRUZ
Santa Cruz
ORURO
Oruro
Sucre
Potosi
POTOSI
CHUQUISACA
Tarija
TARIJA
1,000
3,000
70°
66°
62°
58°
8°
12°
16°
20°
24°
The boundaries, colors, denominations and any other information shown on this map do not imply, on the part of The World Bank Group, any judgment on the legal status of any territory, or any endorsement or acceptance of such boundaries.
JUNE 1994

were from fuels, minerals, and metals. In 1970, the long-term debt to GNP ratio of 49.3 percent was the highest of all lower-middle-income countries, and in 1987 it was the sixth highest at 185.6 percent, higher than that for all other Latin American countries except Nicaragua.

The political situation has been volatile, even by Latin standards, with numerous changes of government since independence in 1825. In the period of modern economic growth, a civilian government was in power from 1951 to 1964, followed by military rule until 1978. The period 1978-82 was exceptionally turbulent politically, with seven different presidents, and the military prevented a left wing coalition headed by Siles Zuazo from assuming power. The latter took office in 1982 and presided over the years of economic collapse. A more right wing government headed by Paz Estenssoro took over in July 1985 and implemented a radical shift in overall economic policy (Morales 1987). In 1989 Paz Estenssoro's party achieved a plurality in the elections, but power was assumed by a rather unusual coalition between the left of center party and a party of the further right under Paz Zamora.

Morales (1987) highlights the fairly severe internal conflicts that contributed to the political instability and, in turn, to the difficulties of economic management. There have been long-standing conflicts between the government and the miners: the government has wanted to use implicit taxes on the nationalized mining sector to pay for government expenditure, while the miners have demanded real wage increase. During the military years, the middle classes became used to consumption raises obtained at the expense of the unions, and were unwilling to give these up on return to civilian rule. The *campesinos'* (peasants') political power increased following land reform, but the government has since neglected the traditional agricultural sector. The *campesinos'* power has also been eroded by the shift toward commercial agriculture in the eastern lowlands. Finally, regional conflicts have arisen, with the prospering eastern regions unwilling to subsidize declining traditional areas in the highlands.

Some of the seeds of the economic problems of the 1980s were sown in the 1970s. The boom in oil, gas, and commodities, along with the discovery of petroleum and gas in Bolivia, led to large public capital inflows equal to 50 percent of export receipts between 1975 and 1978 according to World Bank data. Public investment dominated private investment during this period: 11 percent of GDP versus 6 to 7 percent between 1976 and 1978. The state's large role in the economy, along with political instability, tended to inhibit private sector investment, and private capital outflows took place. According to the World Bank, private capital flight and unrecorded imports amounted to over 60 percent of the value of debt accumulated during the decade 1971–81. However, economic growth was respectable at 5.5 percent per annum during 1971–78.

Bolivia's macroeconomic problems began in 1978/79 when commercial banks became concerned about their exposure and slowed down lending, which led to problems in debt servicing. Thus, the debt crisis hit Bolivia a little sooner than some of the big Latin American debtors. The year 1979 saw a large devaluation, an IMF stand-by agreement, a World Bank structural adjustment loan, and the initiation of negotiations that subsequently led to a commercial debt rescheduling in 1981. However, the political instability prevented the country from following a coherent economic policy. The Siles Zuazo government attempted six stabilization packages between 1981 and 1985. However, these were *ad hoc* and not well coordinated, and the Confederación Obrero de Bolivia (COB), the union movement, opposed them. Many strikes took place and the COB declined the president's overtures to join the government. Some of the measures in the stabilization packages actually fueled the accelerating inflation: the fiscal component was weak, and "dedollarization" (insistence that transactions be denominated in local currency rather than in U.S. dollars) arguably reduced the amount of inertia in the system. The economic difficulties were compounded by agricultural problems in 1983, when the west suffered from drought and the east from floods. Morales (1987) describes this period in more detail.

The economic collapse finally resulted in hyperinflation in 1984/85, the only hyperinflation of the 20th century not caused by war or revolution (Morales and Sachs 1988). According to Morales and Sachs (1988), the government deficit contributed heavily to the hyperinflation. Bolivia's tax base has traditionally been weak; however, the deficit rose because the government was politically unable to cut spending when one of its main sources of funds (foreign capital inflows) dried up rather than because of new spending. Resorting to inflationary finance initially helped the government's position, but eventually eroded the tax base. Economic agents (individuals, firms, and even the parastatals) delayed payments to such an extent that the amounts the government ultimately received became valueless. Some taxes (excise and property) were in nominal terms, hence their value dwindled to almost nothing, as did the value of money received for government services. The overvalued exchange rate, with the overvaluation itself exacerbated by rapid inflation, encouraged smuggling, thereby reducing import tax receipts. Finally, the downturn in economic activity also reduced imports and tax receipts. Although the government ceased debt service to the commercial banks in early 1984, this was insufficient to prevent the final onset of hyperinflation.

Stabilization and Structural Adjustment after 1985

In September 1985, the newly elected centre-right government of Paz Estenssoro implemented a policy package combining elements of both stabilization and structural adjustment. This new economic policy (NPE) occurred at an inauspicious time, only a month before the world tin market collapsed. Nevertheless, the stabilization measures were immediately successful: inflation plummeted within a week or so of the decree. The longer-run structural adjustment measures have had less immediate success. Having been negative every year but one since 1978, economic growth was positive in 1987 and 1988, although this is hard to attribute purely to the reforms.

Since 1985 the government has issued a number of other decrees aimed at strengthening its structural adjustment policies. These include the creation of the Emergency Social Fund in December 1986 and the economic reactivation decree of July 1987.

The NPE included reforms in a number of important areas, including the foreign exchange market, fiscal policy, tariff structure, external financing, public enterprises, and liberalization in three important markets, namely, those for goods, finance, and labor.

The reforms in the foreign exchange market were critical to controlling inflation. The years of very rapid inflation had led to domestic prices being set in U.S. dollar terms and then converted to domestic currency using the spot exchange rate. The exchange rate was sharply devalued to a more realistic rate, and has since been determined by weekly auctions. There is almost no difference from the parallel market rate. The foreign exchange market has also been liberalized. Morales (1987) argues that the latter development played an important role in "destrangulation" of the external sector: it encouraged the repatriation of at least some of the private capital flight from the preceding years, and the government also whitewashed the dollars from the clandestine economy.

Morales and Sachs (1988) maintain that control of fiscal and monetary policy is the other crucial component of successful stabilization. As Bolivia does not have a bond market, the fiscal deficit automatically leads to monetary expansion in the absence of foreign financing. Following the inauguration of the NPE, the government moved to control public expenditure and to raise taxes. It cut public expenditure primarily by shedding employment. The mining parastatal (COMIBOL) suffered the largest cuts—the labor force dwindled from 30,000 in 1985 to 7,000 in 1987—and there were also cuts in the hydrocarbon parastatal (YFPB). Total public employment (including the two parastatals previously mentioned) fell by 58,815 between 1985 and 1987 (CET 1988), a fall of about 25 percent (using figures on total public sector employment from Klinov 1987). On the income side, the government achieved immediate revenue from raising the price of hydrocarbons to world levels—a tenfold price increase— and by collecting back taxes from the mining and hydrocarbon parastatals, which had had an incentive to delay payment during the hyperinflation. More long-run reforms included a national value added tax of 10 percent implemented in 1986, reforms of personal taxes, and a land tax implemented (despite opposition) in 1988 that for the first time requires *campesinos* to pay direct taxes.

Restructuring incentives for trade is a frequent component of structural adjustment plans. The NPE abolished import prohibitions and licensing requirements and set tariffs initially at 10 percent, plus 10 percent of the previous tariff, which was replaced in 1986 by a uniform tariff of 20 percent on almost all items (World Bank unpublished document).

External finance is usually important to ease the transition to stabilization and structural adjustment. In 1985, Bolivia was in arrears to all its creditors and in default to some. Since then the country has become current on payments to multilateral creditors, rescheduled payments to bilateral government creditors, and has tried to negotiate relief on commercial debt. As a small country and the second poorest in the region, Bolivia has tended to receive fairly high levels of aid per capita. Although the NPE received only fairly modest external support, the Emergency Social Fund was a channel for sizeable additional amounts of aid (Newman and others 1990).

The reform of the public sector and the dismantling of much of the system put in place since the 1952 revolution was a far-reaching change. In addition to the cuts in employment, the government also stepped back from its involvement in most parastatals (except COMIBOL and YPFB). It dissolved the Bolivia Development Corporation's holdings and transferred them to regional development corporations, to municipalities, and in some cases privatized them or made them into cooperatives (Morales 1987; World Bank unpublished document). The aim was to promote the private sector, and the ensuing policy debate has emphasized the promotion of small-scale enterprise (Delons and Bour 1988; Sánchez 1988).

Finally, the NPE included provisions for liberalization in various important markets. In the goods market, the government removed price controls, which had been particularly important in the agricultural sector. The government also raised the prices of public services using neighboring country levels as guidelines and deregulated trucking (World Bank unpublished document). In the finance market, it freed interest rates and reduced controls on financial contracts. However, the banks remain weak due to the aftermath of the hyperinflation and real interest rates are still high. This tends to conflict with aims to encourage the private and small-scale sector.

The government made a number of far-reaching changes in the labor market (see Donoso 1988). In addition to public sector labor shedding, the private sector was allowed to freely rescind work contracts. Previously these were of unlimited duration, and any worker hired for longer than a certain period of time became a permanent employee. In an attempt to mitigate some of the effects of the labor shakeout, the government introduced a temporary relocation benefit for fired workers.

Another important change was the consolidation of the wage structure. Since 1971, governments had granted so many bonuses (a bonus is usually equivalent to a month's salary) that the wage actually paid and the base wage bore very little relation to each other. During November 1982 to March 1983, the number of bonuses paid in annual income (in addition to base salary) ranged from 4 in agriculture to 44 in manufacturing (Mercado and others 1988). The previous government had already tried to consolidate wages, but unions persisted in renegotiating the bonuses. After 1985, however, only overtime and Christmas bonuses remained. The government also stepped out of private sector wage negotiation, leaving it up to the employer and employee (or union), whereas previously national negotiations between the government and the unions had taken place. Public sector wage scales were regulated so as not to exceed a certain multiple of the minimum wage. Unlike some of the other stabilization plans in Latin America, wages did not need to be de-indexed as formal indexation had not been especially important in Bolivia. Although the minimum wage had been indexed between November 1982 and February 1985, it had mainly affected some social benefits such as pensions, and direct bargaining between the unions and government had been more important in the wage setting process.

Following the NPE, a number of other decrees were aimed at further structural adjustment. The Emergency Social Fund was set up as a temporary measure to create employment, motivated partly by the rise in unemployment, the increase in the share of the unemployed with previous job experience and the corresponding decline in the share of new job market entrants, and the larger share of heads of household in the unemployed (see PREALC 1985). The decree aimed to set up a two-year program for immediately implementable projects mainly in the large cities and in mining areas, and was divided into three subprograms: infrastructure, housing, and small enterprises. It was subsequently extended, but is scheduled to wind down by the end of 1990. The government hoped that the program would halve the unemployment rate.

In 1987, the government issued the economic reactivation decree, which laid out policies for reactivating the economy (see Doria Medina 1987 and Villegas Quiroga 1987 for a none too sympathetic assessment). The decree was a three-year plan that aimed to increase employment, increase the growth and diversification of exports, raise domestic production behind low and uniform tariffs, enhance the availability and reduce the cost of credit to the private sector, settle the payment schedule on outstanding external commercial bank credit, and increase the supply of housing (World Bank unpublished document). The government was to use a number of tools to achieve these ends, including a public investment program (in conjunction with the Emergency Social Fund); a fund for private sector credit; a tax rebate of 5 percent on traditional exports and 10 percent on nontraditional exports; changes in banking regulations (for example, some limits on lending and restructuring of the three state banks); a debt swap arrangement for outstanding external commercial bank debt using aid money; and the creation of some new institutions, including the National Council for Social Policy, and others in the areas of housing and export promotion (World Bank unpublished document). The government that came to power in 1989 also issued policy statements concerning structural change similar to those of the preceding government.

It is too early to assess the effects of the adjustment program. The stabilization part of the package was immediately successful. Inflation halted within a week or so (Morales and Sachs 1988), and has since remained at 10 to 14 percent per annum, one of the lowest rates in Latin America. The Emergency Social Fund has been relatively successful at reaching its employment targets, if rather slow to begin. By December 1987 it still employed fewer than 10,000 people in a given month, although by June 1988 the figure had risen to 20,000 in a month (Emergency Social Fund unpublished data). This compares to an estimated number of unemployed of 110,000 in the nine department capitals in 1988 (INE 1988b). The package was also relatively successful at targeting poorer individuals (Newman and others 1990).

However, the reactivation measures have had less immediate success. Although the GNP began to rise again in 1987 and 1988, the recovery has been relatively weak to date, and was largely concentrated in construction and manufacturing. A number of problems remain. The trade balance has worsened since 1985 despite the devaluation, although estimates suggest that coca exports more than compensate. The labor market statistics from 1988 and 1989 are worrisome. There is also concern that the Paz Zamora government may be finding it difficult to maintain tight fiscal control.

A number of important obstacles remain in the path of successful adjustment. First, some analysts argue that the exchange rate is still somewhat overvalued, causing Bolivian labor costs to be high relative to those in surrounding countries. One possible cause of this is a "Dutch disease" effect due to drug exports and possibly repatriation of some of the funds from capital flight during the inflationary years that are fueling the construction boom. The narcotics trade exerts an unmeasurable but large effect on the economy: unofficial USAID estimates for 1988 place coca exports at 56 to 87 percent of the value of legitimate merchandise exports, and 6.0 to 9.3 percent of GDP in direct effects. Overvaluation of the exchange rate is also problematic for the trade balance.

Second, Morawetz (1987) cites the problems of low labor productivity in Bolivia, due in part to low levels of human resources, that further increase the problems of export competitiveness.

Third, the opening of the economy to trade led to large contractions in sectors such as milk, paper, and chemicals (Afcha and others 1988), serious in view of Bolivia's very limited manufacturing base. Another problem for the trade sector is that people from neighboring countries with foreign exchange controls and overvalued official exchange rates are using Bolivia's free foreign exchange market. Bolivia's consumer goods market has been flooded with cheap imports from Brazil, Chile, and Peru, whose exporters can obtain bolivianos to exchange for dollars at favorable rates. Comparing Bolivia's current set of policies with the disastrous Southern Cone experiments of the 1970s to liberalize current and capital accounts simultaneously is tempting.

Fourth, the banks continue to experience difficulties, and the tight monetary policy exacerbates the problem of already scarce and expensive credit to the private sector.

Fifth, new institutions created as part of the structural adjustment measures have been slow to commence activities. The Emergency Social Fund took longer to get going than expected, partly because the central bank, which administers the fund, underwent a major reorganization and labor shakeout along with other government agencies. The other institutions created by the NEP have been even slower in getting off the ground.

Finally, additional external finance to support adjustment has been limited. Bolivia is unfortunately considered too small and unimportant to receive the same assistance with restructuring its debt that the big Latin American debtors receive, although efforts to control drug trafficking may lead to greater leverage with some aid donors. The success of the debt buy-back was modest (World Bank unpublished document), but a 1990 donor's meeting was more successful than past exercises in obtaining aid pledges.

Some people are concerned that the rather unusual coalition that formed the incoming government in 1989 may find it hard to maintain the pace of reforms. Observers are carefully examining indicators such as the government's fiscal position.

An in-depth evaluation of the structural adjustment policies will have to await further developments. However, the political costs of the measures undertaken have not been trivial: there have been numerous marches of *campesinos* in the capital, demonstrators confronted by tanks, strikes and blockades by groups such as teachers, and so on. Some early indications of recovery are therefore important to maintain political support for the measures.

The Bolivian Labor Market

Many studies examine Bolivia's labor market. This section summarizes their conclusions (see appendix A for data sources). Note that in the tables presented in this section the years covered are dictated by data availability.

Maletta (1980) describes the evolution of the Bolivia labor force based on the three censuses. Bolivia has undergone many of the same employment changes as other developing countries, namely, a falling share of employment in agriculture, an increase in the size of firms, an increase in the share of salaried employment, and a fall in the overall participation rate as younger age groups stay out of the labor force for education and older people retire. Increased participation of women over time is not obvious, but data on this are only available since 1976. The 1952 revolution occasioned some changes in employment, particularly in that land reform caused the replacement of hired labor by self-employed farmers. Subsequently a trend back to hired agricultural labor has been evident as the focus of production has shifted away from the traditional agriculture in the *altiplano* and toward commercial agriculture in the east.

The country's marked regional differences affect the labor market. Bolivia is divided into nine departments. Although the departments do not correspond exactly to different geographic zones, a crude guide is that La Paz, Potosi, and Oruro are basically western mountain and *altiplano* areas; Cochabamba, Chuquisaca, and Tarija are eastern and southern valleys; and Beni, Pando, and Santa Cruz are eastern lowlands (see figure 3.1).

Migration has followed the shift of economic activity. Between 1900 and 1976, the population decreased in three departments (Cochabamba, Potosl, and Chuquisaca), increased in three (Santa Cruz, Beni, and Pando), with little change in the other three. During 1900-50, migration was mainly toward the four cities that were at the center of traditional activities, namely, La Paz (the capital), Oruro and Potosi (mining centers), and Cochabamba (an agricultural center). Since 1950, there has been a shift toward the provinces of commercial agriculture in the eastern lowlands and a demise in the traditional mining areas, a trend likely to be accelerated by structural adjustment. Thus, in Bolivia, structural adjustment implies substantial geographic mobility.

The cities of La Paz, Santa Cruz, and Cochabamba account for most of the urban population, and together with Oruro are sometimes known as the *Eje Central* (central axis). Since data tend to be consistently available for these cities and not for some of the smaller cities, much of the discussion is based on the *Eje Central*. The *Eje Central* accounts for just under 90 percent of the employed population of the nine department capitals.

Table 3.2 shows some of the aggregate labor force statistics for Bolivia. Participation rates are similar to those in other Latin American

Table 3.2 Labor Market Indicators, Urban Centers, 1980–89

Indicator	1980	1981	1982	1983	1984	1985	1986	1987	1988	1989
	Seven cities (department capitals)									
Population older than 10 (thousands of people)	1,321	1,363	1,416	1,470	1,626	1,686	n.a.	1,830	1,977	1,772
	Eje Central (four cities)									
Population older than 10 (thousands of people)	1,155	1,196	1,246	1,279	1,454	1,501	1,535	1,625	1,730	1,606
Labor force participation rate (percent)	51.2	49.6	41.8	44.8	49.7	44.8	47.1	46.3	48.9	48.7
Unemployment rate (percent)	7.5	6.2	7.5	8.2	6.6	5.7	4.2	5.9	11.5	10.7
Underemployment rate (percent)	9.0	n.a.	4.8	3.4	4.2	2.0	2.2	3.5	7.0	5.3
Percentage of job leavers in unemployed	62.9	68.6	n.a.	67.6	67.1	50.6	49.3	56.6	76.2	66.0
Percentage of salaried employees	58.4	58.9	58.9	58.2	53.8	56.9	57.5	53.8	54.3	n.a.
Hours worked per week	44.6	n.a.	42.0	n.a.	44.6	n.a.	44.1	44.8	44.5	n.a.

n.a. = not available

Notes: The participation rate is the ratio of the economically active population to the population aged over ten years. Job leavers are those who have previously held a job (the underemployed consist of both job leavers and new entrants to the labor force). Underemployment is all those working 12 hours or less per week.

Sources: Hours worked based on author's calculations; other indicators INE (1988c, 1989).

countries. Open unemployment rates (6 to 7 percent) are not particularly high at least until 1988 (unsurprising in view of the lack of any unemployment insurance system), and rates of under-employment are also not especially high.[1]

Table 3.3 gives the sectoral composition of employment for selected years. According to the World Bank (1988), Bolivia has a somewhat lower share of its labor force in agriculture and a somewhat larger share in manufacturing than other countries with similar income levels.

Table 3.3 Sectoral Composition of Employment, Selected Years *(percent)*

Sector	1970	1976	1980	1986
Agriculture	50.6	48.1	46.5	49.9
Mining	4.0	3.3	4.0	3.1
Hydrocarbons	0.3	0.3	0.4	0.5
Manufacturing	9.7	10.1	10.3	8.9
Construction	3.7	5.7	5.5	2.6
Utilities	0.2	0.2	0.4	0.5
Transport	4.0	3.9	5.4	5.6
Commerce	7.2	7.4	7.4	8.2
Finance	0.6	0.6	0.6	0.8
Services	19.7	19.6	19.3	20.0
Tradables	64.6	61.8	61.2	62.4
Nontradables	35.4	37.4	38.6	37.2
Total	100.0	100.0	100.0	100.0

Notes: Tradables include agriculture, hydrocarbons, manufacturing, and mining. All other sectors are considered nontradables. Figures are rounded and therefore may not add exactly to 100 percent.
Source: Ministry of Labor unpublished data.

1. The INE's underemployment measure (working less than 12 hours per week) is not identical with what labor economists might define as underemployment, as some people voluntarily work short hours, while others who work longer hours may be in very low paid jobs or jobs not commensurate with their abilities. However, the latter concept is very hard to quantify empirically.

Table 3.4 provides an overview of different labor market sectors. The state and capitalist sectors correspond roughly to the formal sector, while small enterprises, family businesses, and domestic servants correspond to the informal sector. The table illustrates the small employment share of the private formal sector, which is a third or less the size of the small enterprise and family business sectors combined, and also employs fewer people than the state sector. Family businesses account for the largest share of employment of any sector. There are some variations between cities: La Paz has a larger state sector than the other cities, as well as a larger formal private sector.

Table 3.4 also shows that the state sector has the second highest average age of workers, the highest level of education, the second highest proportion of migrants, the highest mean incomes, and the best coverage by benefits. The domestic sector is the exact opposite, with the lowest age and mean income, and is evidently an entry sector for young female migrants. Family businesses also have a disproportionately large share of female employees, the oldest workers, low wages, and low education. Those women who manage to obtain employment in the state and both enterprise sectors require higher levels of education than men in the same sectors.

Klinov (1987) describes the public sector. This sector is not especially large in Bolivia (11.2 percent of employment) in comparison to other Latin American and industrialized countries (18 percent of employment in 1980). However, the sector grew from 9.3 percent of total employment in 1971 to 14.0 percent in 1985 before falling back below 12 percent in 1986 and continuing to decline in 1987. What is of more concern is the very large share of the public sector in formal sector employment: 60 to 62 percent in 1980. During 1980–85 the growth in public administration alone accounted for 172 percent of the increase in salaried employment, thus indicating the substantial weakness of the private formal sector.

The literature seems to have neglected the private formal sector. Recent policy concern has focused on small-scale enterprises (Morawetz 1987; Sánchez 1988). The formal sector is relatively small, was affected by the hyperinflation, and continues to suffer from the small and fragmented internal market. It continues to have problems resulting from the reduced tariff protection since 1985, which

Table 3.4 Employment, Socioeconomic Characteristics, and Gender Differences, by Labor Market Sector, Selected Cities and Years

Category	State	Capitalist enterprise	Small enterprise	Family business	Domestic	Total
Employment (percent)						
La Paz, 1980	23.6	17.2	16.9	36.8	5.3	100.0
Santa Cruz, 1980	21.0	14.9	27.7	27.7	8.7	100.0
Cochabamba, 1983	21.3	13.8	24.3	33.4	7.2	100.0
Santa Cruz, 1986	15.6	19.5	29.0	32.9	3.0	100.0
Cochabamba, 1986	23.3	12.5	21.7	41.0	1.5	100.0
Socioeconomic characteristics, La Paz 1980						
Average age (years)	36.0	33.0	32.0	38.0	24.0	35.0
Percentage of migrants	65.3	59.7	61.0	60.0	79.9	62.5
Education (years)	11.7	8.6	7.4	5.0	3.6	7.5
Income (pesos)	1,200.0	997.0	861.0	564.0	227.0	835.0
Percentage without benefits	5.4	41.7	79.5	99.9	69.2	63.0
Gender differences, La Paz 1980						
Males (percentage)	27.6	22.2	22.4	27.4	3.9	100.0
Females (percentage)	17.2	8.9	8.1	52.4	13.3	100.0
Mean education (years)						
Men	11.1	8.1	7.3	6.3	5.7	8.2
Women	13.2	10.4	7.7	3.8	3.5	6.3

Source: Cochabamba: Casanovas and Rojas (1988); Santa Cruz: Escobar de Pabón and García (1988); La Paz: Casanovas (1987).
Note: Migrants are those who were not born in the city in which they work. Capitalist enterprises refers to the private formal sector.

combined with the overvalued exchange rate and low labor productivity render domestic labor costs uncompetitively high.

The informal sector has been much more extensively studied, perhaps due to its greater size (see Casanovas 1987; Casanovas and Rojar 1988; CEDLA 1988; CET 1987; Escobar de Pabón and García 1988; INE and UDAPE 1987). The sector is fairly heterogeneous, encompassing small-scale enterprises (INE's definition is fewer than five employees), self-employed workers, family businesses, and (depending on the definition) domestic workers.

The informal sector is very large, both in terms of share of employment and number of economic units.[2] By sector of production, the informal sector is concentrated in services and commerce: 90.7 percent of informal compared to 47.4 percent of formal establishments are in this sector. However, the sheer number of informal sector establishments implies that they nevertheless contribute a large proportion (74.2 percent) of the number of establishments in manufacturing, including small enterprises and family businesses (Casanovas 1987). Informal sector manufacturing establishments produce mainly clothing, textiles, and thread (over 50 percent of the establishments), with the other products in order of importance being furniture, food, pottery, metalworking, shoes, and other (Casanovas 1987).

Relatively little is known about Bolivia's rural labor markets. Ormachea (1988) and Maletta (1980) synthesize what is available, mainly from census data, although migration surveys yield some information. Self-employed farmers on the *altiplano* practice traditional agriculture with relatively small landholdings and traditional farming techniques. The pressure for outmigration is substantial. In the lowlands commercial agriculture is the dominant

---

2. Of the 63,289 economic units listed in the first national survey of economic establishments, 95.1 percent were small (fewer than five employees). If one includes market stands and ambulant commerciants (people who set up on street corners, not in licensed spots, or who walk around selling things) as economic units, 97.8 percent of the 142,469 economic units were small. However, the employment share of the informal sector was smaller: 44.1 percent of the 245,611 workers if market stands, and so on are excluded, 58.4 percent of the 330,407 if they are included. This reflects the much smaller scale of informal compared to formal sector enterprises: 1.4 persons per establishment in the informal sector, versus 44.0 in the formal in 1985 (INE and UDAPE 1987).

form of cultivation. About 76 percent of production in the country as a whole is traditional and 24 percent commercial (Ormachea 1988). Migrant labor is important in commercial agriculture. The crops that require seasonal labor include sugarcane, cotton, rubber, chestnuts, and grapes. The migrant flows can be relatively large: for example, in 1987 seasonal labor requirements were estimated at 12,000 people in Santa Cruz (Ormachea 1988) and around 1,900 in Tarija for sugarcane and 10,000 in Santa Cruz for cotton. These seasonal labor requirements are largely filled by migrants, who often travel fairly long distances: of those in Santa Cruz, over half were estimated to come from other departments. A sizeable fraction of those migrants surveyed were nonagricultural workers.

There have been a number of studies of urban migration (Casanovas and Rojas 1988; Escobar de Pabón and García 1988; Maletta 1980; PREALC 1988). As discussed above, these flows have been large in the past, as the geographic location of economic activity has shifted. Some of the migration has been the usual rural-urban flows accompanying economic development—the urban share of the population was 27.3 percent in 1950 and 41.7 percent in 1976 (Maletta 1980)—but urban-urban migration has also been important and has been growing in recent years. Rural-rural migration is also significant: in addition to seasonal flows, farm families have been encouraged to colonize the eastern lowlands. La Paz and Santa Cruz have been the main urban destinations for migrants. Little is known about recent migration flows to coca growing areas, but USAID unofficial estimates for 1988 suggest that 180,000–210,000 workers are involved in production and another 30,000 to 50,000 in transporting, processing, and exporting; presumably an increase over traditional numbers in this sector.

The domestic service sector is an important entry point for young, female, rural migrants. However, many migrants obtain salaried jobs: 77 percent in La Paz and 80.6 percent in Santa Cruz in 1987 (PREALC 1988), and until 1985, the state sector was an important recipient of migrants. Migrants also tend to be overrepresented in construction. PREALC (1988) argues that the onset of the economic crisis in 1976–80 led to an increased flow of migrants into services; prior to this date services and the informal sector had not been an important point of insertion of migrants contrary to many usual theories of migration.

Stabilization, Structural Adjustment, and the Labor Market

Relatively few studies on adjustments in the labor market in Bolivia in the late 1970s and 1980s are available (see Afcha and others 1988; CET 1988; INE and UDAPE 1987; Morales 1987). It is important to try to separate two sets of factors, namely, the usual cyclical effects on the labor market caused by economic conditions (1982–83 was a recessionary period when the GDP fell over 11 percent) and trend changes following stabilization and structural adjustment policies introduced in 1985. However, separating these events is not easy, especially since data are only available for a relatively short span of years.

The figures in table 3.2 suggest that mainly cyclical factors were at work in affecting participation and unemployment rates. In the recession years (1982–83) participation rates fell (discouraged worker effect), unemployment rates peaked, the percentage of unemployed who had previously worked increased, and hours worked per week fell. Detecting an effect due to stabilization or structural adjustment on these labor market variables is difficult, at least until 1987. The only discernible trend to 1987 is a decrease in the percentage of salaried employees. Thus, despite economic stagnation, unemployment apparently did not rise. However, several of the labor market indicators worsened in 1988 and 1989: unemployment, underemployment, and share of job leavers in the unemployed. This merits close watch in case it represents a delayed response to the structural adjustment measures.[3]

It is interesting to speculate on the role of the Emergency Social Fund in alleviating unemployment. The fund was first suggested in 1985 (PREALC 1985), at a time when the 1982–83 unemployment

---

3. However, some caution is required in interpretation as the INE changed some of its methods in 1988, including a switch from mainframe computer processing to use of microcomputers. The fact that the urban population of working age fell in 1989 suggests data problems unless the shift to rural areas and coca growing areas was quite dramatic.

Table 3.5 Urban Real Wages by Sector, 1970–80, 1982–88

Sector	Ministry of Labor data (1970 = 100)											Ministry of Labor data (Mar. 1982 = 100)					INE data [a] (1982 = 100)		
	1970	1971	1972	1973	1974	1975	1976	1977	1978	1979	1980	Dec. 1982	Dec. 1983	Dec. 1984	Dec. 1985	Dec. 1986	1986	1987	1988
Mining	100.0	102.0	100.0	102.0	82.0	79.0	83.0	81.0	76.0	78.0	76.0	161.8	76.7	117.4	110.0	99.7	76.0	68.3	55.6
Hydrocarbons	100.0	102.0	100.0	102.0	82.0	142.0	189.0	209.0	263.0	248.0	249.0	74.4	48.5	199.8	66.0	66.4			
Manufacturing	100.0	113.0	114.0	123.0	99.0	98.0	114.0	111.0	111.0	114.0	102.0	81.3	113.6	136.3	51.8	58.5	52.5	42.9	31.9
Construction	100.0	119.0	116.0	109.0	97.0	90.0	109.0	115.0	115.0	131.0	121.0	51.5	47.3	92.5	51.9	73.5	101.9	84.7	76.7
Utilities	100.0	87.0	82.0	85.0	69.0	91.0	92.0	93.0	97.0	84.0	84.0	82.9	43.1	88.9	47.0	74.3	64.5	63.9	68.0
Transport	100.0	104.0	102.0	122.0	96.0	96.0	102.0	112.0	120.0	120.0	120.0	56.7	44.8	55.8	68.5	57.9	89.2	71.2	59.0
Commerce	100.0	108.0	105.0	117.0	83.0	79.0	101.0	107.0	114.0	110.0	91.0	69.0	56.9	76.4	48.2	62.5	43.5	43.8	23.5
Finance	100.0	98.0	94.0	73.0	46.0	43.0	42.0	53.0	60.0	59.0	53.0	89.8	65.9	108.9	95.1	129.5	69.4	64.7	47.6
Services	100.0	102.0	100.0	104.0	87.0	70.0	76.0	92.0	89.0	84.0	80.0	63.4	57.1	103.6	47.5	72.1	n.a.	n.a.	n.a.
Public administration												51.9	45.8	64.8	46.0	32.7	69.3	27.9	50.5
Average for all sectors	100.0	114.0	116.0	118.0	94.0	86.0	98.0	107.0	108.0	110.0	100.0	75.2	63.4	99.1	60.4	74.2	58.8	51.8	38.7

n.a. = not available

Note: Tradables include manufacturing, hydrocarbons, and mining.

a. INE data are for *Eje Central* only.

Sources: 1970–80: Delons and Bour (1988); 1982–86: Afcha and others (1988); 1986–88: authors' calculations from INE and Encuesta Permanente de Hogares (EPH) data, deflated using consumer price index of June.

120

data were becoming available. At that time unemployment was rising, and the percentage of job leavers and heads of household among the unemployed was increasing. At the same time, the government anticipated that the labor market measures included in the structural adjustment decrees would create further unemployment. However, the fund did not become significant in terms of job creation until 1987/88.

Table 3.3 shows some disturbing trends in sectoral employment. During 1970–80 the sectoral shifts were of the kind usually associated with economic development, namely, a shift out of agriculture and into industry. This trend was abruptly reversed in the 1980s, with a shift back out of industry into agriculture, commerce, and services. This is of concern if it implies a crowding of displaced workers in relatively low productivity and low remuneration activities. Another way of interpreting these data is to group sectors into tradables (agriculture, mining, hydrocarbons, and manufacturing) and nontradables (all other sectors). On this basis, Bolivia's inward-oriented economic policies prior to 1986 were associated with a continuous shift out of tradables; thereafter the trend was reversed. However, coca production may also be responsible for the increased share of agriculture, and hence of tradables.

Table 3.4 shows the shifts between market sectors in two of the three major cities over time. In both Cochabamba and Santa Cruz, the family business sector gained in relative employment share. In Santa Cruz, which has tended to benefit from structural adjustment, both enterprise sectors (capitalist and small) gained in employment share, but they lost out in Cochabamba.

Table 3.5 presents data on real wages.[4] Note that the data for the hyperinflation years of 1984 and 1985 are particularly unreliable, therefore, apparent sectoral differences in 1984 and 1985 should not be ascribed undue significance. The net effect of the 1970-80 decade was of no change in real wages: the onset of the economic crisis

---

4. I have been unable to obtain the original Ministry of Labor data and have had to rely on indices calculated in secondary sources, namely, Delons and Bour 1988; Afcha and others 1988; Muller and Machicado 1986. It is not possible to link the data for the 1970s and 1980s, since the sectoral data for 1981 are not available in these secondary sources, and it is not always clear which month of the year is being used.

eroded the gains made up to 1978. As concerns sectoral differences, the hydrocarbon sector did relatively well, while commerce and services did relatively badly.

In the early 1980s real wages began to fall substantially. Using the Ministry of Labor data, and assuming that the Muller and Machicado index for 1981 represents a point near to the end of the year and can be linked to the March 1982 base for table 3.5, then at a conservative estimate real wages fell by 20 percent of their 1980 value by the end of 1981, and by a further 25 percent of their March 1982 value by December 1986, that is, by 1986 real wages were around 59 percent of their 1980 (and hence also 1970) value. If instead we use the INE series for the period 1982–86 (and arguably this is better, due to the break in the Ministry series due to the consolidation of the salary structure in 1985), then real wages in 1986 were 52 percent of their 1982 value, and thus 41 percent or less of their value in 1980. Both sets of data agree that real wages fell substantially, and apparently far exceeded the fall in per capita GDP during the same period (around 73 percent of its 1980 value by 1986).

Both the ministry and INE series show similar sectoral patterns of change in real wages. The sectors that fared the worst were manufacturing, transport, public administration, and (according to INE) commerce. Manufacturing obviously suffered from the fall in tariff protection, transport from deregulation, and public administration from the drastic labor shedding. The explanation for commerce is most likely the "crowding" one, namely, that labor shifted into the relatively unremunerative sectors in the informal sector.

Rough, separate estimates of indexes for real wages in the tradable and nontradable sectors show that the tradable sector fared consistently worse during 1982–88. Note, however, that no wage series is available for the agricultural sector, the one tradable sector that was gaining in employment share. Nevertheless, the data do suggest that the shift in incentives for manufacturing due to the change in the exchange rate was not large enough to offset the adverse effects of decreased protection for this sector.

Table 3.6 provides some information on the formal and informal sectors. The informal sectors are defined below the table. The formal

Table 3.6 Share of Employment in Informal Sector, Urban Areas, and Median Earnings, Selected Years
(percent)

Sector	1982[a]	1983[a]	1984[a]	1985[a] ⋯	1988[b]
	Employment share				
Mining	16.1	n.a.	9.3	n.a.	20.6
Manufacturing	59.2	n.a.	66.7	n.a.	68.2
Construction	61.4	n.a.	63.5	n.a.	56.1
Utilities	6.8	n.a.	14.8	n.a.	8.7
Transport	70.8	n.a.	67.7	n.a.	70.3
Commerce	83.6	n.a.	90.6	n.a.	89.9
Finance	40.9	n.a.	29.1	n.a.	40.7
Services	45.5	n.a.	42.8	n.a.	46.4
All sectors	56.9	61.1	60.5	56.3	64.3
	Median earnings				
Informal as percentage formal	54.3	n.a.	69.3	80.0	60.0

n.a. = not available
Notes: The informal sector is defined as self-employed workers, excluding professionals; domestic employees; and employees, employers, and unpaid family workers in establishments with fewer than five workers. Earnings are for primary occupation only. As a percentage of earnings in the formal sector, median earnings in the informal sector were 54 percent in 1982, 69 percent in 1984, and 60 percent in 1988.
a. Includes data for eight cities, all department capitals except Cobija.
b. Cities of *Eje Central* only.
Sources: 1982 and 1984: INE and UDAPE (1987); 1988: author's calculations.

sector includes those working in establishments of six or more people and professionals. The data suggest that there has been a general increase in informalization over time, particularly in manufacturing and commerce. Casanovas (1987) confirms that the number of self-employed workers rose much faster than the size of the labor force during the 1980s: he estimates that the informal sector in La Paz increased from 47 percent of employment in 1976 to 53 percent in 1980 and 58 percent in 1984. We can combine this information with INE and UDAPE (1987) data that indicate that the median size of informal sector establishments actually fell during the 1980s from 2.06 people in 1982 to 1.75 people in 1985, while the median size of private formal sector establishments increased from 13.0 people in 1983 to 40.9 people in 1985. One interpretation is therefore that there was increased concentration in the formal sector as smaller formal sector establishments went out of business and people shifted into the informal sector, particularly into one-person enterprises.

Anecdotal evidence on the shift from formal to informal sector employment, particularly into petty commerce activities, is also available. The mechanism for worker dismissal often encouraged such a shift. The miners and some other public employees who were dismissed were eligible for fairly large severance payments, extending up to two or three years wages for miners (CET 1988). In some cases these payments were made in dollars. Apparently a number of those dismissed used these severance payments to purchase imported consumer goods and set themselves up in trade and commerce.

Figures on formal versus informal sector earnings (see table 3.6, notes) suggest that informal sector earnings rose relative to formal sector earnings during the hyperinflation, but had dropped back again by 1988 (those on fixed wages and salaries would tend to lose out during rapid inflation so this finding is not surprising).

Thus, the evidence suggests a pattern of labor market adjustment during economic crisis, with as yet little in the way of recovery and resumption of economic growth. The consequence of prolonged stagnation and very severe recession in 1982–83 was a fall in participation rates, a fall in the proportion of salaried employment, an increase in informalization of economic activity, and a reversal of the sectoral shifts that usually accompany economic development. However, on a more optimistic note, there seemed to be a reversal of past trends in which labor had consistently shifted out of tradables. Displaced labor from the formal sector has moved into self-employment, into one-person establishments, and frequently into petty commerce activities. The evidence does not suggest that the labor market was rigid and impeded adjustment. In addition, the decline in real wages is particularly important in a relatively poor country such as Bolivia.

Implications of Labor Market Adjustment

Labor Market Adjustment and Income Distribution

Work on income distribution in Bolivia is hampered by the lack of national survey data and the very fragmentary information available for the rural sector. A number of studies are available that deal with poverty (for example, R. Morales 1985, 1987). The INE household surveys can be used to study the distribution of urban income, but the literature is somewhat frustrating in this respect. Afcha and others (1988) compare data for 1982 and 1985, but do not state whether they are using constant or current prices. INE and UDAPE (1987) compare 1982, 1984, and 1985, but in current prices, and only for the informal sector. Finally, the INE is now publishing information on income distribution (INE 1988b), but only since 1988. Moreover, all these studies deal only with the distribution of earned income across individuals.

To give some idea of trends over time, figure 3.2 presents Lorenz curves for 1982, 1985, and 1988 for the distribution of earned income on a personal basis. Variation in income distribution over short periods of time is relatively unusual, yet noticeable changes are evident here. The hyperinflation apparently improved the distribution of income for the vast majority of the population, although the bottom 15 percent lost out slightly and the top 10 percent gained.

Table 3.7 compares the personal distribution of earned income with the household distribution of earned income and the household distribution of total income for 1988. The results show that the distribution of earned income on a household basis is slightly less unequal than on a personal basis, particularly at the extreme deciles.

The inclusion of unearned income also tends to improve income distribution slightly (however, data on unearned income are probably unreliable, especially in the top deciles). Per capita and per household distributions are not consistently different. Apparently household size is not systematically related to household income, unlike in some other countries. Overall, the data suggest that the distribution of

Figure 3.2 Lorenz Curves for Personal Distribution of Earned Income, Selected Years

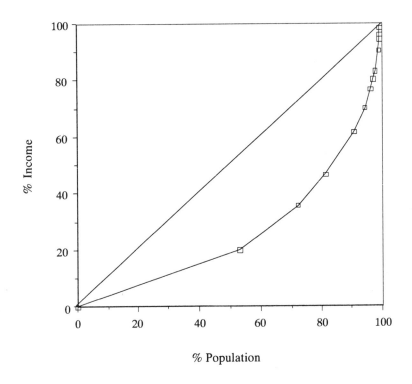

personal earnings on an individual basis is a reasonable guide to urban income distribution.

These data, however, only provide part of the story on income distribution. The shift from labor earnings to other types of income (as evidenced by the much larger fall in real wages than in per capita GDP) would likely worsen income distribution, but the shift in favor of rural areas would have the opposite effect.

Table 3.7 Urban Income Distribution Data, 1988
(percentage of total income accruing per decile)

Decile	Earned income		Total income		Earned income per individual[c]
	Per household[a]	Per capita[b]	Per household[a]	Per capita[b]	
1	1.1	1.0	1.1	1.2	0.9
2	1.9	2.1	2.2	2.1	2.2
3	3.4	2.8	3.4	2.9	3.2
4	3.8	4.0	3.8	4.3	4.6
5	5.0	5.0	5.3	5.3	5.0
6	6.4	7.0	6.2	6.9	6.7
7	8.5	8.1	9.1	8.2	8.5
8	11.7	11.9	11.4	12.4	10.4
9	16.4	16.9	16.6	16.6	15.7
10	41.8	41.2	40.9	40.0	42.8
Bottom 40%	10.2	9.9	10.5	10.5	10.9
Middle 40%	31.6	32.0	32.0	32.8	30.6
Top 20%	58.2	58.1	57.5	56.6	58.5

a. Deciles calculated on the basis of household income.
b. Deciles calculated on the basis of income per capita, for households.
c. Deciles calculated on the basis of individuals' own earnings.
Source: Author's calculations.

Labor Market Adjustment and Regional Development

As indicated earlier, structural economic changes in Bolivia frequently imply regional shifts in employment and economic activity. Between 1900 and 1950 the major shifts were toward the *altiplano*, the center of mining and traditional agricultural activities. Since 1950, and especially since the crisis in minerals, the eastern lowland provinces have gained in importance, both for industry and for commercial agriculture. This has important consequences for migration and for the political economy.

Table 3.8 provides some information on labor force indicators by city. Larger cities tend to have higher participation rates and a higher percentage of nonsalaried workers. Evidently the greater level of

Table 3.8 Labor Force Indicators by City, Selected Years

City	Population over age 10 ('000)		Participation rate (%)		Unemployment rate (%)		Percentage salaried		Percentage in informal sector	Mean monthly earnings as percentage of mean for Eje Central	
	1980	1987	1980	1987	1980	1987	1980	1987	1988	1981	1988
Total											
(7 cities)[a]	1,321	1,830	49.8	46.3	7.3	9.2	59.3	54.3	65.0[b]	100.0[b]	100.0[b]
La Paz	600	789	54.8	49.6	9.6	11.9	56.9	54.2	70.4	81.7	66.4
Cochabamba	193	264	47.4	42.5	7.4	4.8	57.8	56.4	57.6	104.0	123.3
Santa Cruz	250	430	48.0	48.4	2.0	5.3	63.4	53.1	62.6	136.2	143.7
Oruro	112	143	45.0	35.7	7.5	16.7	56.5	47.1	61.0	82.5	80.3
Sucre	58	69	41.3	41.7	11.3	8.2	65.6	60.7	n.a.	n.a.	n.a.
Potosí	69	83	34.7	38.0	1.2	9.1	70.4	60.5	n.a.	n.a.	n.a.
Tarija	39	53	48.5	47.6	4.9	5.1	63.4	55.8	n.a.	n.a.	n.a.
Trinidad	23	n.a.	42.6	n.a.	1.3	n.a.	69.7	n.a.	n.a.	n.a.	n.a.

n.a. = not available

Notes: 1981 data needs weighting. Earnings data are for primary and secondary occupations combined.

a. Includes all department capitals except Cobija and Trinidad.

b. Includes only the four cities of the *Eje Central*.

Sources: Population, participation, unemployment, and percentage of salaried workers: INE (1988c); remainder: author's calculations.

128

overall economic activity in larger centers is better able to support informal sector activities. The most prosperous cities of the *Eje Central* are Santa Cruz and Cochabamba. The *altiplano* cities of La Paz and Oruro have markedly lower levels of earnings per person.

The recession had different effects on different cities. The highest unemployment rates in 1987 were in the three *altiplano* cities, namely, Oruro and Potosí, the two worst hit by the problems in mining, and La Paz, the immediate destination of most *altiplano* migrants. Participation rates in 1987 were the lowest in the two mining cities, Oruro and Potosí, which might suggest discouraged worker effects. Earnings trends suggest that La Paz fared the worst relative to the other cities of the *Eje Central*, again implying substantial immigration to the informal sector in La Paz.

These regional shifts imply some future adjustment problems. The eastern cities are in an area where the transport infrastructure is less well developed and where exporting costs are higher. In addition, the government has apparently encountered difficulties in shifting the burden of taxation to the newer economic activities in the east. In the past, taxing the nationalized mining sector was easier, notwithstanding the occasional clashes between the mining unions and the government. Another somewhat unusual feature is to have the capital city located in an area of declining economic activity.

Labor Market Adjustment and Women

Most experts believe that women tend to be especially disadvantaged during the process of structural adjustment. As more marginal employees, they are more likely to lose their jobs during a recession, at the same time as recession may force more women into the labor market to supplement falling family incomes. A counterargument would be that women are less likely to be located in the public and formal sectors that are worst hit by structural adjustment.

The literature suggests that Bolivian women have a worse position in the labor market than men. Casanovas' (1987) data (table 3.4) show that women are concentrated in lower paying sectors with fewer benefits, and that to be able to break into the formal sector women require more education than men. Fernández (1988) reports that in La

Table 3.9 Urban Labor Market Indicators by Gender, *Eje Central*, 1980–88

Variable	1980	1981	1982	1983	1984	1985	1986	1987	1988
Participation rate (%)									
Men	67.1	n.a.	58.3	n.a.	61.8	n.a.	58.0	59.6	58.6
Women	35.7	n.a.	26.9	n.a.	38.6	n.a.	32.8	35.2	40.0
Unemployment rate (%)									
Men	6.4	n.a.	9.0	n.a.	7.8	n.a.	5.6	6.6	11.5
Women	6.2	n.a.	5.5	n.a.	4.9	n.a.	1.9	4.6	11.5
Underemployment rate (%)									
Men	7.5	n.a.	4.4	n.a.	2.7	n.a.	1.5	2.4	5.1
Women	11.6	n.a.	5.5	n.a.	6.4	n.a.	3.3	5.3	9.5
Percentage of salaried employees									
Men	66.1	n.a.	60.3	n.a.	59.8	n.a.	60.4	57.6	60.2
Women	46.7	n.a.	56.5	n.a.	45.0	n.a.	47.4	47.7	46.4
Men's earnings as percentage of women's earnings	n.a.	205.0	108.09	n.a.	169.9	n.a.	169.7	175.2	199.7
Percentage of women in sector									
Mining & hydrocarbons	4.9	n.a.	n.a.	n.a.	n.a.	n.a.	n.a.	n.a.	18.4
Manufacturing	32.5	n.a.	n.a.	n.a.	n.a.	n.a.	n.a.	n.a.	31.5
Construction	2.0	n.a.	n.a.	n.a.	n.a.	n.a.	n.a.	n.a.	8.9
Utilities	18.9	n.a.	n.a.	n.a.	n.a.	n.a.	n.a.	n.a.	2.5
Transport	6.6	n.a.	n.a.	n.a.	n.a.	n.a.	n.a.	n.a.	7.1
Commerce	66.3	n.a.	n.a.	n.a.	n.a.	n.a.	n.a.	n.a.	65.6
Finance	28.9	n.a.	n.a.	n.a.	n.a.	n.a.	n.a.	n.a.	21.6
Services	42.8	n.a.	n.a.	n.a.	n.a.	n.a.	n.a.	n.a.	45.6
Formal	n.a.	n.a.	n.a.	n.a.	n.a.	n.a.	n.a.	n.a.	25.0
Informal	n.a.	n.a.	n.a.	n.a.	n.a.	n.a.	n.a.	n.a.	49.4
Total	38.3	n.a.	n.a.	n.a.	n.a.	n.a.	n.a.	n.a.	42.8

n.a. = not available

Note: 1981 data need weighting.

Sources: 1980, 1982, 1984, 1986, 1987: INE calculations; 1981, 1988: author's calculations.

Paz, 40 percent of women work as individuals, three-quarters of these in commerce. He also describes the precarious situation of women in El Alto, the poorest suburb of La Paz and destination of most low-income migrants to the city. In El Alto, a 1987 survey showed that 34 percent of working women earned less than Bs 50 a month, at a time when the weekly minimum wage was Bs 200. The survey also showed that women were engaged in additional work in the home designed to supplement their inadequate household incomes. Of households in El Alto, 6 percent grow food (quite a feat in a suburb), 18 percent keep chickens, and 8 percent keep rabbits; all predominantly female activities.

As regards the impact of the recession on women, CET (1988) argues that those subject to dismissal from the formal sector were more likely to be women because of the higher costs of maternity leave and their allegedly lower productivity. However, the biggest group among those dismissed were miners, of whom only 5 percent were women.

Table 3.9 analyzes urban labor market indicators by gender. Female participation rates tend to be lower than those for men, but unlike the rates for men have not generally declined over time. Possibly Bolivia is following (belatedly) the secular trend elsewhere in Latin America for increased female labor force participation. Also, the hyperinflation might have led to increased participation of secondary income earners so that families could make ends meet. The table also shows that female unemployment rates tend to be higher than for men. The latter might be in line with the luxury unemployment view, that is, secondary family workers can more readily afford to be unemployed. Women work on average somewhat shorter hours than men, but this may reflect the choice of part-time work by some female workers. In general, women are overrepresented in family businesses and domestic service, where hours are very long. Fewer women than men are salaried, but unlike men, there was not a substantial fall in the proportion salaried between 1980 and 1988. As far as the relative male-female earnings differential is concerned, there is little evidence of change over time (the 1982 data are an outlier and are perhaps unreliable).

The sectors that are most heavily female are commerce, services, and manufacturing. In 1988, women accounted for half of informal sector but only a quarter of formal sector employment, which explains in large part the much lower average wages of women.

Thus, women are at a disadvantage in the labor market in Bolivia compared to men, as they are in most countries, especially developing countries. Undoubtedly women and children suffered substantially during the economic recession and stagnation; however, there is no evidence that structural adjustment *per se* has had especially adverse effects on women in the labor force in Bolivia.

Labor Market Adjustment, Political Economy, and Effects on Long-Run Economic Growth

Political economy is very important in understanding the persistent inflationary tendencies and problems in adjusting in many Latin American countries, and this is definitely true in the case of Bolivia. We have already referred to the political economy's contribution to the hyperinflation. The political economy of adjustment is a very large topic that this paper can only touch on.

With a relatively strong right wing government in power between 1985 and 1989 that was willing to use displays of police and military power where necessary (although using the Catholic Church as a mediating factor), the population accepted the strong economic measures undertaken in the stabilization and structural adjustment programs. Despite strong unions, the government liberalized the labor market substantially and real wages fell dramatically. However, only time will tell whether the government can maintain the current consensus unless more vigorous economic growth resumes soon. The rise in unemployment in 1988 is a worrisome sign.

As regards the working of the labor market and its effects on the resumption of long-run economic growth, the labor market seems to have been relatively flexible in terms of the substantial sectoral shifts, regional migration, relative wage changes, and real wage declines observed. The blame for lack of resumption of sustained growth does not seem to lie in this sector.

One way to analyze labor market functioning in more detail is to use earnings functions. Table 3.10 contains some simple earnings

Table 3.10 Urban Earnings Functions, 1981 and 1988

Independent variable	Earnings functions coefficients[a]		Variable means[b]	
	1981	1988	1981	1988
Education (years)	0.122	0.0951	8.091	9.694
	(55.399)***	(25.835)***	(4.936)	(4.819)
Experience (years)	0.053	0.0322	21.170	20.511
	(24.435)***	(9.207)***	(14.682)	(14.155)
Experience^2 (years^2)	-0.000640	-0.000308	663.724	621.029
	(17.358)***	(4.911)***	(816.637)	(759.063)
Female dummy	-0.327	-0.234	0.384	0.415
	(16.314)***	(7.457)***	(0.486)	(0.493)
Unmarried dummy	-0.159	-0.022	0.368	0.339
	(7.222)***	(0.639)***	(0.482)	(0.474)
Informal dummy	-0.156	-0.0558	0.339	0.347
	(7.430)***	(1.704)*	(0.473)	(0.476)
Oruro	-0.0334	-0.262	0.849	0.162
	(0.986)	(6.032)***	(0.279)	(0.368)
Cochabamba	0.199	0.136	0.266	0.248
	(8.924)**	(3.528)***	(0.442)	(0.432)
Santa Cruz	0.487	0.339	0.214	0.233
	(20.607)**	(8.720)***	(0.410)	(0.423)
Natural log (hourly wage) (current Bs.)	—	—	2.853	0.183
			(1.002)	(0.977)
Intercept	1.238	-1.153	—	—
	(29.882)**	(16.145)***		
Adjusted R^2	0.478	0.253	—	—
F statistic	663.741**	127.992***	—	—
degrees of freedom	9,6502	9,3364		

— = not applicable
* implies significant at 10 percent level
** implies significant at 5 percent level
*** implies significant at 1 percent level
a. Figures in parentheses are t statistics.
b. Figures in parentheses are standard deviations.
Source: Author's calculations.

functions for 1981 and 1988. (Note that use of the semi-log functional form implies that coefficients represent the effects of a change of one unit in the independent variables as a percentage change of wages.)

The equations are well behaved, with the usual positive effect of education and experience, lower wages for women and those not married, lower wages in the informal sector, and with substantial wage differentials between cities. What is quite striking is the change in the equations over time: between 1981 and 1988 the effect of all personal characteristics declined: the rate of return to a year's education fell from 12 to 10 percent, of a year's experience from 5.3 to 3.6 percent, the male-female differential fell, and the effect of marital status declined and became less significant. The formal/informal differential declined from 16 to 7 percent. The explanatory power of the equations also diminished. One possible interpretation is that the 1980s substantially disrupted the traditional working of the labor market, and particularly of the formal sector (implying falls in the wages of relatively privileged groups such as men, the educated, and those married). The topic merits further investigation elsewhere.

Conclusion

This chapter has covered a great deal of ground and includes a substantial amount of new empirical work using microeconomic data. Few previous studies have systematically attempted to study changes in the labor market or income distribution over the 1980s for Bolivia. However, much work remains to be done. The magnitude of the changes in economic institutions, for example, the somewhat daring attempt to open the capital account, make Bolivia a very interesting case for further study. The chapter has focused instead on micro issues regarding the labor market, themselves of great interest in view of the large changes that occurred in just a few years, and indicative of substantial ability to adjust even in a relatively poor country with substantial economic distortions.

Previous economic studies of Bolivia have tended to focus on the macroeconomic aspects. Bolivia's economic crisis had a rather earlier onset than for other Latin countries (in 1978), although it took seven years for stabilization to be successfully implemented, and the ensuing structural adjustment packages have as yet to yield any worthwhile benefits in terms of substantial growth, let alone employment and real wage increases. The structural adjustment measures took an almost textbook form: freeing of markets for foreign exchange, foreign capital, trade, finance, goods, and (of most concern here) labor; severe public sector employment cuts; and fiscal restructuring. Current causes for concern are the high level of real interest rates, the worsening trade and payments balance, sharply rising unemployment in 1988, and the open capital account. However, the size of the illegal (drug) economy makes it important to qualify analysis based solely on reported economic transactions.

The structure of the labor market prior to the onset of crisis and adjustment reflected previous government policies. Public sector employment dominated the formal sector, and a large, and relatively low-income, informal sector existed. The 1980s sequence of prolonged recession interspersed with hyperinflation, a fairly drastic stabilization, and far-reaching institutional changes designed to encourage structural adjustment has had large effects on the labor market. Sectoral employment shifts, both out of secondary and into primary and tertiary activities and out of formal and into informal activities, have been large, and in the opposite direction from that usually accompanying economic development. Despite prolonged stagnation there was no trend increase in unemployment, fall in hours worked, or fall in labor force participation rates, although a cyclical trough occurred in 1982–83. The labor market adjustment took the form of sectoral shifts and falls in real wages of 40 to 50 percent or more since 1980. The government employment creation program can be given relatively little credit for mopping up surplus labor before 1988. However, it may have served a more important role in 1988 and 1989 as unemployment indicators worsened sharply in 1988 despite modest positive GDP growth, perhaps indicating a second round of labor market adjustments due to structural adjustment.

The changes in the labor market have ramifications elsewhere in the economy. The distribution of earned income has worsened (despite the very short time series for which data are available), losing any improvements that were caused by hyperinflation. Given that the fall in real wages is about twice the magnitude of the fall in real GDP, the likelihood that overall urban poverty has increased is almost inescapable. However, apparently women were not the big losers that some have theorized to be the case in developing countries undergoing structural adjustment. A wide disparity is evident in the experience of different cities and regions of the country during the economic difficulties. The declining areas, including the capital, have fared badly relative to the newer eastern lowland cities. This in turn has political economy ramifications, as the tax base and location of population also has to shift. Finally, regarding the prognostications for future growth, the evidence suggests that the labor market has performed relatively well in adjusting, and that the blame for inadequate recovery lies elsewhere, possibly in some macropolicy decisions, but mainly in the lack of external resources to fuel a successful recovery. Bolivia has followed an almost textbook path in the kinds of adjustment policies adopted. Unless growth resumes in the near future, the social and human costs incurred to achieve these adjustments will not have been worthwhile.

APPENDIX A
SOURCES OF LABOR MARKET DATA

Most of the data on which studies of the Bolivian labor market are based are from urban areas; only the censuses of 1900, 1950, and 1976 cover rural areas as well. This is now changing as the current urban labor force survey was expanded into a Living Standards Measurement Survey, which was expanded to cover rural areas commencing in 1990.

The urban studies are based mainly on data collected by the INE, whose surveys include a household labor force survey conducted annually since 1980, a survey of small establishments conducted several times since 1983, and some special surveys of self-employed workers conducted in La Paz in 1983 and in Cochabamba and Santa Cruz in 1986. Aggregate data collected by the Ministry of Labor used to be published in an annual yearbook. There are also a number of one-time surveys on particular topics, such as the Ministry of Labor's 1980 study (in conjunction with the International Labour Organisation) of migration, studies of migration in particular areas or industries, and studies of displaced workers.

Caution is needed when interpreting the data. The Ministry of Labor's data are based on information from different sectors, and the coverage of the informal sector is particularly weak. Hence its unemployment data (which show a large increase in the 1980s) are particularly suspect, much of the so-called unemployment probably represents a shift into informal sector activities that the ministry simply misses. Similarly, the ministry series on real wages is highly suspect after 1985: as the ministry collects mainly basic salary data (excluding bonuses), the incorporation of the bonuses into the basic salary in 1985 means that the ministry data tend to underestimate the fall in real wages.

The INE household surveys seem more reliable on unemployment and wage data, but also have a couple of disadvantages. One is that the surveys took place at different times of the year, hence an unmeasurable seasonal effect may be present. Another is that the data only go back to 1980; data from earlier surveys between 1976 and 1979 are not readily available.

References

Afcha, G., G. Huarachij, R. Pereira, and F. Valverde. 1988. *La Politica de Shock Antinflacionario y el Mercado de Trabajo: El Caso Boliviano.* La Paz: Unidad de Análisis de Políticas Económicas. Discussion paper for presentation at workshop on anti-inflation policies, Programa Regional del Empleo para America Latina y el Caribe. Santiago, Chile.

Casanovas S., R. 1987. "El Sector Familiar en la Ciudad de La Paz." In J. P. Perez S., R. Casanovas S., J. Alvarado, J. C. Ribadeneira, and M. Chiriboga, eds., *Familia y Trabajo en la Ciudad Andina.* Quito, Ecuador: Centro Andino de Accion Popular.

Casanovas S., R., and A. Rojas R. 1988. *Santa Cruz de la Sierra: Crecimiento Urbano y Situación Ocupacional.* La Paz: Centro de Estudios para el Desarrollo Laboral y Agrario/Centro de Información y Documentación de Santa Cruz.

CEDLA (Centro de Estudios para el Desarrollo Laboral y Agrario). 1988. *El Sector Informal Urbano en Bolivia.* La Paz: Beatriz Cajias.

CET (Centro de Estudios del Trabajo). 1987. *Sector Informal y Movimiento Obrero.* Temas Laborales No. 2. La Paz.

———. 1988. *La Relocalización.* Temas Laborales No. 5. La Paz.

Cottani, J. 1988. "Exchange Rate Trends, 1960–87." Washington, D.C.: World Bank. Draft, processed.

Delons, J. R., and J. L. Bour. 1988. *Empleo, Recursos Humanos e Ingresos en Bolivia: Una Propuesta para la Acción.* La Paz: Unidad de Análisis de Políticas Económicas.

Donoso, S. 1988. "Politicas, Actividades y Estudios sobre Empleo." La Paz: Unidad de Análisis de Políticas Económicas. Draft.

Doria Medina, S. 1987. *La Quimera de la Reactivación: Balance y Perspectivas de la Económica Boliviana*. La Paz: EDOBOL.

Escobar de Pabón, S., and C. L. García. 1988. *Urbanización Migraciones y Empleo en la Ciudad de Cochabamba*. La Paz: Centro de Estudios para el Desarrollo Laboral y Agrario/Centro de Información y Documentación de Santa Cruz.

Fernandez M., M. 1988. "Inserción Laboral, Ingreso y Estrategias Ocupacionales de la Mujer Popular de El Alto de La Paz." La Paz: Centro de Promoción de la mujer "Gregoria Apaza." Draft, processed.

IMF. Various years. *International Financial Statistics*. Washington, D.C.

INE (Instituto Nacional de Estadística) 1988a. *Encuesta Permanente de Hogares 1987*. La Paz: Ministerio de Planeamiento y Coordinación, Area Sociales n. 1–88.

————. 1988b. *Encuesta Permanente de Hogares 1988*. La Paz: Ministerio de Planeamiento y Coordinación.

————. 1988c. *Principales Resultados de la Encuesta Permanente de Hogares 1980-87*. La Paz: Ministerio de Planeamiento y Coordinación.

————. 1989. *Encuesta integrada de Hogares 1989*. La Paz: Ministerio de Planeamiento y Coordinación.

INE (Instituto Nacional de Estadística) and UDAPE (Unidad de Análisis de Políticas Económicas). 1987. *Un Intento de Medición del Sector Informal Urbano en Bolivia*. La Paz: UDAPE.

Klinov, R. 1987. "Public Sector Wages and Employment in Bolivia." Washington, D.C.: World Bank. Draft, processed.

Maletta, H. 1980. *La Fuerza de Trabajo en Bolivia 1900–1976: Analisís Critico de la Información Censal*. Proyecto de Migraciones y Empleo Rural y Urbano BOL/78/P03. La Paz: Ministerio de Trabajo y Desarrollo Laboral.

Mercado S., A. F., M. Fernandez, and T. Reinaga. 1988. "La Relación Precios-Salarios: El Caso Boliviano (1982–1985)." La Paz: Instituto Nacional de Estadistica. Draft, processed.

Morales A., J. A. 1987. *Precios, Salarios y Politica Económica Durante la Alta Inflación Boliviana de 1982 a 1985.* Estudio Diagnostico Debate. La Paz: Instituto Latinoamericano de Investigaciones Sociales.

Morales A., J. A., and J. Sachs. 1988. *Bolivia's Economic Crisis.* Working Paper No. 2620. Cambridge, Massachussetts: NBER.

Morales A., R. 1985. *La Crisis Económica en Bolivia y su Impacto en las Condiciones de Vida de los Niños.* La Paz: UNICEF.

Morales A., R. 1987. *Bolivia: Efectos Sociales de la Crisis y de las Politicas de Ajuste.* La Paz: Instituto Latinoamericano de Investigaciones Sociales. Estudio Diagnostico Debate.

Morawetz, D. 1987. *Exportaciones de Productos Manufacturados de Bolivia: Una Perspectiva mas Optimista?* La Paz: Unidad de Análisis de Políticas Económicas. Processed.

Muller y Asociados. 1988. *Estadísticas Económicas 1988.* La Paz: Instituto Latinoamericano de Investigaciones Sociales.

Muller y Machicado Asociados. 1986. *Características Estructurales del Empleo y la Evolución del Salario.* La Paz. Confidential report. Processed.

Newman, J., S. Jorgenson, and M. Pradhan. 1990. "How Did Workers Benefit from Bolivia's Emergency Social Fund?" Washington, D.C.: World Bank. Processed.

Ormachea, E. 1988. *Apuntes Relativos al Empleo Rural.* Documento de Trabajo Analitico DTA-0176/88. La Paz: Unidad de Análisis de Políticas Económicas.

Programa Regional del Empleo para America Latina y el Caribe. 1985. *Bases para la Formulación de un Programa de Empleo de Emergencia Bolivia 1985–86.* Documento de Trabajo PREALC/268. Santiago, Chile.

————. 1988. *Migración y Empleo en Bolivia: Los Casos de las Ciudades de La Paz y Santa Cruz.* Documento de Trabajo PREALC/321. Santiago, Chile.

Sánchez, C. E. 1988. "La Pequeña y Mediana Empresa Industrial en Bolivia: un Diagnostico y Recomendaciones de Política." La Paz: Unidad de Análisis de Políticas Económicas. Processed.

Villegas Quiroga, C. 1987. *Reactivación Económica en Bolivia: Analisís del D. S. 21660.* La Paz: Centro de Estudios para el Desarrollo Laboral y Agrario.

World Bank. 1988. *World Development Report 1988.* New York: Oxford University Press.

————. 1989. *World Development Report 1989.* New York: Oxford University Press.

4

BRAZIL

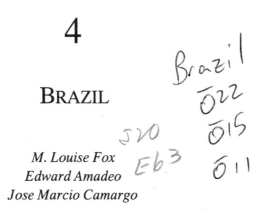

M. Louise Fox
Edward Amadeo
Jose Marcio Camargo

Although the external shocks of the early 1980s presented major challenges for all middle-income countries, most entered the 1990s in a stronger macroeconomic position than they had entered the previous decade. The process of adjustment (painful for all, but especially for the population's poorest segments) resulted in leaner public sectors, an increased decentralization of economic decisionmaking, more competitive economies, and a more favorable debt structure.

This was not the case in Brazil. By following a less orthodox macroeconomic program Brazil experienced significantly less pain than most of its Latin American neighbors during the decade. Its economic growth rate was one of the highest in the hemisphere during the period. However, Brazil ended the 1980s in a significantly worse position than it had begun because of its failure to adjust macroeconomic balances. Inflation remains high, capital outflow continues, growth comes in spurts and is unsustainable, and its debt structure (especially internal debt) is much worse.

In many countries, the adjustment effort's success or failure has depended on the labor market's flexibility and its ability to adjust. This has been especially important in effecting the terms of trade changes required. Was the labor market (or one segment, the labor unions) responsible for the failure of Brazilian macroeconomic policy? This chapter argues that the answer to this question is no. While the democratic process and the role of labor unions in that process complicated the formulation of economic policy during the period, Brazilian labor markets were very flexible, and indeed the external

143

adjustment required was achieved relatively painlessly. What hurt Brazil was the failure of the political process to agree on the size of the public sector and who would pay for the public consumption that segments of the population sought.

Origins and Nature of Brazil's Adjustment Problem

In the two decades before the advent of the debt crisis in the early 1980s, Brazilians had become accustomed both to high rates of economic growth and significant improvements in living standards. In the 1960s, growth averaged 3 percent per capita annually, and between 1970 and 1979 grew at an astonishing 6 percent per capita per annum. During the latter period, the incidence of poverty fell roughly 50 percent, and the severity of poverty (the poverty gap) fell by 25 percent (Fox 1990).

These decades of high growth were also ones of structural transformation. Brazil had started an industrialization and import substitution program in the early 1950s that focused primarily on consumption goods. While imports of consumer goods were reduced drastically, foreign exchange earnings continued to depend on the coffee crop. After 1968, Brazil sought to break its dependence on coffee through a more open trade regime combined with a manufactured export development program financed by large inflows of foreign capital. The result was a substantial increase in the size and diversity of Brazil's international trade, such that manufactured exports grew from 8 percent of total export receipts in 1965 to 30 percent in 1975, while coffee's contribution declined from 45 percent to 10 percent during the same period. Brazil ran a continuous trade surplus from 1968 to 1973.

After the first oil shock, payments for oil imports climbed sharply, up from 11.0 percent of imports during 1967–72, to 22.4 percent in 1974, and 44.4 percent by 1980. Instead of reducing absorption, the government decided to try to grow its way out of this crisis. It opted to borrow abroad at relatively low real interest rates and continue its investment push, primarily in the state enterprise sector, designed to substitute domestic goods for imported capital and intermediate industrial goods. Although Brazil was able to continue to increase both exports and domestic consumption, it was sowing the seeds for the adjustment problems of the 1990s. The heavy borrowing, combined with increases in world interest rates, meant that interest payments rose steadily as a share of export earnings, from 8.2 percent in 1974 to 31.2 percent in 1980.

The decision not to reduce absorption meant that the second oil shock and the subsequent rapid rise in world interest rates in the early 1980s caught the Brazilian economy in a very unstable and vulnerable position. Even before the second oil shock, Brazil's debt had grown to enormous proportions, and new lending was increasingly needed just to cover interest obligations. Thus, the Brazilian growth machine would have faced serious adjustment problems in the 1980s in any event.

Although many people have criticized the policies prevalent during the boom years of the 1970s for the simultaneous increase in inequality, most of the population experienced significant increases in their standard of living.[1] These effects were not uniform, as poverty was reduced by roughly 66 percent in urban areas compared with 50 percent in rural areas, and roughly 70 percent in the southeast compared with just under 50 percent in the northeast. Improvements in social indicators were also more dramatic in the southeast. Nevertheless, Brazil's record on poverty alleviation in the 1970s, even in the least affected areas, is the envy of many countries, and despite having one of the most unequal income distributions in the world, the economic growth of the 1970s was clearly accompanied by significant social mobility (Morley 1982; Pastore and others 1983).

Poverty reduction came primarily through expanded employment in the urban formal sector, where average wages were close to three times the wages in the rest of the economy by the end of the decade. The growth in formal sector employment reflected the government's continuing commitment to an industrialization strategy throughout the 1970s, and was heavily concentrated in the already more developed southeast. Much of this employment was in enterprises that depended on either government subsidies, government protection from domestic or

---

1. Brazil's ability to decrease poverty at the same time that income inequality was rising does not imply that the criticisms of the unequal nature of Brazil's growth strategy are without merit. On the contrary, studies have shown that Brazil's progress in poverty reduction would have been even greater if it had been able to have more distributionally neutral growth (Fox 1990; World Bank 1990).

international competition, or government capital (in the form of equity shares).

The effects of continuing economic improvement and of the expanded opportunities available to the working class, especially the urban working class, changed working class expectations. These changed expectations were given voice as the dictatorship lightened its repression of labor unions in the late 1970s and a politically active labor movement reemerged. The expectations formed during the 1970s about economic growth and the state's role played an important role in the political economy of adjustment policies during the 1980s.

The debt crisis hit Brazil hard. Domestic absorption had to be cut by 4 percent of GDP merely to adjust to the cutoff in foreign capital inflows. At the same time interest rates were rising in real terms, requiring even more belt tightening. Nevertheless, despite the severity of the crisis, most observers believed that Brazil, with its diverse economy and relatively rich resource base, would eventually return to a growth path less dependent on external savings. In 1983, the World Bank estimated that the required adjustment in Brazil would require a savings rate of about 20 to 25 percent of GDP over the next five years (a marginal rate of about 30 percent, assuming a return to growth after a brief period of austerity). Compared with the marginal savings rates of 50 to 60 percent required from Chile during the same period, Brazil was viewed as the country that could be a model for the region in terms of adjustment, growth, and external transfer, with minimal tradeoffs between the three objectives.

What these projections could not highlight, which proved critical in Brazil's failure to adjust, was that in Brazil all the adjustment had to take place in the public sector (the actual owner of the debt), to avoid a large public-private transfer problem and significant crowding out. This adjustment in the public sector had to take place at the same time as the country was opening up the political process to groups that had been disenfranchised for 20 years. Politically, the task was to cut the size of the pie by about 25 percent just as the group standing in line to get a piece was increasing dramatically and its power was growing. Brazil's ultimate failure to stabilize and adjust effectively in the 1980s was in part a result of the emerging democracy's failure to reach a political consensus on who would pay the bill for the excesses of the 1970s.

The Period of Adjustment: The 1980s

Brazilian macroeconomic policy in the 1980s and its outcomes can be divided into three periods: (1) recession, 1981–83; (2) recovery, 1984–85; and (3) boom-bust, 1986–89. Tables 4.1 and 4.2 summarize the quantitative record.

Table 4.1 Macroeconomic Indicators, 1980–87

Indicator	1980	1981	1982	1983	1984	1985	1986	1987	1988
GDP factor cost (1980 = 100)	1.00	0.96	1.00	0.93	0.99	1.07	1.12	1.17	1.18
Agriculture	1.00	1.08	1.08	1.07	1.11	1.22	1.12	1.28	1.30
Industry	1.00	0.91	0.91	0.86	0.91	1.00	1.11	1.12	1.09
Services	1.00	0.98	1.00	0.99	1.03	1.10	1.19	1.23	1.26
GDP market prices (1980 = 100)	1.00	0.96	0.96	0.93	0.98	1.06	1.14	1.18	1.18
Fiscal policy indicators									
(percentage of GDP)									
Revenue	23.7	23.5	23.8	23.2	20.7	21.2	23.4	24.4	22.9
Interest	1.9	2.2	3.3	4.2	6.2	10.9	10.6	9.7	12.5
Government saving	1.1	1.1	-0.4	-1.4	-2.8	-8.0	-7.0	-6.6	-12.6
Debt	n.a.	15.5	19.8	28.4	34.3	36.1	22.7	40.0	n.a.
Inflation (annual rate, percent)*	90	108	106	141	215	235	144	210	673
Real exchange rate	1.0	0.9	0.9	1.2	1.2	1.3	1.1	1.0	0.9
Real interest rate (working capital)	-13.4	25.7	24.6	13.4	36.4	32.1	6.4	30.7	n.a.
Implicit rate of return,									
government debt, overnight									
market (percent)	1.3	18.5	26.5	13.6	17.9	15.9	5.8	7.4	n.a.

n.a. = not available
* GDP deflator, annual rate of change.
** Exchange rate deflated by the cost of living (Brazil) times U.S. WPI (increase = depreciation).
Source: National Accounts: *Conjuntura Economica* (June 1990); Government debt: World Bank (1988, p. 313).

Table 4.2 Changes in Saving and Investment, 1980–88
(millions of 1980 cruzeiros)

Category	Recession 1980–83	Recovery 1983–86	Boom 1985–86	Slowdown 1986–88	Total period 1980–88
Changes in					
consumption	-494	701	960	48	1,215
Government	-28	152	234	347	704
Private	-466	549	726	-298	511
Exports	290	432	-195	574	1,101
Imports	-447	-28	265	-50	-261
Foreign saving	−738	-460	460	-624	-1,361
Domestic saving (GDP - consumption)	-377	879	28	466	996
Investment	-1,115	418	488	-156	-365
GDP	−871	1,580	988	514	2,211

Source: Fox and Morley (1990).

In light of the collapse of foreign exchange reserves and the increase in the trade deficit, only a "hard-option" financial adjustment seemed possible by 1981. During this period, Brazil used tight money policies, some fiscal restraint, quantitative import controls, and an active exchange rate policy to lower demand and squeeze out the resources that were needed for the external transfer.[2] GDP fell by 5 percent between 1980 and 1983. The burden of adjustment fell primarily on the private sector,

2. Throughout the 1980s, imports were tightly controlled by a system of import licensing and quantitative restraints. Thus, the exchange rate was used primarily as an export promotion tool, and Brazil was able to generate the trade surpluses required with small changes in the real exchange rate. In this way, the Brazilian experience contrasts with that of other, more open, economies. Large real depreciations/devaluations were not required in response to the external shocks of the 1980s, and exchange rate policy played a relatively minor role in stabilization/adjustment programs.

as government savings began to turn negative with rising interest costs. In an attempt to control inflation and limit the burden of adjustment on the poor, the government also used a wage control policy of "cascading" adjustment in the formal sector that permitted more than 100 percent indexation of wages at lower wage levels, and less than 100 percent indexation at higher wage levels. The result of these policies was Brazil's deepest recession in 15 years, a 40 percent fall in investment and, by 1983, an annual transfer abroad of 4 percent of GDP.[3]

Brazil was able to achieve external balance and earn the foreign exchange necessary to service its debt quite rapidly. Exports increased from US$20 billion in 1982 to US$27 billion in 1984, reacting to a slow domestic market and better prices abroad. Imports declined from US$19 billion to US$14 billion under the tight regime of quantitative restrictions. The balance of payments shifted from a deficit of US$9.5 billion in 1982 to a small surplus of US$0.4 billion in 1984. Brazil achieved this rapid success largely because of the export promotion policy of the 1970s.

During the recovery period (1984–85), Brazil began to ease interest rates. At the same time, government expenditures on goods and services, wages, and investment returned to the levels of the 1970s, when they had been financed by external debt. Unfortunately, this source of financing was no longer available, and interest payments continued to grow. To finance the expenditures and the consequent deficit, the government was forced to sell more government bonds—eventually forcing interest rates back up—and to print money. These policies led to accelerating inflation and no substantial improvement in investment.

As the recession had left many private sector firms with excess capacity, the previous decline in investment was not yet much of a constraint on growth, and the Brazilian economy responded well to the fiscal stimulus. The government abandoned the policy of cascading wage adjustments, and a policy of exchange depreciation maintained the trade surplus even as internal demand began to expand, providing Brazil with the foreign exchange to continue debt service payments. Once again,

---

3. One would expect that the cascading policy would lead to the compression of salary differentials. In practice, it only had this effect in the public sector, as major private sector and joint public-private companies simply corrected for this policy by paying wage supplements of various kinds to their higher level staff.

earning foreign exchange was not a problem for Brazil. The trick was to get the local currency equivalent of the trade surplus into the government's hands so that the debt could be serviced; a feat that was proving increasingly difficult. Nonetheless, Brazil achieved a marginal savings rate well above the level required for debt service during 1984–85, investment began to recover, and, except for the troubling inflation, Brazil seemed to be emerging from the debt crisis on a "Baker" path.

By the end of 1985 (the start of the third period), the transfer problem was becoming acute. Inflation was accelerating, the velocity of money was increasing, and financing the government deficit by printing money was becoming more and more difficult. Only two possible options were available for solving these problems: reduced government consumption or increased revenues. Both required political consensus. Unfortunately, the coalition government, Brazil's first democratically elected Congress in 20 years led by a politically weak president, was not in any mood to forge this belt-tightening consensus. The opposition, without control of the public purse for so long, mostly sought to benefit its constituencies. Neither was the establishment, represented politically by the president, in any mood to bear the burden of adjustment. All elected officials feared recession and unemployment; the right, because it would strengthen the leftist labor unions, and the left because their voters would suffer and blame them.

This political stalemate dominated Brazil's macroeconomic policies throughout the second half of the 1980s. The outcome was a period of growth (1986), followed by recession (1987–88), followed by a further growth spurt (1989), with inflation held in check only through increasingly unsuccessful wage and price control programs inaugurated roughly once every 18 months, and with private investment crowded out.

The first and most famous of Brazil's stabilization plans was the Cruzado Plan, initiated in February 1986. Its key elements included (a) real wage increases to pacify organized labor; (b) monetary reform and a price freeze; (c) a government-imposed deindexation of the economy, including financial instruments and the exchange rate; and (d) an exchange rate freeze (which implied an appreciation) and a more open import policy to ease shortages. All these measures increased real purchasing power in the short run, increasing aggregate demand. Yet despite the breathing room that the temporarily lower inflation brought in terms of interest savings and seigniorage gains, and the increased tax collections stemming from the reverse Tanzi effect, the government failed to cut government spending.[4] On the contrary, the failure to increase public sector prices prior to the freeze and the real wage increases granted to government workers as part of the package aggravated fiscal pressures. The disequilibrium in the balance of supply and demand became evident by July 1986. Shortages developed, inflation returned, and the plan collapsed. In addition, the import buying spree that was stimulated by the appreciated exchange rate (facilitated by government import policy) had used up reserves. A debt moratorium was finally imposed in 1987.

Brazil undertook two more shock stabilization programs in the 1980s. While both appear to have averted hyperinflation—a constant threat to Brazil as inflation begins to accelerate with each recovery in private aggregate demand—neither permanently reversed the negative trend in government savings. At the same time, a new debt agreement with foreign commercial banks in 1988 led to renewed savings outflows. With the debt service outflow and the government financing needs eating up savings, private investment remained stagnant after a short period of increase during the Cruzado Plan.

Brazil never stabilized financially during the 1980s, constantly opting for inflation over unemployment and consumption over savings. Table 4.2 shows the macroeconomic results of Brazil's economic policy during the second half of the 1980s. On the positive side, Brazil increased domestic income by about 16 percent over the level in 1980, and met the savings targets required to continue servicing its foreign debt, moving quickly from a trade deficit in 1980 to a surplus in 1982. That position was maintained throughout the decade except during the Cruzado Plan boom of 1986.

Both private and public consumption also increased, and although public consumption increased almost 50 percent faster than private consumption, the overall increase did help to protect living standards. However, most of the savings generated during the 1980s were applied to

---

4. As inflation increases, real tax revenue tends to decline even as tax rates remain unchanged because money loses value during the collection process. This is known as the Tanzi effect. When inflation declines and real tax revenues increase, the process is called the reverse Tanzi effect.

debt service; consequently, the level of investment fell from 23 percent of GDP in 1980 to 16 percent in 1984. The private sector's increasing unwillingness to finance government consumption (including debt service payments) led to an inflation level of above 50 percent per month by the end of 1989. This failure to invest can be expected to compromise Brazil's growth prospects for the 1990s.

The Development of the Labor Market in the 1980s

Segmentation in the Brazilian Labor Market

The distribution of employment by sector in Brazil reflects the industrialization of the postwar period. Most Brazilians do not work in agriculture, but in industry, commerce, or services. Out of a total labor force of about 50 million, about 5 million people work directly for the government in public administration positions, and about 2 to 3 million more work in state-owned enterprises.

The Brazilian labor market can be divided into three segments: the formal sector, the informal sector, and the self-employed (table 4.3). Labor law obliges employers to sign identification cards for each worker, which makes the worker eligible for a number of benefits from the state.

Table 4.3 Composition of the Labor Force by Sector, 1986
(percent)

Sector	Formal	Informal			
	Signed contract	*Nonsigned contract*	*Self-employed*	*Without remuneration*	*Either employer*
Agriculture	6.9	33.2	33.2	25.2	3.5
Industry	72.4	15.9	6.6	1.3	3.8
Construction	39.3	27.9	29.6	0.7	2.5
Commerce	42.5	16.3	30.9	3.5	6.8
Services	21.9	40.7	33.2	1.5	2.7
Transport and communication	60.2	11.9	25.1	0.7	2.1
Public administration	52.5	47.0	0.3	0	0.2
Total	38.2	27.9	22.9	7.6	3.4

Source: Saboia (1989).

These include extended health and social security benefits, unemployment insurance, protection from minimum wage laws, paid vacations, a maximum normal working week of 44 hours with time and a half for overtime, and so on. These benefits cost the employer 50 to 70 percent of the direct wage. Employers also pay a 20 percent payroll tax on workers' earnings (matched by an 8 percent payroll tax paid by the workers themselves).

Small business often cannot afford these additional costs, and do not sign their workers' cards. Together with the self-employed, these workers constitute the informal sector. The extent to which workers fall into these categories varies widely by industry. Only a tiny percentage of agricultural workers and a slightly larger percentage of service industry workers are in the formal sector. This contrasts sharply with industrial workers, and above all public sector workers, who are much more likely to be in the formal sector.

Regional differences are also important in the distribution of formal sector workers (table 4.4). São Paulo is the most developed state in the

Table 4.4 Distribution of Formal Sector Employment by State and Sector, Selected States, 1985

State	Sector (percent)				Total nonagriculture formal sector employees (thousands)
	Industry	Services	Commerce	Public administration	
Ceara (NE)	23.2	24.4	12.3	38.4	477
Paraiba (NE)	20.8	18.2	7.9	52.7	235
Pernambuco (NE)	32.1	27.3	11.5	27.8	738
Bahia (NE)	21.8	31.4	14.0	31.1	834
Rio de Janeiro (SE)	24.9	39.0	14.2	21.7	2,711
São Paulo (SE)	41.0	31.4	12.3	13.6	6,780
Total Brazil	32.1	30.9	13.1	22.3	20,172
Percentage of formal sector employment in sector					
São Paulo	43.1	34.2	31.7	20.7	
6 southeast states	81.1	76.0	75.4	57.0	
Rest of Brazil	18.9	24.0	24.6	43.0	

Source: Saboia (1989).

country, accounting for roughly 60 percent of GDP. Of its workers, 54.8 percent were in the formal sector in 1986, while that figure was only 21.8 percent in the poorer northeast. Similarly, 82.6 percent of industrial workers were in the formal sector in São Paulo, compared to only 41.7 percent in the northeast.

Most of Brazil's poor, urban and rural, live in households whose head is not employed in the formal sector (table 4.5). Most heads of poor families are self-employed or sharecroppers, earning income in the agricultural or tertiary sectors, although in urban areas, heads of poor households are also found in significant numbers in manufacturing and construction. However, in the large cities of the southeast, poor southeast, poor households do depend on formal sector earnings from the head. Average formal sector earnings are roughly three times those in the informal sector (including agriculture) (table 4.6).

Table 4.5 Occupational Characteristics of Heads of Poor Households, Selected Areas, 1985
(percentage of poor population in household)

Occupation of head	Brazil	Urban northeast	Urban southeast	Rural northeast	Rural southeast
Technical/administrative	4.4	5.2	6.8	2.7	3.1
Agriculture and mining	39.2	27.6	13.6	85.9	84.9
Manufacturing and construction	10.3	25.8	33.2	5.5	5.1
Commerce and related activities	8.6	12.1	6.7	1.7	.8
Transport and communications	4.6	4.3	5.7	.9	.6
Services	22.4	6.9	12.8	.7	2.6
Others	13.3	18.2	19.5	2.6	3.0
Formal sector employment	17.7	31.8	50.1	5.5	10.9
Share of the poor	100.0	20.2	17.2	33.8	10.2

Source: Fox (1990).

Table 4.6 Average Monthly Earnings of Heads of Households, 1987 *(Cz$)*

Employment status	Northeast (Cz$)	Southeast (Cz$)	South (Cz$)	Northeast/ southeast
Formal sector	23,225	33,812	27,753	0.69
Informal sector	10,511	22,000	20,664	0.47
Self-employed	12,180	30,383	25,263	0.40
Employer	58,121	81,647	82,150	0.71

Note: Employees in the formal and informal sector do not include agricultural laborers or unpaid workers.
Source: Fox (1990).

During the 1980s, rural and urban labor markets became increasingly integrated. Thus, for example, 25 percent of the heads of poor households in the urban southeast work in primary sector activities, and 15 percent of heads of poor households in the rural southeast do not work in agriculture. The agricultural labor force has also become increasing proletarianized during the decade: by 1987 over 50 percent of those earning income in agriculture were employees (even in the northeast, the comparable figure is 48 percent).

Roughly one-fifth of agricultural employees nationwide have signed labor cards (formal sector employment), but this ratio also varies significantly by region, with the level of formalization in the south twice that in the northeast. While most earners in poor households are at the bottom of the earnings distribution, not all low earners belong to poor households. In 1985, roughly 40 percent of those earning the minimum wage in the formal sector were secondary earners in households with per capita incomes in the top 40 percent of the distribution (Alemeida Reis 1989).

The Rise of the Unions

The reemergence of a populist, leftist labor movement in the 1980s was one of the period's great ironies. One of the main goals of the authoritarian military regime that came to power after the coup of 1964 was to subjugate the labor movement under federal control. During the repression of 1964/65, a large number of labor leaders were jailed or exiled, and government control over unions increased. Unions had to be organized by occupation and geographical location, and needed the formal approval of the Ministry of Labor. Approved unions were given sole rights to represent given groups of workers, and national unions were initially outlawed. Unions were tied to the state financially through the provision of compulsory union dues mandated by the state, and restrictive strike laws (which included the identification of "key" sectors where strikes were entirely forbidden) blocked the emergence of independent power centers. While unions did have the right to engage in collective bargaining, these bargains were always subject to a national wage policy, effectively rendering the collective bargaining process at the local level impotent.[5]

As long as the government was able to maintain authoritarian control, the corporatist system worked reasonably well from a macroeconomic perspective. Costly strikes were avoided, real wages rose with economic growth, and inflation was moderate. However, the system began breaking down as the political system began to liberalize during the late 1970s. The very tool that had worked so effectively to control inflation during the period of maximum repression began to be the undoing of the system during liberalization, as unions continued to pressure the government to set federal wage guidelines at a level that would allow workers to make up for past inflation. As the government was both part or full owner of many of the large employers of unionized workers and at the same time was beginning to compete for the political support of the unions, it often acquiesced, having no countervailing organized political pressures for wage moderation.

At the same time, unions began to flout government wage guidelines in their negotiations. The existing institutional framework of labor law, which carried excessive penalties for minor infractions, became useless during the period of liberalization, as the government could not afford the political costs of invoking laws that were widely perceived to be harsh and excessive. Thus, the government simply avoided the existing

---

5. Wage indexation became a key tool of incomes policy. Between 1965 and 1974, an "expected" rate of inflation was imposed as the norm for adjusting nominal wages to inflation. As expected rates invariably lagged real inflation rates, real wages fell, and some downward pressure was exerted on inflation.

structure, and costly and violent strikes began to occur (table 4.7). Labor leaders mobilized workers directly at the factory floor, short-circuiting the formal structure of corporatist state controls on union activity. As mobilization increased, strong local leaders began to attract support from the most important unions in the manufacturing regions, especially the southeast. A Workers' Party (the PT) was formed in the early 1980s, and two centralized national union federations were created, one of which, the *Central Unica dos Trabalhadores* or CUT, was linked to the PT. Consistent data on the growth of unionization and mobilization is sketchy until the mid to late 1980s, so tracking the growth of this movement is impossible, but by 1986, roughly one-third of the nonagricultural labor force in the industrialized southern half of the country belonged to a union (table 4.8).

The unions also adopted a targeting strategy, seeking to bargain at the enterprise level with the largest firms. Agreements made with these firms were used as a basis for all agreements, and became national bargains. Negotiations occurred year round as each occupational group bargained in a different month. Naturally, the bargains made by the best organized unions became the targets for the rest, while the support offered by the central labor federations increased every union's ability to enforce its

Table 4.7 Number of Strikes and Total Number of Workers on Strike, 1985–89

Year	Number of strikes	Total number of workers on strike (millions)
1985	843	6.6
1986	1,493	7.1
1987	2,275	8.3
1988	1,914	7.1
1989	4,167	10.0

Source: Ministry of Labor, Brazil.

Table 4.8 Membership in Workers' Associations, 1986
(percentage of nonagricultural workers)

Sector	Membership
Manufacturing	29.10
Construction	12.30
Other industries	43.36
Commerce	14.79
Services	5.61
Auxiliary services	36.30
Transport and communication	43.37
Social services	25.85
Public administration	20.89
Others	48.56
Total	21.36

Note: Employers are included in the denominator, thus the level of unionism is understated.
Source: PNAD survey data (1986).

demands. As bargains were usually made once a year, the high and very uncertain inflation rate had a huge impact on bargaining. It ensured that unions would aim at wage increases not only large enough to compensate members for any nominal losses since the last agreement, but large enough to ensure that members would not suffer regardless of the prevailing inflation rate in the coming year. The result was built in inflationary pressure.

A bargaining structure in which bargains were made locally but enforced nationally had poor macroeconomic results. The national enforcement ensured that labor markets became very rigid, unable to differentiate between successful and failing firms, occupations with strong demand and weak demand, and so on. Conversely, the local negotiation meant that national macroeconomic concerns were not part of the equation, in contrast to more centralized systems such as that of Sweden.

In sum, unionization became a powerful force affecting economic outcomes during the 1980s. Equally important perhaps, the unions had developed into a sufficiently potent force to ensure that adjustment measures primarily affected those in the informal sector.

The Role of the Labor Market in the Adjustment Process

Brazil's macroeconomic policies of the 1980s produced modest growth in per capita income, external balance, and high inflation. Brazil's labor market structure, policies, or institutions did not prevent the economy from earning the foreign exchange necessary to service its external debt. However, achieving internal stability was another matter. Throughout the 1980s, Brazil struggled in various ways to achieve this goal.

In general, the Brazilian labor market exhibited tremendous flexibility throughout the 1980s (tables 4.9 and 4.10). During recessions, the decline in formal sector output crowded workers into the informal sector, lowering average incomes in this sector. During expansions, wages and employment in the formal sector rose. While unemployment was a major problem during the early part of the decade, both because of the recession and the drought in the northeast, which brought many heads of farm families to the cities in search of work, it declined during the decade as the informal sector was able to continue to absorb new entrants. However, different parts of the labor market gained or lost during different policy regimes.

During the recessionary period (1981–83), the formal sector clearly gained at the expense of the informal sector, while the big loser was agriculture, where roughly 29 percent of the labor force was employed.[6] Two government policies seem to have facilitated this outcome: (a) the guarantee to formal sector workers in lower earnings categories that wages would be overindexed every six months; and (b) the generous government employment policy. Private sector employers did shed some workers in response to falling demand, but some labor stockpiling also occurred, as output fell faster. In contrast, government employment

---

6. Although agricultural output increased overall, earnings in agriculture must have been affected by the drought, which lasted through the 1982 harvest.

increased during the period, so total formal sector employment did not decline.

Table 4.9 Indices of Labor Market Outcomes, 1980–88

Category	1980	1981	1982	1983	1984	1985	1986	1987	1988
Employment growth									
Total	1.00	1.01	1.06	1.04	1.12	1.18	1.22	1.27	1.30
Agriculture	1.00	0.96	1.02	0.95	1.08	1.10	1.02	1.01	1.02
Formal	1.00	1.01	1.03	1.01	1.03	1.11	1.21	1.25	1.31
Informal	1.00	1.05	1.22	1.27	1.38	1.49	1.54	1.69	1.67
Private formal sector +	1.00	0.95	0.95	0.89	0.92	0.98	1.02	n.a.	n.a.
Public sector +	1.00	1.06	1.12	1.16	1.25	1.32	1.43	n.a.	n.a.
Open unemployment (PMD) (%)									
São Paulo	7.20	7.20	5.50	6.80	6.80	5.00	3.40	3.80	3.80
Average, 6 cities	n.a.	n.a.	6.30	6.70	7.10	5.20	3.60	3.70	3.80
Real wages									
Private industry									
(São Paulo, FIESP)	1.00	1.07	1.14	1.06	0.99	1.05	1.17	1.08	0.95
Total formal sector +	1.00	1.01	1.07	0.92	0.87	0.98	1.05	n.a.	n.a.
Government sector +	1.00	0.97	1.03	0.86	0.78	0.99	1.16	n.a.	n.a.
Minimum wage	1.00	0.99	1.01	0.91	0.85	0.86	0.89	0.73	0.76
Real average incomes**									
Formal	1.00*	0.85	1.30	0.92	1.03	1.20	1.65	1.24	0.88
Informal	1.00*	0.85	1.30	0.92	1.03	1.20	1.65	1.24	0.88
Agriculture	1.00*	0.84	0.96	0.77	0.78	0.84	1.16	0.83	0.52
Income differentials									
Formal/informal	3.08*	3.10	3.11	3.25	2.66	2.76	2.50	2.72	3.28
Informal/agriculture	0.63	0.64	0.86	0.75	0.84	0.90	0.90	0.94	1.08
Factor incomes in formal sector									
Labor	1.00	1.03	1.10	0.93	0.88	1.05	1.23	1.16	1.01
Interest	1.00	1.30	1.28	1.28	1.32	1.48	0.84	1.58	1.58
Profit (real)	1.00	0.89	0.86	0.88	0.96	0.99	1.13	1.12	1.15
Profit and interest	1.00	0.93	0.91	0.93	1.00	1.04	1.10	1.17	1.20
Labor productivity	1.00	0.92	0.91	0.89	0.91	0.90	0.95	0.90	0.90

n.a. = not available
*   1979 + RAIS data.
**   Average earnings not corrected for hours worked, main occupation.
Note: Informal sector includes agriculture and is defined as labor force participants not contributing to the social security system.
Source: Fox and Morley (1990).

Table 4.10 Poverty Indicators, 1981–87

Indicator	1981	1983	1985	1987	1988
Incidence of poverty by location					
Brazil total	26.4	32.1	26.2	24.2	26.9
Urban	14.9	21.6	17.1	14.8	n.a.
Rural	46.8	54.2	47.1	46.3	n.a.
Poverty gap index	10.1	13.1	9.9	9.5	10.7
Index of GDP per capita	1.0	0.9	1.0	1.1	1.1
Index of real household income					
Mean	1.0	0.9	1.1	1.2	1.2
Bottom 10 percent	1.0	0.9	1.1	1.1	1.0
Bottom 25 percent	1.0	0.9	1.1	1.1	1.0
Top 10 percent	1.0	0.9	1.2	1.3	1.4

n.a. = not available
Source: Special Tabulation of Household Surveys. For a definition of the poverty line, see Fox (1990).

The evidence on wages is more ambiguous. The minimum wage fell by 10 percent from 1980–85, but real wages in the industrial sector increased. The share of factor income going to labor increased sharply, while the share of nonfinancial profits declined correspondingly. Within the government sector, the employment increase was accompanied by significant real wage compression, which caused average wages in the formal sector as a whole to fall. As overall employment was stagnant in the formal sector and shrinking in agriculture, the informal sector absorbed all the natural increase in the size of the labor force during the recession, and average value added per worker in this sector fell by one-fourth. Reflecting this surge in employment (as well as the decline in agricultural incomes), informal sector incomes fell by almost 10 percent between 1980 and 1983. Somewhat surprisingly, the differential between the formal and informal sector incomes remained roughly constant, increasing by only 5 percent for the period. At the upper end of the income spectrum, profits—specially nonfinancial profits—contracted sharply, as owners of physical capital were hurt by the combination of high interest rates, workers' ability to protect their wages, and sluggish demand.

In short, the government's tight money policy, combined with a wage policy that maintained real wages in the formal sector, in effect protected the middle of the income distribution against both ends. The protection of the middle clearly also benefited the urban informal sector by helping to support demand for its services. Nonetheless, the fall in incomes in the agricultural sector, where the majority of the poor earn their incomes, was combined with the crowding of new labor market entrants into the informal sector, where average earnings are one-third of those in the formal sector. This pushed a significant portion of the population back into poverty, especially in the urban areas in the south and southeast, where most of the urban population is located.

During the recovery period (1984–85), formal public sector workers, holders of capital, and informal (including agricultural) workers improved their positions at the expense of private formal sector workers. The income differential between formal and informal sector workers fell. Public employment continued to swell, while private sector employment kept pace with output growth. In addition, in 1984, when inflation took a sharp jump upward, formal sector workers were left behind. These income losses led workers to demand (and receive in some sectors) a halving of the indexation period in 1985. Although private sector workers did not make real gains, government workers began to recover wages lost during the previous period. The increase in informal sector incomes combined with the increase in formal sector employment, which automatically raises average wages in the economy as the formal sector is the high wage sector, brought a significant decrease in urban poverty and in poverty overall. In this period, growth did trickle down to the poor, reversing some of the adverse effects of the previous period.

The Cruzado Plan resulted in short-run gains for all groups, but it proved unsustainable. Under the plan, interest rates and prices declined while profits and consumption increased. This generated increases in real income across the board. In addition, employment rose, especially in the higher earning formal sector. Labor markets tightened, the earnings differential between the formal and informal sectors narrowed further, and the increased demand relative to the supply of labor sharply increased real earnings in the informal sector. Agricultural incomes also jumped as employment in the sector dropped in response to the urban boom. The poor immediately benefited from the real income gains as poverty dropped below pre-crisis levels.

After the boom, inflation returned in 1987 as the government tried to force the private sector to finance the fiscal expansion. Prices rose and real incomes—both labor earnings and profits—fell. Higher inflation clearly hurt labor incomes, especially in the less organized parts of the formal sector where average earnings fell 35 percent. Informal sector earnings also dropped (almost to 1984 levels), and the incidence of poverty increased again, eroding the gains of the previous period.

From a poverty perspective, the boom and bust of the Cruzado Plan ultimately hurt the poor, as the slowdown that followed the plan lasted through 1988. In addition, the Cruzado Plan's excesses also exacerbated the stabilization and adjustment problem by adding to the debt burden. If Brazil had actually stabilized in 1986 (and this was not an absurd possibility), the poor might have recovered what they had lost relative to the middle class during the recession by the closing years of the decade. The longer stabilization and adjustment was postponed, the worse off the poor became.

During the 1980s, the labor movement had gained a critical voice in policies determining the distribution of burdens resulting from adjustment. The case of São Paulo State is instructive. During the recession, industrial workers were the only group in São Paulo able to avoid real wage reductions while other groups suffered severe cuts and the incidence of poverty increased by 50 percent. In contrast, nonunionized workers did much better, relatively speaking, during the recovery and especially under the Cruzado Plan, when they benefited from the price freeze. Unionized workers were clearly much better able to avoid the pain of adjustment, and they did so through the usual means open to unions: militancy and activism. However, organized labor was not the obstacle to successful stabilization and successful adjustment in 1985; it was the failure of the system as a whole to reach agreement on the distribution of consumption. No doubt the unions' emergence as a powerful actor onto the political scene at a time when increasing democratization made the political system much more open to influence complicated the political economy of adjustment. Unfortunately, at the same time, Brazil realized that an agreement with the labor movement was critical, the political institutions, and perhaps the political will, that would make such an agreement possible were lacking.

Consequences of Adjustment for the Poor

During 1980–87, Brazil's macroeconomic policies hurt the poor less than they might given Brazil's lackluster growth performance. Despite data difficulties and ambiguities, we can conclude with some confidence that if the incidence and intensity of poverty did worsen, it did not worsen very much. The main reason for this appears to be the protection of formal sector wage incomes during the recession, and the expansionist fiscal policies in the postrecession period. In the 1980s, as in the 1970s, output growth was strongly related to poverty reduction. The major factor keeping the economy afloat was government consumption, a significant portion of which was public employment. This fiscal stimulus helped to maintain employment and stimulated some growth in real output. The stimulus appears to have trickled down to the poor most rapidly in 1984–85, when output in the private formal sector also expanded rapidly. But during 1986–88, the poor were not as fortunate, as negative distributional shifts overwhelmed overall income growth, reducing the average incomes of the poorest 10 percent of the population.

By 1988, Brazil's poor were already beginning to pay the costs of the failure to exercise macroeconomic restraint during 1985–87, and these policies will likely bring high future costs for the poor as well. First, the public sector deficit absorbed a large share of private sector savings, crowding out the private sector investment needed for accelerated growth and labor productivity improvements in the 1990s. Second, the high interest rates the government paid on its internal debt constituted a significant and regressive income transfer, as the share of national income going to debt service rose to 10 percent of GDP by the middle of the decade. The household survey data does a very poor job of recording capital income, and thus the effect of this transfer on income distribution is not well documented. Nonetheless, the size of this transfer to holders of government bonds may have been a factor in the deterioration of Brazil's already unequal income distribution that occurred during the late 1980s.

To analyze further the effects of adjustment on the poor, they can be disaggregated into three groups: the rural poor, who are found primarily in the northeast and who constitute 50 percent of the overall poor population; the urban poor in the northeast, most of whom continue to depend on agriculture and/or the informal sector for their incomes; and the urban poor in the south and southeast, who are much more tightly linked to the formal sector. Rural poor households are overwhelmingly agricultural in occupation, and very few have the signed employment cards that provide access to the formal sector (although the rate in the southeast is twice that in the northeast). Urban poor households are much more likely to be headed by persons with formal sector jobs: in the southeast, 50 percent of the poor have a main source of income in the formal sector.

The incidence of poverty changed for all three groups during the 1980s. First, for the first time in two decades, the percentage of the poor living in urban areas increased substantially: by 1985, less than 40 percent of the poor lived in households where the main source of income was agriculture. Second, the percentage of the poor living in the northeast also increased, even though the actual incidence of poverty increased faster in the south and southeast (from a lower base). Apparently the northeast was simply not as efficient in using its (generally higher) growth during the early 1980s to alleviate poverty.

Poverty in the rural northeast is much more strongly affected by supply-side factors such as investment than by adjustment. Agricultural policies that have steadily favored investment and the building of infrastructure—irrigation and so on—have helped to improve the productivity of large farms, as has the switch from crops to livestock. Increased investment and technical change have also encouraged the proletarianization of the rural labor force, as wage labor has in some regions, such as the sugar plantations of the *Zona de Mata*, completely replaced the historically dominant sharecropping relationship. This process has also led to a rise in the use of permanent labor contracts, membership in trade unions, and the incidence of signed employment cards. Although no data is available on the economic effects of these changes on the poor, they are likely to have tightened the link between the economic condition of the country as a whole and the lot of the rural poor, who are now more closely linked to the product markets in Brazil, and even abroad.

In contrast, poverty in urban areas is strongly and negatively related to economic growth. This is especially so of the private formal sector, which produced 70 percent of GDP in 1980 and employed 47 percent of the nonagricultural work force. This relationship is especially strong in the south and southeast. Thus, while the incidence of poverty increased by 50 percent during the 1981–83 recession in the south and southeast, it increased by only 30 percent in the northeast. Similarly, poverty declined much more slowly in the northeast during the boom years of the Cruzado Plan.

Despite the recession and persistent crises, Brazil continued to realize improvements in social indicators. In part, this was because the heavy investments in social infrastructure of the previous decade were delivering their payoff in the 1980s, but also because adjustment did not stop the expansion of social infrastructure in Brazil. Overall mortality rates continued to decline, and the infant mortality rate fell 40 percent between 1980 and 1986. By 1987, over 90 percent of urban households had access to potable water and to electricity. However, the disadvantaged northeast remained far behind, especially in the rural areas.

Conclusion

In the end, Brazil never permanently adjusted internal demand to the external shocks of the 1970s and 1980s. In the 1970s, it borrowed its way through the oil crisis, waiting for oil prices to fall while continuing to invest, increasingly in the public sector. In the 1980s, oil prices did fall, but interest costs increased fast and external sources of finance dried up. Initially, Brazil responded by reducing demand. From 1985 onward, the government switched policies and sought instead to borrow from domestic sources. To do so, it had to pay very high real interest rates, and interest payments became a growing proportion of overall government expenditures.

In the field of trade and the external balance, Brazil's quantitative controls over imports and substantial export promotion incentives allowed the government to switch expenditure as needed. Thus, unlike most middle-income countries, earning foreign exchange was not a problem. Brazil's success in this area is due primarily to its diversified industrial structure and large internal market, which allowed Brazil, more than most middle-income countries, to achieve external balance through expenditure-switching policies instead of expenditure-reducing ones. A large real wage decline was not necessary for Brazil to achieve external balance.

However, some decline in consumption was needed to achieve internal balance. The evidence from the labor and capital markets is that none of the actors with any influence over government policy were prepared to sacrifice their own consumption to achieve this goal, nor under the emerging democracy was capital able to force labor to sacrifice as it did in the 1960s. Capital demanded high real interest rates to stay in Brazil while profits recovered from the recession; workers in the formal sector managed to defend real wage levels more or less continuously until 1988; and wages in the informal sector did fall during the recession of the early 1980s, but then rebounded. Only in agriculture did incomes fall overall, but the difficulty of measuring incomes in this sector makes this comparison problematic.

While Brazil's labor markets have shown significant flexibility and can be expected to do so in the future, the political economy of Brazil's labor market institutions suggests that achieving stability and growth in the future will continue to be problematic. The government has little credibility with the unions, who do not believe that an adjustment program will treat them fairly. Yet adjustment will almost certainly demand some kind of social contract involving both the unions and holders of capital. The alternatives—such as lowering real wages through a recession—are expensive, especially given the decentralized bargaining structure, and politically highly unpopular. Such a policy would also favor financial capital if it were implemented through the standard approach of a tight money policy.

The difficulties of putting together such a social contract are formidable. Experience in Europe suggests that key ingredients in such a deal include (a) a belief that the process itself is fair and that burdens are being shared fairly; (b) a long-term commitment to the process on all sides so that inequities in one deal can be compensated in the next; (c) a crisis serious enough to engage the attention of all parties; and (d) a government that does not seek to load the process of bargaining with too many reforms, for example, a sectorally-oriented industrial policy.

Whether Brazil has the political and institutional resources to manufacture a policy that fits these requirements is an open question.

References

Almeida Reis, Jose Guilherme. 1989. "Salario Minimo e Distribuicao de Renda." In *Perspectivas da Economia Brasileira 1989*. Rio de Janeiro: IPEA/IN.

Fox, M. Louise. 1990. "Poverty Alleviation in Brazil, 1970–87." Internal Discussion Paper (IDP-072). Washington, D.C.: World Bank, Latin America and the Caribbean Region.

Fox, M. Louise, and Samuel A. Morley. 1990. "Who Paid the Bill? Adjustment and Poverty in Brazil, 1980–85." Background paper for *World Development Report 1990*. Washington, D.C.: World Bank.

Morley, Samuel A. 1982. Labor Markets and Inequitable Growth: *The Case of Authoritarian Capitalism in Brazil*. Cambridge, U.K.: Cambridge University Press.

Pastore, Jose, Helio Zylberstajn, and Carmen Silvia Pagotto. 1983. *Mudanca Social e Pobreza no Brasil: 1970-1980. (O que Ocorreu com a Familia Brasileira?)*. São Paulo: FIPE/PIONEIRA

Saboia, J. 1989. "Dualism e Integracao do Mecado de Trabalho." Discussion paper. Rio de Janeiro: Federal University of Rio de Janeiro.

World Bank. 1988. *Brazil: An Assessment of the Current Macroeconomic Situation*. Report No. 7540-BR. Washington, D.C.

_____. 1990. *World Development Report 1990: Poverty*. New York: Oxford University Press.

5

Chile J20
022 E63
015
011

CHILE

Luis A. Riveros

Like other developing countries, at the outset of the 1980s Chile faced persistent internal imbalances and an unsustainable external deficit. This was partly due to internal factors, especially the economic policy of the late 1970s, which sustained a revaluation of the real exchange rate, stimulated low savings and permitted growing external indebtedness. However, the lending cutback of 1982, a sharp drop in the terms of trade, and an increase in international interest rates also played crucial roles in creating a deep recession. The economy was unable to generate a trade surplus quickly in response to these external developments. After a deep recession, export promotion and other policies dealing with the debt problem allowed the Chilean economy to resume sustained growth and internal balance, which was complemented by a return to a democratic form of government in 1990.

The labor market played a key role in the adjustment Chile's economy underwent in the 1970s in the post-recession period of the 1980s. As predicted by standard adjustment models, a decline in real wages occurred as a result of expenditure-reducing and expenditure-switching policies. However, due to rigidities that hindered labor mobility, the economy suffered from persistent high unemployment. These rigidities were mainly associated with labor market segmentation and expectations associated with the lack of an

The author is indebted to Bela Balassa, Albert Berry, Erik Haindl, Susan Horton, Ravi Kanbur, Dipak Mazumdar, Ricardo Paredes, and the participants of workshops held at the University of Toronto and the University of Chile for valuable comments on earlier drafts, and to J. Charoenwattana and J. Lackman for efficient research assistance.

institutional framework for the labor market. As a result of the post-1984 export-led adjustment program and the introduction of more adequate labor market reforms, open unemployment declined, employment in tradables increased strongly, and real wages started to recover.

Without the profound structural economic reforms of the 1970s, rapid achievement of growth and macroeconomic equilibrium after the financial crash of 1982–84 would have been nearly impossible. These reforms permitted flexible and competitive markets, as required to achieve macroeconomic adjustment. Similarly, understanding the precarious situation of labor market variables in the late 1970s is essential in comprehending the effect of the 1980s' crisis on such variables as open unemployment and real wages.

This chapter reviews the Chilean labor market during the structural reforms of the 1970s and the crisis and recovery period of the 1980s. To analyze the effect of macro policies—and given that existing wage differentials and the behavior of both unemployment and investment are central in interpreting the role of the labor market in the adjustment—it adopts a segmented labor market model to study the effect of exchange rate policies on labor market variables. The chapter analyzes the wage determination process in the formal and informal sectors using a model that examines the effect of typical macro policies. The implication is that if labor markets were less segmented, unemployment during the adjustment would have been lower. Given that segmentation is linked to labor market policies, less intervention would have been advisable.

The Economic Setting

Chile's achievement of deep economic reforms in the 1970s radically changed relative prices and reduced state intervention in the economy. During 1970–73, economic policies inspired by socialism produced substantial economic and political strain. A military government took power in September 1973 and instituted deregulation aimed at correcting major price distortions during 1973–75. In a second phase during 1975–76, the government placed greater emphasis on price stabilization while it continued with the structural reforms. Appreciating real exchange rates, high domestic interest rates, and labor market friction created macroeconomic problems during 1976–80 and promoted higher growth of nontradable relative to tradable production. During this third phase, the economy was characterized by growing real wages, high growth, and high unemployment. The 1982–84 financial crisis resulted in a sharp economic decline amid serious balance of payment problems. Following the crisis, sharp devaluations combined with reduced expenditure and other policies aimed at affecting expectations, increasing savings, and promoting exports led to a notable export-led economic expansion. This sequence of phases is paramount in explaining observed labor market outcomes.

The Socialist Experiment, 1970–73

The government of Dr. Allende aimed at making profound changes in Chile's economy that would achieve key improvements in distributive results and growth records. The installation of this economic program, however, involved serious macroeconomic imbalances. During 1971, the budget deficit increased from 2.7 to 10.7 percent of GDP, and credit from the central bank to the public sector increased by more than 110 percent. On the external front, and partly as a result of a sharp drop in the world price of copper, Chile's major export at that time, international reserves dropped dramatically from US$390 million in 1970 to US$161 million in 1971, and the trade balance went from a surplus of US$156 million in 1970 to a deficit of US$16 million in 1971. On top of traditionally high tariff rates, the government decided to introduce significant quantity controls on imports, thereby generating a more recessionary productive adjustment. Moreover, as a result of changes in relative prices, consumption increased by 12 percent and investment dropped some 2 percent of GDP in 1971. This increase in consumption was associated with a sharp growth in real wages of more than 22 percent during 1971, which was achieved mainly through traditional government policies and at the cost of productive investment.

The overheating of the economy that began in 1971 created increasing problems during the next two years. The government considered maintenance of its progressive and revolutionary image to be more important than reducing disequilibria (Larrain and Meller

Table 5.1 Macroeconomic Indicators, 1970–88

Year	GDP growth	Output growth in tradables	Output growth in nontradables	CPI inflation	M1 growth	Gross investment (% of GDP)	Fiscal deficit (% of GDP)	Current account deficit (% of GDP)	Real exchange rate
1970	2.1	1.4	2.9	32.5	66.2	16.4	2.7	-1.2	38.5
1971	9.0	9.2	8.8	22.1	113.4	14.5	10.7	-1.9	35.3
1972	-1.2	-0.8	-1.1	260.5	151.8	12.2	13.0	-4.0	36.7
1973	-5.6	-7.3	-3.7	605.1	362.9	7.8	24.7	-2.7	56.7
1974	1.0	6.6	-0.4	369.2	231.2	21.2	10.5	-2.6	83.8
1975	-12.9	-16.6	-8.4	343.3	257.2	13.1	2.6	-6.8	100.0
1976	3.5	5.3	1.6	197.9	189.4	12.8	2.3	1.5	91.5
1977	9.9	7.8	9.4	84.2	113.5	14.4	1.8	-4.1	83.5
1978	8.2	4.5	9.6	37.2	65.0	17.8	0.8	-7.1	101.6
1979	8.3	7.0	10.0	38.9	57.8	17.8	-1.7	-5.7	105.9
1980	7.8	5.5	10.0	31.2	64.0	21.0	-3.1	-7.1	94.0
1981	5.5	3.8	5.4	9.5	-3.8	22.7	-1.7	-14.5	74.8
1982	-14.1	-11.2	-10.8	20.7	7.3	11.3	2.3	-9.5	81.1
1983	-0.7	0.5	-6.1	23.1	27.7	9.8	3.8	-5.6	98.1
1984	6.3	7.9	5.3	23.0	12.1	15.3	4.0	-10.7	100.8
1985	2.4	2.5	2.4	26.4	11.3	13.9	6.3	-8.3	123.0
1986	5.7	6.7	5.0	17.4	41.4	15.0	2.8	-6.5	139.9
1987	5.7	3.5	6.6	21.5	9.8	17.9	0.1	-4.6	143.5
1988	7.4	6.9	7.7	12.7	82.4	18.1	1.7	-3.0	149.9
1989	10.0	8.1	10.9	17.1	13.2	22.0	0.4	-4.7	151.2

Notes: Tradables includes agriculture, fishing, mining, and manufacturing. Nontradables includes construction and services. CPI inflation corresponds to the December to December change in the corrected CPI. The real effective exchange rate is the real multilateral exchange rate in terms of the wholesale prices of trading partners and Chile's cpi. The average ratio of investment to GDP during 1960–69 was 14.9 percent. M1 growth is the December to December growth of M1.

Sources: Banco Central de Chile (1987); Corbo (1985a); Cottani (1988); Cortazar and Marshall (1980); IMF (various years); World Bank (1990). For 1988 and 1989: Banco Central de Chile (1990).

1990). The fiscal situation deteriorated because the government made no effort to reduce expenditures, while the need for transferring resources to a growing number of public enterprises placed a heavier burden on fiscal expenditures. At the same time, tax collection dropped dramatically, making the fiscal situation even worse. In response to these developments, the total quantity of money increased by 152 in 1972 and 363 percent in 1973 (table 5.1). As a consequence, yearly inflation rates skyrocketed to 261 and 605 percent, respectively, during the same years. Another outcome was the significant drop in GDP of 1.2 percent in 1972 and 5.6 percent in 1973. This was accompanied by a drop in real wages of 11.3 and 38.6 percent, respectively. The current account deficit rose from US$189 million in 1971 to US$387 million in 1972 and US$295 million in 1973, despite heavier import controls. The government insisted that the problem was a plot organized by entrepreneurs and insisted on nationalizing private firms. This increased the political turbulence in 1973, which was already high due to severe shortages and a very critical opposition party.

During the socialist experiment, union activities reached a peak. The increase in real wages in 1971 and the permanent efforts to keep pace with price inflation in 1972 and 1973 were facilitated by a centralized system of wage fixing in which the national union confederation (CUT) played a key role. Unemployment rates reached the lowest historical level in 1972 (3.1 percent), and increased slightly to 4.8 percent despite the significant drop in GDP in 1973. This was due mainly to a significant increase in public sector employment.

The Economic Reforms of the 1970s

The military government that took office in 1973 embarked on an intense program of economic reforms aimed at improving efficiency in the framework of an open economy. Many observers have analyzed the specific targets and policy tools used to achieve those reforms (see Corbo 1985a; Edwards and Edwards 1987; Walton 1985). However, the direct and indirect impacts of the reform program on labor market outcomes have received relatively little attention despite their crucial political impact.

The government deemed that major changes in labor market institutions were necessary in the context of a freer, more deregulated, open economy. The presence of some intervening policies notwithstanding, these changes directly affected wages and employment. Deregulation of output markets, the opening of the economy, and the reduction in the state's economic size affected employment and wages indirectly as vital shifts in the skill composition of the labor demand called for higher labor mobility. A more detailed description of the main reforms follows.

TRADE REFORMS. Chile, like many other developing countries, pursued industrialization based on the creation of a sizable import substituting industry. Major outcomes of this policy were high trade barriers, considerable inefficiency, discrimination against agriculture, and growing government intervention in economic management (Corbo 1986). Paradoxically, employment growth in manufacturing was affected negatively (Corbo and Meller 1984), and labor market segmentation occurred due to the parallel need for labor protection created by the appearance of a strong labor movement. As the failure to achieve an efficient industrial sector required progressively higher protective barriers, average tariff rates reached as high as 105 percent by 1973 (Torres 1982).[1]

The reforms initiated by late 1973 aimed at sharply reversing import substitution through a far-reaching opening up of the economy.[2] The trade opening was expected to produce more investment and employment in sectors with comparative advantages. Two causes account for failure to obtain higher exports and growth of labor-intensive industries after 1973: (a) the tariff reduction program did not begin with a precise final target, thereby creating uncertainty among investors (Riveros 1986); and (b) the exchange rate was used

1. *Ad-valorem* tariff rates ranged from 0 to 750 percent, while import prohibitions applied to 187 tariff classifications, a 90-day import deposit requirement was in effect for 2,800 others, and 2,300 categories required special approval from the central bank.

2. Tariffs were planned to reach an average 60 percent by 1977. By 1975, average tariffs had reached 57 percent while almost all quantitative restrictions were eliminated. In a second stage, a new structure with tariffs ranging from 10 to 35 percent was achieved during the third quarter of 1977. Finally, a more radical reform allowed the average nominal tariff rate to reach a uniform 10 percent by late 1977.

as a stabilization device, particularly after 1978, thereby permitting substantial overvaluation (Corbo 1985b; Edwards and Edwards 1987).[3] However, amid high internal interest rates and growing peso appreciation, the economic authorities decided to open up the capital account. In addition to the macro imbalances so generated (Edwards and Edwards 1987), this policy allowed large firms to adopt more capital-intensive techniques, which also affected the prospects for employment creation in expanding activities.

PUBLIC SECTOR REFORMS. Another set of reforms after 1973 aimed at reducing the state's economic size by reducing both government expenditures and privatization of public firms. The huge fiscal deficit that existed in 1973 is an indicator of the economic importance the state had attained. Another indicator is the share of parastatals in total production, which had been 14 percent of GDP in 1965, but reached 39 percent of GDP in 1973 (Hachette and Luders 1987). Still another indicator is the state's importance as an employer, especially during the socialist experiment of 1970–73, when public sector employment reached about 15 percent of total employment. Total public sector employment grew by 38 percent between 1970 and 1973.

To reduce the state's economic importance, the government implemented a privatization program together with policies aimed at making the central government more efficient. Private firms nationalized during the socialist regime were immediately privatized: by the end of 1974, 202 out of 259 had been returned to their owners (Larrain 1988). In addition, the government quickly sold some state assets, with most bank shares (US$171 million) and a significant part of industrial property (US$58 million) being sold by 1975.[4] As

---

3. After unification of the exchange rate in 1973, an initial 300 percent devaluation, and a series of minidevaluations, the real exchange rate reached a peak value by late 1975. Subsequently, the real exchange rate declined sharply concluding in a 10 percent appreciation in June 1976. Real peso appreciation continued being used as a stabilization device through a system of devaluations that allowed for certain real appreciation. However, inflation did not drop as expected. From June 1979 a nominally fixed exchange rate was implemented and maintained until mid-1982, when dramatic peso devaluations took place in the wake of the world recession. In this analysis, appreciation is represented by a decline in the real exchange rate.

4. This was a year of unprecedented economic decline (GDP fell by 12.9 percent), thus sales were not profitable. At the same time, firms were sold below their book values, although above their stock market value (Larrain 1988).

parastatals' share in GDP dropped from 39 percent in 1973 to a still high 24 percent in 1981, the government initiated further privatization at the time of the 1980s crisis. Owing to active job creation in the public sector in 1971–73 and redundant employment, major job cuts occurred in both the civil service and parastatals between 1973–77, when total public sector employment declined by 24 percent, implying an increase in the unemployment rate of about 3 percent of the labor force.

MARKET DEREGULATION. A top priority of the reform program after 1973 was to improve resource allocation through an efficient price system. Hence, and countering a historical tradition of price fixing, price regulation was almost completely eliminated. After an era in which more than 3,000 prices were set and eventually controlled by the authorities, only 33 commodities remained under government control, most of them utilities. Likewise, interest rates were also deregulated and quantitative constraints for capital market operations were eliminated before 1979. Entrepreneurs facing increased market competition had to improve their productive efficiency, which resulted in several bankruptcies during the period of transformation.

The wave of deregulation also reached the labor market, which was considered a crucial area after a period of acute government intervention and union activism. Deregulation resulted in a fundamental change in wage setting mechanisms and encouraged labor dismissals aimed at eliminating overemployment. Before September 1973, the Labor Law (*Codigo del Trabajo*) governed the institutional functioning of the labor market, and according to this law wage bargaining could be made at the most aggregated level, thereby authorizing unions to form confederations and negotiate with entrepreneurial associations. Immediately after September 1973, collective bargaining and union activities were simultaneously eliminated, which also ousted traditional wage bargaining procedures. Similarly, traditional regulations on job security, which made labor dismissals relatively expensive, were eliminated. After 1973, massive labor dismissals only required a simple administrative authorization from the government. Thus, the new government gave the private sector full power to implement its desired employment wage strategy.

The importance of institutional changes in the labor market after 1973 is revealed by the fact that once almost all unions were virtually eliminated, the government hand picked the leaders for the remaining ones. The most striking result was, however, that during the entire period 1973–79, no new legal provisions governed labor relations, including those in connection with wage bargaining, job security, the right to strike, negotiation of working conditions, and union activities. Although a set of rules for industrial relations was enacted in 1975 (Decree 1005), it did not introduce any significant changes as concerned the functioning of the labor market.

After 1973, minimum wages and nonwage cost regulations were upheld and a wage indexation system was implemented, although it had little effect given the absence of enforcement mechanisms (Edwards and Edwards 1987; Riveros 1986). As discussed later, a major failing of the program was the lack of a labor law during 1973–79, and even of signals about projected legal changes, which created expectations of high future firing and hiring costs, and affected private sector decisions on employment.

Between 1979 and 1982, the government adopted key changes in labor market institutions. In 1979, a new law (DL 2756 and DL 2758) was enacted, establishing new guidelines for unionization and collective bargaining. Countering a tradition in Chile, more than one union was allowed per enterprise, wage bargaining could only be done at the firm level, and the right to strike was curtailed by granting firms the right to hire temporaries. In addition, the law did not restore labor courts that had existed before 1973. Instead it established the principle of voluntary affiliation to unions and banned public employees' right to strike. Finally, the law also instituted a 100 percent wage indexation to past inflation as a floor for any negotiation.

After 1982 the government made several changes to the 1979 labor law. The most important was the elimination of the full indexation clause, which had apparently created substantial problems in connection with the economy's response to the 1982 recession. Other changes included eliminating special authorizations required to hold certain jobs, such as, actors, musicians, and bus drivers. The most important change was the elimination of special privileges traditionally awarded to dock workers, which permitted more competition in hiring labor. Finally, the government eliminated employers' rights to dismiss workers without justification and established severance compensation of one month per year of service for workers hired after 1981.

THE STABILIZATION PROGRAM. The initial phase of the structural reforms was accompanied by a sharp stabilization effort in 1975–76. As table 5.1 shows, as late as 1975 inflation was still above 300 percent per year. To deal with it, the government managed to reduce the fiscal deficit (measured against GDP) from 24.7 in 1973 to 10.5 in 1974 and 2.6 in 1975, mainly by reducing public sector expenditures. This was accompanied by tighter monetary policy, and later on by a deliberate appreciation of the real exchange rate. Inflation was significantly curbed between 1975 and 1978, and continued dropping until 1981 as a result of exchange rate management and the creation of a fiscal surplus instead of the traditional deficit. The effect on unemployment of the across the board reduction in aggregate demand was as important as the drop in real wages. The stabilization effort also affected long-run growth due to its effects on investment and wealth (Edwards 1985).

The 1982 Financial Crisis and the Policy Response

Domestic economic policies introduced at the end of the 1970s were primarily responsible for creating macroeconomic disequilibria that led to unsustainable, high expectations, and ultimately to a disruption in the economic recovery initiated in 1976. The full opening of the capital account when the exchange rate was fixed with the aim of controlling inflation produced substantial difficulties. This combination of policies was still more burdensome in the presence of a binding full indexation of wages to past inflation. Large capital inflows financed an otherwise unsustainable expansion of private consumption and investment. Optimism about future trends was based on the economy's stable growth since 1976, the balanced public budget, the sustained improvement in real wages, and the opening of the economy. However, the economic boom of 1979–81 was basically financed with foreign credit, with few resources being allocated to productive investment. In addition, a poorly controlled financial system was weakened by a deterioration in the quality of its loans to the corporate sector. This was aggravated by the normal practice of granting credits to firms whose ownership was interlocked with that of the lending institutions.

Some indicators reveal the magnitude of the crisis the Chilean economy faced in 1982. Total external debt increased from 2.7 times total exports in 1979 to 4.6 times in 1983. As a share of GDP, the external debt increased from 40 percent to 100 percent during the same years, while yearly interest payments increased from 3 to 10 percent of GDP. At the same time, and due to an early policy reaction to the crisis, the value of imports in real terms declined by more than 40 percent (table 5.2), which precipitated a GDP drop of more than 15 percent in GDP (table 5.1). This GDP drop was accompanied by an

Table 5.2 The External Sector, 1979–87
(billions of current US$)

Category	1979	1980	1981	1982	1983	1984	1985	1986	1987
External debt									
Total	8.49	11.80	15.50	17.10	17.40	18.90	19.30	19.40	19.10
Interest	0.67	0.93	1.46	1.92	1.75	2.02	1.90	1.89	1.70
Debt/exports	2.70	2.40	4.10	4.60	4.60	5.20	5.10	4.60	3.70
Debt/GNP	0.40	0.40	0.50	0.80	1.00	1.10	1.40	1.30	1.20
Exports (f.o.b.)									
Traditionals	2.16	2.62	2.18	2.12	2.34	1.96	2.12	2.10	2.60
Nontraditional	1.68	2.09	1.66	1.58	1.50	1.69	1.68	2.10	2.62
Total	3.84	4.71	3.84	3.71	3.83	3.65	3.80	4.20	5.22
Total*	4.33	4.71	4.41	4.87	4.78	4.92	5.32	5.92	n.a.
Imports (c.i.f.)									
Consumer goods	1.33	2.07	2.73	1.48	1.02	1.04	7.51	7.54	9.01
Capital goods	0.95	1.27	1.45	0.70	0.39	0.60	0.65	0.74	1.10
Total imports	4.71	6.15	7.32	4.09	3.17	3.74	3.27	3.44	4.40
Total imports*	5.81	6.19	6.25	4.25	3.36	4.04	3.59	3.65	n.a.
Terms of trade									
(1980 = 100)	118.50	100.00	84.30	80.40	87.50	83.20	78.50	82.00	77.00

n.a. = not available
* Series is expressed in constant 1980 billions of dollars.
Notes: Data for 1987 are preliminary. Traditional exports include copper and mining. Nontraditional exports are agricultural and industrial products.
Sources: *Boletin Mensual*, Banco Central de Chile; *World Tables* (IBRD); Corbo & Sturzenegger (1988).

even larger decline in aggregate investment, which affected future growth. The magnitude of the external shock is demonstrated by the drop in terms of trade (from 119 in 1979 to 88 in 1983) and the increase in real (LIBOR) interest rates from 2.6 to 4.6 percent (see Corbo and Sturzenegger 1988). The sharp curtailment of capital flows in early 1982 amplified the problem and led the economy into a deep recession in 1982–83.

During 1979–81, the authorities also shifted their attention away from stabilization policies and toward structural adjustment. During this period, the government implemented a series of reforms aimed at changing traditional practices with regard to social policies and administration of social welfare. In 1981, the government made a key change to the social security system, changing it from a pay-as-you-go system to one in which benefits depended only on individual contributions. Also in 1981, the government introduced health system reforms aimed at promoting a private health care system. It also decentralized the education and health systems to make them more responsive to local needs. These changes were important during the recovery from the world recession, as they permitted better targeting of fiscal social expenditures on the poor.

In 1984, a so-called "adjustment without recession" approach resulted in huge reserve losses and further external indebtedness. This policy stimulated aggregate demand to encourage output growth. However, the availability of external financing posited a tough constraint to the planned expansion in aggregate expenditures. The current account deficit almost doubled between 1983 and 1984, while the fiscal deficit also increased considerably (table 5.1). Although unsustainable in the medium run, this approach resulted in a GDP growth of more than 6 percent in 1984, but also resulted in declining exports and a large growth in external payments (table 5.2). What the economy needed to face the recession was sensible policies aimed at encouraging exports and a continuation of the structural reforms.

After 1985, the adjustment program focused on maintaining a high real exchange rate, privatizing public firms, controlling fiscal expenditures; creating mechanisms that allowed conversion of external debt into investment (which has yielded a drop in the total external debt of more than 10 percent), introducing specific incentives for exports, and targeting fiscal social expenditures to the poor. This combination of policies resulted in a resumption of strong economic growth (more than 5.5 percent per annum in 1986–88 and about 10 percent during 1989), with a large expansion of nontraditional exports, investment growth, low inflation, and sharply declining open unemployment. The year 1988 was a culmination of a successful adjustment achieved by accentuating the role of markets in allocating resources.

Labor Market Effects of the Adjustment Program

The economic reforms of the 1970s had major effects on the labor market. One of the most important was the increase in open unemployment rates from an average of about 6 percent of the labor force during the 1960s to more than 16 percent during 1974–81 (table 5.3).[5] Moreover, even with high GDP growth between 1976 and 1981, open unemployment remained at relatively high levels (table 5.3). A related result was the decline in average real wages. In addition, during 1976–81, employment in nontradable activities expanded more rapidly than in tradables, a result not concordant with the outward orientation of the economic program, but explainable in the context of the signals provided by an appreciating real exchange rate (table 5.1). Finally, traditional labor market institutions—like wage bargaining, unionization, and job security laws—were not legally reinstated until 1979, which probably effected expectations and countered employment creation in expanding tradable activities.

Employment and Unemployment Trends

Unemployment rates increased significantly after 1974, causing concern about the social impact of adjustment policies. Unemployment was proportionally higher for the relatively more skilled labor force, as revealed by unemployment rates broken down by education (Riveros and Diaz 1987). Similarly, unemployment rates were higher for older people, possibly because those entering the

---

5. This average includes persons in emergency employment programs (EEP). As discussed later, this calculation yields an economically meaningful unemployment level. If EEPs are not included, the average unemployment in 1974–81 reaches about 13 percent of the labor force.

Table 5.3 Employment and Unemployment, 1970–89

Category	1970	1971	1972	1973	1974	1975	1976	1977	1978	1979
1. *Population (thousands of persons)*										
(a) 12 years and over	6,455.6	6,636.3	6,815.4	6,992.5	7,164.2	7,339.1	7,515.0	7,691.5	7,866.7	8,057.1
(b) Total labor force	2,932.2	2,978.8	3,000.8	3,039.0	3,066.8	3,152.9	3,216.4	3,259.7	3,370.1	3,480.7
(c) Participation rate	45.4	44.9	46.8	43.5	42.8	43.0	42.8	42.4	42.8	43.2
2. *Employment (thousands of persons)*										
(a) Total employment (UCH)	2,766.1	2,865.6	2,907.8	2,893.1	2,784.7	2,727.3	2,705.0	2,796.8	2,891.5	3,000.4
(b) Total employment (INE)	n.a.	2,880.5	2,901.8	n.a.	n.a.	2,777.3	2,820.5	2,981.3	3,003.3	3,257.1
(c) Emergency employment program	—	—	—	—	71.5	172.0	187.6	145.8	133.9	191.0
3. *Unemployment (percent)*										
(a) Castaneda (UCH)	5.7	3.8	3.1	4.8	9.2	13.5	15.9	14.2	14.2	13.8
(b) Corrected (a)	5.7	—	—	—	—	15.5	20.6	19.2	18.0	17.2
(c) INE	n.a.	3.7	3.3	3.3	n.a.	n.a.	12.7	11.8	14.2	13.6
(d) Corrected (c)	—	—	—	—	—	—	17.4	16.9	17.9	17.0
4. *Sectoral employment (thousands of persons)*										
(a) Tradables	1,206.0	1,223.0	1,178.0	1,151.5	1,128.2	1,088.2	1,017.1	1,060.0	1,058.1	1,086.4
Agriculture	625.6	588.0	530.5	500.0	510.0	534.6	486.9	517.4	514.7	512.1
(b) Nontradables	1,560.1	1,642.6	1,729.8	1,741.6	1,656.2	1,575.0	1,536.4	1,571.4	1,705.0	1,799.1
(c) Public sector employment	280.0	325.3	342.0	387.2	360.2	325.5	314.3	295.9	293.3	315.7
(d) Ratio of tradable employment to nontradable employment	0.77	0.74	0.68	0.66	0.68	0.69	0.66	0.67	0.62	0.61

1. Population *(thousands of persons)*										
(a) 12 years and over	8,207.4	8,369.7	8,527.0	8,681.9	8,888.6	9,096.0	9,309.6	9,502.7	9,710.2	9,922.2
(b) Total labor force	3,539.8	3,669.3	3,729.5	3,797.1	3,937.1	4,071.8	4,160.3	4,288.3	4,455.0	4,620.6
(c) Participation rate	43.1	43.8	43.7	43.7	44.3	44.8	44.7	45.1	45.9	46.6
2. Employment *(thousands of persons)*										
(a) Total employment (UCH)	3,122.1	3,269.3	2,971.5	3,091.2	3,185.1	3,420.3	3,582.0	3,748.0	3,911.5	4,163.2
(b) Total employment (INE)	3,270.9	2,943.1	3,215.8	3,349.4	3,537.4	3,895.7	4,010.8	4,110.8	n.a.	n.a.
(c) Emergency employment program	175.6	226.8	502.7	336.3	324.3	233.5	148.5	46.2	—	—
3. Unemployment *(percent)*										
(a) Castaneda (UCH)	11.8	10.9	20.4	18.6	19.1	16.0	13.9	12.6	12.2	10.1
(b) Corrected (a)	16.5	15.1	25.7	30.1	22.9	20.9	18.0	15.2	13.1	10.1
(c) INE	10.4	11.3	19.6	14.6	13.9	12.0	8.8	7.9	6.3	5.3
(d) Corrected (c)	15.0	15.5	25.0	26.2	21.4	19.0	13.6	10.0	7.2	—
4. Sectoral employment *(thousands of persons)*										
(a) Tradables	1,113.3	1,164.6	1,037.1	993.5	1,021.6	1,035.9	1,173.6	1,273.9	1,374.7	1,491.6
Agriculture	518.3	546.9	531.9	510.1	532.7	561.0	570.9	605.2	647.3	657.6
Nontradables	1,840.7	1,950.2	1,734.8	1,655.2	1,867.6	2,060.1	2,212.9	2,343.4	2,496.1	2,671.6
(b) Public sector employment	258.9	281.3	230.5	357.6	356.2	381.6	360.6	349.1	302.7	n.a.
(c) Ratio of tradable employment to nontradable employment	0.60	0.59	0.60	0.57	0.57	0.52	0.53	0.54	0.56	0.56

n.a. = not available
— = not applicable

Note: The Emergency Employment Program existed only between 1974 and 1987.

Sources:
1(a). 1970–83 from Castaneda (1983), 1984–89 projected on the basis of UCH surveys;
1(b). 1970–83 from Castaneda (1983), 1984–89 estimated with the growth rate (March–March) in UCH surveys;
2(a). Banco Central de Chile (1987);
3(a). Castaneda's figures using INE's unemployment rate corrected for rate of participation; 1984–89 based on UCH surveys;
3(b). is 2(a) adjusted by employment emergency program during 1975–88: U-corrected = $(*U) + (EEP*0.88)/(LF)+(EEP*.05)$, where LF = total labor force, U = uncorrected unemployment rate, EEP = number of members;
4(a). estimated based on Riveros (1985a) and Banco Central de Chile (1987);
4(b). 1970–83 from Budnevich and others (1986), 1984–89 based on UCH surveys; figures exclude 88 percent of EEP members (see text);
4(c). Paredes (1987).

labor market were more flexible about accepting lower wages. At the same time, employers considered younger job searchers easier to train, and thus they were more likely to obtain a job. The duration of unemployment also increased dramatically, from an average of six months in the 1960s to more than a year in 1975–79 in the Greater Santiago area (Riveros and Diaz 1987).

Explanations of the persistent high unemployment of the 1970s occupied a prominent place in the literature (for a review see Meller 1984; Riveros 1985b). After a protracted debate, economists reached consensus that alternative explanations have to be combined to provide a consistent theory on the unemployment figures shown in table 5.3.[6]

A first explanation refers to the higher labor force growth seen in the 1970s compared to the 1960s. Although participation rates did not increase, and even declined slightly in 1974–80, labor supply growth was triggered by the post-World War II baby boom (Castaneda 1983). Some estimates showed that this supply effect may have accounted for no more than 3 percent of the higher open unemployment seen in the 1970s (Riveros 1986).

A second explanation refers to the effect of policies on public sector and trade reforms. Figures on public sector employment (table 5.3) show a dramatic decline after 1973, which probably raised total unemployment in the short run. As already mentioned, between 1973 and 1977 public sector employment fell by almost 3 percent of the labor force, while the public sector's wage bill declined by about 3 percent of GDP in 1973–76 (Larrain 1988).[7] Moreover, the elimination of job security amid increased competition in product markets gave rise to a drastic reduction in redundant employment in the private sector (most entrepreneurs declared to a survey carried out through a World Bank study that one of the most beneficial reforms in

6. Statistics presented in table 5.3 adds to total observed unemployment those included in EEP but declaring themselves as "employed" to the surveys (see Riveros 1986). The economic interest of this corrected series is that it permits observation of actual supply pressures on the labor market.

7. According to Paredes (1987), with data taken from Marshall and Romaguera (1981), public employment in 1973 reached about 388,000 persons. Cortes and Sjaastad (1981) suggested a more drastic decline between 1973–76, with public employment declining by more than 6 percent of the labor force.

connection with firms' adjustment was that referring to labor laws). Hence, the array of reforms of the 1970s would have transformed the hidden unemployment that existed before 1973 into open unemployment.

A third explanation refers to the existence of labor market imperfections. The two explanations described above assume that wages did not play any significant role in accommodating a larger labor supply or a decline in labor demand. Although this is a likely short-term outcome, a prolonged period of high unemployment may be ascribed to market imperfections. The basic hypothesis here is that the existence of protected/ unprotected sectors in the labor market— and possibly the expansion of the informal sector during the 1970s— led to increased quasi-voluntary unemployment associated with queuing by informal sector workers for formal jobs. The observed evolution of wage differentials supports this hypothesis, particularly because of the increase in the ratio of minimum wages to average unskilled labor after 1974 (Riveros and Paredes 1989).

A fourth explanation refers to skill mismatches derived from the major productive shifts associated with the structural reforms, which would have produced significant shortages and/or surpluses of industry-specific skills. This is suggested by the presence of a growing tradable/nontradable wage gap for both skilled and unskilled labor, and by increasing returns to the general human capital in economic sectors undergoing expansion (Riveros 1986). Prolonged friction was associated with the wrong signals emanating from both the lack of labor laws and an appreciating real exchange rate. This did not allow expansion of more labor-intensive sectors like agriculture and export manufacturing, which are less intensive in specific skills than typical import substituting activities. The result was a stubborn persistence of wage differentials and lack of labor mobility toward expanding industries.

While employment in tradables did not expand significantly in 1976–81 (table 5.3), employment in nontradables was much more dynamic, growing at an average of 5.8 percent per annum.[8] This

---

8. Employment in tradables grew at an average of only 1.3 percent per annum and employment in agriculture at 0.8 percent per annum.

higher growth was mainly associated with construction activities, private services, and the financial sector. As table 5.1 showed, nontradable production also expanded relatively more during the 1970s (at 7.7 percent per annum in 1976–81, while tradables grew at only 5.7 percent per annum), thus revealing a major problem with the signals provided by exchange rate policies, and later by the opening of the capital account.

Unemployment skyrocketed during the financial crisis, when the corrected rate reached as high as 30 percent of the labor force (table 5.3). This result was basically demand-driven, as participation rates did not change significantly with the recession. In addition, employment in tradable sectors dropped relative to total employment, an outcome probably associated with the increase in urban informal jobs. This caused a decline in urban informal wages, as suggested by the increase in relative unskilled wages. Furthermore, real wages declined as unemployment was increasing.

As a result of the policy stance of 1984, total corrected unemployment fell significantly as employment grew by about 10 percent and emergency employment declined. Nevertheless, as the 1984 program was short-lived, real wages declined by more than 4 percent in 1985, at the time that the real exchange rate further depreciated (table 5.1). The unemployment rate experienced a steady decline since 1984, in a way apparently correlated with the recovery in GDP, which was accompanied by expanding employment and production in tradable industries, and by a notable increase in nontraditional exports (table 5.2). Employment in agriculture and manufacturing mining grew at 6 and 11 percent per year, respectively, in 1985–88, when total employment grew at 6 percent per year. Even though the economy underwent a major adjustment program during 1985–87, output and employment grew considerably in agriculture and manufacturing as a result of strong exports. At the same time, a more deregulated labor market, in which the institutional framework was clearly defined, and the maintenance of high real exchange rates allowed the labor-intensive sectors to expand.

The Performance of Real Wages

There are two basic data sources on wages. First, the National Bureau of Statistics (INE) wage index, which is prepared on the basis of firm-based surveys, provides information about formal sector activities. Second, the University of Chile (UCH) labor force survey for the Greater Santiago area, which collects information on labor incomes once a year, covers both the formal and the informal sectors. Yanez (1987) constructed sectoral wages based upon this information, which are the ones used in this study.

The official (INE) wage index shows a decline in real formal sector wages during the recessionary years of 1975–76, following the dramatic drop of 1973 caused by spiraling inflation (table 5.4, column 2). Figures from the University of Chile's surveys (table 5.4, column 6) indicate a very similar trend, though the earlier decline is more dramatic and the recovery in 1975–81 is stronger, probably because of the more procyclical nature of labor earnings in informal activities. The real minimum wage was relatively stable in 1976–80, but declined sharply during the postcrisis period (1983–87). Note that the minimum wage grew significantly relative to both the equilibrium wage for unskilled labor in the informal sector and the average wage in the economy. Hence, minimum wages were probably important in affecting both average wages (Paldam and Riveros 1987), and the level of employment of less skilled workers (Riveros and Paredes 1988, 1989). The argument here is that increases in the minimum wage increased open unemployment and caused the withdrawal from the labor force of low-skilled people, particularly women and young job seekers.

Average real wages resumed growth during the 1976–81 expansion despite unemployment rates higher than historical averages. Nonetheless, during the growing phase (1976–81), unemployment was declining, which would suggest adequate, though probably slow, allocative work of the labor market. In interpreting observed wage growth in 1976–81, some observers (for example, Cortazar 1983) have suggested a binding role of the indexation mechanism implemented by the military government, whereby the private sector was advised to award workers the same wage increase given to public

Table 5.4 Real Wages, 1970–89
(index, 1980 = 100)

Year	INE Minimum wage (1)	INE Average wage (2)	INE Manufactured wage (3)	University of Chile Unskilled wage (4)	University of Chile Skilled wage (5)	University of Chile Average wage (6)	University of Chile Manufactured wage (7)	Total labor cost (8)
1970	81.0	109.7	97.1	124.1	144.0	12.4	113.9	0.69
1971	106.8	134.1	106.6	133.7	182.9	117.8	135.3	1.09
1972	101.7	119.0	101.2	138.4	157.7	104.3	92.9	1.06
1973	46.2	73.1	68.4	99.0	94.3	58.4	49.6	0.58
1974	90.6	70.2	62.2	94.5	78.4	56.2	53.6	0.53
1975	105.1	62.5	58.3	77.3	66.7	62.8	72.0	0.43
1976	100.1	78.9	78.6	77.0	77.7	71.5	80.4	0.60
1977	84.6	79.9	78.6	80.3	89.5	81.3	84.9	0.88
1978	97.4	85.0	87.4	82.4	97.6	91.0	101.7	1.06
1979	98.3	92.0	94.2	102.6	103.3	99.6	108.1	1.28
1980	100.0	100.0	100.0	100.0	100.0	100.0	100.0	1.45
1981	111.0	108.8	115.5	120.4	117.7	114.4	131.5	2.42
1982	122.2	108.6	110.7	126.6	133.3	133.2	146.7	2.08
1983	93.2	97.0	102.9	80.9	95.2	95.1	111.5	1.30
1984	82.1	97.1	99.0	77.8	89.8	89.4	101.3	1.13
1985	74.3	93.0	97.1	75.6	74.4	75.5	85.1	0.77
1986	78.8	95.0	101.9	64.4	66.6	72.6	78.7	0.78
1987	66.9	93.1	103.2	63.1	65.2	71.4	81.1	0.81
1988	74.2	98.6	109.8	64.5	67.1	72.1	86.3	0.91
1989	75.1	100.6	114.0	65.1	71.2	79.7	91.4	0.97

n.a. = not available
Note: (8) is expressed nominal dollars per hour.
Sources: (1): INE (two legal minimums existed in 1970, one for white and one for blue collar workers; the latter is used here; (2)–(3): INE; (4)–(5): Paredes (1987), May of each year. Unskilled wages are a proxy for informal sector wages and correspond to an average for self-employed workers with less than eight years of schooling. Skilled wages are a proxy for formal sector wages and correspond to an average for blue and white collar workers with more than 8 years of schooling. (6)–(7): Yanez (1987), May of each year. All the wage data have been deflated by the average corrected CPI based on INE, Yanez (1979), and Cortazar and Marshall (1980). (8): Riveros (1988).

sector workers for the period up to 1979. Thereafter, there was 100 percent indexation. The hypothesis that indexation resulted in a growth trend in real wages is a very unlikely explanation, at least for the period 1973–79, when labor laws were lacking, unions were banned, wage bargaining was suspended, job security did not exist, and unemployment was relatively high. The wage indexation scheme prevailing in 1973–79 was ineffective not only because of poor enforcement, but also because the past CPI inflation was normally higher than mandated adjustments (Edwards and Edwards 1987), and the actual (corrected) inflation was even higher than the official level (Cortazar 1983). Moreover, the mandated adjustments were not a legal obligation that could be enforced by the authorities. Possibly, a neoclassical model, that is, one based on the role played by unemployment, inflation, and labor productivity, would be more suitable to explain observed nominal wage trends during this period. However, in 1979–82 when the new labor law was enacted that included a full wage indexation rule, the explanation of a binding indexation postulated by Cortazar is more acceptable, because labor market institutions were allowed and the wage indexation mechanism was established by law.

Real wages declined strongly between 1982 and 1983, partly because of the recession, but also because of the elimination of the legal wage indexation established in 1979. After 1983, and particularly after 1985, average real wages remained basically constant, and increased in the case of manufacturing. This contrasts with wage behavior during the economic expansion of 1976–81. During this period, high unemployment coexisted with growing real wages, probably because in the absence of a legal framework for the labor market, entrepreneurs were unwilling to hire more labor and preferred to expand production on the basis of increasing the number of hours worked and providing more incentives to increase labor productivity. In addition, as other studies have shown (Riveros 1986), the labor market during this period was characterized by substantial skill mismatches, which probably resulted in higher wages for those employed and owners of the specific human capital. In the post-1985 period, by contrast, employment expanded significantly, particularly in the case of tradable industries and agriculture. This was facilitated by the existence of a legal framework and a less severe skill mismatch, given that the activities were basically labor intensive.

Wage Indexation

Analysis of wage indexation in 1976–82 is important in connection with the effect of wages on other macroeconomic variables, particularly inflation and the competitiveness of domestic production. It is also crucial to understand the role of institutions in determining the path of real wages. Our strategy to statistically analyze the effect of wage indexation is to distinguish the period when indexation was unaccompanied by enforcing mechanisms (1974–79) from the period when legal wage indexation was established in combination with a more appropriate legal framework (1979–82).

We used quarterly INE data on wages—the same information Cortazar used for the entire period 1974–81—to estimate a regression equation in which mandated wage increases (M) "explain" the actual change in average wages (W). This model assumes that the performance of wages is entirely explained by government policies. Regression results reveal that in 1973–79 the presumed causality from mandated wage increases to average wage growth is debatable. As table 5.5 shows, the correlation between these variables is high, and the parameter associated with M reaches a value of 1.0. However, when the quarterly inflation rate (P) is included, the effect of M on W does not have any interpretation: it has a negative sign. When the past rate of inflation (P-1) is included instead of actual inflation, the parameter associated with M is still significant, but its effect on average wages is relatively smaller than that of inflation.[9] Hence, the causality role of mandated adjustments in terms of observed wage changes is not easily identifiable using statistical analysis.

The observed effect of mandated adjustments on average wages seems to reflect only the effect of price inflation on wages. Therefore, the performance of wages in the Chilean economy during 1973–79 may be better explained by an economic model that takes inflation and the existence of open unemployment into account. A standard short-run wage setting equation was adopted to test this hypothesis, in which nominal wage growth is explained by price inflation,

9. When we included lagged adjustments (M-1) and actual inflation, both parameters were significant and the values were 0.70 and 0.26, respectively. Alternative lag structures were used with regard to both M and P.

Table 5.5 Wage Indexation Results, 1973.3–1979.2

Specification	Constant	M	P	P-1	R^2	DW
(1)*	4.57 (1.12)	1.00 (7.00)			0.72 (51.20)	1.74
(2)*	6.05 (4.20)	0.60 (-3.65)	1.37 (10.50)		0.97 (93.50)	1.98
(3)*	0.21	0.40 (0.78)	0.65 (3.00)	(5.75)	0.88 (71.70)	2.16

* = Correction for first-order serial correlation was implemented.
Notes: The method of estimation was OLS. The value of the t-test is presented (in parenthesis) under the corresponding parameter. The value of the F test is presented in the R^2 column.

unemployment (U), and the growth in average labor productivity (q). In estimating a regression model, we assume that only the cyclical portion of total unemployment (UC) is actually able to affect market wages (Lopez and Riveros 1988; Riveros and Paredes 1990).[10] We found a significant effect of both unemployment and inflation on observed wage changes in the period 1974.2–1979.2 (table 5.6, row 1). In addition, when the variable M (mandated wage increases) was included in the equation, it produced a nonsignificant coefficient. This evidence suggests that wage setting in this period was driven by economic rather than institutional forces.

Quite another story fits the period 1979.3–1982.2, when wage indexation was included in the labor law enacted in 1979, which also gave rise to unionization and formal wage negotiation. As table 5.6 (row 3) shows, the effect of lagged inflation is significant, but the overall fit is much poorer, while the parameters of unemployment are statistically equal to zero. This suggests that nominal wage behavior in this latter period was probably dictated by institutional indexation rules rather than by economic forces.

10. The estimate of cyclical unemployment was obtained from a regression discussed later, in which total unemployment is set as a function of both structural and cyclical variables. This is a version of the model proposed by Lopez and Riveros (1988) and applied by Riveros and Paredes (1989).

Table 5.6 The Unemployment–Wages Tradeoff

Period	Constant	P	UC	q	R^2	DW
1974.2–79.2						
(1)*	24.1	0.98	-21.1	-0.02	0.97	1.5
	(3.98)	(24.60)	(-3.4)	(-0.32)	(220.30)	
1979.3–82.2						
(2)	9.1	0.23	-4.7	0.04	0.10	1.9
	(0.68)	(0.48)	(-0.4)	(0.14)	(2.92)	
(3)*	1.2	0.97[a]	-1.4	0.37	0.42	1.8
	(0.15)	(3.37)	(-0.2)	(1.61)	(4.41)	

* = Correction for first-order serial correlation was performed.
Notes: The equations were estimated with OLS. The t-values are presented under the corresponding coefficients. The F value is presented under the R^2.
a. The parameter corresponds to the variables P-1.

This wage analysis establishes the importance of institutional labor market intervention policies. Wage indexation created substantial rigidities to accommodate production and employment to a changing external environment, because it was binding at a time when the exchange rate was nominally frozen. Thus, indexation caused a notable increase in wages in terms of the price of tradables (Corbo 1985a).[11] In addition, indexation further segmented the labor market during a period of output and employment growth. If the wrong signals had caused deterioration in employment growth prior to 1979, in 1979–82 overvaluation and the blow to tradables production were a further reason for persistent unemployment.

Relative Wages

The ratio of skilled to unskilled wages is one proxy for the relative wage of the formal to informal sectors. The wage of unskilled workers corresponds to urban self-employed workers with less than eight years of formal schooling, which is a good proxy for the typical member of the informal sector. The ratio between skilled and unskilled wages dropped during the 1970s recession, but increased with the recession

11. Data on dollar labor costs in table 5.4 (column 8) indicate the substantial increase associated with the period under discussion.

of the 1980s (table 5.7). During the former period, the demise of job security probably affected skilled labor more. During the economic recovery period of 1976–81, this ratio increased until 1978, but dropped significantly in 1979–81, probably due to an expansion of informal sector activities. The ratio between the average wage indices of INE and UCH may also be taken as representative of formal-informal wages, given that the former include only relatively large enterprises. As table 5.7 indicates, this ratio also declined with the recession of the 1970s, although not as much as the ratio of skilled-unskilled labor. During 1976–79, the INE-UCH ratio dropped, then increased in 1980, thereby showing a different trend than that displayed by the skilled-unskilled ratio, probably because the skilled-unskilled differential within the formal sector changed.

The ratio of minimum wages to average wages increased significantly in 1973–75, mainly due to an increase in the former. After that period, minimum wages suffered periods of decline (for example, 1975–77, 1978–80, 1982–87) and expansion (1977–78, 1980–82). The behavior of this ratio was basically driven by periodic minimum wage adjustments, which were probably very relevant for unskilled labor employed in the formal sector. This is also suggested by the decline of the relative wage of unskilled labor—which corresponds to the informal sector of the labor market—during periods when the minimum wage was increasing, for instance, 1973–75 and 1978–81, due to the spillovers of unskilled labor from the formal to the informal sector.

The ratio of public to private sector wages declined dramatically in 1970–76, and stayed relatively constant until 1980. After 1973 this result must be linked to the privatization of public firms, which produced a downward bias in the public sector average wage as obtained from labor force surveys. With the recession of the 1980s, public sector wages carried a more substantial burden of the economic adjustment. With regard to the ratio of white collar to blue collar wages, an interesting point is that the decline suffered during the recession of the 1970s was more significant than during the 1980s recession. The ratio's behavior in the early 1970s is also associated with the government's practice during 1970–73 of promoting

Table 5.7 Relative Wages, 1970–89

Year	Skilled / unskilled (1)	Minimum wage / average wage INE (2)	Average wage INE / average wage UCH (3)	Public sector wages / private sector wages (4)	White collar wages / blue collar wages (5)	Tradable[a] / nontradable (6)
1970	116.1	73.8	97.6	144.4	97.4	119.9
1971	136.7	79.6	113.8	138.2	106.6	106.2
1972	113.9	85.5	114.1	126.8	90.5	109.3
1973	95.0	63.2	125.2	116.9	76.2	119.1
1974	83.0	129.1	124.9	106.1	73.8	132.4
1975	86.3	168.2	99.5	109.8	81.5	130.4
1976	101.1	126.9	110.4	99.1	93.7	118.8
1977	111.7	105.9	98.3	106.1	103.3	118.7
1978	119.4	114.6	93.4	106.0	99.7	116.0
1979	101.2	106.8	92.4	108.2	93.0	98.0
1980	100.0	100.0	100.0	100.0	100.0	100.0
1981	98.6	102.0	95.0	91.7	95.7	124.8
1982	105.3	112.5	81.5	91.5	103.0	118.6
1983	118.5	96.1	102.0	68.8	105.0	110.9
1984	115.0	84.6	108.5	107.7	110.3	122.3
1985	98.1	79.9	109.3	106.0	104.0	121.1
1986	103.4	82.9	130.9	101.4	100.0	108.1
1987	103.3	71.9	130.4	104.7	98.3	107.7
1988	104.0	68.6	128.6	103.4	99.1	108.4
1989	109.3	68.1	129.1	102.5	99.6	109.1

n.a. = not available
a. Tradables = manufacturing, nontradables = construction.
Sources: Columns 1–3: table 5.4; columns 4–6: Yanez (1987) and UCH surveys.

relatively higher wage increases for blue collar workers along the lines of traditional distributive policies.

Earning Functions

With the purpose of qualifying the trend displayed by average wage data, it is important to analyze earning functions based on data provided by the University of Chile's labor force surveys. A standard Mincer-type earnings function reveals that the average social rate of return to schooling has increased over time, possibly due to the selectivity bias created by higher unemployment (Riveros 1990). During 1978–81, however, that rate of return did not change significantly. Analysis based on cost-benefit comparisons leads to the conclusion that the private rate of return to schooling has declined over time, particularly in the case of primary and secondary education (Riveros 1990). The rate of return to experience (table 5.8) suggests very stable behavior during most of the period analyzed except for a notable increase in 1978.

Distributive Results

Income distribution deteriorated sharply as a result of the reform program of the 1970s. The social cost of the adjustment was associated with the appearance of higher unemployment and declining real wages (Riveros 1985b). The Gini coefficients for the family income distribution (table 5.9), for instance, increased notably in 1974–76 to decline only slightly afterwards (between 1976 and 1979). Strikingly, during the expansionary years 1979–81—amid a financial boom—the observed income distribution deteriorated further (table 5.7), which is consistent with the persistence of unemployment and low real wage levels that still existed during that period. By

Table 5.8 Earning Functions
(dependent variable: Ln of income, selected years)
$(LnY = \alpha_0 + \alpha_1 S + \alpha_2 X + \alpha_3 X^2 + \alpha_4 LnH + \mu)$

Category	1968	1972	1976	1978	1982	1985
Schooling (S)	0.1374	0.1280	0.1331	0.1572	0.1507	0.1512
Experience (X)	0.0560	0.0518	0.0520	0.0640	0.0581	0.0572
Experience sq. (X^2)	-0.0006	-0.0007	-0.0007	-0.0008	-0.0007	-0.0007
Ln hours worked	0.2227	0.1275	0.3915	0.3498	0.3874	0.4320
Constant	1.3687	0.7684	0.7390	1.9110	3.2151	2.9710
Adj. R-sq.	0.4810	0.4300	0.4210	0.4850	0.4610	0.4720

Notes: Method of estimation is the OLS. All parameters are statistically significant.
Source: Riveros (1990).

Table 5.9 Social Indicators, Selected Years and 1974–88

Years	Gini coefficient (1)	(2)	Income share of 40% poorest (3)	Fiscal social expenditure (% of GDP) (4)	Per capita GDP (1976 US$) (5)
1960	0.4590	n.a.	13.59	n.a.	n.a.
1965	0.4750	n.a.	12.87	n.a.	n.a.
1968	0.4980	n.a.	11.70	n.a.	1,114
1970	0.5010	0.4345	11.50	n.a.	1,137
1974	0.4499	0.4232	n.a.	11.08	1,090
1975	0.4710	0.4127	12.78	10.30	0,933
1976	0.5380	0.4886	n.a.	9.99	0,950
1977	0.5260	0.4762	n.a.	10.56	1,026
1978	0.5197	0.4662	n.a.	10.16	1,091
1979	0.5179	n.a.	n.a.	9.25	1,162
1980	0.5257	n.a.	10.88	10.29	1,231
1981	0.5220	n.a.	11.24	12.80	1,277
1982	0.5390	n.a.	9.95	15.76	1,078
1983	0.5420	n.a.	10.07	15.10	1,052
1984	0.5550	0.5151	9.33	15.40	1,100
1985	0.5320	0.5011	10.13	15.12	1,108
1986	0.5390	0.4997	10.00	14.30	1,119
1987	0.5310	0.4950	10.22	13.97	n.a.
1988	0.5301	0.4897	10.37	14.01	n.a.

n.a. = not available

Notes: The Table includes two alternative Gini coefficients for the family income distribution. To calculate the one in column 1, we ranked households by total household income. To calculate the second one (column 2), we ranked households by the per capita income (Riveros and Weber 1987). However similar conclusions are reached on analyzing both coefficients.

Sources: Columns 1–4: Riveros and Weber (1988); column 5: World Bank (various years).

contrast, the decline seen in the Gini coefficients after 1984 is most likely related to the improved performance of employment and wages under the export-led growth strategy.

The existence of fiscal social expenditures in the form of direct monetary subsidies to the poor makes estimates of Gini coefficients based on only labor incomes subject to debate because they may be downward biased. However, in 1976–79 the need to control inflation and to tighten fiscal expenditures caused a severe decline in social outlays, which apparently increased poverty. After 1980, the increase in social outlays (table 5.7, column 4) is associated with the privatization of the social security system and the emergency employment programs, and does not necessarily mean that more resources were devoted to deal with poverty. Declining social outlays after 1985 are associated with fiscal restraint and improvement in some labor market results, particularly the decline in open unemployment. Although social outlays may have declined in the 1980s, there was an improvement in targeting the poorest groups, which was facilitated by the social sector reforms implemented during the early 1980s. In general, however, problems of access to and financing of the health and education systems are still of paramount importance.

A Model for Adjustment Policies and Labor Market Response

This section discusses and presents estimates of a model aimed at analyzing observed wages and unemployment in the presence of labor market segmentation. In this model, segmentation is defined on the basis of protected and unprotected sectors with regard to the coverage of typical labor market regulations. In considering that protected sectors usually consist of large urban firms and the public sector, the protected/unprotected breakdown overlaps significantly with the traditional formal/informal dichotomy. Given that the enforcement (and enforceability) of certain regulations may prompt asymmetrical wage effects across sectors, this approach to segmentation is appealing from an analytical viewpoint.

The existence of a growing protected/unprotected wage gap during a period of substantial macro adjustment may explain persistent unemployment. The existence of queuing unemployment—informal sector workers queuing for formal sector jobs—is likely to increase during adjustment if the relative degree of labor protection in the formal sector increases. For instance, as suggested by the increase in minimum wages relative to the wages of unskilled-informal labor during the reform period, the relatively larger protection awarded to formal sector workers may have resulted not only in more unemployment, but also in inequitable effects in terms of wages in the unprotected sector.

In a neoclassical labor market, one would expect flexible wages in the face of aggregate expenditure-reducing and expenditure-switching policies. This condition would imply declining wages in terms of the price of tradables that will, in turn, produce labor shifts away from the production of nontradable to tradables. Rigid wages in a neoclassical labor market will result in a lack of mobility, thus leading to standard policies aimed at removing wage distortions, but will not necessarily create systematic changes in wage differentials across certain labor force groups.

In a segmented labor market, adjustment policies would exert an inequitable effect in terms of the observed protected/unprotected wage gap. In particular, nominal wages in the protected sector will be less responsive to a change in tradable prices, thus making a nominal devaluation less effective in achieving a real devaluation. This will hinder interindustrial labor mobility and increase total unemployment. In addition, the deterioration in income distribution in terms of wage gaps will affect the sustainability of adjustment programs. Thus, persistent unemployment, deteriorating income of the poorest segment of the labor market, a decline in the production of nontradables (due to a drop in relative prices), lower employment in protected activities, and implementation of repeated ineffective nominal devaluations are probable outcomes of a segmented market.

A Theoretical Model

The urban labor market is segmented into a protected (formal) sector characterized by government and union intervention in wage setting and by binding minimum wages, and an unprotected (informal) sector, which is basically a neoclassical labor market. The formal sector produces both tradable and nontradable goods using skilled and unskilled labor, while the informal sector produces nontradables with only unskilled labor. (This model follows the basic lines presented in Lopez and Riveros (1989, 1990). Assumptions about the informal sector satisfy two important characteristics of this sector in developing countries (PREALC 1987): it is a low productivity sector mainly concentrated in the services sector.)

The formal market for skilled labor determines a notional equilibrium wage (ws*); the actual equilibrium wage (ws) includes a distortionary factor θ associated with government and union intervention. This wage-setting function is compatible with the case of oligopolistic unions that maximize a utility function that depends on relative wages and membership (Lopez & Riveros 1990). Thus, the actual nominal equilibrium wage is written as:

$$\text{ws} = \theta \text{ws}^* \qquad (1)$$

where $\theta > 1$ (a more general specification of this relationship is explored in Lopez and Riveros 1989). The minimum wage (MW) is binding for unskilled labor in the formal market and we assume some degree of substitution of skilled for unskilled labor. Thus, the formal sector demand for skilled labor (Lds) depends on minimum wages as well as on output prices and wages. The function is:

$$\text{Lds} = \text{Lds}(\text{ws}, \theta, \text{MW}, \text{PT}, \text{PN}, \text{K}) + \text{Lg} \qquad (2)$$

where PT and PN are, respectively, prices of tradables and nontradables, K is capital stock, and Lg is public sector employment. This function is a homogeneous degree one in prices and wages.

The labor supply of skilled workers (Lss) can be written as shown in equation (3):

$$\text{Lss} = \text{Lss}(\text{ws}, \text{MW}, \text{CPI}, \text{N}) \qquad (3)$$

where CPI is the consumer price index (in turn, an average of PT and PN), and N is the working age population.

The formal sector demand for unskilled labor (Ldu) is:

$$\text{Lduf} = \text{Lduf}(\text{MW}, \text{ws}, \text{PT}, \text{PN}, \text{K}) \qquad (4)$$

200 Luis A. Riveros

which depends on ws because of the substitution possibilities between skilled and unskilled labor.

The total supply of unskilled labor (Lsu) in the economy is:

$$Lsu = Lsu(MW, wu, CPI, N, K) \tag{5}$$

where wu is the equilibrium wage in the informal sector. Finally, the demand for labor in the informal sector is:

$$Ldu = Ldu(wu, PN, MW, K) \tag{6}$$

Given MW and Lsu, employment of unskilled labor in the formal sector is determined by equation (4), thus leaving an effective supply to the informal sector that, in combination with Ldu, determines wu. This type of equilibrium follows the concept introduced by Harberger (1971). Given that there will be persons with supply price above wu, but below the (given) MW, there will exist queuing (quasi-voluntary) unemployment.

For empirical purposes, the equilibrium form of the system will be considered. Thus, the system is reduced to two equilibrium wage equations. This will permit concentrating the analysis on the effect of policies on the formal-informal wage gap, thereby circumventing estimation of the underlying structural demand and supply functions, for which employment and labor force data are scarcer. Equilibrium in both the skilled (formal) market and the unskilled (informal) market yields the following expressions:

$$ws = ws(MW, PT, PN, K, Lg, N) \tag{7}$$

$$wu = wu(MW, ws, PT, PN, K, N) \tag{8}$$

Due to the homogeneity properties of the underlying demand and supply functions, equations (7) and (8) are homogeneous degree zero in prices and wages. Hence, for estimating purposes both equations will be written in terms of MW.

Unemployment in this model results from two sources: labor market distortions (that is, wages above notional equilibrium in the formal skilled market and queuing unemployment in the informal market) and cyclical fluctuations in the economic activity (see Riveros and Paredes forthcoming). Hence, a general formulation of an unemployment equation may allow us to derive empirically both components based on aggregate data. In equation (9) both structural and cyclical factors are used to explain aggregate observed unemployment. Given their association with structural unemployment—in turn due to the presence of labor market distortions—the ratio MW/Wu and the value of the distortionary factor θ are included. The growth trend of the labor force (LFT) is also included as a factor associated with the structural unemployment in the economy (this variable is obtained by fitting actual labor force data to a time trend). Among the cyclical factors, we consider unexpected changes in the following variables: GDP (Y), terms of trade (TOT), and the labor force (LFS). Unexpected changes are empirically proxied through the difference between observed values and the fitted values obtained from a regression of the respective variables against a time trend. Thus, the following unemployment equation was estimated:

$$U = U\left(MW/Wu, \theta, LFT, Y, TOT, LFS,\right) \qquad (9)$$

Using equation (9) we estimate cyclical unemployment as the difference between U (total unemployment) and US (structural unemployment). US is calculated as the sum of the shift coefficient and the parameters associated with MW/Wu, θ, and LFT obtained from equation (9), multiplied by the values of the corresponding variable.

Thus, the third equation in the system corresponds to cyclical unemployment (UC), which is:

$$UC = UC\left(Y, PN, PT, ws, wu, Lg, K, N\right) \qquad (10)$$

Equation (10) results from specifying equilibrium wages in both the skilled and unskilled markets, and allowing for the presence of unemployment. This equation is homogeneous degree zero in income, prices, and wages.

Prices of nontradables are endogenously determined. However, to allow a better focus on the labor market issue, we do not include an equation for PN, but we will account for its endogeneity in estimating the structural system (Lopez and Riveros 1989 present a model in which prices of nontradables are simultaneously estimated). PT is determined using the small-country assumption, and is thus equal to the nominal exchange rate multiplied by the world price of tradables.

The model finishes with an investment equation that permits connecting the short run and the long run. Investment responds to a partial adjustment to a desired capital stock level, while the optimal capital stock depends on the interest rate, wages, prices, and growth (Y). Hence, the following investment function is estimated:

$$I = I(i, Pt, Pn, wu, ws, MW, Y) \tag{11}$$

Given the price and income homogeneity properties of the model, we arbitrarily chose to normalize by the minimum wage.[12] Equations (7), (8), (10), and (11) were estimated in rate of changes through 3SLS. The results are presented in table 5.10 below. The appendix defines the variables.

Empirical Results

As a preliminary step, and to obtain the parameters to compute the cyclical unemployment rate, we empirically estimated equation (9). The 2SLS estimates presented below (table 5.10) indicate that the distortionary factor MW/Wu is statistically significant to explain observed unemployment. This result suggests the queuing unemployment is an important component of the structural unemployment and, in turn, of total open unemployment. Labor force and terms of trade are also significant explanatory variables.

---

12. The demand and supply functions are homogeneous degree zero in prices, wages, and income. The wage equations are homogeneous degree one in prices. We also assume the investment and the unemployment functions are homogeneous degree zero in prices and income.

Table 5.10 Open Unemployment Equation (Dependent Variable: Total Unemployment)

Constant	θ	MW/Wu	LFT	Y*	TOT	LFS
870.3	4.57	5.55	0.82	-0.16	0.58	0.09
(1.40)	(0.92)	(1.98)	(2.17)	(-0.85)	(1.68)	(1.99)
	$R^2 = 0.94$		$F = 27.7$		$DW = 2.23$	

Notes: The method is 2SLS. Instruments: government expenditures, working age population, domestic credit and lagged values, endogenous variables: MW/Wu and Y*. θ was proxied by the monetary value of nonwage labor costs. LFT is the fitted value of a labor force series regressed against time; LFS is the "shock" defined as the difference between the observed labor force and LFT. Y* is the output shock, which was obtained similarly to LFS. TOT is the structural trend in terms of trade, which is a fitted value against a time trend.

Using these econometric results, we decompose total unemployment into its structural and cyclical components. The results are presented in figure 5.1. An interesting feature is that structural unemployment has been relatively high. After 1975, structural unemployment increased, but then fluctuated less. Cyclical unemployment was historically low, and at times negative, indicating excess vacancies probably produced by skill mismatch. The relative importance of cyclical unemployment increased in the 1980s.

The econometric results for the system of four equations indicate satisfactory overall fits and right sign of the key coefficients (table 5.11). This suggests that a segmented labor market is an appropriate way to analyze the statistical information concerning wages, unemployment, and the role of macro policies.

In the case of the skilled wages equation, most parameters are significant using a 90 percent confidence interval. The effect of the distortionary factor θ appears prominent, which suggests the potential impact of exogenous intervention in raising effective market wages. The effect of changes in the price of tradable and nontradable goods (PT and PN) indicates the positive response of formal sector nominal wages to inflation. This contrasts with the negligible effect observed in the case of informal sector wages. This is particularly important with regard to PT, which reflects the direct effect of nominal devaluations. This finding suggests the extent of relative wage rigidity in the formal sector, which is at the root of an inequitable impact of exchange rate policies in the presence of segmentation. This observed asymmetric effect cannot be easily explained in the context of an integrated labor market and suggests the need for appropriate corrective policies.

Income growth and the price of nontradables exert a positive effect on formal sector wages, possibly due to unions' ability to transform most of the increases in market output prices into wage gains. The

Figure 5.1 Components of Total Unemployment, 1963–85

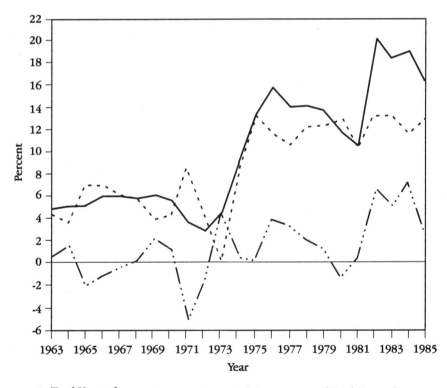

────── Total Unemployment   - - - - Structural Component of Total Unemployment
───·· Cyclical Component of Total Unemployment

Table 5.11 A Segmented Labor Market During Adjustment, 1960–85
(2SLS estimates)

---

ws = 6.70 + 0.99 (θ) + 0.50 Yg + 0.53 PTg + 0.38 PNg -2.78 I_1 -1.06 Lg
     (1.66) (5.25)   (1.34)   (2.41)   (1.41)   (-1.15)   (-3.72)
                   R^2 = 0.79   DW = 2.13
                   F   = 11.2

wu =-11.4 + 2.00 Yg -0.94 PTg -0.004 PNg + 3.74 I_1 -0.02 Lg -0.72 LCg
     (-1.42) (3.23)   (-0.59)   (-0.01)   (1.56)   (-0.07)   (-1.61)
                   R^2 = 0.73   DW = 1.79
                   F   = 8.74

UC = 7.32 -1.75 Yg + 0.92 PTg + 0.52 PNg -0.79 I - 0.51 Lg + 0.32 LCg + 0.67 wu
     (1.39)(-3.38)   (2.40)   (1.81)   (-1.52) (-1.68)   (3.04)   (1.99)
                   R^2 = 0.42   DW = 1.99
                   F   = 2.55

I = 10.4 + 0.27 PT/PN - 0.02 ws-1 + 0.22 wu-1 + 0.30 M1g -0.34 M1D -0.11 YS-1
     (-1.34) (1.32)   (-0.04)   (0.06)   (3.53)   (-3.68)   (-2.59)
                   R^2 = 0.52   DW = 1.82
                   F   = 5.12

Notes:
Prices, wages, and income are defined in growth rates (relative to minimum wages).
Capital growth, nonwage labor costs, and money are expressed in real terms.

ws	=	wages of skilled workers	Yg =	aggregate expenditures
wu	=	wages of unskilled workers	Kg =	capital stock
(θ)	=	real nonwage costs of labor	Lg =	public sector employment
PTg	=	price deflator of tradable goods	M1g =	M1
PNg	=	price deflator of nontradable	M1D =	dummy (1 = 1960–73)
		goods	Ig =	investment
LCg	=	total labor costs [ws + (0)]	UC =	cyclical unemployment
ws-1	=	lagged (1 year) ws	YS-1 =	lagged income shock
wu-1	=	lagged (1 year) wu		

Instruments: public expenditures, working age population, lagged values.

growth in capital stock affects ws negatively, possibly because skilled workers are substituted for new capital. However, the parameter in this case is not statistically significant. Finally, the effect of public sector employment on ws is negative, which indicates that the public sector's share in the wage index is high, and that expansion in public sector employment takes place only at the cost of lower wages in terms of the minimum wage.

The wu equation indicates that growth of prices and formal sector wages is not relevant in explaining change in equilibrium wages in the informal market. The factor relatively more important is income growth, which displays a highly significant elasticity. In comparing the coefficients obtained in both the ws and wu equations with respect to aggregate income, we conclude that contractionary policies would affect unskilled labor in the informal sector relatively more than labor in formal activities. These results are in line with those Lopez and Riveros (1989) found in a comparative study covering four countries.[13]

In the case of the cyclical unemployment equation, the results indicate that expenditure growth as well as the expansion in public sector employment and the growth in the capital stock negatively affect unemployment. A positive impact derives from both tradable prices and wages; moreover, when the regression was performed with the ratio PT/PN (the real exchange rate), the parameter was significant and positive, indicating that switching policies create more cyclical unemployment likely due to both rigidities in moving labor across sectors and higher wage rigidity in the formal sector. The total effect of a devaluation on unemployment must also account for the effect on skilled wages and their impact on total unemployment.

The investment equation reveals a significant impact of the growth in M1, a variable we included as a proxy for the real interest rate.[14] Furthermore, a dummy variable on this coefficient (M1D = 1 for the period 1960–73) was significant and negative, implying that due to higher government intervention, the role of the interest rate on aggregate investment was probably very low or zero. The other variable that affects investment is the lagged income shocks, defined as the difference between observed aggregate income and a fitted time trend. The relative price of tradables to nontradables is positive and

13. In both wage equations we included the rate of growth of the labor force, but the results were not significant. We tested for structural differences in the equations for the periods 1960–73 and 1976–1981, but we did not find evidence in support of the idea of a different distribution of the data.

14. Due to control of the interest rate during most of the 1960s and early 1970s, this variable is not reliable for measuring the opportunity cost of capital. We also use the investment deflator, but the result was not significant.

significant at 90 percent. However, wages do not appear to affect investment growth or output prices when included separately.

A devaluation increases the formal/informal wage gap. A similar result is associated with an output decline. The implication is that due to the prevailing labor market structure, typical adjustment policies exert a negative equity impact. This evidence also indicates that adjustment policies based on nominal devaluation increase cyclical unemployment. Likewise, contractive policies negatively affect investment and a real devaluation seems to encourage it, but labor market variables do not play a direct role. However, if labor market segmentation makes a nominal devaluation more ineffective in reaching a real devaluation—in the case of prices of nontradables highly responsive to the increase in formal sector wages—the labor market would play a direct role.[15] In sum, the adoption of a segmented labor market approach allows us to highlight the distributive consequences of adjustment policy, which may also contribute to more persistent unemployment. In general, this evidence suggests that the political sustainability of typical adjustment programs is strongly related to the prevailing labor market structure and labor market intervention policies.

Conclusion

This chapter has analyzed the key role of the labor market in the adjustment of the Chilean economy in the 1980s. To explain the performance of the labor market during the structural adjustment of the 1980s, consideration of the deteriorating situation in terms of unemployment and wages in the late 1970s was deemed necessary. The impact on labor market variables of a series of structural reforms aimed at reducing the state's economic size, deregulating product and factor markets, and opening the economy to foreign trade were of paramount importance in the 1970s. Moreover, the absence of labor laws and the use of the exchange rate as a stabilization device gave signals that prompted lower employment growth, higher growth of

---

15. Lopez and Riveros (1989) measured this effect, and calculated the elasticity displayed by PN with respect to prevailing labor market distortions. In the case of Chile it was found that the degree of ineffectiveness associated to a nominal devaluation due to labor market distortions is small.

nontradables, decreasing savings, and increasing external indebtedness.

After 1984 the Chilean economy underwent a major macro adjustment, whose success was partly expedited by the deep reforms of the 1970s. The postcrisis policy was characterized by the achievement of significant real devaluations, further privatization, targeting of social expenditures to the poor, and export promotion and financial policies to deal with the external debt and to increase investment. The results in terms of the labor market were a dramatic decline in open unemployment, a slight increase in real wages, and significant growth of employment in tradables.

The characteristics of the Chilean labor market provide support to a model of labor market segmentation associated with the degree of protection awarded to formal sector workers. Econometric analysis indicates that expenditure-switching and expenditure-reduction policies reduce real informal sector wages relative to formal sector wages, thereby negatively affecting income distribution during periods of adjustment. Relative wage rigidity in the formal sector and the increase in the formal-informal wage gap hinder labor mobility and make unemployment more persistent. This suggests that the persistence of open unemployment is associated with the prevailing labor market structure, which is also at the root of a slower adjustment to macro policies.

Three important implications can be extracted from this case study. First, macroeconomic adjustment should be accompanied by deregulation of the labor market to minimize the adverse and inequitable effects stemming from expenditure-reduction and expenditure-switching policies. This essentially implies that wage indexation and other policies aimed at protecting formal sector incomes should be carefully considered. Second, the role of skills is important in terms of the structure of the labor market and its response to macroeconomic policies, which demonstrates the importance of including skill enhancement in structural adjustment policies. This also implies that an increase in labor mobility may be achieved not only through legal and institutional reforms, but also by providing informal sector workers with skills. Third, high open unemployment is strongly linked to queuing for formal sector jobs, which in turn derives from relatively high formal sector unskilled wages. In periods of transition, open unemployment will be linked not only to shifts in production, but also to higher queuing unemployment due to a relatively larger wage distortion. This suggests that policies aimed at dealing with unemployment must pay attention to the regulatory framework existing in formal labor markets.

APPENDIX
EMPIRICAL DEFINITION OF VARIABLES

Wages of Skilled Workers (Ws):
Index computed from the labor force surveys of the University of Chile, which considers blue and white collar workers with more than eight years of schooling.

Wages of Unskilled Workers (Wu):
Index computed from the labor force surveys of the University of Chile, which considers self-employed workers with less than eight years of schooling.

Nonwage Labor Cost (θ):
Fringe benefits, social security contributions, regular bonuses, and vacation periods expressed as a proportion of wages (source: labor law and Price-Waterhouse: *Doing Business in Chile*, 1979, 1983).

Price of Tradables (PT):
Price deflator obtained from national accounts (central bank) for agriculture, manufacturing, and mining.

Price of Nontradables (PN):
Price deflator obtained from national accounts (central bank) for services and construction.

Aggregate Expenditures (Y):
GDP at market prices (national accounts).

Investment (I):
Fixed gross domestic investment (national accounts).

Unemployment (U):
Unemployment rate (number of unemployed divided by the total labor force). Table 5.3. Unemployed people are those that declared themselves to be involved in job search during the week of reference for the surveys.

Labor Force (L):
Employed plus unemployed population 12 years and older. Table 5.3.

Terms of Trade (TOT):
Ratio of export prices to import prices.

References

Banco Central de Chile. 1987. *Indicadores Economicos y Sociales 1960–85.* Santiago.

_____. 1990. Boletin mensual No. 748. Santiago. June

Budnevich, C. and others. 1986. "Trimestralizacion de las series nacionales de Emples." Technical Note, Estudios de Economica, University of Chile, 13(1):155–165.

Castaneda, T. 1983. *Evolucion del Empleo y Desempleo y el Impacto de Cambios Demograficos Sobre la Tasa de Desempleo en Chile: 1960–1983.* Documento Serie Investigacion No. 64. Santiago: University of Chile, Department of Economics.

Corbo, V. 1985a. "Reforms and Macroeconomic Adjustment in Chile During 1974–1984." *World Development* 13(8).

_____. 1985b. "The Role of the Real Exchange Rate in Macro-Economic Adjustment: The Case of Chile 1973–82." Discussion Paper DRD145. Washington, D.C.: World Bank.

_____. 1986. "Problems, Development Theory and Strategies of Latin America." Discussion Paper DRD190. Washington, D.C.: World Bank.

Corbo, V., and P. Meller. 1984. "Trade and Employment in Chile in the 60s." *American Economic Review* 69(2).

Corbo, V., and F. Sturzenegger. 1988. "Stylized Facts of the Macroeconomic Adjustment in the Indebted Countries." Washington, D.C.: World Bank. Processed.

Cortazar, R. 1983. "Wages in the Short Run: Chile 1964–1981.'" Notas Tecnicas No. 56. Santiago: Corprociao Investigaciones Economics Pro Latinoamerica (CIEPLAN).

Cortazar, R., and J. Marshall. 1980. *Indice de Precios al Consumidor en Chile 1970–1978.* Santiago: Corprociao Investigaciones Economics Pro Latinoamerica (CIEPLAN).

Cortes, H., and L. Sjaastad. 1981. "Proteccion y Empleo." *Cuadernos de Economia* (54-55). Universidad Catolica de Chile.

Cottani, J. 1988. "Exchange Rate Trends for Fifty-One Developing Countries. 1960–1986." World Bank, Debt and Macroeconomic Division. Washington, D.C.: World Bank. Processed.

Edwards, S. 1985. "Economic Policy and the Record of Economic Growth in Chile 1973–1982." In Gary M. Walton, ed., *The National Economic Policies in Chile, Contemporary Studies in Economic and Financial Analysis*, vol. 51. New York.

Edwards, S., and A. Edwards. 1987. *Monetarism and Liberalization, The Chilean Experiment.* Cambridge, Massachusetts: Ballinger.

Hachette, D., and R. Luders. 1987. "Aspects of the Privatization Process: The Case of Chile 1974–85." Washington, D.C.: World Bank. Processed.

Harberger, A. 1971. "On Measuring the Opportunity Cost of Labor." *International Labor Review* 130.

IMF. Various years. *International Financial Statistics.* Washington, D.C.

Larrain, F. 1988. "Public Sector Behavior in a Highly Indebted Country: The Contrasting Chilean Experience 1970–1985." Washington, D.C.: World Bank. Processed.

Larrain, F., and P. Meller. 1990. "The Socialist-Populist Chilean Experience 1970–73." Santiago. Processed.

Lopez, R., and L. Riveros. 1988. "Wage Responsiveness and Labor Market Disequilibrium." PPR Working Papers WPS85. Washington, D.C.: World Bank.

——————. 1989. "Macroeconomic Adjustment and the Labor Market in Four Latin American Countries." In G. Standing, ed., *Towards Social Adjustment: Labor Market Concerns in Structural Adjustment.* Geneva: ILO.

——————. 1990. "Do Labor Market Distortions Cause Overvaluation and Rigidity of the Real Exchange Rate?" PRE Working Papers WPS 485. Washington, D.C.: World Bank.

Marshall, J., and P. Romaguera. 1981. *La Evolucion del Empleo Publico en Chile 1970–78.* Notas Tecnicas no. 26. Santiago:

Corprociao Investigaciones Economics Pro Latinoamerica (CIEPLAN).

Meller, P. 1984. "La Evolucion del Empleo y Desempleo En Chile." Santiago: Corprociao Investigaciones Economics Pro Latinoamerica (CIEPLAN). Processed.

Paldam, M., and L. Riveros. 1987. "The Causal Role of Minimum Wages in Six Latin American Labor Markets." DRD270. Washington, D.C.: World Bank.

Paredes, R. 1987. "Stylized Facts on Adjustment and Labor Market Trends in Chile." Santiago: University of Chile. Processed.

PREALC. 1987. *Modelos de Empleo y Politica Economica.* Santiago: International Labor Office.

Riveros, L. 1985a. "Desempleo, Distribucion del Ingreso y Politica Social." *Estudios Publicos* 20.

_____. 1985b. "Una Revision de la Literatura sobre el Mercado laboral Chileno en los Anos 1970." *Estudios de Economia* 12(2):17–36.

_____. 1986. "Labor Market Maladjustment in Chile: Economic Reforms and Friction Among Sub-Markets." *Analisis Economico* 1(1).

_____. 1988. "International Comparisons of Wage and Non-Wage Costs of Labor." Washington, D.C.: World Bank. Processed.

_____. 1990. "The Economic Return to Schooling in Chile. An Analysis of its Long Term Fluctuations." *Economics of Education Review* 9(2):111–121.

Riveros, L., and A. Diaz. 1987. "Desempleados y Tiempo de Desocupacion: Gran Santiago 1970–1983." In C. Clavel, ed., *Empleo Recopilacion de Articulos.* Santiago: University of Chile, School of Economics.

Riveros, L., and R. Paredes. 1988. "Measuring the Impact of Minimum Wage Policies on the Economy." PPR Working Papers WPS101. Washington, D.C.: World Bank.

_____. 1989. "Political Transition and Labor Market Reforms." Washington, D.C.: World Bank. Processed.

_____. 1990. "Factores Estructurales y Ciclicos y la Composicion del Desempleo Abierto en Chile." *Revista de Analisis Economico* 5(1), Instituto Latinoamericano de Doctrina Economicos y Social (ILADES). Santiago.

Riveros, L., and C. Weber. 1987. "Structural Economic Reforms, Financial Stress and Targeting the Poor: Trends in Income Distribution and Social Expenditures in Chile 1974–1981." Washington, D.C.: World Bank. Procssed.

Torres, C. 1982. *Evolucion de la Politica Arancelaria: Periodo 1973–1981.* Report No. 16. Santiago: Central Bank.

Walton, Gary M., ed. 1985. *The National Economic Policies in Chile, Contemporary Studies in Economic and Financial Analysis,* Vol. 51. New York.

World Bank. 1990. "Chile's Country Economic Memorandum." Washington, D.C.

_____. Various years. *World Tables.* Baltimore, Md.: Johns Hopkins University Press.

Yanez, J. 1979. *Una Correccion del Indice de Precios al Consumidor Durante el Periodo 1971–1973.* Serie Investigacion No. 34. Santiago: University of Chile, Department of Economics.

_____. 1987. "Un Indice de Remuneraciones para el Gran Santiago." Santiago: University of Chile, Department of Economics. Processed.

6

Costa Rica
ō22
ōıS
ō11

COSTA RICA

T. H. Gindling
Albert Berry

J20
E6 3

The Costa Rican economy fared better during the 1980s than many others faced with the need to adjust to serious balance of payments and fiscal crises. Its performance during the last few years of the decade suggests that it may be on a new sustainable growth path. Wages have reattained their precrisis levels and unemployment is once again low. Although the crisis caused both wages and unemployment to deteriorate rapidly, the recovery was relatively quick. The policies introduced to produce structural adjustment were deliberately "gradualist" in nature, and the public's reaction was tolerant and relatively supportive. As the outcome qualifies Costa Rica's experience as a success story, at least in a relative sense, an examination of the economic, social, or political structure and setting or the steps taken to deal with the crisis should be of interest.

Costa Rica's Precrisis Experience

This section reviews the relevant precrisis experience of Costa Rica in the areas of macroeconomic performance and labor market institutions and functioning.

The Macroeconomic Side

Costa Rica is in many respects unique in Central America and unusual in Latin America as a whole. While its per capita GDP puts it

---

The authors would like to thank Susan Horton, Dipak Mazumdar, Juan Diego Trejos, and participants in the Toronto and Warwick conferences on labor markets and structural adjustment for helpful comments and Karen Turner for excellent research assistance. More detailed discussions of many aspects of the methodology used in this paper are available in Gindling and Berry (1991).

among the lower middle-income developing countries (World Bank classification), many of its social indicators compare favorably to those of the upper middle-income bracket. Life expectancy is higher and infant mortality and fertility rates lower than in most countries in the upper ranges of the middle-income developing countries (Gindling and Berry 1991). The stability and competitiveness of its political system is unique within the region. For most of this century, the country's governments have been chosen in competitive elections, and have typically had a high level of popular support and legitimacy (Seligson and Muller 1987).

Economists believe that the exceptional performance of social indicators in Costa Rica is largely the result of social and economic policies begun in the early 1940s by the government of Calderon-Guardia, and fully institutionalized after a social democratic "revolution" in 1948. Policies introduced or strengthened after 1948 include minimum wage and other worker protection legislation, a comprehensive social security system (which includes a government-financed health care system as well as a pension program), nationalized banking and insurance systems, elimination of the army, and a pattern of state intervention in the economy designed to encourage a more equitable distribution of income.

From 1950 to 1980, GDP grew at an average annual rate of 6.2 percent (3.0 percent in per capita terms), placing Costa Rica among the fastest growing economies in Latin America. Much of this growth was fueled by expansion of traditional primary product exports, chief of which were coffee, bananas, meat, sugar, and cocoa. In the early 1960s these products accounted for over 20 percent of the GDP and 80 to 90 percent of all export earnings (Celis and Lizano 1990). The growth of export agriculture coincided with an increase in farm size; a decrease in the number of landowners and in the rural labor force, but an increase in the share of workers who were landless; and substantial migration from rural to urban areas, especially San José. By 1980, Costa Rica's agricultural subsistence sector had virtually disappeared, and the share of the labor force in agriculture had fallen to below 30 percent. Still, the economy remained vulnerable to shifts in the prices of its principle exports (particularly coffee); an important focus of concern and policy.

In the 1960s, in part because of this perceived vulnerability, Costa Rica instituted a policy of import-substituting industrialization. The Central American Common Market (CACM), established in 1962, enlarged the market for Costa Rica's import-substituting products by lowering or eliminating barriers to trade between the Central American countries and instituting a common external tariff on imported manufactured products. The import substitution undertaken at the regional level provided an engine for growth and industrialization in Costa Rica (Bourguignon 1986). As the most developed member of the CACM, Costa Rica was well placed to achieve a significant surplus in manufactured goods trade within the CACM. Manufacturing output rose from 12 percent of GDP in 1960 to 22 percent in 1979, due in part to the increase in manufactured exports to other CACM countries. Costa Rica's main exports within the CACM were processed foods, domestic appliances, textiles and clothing, and other metal products.

However, the growth of manufacturing within the CACM produced its own problems. For one thing, policies used to encourage that growth (low import duties on capital equipment, an overvalued exchange rate, low interest rates on loans from the nationalized banking system, and so on) also encouraged capital intensity in the sector, so that manufacturing employment grew at a much slower rate than manufacturing output. Second, the health of Costa Rican manufacturing depended on the economic and political conditions in the CACM. As the 1969 "football war" between El Salvador and Honduras showed, the foundations of the political cooperation necessary to maintain the CACM were weak. Third, the new industries were heavily dependent on imported inputs, so the contribution to net exports was less than it appeared and the import-substituting manufacturing sector was quite vulnerable to swings in international prices, just as the exporting agricultural sector had always been. Each dollar of manufacturing output required an estimated 60¢ (Cespedes and others 1985) to 80¢ (Gonzalez-Vega 1984) worth of imported inputs.

A looming structural problem lay in the rapid growth of the public sector (Gonzalez-Vega 1984), a growth whose roots lay in the social welfare state established in the late 1940s. When, as part of the import-substituting industrialization strategy, the state became increasingly

Table 6.1 Selected Macroeconomic Indicators, 1970–89

Year	GDP (millions of 1966 colones)	Growth rate: GDP (percent)	Growth rate: agriculture (percent)	Growth rate: manufacture (percent)	Terms of trade	Inflation rate[a] (% change in CPI)	Absorption	Exports of goods and nonfactor services	Exports as % of GDP	Imports of goods and nonfactor services	Imports as % of GDP	Resource balance as % of GDP (current prices)	Relative price of exports[b]
1970	5,573.5	7.5	n.a.	n.a.	93.5	4.7	5,877.3	1,904.2	34.2	2,208.0	39.6	-6.77	0.83
1971	5,951.3	6.8	n.a.	n.a.	n.a.	3.1	6,268.5	2,059.3	34.6	2,376.5	46.5	n.a.	n.a.
1972	6,438.0	8.2	n.a.	n.a.	n.a.	4.6	6,412.3	2,410.7	37.4	2,385.0	37.0	n.a.	n.a.
1973	6,934.3	7.7	n.a.	n.a.	n.a.	19.9	6,880.8	2,586.4	37.3	2,532.9	36.5	n.a.	n.a.
1974	7,318.8	5.5	n.a.	n.a.	n.a.	30.6	7,315.7	2,774.2	37.9	2,771.1	37.9	-14.98	0.87
1975	7,472.5	2.1	3.0	3.2	73.7	12.4	7,321.1	2,719.5	36.4	2,568.1	34.4	-8.49	0.83
1976	7,885.1	5.5	5.3	5.6	86.2	3.5	8,061.5	2,866.9	36.6	2,983.6	37.8	-6.00	0.79
1977	8,586.9	8.9	2.2	12.0	102.2	4.2	9,217.9	3,100.7	36.1	3,731.7	43.5	-5.47	0.85
1978	9,125.1	6.1	6.4	7.9	92.0	6.0	9,727.9	3,408.9	37.4	4,011.7	44.0	-7.85	0.75
1979	9,575.8	4.8	0.5	2.6	84.9	9.2	10,184.5	3,520.0	36.8	4,128.7	43.1	-10.27	0.73
1980	9,647.8	0.7	-0.5	0.8	85.1	18.1	10,267.7	3,367.1	34.9	3,987.0	41.3	-10.34	0.76
1981	9,429.6	-2.3	5.0	-0.5	70.5	37.7	8,625.0	3,741.5	39.7	2,936.9	31.1	-4.91	1.09
1982	8,742.6	-7.6	-4.8	-12.1	72.7	90.1	7,610.2	3,537.3	40.5	2,404.9	27.5	0.41	1.10
1983	8,992.9	2.8	3.9	1.8	78.2	32.6	8,287.1	3,490.9	38.8	2,785.1	31.0	-0.75	0.93
1984	9,714.5	7.7	9.6	9.9	80.3	12.0	8,912.3	3,884.5	40.0	3,082.3	31.7	0.41	0.86
1985	9,784.6	0.7	-5.7	2.0	82.9	15.1	9,322.1	3,729.4	38.1	3,266.9	33.4	-1.75	0.81
1986	10,326.3	5.5	4.8	7.3	102.2	11.8	10,303.0	3,864.7	35.5	3,841.4	35.3	-0.85	0.84
1987	10,885.3	5.4	4.0	5.5	93.3	16.9	11,100.0	4,546.5	40.6	4,761.2	42.5	-4.48	0.75
1988	11,204.4	2.9	5.4	2.1	92.5	20.8	10,992.4	4,987.5	43.2	4,775.5	41.4	-1.19	0.77
1989	11,540.5	3.0	n.a.	n.a.	n.a.	16.5	n.a.	n.a.	n.a.	n.a.	n.a.	n.a.	n.a.

n.a. = not available

a. Percentage change in the consumer price index of low- and medium-income families in San José, calculated on the basis of the annual average price index.

b. The relative price of exports to the GDP, as derived from comparison of the current price and constant (1966) price series for these variables in the national accounts.

Sources: ECLA (various years); World Bank (1977, 1988). The source of the data cited in all these publications is the Central Bank of Costa Rica (BCCR).

involved in the production of goods, public employment increased rapidly. The government was under political pressure to employ the increasing flow of educated workers into the public sector at relatively high wages (Gonzalez-Vega 1984). Along with increased government spending went rising fiscal deficits, which were financed increasingly by borrowing on the international credit markets.

While Costa Rica's rapid growth during the 1960s and 1970s was achieved with reasonably typical gross domestic investment rates and marginal output capital ratios, the country's low rate of national savings and high share of investment financed with foreign savings was atypical, at least compared to other Latin American countries. At the beginning of the 1970s, 40 percent of gross investment was financed by foreign savings, and by 1977–80, 46 percent was. The ratio exceeded 50 percent in 1974 and 1975.

The 1974 oil price hike worsened Costa Rica's terms of trade enough to threaten a recession. To offset this contractionary impulse the government pursued expansionary monetary and fiscal policies, financing the resulting fiscal deficits by borrowing on the international capital markets. Between 1975 and 1977 a sharp, fortuitous rise in the price of coffee (by over 100 percent) pushed the overall terms of trade up by 40 percent, raised export earnings, and increased government revenues (see tables 6.1–6.2). This coffee boom appeared *ex post* to "justify" the government's expansionary policies in 1974–75 and also invigorated private spending, pushing absorption up by 24 percent between 1975 and 1977 (table 6.1). Imports skyrocketed during 1975–77, then remained high when the terms of trade returned to more normal levels. The result by 1979–80 was a current account deficit exceeding 50 percent of exports of goods and services, up from an average of 33 percent during 1957–69. The government again borrowed extensively in the international capital market, encouraged by the easy availability of credit and the low real interest rates (Gonzalez-Vega 1984, p. 315), and was soon facing a major debt crisis.

For purposes of macroeconomic analysis, it is useful to divide the period beginning in 1978 into three phases: expanding crisis with ineffective expansionary policy (1978–82), stabilization (1982–83), and recovery with structural adjustment (1983 onward).

Table 6.2 Selected Indicators of Internal and External Finance, 1975–88

Year	Exchange rate[a] (colones/US$) Yearly average	July	Absolute figures (US$ millions) Current accounts balance	Balance of payments	Net capital flight[b]	Net direct foreign investment	US aid	As a percentage of the GDP Government spending	Fiscal deficit	Money supply	Debt Public	Private
1975	8.6	8.6	-217.6	20.9	n.a.	69.0	n.a.	13.6	-0.21	30.3	421.3	
1976	8.6	8.6	-201.5	59.1	n.a.	63.3	n.a.	13.7	-0.66	38.4	535.9	
1977	8.6	8.6	-225.0	107.9	-4.6	63.2	n.a.	13.3	0.05	39.4	725.4	
1978	8.6	8.6	-387.7	-26.8	33.1	47.1	8.2	14.2	-0.82	43.6	949.9	
1979	8.6	8.6	-601.6	-100.4	-89.7	46.0	17.2	14.9	-2.50	41.4	1,309.1	
1980	9.3	8.6	-658.6	-172.8	110.3	48.1	15.9	15.3	-3.10	41.6	1,697.4	411.9
1981	21.2	14.5	-420.3	-111.5	-277.1	66.2	17.4	15.2	-1.60	56.5	2,206.4	371.5
1982	39.8	65.5	-246.0	139.9	-230.5	26.3	57.0	15.5	-1.10	42.0	2,429.2	381.2
1983	41.6	45.3	-309.7	-58.1	248.5	55.1	216.5	16.2	0.36	43.4	3,226.2	348.2
1984	44.4	43.6	-263.9	97.7	-126.4	51.9	186.2	16.3	0.26	40.3	3,289.5	316.6
1985	50.5	50.9	-365.9	99.8	n.a.	63.2	220.1	15.2	0.94	38.4	3,579.5	301.6
1986	56.1	56.1	-187.8	54.8	n.a.	57.3	154.5	15.9	0.47	37.2	3,575.0	306.4
1987	62.8	62.3	-399.5	-76.7	n.a.	89.5	180.1	15.3	0.36	37.6	3,623.0	345.1
1988	75.9	75.9	105.7	n.a.	n.a.	n.a.	n.a.					

a. Free-rate for July. The yearly average corresponds to an average over the course of the year of the effective exchange rates between current inpayments and outpayments in the balance of payments.

b. Using a technique developed by Morgan Guarantee Trust. A negative entry means a net inflow of capital, a positive entry means a net outflow of capital (capital flight).

Sources: World Bank (1988, various years); Glower (1986); Sanford (1989); Central Bank of Costa Rica data.

Between 1978 and 1981 Costa Rica's terms of trade fell by a third to a little under the precoffee boom lows of 1974–75 as the price of coffee fell by 61 percent between 1977 and 1981 and the 1979 oil embargo increased the price of imports (see table 6.1). Political turmoil and economic recession cut demand for Costa Rica's previously substantial exports to CACM countries. Despite shrinking export markets (especially for industrial products) and stagnant banana exports, the export quantum continued upward until 1981, but the purchasing power of exports fell by 20 percent. Balance of payments deficits became increasingly difficult to finance as international interest rates rose, international banks curtailed credit availability, and private direct foreign investment declined.

Largely in response to popular pressure, the Carazo government (1978–82) attempted to stimulate the failing economy using the same recipe applied successfully in 1975–77: a high level of aggregate demand and relatively stable prices. This attempt probably contributed to the severity and length of the crisis (Gonzalez-Vega 1984). Government spending was increased, especially on heavy infrastructure, thereby increasing the fiscal deficit and public sector borrowing on the international capital markets. Import duties on consumption items were cut further, which increased imports and the balance of payments deficit, but held the consumer price index to an annual average increase of only 11 percent during 1977–80. Refusal to devalue the colon in the face of a looming balance of payments crisis encouraged capital flight and speculative importing (table 6.2). The public foreign debt, previously growing but manageable, ballooned out of control, more than doubling between 1978 and 1981 (Carrillo 1988). The failure to reach an agreement with the IMF in early 1980 increased capital flight, and prefaced a reluctant but massive devaluation (from a rate of 8.6 colones per dollar to 21.8) near the end of 1980, which in turn led to rapidly accelerating inflation. With a devaluing currency, falling export earnings, and little or no access to foreign public or private capital without an IMF agreement, a moratorium was declared on servicing the public sector's external debt (Rodriguez 1987).

Between 1979 and 1982, the GDP fell by over 9 percent. Industrial production, which fell by 12 percent in 1982, was hit especially hard by the breakdown of the CACM and by the rise in imported input prices when the devaluation finally came. As inflation increased from 9 percent in 1979 to over 90 percent in 1982, real wages fell by nearly 40 percent, the unemployment rate rose from 5 to 8 percent of the national labor force, and the underemployment rate rose from 3 to 7 percent.

The economy hit bottom in mid-1982; 1983 saw a mild upturn, a sharply reduced inflation rate, and a significant recovery of real earnings. The reversal occurred as the new government of Partido Liberacion Nacional's (PLN) Alberto Monge took office. Monge and the PLN, with strong ties to the unions and past social legislation, were in a better position to command union and popular confidence and to call for short-term sacrifices than was the business-supported Carazo.

In summer 1982, Monge instituted a "100-day stabilization plan" that included an appreciation of the colon, together with controls on the outflow of capital and unification of the official and free-market exchange rates;[1] income, sales, and consumption tax increases of 60 to 170 percent; decreases in subsidies (by 50 to 80 percent in the case of public transportation) and increases in the prices of public utilities (that of fuel increased by 80 percent, of electricity by 80 to 90 percent); a public sector wage freeze; and a credit restraint/contraction of the money supply (*Latin American and Caribbean Contemporary Record* 1983; Nelson 1989). In December, 1982 a letter of intent was signed with the IMF. Large infusions of American aid, which rose from virtually zero in 1979 to US$216 million in 1983, mitigated the damping effects of the public sector's large foreign debt (Rivera Urrutia and others 1986).

Despite the apparent harshness of the stabilization measures, there was relatively little public protest. Seligson and Muller (1987) report that optimism about future economic conditions was higher in 1982 than at any time during the previous seven years. Nelson (1989, p. 148) reports that by "mid-1982, all groups were paying dearly for unplanned adjustment, and many were willing to acquiesce to any

---

1. Capital controls were accomplished by closing the exchange houses and controlling all currency exchange within the nationalized banking system. All foreign exchange earnings from exports or tourism had to go through the central bank.

plausible policy that signaled the resumption of government control over the situation." Nelson also notes that austerity policies were biased in favor of the poorer segments of society. Businesses and medium and large agricultural interests bore the largest share of the substantial tax and utility price increases. According to the national accounts, general government revenues as a share of GDP rose from 21.2 percent in 1982 to 26.3 percent in 1983.

Terms of trade stabilized in 1982 and improved thereafter through 1986, then slipped back again. In 1988 they were at about the 1980 level. The price of coffee began to rise in 1984 and experienced a 47 percent increase in 1986, before falling 53 percent in 1987. Real wages and earnings regained their 1979 levels between 1986 and 1988. GDP began to grow in 1983 and achieved rates of at least 3 percent each year through 1989, except for a slump in 1985, caused in part by decreased agricultural subsidies to basic grains with a consequent drop in agricultural production, a temporary cutoff of U.S. aid, and a drop in banana exports (Standard Fruit abandoned production on the Pacific Coast due to labor troubles, high export taxes, and crop disease). Average growth between 1982 and 1989 was 4 percent.

In 1984, under pressure from USAID, the IMF, and the World Bank, Costa Rica initiated one of the most comprehensive structural adjustment programs in Latin America (Rivera Urrutia and others 1986). The program included the following:
- selling state-owned production enterprises (by 1988 only four remained);
- a 1987 agreement with the IMF to limit the increase in public sector salaries;
- a new CACM tariff regime instituted in January 1986 to replace the 1963 regime, whereby the mean tariff was cut from 53 to 20 percent and the standard deviation from 62 to 21 percent (according to a 1987 IMF stand-by agreement further tariff unification is to continue until January 1991);
- a 1987 tax reform that lowered the maximum marginal income tax rate to 25 percent and increased the threshold for contributions, instituted a 30 percent flat corporate tax rate, and increased sales, property, social security, and stamp taxes;

- a loosening of the monopoly of state-owned banks, and hence of government control over the provision of credit, and a reduction in subsidized credit (although the program for subsidized credit to small farmers was expanded);
- a reduction of some agricultural subsidies, together with elimination of all quantity restrictions on agricultural imports;
- a program to promote nontraditional exports to third markets via creation of free trade zones, tax breaks, import duty exemptions, and production and marketing extension services.

The free trade zones are designed to encourage "draw-back" or *maquila* industries, which can import and export duty free and benefit from tax breaks. Over 75 percent of the participating firms are in the textile industry, and over 15 percent are in electronics (CENPRO 1986). According to the Central Bank of Costa Rica, value added in draw-back industries now accounts for 12 percent of the value added of nontraditional exports.

The administrations of both Monge and Arias emphasized that the structural adjustment program should be implemented gradually in an attempt to minimize disruption. If the results have matched the plans, a gradual rather than a rapid shift in the structure of production toward exports (in particular nontraditional exports) should have occurred. After falling by 15 percent during 1980–83, the current dollar value of exports (f.o.b.) had by 1989 climbed to 40 percent above the 1980 level, while the value of imports, just equal to exports in 1988, only surpassed the 1980 level when they jumped by 20 percent in 1989. (In 1980 the import/export ratio was 1.37.) Meanwhile, with interest charges high, current account deficits and the public foreign debt remained high. By the end of 1987, the stock of debt was roughly equal to the GDP and interest payments amounted to 6 percent of GDP and 18 percent of export earnings. This heavy debt overhang was made tolerable by a continued high level of U.S. aid and IMF balance of payments support. The U.S. aid came with stringent conditions, including Costa Rican support for the Reagan administration's policy toward Nicaragua.

Recently, the debt burden has been eased somewhat. In 1990 Costa Rica negotiated a buy-back of US$1.8 billion of its foreign debt. This buy-back was financed in part with a US$250 million "bridge" loan arranged and financed by central banks in the United States, Taiwan, Mexico, and Venezuela (*Tico Times*, May 25, 1990).

In the crisis years of the early 1980s the (current price) gross investment rate appears to have held up surprisingly well, never falling below about 23 percent, although the fixed investment figures did show a more marked decline (from an unweighted average of 23.9 percent over 1977–80 to 19.5 percent over 1982–84) and the inventory change estimates may be invalid (table 6.3). The share of investment financed by foreign savings fell from a local peak of over 50 percent during 1979–82 to under 40 percent by 1984–85. The dramatic decrease in real investment (in constant 1966 prices) from a peak of 28.5 percent of GDP in 1980 to a low of 14.6 percent in 1982 was due to a sudden change in the relative price of investment goods, not to a major decline in either the current price investment and savings rates or to the national savings rate (which in fact rose from 11.5 percent during 1975–80 to 13.8 percent during 1981–85), but when foreign savings fell and capital goods became much more costly, maintaining a high real investment rate was not feasible given the traditionally very low national savings rate.

Labor Market Overview

From the early 1960s to the late 1970s, opportunities for the average Costa Rican worker improved markedly. The share in agricultural employment, the lowest paying sector, decreased steadily from 49.1 percent in 1963 to 38 percent in 1973 and 30 percent in 1979, while the proportion of professionals and technicians rose steadily, and the share in the high paying public sector increased from 13.3 percent in 1963 to 15.3 percent in 1973 and nearly 19 percent in 1980 (1963 census; 1973 census; 1979/80 household surveys). The unemployment rate typically hovered around 5 to 6 percent. Incomes and real wages increased by more than 60 percent between 1963 and 1979. A temporary decline between 1972 and 1975 due to the recession caused by the first oil embargo was more than offset by a 25 percent "coffee boom" increase between 1976 and 1979. The incidence of poverty fell. Improvements on all fronts came faster with the coffee boom, which produced growth spurts in both agricultural and manufacturing production (9.1 percent and 22 percent,

Table 6.3 Gross Savings and Investment as a Percentage of GDP, 1970–88 (constant 1966 prices)

Year	Gross investment	Investment in fixed capital			Change in inventories	Gross investment	Gross investment in fixed capital	Foreign savings as percentage of gross savings	Foreign savings	National savings		
		Total	Construction	Machines & equipment						Total	Public	Private
1970	20.23	19.34	9.23	10.11	0.91	20.53	19.46	37.8	7.8	12.7	n.a.	n.a.
1971	23.52	21.08	n.a.	n.a.	2.44	24.34	22.12	46.2	11.2	13.1	2.7	10.4
1972	20.15	20.40	n.a.	n.a.	-0.25	22.03	21.91	41.4	9.1	12.9	2.9	10.0
1973	22.20	20.54	n.a.	n.a.	1.66	23.99	22.16	35.0	8.4	15.6	3.6	12.0
1974	22.84	21.36	9.64	11.72	1.48	26.74	24.02	62.4	16.6	10.1	5.4	4.7
1975	20.38	20.66	9.70	10.96	-0.28	21.64	21.99	51.3	11.1	10.5	4.7	5.8
1976	24.43	24.22	11.57	12.65	0.21	23.66	23.44	35.3	8.4	15.3	4.3	11.0
1977	27.54	25.00	11.40	13.60	2.54	24.27	22.36	30.3	7.4	16.9	4.2	12.7
1978	25.48	25.44	10.96	14.48	0.37	23.46	23.03	43.9	10.3	13.2	3.4	9.8
1979	26.87	27.95	12.42	15.53	-1.08	25.31	26.17	54.0	13.7	16.6	0.3	11.3
1980	28.54	25.13	12.56	12.56	3.41	26.57	23.90	55.8	14.9	11.7	-1.0	12.7
1981	18.18	19.31	9.66	9.64	-1.13	29.03	24.06	52.3	15.2	13.8	1.2	12.6
1982	14.62	15.03	8.15	6.88	-0.41	24.69	20.32	49.9	12.3	12.4	-0.8	13.2
1983	18.91	15.82	8.28	7.54	3.09	24.71	17.99	44.0	10.8	13.9	10.2	3.7
1984	19.42	18.48	9.88	9.29	0.95	22.61	20.05	31.4	7.1	15.5	8.3	5.9
1985	20.78	19.33	9.50	9.83	1.45	25.42	19.32	29.5	7.5	15.8	n.a.	n.a.
1986	25.76	20.49	9.34	11.15	5.27	25.20	18.66	15.2	3.8	21.4	n.a.	n.a.
1987	28.77	21.32	8.63	12.67	7.45	28.25	19.59	31.2	8.8	19.4	n.a.	n.a.
1988	25.69	19.53	8.74	10.79	6.16	26.04	18.11	n.a.	6.0	20.1	n.a.	n.a.

n.a. = not available
Source: ECLA (various years).

228

respectively, between 1976 and 1979). Total employment increased at an average annual rate of 4.7 percent per year and the labor force at 4.0 percent, pushing the unemployment rate to a low of about 4.0 percent in 1979. Employment in the public sector increased rapidly from some 16 percent of total employment in 1976 to 18.3 percent in 1978, or by an average of over 11.0 percent per year, before slowing in 1979.

The labor market began to show signs of a downturn in 1979. Although open unemployment did not rise, underemployment moved up sharply. The late 1980 devaluation was followed by a sharp increase in inflation, a huge drop in real wages and earnings (about 35 percent between 1980 and 1982), and an apparent "additional worker" effect as secondary family workers entered the labor force. The proportion of the labor force not heads of households increased from 50 to 51 percent during 1977–80 to 53 to 54 percent in 1981–82, and the share of women appears to have risen somewhat more rapidly than the average increase in other years. The number of new entrants to the labor force doubled between 1980 and 1981. During 1979–82, the influx of secondary family workers pushed the labor force up at an average of 4.3 percent per year, while employment grew at only 2.6 percent per year (table 6.4) so the unemployment rate rose steadily to a peak of 9.4 percent in 1982.

While employment did not increase as fast as the labor force, that it increased at all is surprising, given the contraction of both agricultural and manufacturing output. An important ameliorating factor as the crisis set in was the 8.8 percent increase in public sector employment (almost all of it in the central government) between 1979 and 1981, which accounted for most of the employment increase in that interval, and reflected the Carazo government's attempt to spend its way out of the impending crisis and to keep the unemployment rate at manageable levels (table 6.4). Salaried employment also increased in small repair firms and for domestic servants (interview with Juan Diego Trejos). The increase in employment from 1979 to 1981 was entirely composed of wage earners (the number of self-employed workers and owners actually decreased by 6.2 percent between 1970 and 1981).

Table 6.4 Labor Market Indicators, 1976–88

Year	Labor force (seasonally adjusted) (1)	Employment (seasonally adjusted) (2)	Percentage of labor force that was: Unemployed (3)	Under-employed (open) (4)	Female (5)	Non-household head (6)	Percentage of employment in: Public sector (7)	Rural areas (8)	Agriculture (9)	Real wages: Paid workers only (10)	All workers (11)	Real earnings: Paid workers only (12)	All workers (13)
1976	664.7	635.3	4.42	9.43	23.8(2)	50.8(2)	15.9(2)	50.0	34.2	5.7	n.a.	1,061(2)	n.a.
1977	697.3	662.6	5.07	10.30	23.6	51.0	16.7	54.2	34.4	6.4	n.a.	1,199	n.a.
1978	737.7	704.0	4.56	9.87	25.9	50.8	18.3	55.0	33.5	6.9	n.a.	1,314	n.a.
1979	748.9	718.3	4.09	15.50	25.7	50.8	18.6	53.1	31.0	7.4	n.a.	1,401	n.a.
1980	779.7	738.0	5.34	17.17	25.8	50.2	18.8	52.5	29.5	7.2	7.3	1,346	1,353
1981	819.3	751.6	8.27	20.30	26.9	53.0	18.6	55.1	31.9	6.3	6.3	1,141	1,161
1982	849.0	777.3	8.45	22.80	27.2	54.0	17.3	52.2	29.8	4.8	5.0	865	899
1983	844.3	776.0	8.09	17.70	25.6	52.1	18.8	50.9	30.3	5.7	5.8	1,030	1,051
1984(2)	853.1	790.7	8.00	16.83	26.8	51.3	19.7	52.2	30.4	5.9	6.3	1,162	1,223
1985(2)	901.9	846.6	6.14	15.46	26.0	52.7	18.8	49.9	31.2	6.9	7.1	1,230	1,286
1986(1)	962.2	909.8	5.45	16.63	28.0	53.1	20.1	50.8	26.9	7.4	7.4	1,339	1,375
1987(1)	992.7	941.5	5.15	8.82	28.3	55.0	15.9	46.1	28.1	8.1	8.2	1,433	1,491
1988(1)	1,021.0	970.0	5.00	8.91	29.2	53.8	17.1	46.2	28.1	7.6	7.7	1,414	1,427

Sources and methodology Except where indicated, data are averages across observations for March, July, and November. Numbers in parentheses indicate years or variables in which observations were only available to us for one or two rather than the usual three months. The data are from the household surveys of employment and unemployment. For columns 1–8, 12, and 13, missing figures for any of the three months were filled in on the basis of the observed average seasonal differences over 1977–83 (when data were available for each of March, July, and November), as follows, and in each case setting July = 100.

Labor force:	Mar. 97.5	Nov. 107.0
Employment:	Mar. 97.6	Nov. 108.4
Female share of labor force:	Mar. 98.1	Nov. 109.1
Nonhousehold head share of labor force:	Mar. 102.9	Nov. 106.1
Public sector share of labor force:	Mar. 98.9	Nov. 93.3
Rural sector share of employment:	Mar. 101.6	Nov. 104.6
Agriculture share of employment (July data not available):	Mar. 100.0	Nov. 113.3

By the time of the devaluation, the Carazo administration seemed to have given up its holding action against the recession, and public sector employment fell between July 1981 and the end of 1982. Growth in total employment between July 1981 and July 1982 was driven by a 6 percent increase in rural employment as agricultural production grew by almost 5 percent, while nonwage employment grew faster than wage employment (4.4 percent as opposed to 3.9 percent). Whereas the increase in public sector employment between 1979 and 1981 occurred mostly in the central government, the decrease between July 1981 and July 1982 took place primarily in autonomous and semi-autonomous enterprises (in transportation, commerce, construction, and utilities).

About the time that Monge (June–July 1982) instituted his 100-day plan to stabilize and revive confidence in the economy, real public sector salaries and real minimum wages rose because they were indexed to the inflation rate of the past period. With inflation slowing down, the indexing mechanism pushed nominal salaries up faster than prices. In addition, more frequent adjustment of these institutionally set salaries worked in the same direction. The increased real wage probably had a dampening effect on the participation of secondary workers: the share of nonhousehold heads in the labor force dropped to its precrisis levels. Another large increase in public sector employment between July 1982 and July 1983 accounted for more than the total increase in employment. The Monge government thus mitigated the negative welfare effects of the stabilization package through increases in public sector employment, public sector wages, and the minimum wage helped by the sharp increase in U.S. aid in 1983.

From 1983 to 1987, labor incomes continued to rise. Real wages and real earnings regained their 1980 levels by 1986. The proportion of younger and older people in the labor force resumed its earlier downward trend, while the proportions of women and of nonhousehold heads, after dropping from their 1981–82 peaks, resumed their previous upward trends (table 6.4). Unemployment fell to the low levels of the late 1970s, as did the average duration of unemployment spells. In 1985 rural employment experienced a temporary decline, related to a 5.7 percent decrease in agricultural production probably due to the elimination of subsidies to rice and sorghum producers (a structural adjustment policy), and to the withdrawal of Standard Fruit from the Pacific coast. Employment in the public sector remained high through 1986 and beyond.

Labor Market Institutions in the Adjustment Process

Addressing the economic crisis in Costa Rica required a sufficient reduction of aggregate demand to narrow the gap between absorption and production, and a sufficient resource shift toward tradables to rectify the balance of payments disequilibrium. The key components of many stabilization plans are expenditure reduction and devaluation. Since absorption must fall, incomes must probably also fall. The objective is to limit that fall to the level essential to achieve the adjustment. Inflexible labor costs may mean that expenditure reduction will result in unemployment of workers attached to the rigid wage sector or in underemployment or misallocation of labor among sectors; outcomes that might be avoided if real wages are flexible. For output composition to change some labor shift between sectors may be important, which may require a change in relative wages, a lack of barriers to movement, or both.

Labor Market Institutions and Real Wages

Many of the labor market institutions that one might expect to protect workers from falling real wages are firmly implanted in Costa Rica. Relatively well enforced minimum wages are generally considered to be the key institution influencing real wages in the private sector.[2] Public sector wages, clearly important given the quantitative significance of public sector employment, are also likely to be resistant to sharp declines.

In examining the impact of labor market institutions on short-run stabilization, we are particularly interested in two periods: the aftermath of the drastic devaluation of the colon (December 1980 to mid-1982), and the period of government expenditure reduction, tax increases, and appreciation of the colon (mid-1982 to 1984). The

---

2. Minimum wages are legislated for over 130 different industrial classifications, each with up to 9 occupational categories. Over 500 separate minimum wages can be legislated.

proximate determinant of real wage movements during these periods was the rate of inflation together with mechanistic wage setting rules. The 34 percent decline in real wages during 1980–82 occurred because accelerating inflation eroded the protective effect of these rules. Both minimum wages (a key to private sector wage setting) and public sector salaries are indexed to the change in price level since their last adjustment. Under such an arrangement, real wages fall in times of accelerating inflation, stabilize below pre-inflation levels if inflation stops accelerating but stays high, and rise when inflation slows. The fiscal crisis experienced by the government probably accounted for the upswing in real public sector salaries being somewhat slower than in the private sector. An assessment of the role of devaluation and exchange rate policy as determinants of real wages is made difficult because their effects occur primarily through their impacts on inflation and may easily be disguised by and confused with the intermediating role of inflation and the mechanisms it sets in motion (see Gindling and Berry 1991 for a more detailed discussion of these issues).

The influence of unions in Costa Rica has traditionally been limited mainly to the public sector; private sector unionization has been significant only among banana workers. Union influence reached its peak at the end of the 1970s, since when it has declined dramatically. A turning point was a 72-day strike against Standard Fruit's banana operation on the Pacific Coast in 1984, which relied heavily on 48 sympathy strikes by other private sector unions, and the prestige of the most powerful private sector union leaders rested on a successful conclusion. When Standard Fruit closed its operations and abandoned Costa Rica, the power of the remaining private sector unions declined dramatically and the union movement divided (Donato and Rojas 1987). Meanwhile, the government's fiscal problems overwhelmed the public sector unions. Monge's mandate to "do something" created a sense of purpose in the government that precluded unified action against it, while the public sector union movement was by then suffering from disunity and confusion spawned by the economic crisis. With the 1987 accord with the IMF, in which the Arias administration agreed to avoid increases in the average public sector wage, union influence waned further.

In summary, the sharp decline in real wages between 1980 and 1982 and a direct assessment of the major labor market institutions suggest that these institutions did not significantly limit downward flexibility of real wages during the crisis. They may actually have pushed wages below the levels that might have resulted under many other institutional arrangements. In a sense, real wages fell because these institutions failed to perform their planned function. By this failure, they may have provided the government with an easy, apparently neutral, mechanism whereby real wages could be pushed down when the state of the economy most required it.

Sectoral Employment Shifts

We distinguish here four important sectors. *Importables* are those tradable goods for which the likely alternative sources are imports and domestic production, the latter often protected from foreign competition by policies of import-substituting industrialization. The approximation used here includes all private sector production of manufactured goods plus basic grains (rice, sorghum, maize, and beans), all of which have been heavily protected.[3] *Exportables* are those tradables exported to non-CACM countries or consumed at home, including agricultural products and services (with the exception of basic grains) plus mining. *Private nontradables* include the activities of construction, basic services, commerce, and services (UIIC two-digit classifications 40 to 96). The *public sector* is defined here to include the central and municipal governments and autonomous and semi-autonomous enterprises (parastatal enterprises). Although primarily composed of nontradable services such as public utilities, education, insurance, banking, pensions, and medical services, it also includes production of some import substitutes (such as cement and fertilizers) and even the processing of some exports (sugar, coffee, and

---

3. A dilemma in the distinction between the export and import categories arises from the country's exports of significant amounts of manufactured goods to other CACM countries, although these items would otherwise be, and since the demise of the CACM have become, importables. The main items in a group we refer to here as the CACM importables are processed foods, textiles, petrochemical products, and electrical machinery. Unfortunately, because by the late 1980s some processed foods and textiles are nontraditional exports, treating CACM importables systematically as a separate category is not possible.

so on). The presence of these latter activities means that this is not a purely nontradables category.

The total current dollar value of merchandise exports increased with the coffee boom from 1975 to 1977, eased up during the rest of the decade, fell sharply in 1982, and then grew back to a new high in 1989, 40 percent above the earlier 1981 peak (table 6.5). This growth path of the export quantum was rather different, however (table 6.1), with good growth through 1978 and very little (only 10 percent) from then through 1986, followed by a 30 percent burst in the next two years. By 1983–85, the colon price of exports (abstracting from export taxes and subsidies) was back down to its precrisis 1978–79 level and well below that of 1975–77, so the stagnation of export quantum was not surprising given the absence of a maintained increase in the relative price of exports.

In the late 1970s, current dollar exports in each of traditional exports, exports to the CACM, and other nontraditional exports grew fairly rapidly. During the heart of the crisis, the big loss of export revenues occurred in the CACM category; the downward trend continued through the rest of the decade. Rising revenues during 1983–87 came from both traditional exports, whose prices were now moving up, and from nontraditional exports, which leapt from 166 million in 1983–84 to 372 million in 1987. By 1987, the nontraditional category provided fully one-third of total export revenues. If the post-1983 adjustment policies deserve credit for this impressive performance, they might be considered an overall success.[4] While the relative price of exports as a whole continued to fall from its peak in 1980–81, the price incentive for these new exports, with the tax relief for nontraditional exports and draw-back incentive systems in place, may have been strong. In any case, as the policies of short-term stabilization gave way during 1984–1987 to those of longer-term structural adjustment, the composition of exports did change in a manner consistent with the goals of the Costa Rican government.

While export and import trends determine the achievement of external payments balance, trends in the production of exportables,

---

4. Given the high import content of these exports (as much as 80 to 90 percent of material inputs used), the benefits from this growth of nontraditional exports are somewhat less than they appear.

Table 6.5 Merchandise Exports by Category and Sectoral Price Deflators, 1975–87

Category	1975	1976	1977	1978	1979	1980	1981	1982	1983	1984	1985	1986	1987
GDP (millions of 1966 colones)	7,472.5	7,885.1	8,586.9	9,125.1	9,575.8	9,647.8	9,429.6	8,742.6	8,992.9	9,714.5	9,784.6	10,326.3	10,817.6
Total exports (US$ millions)	493.6	592.9	828.0	865.0	942.1	1,000.9	1,008.6	869.8	852.5	997.5	939.1	1,084.8	1,113.5
Traditional exports (US$ millions)	345.0	391.4	560.0	585.9	624.1	581.0	599.9	545.0	532.6	604.6	599.9	694.3	643.9
Exports to the Central American Common Market (CACM) (US$ millions)	n.a.	130.6	173.8	178.7	175.4	270.3	238.0	167.2	198.2	192.9	143.5	98.9	98.0
Other exports (US$ millions)	n.a.	70.9	94.2	100.4	142.6	149.6	170.7	157.6	121.7	200.0	195.7	291.6	371.6
Nontraditional exports to third markets (US$ millions)	n.a.	n.a.	n.a.	n.a.	n.a.	n.a.	n.a.	104.2	92.4	137.4	163.7	240.2	312.9
Maquila exports (value added) (US$ millions)	n.a.	n.a.	n.a.	n.a.	n.a.	n.a.	n.a.	10.8	16.9	26.1	34.5	34.2	42.9
GDP price deflators (1966 = 100)													
Agriculture	215.5	264.4	358.8	355.0	366.7	424.6	720.4	1,373.6	1,573.1	1,737.0	1,985.8	2,664.4	2,553.4
Manufacturing	215.9	242.5	264.1	276.2	301.1	363.3	512.9	1,061.1	1,485.8	1,746.0	2,040.6	2,292.5	2,479.5
Services	233.8	271.2	310.8	348.4	387.1	460.6	601.4	1,063.9	1,375.8	1,643.1	2,055.4	2,404.3	2,791.5
GDP	224.9	262.2	306.6	330.9	361.2	429.2	605.6	1,115.3	1,438.0	1,678.0	2,022.8	2,401.3	2,639.1
Prices relative to GDP													
Agriculture	0.958	1.008	1.170	1.073	1.015	0.989	1.190	1.232	1.094	1.035	0.982	1.110	0.968
Manufacturing	0.960	0.925	0.861	0.835	0.834	0.846	0.847	0.951	1.033	1.041	1.009	0.955	0.940
Services	1.040	1.034	1.014	1.053	1.072	1.073	0.993	0.954	0.957	0.979	1.016	1.001	1.058

n.a. = not available

Note: The distinction between traditional and nontraditional exports to third markets (not the CACM) is based on the laws defining nontraditional exports to these markets. Prior to 1982, the data necessary to distinguish these categories are not available.

Sources: World Bank (1977, 1988); in addition, some figures on CACM exports are from SIECA, *Estadísticas Analíticas del Comercio Intracentroamericano* (various issues).

236

importables, and nontradables are of equal interest in assessing stabilization and adjustment policies, as they largely determine trade flows in the longer run, when shorter-term influences have averaged out. If one focuses on production of exportables and on the increasing number of products with export competitiveness, Costa Rica has managed a reasonably successful adjustment since 1980. If one focuses on tradables, this is not the case: after an increase in 1980–82 associated with the fall of GDP, their share in output fell (table 6.6). The public sector share of value added rose smoothly (from 9.9 to 11.2 percent) during 1976–82, then gradually declined to 9.7 percent with the stabilization and structural adjustment programs of 1983–87. An upward trend in the share of private nontradables was broken only by a sharp fall in 1981.

In terms of labor immobility among sectors, the biggest problem for successful adjustment would have been barriers to movement into the exportables sector, and in particular, into the production of nontraditional exports. Employment trends by trade-related sector are somewhat different from those for value added (table 6.7), but there are no strong hints of such immobility. Employment in exportables decreased as a share of total employment from 1976 to 1980, increased significantly in the crisis years, fell with the appreciation of the colon in 1983, and stayed about constant thereafter: what was probably a downward secular trend up to about 1980 (recall that this sector includes much of agriculture) has been at least temporarily stopped. The employment share of the importables sector trended down until 1981, rose through 1983, and then held about constant. The share of private nontradables fluctuated only slightly during 1976–88, while that of the public sector continued its earlier upward trend until about 1980, then leveled off (with a dip in 1982).

In general, these data suggest a reasonable degree of mobility between sectors. Whether it was due to the devaluation or not, employment in exportables rose significantly during 1980–82, while that in the public sector fell. Such observed changes in employment structure could have occurred without worker mobility, however. Thus in the 1981–82 post-devaluation period, the dramatic increase in exportables sector employment could have been due to new entrants joining that sector. Much of the increase in exportables sector

Table 6.6 Value Added by Trade-Related Sector, 1975–87

Sector	1975	1976	1977	1978	1979	1980	1981	1982	1983	1984	1985	1986	1987
In millions of 1966 colones													
Exportables	1,460	1,458.0	1,502.0	1,603.0	1,599.2	1,591.9	1,671.6	1,627.3	1,637.9	1,791.2	1,697.1	1,788.5	1,894.9
Importables	1,558	1,545.8	1,827.3	1,996.8	2,047.8	2,013.1	2,097.9	1,761.5	1,812.6	2,052.6	2,081.4	1,864.7	2,024.8
Private nontradables				4,459.6	4,795.5	4,825.4	4,511.7	4,179.4	4,341.9	4,669.6	4,802.6	5,078.6	5,407.8
Public sector				881.1	932.7	966.7	984.3	955.8	940.5	954.6	959.4	978.6	1,003.0
Processed foods		725.3	833.1	927.1	972.3	922.3	952.5	876.1	927.7	1,048.6	1,081.3	1,172.3	
Textiles		276.3	295.5	295.6	282.3	284.6	282.7	316.9	328.1	320.1	316.3	302.1	
Petrochemical products		279.5	327.7	364.5	368.7	397.2	406.2	307.4	300.1	341.3	339.4	381.8	
Electrical machinery		114.5	140.8	156.9	166.6	191.5	155.6	108.3	80.2	89.8	90.0	103.0	
As a percentage of total value added													
Exportables				17.9	17.1	16.9	18.0	19.1	18.8	18.9	17.8	18.4	18.3
Importables				22.3	21.8	21.4	22.6	20.7	20.8	21.7	21.8	19.2	19.6
Private nontradables				49.9	51.2	51.3	48.7	49.0	49.7	49.3	50.3	52.3	52.3
Public sector				9.9	9.9	10.3	10.5	11.2	10.8	10.1	10.1	10.1	9.7
Processed food				10.4	10.4	9.8	10.3	10.3	10.6	11.1	11.3	12.1	
Textiles				3.3	3.0	3.0	3.1	3.7	3.8	3.4	3.3	3.1	
Petrochemical products				4.1	3.9	4.2	4.4	3.6	3.4	3.6	3.6	3.9	
Electrical machinery				1.8	1.8	2.0	1.7	1.3	0.9	0.9	0.9	1.1	

Note: Exports are defined to include agriculture and mining minus basic grains (rice, beans, sorghum). Importables are defined as manufacturing and basic grains. Disaggregated data on manufactured goods are available only in current colones; these figures were converted into 1966 colones using the GDP price deflator. Value added in agricultural goods is reported in 1966 colones. Private nontradables are defined as elasticity, construction, transportation, finance, durables, plus other services. The public sector is defined as the central government, municipal governments, and state-owned enterprises. The public sector and private nontradables value added are reported in 1966 colones.

Sources: World Bank (1977, 1988); Central Bank of Costa Rica, *Cuentas Nacionales de Costa Rica* (various issues).

Table 6.7 Employment by Trade-Related Sectors, 1976–83, 1985–88 (July)

Sector	1976	1977	1978	1979	1980	1981	1982	1983	1985	1986	1987	1988
					Number of workers							
Exportables	178,601	179,076	173,306	180,472	175,542	180,771	197,525	181,378	188,633	199,672	213,250	223,067
Importables	125,306	138,826	138,780	136,734	139,545	130,052	145,537	160,691	167,502	180,822	206,632	202,113
Private nontradables	208,252	220,273	246,050	259,270	267,914	269,809	278,944	278,993	309,334	323,093	348,921	352,927
Public sector	102,666	114,917	128,856	130,448	142,271	141,692	134,281	145,254	157,792	183,738	150,513	167,501
Processed foods	22,606	25,656	26,850	31,387	31,185	29,862	29,807	28,142	34,878	38,002	37,081	36,126
Textiles	26,086	32,883	32,143	28,867	31,249	27,574	35,053	39,226	38,326	52,822	54,600	55,867
Petrochemical products	8,765	9,186	7,450	11,146	11,019	12,285	10,774	15,065	12,640	17,107	16,037	14,675
Electrical machinery	9,159	11,483	9,802	12,765	13,337	10,405	9,776	13,333	11,562	16,768	15,890	13,956
					As a percentage of total employment							
Exportables	30.9	29.1	26.6	25.5	24.2	25.0	26.1	23.7	22.9	22.5	23.2	23.6
Importables	21.7	22.5	21.3	19.3	19.2	18.0	19.2	21.0	20.3	20.4	22.5	21.4
Private nontradables	36.0	35.7	37.8	36.7	36.9	37.4	36.9	36.4	37.6	36.4	38.0	37.3
Public sector	17.8	18.6	19.8	18.5	19.6	19.6	17.8	19.0	19.2	20.7	16.4	17.7
Processed food	3.9	4.2	4.1	4.4	4.3	4.1	3.9	3.7	4.2	4.3	4.0	3.8
Textiles	4.5	5.3	4.9	4.1	4.3	3.8	4.6	5.1	4.7	6.0	5.9	5.9
Petrochemical products	1.5	1.5	1.1	1.6	1.5	1.7	1.4	2.0	1.5	1.9	1.7	1.6
Electrical machinery	1.6	1.9	1.5	1.8	1.8	1.4	1.3	1.7	1.4	1.9	1.7	1.5

Notes: For the definition of the sectors see table 6.6. Figures for public sector employment in 1987 and 1988 are probably biased downward relative to those of earlier years, as the definition of the public sector was narrowed between the household surveys of 1986 and 1987. Accordingly, one or more of the other categories would be upwardly biased. The main candidate is private nontradables, since most government employment consists of the provision of services (Gindling and Berry 1991). Public sector construction also fell sharply between 1986 and 1987, probably due to this reclassification. Since construction also is a nontradable, it seems unlikely that the figures for private tradables rises spuriously between 1986 and 1987 due to the change in the definition of the public sector.

Source: Calculations based on the household surveys of employment and unemployment for July of each year. For 1976–78, employment in agriculture was not available separately for basic grains and other products. We have estimated employment in basic grains for those years by assuming the same proportion of all agricultural workers were so engaged as in 1979.

employment may have been of relatively lower-skilled workers, whose behavior might indicate the degree of mobility of the higher skilled workers needed in the nontraditional export sectors. It is difficult to know how much or what sort of labor reallocation would be required for a given process of structural adjustment to be effective. Accordingly, one must consider direct evidence on impediments to mobility, including sector-specific wage rigidity and public policies that could increase the costs of mobility.

Sectoral Wages

The evolution of real wages in Costa Rica during the crisis period leaves no room for doubt that considerable downward flexibility exists in the short run, both on average and for each category that can be singled out. However, as real wages recovered rather quickly and mechanically, one could argue that long-run downward rigidity does exist. Efficient reallocation of labor is more likely to be impeded by rigidity of relative wages between sectors, so testing for such rigidity is important, if possible in both the short and the longer run. In assessing potential relative wage rigidity across trade-related sectors, the details of wage setting processes are of obvious relevance, together with statistical evidence on wage and earnings trends for workers in those categories. Evidence on formal-informal sector earnings gaps and how they have changed over time may be relevant to this question.

Gindling (1991) and Pollack and Uthoff (1986b) found wage differentials of 20 to 30 percent between the private formal and informal sectors and of 10 to 20 percent between the public formal and private formal sectors, after controlling for human capital characteristics and selectivity bias. The gap between private formal and informal sector wages for observationally identical individuals increased during the crisis when real wages were falling sharply, and then decreased (though perhaps not monotonically) between 1982 and 1985, when real wages were rising. Since informal sector wages fell more sharply during 1980–82 than formal sector wages, one could argue that the latter, however sharp their descent, were more "protected" from those of the informal sector at the height of the crisis than previously or subsequently. As the share of workers who fall in the formal category is higher in the nontradables (public and private together) than in the tradables sector (Gindling and Berry 1991), one might anticipate more rigidity in nontradables than in tradables wages, but such evidence permits only tentative hypotheses.

Public sector wages/salaries have, on average, been higher than those in the private formal sector for individuals with comparable human capital, and it would not have been surprising if they had fallen less during the crisis. The public sector is the only highly unionized one, and the government is in any case sensitive to the charge that it is not paying its workers a "just wage," a charge most likely to come from the politically powerful college educated group, most of whom work in the public sector. Unfortunately, the behavior of public sector wages during and after the crisis is unclear due to inconsistent pieces of evidence (Gindling and Berry 1991). It is clear that with job security high in the public sector, good working conditions, and other nonwage benefits, people would tend to think twice before leaving the public employ.

Meanwhile, the minimum wage system could affect the relative wages of the exportable, importable, and nontradable sectors either through differential adjustment or differential coverage, but Pollack and Uthoff (1986a) found no evidence of the former for 1976–82. Enforcement is at best partial among small firms of the informal sector, as reflected in the high share of salaried workers in agriculture (from which most exportables come) earning below the minimum wage.

While the background information on labor market institutions just reviewed provides some grounds for worry that sectoral wage rigidities could hamper adjustment, it needs to be complemented by direct evidence on wage patterns and trends. Household survey data reveal that average wages/earnings are lowest in the exportables sector, in the middle range for the importables and nontradables sectors, and highest in the public sector (Gindling and Berry 1991). The lower exportables sector wages could be due partly to their being less protected than those in the other sectors and/or to a lower average level of human capital. When one controls for human capital (see Gindling and Berry 1991) average pay remains lowest in the exportables sector, and although pay is, on average, higher in the public sector than in the importables and private nontradables sectors, it is not systematically or substantially so (tables 6.8 and 6.9). Although most of the difference in average pay between the public sector and the importables and private nontradables sectors is due to the higher average levels of experience and education of the former group, the gap between the exportables sector and the other three is not fully explained by such human capital differences. It must reflect either market segmentation or compensating nonmonetary benefits between the exportables sector (many of whose workers live in rural areas) and the rest of the economy.

Prior to 1980, real wages/earnings rose in all four of these sectors, whether one adjusts for changes in human capital or not. Between 1980 and 1982, wages (unadjusted for human capital) fell sharply in all sectors, but less in exportables and the public sector than elsewhere. Thus, paid wages in the importables and nontradables sectors were not at all inflexible either in absolute terms or relative to those in the exportables sector. Although due to data problems there is some ambiguity as to the trends in public sector pay, there is certainly no clear suggestion of downward rigidity.

In the period of wage increases since 1982, all sectors have gained significantly: all reached the 1980 level in either 1986 or 1987. The increases were fastest for importables and private nontradables, the two biggest losers during 1980–82. By 1987–88, the average wage differentials across the four sectors were almost identical to what they had been in 1979–80. Adjusting for changes in human capital all three of the other sectors had gained somewhat on exportables since 1982, and the 1979–80 differentials had been approximately restored here too.

Income Distribution, Poverty, and Unemployment

Income distribution in Costa Rica has traditionally been unequal, but substantially less so than in such countries as Brazil. Estimates of the Gini coefficient of household income (with households ranked by income, not per capita income) have typically fallen in the range

Table 6.8 Average Real Earnings and Real Wages by Trade-Related Sector, Controlling for Human Capital Characteristics, 1976–83, 1985, 1987–88 (July figures)

Sector	1976	1977	1978	1979	1980	1981	1982	1983	1985	1987	1988
Wages (1975 colones per hour) for all workers, including self-employed and owners											
Exportables					6.01	4.82	3.95	5.05	5.82	6.24	5.54
Importables					6.47	5.81	4.40	5.39	6.34	7.65	6.72
Private nontradables					7.23	5.94	4.93	5.65	6.95	7.88	7.45
Public					6.68	6.09	4.65	5.99	6.66	7.63	6.87
Wages of all workers as a proportion of those in exportables											
Exportables					1.00	1.00	1.00	1.00	1.00	1.00	1.00
Importables					1.08	1.20	1.12	1.07	1.09	1.23	1.21
Private nontradables					1.20	1.23	1.25	1.12	1.19	1.26	1.34
Public					1.11	1.26	1.18	1.19	1.14	1.22	1.24
Wages (1975 colones per hour) of paid workers											
Exportables	4.58	5.45	5.07	4.38	5.39	4.39	3.73	4.92	5.49	5.51	5.14
Importables	4.87	5.92	6.39	6.78	6.29	5.65	4.04	5.32	6.29	7.09	6.62
Private nontradables	4.99	5.88	5.86	6.47	6.53	5.32	4.12	5.07	6.08	7.36	6.62
Public	5.98	7.65	6.95	7.42	6.71	6.02	4.63	6.00	6.58	7.56	6.68
Wages of paid workers as a proportion of those in exportables											
Exportables	1.00	1.00	1.00	1.00	1.00	1.00	1.00	1.00	1.00	1.00	1.00
Importables	1.06	1.09	1.26	1.55	1.17	1.29	1.08	1.08	1.15	1.29	1.29
Private nontradables	1.09	1.08	1.16	1.48	1.21	1.21	1.11	1.03	1.11	1.33	1.29
Public	1.30	1.40	1.37	1.69	1.24	1.37	1.24	1.22	1.20	1.37	1.30

(Table continues on the following page.)

Table 6.8 (continued)

Sector	1976	1977	1978	1979	1980	1981	1982	1983	1985	1987	1988
Earnings (1975 colones per month) of all workers, including self-employed and owners											
Exportables					1,121.2	916.1	720.5	936.2	1,096.6	1,186.0	1,282.7
Importables					1,275.1	1,080.9	813.5	1,021.3	1,217.7	1,425.8	1,390.2
Private nontradables					1,388.8	1,119.5	879.8	1,054.8	1,324.6	1,481.2	1,368.6
Public					1,331.1	1,207.5	915.3	1,156.5	1,295.0	1,478.8	1,356.2
Earnings of all workers as a proportion of those in exportables											
Exportables					1.00	1.00	1.00	1.00	1.00	1.00	1.00
Importables					1.14	1.18	1.13	1.09	1.11	1.20	1.08
Private nontradables					1.24	1.22	1.22	1.13	1.21	1.25	1.07
Public					1.19	1.32	1.27	1.24	1.18	1.25	1.06
Earnings (1975 colones per month) of paid workers											
Exportables	838.2	1,003.8	988.7	804.1	1,064.5	868.1	667.0	938.5	1,072.4	1,099.5	1,072.9
Importables	1,006.6	1,247.3	1,330.1	1,388.3	1,279.6	1,104.9	801.7	1,044.0	1,239.4	1,441.9	1,329.0
Private nontradables	986.7	1,164.8	1,160.1	1,252.8	1,269.4	1,017.0	750.3	976.3	1,095.5	1,431.8	1,279.3
Public	1,159.0 / 1,322.9	1,473.8	1,366.9	1,421.1	1,329.7	1,186.9	902.1	1,148.4	1,273.4		1,453.6
Earnings of paid workers as a proportion of those in exports											
Exportables	1.00	1.00	1.00	1.00	1.00	1.00	1.00	1.00	1.00	1.00	1.00
Importables	1.20	1.24	1.35	1.73	1.20	1.27	1.20	1.11	1.16	1.31	1.24
Private nontradables	1.18	1.16	1.17	1.56	1.19	1.17	1.12	1.04	1.02	1.30	1.19
Public	1.38	1.47	1.38	1.77	1.25	1.37	1.35	1.22	1.19	1.32	1.23

Wages (1975 colones per hour) of all workers, including self-employed and owners, as a proportion of average wages										
Exportables	0.86	0.85	0.80	0.90	0.85	0.87	0.91	0.89	0.84	0.82
Importables	0.91	0.92	1.01	0.97	1.02	0.97	0.98	0.97	1.03	1.00
Private nontradables	0.94	0.91	0.93	1.08	1.05	1.09	1.02	1.07	1.06	1.11
Public	1.12	1.19	1.10	1.00	1.07	1.03	1.08	1.02	1.03	1.02
Wages of all workers as a proportion of average wages										
Exportables			0.71	0.86	0.83	0.91	0.93	0.90	0.80	0.82
Importables			1.10	1.01	1.07	0.99	1.01	1.03	1.03	1.05
Private nontradables			1.05	1.05	1.01	1.01	0.96	1.00	1.07	1.05
Public			1.20	1.08	1.14	1.13	1.14	1.08	1.09	1.06
Earnings (1975 colones per month) of paid workers as a proportion of average earnings										
Exportables	0.81	0.79	0.79	0.87	0.85	0.87	0.90	0.88	0.85	0.95
Importables	0.97	0.99	1.06	0.99	1.00	0.98	0.98	0.98	1.02	1.03
Private nontradables	0.95	0.92	0.92	1.08	1.04	1.06	1.01	1.06	1.06	1.01
Public	1.12	1.17	1.09	1.03	1.12	1.10	1.11	1.04	1.06	1.00
Earnings of paid workers as a proportion of average earnings										
Exportables			0.67	0.86	0.84	0.87	0.92	0.93	0.81	0.86
Importables			1.16	1.04	1.07	1.05	1.03	1.07	1.06	1.06
Private nontradables			1.05	1.03	0.99	0.98	0.96	0.95	1.05	1.02
Public			1.19	1.08	1.15	1.18	1.13	1.10	1.07	1.06

Source: Calculated from wage and earnings equations estimated for each sector using the average values of education, experience, and log of hours worked for each year. Nominal real wages and earnings (excluding fringe benefits) are deflated by the July San José cost of living index for lower- and middle-income families.

Table 6.9 Wage and Earnings Equations, 1976–83, 1985, 1987–88

Sector	1976	1977	1978	1979	1980	1981	1982	1983	1985	1987	1988
Hourly wages as dependent variable, paid workers only											
Intercept	-0.1136	0.001252	-0.11565	0.09484	0.2871	0.3671	0.7327	1.3817	1.915	2.284	2.5026
Education	0.114	0.1052	0.1485	0.1426	0.1348	0.1382	0.1341	0.1151	0.1146	0.1147	0.123
Experience	0.03572	0.05485	0.05637	0.05111	0.0505	0.05362	0.05327	0.04881	0.14297	0.0428	0.03911
Experience squared	-0.00036	-0.00073	-0.00070	-0.00062	-0.00063	-0.00065	-0.00064	-0.00059	-0.00050	-0.00051	-0.00045
Sex	0.2847	0.3275	0.2886	0.353	0.3318	0.3101	0.3416	0.3407	0.25855	0.2696	0.1945
R-Squared	0.28	0.43	0.46	0.462	0.472	0.459	0.421	0.379	0.4055	0.2632	0.356
Monthly earnings as dependent variable, paid workers only											
Intercept	4.1944	3.0631	2.8634	2.9932	3.1971	3.4728	3.9097	4.413	5.0388	5.321	5.306
Education	0.1321	0.1054	0.1463	0.1408	0.13325	0.1334	0.13	0.1116	0.1098	0.116	0.1148
Experience	0.04332	0.05928	0.05949	0.05403	0.048835	0.0504	0.05498	0.0485	0.045	0.04651	0.04252
Experience squared	-0.00050	-0.00080	-0.00076	-0.00067	-0.00059	-0.00060	-0.00065	-0.00060	-0.00054	-0.00058	-0.00052
Sex	0.2998	0.3486	0.3165	0.3713	0.3627	0.347	0.3874	0.3951	0.2846	0.3284	0.2691
Log of Hours	0.2319	0.5646	0.5937	0.6136	0.6173	0.5743	0.5391	0.5828	0.5623	0.5601	0.6199
R-Squared	0.327	0.499	0.515	0.526	0.494	0.497	0.45	0.426	0.42	0.3674	0.372

Hourly wages as dependent variable, all workers

Intercept	0.3437	0.4845	0.8232	1.474	1.989	2.171	2.503
Education	0.1325	0.1314	0.1277	0.1079	0.1091	0.121	0.113
Experience	0.04643	0.04756	0.05	0.04579	0.04183	0.0464	0.03911
Experience squared	-0.00055	-0.00055	-0.00056	-0.00055	-0.00048	-0.00055	-0.00045
Sex	0.3217	0.2966	0.3308	0.3474	0.2397	0.3133	0.1945
R-Squared	0.4021	0.386	0.332	0.299	0.319	0.3701	0.251

Monthly earnings as dependent variable, all workers

Intercept	3.1686	3.307	3.598	4.245	4.9812	4.978	5.0879
Education	0.1341	0.1383	0.1352	0.1171	0.11402	0.1212	0.1188
Experience	0.05271	0.05641	0.0577	0.05175	0.04586	0.04874	0.04547
Experience squared	-0.00067	-0.00070	-0.00071	-0.00064	-0.00055	-0.00057	-0.00055
Sex	0.3488	0.3356	0.3626	0.3663	0.2734	0.3395	0.2806
Log of Hours	0.6189	0.5973	0.6092	0.6121	0.5677	0.6337	0.6644
R-Squared	0.531	0.534	0.519	0.482	0.481	0.4612	0.448

Note: In all cases the natural logarithm of the dependent variable is used. All coefficients are significant at 1 percent.
Source: Household surveys of employment and unemployment.

0.43–0.50.[5] Some authors suspect that income distribution was worsening during the crisis years of the early 1980s (for example, Trejos and Elizalde 1986), but no reliable data are available to clarify the changes in household distribution at this time. The distribution of income among earners (substantially less unequal than that among households, with Gini's usually in the range 0.35–0.40), can be traced more successfully. They suggest little change during 1976–80, possibly a mild worsening during 1980–82, and then a rather marked improvement in the next two years (CEPAL 1987, table 6.1). As for the key period of macroeconomic crisis, although the earner data indicate some worsening, some less solid household data suggest the opposite, so the case cannot be considered closed on this point.[6] The marked increase in nonhousehold heads as a share of employed workers would by itself produce some worsening in the earner distribution, but might simultaneously improve household distribution. (Our figures, however, show a higher share of household labor income coming from household heads in 1982 and 1983 than in earlier or later years. The reason for this apparent anomaly is not clear.) The sharp drop in real wages in the formal and public sectors during the crisis would be expected to lower labor income most sharply for the deciles toward the middle and the top of the distribution. As those incomes rebounded in later years, the shares move back up again. Since none of the trends suggested by the data can be accepted with great confidence, one cannot rule out the possibility that household distribution worsened during 1980–82. In particular, the capital share would have risen at this time, implying an increasing concentration that would go unrecognized in data that either does not include at all or seriously understates capital incomes.

All sources that have measured poverty trends during the crisis show the expected sharp increase during 1980–82, with recovery in

---

5. Most surveys exclude nonlabor income, and thus understate income inequality, but two (1971 national level, and 1974 urban level), which aimed at inclusion of all incomes and whose underreporting seems to have been relatively small, produced Gini coefficients of around 0.45 (CEPAL 1987, tables 4, 5.1, and 5.2).

6. Altimir (1984) reports a decline in the Gini coefficient among households (ranked by per capita income) from 0.376 to 0.346 between July 1979 and June 1982, with significant share increases for each of the bottom deciles (from 2.0 to 2.6 for the lowest deciles).

later years back to or near the turn of decade figures. It is of interest to know which households defended themselves best at this time, and how the safety nets in place in Costa Rica performed. With a relatively high poverty line (188 1980 colones per capita per month in urban areas and 166 in rural areas), the incidence of poverty among households rose from 48 percent in 1980 to 78 percent in 1982, then fell back to about 45 percent by 1987–88. The increase was very similar for female- and for male-headed households, with poverty incidence typically 10 to 15 percentage points higher for the former. Incidence rose much less than average for households headed by self-employed people, whereas in 1980, the incidence was much higher than for households headed by paid workers (56 percent to 40 percent). At the peak of the crisis in 1982, the figures were identical at 72 percent. Thereafter a gap reappeared, though smaller (6 to 8 percentage points in 1986–88). Possibly the incomes of self-employed heads of households fell less than those of paid workers; we know that the latter fell very sharply.

Prior to the crisis, unemployment was low, averaging under 5 percent nationally each year during 1976–79. It was heavily concentrated among younger workers. Persons with a high school education had the highest unemployment rate, while those with no education or a college education had the lowest rates. The female rate exceeded that for men, and nonhousehold heads suffered a higher rate than heads of households. The crisis raised unemployment rates for all groups, but most notably for household heads and for men (substantially overlapping groups). As noted earlier, the crisis saw an increase in the labor force share of secondary family workers (nonhousehold heads), making it striking that this group's share of unemployment fell. These various trends reversed themselves with the recovery and structural adjustment. The underemployment rate took a year or so longer than the (open) unemployment rate to return to precrisis levels (table 6.4).

Public Expenditure on Education and Other Social Services

Public spending on education fell sharply in real terms during the economic crisis (35 percent between 1980 and 1982 when current price spending is deflated by the GDP deflator). With the upturn spending has recovered somewhat, though the 1987/88 average was still 15 percent below the 1980 level. The drop in spending on education was not translated into a fall in education services, at least as far as the available data indicate. The number of educational institutions and the staff at the Ministry of Public Education continued to grow, albeit more slowly than before 1980. Real public spending on education fell initially because salary levels fell during the economic crisis, reflecting the fall in real salaries in the economy as a whole. Public spending on materials, machinery, buildings, and capital have also fallen dramatically since 1980, explaining the continued fall in total expenditures during the period of economic recovery. If not reversed, this trend will sooner or later have negative consequences on the quality of education in Costa Rica (Gindling and Berry 1991).

Stabilization and structural adjustment influence the effective demand for education as well as the supply. During the crisis years from 1980 to 1983, total enrollment in formal schooling decreased instead of recording the expected increase (Gindling and Berry 1991). The most striking decrease, 24 percent in secondary enrollment between 1980 and 1985, was probably due in part to former or potential secondary and technical school students entering the labor force as secondary workers to help maintain family incomes.

The reduction in overall government spending brought a decrease in spending on most social programs, both in absolute terms and as a proportion of the GNP. Spending on health declined sharply from its 1980 high. As with education, the decrease was not reflected in a large immediate decline in the level of health services, although there were declines in some services (days in hospital, number of consultations) and in the number of health care establishments in 1982.[7] However, investment in equipment and buildings fell in the face of the need to meet day-to-day costs, so the major effects of the decline in overall health spending will probably be felt only after a lag.

---

7. Days spent in hospital may have fallen for exogenous reasons. The drop in the number of health care establishments was primarily due to a drop in temporary health centers (mobile units and *puestos de salud*).

Women and the Crisis

Women accounted for about 25 percent of the Costa Rican work force at the beginning of the 1980s and probably closer to 30 percent by 1988 (table 6.4). Most of the rise was probably the result of secular forces, but the crisis years did seem to produce a slightly faster than normal increase. The male/female earnings differential increased with the economic crisis and then fell with the recovery. However, Gindling (forthcoming) argues that this decrease in women's relative earnings was due primarily to the lower educational level (and correspondingly lower earnings) of new entrants than of women already in the work force. After the recession, the earnings differential fell back to its previous level, and appeared to be continuing its downward secular trend.

By entering the labor force during the recession, women helped to shore up falling family incomes. New labor force entrants seemed to find jobs at least as easily as men, judging from the fact that the female share of unemployment fell even as their share of the labor force was rising (Gindling forthcoming).

Conclusion

Costa Rica's recovery from the sharp downturn of 1980–82 has been relatively good, with output, wages, and unemployment recovering to precrisis levels faster than in many other countries. The net resource inflow to Costa Rica (imports of goods and nonfactor services minus exports of goods and nonfactor services) fell from over 10 percent of GNP in 1978–80 to about 1 percent during 1983–88 taken as a whole. The fiscal situation was greatly improved and inflation brought down to about 15 percent or below from 1984 on. The gross fixed investment ratio, after falling from its very high level of about 25 percent in 1980 (constant 1966 prices) to 15 percent in 1982, gradually climbed back up to average a little over 20 percent during 1986–88 (table 6.3). All this suggests that the Costa Rican model for stabilization, adjustment, and recovery was a good one.

Success, if that is what it is, has, of course, not come without a price. All wages fell sharply, in most cases by 25 to 40 percent during the crisis years 1980–82. Tradables sector wages fell by about the same amount as those in the nontradables sector. Unemployment and poverty incidence rose for all groups, but less for female-headed households and for households headed by self-employed workers than for other groups. Secondary workers entered the labor force in significant numbers, and did not appear to have unusual difficulties in getting jobs. Enrollment in secondary schools fell markedly. However, the crisis was not drawn out. Real wages recovered quickly to precrisis highs by 1987, unemployment and underemployment returned to precrisis lows, and primary and university enrollments resumed their upward trends. Secondary enrollment, however, remained far below the 1980 level.

For some time the main doubt was whether enough structural adjustment had taken place to permit sustained growth. The initial balance of payments adjustment came mainly via the sharp curtailment of imports, whose 1985–86 average was still 16 percent below that of the peak years 1978–80. By 1987–88 they exceeded the 1978–80 level by 18 percent. The level of exports (of goods and nonfactor services) rose by under 10 percent between local peaks in 1979 and 1986, but a boom in 1987–88 put the 1988 figure 42 percent above that of 1979. The brightest spot on the export front has been the rapid growth during the recovery of nontraditional, non-CACM exports, a growth that more than offset the sharp reduction in the latter category, at least in terms of gross foreign exchange revenues. By the late 1980s, therefore, there were grounds for optimism that the trade imbalance was on its way to being brought under control.

Note that taking the postcrisis period as a whole, adjustment of the balance of payments was not sought by the broad price incentive of a sustained high exchange rate. Though the 1980 devaluation was sharp, the real exchange rate eroded fairly quickly, so that by the latter half of the 1980s it was at about the same level as in the mid-1970s. A main push was provided by incentives to nontraditional exports, and as noted earlier, these have become the dynamic component of exports.

Given the record of low national savings, the generation of high domestic investment without the large foreign savings inflows of the 1970s was destined to be a serious challenge. Here too the outcome thus far is encouraging. The national savings rate, which averaged just

13 percent during the 1970s, exceeded 20 percent during 1986–88 (table 6.3).

An interesting question is whether the rapid return to relatively high wages discouraged overall labor absorption. The evidence from the unemployment rate suggests not. Indeed, it may be that the quick recovery of real wages contributed to the smooth macroeconomic recovery by keeping aggregate demand up. On the question of whether wage setting procedures discouraged intersectoral mobility, taking an adequate reading is harder. Public sector wage policies do appear to have pushed wages in that sector above those of the private sector (for comparable workers) and differential enforcement of minimum wage laws does presumably contribute to the wage gap between the formal private sector and the informal sector. However, these factors certainly did not prevent wages in the protected sectors from falling sharply in response to the devaluation/stabilization events of 1980–82, nor greatly widen the wage gap in relation to the relatively unprotected exportables sector workers. The quick and complete wage recovery is probably due mainly to these institutional mechanisms. The fact that recovery was as complete in the less protected as in the more protected sectors does not mean that the "protective" wage institutions were unimportant. In Costa Rica, social resistance to low wages appears to be greater than in many other countries, so informal sector wage movements might follow those of the formal sector more than in most countries.

We have found no evidence that wages in the importables, nontradables, or public sectors are inflexible relative to those in the exportables sector, nor that labor mobility across sectors was seriously limited. Some data suggest that the flexibility of relative wages and the mobility of workers in the aftermath of the devaluation was particularly marked during 1980–82, though given the lack of direct information, there is inevitable ambiguity on these points.

It is ironic that the institutions designed to limit downward wage flexibility in Costa Rica not only were ineffective during 1980–82 because the mechanisms were not designed to deal with rapidly accelerating inflation, but that they may have facilitated the wage declines by making them an automatic result of those impersonal mechanisms. Any surmise as to the effect of the institutions depends, however, on one's interpretation of how decisionmakers use the existing mechanisms, and what political pressures they are subjected to.

If Costa Rica continues on a satisfactory growth path for a few more years, its crisis management and adjustment strategies will have been judged successful. Several factors have probably contributed. Perhaps the most general has been a relatively satisfactory sharing of the burden of crisis/adjustment such that no groups remained so disgruntled as to pursue highly disruptive tactics. Strong political leadership at a crucial time (1982–86) by an individual with a prolabor history but a recognition of the need for belt-tightening may have been important here. Also of note was the decline of union influence since 1980, both in the private sector, where it was never strong, and in the public sector. That this decline created no more of a furor than it did may be associated with the rapid recovery of real wages, and it is not clear in the context of the Costa Rican institutions that produced that wage recovery that the unions' weakness was an important contributor to adjustment. The rapid real wage recovery may have prevented some potential negative multiplier effects that might otherwise have prolonged or deepened the crisis.

Another special feature was the country's small size. This may have made it easier to enter new foreign markets, and certainly facilitated access to foreign aid. Perhaps the over 25 percent fall in per capita absorption between 1980 and 1982, coming off a peak only achieved for a few years, eased the trauma. Total absorption in 1982 was the same as in 1976, and absorption per capita was only 16 percent lower and private consumption per capita only 11 percent lower.

On the trade side, the absence of a worsening of the terms of trade during the crisis/adjustment period was a bit of luck, given the sharp fluctuations experienced in the 1970s. In terms of policy, the use of special incentives to chosen categories of exports may have been both an efficient way to stimulate exports and an approach to minimize social costs, if a more devalued exchange rate would have either promoted a higher rate of inflation or tended to push real wages lower.

The broad question that emerges from the Costa Rican experience is whether it provides a valuable model to be pursued by other countries in comparable situations. Certainly the outcome was better than most. It is not yet clear which among the relatively good access to foreign finance, the considerable social consensus, the sharp decline but sharp recovery of real wages, the targeted support for new types of exports, or the quick action on the fiscal problem after 1982 were central to the relative success achieved. When the effect of each of these factors has been better sorted out, the policy implications of this case will hopefully come into focus.

References

Altimir, Oscar. 1984. "Poverty, Income Distribution and Child Welfare in Latin America: A Comparison of Pre- and Post-Recession Data." *World Development* 12(3):261–282.

Bourguignon, François. 1986. "Income Distribution and External Trade: The Case of Costa Rica." Paris. Processed.

Carillo C., Mario Alberta. 1988. "Las formas de financiamiento estatal en el desarrollo económico reciente de Costa Rica." Working Document No. 117. Instituto de investigaciones en Ciencia Economica.

Celis, R., and E. Lizano. 1990. "Development in Costa Rica: The Key Role of Agriculture." Paper prepared for the IFRRI Conference of Agriculture and the Road to Industrialization, Taipei.

CENPRO (Centro de la Provición de Exportaciones). 1986. "Analisis del Potential de Exportaciones no Tradicionales de Costa Rica." San José. Processed.

CEPAL (Comisión Económica para America Latina). 1987. *Antecedentes Estadisticos de la Distribución del Ingreso en Costa Rica: 1958–1982.* Santiago, Chile: United Nations.

Cespedes, Victor Hugo, Runolfo Jiminez, and Alberta DiMare. 1985. *Costa Rica: Recuperación sin Reactivación.* San José: Academia de Centroamerica.

Donato, M. Elisa, and B. Manuel Rojas. 1987. *Sindicatos Politica y Economia: 1972–1976.* San José: Editorial Alma Mater.

ECLA. Various years. *Statistical Yearbook for Latin America and the Caribbean.*

Gindling, T. H. 1989a. "Crisis economica y segmentación en el mercado de trabajo urbano de Costa Rica." *Revista de Ciencias Economicas* (University of Costa Rica) 9(1): 77–93.

_____. 1989b. "Women, Earnings and Economic Crisis in Costa Rica." Paper presented at the International Congress of the Latin American Studies Association, Miami, December.

_____. 1991. "An Investigation into Labor Market Segmentation: The Case of San José, Costa Rica." *Economic Development and Cultural Change* 39(3): 585–606.

_____. Forthcoming. "Women, Earnings and Economic Crisis in Costa Rica." *Economic Development and Cultural Change.*

Gindling, T. H., and Albert Berry. 1991. *The Labor Market in Successful Adjustment: Costa Rica.* Processed.

Gonzalez-Vega, Claudio. 1984. "Fear of Adjusting: The Social Costs of Economic Policies in Costa Rica in the 1970's." In Donald Schulz and Douglas Graham, eds., *Revolution and Counterrevolution in Central America and The Caribbean*, pp. 351–384. Boulder, Colorado: Westview Press.

Latin American and Caribbean Contemporary Record. 1983. New York: Holmes and Meier.

Nelson, Joan. 1989. "Crisis Management, Economic Reform, and Costa Rican Democracy." In Barbara Stallings and Robert Kaufman, eds., *Debt and Democracy in Latin America,* pp. 143–162. Boulder, Colorado: Westview Press.

Pollack, M., A. Uthoff. 1986a. "Wages and Price Dynamics in Costa Rica: 1976–1983." Monograph on Employment No. 51, Santiago, Chile: PREALC/ECIEL.

_____. 1986b. "Inflación, salario minimo y salarios nominales 1976–1983." *Revista de Ciencias Economicas* (University of Costa Rica) 6(1): 57–78.

Rivera Urrutia, Eugenio, Ana Sojo, and José Roberto Lopez. 1986. *Centroamerica: Politica Economica y Crisis.* San José: Editorial DEI.

Rodriguez V., Adrian. 1987. "La deuda pública externa de Costa Rica: Cresimiento, moratoria y renegociación." *Revista de Ciencias Economicas* (University of Costa Rica) 7(2):12–35.

Seligson, Mitchell, and Edward Muller. 1987. "Democratic Stability and Economic Crisis: Costa Rica, 1977–1983." *International Studies Quarterly* 31: 301–326.

Trejos, Juan Diego, and Maria Laura Elizalde. 1986. "Ingreso, desigualdad y empleo: Evidencias recientes sobre las caracteristicas y evolucion del perfil distributivo en Costa Rica." *Revista de Ciencias Economicas* 6(2): 87–104.

World Bank. 1977. "Economic Positions and Prospects of Costa Rica." Report No. 1666–CR. Washington, D.C.

_____. 1988. "Costa Rica: Country Economic Memorandum." Report No. 7481–CR. Washington, D.C.

_____. Various years. *World Debt Tables.* Washington, D.C.

7

CÔTE D'IVOIRE

Richard Blundell
Christopher Heady
Rohinton Medhora

The Government of Côte d'Ivoire introduced a structural adjustment program in 1981 in response to the growing balance of payments and budget deficits. By 1980, the balance of payments deficit on current account had reached 17.4 percent of GDP and the budget deficit had reached 11.9 percent of GDP. This situation represented a severe deterioration from five years earlier, when the corresponding figures were 8.2 percent and 2.2 percent, and was accompanied by a rapid increase in external indebtedness.

A major cause of these deficits was an increase in public expenditure, particularly investment, that was stimulated by the revenues generated in the coffee and cocoa boom of 1975–77, but was financed by foreign borrowing after the boom ended. The balance of payments situation was aggravated by inflation that was more rapid than in Côte d'Ivoire's main trading partners. This was particularly serious because Côte d'Ivoire is a member of the Western Africa Monetary Union (UMOA), and so cannot independently devalue its currency.

The aims and instruments of the structural adjustment program are set out in the statements of development policy that the government produced in the context of each of the three World Bank structural adjustment loans (1981, 1983, and 1986). The overall strategy was

The authors would like to thank Rob Alessie, Paul Baker, Paul Glewwe, Costas Meghir, John Newman, Valerie Kozel, and K. Yao and the editors for many helpful comments, and Tindara Addabbo for excellent research assistance.

first to eliminate the large deficits and then to restructure the economy with a shift toward the traded sector.

The elimination of the deficits—the stabilization phase—was achieved mainly by a dramatic cut in public investment, from 11.6 percent of GDP in 1980 to 3.2 percent in 1985, and a freeze of public and minimum wages. By 1985, both deficits had been turned into small surpluses, but at the cost of a severe recession: from 1980 to 1984, per capita GDP fell by 26.2 percent and per capita private consumption fell by 22.6 percent (Glewwe and de Tray 1988).

The stabilization phase took place in the context of favorable international economic developments. The U.S. dollar and several other currencies appreciated relative to the franc, allowing firms to increase exports at a time of depressed domestic demand. The main goals of the restructuring program were to reduce government support for inefficient sectors of the economy, increase the relative prices of traded goods, and shift the internal terms of trade in favor of the rural sector. Unfortunately, the international economic environment had changed by 1985, and the CFA franc increased in value against the currencies of its main trading partners. This counteracted some of the policies that were intended to enlarge the economy's traded sector.

Another difficulty that inhibited restructuring was the severe shortage of credit that developed. Lorch (1989) reports that medium- and long-term loans to modern manufacturing enterprises declined by 42 percent between 1984 and 1987. This was compounded by the state's policy of paying suppliers only when it wanted to place the next order.

In the light of these adverse circumstances, it is not surprising that the restructuring phase was not as successful as the stabilization phase. However, some evidence indicates that the losses of public enterprises are being brought under control (World Bank 1987). The government has also introduced some policies to alter incentives. The measures used to increase the relative prices of traded goods were changes in tariffs and an export subsidy scheme aimed at producing a uniform rate of effective protection (about 40 percent) for manufactured goods. This was essentially an attempt to mimic a devaluation, but it was partly offset from 1985 to 1988 by the appreciation of the CFA franc.

The government planned to redress the urban-rural imbalance by holding down wages in the urban areas while increasing agricultural prices. Some evidence suggests that urban real wages did decline around 20 percent, and although many of the increases in agricultural prices did no more than keep up with inflation, there is also evidence of a 10 percent increase in the relative price of traded goods (Berthelemy and Bourgignon 1989, p. 424).

Most of the analysis in this chapter deals separately with the urban and rural areas of Côte d'Ivoire. There are two main reasons for this separate analysis. First, the structural adjustment program had a much greater direct impact on the urban areas, which include virtually all the manufacturing sector. Second, the structure of the labor markets, the returns to education and experience, and data availability in the two sectors are very different.

The Macroeconomics of Côte d'Ivoire

As a member of the franc zone, Côte d'Ivoire's recent macroeconomic history and experience with adjustment make it an interesting country to study. By belonging to the UMOA, one of the two monetary unions in francophone Africa, Côte d'Ivoire enjoys certain privileges and operates under certain institutional and historical constraints that most developing countries do not.

The UMOA is a complete monetary union that has evolved, since independence in the early 1960s, from France's colonial governing institutions in its African territories. Membership in the UMOA is fluid. Today, Benin, Burkina Faso, Côte d'Ivoire, Mali, Niger, Senegal, and Togo belong. Mauritania left the union in 1973. Mali joined in 1984 and the possibility now exists that other, nonfrancophone countries might join. "Completeness" involves having a common currency (the CFA franc) issued by a common central bank (Banque Centrale des Etats de l'Afrique de l'Ouest [BCEAO]), and partially pooled international reserves. The link with France is in the form of a fixed exchange rate with the French franc (CFAF 50 = F 1 since 1948), a guarantee of convertibility of the CFA franc by the French Treasury, and French representation in the policy decisions and operations of the BCEAO. (For a more detailed and analytical account of the UMOA see Bhatia 1985; Guillaumont 1984; Medhora 1989; Neurrisse 1987; Vinay 1980.)

Thus, other things (such as export price shocks and world interest rate changes) being equal, Côte d'Ivoire's membership in the UMOA may give it certain advantages in dealing with crises. By not having complete control over the common central bank, monetary policy may be less subject to political pressure. By having access to its partners' international reserves, country-specific short-term balance of payments problems can be smoothed over. The foreign exchange constraint is made even less onerous by the French guarantee of convertibility: in practice a promise by the French Treasury to augment, at a small cost and without explicitly stated conditions, the union's pooled reserves maintained in an operations account in Paris.

However, none of these factors were enough to prevent Côte d'Ivoire from sharing in the developing countries' economic malaise of the late 1970s, leading to the use of World Bank and IMF resources, debt rescheduling, and being classified by the World Bank as a severely indebted middle-income country.[1] We argue that the UMOA's structure was not equipped to deal with the types of shocks that its largest member faced, and that membership limited the policy options available to implement structural adjustment programs.

By African standards, Côte d'Ivoire's postindependence economic history has been enviable, with rising standards of living and low inflation rates (table 7.1). An open trade regime, risk free foreign investment (due to the unchanged parity and guarantee of convertibility), and free movement of factors of production within the union made the Côte d'Ivoire paradigm receive much favorable attention in textbooks on planning.[2]

Through most of the 1970s, the level of economic activity was driven by growing public outlays in the form of investment and

---

1. A severely indebted middle-income country is defined as one with a debt:GNP ratio above 50 percent, a debt:exports ratio above 275 percent, an accrued debt service:exports ratio above 30 percent, and an accrued interest:exports ratio above 20 percent.

2. Devarajan and de Melo (1987) find that for the period 1960–82, and especially for the subperiod 1973–82, the franc zone countries had GNP growth rates that compare favorably to those of other countries, especially other Sub-Saharan African countries. They attribute this to membership in the franc zone.

Table 7.1 Basic Economic Indicators, 1970–87

Year	GNP per capita (current US$)	Public investment (CFAF billions)	Inflation[a] (%)	Real GDP (CFAF billions, 1980 prices)	Industrial production[b] (1985=100)	Real investment[c] (1986=100)
1970	270	n.a.	9.4	n.a.	24.0	n.a.
1975	500	6.0	11.4	1,491.7	47.8	58.4
1976	580	11.0	12.1	1,670.7	59.7	100.1
1977	670	64.4	27.4	1,749.3	69.5	207.6
1978	820	108.8	13.0	1,922.5	80.0	320.6
1979	980	78.5	16.6	2,022.4	82.3	259.7
1980	1,170	32.7	14.7	2,149.9	94.8	143.3
1981	1,130	23.1	8.8	2,179.9	95.7	113.8
1982	960	16.4	7.3	2,245.4	105.1	76.4
1983	760	15.4	5.9	2,045.6	89.5	72.3
1984	660	24.7	4.3	n.a.	97.0	78.8
1985	630	24.4	1.8	n.a.	100.0	76.8
1986	700	25.7	7.3	n.a.	108.1	100.0
1987	750	13.3	0.4	n.a.	108.1	78.6

n.a. = not available
a. The inflation rate is for the consumer price index rate of change.
b. The industrial production index includes the mining, manufacturing, and energy sectors.
c. The real investment index excludes the petroleum refining sector.
Sources: GNP: World Bank (various years); investment: Lorch (1989); inflation and industrial production: IMF (various years).

government consumption and buoyant prices for the country's principal exports, coffee and cocoa. During the decade, government consumption expenditures grew sixfold (table 7.2), and public investment grew from CFAF 5.1 billion in 1974 to CFAF 78.5 billion in 1979. Total real investment quadrupled between 1975 and 1979, industrial production quadrupled between 1970 and 1981, while real GDP rose 40 percent between 1975 and 1981.

During the 1970s, Côte d'Ivoire shared in the boom brought about by high coffee and cocoa prices. Although some of the dollar gains in these prices were tempered by the strength of the French franc against the U.S. dollar, even in CFAF terms, export unit values had more than

Table 7.2 Investment, Government Expenditure, and Trade, 1970–87

Year	Gross fixed capital formation (CFAF billions)	Government consumption (CFAF billions)	Terms of trade (1985 = 100)	Current account (US$ millions)
1970	83.9	64.9	n.a.	-37.9
1975	199.4	141.8	83.6	-379.0
1976	247.2	180.3	120.1	-249.3
1977	397.7	209.7	151.8	-177.3
1978	529.0	290.4	126.4	-839.3
1979	526.7	353.8	123.4	-1,383.3
1980	523.6	362.4	104.3	-1,826.5
1981	558.4	403.6	88.1	-1,411.4
1982	539.5	449.4	90.3	-1,017.3
1983	527.7	463.6	95.5	-931.2
1984	352.6	448.6	104.0	-58.2
1985	359.3	437.1	100.0	63.6
1986	386.2	491.7	108.0	-138.4
1987	n.a.	n.a.	95.4	n.a.

n.a. = not available
Sources: Same as table 7.1.

tripled between 1970 and the peak year, 1977. To be sure, the oil shocks of the 1970s had contributed to a rise in the price of imports, but in 1977, Côte d'Ivoire's terms of trade stood at their highest historic value (table 7.2).

The crunch began in 1978 with a collapse in the price of coffee, followed, three years later, by a fall in cocoa prices. There was no similar let-up in import prices or volume, so that the current account, which had always been negative (but manageable), worsened considerably between 1977 and 1980. By the early 1980s, the international reserves accumulated during the boom years had fallen sharply.

It is during times like these that membership in the UMOA is supposed to ease the strain, via access to pooled reserves, and ultimately, the French Treasury. However, given the circumstances, these arrangements could not have insulated Côte d'Ivoire from external events. The collapse in raw materials prices was universal, and also affected the other members of the union, notably Senegal. So was the rise in oil prices. With most members (and certainly the two largest) in distress at the same time, reserve pooling, by its very nature, will not work. Instead, in 1980 the overdraft facility with the French Treasury was used for the first time. What had previously been a guarantee on paper in the statutes governing the BCEAO and its relations with the French authorities was now being tested.

In principle, a crisis management scheme is supposed to be implemented when the BCEAO's external reserves fall for three consecutive months to less than 20 percent of its short-term liabilities. That threshold was crossed in mid-1980, at which point the statutes require the governor of the BCEAO to meet with the Council of Administration, review the situation, and take all appropriate measures; however, what these measures should be is not spelled out. Whether the BCEAO has all the powers needed to act in a situation such as this is not clear. Although the BCEAO's discussions with the French authorities are usually confidential, there is little doubt that the lack of explicitly stated conditionality on the use of the overdraft facility led the French to advise Côte d'Ivoire to do what every other country in its circumstance did: approach the World Bank and the IMF.

Thus, membership in the UMOA can smooth out short-run, isolated, country-specific external shocks. But in the face of a shock common to all members, coupled with largely autonomous fiscal policies, membership confers no special privileges on the countries. However, membership does affect the implementation of a structural adjustment program, as discussed next.

Structural Adjustment

As stated earlier, World Bank/IMF-supervised structural adjustment in Côte d'Ivoire has seen roughly two phases. The first started in 1981, and the priority here was stabilization. The second evolved during 1985, is ongoing, and has the longer-term goal of restructuring, and ultimately, sustainable growth.

Stabilization meant curtailing public spending and depreciating the real exchange rate, but without the aid of a nominal devaluation. This makes the literature on devaluation—especially the debate on whether a devaluation will be contradictory or not—a moot point (for a recent review of the literature see the contributions of Arida and Taylor and Edwards and van Wijnbergen to Chenery and Srinivasan 1989). Rather, the discussion jumps to how else to stabilize. One possibility is the "classical" adjustment process, where aggregate expenditure is curtailed by sharp cuts in public spending. Another is to use fiscal proxies—such as tariffs and subsidies—to mimic a devaluation. Côte d'Ivoire has used both, with mixed results.

The monetary union and the free flow of capital within it precludes interest rate increases in one country only. Instead, a credit ceiling was imposed. Public gross fixed investment fell from 11.6 percent of GDP in 1980 to 3.2 percent in 1985, and investment in parastatals returned to preboom levels (Lorch 1989). Public sector and minimum wages were also frozen.

Crucial help came exogenously in the form of the strength of the U.S. dollar against the French franc between 1980 and 1984, as shown in table 7.3. The net result was a real effective exchange rate depreciation and an improved export performance. Between 1980 and 1984, the French franc halved in value with respect to the U.S. dollar, which accounted for about three-quarters of the 40 percent fall in the real effective exchange rate index.

The mild recovery in exports and production was reversed starting in 1986. Cocoa prices fell once more, as did the U.S. dollar, the currency appreciated again, and the economy was thrown into another recession.

Another feature of most structural adjustment programs is a nominal devaluation. While much of the structuralist literature comes out in favor of a tariff-subsidy scheme over nominal devaluation, this system has certain practical limitations.[3]

---

3. See Taylor (1981, 1983) for the potential effects of a contradictory devaluation. Islam (1984) shows that a tariff-subsidy scheme is preferable to a devaluation. Pegatienan Hiey's (1987) simulations show that a heterodox package that includes import quotas, tariffs, and easy money is less deflationary than an orthodox one that features absorption-reducing policies and tariff liberalization. Laker (1981) reviews the literature on fiscal proxies for devaluation in a historical context.

First, tariffs and subsidies are almost never uniform and universal, as would be necessary to mimic a devaluation perfectly. Capital account transactions will be exempt, and a dual or more exchange rate system is the more likely result. The danger of allocative inefficiencies, loopholes, and corruption then arises. Administering the system can introduce further corruption and delays in payments to exporters. Finally, export subsidies during structural adjustment may require a budgetary outlay at precisely the time when the government budget is under pressure.

If despite this such a system is put in place and run efficiently, there is always the risk that an exogenous event (such as French or American policies that affect their bilateral exchange rate) will wipe out—quickly and completely—the effects of tariffs and subsidies.

Table 7.3 Exchange Rates and Foreign Debt, 1970–87

Year	Real effective exchange rate index	Nominal effective exchange rate index	CFAF:$ index	Debt/X
1970	n.a.	n.a.	161.2	n.a.
1975	n.a.	n.a.	208.2	n.a.
1976	n.a.	85.2	186.7	n.a.
1977	n.a.	83.8	181.4	n.a.
1978	123.3	86.8	197.8	n.a.
1979	135.7	92.4	209.6	n.a.
1980	138.5	95.6	211.2	159.4
1981	118.7	88.3	164.9	226.7
1982	108.2	84.2	136.3	275.0
1983	104.1	87.7	117.5	307.4
1984	99.7	91.4	102.3	259.4
1985	100	100	100	306.1
1986	116.9	118.5	128.9	301.9
1987	128.0	135.4	148.4	360.9
1988	127.2	147.6	149.9	415.8

n.a. = not available
Notes: Debt/X is the ratio of total external debt to exports of goods and services. For first, second, third, and fourth columns, an increase implies appreciation.
Sources: Second, third, and fourth columns: IMF (various years); debt/x: World Bank (various years).

Since the introduction of the new trade regime in 1986, Côte d'Ivoire seems to have undergone most of these problems. For political and administrative reasons, as well as the country's commitments to its regional trading partners, the government has not reached its goal of a uniform tariff structure with 40 percent effective protection for all industries. Some evidence of import fraud, smuggling, and *ad hoc* exemptions for favored enterprises has surfaced.

The export subsidy has not worked. To stay within the budget deficit limits set during structural adjustment, pay-outs have been limited to tariff revenues. As a result, ten firms received 75 percent of the payments, and Lorch (1989) reports that their production, investment, and export performance have been worse than that of nonrecipients. Moreover, the subsidy is not large enough to offset high start-up costs, payment delays, and ultimately, the strength of the CFA franc thanks to the weakness of the dollar. The average subsidy of 13 percent of the value of exports in 1986 was more than offset by the 20 percent depreciation of the U.S. dollar with respect to the French franc in that same year.

In sum, the new trade regime has yet to prove itself, and so long as exogenous exchange rate movements keep occurring, it may never get a chance to do so. Nominal devaluation may be faster to work than a tariff-subsidy scheme, but is unlikely under current conditions.

The government might consider other options as yet unused. A foreign exchange "tax" may deter imports by driving up the cost of foreign exchange for traders. However, it would not solve any of the problems that export subsidy recipients face. In any case, how the rest of the UMOA would react to such a move is unclear. A group devaluation would necessarily be too much for some members and too little for others.

The Urban Labor Market

Côte d'Ivoire is relatively highly urbanized for a country at its level of per capita GNP (US$730 in 1986), with 45 percent of the population in urban areas, of whom 34 percent live in the capital, Abidjan. Despite this, 65 percent of the total labor force were engaged in agriculture in 1980, while 8 percent worked in industry and 27 percent in services (World Bank 1988).

The structure of the labor market in urban areas is fairly complex. Fields (1989) found that in 1986, 38.6 percent were wage employees, 31.1 percent were self-employed in business, and 25.1 percent were self-employed in agriculture.[4] Of the employees, 44.6 percent were employed in the public sector, 28.8 percent were employed in the formal private sector, and 45.5 percent were employed in the informal private sector.[5] Fields defines all self-employed workers as being in the informal sector, while employees are included in the formal sector if one of the following apply: a union is present in the work place; wages are subject to minimum wage legislation, employees have a formal employment contract; employees are entitled to paid holidays, paid sick leave, a retirement pension scheme, or free or subsidized medical care; or employees have access to social security benefits. However, the term informal is often used in a less precise manner to indicate activities that escape some or all taxes and government regulation.

This complexity of the labor market is reflected in the need to use different data sets to analyze different aspects of the market. On the one hand, the Banque des Données Financières has collected data on modern manufacturing firms (formal sector manufacturing firms that use modern technology) for a number of years. This data set has the advantage of providing detailed data for a period that includes the boom of the 1970s and the periods of stabilization and restructuring, but its disadvantage is that it excludes informal and nonmodern manufacturing, services, and agriculture. On the other hand, data from the Living Standards Measurement Survey (LSMS) includes all types of employment, but has only been collected since 1985, and was, unfortunately, discontinued in 1989, just before the staggering 50 percent reduction in the procurement price of coffee. This is even

---

4. Some workers had more than one status, thus the percentage of the urban work force who were in employment in the seven days before the survey is slightly less than the sum of these percentages. The remainder were not working.

5. These percentages add up to more than 100 because some people worked in more than one sector.

more critical for our discussion of rural labor markets and distribution that follows later.

The Modern Sector

The structural adjustment program has affected the urban sector the most. As most government expenditure and employment occurs in urban areas, they have been most severely affected by the program's stabilization phase. In addition, the change in tariff structures and the export subsidy scheme were designed to stimulate manufacturing industries producing tradable goods, and these are concentrated in urban areas.

Table 7.4 presents figures on employment in modern manufacturing by industry group, excluding petroleum. The table shows how total employment in modern manufacturing grew during the investment boom and then fell during the structural adjustment period. This fall in employment continued during the restructuring despite the government's efforts to increase incentives for the production of traded goods, most of which are produced within manufacturing. This might have been due to Côte d'Ivoire's decreasing international competitiveness produced by the high value of the CFA franc, or by firms' slow response to changed incentives. Although the changes in incentives failed to raise employment in manufacturing, one can obtain some idea of industry's responsiveness to changed incentives by looking at the changes in each industry's share of employment.

Two policies changed incentives within the manufacturing sector: the restructuring of protection and the export subsidy scheme. The restructuring of protection started in 1985 and was aimed at producing a uniform rate of effective protection. Lorch (1989) reports that uniformity was not fully achieved, but a general movement in that direction occurred. Food and textiles were both heavily protected before 1985, and so suffered a reduction in protection. Table 7.4 shows that both these industries experienced a fall in their employment share after 1985. Chemical and rubber products and mechanical and electrical goods were both receiving average protection before 1985, and so were little affected by the changes: the employment share of chemical and rubber products rose,

Table 7.4 Employment in Modern Manufacturing, 1974–87
(number of workers)

Sector	1974–75	1976–78	1979–81	1982–84	1985–86	1987
Food processing	22,278 (41.1%)	30,957 (40.8%)	40,840 (45.8%)	40,632 (47.4%)	38,451 (45.9%)	35,384 (44.8%)
Textiles, garments, etc.	8,041 (14.8%)	13,901 (18.3%)	14,866 (16.7%)	14,359 (16.8%)	13,897 (16.6%)	12,709 (16.1%)
Wood processing	8,632 (15.9%)	9,958 (13.1%)	8,984 (10.1%)	7,314 (8.5%)	7,701 (9.2%)	7,158 (9.1%)
Chemicals and rubber	7,246 (13.4%)	9,104 (11.9%)	11,692 (13.1%)	12,783 (14.9%)	14,275 (17.0%)	15,058 (19.1%)
Mechanical, electrical	5,662 (10.5%)	8,533 (11.2%)	9,030 (10.1%)	7,272 (8.5%)	6,178 (7.4%)	5,435 (6.9%)
Others	2,323 (4.3%)	3,588 (4.7%)	3,793 (7.2%)	3,339 (6.9%)	3,335 (7.0%)	3,188 (7.9%)
Total	54,182	75,952	89,206	85,699	83,836	78,932

Notes: Employment in petroleum is excluded. Figures in parentheses are percentages of total.
Source: Lorch (1989, table 9). Calculated from Banque des Données Financières data.

while that of mechanical and electrical goods fell slightly. Finally, wood processing and construction materials (an important part of other industries) were both lightly protected before 1985. They would have benefited from increased protection, and table 7.4 shows that both industries experienced an increase in employment share. These findings are consistent with the view that firms responded to changes in incentives, and that the labor market was sufficiently flexible to reallocate labor.

However, these changes in relative employment could have been the result of other events. For example, the government introduced an export subsidy scheme in 1986 that lasted until 1988. This scheme was intended to apply to all exports to offset the anti-export bias of import duties. The idea was to use import and export taxes to simulate a devaluation in the face of the fixed exchange rates in the franc zone. However, Lorch (1989) reports that the subsidy was only implemented selectively, and almost all the recipient firms were in four industries: food, textiles, wood, and chemical and rubber products.

Table 7.4 also shows that employment share fell in both food and textiles. These were both industries that had suffered from reduced protection from imports. Wood processing experienced an increase in employment share, but that could equally well have been due to the improved protection from imports. However, chemical and rubber products provide an example of an industry that did not benefit greatly from tariff reform, but that did expand employment share. Perhaps the export subsidy is part of the explanation for this.

This discussion has shown that the changes in employment share are consistent with firms responding to changes in incentives. Another piece of evidence supporting that view is provided by a more detailed analysis of the Banque des Données Financières data. Lorch (1989) examined the data at the four-digit level and allocated each product category into a high tradability group or low tradability group depending on whether imports plus exports exceeded half domestic production. He then compared the performance of the two groups. His results are presented in table 7.5.

Table 7.5 shows that the high tradability group improved its relative performance in every indicator after 1985, despite the high international value of the CFA franc. This suggests that the efforts to increase the resources devoted to the production of tradable goods had some effect. However, data on the relative employment growth of the two groups is not easily available.

As mentioned above, the shortcoming of the Banque des Données Financières data is its limited coverage, which might produce misleading results. For example, the reduction in modern manufacturing employment might not imply a reduction in total manufacturing employment if informal manufacturing enterprises expanded rapidly. Thus, to examine overall employment in the urban sector more fully, we use the LSMS data. However, these data only relate to the restructuring period, and the sample size is too small to provide a detailed analysis of employment by industry.

The LSMS started in 1985 and is designed on a semipanel basis, so that half the households interviewed one year are reinterviewed the next. Ainsworth and Muñoz (1986) describe the survey's design,

Table 7.5 Relative Performance of High and Low Tradability Groups, 1979–88
(percent)

Growth rate	1979–81	1982–84	1985–88
Growth rate of number of firms			
Low tradability	6.9	2.5	-4.5
High tradability	4.9	-0.7	-2.1
Nominal investment growth rate			
Low tradability	-38.0	-8.5	8.4
High tradability	5.0	0.8	19.2
Nominal value added growth rate			
Low tradability	13.4	11.8	-4.7
High tradability	15.0	6.6	1.3
Nominal production growth rate			
Low tradability	14.7	10.1	1.3
High tradability	10.8	8.5	8.9
Real production growth rate			
Low tradability	7.7	-1.6	0.8
High tradability	3.1	-1.6	5.7

Source: Lorch (1989, table 18). Calculated from Banque des Données Financières data.

Newman (1987) presents the main labor market data for 1985, and Fields (1989) provides a descriptive analysis of the data for 1985 and 1986. This analysis will concentrate on the people in the LSMS panel for 1985/86 (those people who were interviewed in both 1985 and 1986). After the removal of people under seven years of age and data with reporting errors, we are left with 1,373 individuals. In 1985, 39 percent of these people worked in the 12 months before the survey. Between 1985 and 1986, 21 percent of the labor force stopped working and 17 percent joined the labor force, a net reduction of 4 percent. If we look within the work force at the number of employees, 24 percent left and 17 percent joined. This reduction in employment is consistent with the analysis of the Banque des Données Financières data.

Table 7.6 shows the distribution of the labor force between wage employment and the two types of self-employment for individuals who worked in 1985 and 1986 (stayers), those who did not work in 1985 but did in 1986 (joiners), and those who worked in 1985 but not in 1986 (leavers). The first two columns show a slight move from both wage employment and self-employment in business toward self-employment in agriculture for those who worked in both years. However, the shift toward self-employment in agriculture is much more obvious in the joiners (who disproportionately joined agriculture) and the leavers (who disproportionately left business).

To examine interindustry movements between 1985 and 1986—movements that may in part have been due to structural adjustment—we have analyzed the industry of each person's main employment as indicated in the LSMS. We have defined the main employment as the main employment during the last 7 days, or for those not employed during the last 7 days, the main employment during the past 12 months. This analysis is based on people in the panel.

The LSMS identifies 30 different industries. However, as we are interested mainly in analyzing structural adjustment and the movement between the traded and nontraded sectors, we have aggregated these industries into four groups: (a) agriculture, forestry, and fishing; (b) manufacturing (presumed mainly tradable); (c) services, commerce, and utilities (presumed mainly nontradable); and

Table 7.6 Employment Status of Stayers, Joiners, and Leavers *(percentage of labor force)*

	Stayers		Joiners	Leavers
Type of employment	1985	1986	1985–86	1985–86
Wage employment	39	37	29	35
Self-employment in agriculture	25	29	39	21
Self-employment in business	36	34	32	44

Source: Living Standards Measurement Survey.

(d) other industry. The reasons for keeping other industry separate is that we are not sure what this category includes as it expanded enormously between 1985 and 1986.

The modern sector might have reacted differently to structural adjustment than the informal sector. Thus, table 7.7 presents data on the industrial distribution of employees and self-employed workers. It shows a large apparent movement from manufacturing and services into other industry among employees, the group that includes modern sector workers. This could well be the result of coding changes rather than real changes. The figures for the self-employed are not contaminated by this possible error, and here we see a slight increase in manufacturing employment. However, the numbers here are small.

Although the LSMS data relate to a relatively small number of individuals, they provide an interesting addition to the Banque des Données Financières data. First, they confirm the general reduction in employment, particularly wage employment. Second, the evidence of growing self-employment in manufacturing shows that the Banque des Données Financières data is becoming less representative of the urban labor market as a whole.

Table 7.7 Industrial Composition by Employment Status, 1985 and 1986
(percent)

	Employees		Self-employed	
Industry	1985	1986	1985	1986
Agriculture	3.8	1.0	45.1	45.1
Manufacturing	19.0	9.2	5.8	7.9
Services	74.9	60.0	47.9	46.7
Other	2.4	29.7	1.2	0.3

Source: Living Standards Measurement Survey.

Informalization, Self-Employment, and Nonagricultural Family Enterprises

The LSMS data showed an increase in self-employment in manufacturing despite a reduction in the number of wage employees in the formal manufacturing sector. Lorch (1989) also observed this move toward informal employment. He used the Banque des Données Financières data to suggest a movement of firms from the formal to the informal sector. He also proposes a number of reasons for this growth in informal manufacturing. First, he suggests that informal enterprises were less affected by the economic situation of the 1980s: they were less likely to produce internationally traded goods, and so suffered less from the period of overvaluation of the CFA franc; they were never able to obtain cheap credit, and therefore did not suffer from the reduction in credit availability; they had been less reliant on public investment projects for the sale of their products; and their informal labor contracts meant that they could cut wages instead of employment. Second, he suggests that many formal firms had an incentive to become informal. Many of the advantages of formality, such as cheap credit, had disappeared, while the advantages of informality, particularly lower labor costs and avoidance of taxes and regulations, remained. This incentive became particularly persuasive for firms that were suffering financial distress as a result of the structural adjustment program.

Much less data are available for informal firms than for formal firms. However, the LSMS data include information on nonagricultural, urban self-employment, and Vijverberg (1988) has analyzed these data. In Abidjan, 20.7 percent of males and 62.7 percent of females in the labor force report nonagricultural self-employment. The corresponding figures for other urban areas are 24.8 percent and 49.7 percent, respectively.

In Abidjan, these enterprises employ some paid workers, an average of 1.59, but far fewer in other urban areas (only 0.19 on average). The distribution of enterprises between industry groups is very similar in Abidjan and other urban areas: approximately 14 percent are in manufacturing, 14 percent in services, 45 percent in food commerce, and 27 percent in nonfood commerce. An important aspect of nonagricultural self-employment is that it provides substantial employment for non-Ivorians. In Abidjan, 31.4 percent of Ivorian workers were self-employed in nonagriculture, but the figure was 65.3 percent for non-Ivorians, including 31.1 percent of workers from Burkino Faso and 75.8 percent of workers from Mali. The figures for other urban areas are similar.

Wage Determination and Real Wage Growth

The available evidence indicates significant returns to training, education, and experience within the urban sector during the period of structural adjustment both for public and private sector workers. Table 7.8 documents the data from the 1985 LSMS. The traditional schooling system in Côte d'Ivoire includes six years of elementary school, four years of junior high school, three years of senior high school, and a university program. Table 7.8 presents the average years of schooling for each level of education. Of the six or more years of total schooling, only a very small part is university training, while most of it is elementary education. The LSMS data allow differentiation of total experience into experience related to the current occupation and other general experience. Occupation-specific experience is broader than tenure on the current job, as it includes work experience in previously held jobs that have the same job description as the current one.

Table 7.8 reveals that public sector employees are on average better educated, with an average of 9.2 years of education, versus 5.3 years in the private sector. In addition, more public sector employees hold school diplomas. There are no non-Ivorians in the public sector, and 25.9 percent of the public sector labor force is female, compared to 14.9 percent in the private sector. Total experience (the sum of general and specific experience), measured as age minus years spent in school and technical training minus five (the age of which they normally start school), averages about 20 years in both sectors. Occupation-specific experience, however, is much lower in the private than public sector.

Table 7.9 presents some estimates of returns. Note that while real wages in the private sector have risen, the reverse is true for the public sector. Non-Ivorians earn a higher wage in the private sector, as do women. However, the returns to basic education are higher in the public sector. Occupational experience and higher levels of education appear to yield a higher return in the private sector.

Table 7.8 Summary Statistics on Wages and Human Capital

Symbol	Category	Private sector (N =301) Mean	Private sector (N =301) Standard deviation	Public sector (N = 212) Mean	Public sector (N = 212) Standard deviation
LNW	Log of hourly wage rate (CFAs)[a]	5.557	1.29	6.577	0.99
	General background				
AGE	Age in years	32.554	10.16	35.565	8.70
GEXPER	General work experience	13.135	9.36	9.705	8.85
EXPOCC	Occupation-specific experience	7.399	7.58	11.116	8.23
YRS-APP	Years apprenticeship	1.166	2.20	0.241	1.08
YRS-TEC	Years technical training	0.734	1.58	1.462	11.61
RRR	Reading, writing, and arithmetic skills[b]	1.973	1.37	2.637	0.94
NAT	Non-Ivorian %	0.275	0.44	0.000	0.00
FEMALE	Female %	0.149	0.35	0.259	0.44
	Years of schooling				
TRSCHL	Total years of schooling	5.269	4.94	9.179	5.26
YRS-EL	Years of elementary schooling	3.561	2.84	5.132	2.08
YRS-HI	Years junior high school	1.215	1.69	2.472	1.80
YRS-H2	Years senior high school	0.322	0.89	0.859	1.29
YRS-UN	Years university	0.169	0.83	0.717	1.87
	Diplomas obtained				
DIP-E1	Elementary school diploma %	0.478	0.50	0.830	0.38
DIP-H1	Junior high school diploma %	0.182	0.38	0.491	0.50
DIP-UPP	Higher diploma %	0.089	0.28	0.236	0.43
DIP-TEC	Technical diploma %	0.202	0.40	0.472	0.50

a.   Wages are measured in CFAs; 50 CFA = 1 FF; 1 OFF = US$1 in 1985. The averages reflect CFA 595 in the private sector and CFA 1,173 in the public sector.
b.   This index is zero for the completely illiterate and increases by 1 for every skill acquired.
Source: van der Gaag and Vijverberg (1989).

Table 7.9 The Determination of Cross-Sector Wages

(a) Real wages (1979 = 100)	Public	Private
1979	100.0	100.0
1984	95.6	113.4

(b) Coefficient from log wage regressions

	Public		Private	
CONST	2.841	(7.87)	3.452	(14.65)
NAT (1 if non-Ivorian)	n.a.		0.285	(2.20)
SEX (1 if female)	-0.125	(-1.04)	0.141	(0.97)
DIP-EL	0.801	(2.50)	0.395	(1.92)
DIP-HI	0.424	(2.14)	0.617	(2.40)
DIP-UPP	0.621	(2.10)	0.221	(0.45)
DIP-TEC	0.002	(0.02)	0.031	(0.17)
YRS-HI	0.205	(0.408)	0.012	(0.21)
YRS-UNI	0.206	(5.66)	0.300	(4.21)
YRS-TEC	0.036	(1.34)	0.098	(2.42)
YRS-APP	0.067	(1.85)	0.008	(-0.31)
EXP-OCC	0.087	(4.79)	0.116	(7.32)

n.a. = not available
Note: The figures in parenthesis are asymptotic t-statistics. Symbols are those used in table 7.8.
Source: van der Gaag and Vijverberg (1989).

Table 7.10 shows that during the stabilization period, when a recession occurred, real wages were flexible downward. This simple analysis at the occupational level, first identified by Lavy and Newman (1989), points out how misleading aggregate data can be, since although average real wages increased over this period, once they adjusted for occupation, they showed that real wages fell substantially. Moreover, Lavy and Newman (1989) found additional evidence that new hires were paid very much less than retained workers, although even retained workers saw a shift down in their experience-wage profile during this period.

Rural Labor Markets

In contrast to the urban sector, the rural sector was not initially subject to any direct effects of structural adjustment. For example, until very recently the procurement prices for coffee and cocoa had hardly changed in real terms. The prices of other crops, particularly subsistence crops, did vary, but as they are not under direct government control, ascertaining whether these changes were a result of the structural adjustment program is difficult. Nevertheless, the response to these price changes should indicate rural households' overall ability to adapt to price reforms induced by structural adjustment.

More than half the labor force works in rural areas, and agriculture produces almost all the country's exports. Moreover, the recent change in coffee prices suggests that the adjustment program will soon lead to a closer linkage between procurement prices and world prices. Therefore, considering the effects of price changes on labor supply in the rural sector, and in agriculture in particular, is a worthwhile exercise. We therefore present some results obtained by Alessie and

Table 7.10 Wage Flexibility During Stabilization, 1979 and 1984

	1979		*1984*	
Professional category	*Percentage share of employment*	*Average wage (CFAF 1,000 per month)*	*Percentage share of employment*	*Average wage deflated (CFAF 1,000 per month)*
Director	1.8	345	2.4	384
Upper management	3.7	341	5.4	305
Middle management	2.8	181	3.6	161
Technical employee	6.4	110	11.8	97
Skilled worker	16.6	56	24.6	52
Unskilled worker	68.9	31	56.0	28
Apprentice	0.2	20	0.2	17

Source: Lavy and Newman (1989).

others (1990) on the price responsiveness of participation in agricultural work by young people. Since for young people the choices are essentially between work, schooling, and migration, we investigate the interplay between work and schooling.

Agricultural Enterprises and Household Production

Fields (1989) used LSMS data to show that in 1986, 86.2 percent of rural workers were self-employed in agriculture, and as few as 1.4 percent were wage employees.[6] The remainder of the workers were self-employed in nonagriculture. Vijverberg (1988) demonstrated that approximately 90 percent of these enterprises are in the same household as an agricultural enterprise. The rural sector can therefore be seen as consisting predominantly of household farms, frequently combined with other small businesses, using very little outside labor.

In rural areas, the small, nonagricultural enterprises provide employment for around 10 percent of the women and 6 percent of the men. Looking at it by country of origin, they provide employment for some 6 percent of Ivorians and 23 percent of non-Ivorians (including 10 percent of those from Burkino Faso and 49 percent of those from Mali). Of rural, nonagricultural enterprises, more than half are engaged in food commerce and another quarter are engaged in other commerce. Fewer than 15 percent are engaged in manufacturing. Typically these enterprises do not employ any paid workers (the average number of paid workers is 0.12). They therefore share the urban small enterprises' role of providing employment for non-Ivorians. Their industrial composition is also similar to the urban small enterprises; however, they provide employment for fewer people.

To investigate price responsiveness and working patterns, we need to look closely at the activities of those engaged in agriculture. Glewwe and de Tray (1988) assessed the proportions of farmers who grow each of the main traded crops: 34.4 percent grow cocoa, 37.5 percent grow coffee, 31.6 percent grow rice, 16.0 percent grow oil

---

6. There are reasons to believe that the figure of 1.4 percent understates the proportion of outside workers. First, the sampling frame in rural areas might well underrepresent both wage workers and sharecroppers as these groups often live outside the villages. Second, the questions in the LSMS do not always allow the identification of sharecroppers.

palm, 12.6 percent grow pineapples, 8.7 percent grow rubber, 2.2 percent grow coconut, and 2.2 percent grow sugar. Cotton is grown almost exclusively in the northern savannah region, while the tree crops are predominantly grown in the east and west forest regions. In addition to growing cash crops, most farmers produce subsistence crops such as cassava, yams, sweet potatoes, maize, millet, and sorghum. Thus, separating out farmers who produce traded crops from those who produce nontraded crops is impossible. The LSMS provides data on the output composition of each farm, but the lags involved in changing the output mix, particularly when tree crops are involved, mean that changes cannot be observed in two years of data. Inputs will respond much more rapidly than outputs, but the LSMS does not ask how much time is devoted to the cultivation of each crop. This means that we cannot determine whether resources have been reallocated toward the production of traded goods within the rural sector. We can only ask whether structural adjustment resulted in an increase in labor supply to agriculture.

Schooling and Work in Agricultural Household Enterprises

Table 7.11 presents, for each year of LSMS panel data, the proportion of individuals who report having worked in the preceding 12 months by age group. The general picture is that between the ages of 24 and 60, roughly 95 percent of individuals report some labor market activity. During the two years, overall reported labor market activity increased. This increase was concentrated among those age groups with the lowest percentage of workers, namely, among those aged under 12 and over 60. A somewhat curious feature is that we observe a slight fall in work activity for the 12 to 18 age group.

The above description of the data has concentrated on individuals' rates of participation. However, to gauge price responsiveness we are interested in movements of individuals between the states of working and not working. Table 7.12 shows the numbers and proportion of individuals according to their working status in each year. The general pattern of labor market transitions shows that between the ages of 19 and 60 the numbers of individuals leaving or entering the work force are very small. The vast majority of changes in working status are concentrated among those individuals aged 18 and under. Since work

Table 7.11 Rural Labor Force Participation, 1985 and 1986
(percentage of panel sample)

Age group (1985)	Percentage of panel sample		Number of observations
	1985	*1986*	
7–11	22.5	41.3	417
12–18	71.9	69.8	391
19–23	86.2	90.0	130
24–30	94.2	96.7	154
31–40	96.8	96.7	217
41–50	97.4	96.1	230
51–60	95.1	94.5	182
Over 60	66.5	73.2	209
Total	71.4	76.0	1,930

Source: Living Standards Measurement Survey.

Table 7.12 Work Status Transitions, by Age, 1985 and 1986
(number)

Age group (1985)	Do not work either year	Worked 1985 only	Worked 1986 only	Worked both years
7–11	202	43	121	51
	(48.4)	(10.3)	(29.0)	(12.2)
12–18	53	65	57	216
	(13.6)	(16.6)	(14.6)	(55.2)
19–23	9	4	9	108
	(6.9)	(3.1)	(6.9)	(83.1)
24–30	3	2	6	143
	(2.0)	(2.3)	(3.9)	(92.9)
31–40	4	4	3	206
	(1.8)	(1.8)	(1.4)	(94.9)
41–50	3	6	3	218
	(1.3)	(2.6)	(1.3)	(94.8)
51–60	5	5	4	168
	(2.8)	(2.8)	(2.2)	(92.3)
Over 60	45	11	25	128
	(21.5)	(5.3)	(12.0)	(61.2)
Total	324	140	228	1,238
	(16.8)	(7.3)	(11.8)	(64.2)

Note: Figures in parenthesis are row percentages.
Source: Living Standards Measurement Survey.

activity for this group is likely to result in reduced schooling, we turn briefly to discussion of the schooling system in Côte d'Ivoire.

The school system, inherited under colonial rule, follows the French system.[7] Six years of elementary education lead to the Certificat d'Etudes Primaires (CEPE), awarded on the basis of a nationwide examination. The CEPE is a prerequisite for entrance to secondary school, although because secondary school places are scarce, the score required to gain entrance is often higher than that required to obtain the CEPE certificate. Four years of lower secondary education lead to the Brevet d'Etudes du Premier Cycle (BEPC), which, if successfully completed, allows the student to enter three years of upper secondary education leading to the Baccalaureate. Alternatively, those students who have a CEPE or who successfully complete some or all of their lower secondary education can enter various training programs. One feature of the Ivorian education system is that many students at all levels repeat grades, thus the number of years for which students are enrolled will on average exceed the numbers outlined above.

Table 7.13 shows for our sample the percentage of individuals who attended school in 1985 and 1986 broken down by age and sex. Overall, the table shows a steady fall in attendance between the ages of 12 and 16, with a distinct drop for those aged 17 or over in 1985. As we might have expected, school attendance falls for all age groups from 1985 to 1986. Looking at the pattern of attendance across the sexes, attendance rates are significantly lower for females than for males. Note that of our sample, no 18-year-old females attended school.

A variety of factors may influence households' decisions on whether to send children to school. One such factor is the distance that students must travel, since time and travel costs will increase the further students have to travel to attend school. However, primary schools in the Côte d'Ivoire tend to be neighborhood schools. Some 85 percent of our sample have primary schools located close by, while the remainder are all within eight kilometers of the nearest primary

---

7. We are grateful to Paul Glewwe for providing information on Côte d'Ivoire's education system.

Table 7.13 School Attendance, 1985 and 1986

Age (1985)	Both sexes (percentage of panel sample)		Boys (percentage of panel sample)		Girls (percentage of panel sample)		Number of observations		
	1985	1986	1985	1986	1985	1986	Total	Boys	Girls
12	68.4	64.5	73.1	67.3	58.3	58.3	76	52	24
13	57.7	53.9	66.7	64.4	45.5	39.4	78	45	33
14	40.0	36.5	5.0	44.4	18.8	18.8	52	36	16
15	29.1	25.5	35.7	32.1	22.2	18.5	55	28	27
16	29.3	21.9	36.0	28.0	18.8	12.5	41	25	16
17	12.8	10.3	16.7	12.5	6.7	6.7	39	24	15
18	12.0	10.0	20.0	16.7	0.0	0.0	50	30	20
Total	40.2	36.3	47.9	43.3	27.8	25.2	391	240	151

school. This is not the case for secondary schools, which are located in urban areas. Of our sample only 10 percent live within 10 kilometers of a secondary school and some 60 percent live more than 20 kilometers from a secondary school, with a mean distance from a secondary school of 27 kilometers. One effect of the distance to secondary school is the phenomenon of "child fostering" found in West Africa. Children commonly live with friends or relations, so that they can attend school (Ainsworth 1989).[8]

The vast majority of students in Côte d'Ivoire attend public schools, which do not charge tuition. Some private schools are available, but most are located in urban areas. Table 7.14 breaks down school attendance by type of school. The table shows that within our sample, some 20 percent of individuals aged 13 to 16 remained in education after obtaining their CEPE certificate in 1985.

Turning our attention to work activity, table 7.15 shows that the slight fall in work activity is concentrated among those individuals aged 13 to 16 in 1985. In general, a higher percentage of females than males are engaged in work activity.

8. Such "fostered" children are probably not included in the rural panel sample.

Table 7.14 Type of School Attended, 1985 and 1986

| | Percentage of panel sample | | | | |
| | | | | | |
Year/age	None	Primary school	Lower secondary	Higher secondary	Number of observations
1985					
12	31.6	59.2	9.2	—	76
13	42.3	44.9	12.8	—	78
14	59.6	21.2	19.2	—	52
15	70.9	9.1	20.0	—	55
16	70.7	7.3	22.0	—	41
17	87.2	2.6	5.1	5.1	39
18	88.0	2.0	6.0	4.0	50
1986					
12	35.5	44.7	19.7	—	76
13	46.2	37.2	16.7	—	78
14	63.5	15.4	21.2	—	52
15	74.6	5.5	20.0	—	55
16	78.1	2.4	19.5	—	41
17	89.7	2.6	2.6	5.1	39
18	90.0	2.0	4.0	4.0	50

— = not applicable

Note: The survey does not ask what type of school panel individuals attend. However, since obtaining a CEPE diploma is a prerequisite for attending lower secondary school and a BEPC diploma is a prerequisite for higher secondary school, we assume that individuals holding diplomas attend the appropriate establishment.

Source: Living Standards Measurement Survey.

So far we have only considered our sample's rates of participation in work and school. We are, however, primarily concerned with examining movements of individuals between the states of working and not working and attending school and not attending school. In particular we wish to examine the relationship between the two decisions since, to the extent that work activity may reduce school attendance, the two are closely related. Table 7.16 cross-tabulates the number of individuals in our sample according to their work and education status in both years. Within the sample, nearly 60 percent did not attend school in either year. In terms of work status transitions,

Table 7.15 Individuals Working, 1985 and 1986

Age	Percentage of panel sample						Number of observations		
	Both sexes		Males		Females				
(1985)	1985	1986	1985	1986	1985	1986	Total	Males	Females
12	46.1	48.7	46.1	51.9	59.3	41.7	76	52	24
13	64.1	59.0	64.4	66.7	63.6	48.5	78	45	33
14	73.1	59.6	66.7	52.8	87.5	75.0	52	36	16
15	87.2	83.6	89.3	85.7	85.2	81.5	55	28	27
16	82.9	80.5	84.0	80.0	81.3	81.3	41	25	16
17	84.6	92.5	83.3	87.5	86.7	100.0	39	24	15
18	86.0	88.0	86.7	80.0	85.0	100.0	50	30	20
Total	71.9	69.8	69.2	68.7	76.2	71.5	391	240	151

Table 7.16 Cross-Tabulation of Work and School Status of Sample, 1985 and 1986

Status	Work both years	Work 1985 only	Work 1986 only	Not work either year	Total
School both years	20	47	28	44	139
School 1985 only	6	0	8	4	18
School 1986 only	1	2	0	0	3
Not attend either year	189	16	21	5	231
Total	216	65	57	53	391

15 percent entering the work force in 1986 were recorded as not working in 1985. More interesting, nearly 20 percent of the sample left work in 1986. Of those individuals who changed their working status, the majority did so while attending school in both years.

Labor Supply and Agricultural Prices

Most households are engaged in agricultural production, therefore, analyzing labor supply decisions in the context of agricultural household models is appropriate (see Singh and others 1986). These models represent behavior as the result of collective household decisions about production, labor supply, and consumption. In general, these decisions are interdependent and must be modeled simultaneously. However, under the assumption of complete competitive factor and product markets, the decisions have a separable or recursive structure. Production decisions are made on the basis of profit maximization, as a result of which the household receives profit income. The household labor supply and consumption decisions are then made to maximize collective utility, given consumer prices, wages, and profit income (appendix A provides a formal basis for the following discussion).

In the "separable" model, agricultural producer prices will only affect household labor supply through their effect on profit income. Increased output prices will raise profits, and thus (assuming that leisure is a normal good) reduce household labor supply. This reduction in household labor supply is consistent with the production decision to increase output and labor input in response to increased prices: the difference between labor input and household labor supply is covered by labor market transactions.

Possible reasons for allowing a more general specification than the separable model will be discussed later, but first we must consider how the separable model would allow analysis of the incentive effects of structural adjustment. The discussion in the previous paragraph suggests that increases in agricultural prices will reduce household labor supply, but this was based on the implicit assumption that wages were constant. In reality, one would expect the increased demand for labor that follows from increased agricultural prices to result in increased wages. These increased wages will have both income effects and substitution effects. The substitution effects will increase labor supply, while the direction of the income effect will depend on whether the household is a net buyer or net seller of labor. In either case, the income effect will be proportional to the extent of net labor purchases (or sales), and so will be small for the typical Ivorian farm household, which buys or sells relatively small quantities of labor. Thus, for farm households the substitution effect of wage increases can be expected to dominate their income effect and provide the main route through which increased agricultural prices might stimulate labor supply.

This argument suggests that the effect of output price changes on labor supply cannot be captured by simply looking at a model that takes the wage rate as an exogenous variable. This cannot capture the effect of product prices on wages, and so omits the only way in which increased product prices can increase labor supply. The analysis requires the addition of a relationship between producer prices and the wage rate. This relationship should include the producer prices of all crops produced by labor from the local labor market in order to reflect the role of prices in determining the demand for labor. However, as many of the crops have long periods of production, the demand for current labor will depend in part on expected future prices for the product. Ideally, therefore, the expectations of future prices should also be included.

Although "structural" estimation would reveal more detailed information about household behavior and labor market response, the estimation of a reduced form, which combines the wage and labor supply relationships, can provide the answer to our main question: does labor supply respond to structural adjustment? This can also be estimated without using data on market wage rates; a considerable advantage in Côte d'Ivoire as few data on rural wage rates are available, and those available are of doubtful quality. Finally, as shown below, the distinctions in the structural model become blurred as soon as the assumption of complete (and perfect) markets is relaxed.

The separable model is based on the assumption of complete perfect markets. The labor market might violate this assumption in two main ways. First, the labor market may be very thin, or even nonexistent, so that households may have difficulty in either buying or selling labor. Second, hired labor may not be a perfect substitute for household labor because of greater supervision needs.

With regard to the first violation, our data suggest that very little labor market activity takes place: landless laborers frequently obtain access to land through sharecropping rather than wage labor. On the second issue, obtaining empirical evidence about the substitutability between household labor and hired labor is much more difficult, but the possibility of the two types of labor being less than perfect substitutes has some plausibility.

The implication of both possible violations is that household labor supply does not depend on the market wage, but on a shadow wage that reflects the marginal value of extra household labor. This shadow wage will be influenced by the market wage, if a labor market exists, but will also depend on factors that influence the supply and demand for labor within the household. On the demand side, output prices and the amount of available land would be expected to increase the shadow wage. On the supply side, an increase in the number of household members who are prepared to work will reduce the shadow wage.

Note that farm profits in these circumstances are no longer well defined because of the difficulty of valuing household labor. One can define a shadow profit, based on the shadow wage, and its value will depend on the variables already included. Thus, there is no need to include a separate term for profits in the reduced form equation and we shall simply incorporate nonfarm income.

The producer price index should now represent the prices (ideally including expected future prices) of products produced by this particular household, because it is those prices that determine the demand for labor by this particular household. This suggests that each household should have its own producer price index with weights that reflect the relative importance of the different crops that it produces. There is, therefore, the possibility of considerable variation in incentive changes between households. Our research makes use of this variability by constructing household-specific Divisia price indices (see Alessie and others, 1990) that reflect the relative importance of different crops in each household's total output.

We derive separate composite price indices for both gross production and the production of cash crops. Our approach to the construction of both indices is as follows. First, we calculate for each year average regional prices for each crop.[9] These average prices are then weighted according to the share of each crop in the individual household's production in 1985, thus forming household-specific composite indices of price changes based on first period weights. In calculating these price variables we look only at households located in rural areas, which are in turn divided into five regions.[10]

Having calculated average regional prices we derive composite Divisia price indices for each agricultural household 'h' using the following formula:

$$P = \sum_i w^o_{ih} \Delta \ell n \, p_i$$

where w^o_{ih} = first period value share of commodity i in total gross (cash or gross) crop production for household h.

As equation (1) shows, whereas the value shares are household specific, the price ratios vary only with region. As mentioned above, we calculate two price indices that vary according to the value shares in production by which they are weighted. For the gross production index (PRODIND), the value of production is defined as the amount of the harvest sold, plus the value of replacement capital such as seeds,

---

9. The five regions are: (a) NORTH, north of Kassou Lake; (b) SW1, between Buyo Reservoir and the Guinean and Liberian borders; (c) SW2, central southern area to the southwest of Kassou Lake; (d) SE1, north of Abengourou; (e) SE2, Abidjan hinterland to the south of Abengourou.

10. The LSMS collects information on the quantities sold and the price received for a total of 22 crops. In the case of nine of these crops it is not possible to construct crop price indices either because the value share of the crop in total production was rather small, or because insufficient price information was available because the price of the crop was generally reported in nonmetric units. These crops are rubber, coconut palm, wood, tobacco, pineapple, sugarcane, taro, sweet potato, and millet. The remaining crops used in the construction of our price indices are as follows:

1. Cocoa   4. Plantain   7. Cotton   10. Yam   13. Vegetables
2. Coffee   5. Fruit trees 8. Peanut   11. Maize
3. Oil palm 6. Cola nut   9. Cassava   12. Rice

For the above crops we calculate average regional prices for five regions. In calculating average prices for each crop we exclude those observations where the quantities sold were reported in nonmetric units, and where it was therefore not possible to calculate metric unit prices. Also excluded were some outlier observations. Selection of outliers is based upon a 95 percent confidence interval rule. Note that we were unable to take account of any seasonal variation in prices because we do not know at what time of year crops were harvested and sold.

the value of any harvest given away, and the value of home production. For the cash crop index (CASHIND), the value of net cash crop production equals the value of cash crops, where cash crops are defined as coffee, cocoa, cotton, and cola nut.[11] Constructing this second index was necessary because of the wide dispersion in prices of subsistence crops observed within regions (this dispersion is due, in part, to the fact that we have few observations for some subsistence crops). For cash crops, however, prices are generally controlled, and hence more uniform, thus yielding a more reliable crop price index. Note that in calculating these indices we include only the value of primary production. We are unable to include the value of processed items as insufficient price information is available, and similarly we do not include animal products within the indices.

Table 7.17 shows the regional mean values of the price change indices. It indicates clearly that the prices of cash crops do not change by as much as the prices for gross production. With the exception of the north region, the gross production index shows a larger increase than the cash crop index, indicating an increase in the relative prices

Table 7.17 Regional Mean Price Indices of Production

| Category | Region | | | | | |
	Total	North	SWl	SW2	SEl	SE2
Gross production PRODIND	0.29	-0.17	0.23	0.45	0.76	0.27
	(0.42)	(0.27)	(0.19)	(0.27)	(0.39)	(0.30)
Cash production CASHIND	0.03	0.01	0.04	0.03	0.03	0.03
	(0.02)	(0.01)	(0.02)	(0.02)	(0.03)	(0.01)

Note: Standard deviations in parentheses.

11. Details of the LSMS questions used in the construction of the price weights are as follows: the value of net production is taken to be the value of crops sold (Sec 9B Q4,5); the value of gross production is the sum of net production plus the value of any seeds retained (Sec 9b Q7); the value of any crops exchanged in return for labor (for all goods except coffee and cocoa Sec 9B Q9); and the value of any crops used for home consumption (Sec 128 Q3–5).

of subsistence crops. This means that incentive changes in agriculture have favored nontraded goods, the opposite of what is required for structural adjustment. The difference in the cash crop index observed in the north region is to an extent explained by the fact that the government raised the procurement price for cocoa and coffee not grown within the region.

Labor Force Transitions and Agricultural Price Changes

In this section we estimate the determinants of transitions in and out of the labor market using the model and price indices just described. Empirical studies of individual participation in work are usually restricted to the use of cross-sectional data due to the lack of panel data in developing countries. Alessie and others' (1990) study was therefore in the almost unique position of being able to exploit the repeated observations on each individual across pairs of years in the Côte d'Ivoire panel survey. This enabled us to assess directly the degree of history dependence in work behavior, as well as the benefits of panel data over cross-sectional data in investigating such behavior. As many decisions are based on longer horizons than two years, the models we consider, based on those discussed above, attempt to exploit the richness of the cross-sectional data to capture long-term influences, leaving the panel data to provide information on short-run transitions and history dependence.

The cross-sectional data in the Côte d'Ivoire survey provide ideal instruments for measuring longer-run influences. For example, we can use the consumption expenditure records as a measure of life-cycle income or wealth of the household unit. Moreover, the effect of local constraints on behavior can be captured via the extensive information on infrastructure variables. Equally, the short-run effects of price changes, a central focus in this research, can be identified through the cash crop (CASHIND) and total product (PRODIND) price indices constructed for each household as described earlier. The empirical models presented in this section will therefore attempt to exploit all the cross-sectional information that may explain the work status of young people living in rural households. Through the use of the panel, we can also assess the importance of price changes not easily identified in cross-sectional analysis.

For the individuals in the sample, the initial period's work status can take three easily recognizable states that relate directly to the sample split described in table 7.16. First, we may consider the likelihood of an individual being in work conditional on having worked in the first period. In table 7.16, this would refer to the sum of the first two columns (216 + 65), which shows that of the 281 young people in our panel who worked in 1985, 216 were engaged in some work in 1986. From these we may split out the 73 (20+47+6) who were engaged in some education in the first period. A comparison of these two groups will enable us to assess whether being involved in some education in the initial period influences the decision to keep working in the next period. This is an example of the type of history dependence that is critical to the issues under analysis. In particular, we will wish to know whether the reactions to price incentives across these two groups differ. Finally, we may consider those individuals who move into work from full-time education in the first period. In summary, by conditioning on past period behavior, we can assess the importance of history dependence in individual work behavior. This modeling approach is detailed in appendix B (see also Heckman 1981; Nakamura and Nakamura 1985).

Our results in this section describe a binary model of current work status conditional on past work and schooling behavior.[12] This should be interpreted as a reduced form transition model since we do not estimate the direct effects of current period schooling behavior on work status or the effects of current period decisions over work and schooling by other household members.

For the cash crop price change variable CASHIND, we might expect a strong positive effect on the probability of work in the second period if incentives are having a strong effect on work activities. However, given the reduced form nature of this equation, the

---

12. There are, in principle, two primary measures of work status available in the panel survey. These relate to working behavior in the past week or during the past year. In our studies we use both measures, but in this report we present results for the latter definition alone as these were not only similar to those for the past week definition, but are generally more precisely determined. This is encouraging since it suggests our results are not unduly affected by seasonal work patterns. The results presented here also use a similar past-twelve-month measure for schooling behavior.

cash crop price variable CASHIND will also capture the income effects of an output price change.

Following the arguments detailed earlier, we attempt to capture a longer-run or life-cycle measure of other income and wealth with the use of consumption expenditures. Again, this is likely to be a current period endogenous variable, so to allow for such endogeneity in this reduced form model, we use a consumption measure from the first survey, FOOD(1). In turn, this is restricted to cover food expenditures only, since they appear to not only make up the largest share of a household's budget, but also appear to be the best measured consumption item. These expenditures include the value of home production. In the conditional probability models of state dependence used here, these income and other household decision variables in the first period will only be important insofar as they capture longer-run effects not captured by the initial period work status variables.

The results for the subsample of individuals who are working during the first period are presented in table 7.18. The descriptive statistics relating to each variable and further details of variables used are provided in Alessie and others (1990). The precision and sign of the CASHIND variable are comforting. In all the results set down here, we have tried to present a reasonably parsimonious parameterization of each model specification. Indeed, a general feature of our results was the dominating importance of the cash crop price effects measured through CASHIND over the general index PRODIND. This probably reflects possible measurement problems in the prices of noncash crops.

Turning to the other factors, we started with household variables that might be important in determining this conditional probability. In particular, we found the individual's age (AGE) and the number of other household workers (OTHWK) were of some importance. Since we are deliberately not attempting to model the simultaneous work status decisions of all family members at this stage, we use the number of other household workers as recorded in the first survey denoted by (1). A variable measuring land size was also included in preliminary models, but this was never found to play a role once regional effects were allowed for. As mentioned earlier, initial period food expenditures FOOD(1) were added to capture any longer-run income

Table 7.18 State Dependent Work Behavior

Variable	Coefficient	Standard error	T-statistic	P-value
CONSTANT	-2.579169	0.971435	-2.655008	0.007931
CASHIND	15.965741	5.782105	2.761233	0.005758
AGE	0.354416	0.059647	5.941882	0.000000
OTHWK(1)	-0.085246	0.048298	-1.765000	0.077564
FOOD(1)	-0.450348	0.255106	-1.765341	0.077506
RELIG	0.428714	0.377991	1.134193	0.256714
REGDSW1	-1.999087	0.591587	-3.379194	0.000727
REGDSW2	-2.353115	0.516375	-4.556985	0.000005
REGDSE1	-1.406769	0.568329	-2.475273	0.013313
REGDSE2	-1.256331	0.596177	-2.107313	0.035090

Notes: obs = 281, logL = -103.235.

effects not reflected in the discrete state conditioning variable. The negative coefficient confirms such an effect. In addition to these factors we felt the individual's religion may be important, and in table 7.18 we have retained the coefficient on RELIG, a dummy variable that is unity if the individual is Muslim.

Location variables could play an important role in both shaping preferences and identifying constraints. The regional dummies (REGDSW1-REGDSE2) are clearly important, although some further grouping looks possible. Finally, we tried a number of infrastructure variables and a variable indicating the sex of the individual. These turned out to be of little significance for this transition.

We argued above that it was of some interest to analyze the behavior of the subset of 73 individuals from this group who had not only been working in the first period, but who had also been in education during the first year. Table 7.19 reports the results for this subgroup. These show a similar overall pattern, but an even stronger cash crop price effect. Note that in this smaller sample we were able to group the dummies for SW regions with the base region. We also considered the group of individuals who were wholly engaged in

Table 7.19 Working Behavior for Those Engaged in Some Education

Variable	Coefficient	Standard error	T-statistic	P-value
CONSTANT	-2.958848	2.099278	-1.409460	0.163459
CASHIND	38.182585	11.462775	3.331007	0.001422
AGE	0.183416	0.142478	1.287326	0.202540
OTHWK(l)	-0.165548	0.079879	-2.072476	0.042184
FOOD(l)	-1.026199	0.618155	-1.660099	0.101705
RELIG	1.362558	0.622839	2.187657	0.032289
REGDSEl	0.039072	0.526423	0.074222	0.941061
REGDSE2	1.220068	0.513474	2.376103	0.020445

Notes: obs = 73, -logL = 33.395.

Table 7.20 The Exit From Full-time Education to Work

Variable	Coefficient	Standard error	T-statistic	P-value
CONSTANT	1.714820	1.629952	1.052067	0.296187
CASHIND	-14.462155	9.713291	-1.488904	0.140756
AGE	-0.016953	0.102740	-0.165006	0.869388
OTHWK(l)	-0.186352	0.081931	-2.274508	0.025827
FOOD(l)	0.915047	0.652827	1.401668	0.165189
RELIG	-0.533052	0.458154	-1.163477	0.248368
REGDSW1	-0.130967	0.913481	-0.143371	0.886386
REGDSW2	-0.942830	0.862473	-1.093171	0.277859
REGDSEl	-0.645450	0.894543	-0.721542	0.472846
REGDSE2	-1.884299	0.936895	-2.011217	0.047938

Notes: obs = 84, -logL = 40.655.

education in the first period. Results for this group are presented in table 7.20, and contrast distinctly with those discussed so far. The cash crop price effect is negative, suggesting a more dominant income effect of price movements for this group of individuals. These results show that labor force participation is generally responsive to price incentives. However, people with different work and education histories respond differently.

Distribution, the Role of Women, and Migration

This section considers the effects that structural adjustment has had on the distribution of income, the role of women, and the migration between urban and rural areas.

Income Distribution and Poverty

The collection of the first year of LSMS data in 1985 constituted the first attempt to provide a comprehensive measure of income distribution and poverty in Côte d'Ivoire. Berthelemy and Bourgignon (1989, p. 20) mention some estimates based on partial evidence in the 1970s, but they are not comparable with the Gini coefficient of 0.44 for consumption expenditures per adult equivalent that Glewwe (1987) calculated from the LSMS data. Thus, arriving at any definite conclusions about the effects of structural adjustment on income distribution and poverty is impossible. The analysis is necessarily speculative, using data from 1985 and later to infer what the effects of structural adjustment are likely to have been.

Glewwe and de Tray (1988) and Kanbur (1989) analyze the likely effects of structural adjustment on poverty. Glewwe and de Tray show that 92.3 percent of the poorest decile and 87.5 percent of the poorest three deciles are in households whose head is engaged in agriculture. Thus, most poverty is in agriculture, where there has been little change in real procurement prices for cash crops. As shown in the previous section, the prices of subsistence crops in areas other than the north increased between 1985 and 1986; however, whether these changes were part of a price trend or a result of the structural adjustment policies is not clear. Much of the analysis is therefore in terms of the consequences of possible future policies rather than the effects of actual policies that have been implemented.

Regional factors are very important in Côte d'Ivoire, particularly for poverty. The most important distinction is between the east and west forest areas on the one hand, and the northern savannah on the other. The forest regions grow cocoa and coffee as their major export crops, but these cannot be grown in the north. Cotton is the only export crop grown in the savannah.

Largely as a result of these differences, the north is particularly poor, with 56.8 percent of the poorest decile of the population and 40.1 percent of the poorest three deciles, although only 18.9 percent of the population live there. An increase in export crop prices will only benefit poor northern farmers if it includes cotton. However, Glewwe and de Tray (1988) show that higher producer prices for cotton would benefit 28 percent of the poorest decile and nearly 20 percent of the poorest three deciles. If this was accompanied by increased prices for coffee, cocoa, and oil palm, the benefit would spread to include 66 percent of the poorest decile and nearly 70 percent of the poorest three deciles. Such price increases would also benefit richer farmers and might even increase rural inequality. However, as rural incomes are on average lower than urban incomes, they could well reduce overall inequality and would certainly reduce poverty.

This means that a well-designed policy of price increases could benefit a high proportion of the poor, although any reduction in fertilizer subsidies to cotton farmers would have an opposite effect.

The urban sector experiences relatively little poverty, but has experienced considerable changes as a result of structural adjustment. One possible cause of poverty in urban areas is unemployment, and the reductions in employment in formal manufacturing suggest that unemployment could have increased, and this is supported by the data on unemployment. Newman (1987) reports that the LSMS data for 1985 revealed a national unemployment rate of 2.94 percent, which is somewhat higher than the figure of 2.5 percent for 1975 reported by the World Bank (1987). Also, Berthelemy and Bourgignon (1989, p. 95) report an increase in modern sector unemployment from 59,100 in 1983 to 86,400 in 1985.

The unemployment rate is virtually zero in rural areas, was about 11 percent in urban areas in 1985, and is highest in Abidjan (the area with the least poverty), at about 20 percent. Most of the unemployed are under 30 years old and may well be members of households that can support them without falling below the poverty line. This is supported by the fact that fewer than 1 percent of the heads of the poorest 10 percent of households are unemployed, while almost 75 percent of them are self-employed (Glewwe and de Tray 1988, table 6). Thus, urban poverty results from the poor earnings of the self-employed, rather than unemployment. However, both of these can be the result of low demand in the urban labor market.

Unfortunately, no data on the effects of structural adjustment on the earnings of the self-employed are available, but some more detailed idea of the effects of structural adjustment on urban unemployment can be obtained by looking at the people in the LSMS panel who stopped working. Of the people who left the urban labor force between 1985 and 1986, around 36 percent were aged 18 or less, 37 percent were women between the ages of 19 and 59, and 8 percent were aged 60 or over. Many of the young people might be returning to full-time education, many of the women may be leaving because of household responsibilities, and the people over 60 may be retiring. The remaining 19 percent are men aged 19 to 59. Of those, the majority had been employees in 1985 and were either looking for work or waiting to start a new job. It is therefore likely that most of these adult men were either dismissed or laid off temporarily.

This confirms that the reduction in formal employment has indeed caused unemployment. The importance of this unemployment for poverty depends, in part, on the speed with which people can find new jobs. We can get some idea of this by looking at people who were unemployed.

If we look at the 1986 employment status of those unemployed in 1985, 81 percent of them were still without a job, although 42 percent had stopped looking for work. Of the people who found work, 50 percent were employees (although some of them were also self-employed in business or agriculture). This is higher than the proportion of the overall urban work force who were employees (about 37 percent), and is interesting because it shows that self-employment cannot be regarded as the single major route into the labor market.

This shows that the unemployed have considerable difficulty in finding employment, and therefore that job losses can cause considerable hardship, although one could argue that these are the people who can afford not to enter self-employment. It is also evidence of a generally weak level of demand in the urban labor market, which can be expected to limit the ability of the self-employed (the main sufferers from poverty) to improve their standard of living.

Fertility and the Role of Women

Women's labor force participation has a different pattern from that of men. Their participation rate in rural areas is almost as high as men's, but it is substantially lower in urban areas, particularly in Abidjan. Also, the form of participation is different: women are much less likely to be employees and are mainly engaged in self-employment in business or agriculture. These differences mean that they are likely to be differently affected by structural adjustment that affects the balance between sectors.

Turning first to the distinction between male and female wage rates, table 7.21 provides the results of wage determination by sex. The differences in nationality and junior high school coefficients are particularly noticeable, with non-Ivorian women attaining a higher wage, other things being equal. The nature of returns to education and experience also differ by gender. However, it is comforting to find that there are significant returns for both men and women. The sample size confirms the much lower participation rates among urban women in wage labor (the employee sector). Much of this is due to their interrupted work patterns caused mainly by child rearing. The experience coefficients in table 7.21 point clearly to the effects on female wage rates of lost work experience. If we couple this with the earlier drop out of women from education, the implications for the relative economic position of women are critical. This would be especially so if under structural adjustment the returns to human- and job-specific capital increase.

Fertility has a major effect on participation for women, and in turn, a major effect, through experience, on their returns from the labor market. Table 7.22 presents some estimates of the impact of certain critical factors on the number of children ever born. The difference of income and schooling effects across urban and rural sectors provides more support for our decision to split the analysis along these lines. Descriptive statistics for these women are provided in appendix C,

Table 7.21 Wage Equations for Men and Women

Symbol	Men	Women
Sample Size	414	100
NAT	-0.214 (1.96)	0.558 (2.03)
YRS-EL	0.041 (0.99)	-0.113 (0.81)
YRS-Hl	0.079 (1.67)	0.164 (1.72)
YRS-H2	0.074 (0.64)	-0.260 (1.20)
YRS-UN	0.211 (5.64)	0.936 (1.41)
BASICED	0.109 (1.58)	0.109 (0.46)
DIP-EL	0.528 (3.07)	0.683 (1.52)
DIP-Hl	0.523 (2.75)	0.615 (1.88)
DIP-UPP	0.223 (0.68)	1.489 (2.08)
DIP-TEC	0.059 (0.47)	-0.173 (0.76)
YRS-TEC	0.073 (2.32)	0.102 (1.61)
YRS-APP	0.004 (0.19)	0.128 (1.03)
Exp.	0.117 (8.51)	0.093 (2.79)
Exp^2	-0.002 (4.27)	-0.002 (1.77)
Const	3.537 (17.94)	4.554 (11.36)
R^2	0.673	0.655

Note: See table 7.8 for definitions of symbols.
Source: van der Gaag and Vijverberg (1989).

tables 7.C1(a) and 7.C1 (b). The most impressive aspect of table 7.22 is the strong impact of education on family size among urban women. However, for rural women the income effect appears to dominate. This partly reflects the lower education levels of women in the rural sector, but may also suggest a different allocation of work activities in the two sectors.

Table 7.22 Children Ever Born

Variable	Urban women	Rural women
Age	0.4891	0.4106
	(0.0308)	(0.0285)
Age^2	-0.0046	-0.0036
	(0.0004)	(0.0003)
School years	-0.0990	-0.0633
	(0.0168)	(0.0391)
Log (income)	-0.0842	0.5827
	(0.1286)	(0.1444)
Constant	-5.2096	-12.0359
	(1.588)	(1.810)
R^2	0.528	0.363
N	597	847

Notes: Income refers to permanent income per adult; asymptotic standard errors in parentheses.
Source: Ainsworth (1989).

Migration and Economic Incentives

Evidence on the extent and determinants of migration is scarce. The LSMS panel does provide some distinction between those who remain in their local area and those who leave, including some information on reasons for leaving. However, it does not provide employment and income measures for those who leave (table 7.23). As a result, measuring the effect of economic incentives on migration seems a difficult task. However, for those in employment before migration Vijverberg (1989) provides a rather innovative analysis that lends some strong support to the hypothesis of clear economic incentives to migrate. Although these results are preliminary, the importance of this transition for countries undergoing adjustment places a high value on any information about the nature of economic incentives on migration (table 7.24). In table 7.24, the wage-gap and prof-gap variables refer to the estimated gap in wage and profits, respectively, between the actual and expected returns to working. The returns to labor in household enterprises is measured by its contribution to enterprise profits. The expected return is calculated

Table 7.23 Characteristics of LSMS Panel Members, Aged 12 to 65, by Participation and Migration Status

	Participants			Nonparticipants		
Category	Abidjan	Other urban	Rural	Abidjan	Other urban	Rural
A. Per capita consumption expenditures (CFA 1,000)*						
Migrants	687	359	262	514	314	215
	(781)	(249)	(153)	(469)	(166)	(163)
Nonmigrants	702	416	257	633	395	212
	(722)	(350)	(200)	(633)	(302)	(179)
B. Reason for migration among migrants (percent)						
Work (self/family)	28.6	41.2	26.7	50.0	40.2	30.3
Marriage	14.3	8.8	20.0	11.5	6.5	28.3
School	0.0	5.9	0.0	11.5	26.2	13.1
Other/unknown	57.2	44.1	53.3	26.9	27.1	28.3
Total	100.0	100.0	100.0	100.0	100.0	100.0
C. Destination of migrants (percent)						
City	42.9	50.0	53.3	34.6	54.2	54.2
Town	0.0	26.5	13.3	26.9	28.0	11.0
Large village	0.0	14.7	6.7	7.7	9.4	17.9
Small village	14.2	2.9	20.0	7.7	6.5	5.5
Camp	0.0	2.9	0.0	7.7	.9	11.7
Other/unknown	42.9	2.9	6.7	15.4	.9	1.4
Total	100.0	100.0	100.0	100.0	100.0	100.0
Number of observations						
Migrants	7	34	15	26	107	145
Nonmigrants	246	221	205	389	440	1,720

* Annual, modified by equivalence scale (Glewwe 1987).
Source: Vijverberg (1989).

Table 7.24 A Probit Model of the Determinants of Migration

Variable	Coefficient	T-statistic
Constant	-1.190	(2.76)
Education (years)	0.033	(1.11)
Age	-0.009	(1.01)
Female	-0.010	(0.05)
Head of household	0.109	(0.41)
Household size	0.006	(0.40)
Wage	-0.070	(2.20)
Wage gap	0.346	(2.07)
Profession	-0.113	(3.03)
Profession gap	0.110	(1.90)

Notes: Data as in table 7.23.
Source: Vijverberg (1989).

using standard wage and unit profit regressions. The strong positive effect, especially for the wage-gap variable, indicates the potential importance of economic incentives in migration trends. If we add to this the similarity, in characteristics, between migrants who were participants (and therefore used in table 7.23) and those who were not in work, we might expect migration to respond quite significantly to the relative returns to work across different areas in Côte d'Ivoire. Taken together with our results exported earlier that showed the movement into agricultural self-employment, in which output prices have maintained their real value, it suggests that labor markets in Côte d'Ivoire have responded quite generally to relative returns available in different labor market sectors and locations.

Conclusion

We have argued that any analysis of structural adjustment in Côte d'Ivoire must distinguish between the rural and urban areas. Until recently the rural areas were hardly affected by structural adjustment. This means that the analysis has had to be in terms of the likely consequences of future agricultural price changes. Our analysis showed that labor supply in rural areas is responsive to such incentives. We have also seen that price increases of four main crops can help the majority of poor people. Thus, a price increase can increase output and reduce poverty. However, in the context of the recently announced coffee procurement price reductions, our results suggest a reduction in labor supply and an increase in poverty.

By contrast, the urban sector has been affected by a combination of structural adjustment and external shocks for longer. Formal employment has fallen while informal employment and self-employment has risen. There is some evidence that those industries favored by government policy, such as those producing goods that are heavily traded internationally, have performed better than average, and some have even increased their labor force. Thus, the labor market has succeeded in reallocating labor between industries, and the evidence suggests that this has involved a reduction in the real wages of most workers. The urban labor market continues to suffer from a low level of demand and the unemployed have difficulty finding work. Urban poverty has therefore probably increased during the period of structural adjustment.

Our analysis suggests that structural adjustment has resulted in a move of the labor force into agriculture. There is also some evidence of a shift in urban employment from services into manufacturing. There is no particular reason to suppose that an increase in the production of manufactured tradable goods is not sustainable in the long run. There are, however, some doubts as to whether agricultural exports can be expanded without serious reductions in world prices. These doubts center mainly on cocoa and coffee exports, whose significance has been greatly reinforced by the recent reduction in procurement prices. If agricultural exports were increased through diversification, the shift in resources into agriculture might be beneficial in the long run.

The other possible long-run problem of structural adjustment is the diversion of young people out of education and into work at too early a stage. The paper by Alessie and others (1990) suggests that this may not be a severe problem: the young people who respond to incentives are those who are maintaining some contact with school, while the decision to leave school completely does not seem to be strongly influenced by current prices. As reentry into full-time education is reasonably easy for those who maintain contact, this suggests that households may not be sacrificing their children's long-term interests for the sake of exploiting short-term price movements.

APPENDIX A
THE LABOR SUPPLY MODEL

The separable model of labor supply can be expressed as:

$$L_s = F(cp, w, I, z) \qquad (A.1)$$

where L_s is a measure of labor supply, cp is an index of consumer prices, w is the market wage rate, I is profit and other nonlabor income, and z is a vector of household characteristics.

Market wages are given by:

$$w = G(pp, x) \qquad (A.2)$$

where pp is an index of product prices, and x is a vector of other factors that affect wages.

This produces a reduced form:

$$L_s = H(cp, pp, I, z, x) \qquad (A.3)$$

In the nonseparable model, labor supply is given by:

$$L_s = f(cp, I, w, pp, LAND, z) \qquad (A.4)$$

where LAND is the quantity of land available to the household.

Once again one can substitute out for wages in the case where there is a labor market, resulting in:

$$L_s = h(cp, I, pp, LAND, z, x) . \qquad (A.5)$$

The nonseparable model has additional terms in both the structural equation (A.4) and the reduced form equation (A.5). A comparison of equations (A.4) and (A.1) shows the addition of producer prices and land, while a comparison of equations (A.5) and (A.3) shows the introduction of land.[1]

---

1. It is possible that the area of land is also a choice variable of the household. In that case, a full analysis of labor force participation would also require the modeling of land area decisions.

Appendix B
The Statistical Model of Transitions

The most natural statistical model for describing such relationships takes the form of a state-dependent discrete transition model in which current period work status is related directly to a vector of characteristics "z_i" for individual "i", conditional on last period's work status. If there were only two initial states, work and nonwork, described by whether an index S_i^0 equals unity or zero, then the probability of being observed in work in the current period $\left(S_i^0 = 1 \right)$ would be given by:

$$\Pr\left[S_i^1 = 1 \right] = F\left(z_i' \beta \right) . \Pr\left[S_i^0 = 1 \right] + F\left(z_i' \gamma \right) . \Pr\left[S_i^0 = 0 \right] \tag{B1}$$

where $F(.)$ describes each discrete state-dependent probability and ß the parameters of staying in work conditional on working in the initial period while γ the parameters of the transition probability into work.

If β and γ, the parameters of the two possible transitions into work in equation (Bl),were equal, there would be no state dependence. Indeed, apart from variables that may change from one period to the next, $\Pr[S^0=l] = \Pr[S^1=l]$. In this case cross-sectional data alone could be used to estimate the underlying parameters since $\Pr[S=l] = F\left(z' \beta \right)$. However, with state-dependence the repeated observations available on each individual in panel data is required. Since we have stressed the policy importance of state-dependence in our general model of work and schooling this issue will become an important aspect of our empirical results.

APPENDIX C
DESCRIPTIVE STATISTICS FOR THE FERTILITY ANALYSIS

Table 7.C1(a) Sample Means and Standard Deviations for Fertility Analysis, by Location

Variable	All Women Mean	SD	Urban Mean	SD	Rural Mean	SD
Children ever born	3.91	3.30	3.14	3.05	4.46	3.37
Age	34.31	15.07	30.38	12.93	37.07	15.85
Years of Education	1.69	3.43	3.40	4.47	0.48	1.59
Dummy, 1–6 years	0.136	0.343	0.194	0.396	0.094	0.292
Dummy, 1–2 years	0.029	0.168	0.027	0.162	0.031	0.173
Dummy, 3–6 years	0.107	0.309	0.168	0.373	0.064	0.244
Dummy, 7+ years	0.107	0.309	0.243	0.429	0.011	0.103
Urban dummy	0.41	0.49	1.00	0.00	0.00	0.00
Ln permanent income/adult	12.59	0.82	13.09	0.72	12.24	0.68
Ln current income/adult	12.29	1.43	12.81	1.33	11.92	1.39
Ln nonlabor income/adult	8.31	3.32	10.10	2.52	7.04	3.23
N	1,444		597		847	

Table 7.C1(b) Sample Means and Standard Deviations for Fertility Analysis, by Age

	Age 15–24		Age 25–34		Age 35+	
Variable	*Mean*	*SD*	*Mean*	*SD*	*Mean*	*SD*
Children ever born	1.13	1.28	3.90	2.27	6.06	3.29
Age	19.53	2.73	28.94	2.73	48.74	11.38
Years of Education	3.06	3.88	2.26	4.20	0.31	1.56
Urban dummy	0.53	0.50	0.45	0.50	0.30	0.46
Ln permanent income/adult	12.65	0.77	12.77	0.88	12.44	0.79
Ln current income/adult	12.44	1.00	12.47	1.52	12.04	1.62
Ln nonlabor income/adult	8.76	2.99	8.42	3.17	7.89	3.59
N	473		355		616	

References

Ainsworth, M. 1989. *Socioeconomic Determinants of Fertility in Côte d'Ivoire.* Living Standards Measurement Study Working Paper No. 53. Washington, D.C.: World Bank.

Ainsworth, M., and J. Munoz. 1986. *The Côte d'Ivoire Living Standards Survey: Design and Implementation.* Living Standards Measurement Study Working Paper No. 26. Washington, D.C.: World Bank.

Alessie, R., P. Baker, R. Blundell, C. Heady, and C. Meghir. 1990. "The Working Behaviour of Young People in Rural Côte d'Ivoire." UCL Discussion Paper 90-01, January. London: University College London.

Berthelemy, J. C., and F. Bourgignon. 1989. "Growth and Crisis in Côte d'Ivoire." Paris: DELTA. Processed.

Bhatia, Rattan J. 1985. *The West African Monetary Union, An Analytical Review.* IMF Occasional Paper No. 35. Washington, D.C.: IMF.

Chenery, Hollis, and T. N. Srinivasan. 1989. *Handbook of Development Economics,* vol. II. Amsterdam: North Holland.

Deaton, A., and D. Benjamin. 1987. "Household Surveys and Policy Reform: Cocoa and Coffee in the Côte d'Ivoire." Research Program in Development Studies Discussion Paper No. 134. Princeton, New Jersey: Princeton University.

Devarajan, Shantayana, and Jaime de Melo. 1987. "Evaluating Participation in African Monetary Unions: A Statistical Analysis of the CFA Zones." *World Development* 15: 483–496.

Fields, G., 1989. "Labor Market Policy and Structural Adjustment in Côte d'Ivoire." Washington, D.C.: World Bank.

Glewwe, P. 1987. *The Distribution of Welfare in the Republic of Côte d'Ivoire in 1985.* Living Standards Measurement Study Working Paper No. 29. Washington, D.C.: World Bank.

Glewwe, P., and D. de Tray. 1988. *The Poor during Adjustment: A Case Study of Côte d'Ivoire.* Living Standards Measurement Study Working Paper 47. Washington, D.C.: World Bank.

Heckman, J. J. 1981. "Heterogeneity and State Dependence." In S. Rosen, ed., *Studies in Labor Markets,* pp. 91–139. Chicago: University of Chicago Press.

IMF. Various years. *International Financial Statistics.* Washington, D.C.

Islam, S. 1984. "Devaluation, Stabilization Policies, and the Developing Countries." *Journal of Development Economics* 14: 37–60.

Kanbur, R. 1989. "Poverty Alleviation Under Structural Adjustment: A Conceptual Framework and Its Application to the Côte d'Ivoire." Washington, D.C.: World Bank. Processed.

Laker, John F. 1981. "Fiscal Proxies for Devaluation: A General Review." *IMF Staff Papers* 28: 118–143.

Lavy, V., and J. Newman. 1989. "Wage Rigidity: Micro and Macro Evidence on Labor Market Adjustment in the Modern Sector." *The World Bank Economic Review* 1(1): 97–117.

Lorch, K. 1989. "Côte d'Ivoire: Industrial Competitiveness During Economic Crisis and Adjustment." Washington, D.C.: World Bank. Processed.

Medhora, Rohinton. 1989. "The West African Monetary Union: Institutional Arrangements and the Link With France." Toronto: University of Toronto. Draft.

Nakamura, A., and M. Nakamura. 1985. "Dynamic Models of the Labor Force Behaviour of Married Women That Can Be Estimated Using Limited Amounts of Past Information." *Journal of Econometrics* 27(2): 273–298.

Neurrisse, Andre. 1987. *Le Franc CFA.* Librairie General de Droit et de Jurisprudence .

Newman, J. L. 1987. *Labor Market Activity in Côte d'Ivoire and Peru.* Living Standards Measurement Study Working Paper 36. Washington, D.C.: World Bank.

Newman, J. L., and P. Gertler. 1988. "Female Farm Work and Home Work in Rural Côte d'Ivoire." Welfare and Human Resources Division. Washington, D.C.:World Bank. Processed.

Pegatienan Hiey, Jacques. 1987. *Ivory Coast, Stabilization and Adjustment Policies and Programs.* Country Study No. 16. Helsinki, Finland: World Institute For Development Economics Research.

Singh, I., L. Squire, and J. Strauss, eds. 1986. *Agricultural Household Models.* Baltimore, Md.: Johns Hopkins University Press.

Taylor, Lance. 1981. "IS/LM in the Tropics: Diagrammatics of the New Structuralist Macro Critique." In William R. Cline and Sidney Weintraub, eds., *Economic Stabilization in Developing Countries.* Washington, D.C.: Brookings Institution.

_____. 1983. *Structuralist Macroeconomics, Applicable Models For the Third World.* New York: Basic Books.

van der Gaag, J., and W. Vijverberg. 1989. "Wage Determinants in Côte d'Ivoire: Experience, Credentials and Human Capital." *Economic Development and Cultural Change* 37(2): 371–381.

Vijverberg, W. 1988. *Nonagricultural Family Enterprises in Côte d'Ivoire: A Descriptive Analysis.* Living Standards Measurement Study Working Paper 46. Washington, D.C.: World Bank.

_____. 1989. *Labor Market Performance as a Determinant of Migration.* Living Standards Measurement Study Working Paper 59. Washington, D.C.: World Bank.

Vinay, Bernard. 1980. *Zone Franc et Cooperation Monetaire.* Paris: Ministry of Cooperation.

World Bank. 1987. "The Côte d'Ivoire in Transition: From Structural Adjustment to Self-Sustained Growth." Washington, D.C.

_____. 1988. *World Development Report 1988.* New York: Oxford University Press.

_____. Various years. *World Debt Tables.* Washington, D.C.

8

Egypt *J60* *E43*

Egypt
022
015
011

Ragui Assaad
Simon Commander

What happens in the labor market is critical for the aggregate efficiency of adjustment. However, common assumptions include not only *ex ante* full employment, but also relatively frictionless adjustment mechanisms, particularly as regards labor mobility (Corden 1989). A standard framework accommodates some adjustment costs, but the switching assumptions yield the same levels of aggregate employment. Wage rigidity is assumed to be absent if the *ex ante* employment level is to be undisturbed.

Some of the problems that arise with such a framework for applied work include the following. First, with the normal two goods, four factors model, the key price relationship is that of tradables/ nontradables or the real exchange rate, but this assumes free trade, or at least low to constant tariffs. Two independent, domestic, relative prices exist: the price of exportables relative to importables, and the price of importables relative to nontradables where the former depends on the terms of trade and tariffs, and the latter on the exchange rate and domestic money supply (Collier 1988). Second, one normally assumes that capital is sector-specific in the short-medium term, but that labor is mobile. Wages are also held to be flexible. If wage rigidity obtains in the covered or formal sector, this would imply a sharper fall in real wages in the uncovered sector. If, however, real wage flexibility exists alongside segmentation and hence a lack of mobility, a real devaluation will require a correspondingly higher level of real wage decline in both sectors and unemployment in

Table 8.1 Macroeconomic Indicators, 1973–88

Indicator	1973	1974	1975	1976	1977	1978	1979	1980	1981	1982	1983	1984	1985	1986	1987	1988
Rate of growth																
GDP[a]	0.8	2.7	9.1	15.3	13.5	5.9	6.2	10.3	3.8	10.1	7.6	6.2	6.7	2.7	2.5	3.2
Tradables output[a]	0.6	-1.4	10.9	8.5	10.5	11.5	7.1	13.8	4	5.8	5.9	8.5	1.5	n.a.	n.a.	n.a.
Nontradables output[a]	20.1	16.1	9.3	20.5	9	5.9	12.4	15.9	8.1	6.4	4.2	4.7	2.3	n.a	n.a	n.a.
CPI	4.2	12	11.6	11.2	10.8	13.6	7.4	23.4	14.7	15.7	22.1	10.3	14	23.7	20	18.9
Real interest rate	0.6	-6.5	-6.2	-3.9	-8.6	-5.3	-0.7	-9.9	-3.5	-5.6	-5.6	0.6	-5.3	-10.2	-6.4	-5.3
Shares of GDP																
Budget deficit	-10.1	-20.5	-28.6	-18.8	-16.9	-23	-26.9	-15.8	-25.3	-19.1	-23.1	-22	-22.8	-17.1	-20.0	-19.8
Current account deficit	0.2	-14.4	-18.2	-7.9	-6.8	-5.4	-10.6	-6.4	-9.5	-11.8	-6.8	-7.5	-10	-9.7	-6	-3.1
Remittances	1.3	1.7	2.7	4.4	4.2	7	13.5	11.4	11.5	6.5	9.2	9.7	7.4	5.4	4.6	4.1
Gross fixed investment	21	16	25	22	22	27	30	27	29	27	24	22	22	18	18.5	19
Terms of trade[b]	96	96	83	83	82	74	93	100	102	93	93	89	88	76	57	n.a.
Real effective exchange rate[b]	164	155	159	176	183	178	95	100	116	139	166	199	226	240	255	281

n.a. = not available
a. 1980 prices.
b. 1980 = 100.
Sources: Central Agency for Public Mobilization and Statistics (CAPMAS), Government of Egypt, and World Bank.

the uncovered sector.[1] The output effect in the tradables sector will consequently be constrained by the capital/labor slack. This appears to be recent Egyptian experience. Further, if labor does not move into the tradables sector, investment incentives will be weak given that the marginal physical product of extant capital does not increase. In such cases, the only stimulant to new investment is the relative price increase for output over capital. When—as in the Egyptian case—the adjustment path is marked by wage flexibility alongside constraints on mobility and an inability to correct fundamental macroeconomic imbalances, the costs of that partial adjustment on both the wage and employment sides become correspondingly higher.

Some Macroeconomic Features of the Egyptian Economy

Under the impetus of an oil windfall in the early 1970s and higher transfers into the Egyptian economy, growth accelerated significantly over trend attaining around 10 percent per annum from 1973 through 1982 (table 8.1). Since then deceleration has occurred, which has been associated with strong adverse terms of trade shocks equal to 11 percent of GDP between 1982 and 1987. Since 1986 per capita consumption growth has turned negative, real investment has fallen off sharply, while the degree of fiscal adjustment required of the economy has been made more profound by the large external debt overhang. By 1988 aggregate external debt exceeded 115 percent of GDP, with debt service amounting to over 60 percent of exports. Current projections suggest little likelihood of GDP growth surpassing 3.5 percent per annum over the medium term. Moreover, the economy remains marked by profound domestic and external imbalances, with the current account deficit exceeding 10 percent of GDP and the fiscal deficit extending to over 20 percent of GDP through the 1980s. Conservatively estimated, domestic inflation rates have ranged from 15 to 25 percent per annum. Real wages have fallen to roughly 80 percent of 1982 levels, and open unemployment, though consistently rising from 1960 onward, appears to have grown rapidly between 1976 and 1986. Census data indicate that the unemployment rate

---

1. Such a result could be achieved through job security, other nonwage benefits and particular institutional features of the labor market.

more than doubled from 5.3 percent in 1976 to 12.4 percent in 1986 (CAPMAS 1976, 1986).

The policy response to external shocks—declining export revenues, falling remittances, and lower real transfers into the economy—have been spasmodic and inconsistent. Agreement with both the IMF and the World Bank, particularly on the pace of economic reform, has been largely absent. A managed adjustment path remains particularly difficult given the scale of controls and price fixing rules operating in the economy. Such controls include not only administered prices and forced deliveries for the major agricultural sector tradables—cotton and rice—but also particular labor market interventions. These interventions include centralized determination of the floor for wage increments, constraints on hiring and firing for enterprises with more than ten employees, and the massive presence of the consolidated public sector in the employment of Egyptians. Equally, the widespread use of subsidies on wage goods (with total subsidies accounting for at least 5.5 percent of GDP in 1988) and the use of the public food ration and subsidy system for basic income support raises direct, short-run tradeoffs between fiscal pressures and a historical commitment to low-cost wage goods.

Gradualism has been the dominant adjustment method. The fiscal deficit had been trimmed somewhat to some 20 percent of GDP by 1988, subsidies on both food and energy had been reduced through a combination of price increases and falling import costs, while the range of goods attracting subsidies had been cut.[2] In all, subsidies have been reduced by over 8 percent of GDP during the past six years. As for the majority of developing countries, public expenditure reductions have fallen mostly on capital outlays, with rapid growth in interest payments marking the current expenditure side. Gross domestic investment fell by about 1.3 percent per annum between 1982 and 1987, with drastic declines in 1986 and 1987. While real wage decline and fiscal contraction have achieved some demand dampening, aggregate consumption has risen to over 90 percent of GDP from around 85 percent through the 1980s.

---

2. The size of the wedge between domestic and border prices for energy is such that over 300 percent upward adjustment of nominal prices has still left petroleum products at around 30 percent of border prices.

A more active exchange rate policy has resulted in greater consolidation of transactions in the so-called free market or commercial pool, which has depreciated by 20 percent since 1982. A weighted index for the real effective exchange rate indicates, however, an appreciation of over 40 percent between 1982 and 1987/88. Further measures—such as foreign earnings retention—designed to stimulate exports have resulted in some positive response for nonoil exports, but despite explicit policy measures to raise agricultural prices and limit the share of output taken in forced deliveries, output of the major exportable—cotton—has been held back by producer prices ranging from 30 to 40 percent of international prices, as well as low relative returns to both cotton and rice, the other main exportable.

Although the size of the real wage decline in the economy in recent years suggests gains in external competitiveness (real wages being a counterpart of the real exchange rate), the absence of appropriate fiscal and monetary policy, combined with powerful market rigidities and a reduction in the size and short- to medium-term scope for expansion of the market sector, has tended to dampen any shift into exportables. As will become clear, labor market rigidities, in particular, the consequences of an expanded public and government sector for labor mobility and output mix, remain key features yet to be addressed in a sustained adjustment program.

Windfall, Economic Liberalization, and the Labor Market

Economists have argued that the post-1973 boom and the government's economic liberalization measures (*Infitah*) provide a classical Dutch disease story (Dervis and others 1984). Under the standard argument of a relative price effect, and hence appreciation of the real exchange rate, the oil and associated activities' windfall effectively contracted the nonbooming tradables sector, bolstered output from the nontraded goods sector, and, finally, as the windfall petered out, left the economy exposed to massive external and domestic account imbalances. This outcome on the external account side was derived from contraction in the nonoil exportables subsector and from rigidities that constrained the transfer of resources postwindfall into the nonoil tradables sector. Further, as the windfall accrued primarily to government and the elasticity of expenditure to permanent revenue exceeded unity with no consumption smoothing, the level of fiscal imbalance was likewise exaggerated, with public expenditure cuts incommensurate to the subsequent decline in income. The presence or absence of such a Dutch disease effect is important not only for understanding the macroeconomic story (and hence the required adjustment), but also for the particular labor market response that might be expected.

In labor market terms a Dutch disease model can generate a number of outcomes. In the first place, the expenditure effect combined with resource movement will generate shifts in sectoral labor allocation (Corden and Neary 1982). The most obvious would occur as labor moves into the booming sector. If that sector—as is habitually the case with oil-generated booms—is an enclave, then the derived demand for labor and materials from the domestic economy will be low given both the capital and import intensities of the enclave. However, the conventional weak employment shifts that might be expected need to be qualified somewhat. In the Egyptian case, the regional nature of the oil boom had significant implications for the demand for labor. One component of *Infitah* was the liberalization of rules regarding the rights of Egyptians to work abroad. This resulted in a rapid growth in migration to other Arab states, with remittances increasing more than 14-fold (in real terms) between 1973 and 1980. Thus, the counterpart of one major component of the growth in exogenous resources into the economy was an outflow of labor. In this respect, the regional spillover effects resulted in labor being bid away from the nonoil sectors, particularly agriculture. This caused upward pressure on the wage level, and in the late 1970s/early 1980s led to severe skill mismatching in segments of the labor market (Hansen and Radwan 1982).

The effects of expenditure growth, public expenditure growth in particular, complemented the growth in regional derived demand for labor from the oil sector. If, on standard assumptions, output in the tradables and nontradables sectors is a function of the real product wage, then a windfall will drive up the wage rate when measured in traded goods, at the same time raising the relative price of nontraded to traded goods. As output in the nonbooming tradables sector is likely to be inversely related to the wage rate, this would result in a change in the composition of aggregate output, with a declining share in that sector. For many developing economies this is likely to have an impact on the agricultural sector, especially the exportables subsector.

If the booming sector is indeed an enclave, this would result in deteriorating intersectoral terms of trade for agriculture with likely widening in the rural-urban wage gap. Dynamically, one might expect this to yield accelerated internal migration. However, if—as with Egypt—the booming sector (regionally construed) does bid away labor and a significant share of that labor originates in agriculture, the effect on the nonoil exportables sector will be similar, but the adverse terms of trade shift against agriculture will be absent. The derived labor demand from the enclave will raise the real wage, with the ultimate employment outcome depending on the relative labor demand schedules for the nontradables sector compared to nonoil tradables. In the case of Egyptian agriculture, disentangling these effects is complicated by joint production of tradables and nontradables and the system of forced deliveries. Even if we assume weak resource movement, the spending effect of a windfall would itself be a sufficient condition for raising the real wage. However, if the share of the nontraded goods output in the consumption basket exceeds its contribution to a weighted average of the supply elasticities of the two sectors (that is, excess demand for the nontraded good), then a windfall might result in a fall in the wage and unemployment. When the reverse relationship holds, the outcome would be a rising consumption wage and labor scarcity (Neary and van Wijnbergen 1986).

The latter pattern appears to have characterized the Egyptian experience in certain respects. Real consumption wages rose significantly between 1973/74 and 1982/83, and in certain sectors significant labor shortages and skill mismatching, exaggerated by the structure of external migration, emerged. On a macro plane, however, some expected results were absent. Contrary to standard models, a current account surplus with parallel reserve inflows did not materialize. This can be attributed to the strong pulling-in of imports that followed a period of repressed demand and was financed through own-exchange imports. Moreover, as citizens were allowed to hold foreign currency balances, the appreciation was associated with capital outflow (Braga de Macedo 1982). Nevertheless, with a fixed exchange rate, a strong parallel market for foreign exchange, and legalized holdings of foreign money balances a number of Dutch disease features resulted. Nonoil exports fell in real terms, while a declining exchange rate had predictable current account consequences The distribution of gross investment likewise reflected not only a shift of resources in the oil sector, but some decline in the share of nonoil tradables in aggregate investment.

In looking at the resource allocative effects of the windfall, it is critical to accommodate explicitly the impact of tariffs and the trade regime on the distribution of investment across exportables, importables, and home goods subsectors. Here the free trade assumptions of the standard model lack relevance, so that investment can be hypothesized to respond not only to decline in the exchange rate and the domestic real interest rate, but to their combination with actual tariff levels. In the Egyptian case, despite some liberalization after 1973, the government maintained a wide range of quantitative restrictions and tariffs, with periodic notification. This resulted in a somewhat different set of outcomes than that generated from a standard Dutch disease model. Protection changed the impact on the nonoil tradables sector significantly.

Prior to considering the dynamic results of the boom, it would be useful to indicate the scale of expenditure effect associated with the windfall. In this context, the combination of oil revenues, tourism, Suez Canal earnings, and remittances shifted the share of exogenous resources from around 6 percent of GDP in 1974 to 45 percent by 1980/81 (World Bank 1983).[3] Oil and Suez Canal revenues alone accounted for a quarter of GDP growth in this period. The principal revenue source—oil—accounted for nearly a fifth of GDP by 1980 and was captured almost exclusively by the state. Exogenous revenues had increased from under 10 percent to 35 percent of total government revenues by 1980, while real government expenditure expanded by around 10 percent of GDP. Among other developments, this was associated with a powerful growth in the share of the labor force employed by the state with, until 1982, implicit wage

---

3. This excludes substantial concessional capital inflows.

indexation.[4] In addition, commitments were maintained with regard to guaranteed employment for graduates, the formal abrogation of which has not yet occurred. Alongside the growth in public spending, the period was also marked by a major increase in private investment, which rose from just over 1 percent of GDP in the early 1970s to 5 to 6 percent during 1978–82. Figure 8.1 indicates aggregate investment growth and the rising share of private investment.

Figure 8.1 Total Investment, 1973–86
(public, private and total, 1973 prices)

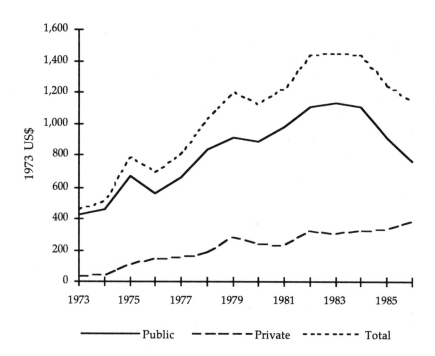

Source: CAPMAS.

---

4. Indexation was of an *ex post* type, namely: $w_t = \alpha_1 + \alpha_2 p_{t-1}$.

Measuring the relative price effects of the windfall is rendered complex by the presence of administered prices and controls, which are most pronounced for nontradables, such as housing, electricity, and transport, but also significant with regard to key tradables prices, such as wheat.[5] Official price series thus appear to demonstrate a far stronger rate of increase for tradables over nontradables prices through the windfall and beyond.[6] This reflects the weight of price controls on nontradables. Calculations of accounting prices, based on output values and hence measuring gross resource cost, indicate that alongside very high variance, median values for nontradables significantly exceeded unity, while those for tradables fell slightly below one (World Bank 1983).[7] This might imply a tradables/ nontradables price relationship the inverse of that apparently signified by official price series. The range of variance over the accounting ratios also points to difficulties in netting out these effects in the absence of reliable consumption weights. Rather, following Shafik (1989), the resource allocative consequences of the windfall are best mapped *ex post*, where sectoral shifts in private investment and labor are interpreted (with some caveats) as a response to relative factor returns in the three subsectors.

The oil windfall clearly provoked an investment boom, with real total investment trebling between 1973/74, and peaking in 1982/83 (figure 8.1). In a standard Dutch disease framework, one would expect rising investment in the booming sector and nontradables, with each round of investment further appreciating the exchange rate and aggravating the current account position. This would be further exaggerated if the speed of adjustment to desired capital stock levels

---

5. Ratios of shadow to market prices indicate, for example, that in 1980 for energy the mean ratio (unweighted) was around 7, with high subsidy urban consumer goods—butagas, rice, vegetable oil, and wheat (unweighted mean: 4.75)—being offset by heavily taxed goods, such as tea, coffee, and tobacco (unweighted mean: 0.5).

6. In 1973 terms, the index for tradables (drawn from official data) moved to 260 in 1980, 474 in 1985, and 792 by 1988; for nontradables 195, 324, and 497, respectively.

7. The accounting ratio being defined as the ratio of the shadow price to its market price, with shadow prices calculated using international prices for traded inputs and shadow factor prices for primary resources. An accounting ratio of one indicates nondistortion.

was strongly associated with foreign exchange availability and the supply of domestic capital goods was constrained. In the Egyptian case, moreover, one can assume that controlled price domestic capital goods are consumed almost entirely by the public sector. This implies that private sector demand for capital goods was largely satisfied through own-exchange imports. An index for components of aggregate investment shows a strong acceleration in imported capital goods prices as also for the construction component (appendix figure 8.A1). Consequently, the aggregate index grows much more rapidly than the GDP deflator. There are good reasons, however, for supposing that the GDP deflator has a downward bias. Note also that despite high levels of savings held in foreign currency with correspondent banks abroad, the banking sector was very liquid through the 1970s. This promoted a relatively expansive path for net credit to the private sector. Total domestic credit to the economy grew by over 16.5 percent per annum in real terms between 1973 and 1981, with private sector credit growing by over 18 percent per annum.

Investment was thus buoyant for a number of reasons. First, the elasticity of capital and intermediate goods imports to foreign exchange availability was high. The windfall raised that availability. Second, borrowing at significantly negative real interest rates (see table 8.l) from the domestic banking system to finance own-exchange imports was feasible. Third, while conservative in relation to the standing of borrowers, net credit expansion was significant and facilitated the investment boom. Fourth, following a period of stagnation and collapse in private investment, the liberalization after 1973 promoted a surge in private investment. The shift in expectations and the low base from which private investment expanded are significant factors in explaining the rate of increment. Fifth, the government enacted laws that eased foreign investment rules, such as Law 43 of 1974, and later, Laws 159 and 230. In reality, such rule changes stimulated domestic investment more than foreign direct investment. Sixth, with cost-plus pricing rules dominating Egyptian industry and with protection, the weak competitive features of the closed market raised desired capital stock levels via profitability and aggregate demand effects in the economy. With the prevailing interest rate structure, this yielded a relatively capital- and import-intensive structure of investment. Private investment in import substituting industry expanded significantly, but tended to be very capital intensive, particularly for the limited number of Law 43 enterprises that were established (Hansen and Radwan 1982).[8] The incremental capital/labor ratio in these projects were over double the average for the economy as a whole. Between 1978 and 1988, Law 43 enterprises generated less than 10 percent of total employment creation in the private sector, principally in manufacturing (Handoussa 1989).[9]

Note that tariff protection was both higher and more significant for the private sector than for the public sector. In the latter case, a substantial part of public sector industry—including cotton textiles— faced negative effective protection rates by the early 1980s, which demonstrates the perversity of the tariff and domestic pricing structure (World Bank 1983). Decomposing the effects of price controls and tariffs shows that the former had the most powerful effect on the level of (dis)protection. The reverse was true for the private sector, where price controls have been less apparent. Public sector industry tended not only to be marked by low efficiency levels (Handoussa 1983), but also by incoherent pricing rules at both enterprise and economywide levels. Anomalies emerged so that the public sector cotton textile industry faced negative protection, while the private textile sector benefited from protection, largely via tariffs. Consequently, investment was not as skewed toward nontradables as might be expected in a Dutch disease framework. Figures 8.2 and 8.3 show that while nontradables investment increased to a limited extent for the public sector, this was not the case for the private sector. Apart from rapid expansion of investment in the booming sector, that in nonoil tradables experienced steady growth through the 1970s. Indeed, private investment in import-substituting industry doubled as a share of private investment from around 11 percent for 1972/74 to some 22 percent between 1978 and 1981. This was reversed somewhat after 1980 (Shafik 1989).

---

8. The largest share of Law 43 investments has been in the financial sector.

9. At least a third of total investment under Law 43 projects has actually been mobilized from the public sector, either by way of direct equity stakes or long-term financing from public sector financial institutions.

Figure 8.2 Public Investment, 1973–81
(by subsector, 1973 prices)

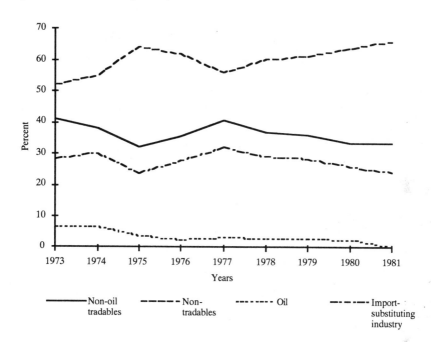

Source: CAPMAS.

The labor market consequences of the boom were marked by two
main features, the expansion of public employment and the relatively
weak employment multiplier from incremental investment in both the
domestic oil sector (as expected) and the import-substituting import
sector. In the latter, employment remained broadly constant (see table
8.2). The sharp decline in the share of the nonoil tradables sector can
be largely attributed to developments in agriculture. In terms of
investment, output, and employment, agriculture was subject to the
greatest contraction. As significant, the composition of output in the
primary sector shifted in a major way against exportables. The
available evidence indicates clearly the extent to which the major
tradables had negative effective protection rates through most of the
period 1973–85, whether using official or equilibrium exchange rates.

Figure 8.3 Private Investment, 1973–81
(by subsector, 1973 prices)

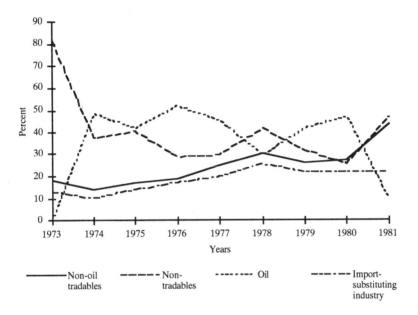

Source: CAPMAS.

For cotton, the effective protection rate using the official exchange
rate and expressed as a share of value added at border prices was
negative over a range of 22 to 200 percent in this period. Using an
equilibrium exchange rate measure, effective protection was generally
negative and in excess of 55 percent. Similarly high rates of net
taxation held for rice and wheat, with producers subject to taxation
through both direct and indirect price interventions (Dethier 1989). A
weighted output price ratio for the main tradables against the principal
nontradables shifted downward from 2.5 between 1965 and 1969, to
2.0 between 1975 and 1979, and 1.8 between 1980 and 1985.
Producers of fodder crops, horticultural produce, and other
noncontrolled outputs (including birseem and wheat straw, the main
types of livestock feed) benefited either from positive effective

Table 8.2 Structure of the Labor Force, 1973–86

Category	Number of people (millions)			Annual compound growth rate (percent)		Share of total (percent)			Share of increase (percent)	
	1973	1982	1986	1973–82	1982–86	1973	1982	1986	1973–82	1982–86
Economic sector										
Agriculture	4.7	4.3	4.2	-1.1	-0.4	50.5	36.8	32.7	-19.0	-5.0
Mining and quarrying (includes petroleum)	0.0	0.0	0.0	3.8	19.2	0.2	0.2	0.4	0.0	2.0
Manufacturing[a]	1.3	1.7	1.4	2.9	-3.7	13.9	14.4	11.2	17.0	-18.0
ISI[b]	(0.7)	(0.7)	(0.7)	0.2	0.8	(7.4)	(6.1)	(5.6)	(0.7)	(1.8)
Construction[a]	0.3	0.6	0.8	9.5	6.7	2.8	5.3	6.2	15.0	15.0
Services[c]	2.9	4.3	4.8	4.6	2.3	31.0	37.6	37.1	64.0	33.0
Transport	(0.4)	(0.6)	(0.6)	5.5	0.5	(4.1)	(5.3)	(4.9)	(10.5)	(1.0)
Total employment	9.1	10.9	11.2	2.0	0.8	98.5	94.3	87.6	78.0	27.0
Government	(1.5)	(2.0)	(2.4)	3.6	4.3	(15.9)	(17.7)	(18.9)	(25.1)	(30.2)
Public enterprise	(0.9)	(1.2)	(1.2)	3.9	0.3	(9.3)	(10.6)	(9.7)	(15.9)	(1.0)
Private (10 or more employees)	(0.2)	(0.3)	(0.3)	4.5	7.7	(1.8)	(2.2)	(2.7)	(3.6)	(7.1)
Unemployment	0.1	0.7	1.6	17.0	22.1	1.5	5.7	12.4	22.0	73.0
Total domestic labor force	9.3	11.6	12.8	2.4	2.6	100.0	100.0	100.0	100.0	100.0
Workers abroad[d]	0.1	0.6	1.2	23.7	23.4	0.8	5.2	9.4		

Notes: Includes individuals 12 to 64 only. Labor force proportions for 1973 and 1982 were calculated from the respective Labor Force Sample Surveys and applied to labor force estimates based on census results, to achieve comparability with 1986 census data.
a. The share of manufacturing seems to be understated and that of construction overstated in 1986.
b. ISI (import-substitution industrialization) includes all public and private (10+ employees) manufacturing.
c. Services include utilities, commerce, finance, insurance, real estate, transport, communications, community, and social and personal services.
d. The estimate of the number of Egyptian workers abroad in 1986 is the same as the figure Ferghany (1988) provides for early 1985. No estimate is available for 1986.
Sources: CAPMAS, *Labor Force Sample Surveys* for 1973 and 1982, *Population Census 1986, Wage and Hours of Work Bulletin, Permanent Employees in the Government and the Public Sector* for 1982 and 1986; other government employment data from Hansen and Radwan (1982, table A.1); public enterprise data from Public Enterprise Information Center, Cairo; migration data from Ferghany (1988).

protection and/or significantly lower taxation rates. This was particularly true for the livestock industry.

One consequence of the agricultural taxation policy and the relative price structure thereby generated was to induce particular patterns of technical change. First, the demand for crop labor (given higher demand, particularly for adult male labor, in tradables relative to nontradables) fell to some degree. Second, linked to the growth in outmigration from the sector to other Arab countries, after 1980, the government introduced an explicit set of policy measures—including discriminatory interest rates and direct credit allocations—whose objective was to induce capital/labor substitutions in production (Commander 1987). Thus, within agriculture resources shifted away from exportables, with labor reallocations to the import-substituting livestock and home goods sectors. The net effect of protection for the livestock subsector, with the growth in nonfarm employment and income as well as expanded external migration, offset domestically— up to 1984—the shift out of the exportables subsector. This allowed for a strong positive real wage effect, even as the move out of tradables had adverse implications for the trade balance.

As expected, the general investment boom was translated into rapid growth in the construction sector, whose share of the total labor force nearly doubled from 2.8 percent to 5.2 percent between 1973 and 1982. Moreover, the employment elasticity of output was high relative to other subsectors (table 8.3). However, the most important factor explaining the relative growth in nontradables employment can be attributed to the expansion of government and public employment, which grew by more than 3.5 percent per annum between 1973 and 1982, a full percentage point above the rate of growth in the total labor force. Compared with the pre-boom period, total public employment more than doubled, absorbing more than 40 percent of net labor force growth in this period. This expansion came on top of an earlier, sustained growth in public employment; a key feature of the Nasser period (Abdel Fadil 1980). This had important longer-run consequences by compressing the market sector of the economy, while also shifting resources into the importables and home goods subsectors. Allied to the wage setting mechanism and the graduate

Table 8.3 Growth in Value Added and Employment by Sector, 1973–1986

(1981/82 prices; annual growth rates in percent)

Sector	Value Added		Employment		Employment elasticity of output	
	1973–82	*1982–86*	*1973–82*	*1982–86*	*1973–82*	*1982–86*
Agriculture	2.5	2.3	-1.1	-0.4	-0.4	-0.2
Manufacturing	7.3	4.9	2.9	-3.1	0.4	-0.6
Construction	10.0	2.8	9.5	6.7	1.0	2.4
Services	6.3	4.1	4.6	2.3	0.7	0.6
Transport	15.0	6.8	5.5	0.5	0.4	0.1

Source: World Bank data.

employment guarantee scheme, this strongly affected the response of the labor market to the recession after 1982.

As regards the scale of migratory flows to the Gulf and other oil-rich economies in the region, estimates vary widely. By the early 1980s, possibly as many as one million Egyptians were working in other Arab countries (Amin and Awny 1985), implying a domestically available labor force roughly 9 to 10 percent below the potential upper bound. Other survey-based estimates (see table 8.2) point to no more than 200,000 Egyptians abroad in 1976, rising to 1.2 million in 1985 (Ferghany 1988). The bulk of the labor that was bid away from the domestic economy originated from agriculture and construction. The growth in external migration extended beyond the boom years, driven in the more recent period by demand from Iraq.

The period from 1973 to 1982 was thus associated with a combination of external migration, growth in public employment, consistent expansion of the informal sector, and broad stability in the share of employment in the import-substituting industry sector. The organized private sector (more than ten employees) also expanded rapidly, albeit from a very small base, but accounted for under 4 percent of net labor force growth in this period (table 8.2). These developments allowed for high levels of aggregate employment in the economy in the 1970s. Despite labor force growth of around 3 percent per annum, open unemployment (adjusted for seasonality) ranged between 3 and 5 percent in the mid-1970s and early 1980s (CAPMAS various years). The windfall was most clearly associated with reduced employment and relatively weak growth in the agricultural sector (tables 8.2 and 8.3). The agricultural labor force declined by 1.1 percent per annum and from 50 percent of the labor force in 1973 to under 37 percent by 1982. Seasonal employment variability fell, with peak period upswings in labor demand being filled by more female and child labor (Richards and Martin 1983). Furthermore, adverse shifts in the terms of trade against agriculture did not result, as the important livestock subsector benefited from positive protection.

With greater internal mobility and a rapid growth in nonfarm labor income, the boom period witnessed a narrowing of wage differentials (a phenomenon extended in the post-boom period) across sectors. Although the share of households below calorie and protein cutoff levels was significantly higher in rural than in urban areas—7.9 percent of rural households compared to 4.3 percent of urban households in 1981/82 (Alderman and von Braun 1984)—the data indicate a very major fall in the share of the rural population in poverty (Adams 1985). Even so, survey data for 1984 suggest that roughly 25 to 33 percent of small-farm households (those with less than three acres) had incomes on or below a household adjusted poverty line (Commander 1987).

Wages through Boom and Recession

With a windfall and an appreciation in the real exchange rate, upward pressure on the real wage would be expected. The degree to which this occurs depends on relative supply elasticities and consumption weights. Both spending and resource movement effects would promote wage expansion. This appears to be valid in the Egyptian context.

Available wage data reveal that real wages rose substantially between 1973 and 1982, except in the government sector, which remained broadly constant (figures 8.4 and 8.5). The strongest upward movement was for agriculture, where real wages rose by 11 percent per annum, thereby trebling during 1973–84. The rate of

Figure 8.4 Real Wage by Sector of Economic Activity
(LE per week, 1973 prices)

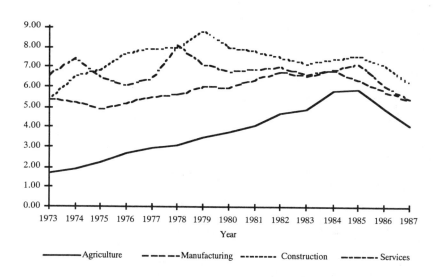

Sources: CAPMAS *EWHW Bulletin*; Assaad (1990) for construction wages; Handoussa (1988) for government wages; Ministry of Agriculture for agricultural wages.

increase would be further enhanced if reductions in the standard working day were incorporated. In the case of agriculture, the rate of growth in the real wage can be largely attributed to labor supply shocks with labor being bid away to both the regional labor market and the urban construction sector (Richards and Martin 1983).[10] Hansen (1987) has rightly argued that in the Egyptian context, mobility and search costs are low, which facilitates labor transfers out of the sector. Consequently, during periods of growth agriculture releases labor to the rest of the economy, acting as a reservoir during recessions. Linked to external migration, this has resulted in a

10. The construction sector largely uses agricultural workers for temporary unskilled work. With the boom, the temporary nature of the work was diluted, and recent survey data show that over 40 percent of permanent unskilled construction labor originated in agriculture (Assaad 1990).

Figure 8.5 Real Wages by Sector of Ownership
(LE per week, 1973 prices)

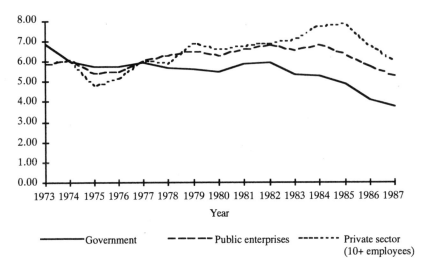

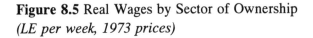

Sources: CAPMAS; Handoussa (1988).

procyclical movement of wages where wages move above value added
trend in boom years and below it in the troughs. The fact that
agricultural wages continued to increase to 1985 can in part be
attributed to relatively strong external demand for labor from Iraq and
Jordan in the 1980s.

One consequence of the relative acceleration in agricultural wages
was a major narrowing in wage and income differentials across the
sector. For other sectors, wage growth was significant, particularly in
private construction and manufacturing. The government and public
enterprise sector shows some wage drift, but was mainly characterized
by implicit indexation to the cost of living. With the organized private
sector bound by publicly determined wage setting rules, this meant
that private sector wages effectively tracked those of the public
enterprise sector up to 1982.

The upward trend in real wages was drastically reversed post
1982/84. Indeed, in construction the downturn came as early as 1979.
By 1987 construction wages were below 1974 levels. The declining

trend in other competitive markets—such as agriculture—is likely to be sustained, albeit with some lag. As the growth in agricultural wages was associated with regional migration, the consolidation of the livestock subsector, and an expansion in rural nonfarm, particularly public, employment, all of which have contracted, this explains the 16 percent per annum decline since the peak in 1985.[11] For the government and public sector, the trend has been unequivocally downward, with real wages for government employees less than half their 1973/74 levels. The contraction has been most severe for white collar workers (see figure 8.6) and has been accompanied by higher turnover levels and multiple job holding (Handoussa 1988). Apart from a contraction in differentials across skill levels, a narrowing of wages between the public and private sectors has also occurred, as in the manufacturing sector. Most striking has been the sharp reduction in the differential between nonagricultural and agricultural wages (see figures 8.4 and 8.5).

Given the size of the public sector and the relationship of the organized private sector's wage policy to public sector wages, the wage setting mechanism is clearly critical. Here, a number of factors are pertinent. First, the wage path from the early 1960s appears to have been determined independently of productivity, being structured by noneconomic considerations. For manufacturing wages over the period 1973–81/82, there appears to be a negative association with a productivity term—measured as labor productivity—with the level of money wages given by consumer prices and policy (annual growth in nominal wage costs per unit of output in manufacturing almost exactly tracked the CPI between 1974 and 1982). With the limited information that is available and taking the nonfinancial public enterprise sector as a whole for the years 1973–83/84, until 1980/81,

---

11. By 1981/82, 18 to 20 percent of rural sector employment was public employment (CAPMAS various years).

Figure 8.6 Real Wages by Sector of Ownership and White Collar/Blue Collar Status
(LE per week, 1973 prices)

Sources: CAPMAS; Handoussa (1988).

wages and productivity clearly moved broadly together, with wage increases significantly exceeding cost of living adjustments. At that point, productivity growth began to lag wages, which in turn lagged the cost of living. However, from the early 1980s onward, the widespread use of incentive payments in some public enterprises and in the private sector has meant that base wages can be a considerable distance from actual wages, making meaningful estimation yet more problematic.

Attempts to estimate either a basic or augmented Phillips curve equation have been largely fruitless. Standard, underlying wage equations relate nominal wage growth negatively to the rate of unemployment and as a positive function of the rate of consumer price change with the latter term commonly lagged. Estimating a nominal wage equation for manufacturing over the period 1972 to 1984 for Egypt, the unemployment term has not only the wrong sign,

levels of capacity utilization and rising underemployment, where the latter is defined as the gap between desired and actual work time at prevailing wages. This is clearly the case in construction, and we can assume that the broad behavior of that sector is generally mimicked in other flexible markets.

Flexible Market Adjustment: Construction

The dynamics of the Egyptian construction sector can be derived from the level of aggregate investment in the economy and from labor supply variations stemming from outmigration and subsequent return migration. At the same time, the sector is important in terms of its relationship with the agricultural labor market (see Assaad 1990 for a more detailed account of the 1988 Construction Workers Survey, on which this section is based).

Sectoral output has been strongly procyclical, varying directly with changes in aggregate investment. Investment demand has accounted for 90 to 95 percent of construction output at any given time, while the latter provides the largest (47 to 53 percent) component of gross fixed investment. Consequently, the fall in investment from 28 percent of GDP during 1978–82/83 to below 20 percent between 1986/88 was directly translated into a reduction of real value added in the sector.

Employment in construction expanded substantially in the boom years despite large-scale migration to other Arab countries. This migration resulted in skill mismatching and selective labor shortages, which further forced wages up, inducing a stronger internal migratory shift of workers out of agriculture. After 1983 (figure 8.9) falling value added did not—at least superficially—throttle off employment. However, the apparent fall in value added per worker conceals the principle response: lower levels of labor force utilization. For construction, the employment cycle involves partial utilization of the available labor force in periods of slow growth, giving way to rapid upturns in labor demand during periods of higher, investment-led growth. Underutilization of labor is replaced by shortages, which are exacerbated by migration abroad in the boom years. The lagged supply response in turn delivers underemployment as the downside of the cycle emerges. Labor is in effect variable capacity under conditions of fixed coefficient production technology.

Figure 8.9 Trends in Construction Employment and Real Value Added *(index, 1980/81 = 100)*

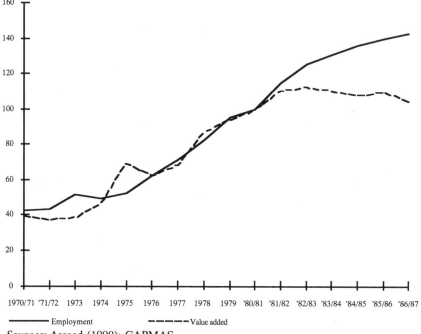

Employment ——————   Value added – – – – –

Sources: Assaad (1990); CAPMAS.

A simple distribution of construction labor by private and public sectors indicates that by 1984, roughly 20 percent of the labor force were in the public sector. That sector is marked by the dominance of large general contracting firms. In contrast, over 75 percent of the labor force was in the small-scale (less than 10 employees) private sector. This subsector accounts for an even larger proportion of site labor (90 percent) and is marked by its flexible wage and employment structure. Downturns in the investment cycle are transmitted directly to this subsector. In other words, adjustment costs are squeezed largely out of the private, small-scale subsector segment. A similar effect occurs more generally with the entire informal sector.

A look at contracts in construction reveals, as expected, a dual market. At least 90 percent of public sector workers have formal contractual arrangements, with over 70 percent guaranteed permanent employment. In contrast, 97 percent of private sector workers are hired on a casual basis without any formal contractual arrangement. It is these workers who carry the brunt of adjustment. The period of effective labor shortages of the 1970s has been conclusively reversed. By 1988, casual construction workers on average could expect to work no more than two-thirds of their available labor time (table 8.5). Urban workers fared slightly worse than their rural counterparts, as did skilled workers compared with the unskilled. In short, the windfall-generated labor scarcities and low frictional unemployment have given way to a labor supply glut and longer unemployment spells, ranging from about 15 days on average for laborers to nearly 55 days for craftsmen and assistants.

The impact on wages has been profound. All subsectors show rapidly falling real wages after 1984. While between 1972 and 1982 real wages climbed by 4.5 percent per annum, in the private sector real wages fell by 3.8 percent per annum between 1982 and 1987, and more than 9 percent per annum after 1986 (figure 8.10).

Table 8.5 Average Employment and Unemployment Spells for Casual Wage Workers in Construction, 1988

Category	Average employment spell (days)	Average unemployment spell (days)	Employment ratio[a] (percent)	Number of observations
Skill level				
Craftsman	80.4	52.9	60	262
Assistant	69.9	56.3	55	96
Apprentice	103.7	36.1	74	58
Laborer	46.7	14.6	76	141
Urban/rural status				
Urban	81.1	44.6	65	335
Rural	59.4	23.8	71	222
Total	72.5	36.3	67	557

a. Employment ratio = E/(E+U), where E = the average employment spell and U = the average unemployment spell.
Source: Assaad (1990).

Figure 8.10 Real Wages in the Construction Sector
(1973 LE/week)

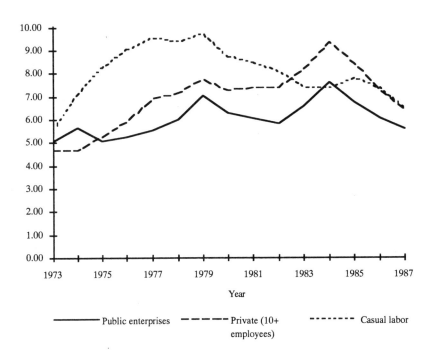

Sources: Assaad (1990); CAPMAS.

Accommodating "capacity" change and assuming near full
employment in 1982 and (optimistically) 70 percent employment in
1987, the rate of decline in monthly earnings rises to 11 percent per
annum.

The evidence presented above indicates unequivocally the nature of
the adjustment mechanism in a flexible market with fixed technology
and limited factor substitutability. Falling labor utilization runs
alongside substantial downward pressure on the real wage. These
signals constrain the inflow of migrant labor from both upper Egypt
and agriculture. Survey data show that exit patterns from construction
differ widely by skill category, but that for unskilled labor, movement
out of the sector was toward services and to a lesser extent agriculture.

With a lag—and under current sectoral supply elasticities—this translates into expanded unemployment and underemployment in the receiving sectors.

Conclusion

The oil and associated revenues windfall facilitated the maintenance of a near-full employment economy. This was achieved in part through growth, in part through regional migration, in part through maintaining rapid growth in the government and public sector work force. In the latter sector, wages were driven primarily by adjustment to the cost of living. These policies established major rigidities in the labor market and effectively squeezed the cost of adjustment to lower external transfers into the economy onto, in the first instance, the small-scale manufacturing and informal sectors, and subsequently agriculture. In all cases, the highest costs—as manifested in unemployment and income dependence—have been placed on new entrants and women in the labor force.

Egyptian statistics grossly underestimate the rate of female labor force participation, and hence the aggregate activity rate (see Commander 1987). Nevertheless, within this truncated measure, women's share in unemployment in 1986 was twice as high as their share in the labor force (23.5 percent to 11.6 percent respectively). The female unemployment rate is strongly correlated with the recruitment of graduates in the public sector, given the limited employment opportunities for educated women elsewhere in the economy. Women are also more able to stay in the queue for government employment as they are generally secondary earners in the household.

The windfall gains of the 1970s were largely appropriated directly by the state. The fiscal expansion this facilitated had predictable Keynesian effect, but the accompanying structure of macroprices—the exchange and interest rates—compressed traditional exportables and skewed investment toward relative capital intensity. The exportables subsector of agriculture was the lagging sector. Given the trade regime, deindustrialization did not result. Moreover, the strong public spending effect was not necessarily associated with a crowding out of private investment. The latter grew strongly in both absolute and relative terms, admittedly from a low base. Shafik (1989) argues that over 40 percent of public investment was allocated to infrastructure through the windfall period, and in an appropriately specified model, this yields strong complementarities: a crowding-in effect with private investment (Chhibber and van Wijnbergen 1988 reach similar conclusions for Turkey).

The employment effects of the windfall were limited, as indicated by tables 8.2 and 8.4. The organized private manufacturing sector expanded employment roughly two percentage points above aggregate labor force growth during 1973–82, but most of the growth was in services and construction. The organized private manufacturing sector grew at only 1.8 percent per annum during the same period. A rising capital/labor ratio, alongside low productivity of capital, has meant that the employment multiplier from private investment in manufacturing was low. There was a stronger employment multiplier in the small-scale private sector, the precise magnitude of which is hard to capture with available data. For public sector manufacturing, employment grew at 4 percent per annum between 1973–82. Productivity per worker declined significantly after 1979, despite the fact that hiring rules for public enterprises were more flexible than elsewhere in the public sector.[16] Wage growth was determined independently of productivity. For the government sector, indexation to the cost of living appears to have held until the early 1980s. Thereafter, wages have been sharply reduced, but the sector still remains massively overmanned (Hansen and Radwan 1982 suggest overmanning of at least 40 percent in the mid-1970s; the trend has obviously been rising).

However, the demand for government and public sector employment cannot be attributed to the wedge between public wage rates and the supply price of labor. Government wages are low, in both absolute and relative terms. Nonwage benefits probably continue to drive the demand for government employment. The effect on the reservation wage is not obvious. Anecdotal evidence suggests that government employment is often akin to ghost employment. Where

16. Productivity per worker is measured for the entire nonfinancial public enterprise sector, and hence does not accurately reflect productivity in the public manufacturing sector.

this is the case, the ultimate effect may be to lower the effective reservation wage, but the lack of solid information on the dynamics of the multiple job-holding market compromises any conclusions.

The expansion of the public sector in the windfall reflected strong procyclical government expenditure policy and was largely dissociated from underlying permanent revenue. Further, strong employment growth was maintained countercyclically up to 1985. This was partly a function of the graduate employment guarantee scheme. The latter—under recent queueing conventions—alone yields an annual growth rate of over 4 percent for government employment. Almost full employment has, until recently, been the outcome of the combination of this expansion and sizeable external migration. Neither option is sustainable. The recent acceleration in unemployment is in effect the gap between the falling rate of growth in private sector employment and the now constrained ability of the public sector to absorb the residual.

Adjustment measures for reducing fiscal imbalances involve demand dampening. Austerity, falling real wages, and currency depreciation boost external competitiveness. Adverse employment effects would, in theory, be counteracted over the medium term by expansion of tradables output. In agriculture, at least, the exportables subsector has higher labor demand.

Positive real interest rates and trade regime reforms could stimulate switching toward higher labor intensity, but this scenario is impaired by a number of factors. First, the relative price swing toward tradables has been too small. In agriculture, for example, relative prices still favor nontradables. Second, the tariff structure and interest rates continue to deliver a bias toward capital. Third, even assuming more coherent macroeconomic adjustment policies, the labor mobility assumptions will not hold. The expansion of government employment locks over 28 percent of the labor force into the nonmarket sector, at least on a first job basis. Aside from the productivity implications, any hypothesized shift of labor into tradables production would be severely constrained. A combination of public employment and the educational system yields a labor force inappropriately matched, in terms of both skills and expectations, to the requirements of structural adjustment.

This analysis of the response of the Egyptian labor market to boom and recession indicates a range of employment and wage setting mechanisms. The public sector and formal private manufacturing sector are characterized by relatively inflexible employment rules. Minimum wages are almost meaningless, but hiring and firing rules enforced by the Labor Office restrict turnover, and in the case of the private sector, create positive incentives for *de facto* small-scale units. Combined with the interest rate and tariff structure, this results in the organized private sector being characterized by high capital/labor ratios. In the case of both the public enterprises and the organized private sector, real wages have fallen sharply since 1985. Wage flexibility may hold, but employment is regulated only via the rate of recruitment, and in the case of the public sector, that rate is itself not necessarily a decentralized variable. For the nonorganized sectors, markets have more standard competitive properties, albeit with nominal wage inertia. The dominant features of the adjustment process to date, particularly the reductions in the public wage, result in further downward pressure on the wage in flexible markets. The elasticity of earnings in the latter with respect to the nonabsorption of labor in other sectors of the economy is significant and negative. In due course this yields a fall in aggregate demand, but at a high cost. Unemployment and sharply falling disposable income can only be exaggerated (in the absence of new growth in net transfers into the economy) by leaving the present labor market rigidities untouched.

APPENDIX

Figure 8.A1 Egypt Investment Deflator and its Components, 1973–87
(index, 1973 = 100)

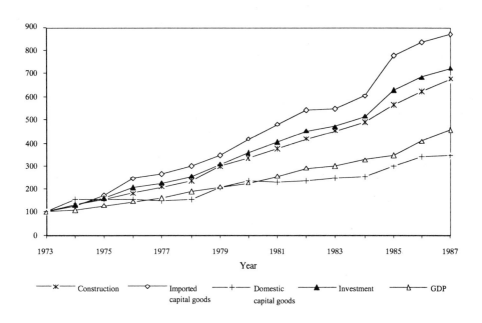

References

Abdel Fadil, M. 1980. *The Political Economy of Nasserism: A Study in Employment and Income Distribution in Urban Egypt, 1952–1972.* Cambridge, U.K.

Adams, R. H. 1985. "Development and Structural Change in Rural Egypt, 1952 to 1982." *World Development* 13(6): 705–723.

Alderman, H., and J. von Braun. 1984. *The Effects of the Egyptian Food Subsidy Systems on Income Distribution and Consumption.* Report 45. Washington, D.C.: International Food Policy Research Institute.

Amin, G., and E. Awny. 1985. *International Migration of Egyptian Labour.* Report MR 108e. Ottawa: International Development Research Center.

Assaad, R. 1990. *The Structure of the Construction Labor Market and its Development since the Mid-1970s.* Working Papers in Planning No. 85. Ithaca, New York: Cornell University.

Braga de Macedo, J. 1982. "Currency Diversification and Export Competitiveness: A Model of the Dutch Disease in Egypt." *Journal of Development Economics* 11(3, December): 287–306.

CAPMAS. 1978. *Population Census, 1976.* Cairo.

_____. 1988. *Population Census, 1986.* Provisional Results. Cairo.

_____. Various years. *Labor Force Sample Survey.* Cairo.

Chhibber, A., and S. van Wijnbergen. 1988. "Public Policy and Private Investment in Turkey." Washington, D.C.: World Bank. Processed.

Collier, P. 1988. "Macroeconomics and the Labor Market." Oxford, U.K. Processed.

Commander, S. J. 1987. *The State and Agricultural Development in Egypt since 1973.* Ithaca, New York: Ithaca Press.

Corden, W. M. 1989. "Macroeconomic Adjustment in Developing Countries." *World Bank Research Observer* 4(1): 51–64.

Corden, W. M., and J. P. Neary. 1982. "Booming Sector and Deindustrialization in a Small Open Economy." *Economic Journal* 92(December): 825–848.

Dervis, K., R. Martin, and S. van Wijnbergen. 1984. *Policy Analysis of Shadow Pricing, Foreign Borrowing and Resource Extraction in Egypt.* Staff Working Paper No. 622. Washington, D.C: World Bank.

Dethier, J. J. 1989. *Trade, Exchange Rate and Agricultural Pricing Policies in Egypt,* 2 vols. Washington, D.C.: World Bank.

Ferghany, N. 1988. *In Pursuit of Livelihood: A Field Study of Egyptian Migration.* Beirut, Lebanon: Centre for Arab Unity Studies. In Arabic.

Handoussa, H. 1983. *Public Sector Employment and Productivity in the Egyptian Economy.* Geneva: International Labour Organisation.

_____. 1988. "The Burden of Public Service Employment and Remuneration: A Case Study of Egypt." Geneva: International Labour Organisation. Processed.

_____. 1989. "Egypt's Investment Strategy, Policies and Performance since the Infitah." Processed.

Hansen, B. 1987. "A Full Employment Economy and its Responses to External Shocks: The Labor Market in Egypt from World War 2." Washington, D.C.: World Bank. Processed.

Hansen, B., and S. Radwan. 1982. *Employment Opportunities and Equity in Egypt.* Geneva: International Labour Organisation.

Neary, J. P., and S. van Wijnbergen, eds. 1986. *Natural Resources and the Macroeconomy.* Oxford, U.K: Blackwell.

Richards, A., and P. Martin, eds. 1983. *Migration, Mechanization and Agricultural Labor Markets in Egypt.* Boulder, Colorado: Westview.

Shafik, N. 1989. "Private Investment and Public Policy in Egypt, 1960–1986." Oxford University, D. Phil. thesis.

World Bank. 1983. *Egypt: Issues of Trade Strategy and Investment Planning.* Report 4136-EGT. Washington, D.C.

9

GHANA

P. Beaudry
N. K. Sowa

The predominant view underlying Ghana's Economic Recovery Program (ERP), initiated in 1983, is that the country was most likely to achieve sustained growth by relying on market forces. Ghanaian policymakers believe that changes in relative prices, which are central to the ERP, incite economic agents to reallocate resources as indicated by market signals. However, the success of such a program depends primarily on the extent to which labor is allocated through the market mechanism. If wages and labor mobility are insensitive to changing market conditions, the ERP is unlikely to achieve its goal of structural adjustment. This chapter examines whether the ERP's reliance on market forces to reallocate and absorb labor was well-founded, and whether the improvements in the Ghanaian economy since 1983 were helped or hindered by the actual functioning of the labor market. This chapter also examines the relative impact the ERP has had on the different segments of the labor market.

Most of our labor market analysis relies on data from the first round of the Ghana Living Standards Survey (GLSS), which was collected in 1987–88. This data set contains information on 1,526 households that encompass 7,637 individuals. The data set is especially well-suited for our analysis as its coverage of both the allocation of time and of the sources of household income are particularly extensive (for information on the design of the GLSS see

---

The authors would like to thank Harold Coulombe, who provided excellent research assistance for this chapter, and S. Horton, L. Dudley, A Martens, and R. Kanbur for their helpful comments.

Scott and Amenuvegbe 1989). However, because this data set consists of only one cross-section, many of the central questions associated with the adjustment process can only be addressed indirectly.[1] Therefore, we have also used aggregate time series data on earnings and employment to complement the household survey data when relevant. These data come mostly from the Statistical Service of the Republic of Ghana.

Historical Background

Ghana's 1983 economic crisis was a culmination of several years of decline. Some authors place the start of the decline soon after independence, which was granted in 1957, while others place it in the 1970s. Indeed, some writers even think the decline started in the pre-independence era, but only became acute, and therefore apparent, in the postindependence era.

Nevertheless, at independence Ghana still had a vibrant economy. The country was a world leader in the production of cocoa, and gold and timber exports were also good sources of foreign exchange earnings. It had a huge buildup (about US$269 million) of external reserves, and the balance of payments was not problematic. At this time, expansion/contraction in the money supply was tied to a surplus/deficit of the balance of payments. Thus, the government avoided indiscriminate expansions in the money supply and held inflation in check. The external value of the currency was relatively strong, and was exchanged at par with the pound sterling.

Soon after independence, the Nkrumah government began a number of projects aimed at import substitution and semi-industrialization. The government embarked on developing infrastructure, such as roads, electricity, and piped water, in the belief that such development would attract foreign investors into the country. Basic education was made free and compulsory for all children of school-going age.

Not long after these projects began, the price of Ghana's chief foreign exchange earner, cocoa, started to fall on the world market. By

---

1. Since the GLSS data were collected between September 1987 and March 1988, the sample does not provide a completely representative sample of yearly activities, and may therefore bias some of our inferences.

the mid-1960s, the country's net reserves were in deficit. The government borrowed heavily from the banking system to finance its growing fiscal deficit, which caused expansions in the money supply that were not matched by growth in production. Thus, from an inflation rate of virtually zero at independence, the rate had climbed to 20 percent by 1965. The falling price of cocoa and the bad reserve position meant a shortage of foreign exchange. The first obvious symptoms of the decline in the economy appeared in 1964, when queues started forming in shops and even at stadiums (which were used as market places) for basic imported commodities like sugar, milk, and soap. These harsh economic conditions precipitated the 1966 coup that toppled the Nkrumah regime.

Unfortunately, the various governments that followed Nkrumah did not implement programs for long-term solution of the economy's problems. Successive governments persisted in providing *ad hoc* solutions to satisfy the public's demand for consumables. This lack of proper economic direction was probably one of the main internal causes of the decline in the economy that led to the crisis of 1980s.

Ghana's economy depends heavily on agriculture, and is therefore affected by uncontrollable factors like the weather. Agriculture contributes about 47 percent of the GDP and employs about 53 percent of the labor force (much of the data for this section are drawn from World Bank 1984b). Cocoa earns about 70 percent of the country's foreign exchange. Since the 1970s, bad weather and inappropriate policies have led to a decline in cocoa output. By the beginning of the 1980s, cocoa output had dwindled to about half of its 1960 level. Table 9.1 provides some salient macroeconomic indicators for 1978 onward. The price distortions that affected the whole economy were particularly harsh in the cocoa sector. The government, through the Cocoa Marketing Board, determines the price of cocoa based on the world price and the exchange rate of the cedi. Thus, when for a long period the cedi remained at a fixed rate and was grossly overvalued, cocoa farmers were grossly underpaid. Furthermore, as the world price fell, Ghana's foreign exchange earnings fell, exacerbating the decline in farmers' earnings. These factors led some of the farmers to shift away from cocoa to other agricultural products. Some of the farmers also smuggled cocoa

Table 9.1 Macro Indicators, 1978–88

Indicator	1978	1979	1980	1981	1982	1983	1984	1985	1986	1987	1988
GNP per capita (percent growth)	0	-5.0	-2.9	-5.8	-10.0	-7.1	7.6	1.5	2.0	1.0	n.a.
Inflation (percent growth)	73	55	50	117	22	122	40	10	25	36	37
Money (percent growth)	69	16	34	51	23	40	54	46	48	45	13
Cedi end year exchange rate (per dollar)	2.75	2.75	2.75	2.75	2.75	30	50	60	90	115	227
Government balance (cedis millions)	-1,772	-1,696	-1,646	-4,440	-5,136	-4,514	-4,053	-5,453	-2,966	8,911	4,894
Trade balance (US$ millions)	112.5	262.6	195.3	-243.6	18.3	-60.6	32.9	-36.3	60.9	-124.7	n.a.
Cocoa production (thousand tons)	265	281	254	220	179	158	175	220	225	234	289
Terms of trade (1980 = 100)	185.6	149.0	100.0	79.8	69.2	89.5	104.5	99.7	83.2	n.a.	n.a.
Net capital formation (1975 cedis millions)	205.8	122.5	275.7	312.2	15.4	14.9	125.9	191.8	180.3	222.5	n.a.
Debt service (percent of exports)	6.5	6.0	8.3	7.2	9.6	23.3	16.4	15.6	16.7	19[a]	n.a.

n.a. = not available

Note: Cocoa production is for the season beginning in the year indicated.

a. = estimate.

Sources: IMF *International Financial Statistics;* World Bank 1984a; Ghana Statistical Service *Quarterly Digest Statistics;* World Bank *World Debt Tables.*

across the borders to the Côte d'Ivoire where they obtained higher prices for their produce.

The relative price of maize and other food crops rose relative to cocoa and some factors shifted into the production of these other crops. However, the main effect was an outward migration. Between 1970 and 1980, agricultural production declined at the rate of about 0.2 percent per annum. Note, however, that even though production declined, the sector's share of gross domestic output increased from 41 percent in 1960 to about 51 percent in 1982. The increase in agriculture's share occurred because other sectors of the economy declined at even faster rates than agriculture. Between 1960 and 1982, the rates of growth of the other sectors were -2.4 percent for industry, -1.5 percent for manufacturing, and -7.5 percent for services.

With Ghana being at an early stage of development, manufacturing and industry have never been large sectors of the economy. Manufacturing is usually undertaken on a small scale and employs only a limited proportion of the labor force. Manufacturing employed about 10 percent of the labor force in 1960, and about 12 percent by the early 1980s. This sector comprises mainly small-scale, light, nondurable consumer goods industries, including food processing, textile, and basic metal processing industries. The big establishments in this sector are mostly state-owned. The main problem that plagued manufacturing was a lack of raw materials and spare parts due to the shortage of foreign exchange. This shortage was in turn largely related to the problems in agriculture. In addition, the state-owned enterprises were grossly mismanaged to the extent that instead of earning income for the state, most of them depended on government subvention for their salaries.

These problems in manufacturing manifested themselves in shortages on the market, and led to inflation. By the early 1980s, the foreign exchange shortage and the import restrictions exacerbated the shortage of consumables on the local market and worsened inflation.

Between 1960 and 1982, government revenue as a percentage of GDP dropped from 17.5 to 5.6. This fall resulted largely from the tax base being heavily dependent on cocoa exports, which were falling. Despite falling revenues, expenditures increased and the budget was consistently in deficit. The government kept on borrowing from the banking system to finance the deficit. This by itself was not surprising because the financial system was not developed enough to allow the government to borrow from any other source. Unfortunately, high government borrowing crowded out private sector borrowing and thus further depressed the private sector's chances for growth. Furthermore, this borrowing was accompanied by a high level of monetary expansion that fueled inflation.

In 1972, when the military government of the National Redemption Council led by General Archeampong repudiated some of Ghana's external debts, the country was blacklisted as not creditworthy. Thus, for most of the 1970s and early 1980s, Ghana could not attract external loans. Whereas the lack of external funds was part of the reason why imported spare parts and raw materials were not available, it also meant that Ghana had a relatively light debt burden. In 1970, its debt service was 1.1 percent of the GNP and 5.0 percent of exports; by 1982, these ratios were 0.2 and 6.8 percent, respectively. Thus, at the time the government introduced the ERP, Ghana did not have much of a debt burden. Other low-income countries in Sub-Saharan Africa had, on average, a debt to GNP ratio of 13.4.

In 1982, further shocks compounded Ghana's long-run problems (inflation, declining terms of trade, overvalued currency, and political instability). The country was hit by the worst drought in its history; bush fires destroyed farms and crops; and almost every conceivable item—food, water, electricity, and so on—was in short supply. These problems were exacerbated when about a million Ghanaians were repatriated from neighboring Nigeria. The plight of these refugees and the near famine situation in Ghana drew the attention of the international community.

In an effort to solve some of these problems the government, with the help of the IMF and the World Bank, instituted the Economic Recovery Program.

Consequences of the Crisis

The immediate consequence of Ghana's economic decline was the general impoverishment of the nation as a whole. Most indicators point to a drop in the standard of living. Per capita GDP, in constant 1975 prices, dropped from a level of c634 in 1971 to c395 in 1983.

Most people could not afford the basic necessities of life. By 1983, the near famine situation caused most people to develop "Rawling's chain" (protruding clavicles). *Kalabule*—a situation in which suppliers take advantage of consumers during periods of scarcity—became the order of the day.

The index of food production per capita with 1971 as 100 dropped to about 72 in 1982. Rough estimates (Green 1987, table 20) show a great increase in poverty: the number of urban people below the poverty line increased from 30 to 35 percent in the late 1970s to 45 to 50 percent by the mid-1980s. For rural people, the situation was even worse. The percentage of people living under the poverty line in rural areas increased from some 60 to 65 percent in the late 1970s to 67 to 72 percent by the early 1980s.

The crisis also manifested itself in the deterioration of human capital. Health standards, which had generally improved during 1960–80, deteriorated severely in the early 1980s. Life expectancy at birth increased from 46 years in 1970 to about 55 years by the end of the 1970s, and then dropped to 53 years in the beginning of the 1980s. The daily calorie supply as a percentage of requirements dropped from 88 percent in the 1970s to 68 percent in 1983. The drop in health indicators in the 1980s was due mainly to a shortage of drugs, food, and other supplies, and also to the "brain drain" in the medical profession.

Education likewise had generally improved since independence, in that the number of school-age children who went to school had increased. However, the quality of education dropped due to the shortage of textbooks and other educational equipment and to the emigration of teachers.

Another significant consequence of the economic crisis of the 1970s and 1980s was its effect on manpower development and labor. The high rates of inflation were not matched by increases in the nominal wage. Thus, over the years workers saw their real incomes being eroded. This affected mainly those on wage incomes, and caused most of them to take on second and third jobs. The most common second job was trading. At the height of the *kalabule* period, those who benefited most were traders. The trading was not necessarily in actual wares. Some people made huge profits just by knowing someone in a position to give them chits for obtaining essential commodities.[2] These chits were then sold to the actual traders for cash. Such dishonest acts did not encourage manpower development in the country. School dropouts who turned themselves into "businessmen" became better-off than their counterparts who continued their schooling. Skilled personnel like doctors, engineers and teachers, who could not engage in these acts of *kalabule*, fled, mainly to other African countries and Asia. Nigeria was the main beneficiary of the Ghanaian brain drain, though most of the medical doctors ended up in Saudi Arabia. Estimates suggest that Saudi Arabia had more Ghanaian doctors than Accra. Most teachers went to Nigeria, as the oil boom in that country in the 1970s led to the establishment of new schools. By the beginning of the 1980s, Ghanaians of every class and skill were leaving in droves for Nigeria. When an economic crisis hit Nigeria in the 1980s, the government expelled almost a million Ghanaian refugees.

Summary of Policies Under the ERP

The government of the Provisional National Defense Council launched the Economic Recovery Program in April 1983 as a medium-term plan with the following objectives (Government of Ghana 1983, pp. 15–16):

1. to restore incentives for production of food, industrial raw materials and export commodities and thereby increase their output to modest but realistic levels;

2. to increase the availability of essential consumer goods and improve the distribution system;

3. to increase the overall availability of foreign exchange in the country, improve its allocation mechanism and channel it into selected high priority activities;

4. to lower the rate of inflation by pursuing prudent fiscal, monetary and trade policies;

5. to rehabilitate the physical infrastructure of the country in support of directly productive activities; and

6. to undertake systematic analyses and studies leading towards a major restructuring of economic institutions in the country.

---

2. One of the methods of rationing scarce commodities was by issuing notes of rights to purchase.

In pursuit of the above objectives, the government introduced the following policies:

- The exchange rate policy was aimed mainly at regularizing the external value of the cedi. In the beginning this involved large devaluations, and later flotation of the currency for the rate to be determined at an auction through market forces.

- The fiscal policy was aimed principally at eliminating the high budget deficits. This policy included widening the tax net and cutting government expenditure.

- The investment policy was aimed at encouraging foreign investors through a system of incentives provided by a new investment code.

- The prices and incomes policy was aimed at removing distortions in the economy. The pricing policy involved eliminating price controls, whereas the incomes policy was intended to adjust workers' incomes to prevent the erosion of real income by inflation.

- The divestiture policy involved the selling of some state-owned enterprises.

- The agricultural policy aimed at increased production of food, selected raw materials, and export crops.

The Macroeconomy Since the ERP

A useful first step is to distinguish between the ERP's stabilization impacts and its adjustment impacts. As table 9.1 shows, between 1983 and 1985 inflation fell from 122 percent to 10 percent per annum and GNP growth per capita rose from -7.1 percent to 1.5 percent annually. Such drastic changes certainly reflect a period of effective stabilization. However, these macroeconomic improvements were probably caused by good weather following the drought of 1983. For example, cereal production tripled between 1983 and 1984 and the production of starchy staples rose 40 percent. Nevertheless, since 1985 per capita GNP growth has been maintained at 1 to 2 percent annually. This period of sustained growth in GNP is in sharp contrast with the five years of continual decline preceding the ERP, thus 1985 may be considered the beginning of the program's adjustment phase. Besides growth, the other most notable changes following the implementation of the ERP were the achievement of a trade surplus in 1986 and a government budget surplus in 1987.

The performance of investment under the ERP has also been relatively successful (table 9.1): in 1983, the ratio of net capital formation to GNP was less than 0.5 percent, but by 1987 it had reached close to 4.0 percent. Improvements in the legal regime governing private investment have probably been an important factor. For example, the 1984 Petroleum Exploration and Production Law, the new investment code of 1986, and the 1986 Minerals and Mining Law all created generous incentives to prospective investors.

The ERP's lasting effect on inflation has been much less impressive than its effect on growth. Inflation has been accelerating since 1985 and had reached almost 40 percent per year in 1988. This reflects the large increases in the money supply, which averaged more than 30 percent per year between 1983 and 1987. Moreover, the monetary dynamics underlying this inflationary spiral may be difficult to reverse.

The continual depreciation of the cedi is likely to be at the center of this spiral. The cedi depreciated by more than 800 percent between 1983 and 1988, which caused a rapid increase in the price of many goods, especially in urban areas. The monetary authorities' need to finance the fiscal deficit before 1987 had forced them to respond to the price increases by printing money. The resulting expansion of the money supply led to further depreciation of the cedi, and consequently further pressures for price increases.

Overall, the ERP's macroeconomic aspects have been relatively successful. However, the extent to which the ERP has provoked real structural adjustment in the allocation of labor is unclear. The following sections will try to address this question, but first we will examine the characteristics of the labor market.

Characteristics of the Labor Market

This section provides basic information on the structure of Ghana's labor force (for an earlier study of the Ghanaian labor market see

Ewusi 1978). Table 9.2 presents estimates of labor participation rates. To avoid omitting certain segments of the labor force, we have chosen a restrictive definition for an economically inactive person. The population of working age encompasses everyone aged seven or older, and a person is classified as inactive if either (a) the person is a student, or (b) the person has neither worked nor looked for work in the preceding week for reasons of sickness, age, household work, or unwillingness to work.[3] All other individuals are considered active.

The table indicates that for people older that 25, participation rates are slightly higher for men than for women. For the prime-age males category (25–60 years of age), the participation rates exceed 80 percent. This is quite close to the level Ewusi (1978) recorded using the 1970 population survey. Overall, the data indicate that 42 percent of the population over seven years of age is economically active.

As table 9.2 suggests, the problem of child labor is still severe in Ghana, especially for females. In rural areas, 30 percent of girls aged 7 to 16 were reported to be economically active, and are therefore not enrolled as students. The level for boys of the same age group is 21 percent. In urban areas the problem is somewhat less severe: 14 percent of girls and 8 percent of boys are economically active. These high figures reflect many households' inability to live on the earnings of the head of the household only. As a result, the children are put to work to supplement household income. Furthermore, the costs of books and school uniforms are often very high relative to household income, which is a further disincentive to school enrollment.

Table 9.3 breaks down the active population by employment sector, level of education, and sex. Household farming is by far the largest sector of employment, followed by household businesses. Public sector employment and employment in the private sector outside the household total only 17 percent of employment. The remaining 83 percent of the employed population work in household businesses or farms.

---

3. A residual category, "other reasons" for neither working or searching, also qualified the person as inactive.

Table 9.2 Labor Participation Rates by Age and Sex

Age	Location	Male	Female	Total
7–16	Urban	8.3	13.9	11.2
	Rural	21.4	29.5	25.2
17–25	Urban	60.0	55.7	57.9
	Rural	69.5	74.6	72.3
26–45	Urban	89.3	76.8	82.2
	Rural	89.4	85.0	87.0
46–60	Urban	83.7	73.1	78.7
	Rural	87.7	76.5	81.4
>60	Urban	55.0	32.5	43.8
	Rural	70.0	55.5	63.3
Total	Urban	39.2	38.0	38.6
	Rural	41.7	46.4	44.1
Total		41.0	43.9	42.5

Source: Authors' calculations from the Ghana Living Standards Survey (1987–88).

The government sector, the state sector, and, to a less extent, the private nonhousehold sector all employ a much higher percentage of educated workers than the household sectors (business and farming). Of those working on household farms, 75 percent have either not received any formal education or have received only a primary education, while in the government sector this group represents only 14 percent of the work force. The government is particularly important in the employment of highly educated Ghanaians: over 50 percent of those with a postsecondary education work for the government.

The last two columns of table 9.3 compare the sectoral composition of employment for men and women. Not included in this table is the difference in education between men and women: women have on average received less education than men; fewer than 30 percent of women have been educated beyond the primary school level, while almost 50 percent of men were educated beyond this level. This result accords with the finding noted previously that girls are more likely

Table 9.3 Employment Sector by Level of Education and Sex (percent)

Sector	Education						Sex		Total
	None	Primary	Middle school	Secondary	Post-secondary	Koranic	Male	Female	
Government	12.6	*1.4	52.6	14.0	18.6	*0.9	71.9	28.1	
	1.7	1.0	11.7	33.7	53.3	9.5	10.5	3.9	7.0
State	19.6	*6.5	58.7	*4.4	*8.7	*2.2	80.4	19.6	
	0.6	1.0	2.8	2.3	5.3	4.8	2.5	0.6	1.5
Private	30.2	14.9	46.5	5.1	*1.4	*1.9	76.7	23.3	
	4.1	10.4	10.4	12.4	4.0	19.1	11.3	3.1	7.0
Household farming	65.8	9.9	22.5	1.2	0.6	*0.1	47.8	52.2	
	65.7	51.3	37.3	21.4	13.3	9.5	52.5	52.2	52.3
Household business	48.7	9.5	37.2	2.2	1.1	1.9	26.2	73.8	
	14.0	14.3	17.9	11.2	6.7	42.9	8.4	21.4	15.2
Household business and farming	48.7	14.8	33.9	1.4	*0.6	*0.6	37.9	62.1	
	10.7	16.9	12.3	5.6	2.7	9.5	9.1	13.6	11.5
Unemployed	32.7	9.5	43.5	7.1	6.6	*0.6	50.0	50.0	
	3.4	5.2	7.6	13.5	14.7	4.8	5.8	5.2	5.5
Total	52.4	10.1	31.5	2.9	2.5	2.9	47.7	52.3	100.0

*Fewer than five observations.

Note: The first row in each sector gives the percentage in that sector that corresponds to a particular educational level, while the second shows the percentage with that level of education that work in the sector. For example, in cell 1, 12.6 percent of government employees has no formal education, while 1.7 percent of those with no formal education work for the government. N = 3063

Source: Authors' calculations from the GLSS.

369

than boys to become economically active before the age of 16. The lower levels of educational achievement for women may help to explain the much lower percentage of women in the government, state enterprise, and private nonhousehold sectors. By contrast, women are much more likely than men to be self-employed in business activities. Over 33 percent of women—compared to 17 percent of men—work in household business.

One of the surprising figures in table 9.3 is the high level of unemployment. At 5.5 percent of the active population, this figure is higher than official figures, and therefore requires some explanation. Table 9.4 provides information on this group. Within the group we classified as unemployed, only 26 percent were actually searching for a job. This is the group usually referred to as the unemployed. Among the others classified as unemployed, 37 percent said they were not searching for a job as they were either waiting to start a new job or waiting to receive an answer from an employer, while the remaining 37 percent said they were not searching for a job because they did not believe jobs were available. This last group, often referred to as discouraged workers, represents about 2 percent of the total active population.

Table 9.4 Unemployment Status
(percentage of unemployed)

Sex	Location	Searching for job	Waiting for job	Discouraged
Male	Urban	46.2	43.6	10.3
	Rural	24.4	35.6	40.0
Female	Urban	23.8	35.7	40.5
	Rural	11.9	33.3	54.8
Total	Urban	34.6	39.5	25.9
	Rural	18.4	34.5	47.1
Total		26.2	36.9	36.9

Source: Authors' calculations from the GLSS.   N=168

Notwithstanding the difficulties associated with measuring the unemployment rate properly, many people consider the level of unemployment to be an inappropriate measure of the underutilization of labor. One better measure of underemployment may be the fraction of the employed wanting more work. Table 9.5 indicates that only 4 percent of employed women and 5 percent of employed men were actually searching for more work during the previous week. Correspondingly, almost 80 percent of employed people considered that they had enough work. Another 11 percent of the working population indicated that they were not searching for additional work since they did not believe that any was available. Together, the figures on unemployment and underemployment do not indicate that finding work is an extremely critical problem for most Ghanaians.

Table 9.6 presents data on household labor income (the definition of "wage" under table 9.10 corresponds to labor income). The male-female distinction in this table refers to the sex of the head of household. The average household labor income per month includes income received from both main and secondary jobs for all members

Table 9.5 Underemployment
(percentage of employed)

Sex	Location	Search for additional work	Enough work	Discouraged	Others
Male	Urban	6.4	72.3	11.7	9.6
	Rural	4.6	79.6	9.7	6.2
Female	Urban	4.1	72.1	11.9	11.9
	Rural	3.4	78.0	11.8	6.9
Total	Urban	5.3	72.2	11.8	10.7
	Rural	3.9	78.7	10.8	6.5
Total		4.3	77.1	11.1	7.6

Source: Authors' calculations from the GLSS. N=2895

of the household.[4] Urban households earn, on average, 50 percent more labor income than rural households. Similarly, male-headed households earn up to 50 percent more than female-headed households in the same geographical region.

The fourth column of table 9.6 helps assess the relative importance of labor income by showing labor income as a percentage of total income. Total income was calculated by summing labor income, business income (profits), and net farming income (these figures should be considered as only indicative, since double counting and undeclared income is likely). Nevertheless, the data indicate that labor income is an important source of income for all the categories shown in table 9.6, with labor income being most important in urban areas, especially Accra.

Table 9.6 Household Labor Income by Sex of Head of Household and Region

Region	Sex of head of household	Household labor income per month (cedis)	Labor income as percentage of total income	Number of earners per household	Average income per earner (cedis)	Household size	Number in sample
Accra	Male	14,287	88	1.4	10,205	4.5	99
	Female	8,311	89	1.0	8,311	3.4	28
Urban	Male	14,116	50	1.0	14,116	4.9	249
	Female	10,652	71	0.8	13,315	4.3	116
Rural Coastal	Male	9,053	39	1.5	6,035	4.9	137
	Female	6,707	28	1.2	5,589	4.1	71
Rural Forest	Male	9,025	33	1.3	6,942	5.3	390
	Female	5,146	38	0.8	6,432	4.6	183
Rural Savanna	Male	6,748	43	1.3	5,191	6.2	216
	Female	6,965	54	0.8	8,707	4.8	38

* Urban refers to households in towns with a population over 5,000 other than Accra.
Source: Authors' calculations from the GLSS.

4. Household sector workers were also asked how much money they received for their work. The answer to this question is considered to be labor income.

One possible explanation for the male-female household income differential observed in table 9.6 is that female-headed households have fewer contributors to total labor income as indicated in the fifth column of table 9.6. The sixth column shows household income divided by the average number of contributors. The sex-related differential is almost eliminated in this weighted data. Although female-headed households may be poorer, the results suggest that this differential may be related mainly to a labor supply effect rather than to limited opportunities.

Table 9.7 examines the determinants of monthly labor earnings more closely by decomposing individuals' earnings into hourly wages, hours worked per week, and weeks worked per year. At the individual level, women again have monthly labor earnings below those of men (except women in urban areas other than Accra). However, women also work less in remunerated employment than men, both in terms of hours per week and weeks per year. Once labor earnings are scaled to hourly earnings, the sex-related wage

Table 9.7 Personal Earnings from Main Job by Sex and Region

Region	Sex	Monthly earning (cedis)	Hours worked	Weeks per year worked	Hourly earning (cedis)
Accra	Male	12,459	50.3	41.9	89.2
	Female	6,557	40.3	37.3	88.1
Urban	Male	10,102	40.9	42.2	90.1
	Female	11,514	33.8	40.5	101.7
Rural Coastal	Male	4,119	32.2	39.0	44.3
	Female	3,732	30.8	37.5	45.5
Rural Forest	Male	5,720	35.6	42.2	65.1
	Female	4,712	28.9	40.3	45.2
Rural Savanna	Male	5,482	38.2	44.3	65.9
	Female	4,861	33.2	39.7	44.7

Source: Authors' calculations from the GLSS.

differentials are considerably reduced. In particular, women in Accra earn almost the same per hour as men, although their monthly earnings are on average nearly half those of men.

One interesting aspect of the average hourly earnings figures in table 9.7 is the extent to which they are similar in Accra and other urban areas and again for different rural areas. This suggests that migration may play an effective role in equilibrating wages between these different local labor markets (the urban rural wage differential observed in this table is much smaller than that usually observed; see Squire 1981 for some comparisons). Consequently, this provides some indirect preliminary support for the notion that relying on migration to respond to the changes in relative wages caused by the adjustment program may be reasonable.

Tables 9.8 and 9.9 provide further information about the determination of wages and the labor supply. Table 9.8 indicates that hourly earnings are on average highest for people working in the household business sector. This may be because many household businesses are in urban areas, where the average hourly wage is much higher than in rural areas. Employees of the government and of state enterprises also tend to receive higher hourly pay than the average worker. Again, this may reflect a composition rather than a sector effect. Table 9.9 shows that workers with more formal education

Table 9.8 Personal Labor Earnings and Hours Worked on Main Job by Sectors

Sector of employment	Hourly earnings (cedis)	Weekly hours worked
Government	96.0	40.2
State	91.2	46.6
Private	52.2	45.4
Household farming	39.6	31.5
Household business	105.8	36.9
Household business and farming	68.6	29.8

Source: Authors' calculations from the GLSS.

Table 9.9 Personal Labor Earnings and Hours Worked on Main Job by Education

Level of education	Hourly earnings (cedis)	Weekly hours worked
None	56.9	34.5
Primary	53.1	33.0
Middle	68.1	36.7
Secondary	164.8	40.0
Postsecondary	130.6	33.3
Koranic	60.3	40.3

Source: Authors' calculations from the GLSS.

receive higher hourly earnings. Since both the government and the state enterprise sector employ a large percentage of educated workers, this could be the cause of this sector effect. However, any reliable appraisal of these different explanations requires multivariate analysis, which is undertaken in the following section. Note that in none of the tables 9.7, 9.8, or 9.9 does a strong link emerge between wages and hours worked. This suggests that labor supply elasticities are quite small.

The preliminary information extracted from the GLSS provides some insight into the functioning of the labor market. Although Ghanaian workers are mainly concentrated in the household sectors, especially in farming, market forces are apparent in the allocation and remuneration of labor. For example, hourly earnings are quite similar within rural areas and within urban areas, most people seem to be able to find a sufficient amount of work, and, on the basis of hourly earnings, women do not seem to be paid less than men.

The Determinants of Earnings and Labor Supply

This section examines the determinants of labor earnings and labor supply in more detail. Table 9.10 examines the determinants of hourly earnings for all individuals that reported labor income. Following the human capital literature (see Mincer 1974 for an

Table 9.10 Hourly Wage for the Main Job

Dependent variable	(1) HWM estimate	Standard error	(2) HWM estimate	Standard error	(3) HWM estimate	Standard error
Experience	0.029	0.007*	0.020	0.008*	0.023	0.007*
Experience squared	-0.0003	0.0001*	-0.0001	0.0001	-0.0003	0.0001*
Primary	0.038	0.021*	0.032	0.021	0.026	0.020
Middle	0.070	0.032*	0.056	0.032*	0.026	0.031
Secondary	0.176	0.044*	0.140	0.044*	0.102	0.042*
Teaching technical ed.	0.105	0.076	0.065	0.075	0.061	0.072
Postsecondary	0.118	0.085	0.125	0.084	0.058	0.081
Professional vocational ed.	0.252	0.150*	0.194	0.148	0.125	0.143
Accra	0.353	0.134*	0.133	0.137	-0.154	0.136
Urban	0.794	0.101*	0.577	0.105*	0.343	0.104*
Rural-coastal	-0.010	0.111	-0.095	0.111	-0.156	0.108
Rural-forest	0.197	0.094*	0.126	0.093	0.192	0.090*
Ghana national	0.241	0.106*	0.256	0.104*	0.270	0.100*
Migrant	-0.130	0.066*	-0.120	0.065*	-0.118	0.063*
Head of household	0.298	0.079*	0.283	0.078*	0.259	0.075*
Women	0.060	0.074	0.084	0.073	-0.058	0.074
Seasonal	0.528	0.114*	0.529	0.114*	0.387	0.111*
Tenure			-0.014	0.003*	0.010	0.004*
Tenure government			0.049	0.007*	-0.005	0.010
Tenure private business			0.026	0.009*	-0.002	0.011
Tenure household business			0.014	0.004*	-0.020	0.005*

Union		0.589	0.215*
Government		1.101	0.202*
Private business		0.484	0.162*
Household business		0.904	0.126*
Pension		0.066	0.152
Mining		0.598	0.223*
Manufacturing		0.317	0.127*
Service		0.284	0.109*
Construction		0.249	0.171
No. obs.	1,801	1,801	1,801
R^2	0.157	0.185	0.255

HWM = log of hourly wage on main job
* Significantly different from zero at 90 percent confidence level
Ghana national = 1 if the individual has Ghanaian citizenship, otherwise 0
Migrant = 1 if the individual has moved within the last five years, otherwise 0
Head of household = 1 if the individual is the head of the household, otherwise 0
Women = 1 if the individual is a female, 0 if a male
Seasonal = 1 if the individual has worked less than 20 weeks in the last 12 months, otherwise 0
Union = 1 if the individual has worked in a unionized firm, otherwise 0
Pension = 1 if the individual has a pension plan, otherwise 0
Tenure government = tenure in the government
Tenure private business = tenure in the formal private sector
Tenure household business = tenure in the informal business sector

introduction), column (1) of table 9.10 presents the estimated coefficients for a regression of hourly earnings on a set of individual characteristics. Most of the results are standard. The first two coefficients represent the effect on wages of total labor market experience: this effect is positive and decreasing. The next five coefficients represent the effect on wages of a year of education at different levels of schooling. All these coefficients indicate a positive return to education. The highest returns to education are associated with formal secondary education. Postsecondary education, including teaching and technical education, show large positive returns, but the coefficients are not significantly different from zero at the 90 percent confidence level. The variable denoted prof-voc is also an education variable. This dummy variable is equal to 1 if the individual has completed a professional or vocational training program. The returns to this type of training are also positive.

The next set of variables is included to capture differences in wages that arise due to geographical considerations. Such differences can result from either different costs of living or from different local labor demand conditions. The latter source of differentials can be maintained in the long run only if migration flows are unresponsive. The four geographical dummy variables included in the regression are mutually exclusive. The residual category is rural savanna. The largest location differential is associated with living in urban areas other than Accra (towns over 5,000 in population). The results of this regression also indicate that living in Accra is associated with a premium when compared to living in rural areas (however, this result is not robust). Among rural areas, the differences are not very large. Working in the forest region, which is the cocoa production region, is nevertheless associated with a small premium compared to the other two rural regions. Although the rural savanna region is very poor, these results indicate that the rural coastal region may be even poorer.

A final set of individual-specific dummy variables capture earning differentials due to information networks or discrimination. Ghanaian nationals and heads of household are shown to receive higher than average hourly earnings, while recent regional immigrants (those who have lived in their current place of residence for less than two years) receive lower than average earnings. Further confirming our previous observations, women are not observed to receive lower hourly earnings than men. Finally, seasonal workers (individuals working less than 20 weeks a year) receive higher than average hourly wages. This last result suggests that seasonal workers enter the market only in good times and leave in bad times, indicating a relatively frictionless labor market.

To examine the link between employment-specific capital and earnings, column (2) of table 9.10 includes a set of tenure variables. The tenure variable is the number of years that individuals have worked in their current job. This variable is also allowed to interact with sector dummies: the public sector, the private nonhousehold sector, and the household business sector, with the household farming sector omitted. In most sectors, the hourly wage has a positive correlation with tenure, but contrary to standard expectations concerning tenure variables, the estimates do not indicate a positive tenure profile for household farm sector workers. Most learning in the household farming sector jobs is therefore possibly of the general human capital type, and consequently may make labor mobility in this sector relatively inexpensive.

Column 3 of table 9.10 adds a set of employer-specific variables to our individual-specific set of explanatory variables. Assuming the labor market was without friction and that employees had no aggregate preferences with respect to types of employment, then employer-specific variables should not be expected to have any explanatory power. However, many of our employer-specific variables are observed to have large and significant effects on hourly earnings. These effects may represent either compensating wage differentials or labor market distortions. The large and significant effect of unions on wages is a common example of an interference with market forces, however, this interpretation is sometimes debated (see Lewis 1986). The increase in wages associated with unionization is estimated to be close to 60 percent. This estimate is much larger than similar estimates for industrialized countries, which are usually of the order of 10 to 20 percent (Lewis 1986). Comparing wage differentials associated with sectors of employment, we find that all sectors of employment receive a premium relative to the household farming sector. The premium is highest among public sector employees, followed by household business employees, and finally by private sector employees. However, a fraction of these premiums are likely to be a compensation for the loss in direct consumption associated with household farming.

Similar to the sector effects, the industry dummies also indicate a negative wage differential for agricultural employees (the agricultural industry is the residual category). The employees of the mining industry are observed to receive the highest industry-related differential. This last observation accords quite well with a compensating differential interpretation of industry effects. However, the other industries—manufacturing, services, and construction—do not exhibit major interindustry differentials. The final employer-specific variable included in this regression is a pension dummy. This variable indicates whether the employee is covered by a pension plan, and it is included to capture the notion of a formal employment relationship. This variable is not observed to have a significant effect on wages, which may be due to its correlation with other variables.

The inclusion of employer-specific variables in our earnings equation has changed some of the estimated coefficients of the individual-specific variables. For example, the Accra dummy is no longer significant once employer variables are taken into account. This suggests that the previous premium we associated with living in Accra was probably caused by the greater likelihood of being employed in high paying sectors rather than an across-the-board compensation. Moreover, this result indicates that migration may be eliminating geographical earnings differentials. Another consequence of the introduction of the employer variables has been the reduction in the returns to schooling. This may be caused by either differential returns to education in different jobs, or by education being used as a selection device in certain jobs. The examination of sector-specific earnings functions will help assess the plausibility of each of these explanations.

In brief, these first regression results indicate that hourly labor earnings conform relatively well to a combination of human capital theory, the theory of equilibrating migration flows, and to the theory of compensating differentials, that is, returns to human capital are positive, regional differences are not extremely important, and compensating differentials are related mostly to being off the farm, especially in the mining industry.

Labor Supply

In order to further depict the overall functioning of the Ghanaian labor market, an examination of labor supply decisions is useful. Table 9.11 presents estimates of the determination of weekly hours worked on the main job. The examination of hours worked in both main and secondary jobs will be discussed later.

Column (1) of table 9.11 presents estimates of a labor supply function using ordinary least squares (OLS). The estimated elasticity of labor supply with respect to hourly earnings is negative. However, this estimate may be severely biased, since unobserved individual heterogeneity is likely to be correlated with hourly earnings. Column (2) therefore presents results from a two-stage least squares (2SLS) estimation of the same labor supply function.[5] These results indicate a positive and significant effect of hourly earnings on the supply of labor, although the effect is quite small. The other results of column (2) worth noting are that women work significantly fewer hours per week than men, and that workers in Accra work on average more hours a week. Column (3) presents estimates for a reduced-form labor supply function, that is, the hourly earnings variable is replaced by the earnings function. These results suggest that our positive estimate of the elasticity of labor supply is most likely the result of the lower wage farmers receive and the lower hours worked by farmers (this aggregation bias will be discussed further).

Main and Secondary Jobs

Both tables 9.10 and 9.11 have examined the determination of hourly earnings and hours worked for main jobs only, however, almost 30 percent of the people in our sample reported earnings from a secondary job. Therefore, column (1) of table 9.12 presents estimates of the determination of total monthly earnings from both main and secondary jobs (using the extended set of variables), and

---

5. The set of instruments used for this estimation are the employer-specific variables and the tenure variables.

Table 9.11 Hours Worked per Week on Main Job

Dependent variable	(1) HRS estimate	Standard error	(2) HRS (2SLS) estimate	Standard error	(3) HRS estimate	Standard error
HWM	-0.150	0.011*	0.194	0.039*	0.001	0.004
Experience	0.007	0.003*	-0.003	0.004	-0.0001	0.00005*
Experience squared	-0.0001	0.00004*	-0.00001	0.0001		
Primary	-0.008	0.009	-0.021	0.012*	-0.016	0.010
Middle	0.025	0.014*	0.001	0.018	0.002	0.015
Secondary	0.032	0.020	-0.029	0.026	-0.019	0.020
Teaching technical ed.	0.005	0.034	-0.031	0.043	-0.027	0.035
Postsecondary	0.030	0.038	-0.011	0.048	-0.001	0.039
Professional vocational ed.	0.068	0.067	-0.018	0.085*	-0.018	0.070
Accra	0.296	0.060*	0.175	0.077*	0.046	0.066
Urban	0.142	0.046*	-0.131	0.065*	-0.109	0.050*
Rural-coastal	-0.169	0.050*	-0.165	0.063*	-0.165	0.053*
Rural-forest	-0.071	0.042*	-0.139	0.053*	-0.090	0.044*
Ghana nat.	0.203	0.047*	0.120	0.060*	0.188	0.049*
Migrant	-0.028	0.030	0.016	0.038	0.004	0.030
Head of household	0.136	0.035*	0.033	0.046	0.070	0.037*
Women	-0.169	0.033*	-0.190	0.042*	-0.174	0.036*
Seasonal	-0.142	0.051*	-0.321	0.068*	-0.227	0.054

Tenure	0.002	0.002
Tenure government	-0.00003	0.005
Tenure private business	0.005	0.005
Tenure household business	0.003	0.003
Union	-0.073	0.105
Government	-0.001	0.098
Private business	0.123	0.079*
Household business	-0.098	0.061
Pension	0.171	0.074
Mining	0.080	0.108
Manufacturing	0.165	0.062*
Service	0.290	0.053*
Construction	0.330	0.083*
No. obs.	1,801	1,801
R^2	0.179	0.138

No. obs.	1,801
R^2	0.074

HRS = log of hours per week worked on main job
HWM = log of hourly wage on main job
* Significantly different from zero at 90 percent confidence level
See table 9.10 for definitions of other dependent variables.

383

Table 9.12 Monthly Wages and Hours Worked on Main and Secondary Jobs

Dependent variable	(1) WMS estimate	Standard error	(2) HRSSM estimate	Standard error
Experience	0.028	0.007*	0.002	0.003
Experience squared	-0.0004	0.0001*	-0.0001	0.0001*
Primary	0.027	0.018	-0.013	0.009
Middle	0.011	0.027	-0.0001	0.014
Secondary	0.056	0.038	0.019	0.020
Teaching technical ed.	0.036	0.063	-0.030	0.033
Postsecondary	0.075	0.072	-0.001	0.038
Professional vocational ed.	0.091	0.127	-0.018	0.067
Accra	0.017	0.122	0.004	0.064
Urban	0.246	0.093*	-0.129	0.049*
Rural-coastal	-0.160	0.098	-0.164	0.052*
Rural-forest	0.179	0.081*	-0.045	0.043
Ghana national	0.530	0.089*	0.171	0.047*
Migrant	-0.117	0.056*	-0.016	0.029
Head of household	0.303	0.067*	0.076	0.036*
Women	-0.210	0.066*	-0.178	0.035*
Seasonal	-0.203	0.099*	-0.228	0.052*
Tenure	0.013	0.003*	0.002	0.002
Tenure government	-0.007	0.009	-0.0003	0.005
Tenure private business	-0.007	0.010	0.002	0.005
Tenure household business	-0.012	0.005*	0.001	0.002
Union	0.362	0.192*	-0.116	0.102
Government	1.313	0.188*	0.195	0.099*
Private business	1.121	0.152*	0.330	0.080*
Household business	1.370	0.123*	0.121	0.065*
Pension	0.094	0.136	0.123	0.072*
Mining	0.230	0.202	-0.006	0.107
Manufacturing	-0.040	0.119	0.061	0.063
Service	0.128	0.104	0.158	0.055*
Construction	0.145	0.158	0.217	0.083*
Second job	0.505	0.087*	0.322	0.046*
No. obs.	1,807		1,806	
R^2	0.379		0.180	

WMS = log of monthly wage on main and secondary job
HRSSM = log of total hours on main and secondary job
* Significantly different from zero at 90 percent confidence level
See table 9.10 for definitions of other dependent variables.

column (2) presents results for total hours worked per week on both jobs (using the reduced form estimates). The sample remains that of all workers, irrespective of whether or not they had a second job.

The regression results for total monthly earnings closely resemble those for hourly earnings; however, a few differences are apparent. First, women receive considerably lower monthly earnings than men, even though their hourly wages were not observed to be below average. Second, the earnings differential associated with unionization on the main jobs is considerably reduced when total monthly earnings are considered instead of hourly wages. Third, workers in all sectors other than the household farming sector receive similar monthly earnings, in particular, public sector employees are no longer observed to receive a premium. Finally, individuals with a second job receive on average 50 percent more monthly earnings than workers with only one job.

The size of the income effect associated with a secondary job warrants closer examination. Economic theory predicts that in a well-functioning labor market, the income effect of a second job should be the result exclusively of the greater number of hours worked. From column (2) in table 9.12 we observe that most of the income effect associated with a second job is possibly the result of an hours effect, that is, the size of the hours effect and the size of the income effect are not significantly different. Consequently, hourly earnings are possibly similar on both jobs. This observation, combined with a previous observation about individuals' general lack of desire for more work (table 9.5), supports a competitive interpretation of labor allocation.

Sector-Specific Earnings Functions

To examine whether different segments of the labor market behave differently, tables 9.13–9.15 present estimates of earnings functions and labor supply functions for specific subsamples. Table 9.13 presents results for the household farming sector, while tables 9.14 and 9.15 present results for the formal and informal segments of the labor market, excluding the household farming sector. In table 9.14, a job has been defined as formal if either (a) it is a public sector job, (b) it is a unionized job, (c) it is covered by a pension plan, or (d) it is covered by social security benefits. For all three tables, column (1)

Table 9.13 Household Farming Sector

Dependent variable	(1) HWM estimate	(2) HRS estimate	(3) WMS estimate	(4) HRSSM estimate
HWM		-0.083		
Experience	0.034*	0.006	0.043*	0.003
Experience squared	-0.0003*	-0.0001	-0.0005*	-0.0001*
Primary	0.081*	-0.037	0.036	-0.043*
Middle	0.010	0.022*	0.040	0.018
Secondary	0.017	0.043	0.012	0.042
Teaching technical ed.	0.086	-0.056	0.044	-0.070
Postsecondary	-1.635	-0.592	-1.667	-0.470
Professional vocational ed.	0.317	0.122	0.333	0.148
Accra	-0.933	-0.119	-0.713	-0.034
Urban	0.203	-0.300*	-0.055	-0.311*
Rural-coastal	-0.173	-0.142*	-0.219	-0.142*
Rural-forest	0.275*	-0.057	0.298*	-0.073
Ghana national	0.343*	0.109	0.488*	0.082
Migrant	-0.188*	-0.086	-0.221*	-0.067
Head of household	0.275*	0.072	0.308*	0.048
Women	-0.046	-0.246*	-0.297*	-0.249*
Seasonal	1.594*	-0.235*	0.276	-0.365*
Tenure	0.005		0.008	0.001
Tenure government				
Tenure private business				
Tenure household business				
Union				
Government				
Private business				
Household business				
Pension				
Mining				
Manufacturing				
Service				
Construction				
Second job			1.464*	0.509*
No. obs.	734	734	735	735
R^2	0.156	0.117	0.220	0.139

HWM = log of hourly wage on main job
HRS = log of hours worked on main job
WMS = log of monthly wage on main and secondary job
HRSSM = log of total hours on main and secondary job
* Significantly different from zero at 90 percent confidence level
See table 9.10 for definitions of other dependent variables.

Table 9.14 Formal Sector

Dependent variable	(1) HWM estimate	(2) HRS estimate	(3) WMS estimate	(4) HRSSM estimate
HWM		-0.031		
Experience	0.020	0.001	0.013	0.0002
Experience squared	-0.0004*	0.00003	-0.0003*	-0.000004*
Primary	-0.106*	0.029	-0.033	0.032*
Middle	0.155*	-0.025	0.055*	-0.054*
Secondary	0.205*	-0.047	0.094*	-0.076*
Teaching technical ed.	0.075	-0.037	0.034	-0.025
Postsecondary	0.047	0.007	0.062*	0.011
Professional vocational ed.	0.028	-0.013	0.028	0.003
Accra	0.098	0.139*	0.223*	0.112
Urban	0.215	0.020	0.137	0.004
Rural-coastal	0.263	-0.241*	0.035	-0.203*
Rural-forest	0.215	-0.032	0.197*	0.055
Ghana national	0.015	0.044	0.081	0.082
Migrant	0.015	-0.004	0.023	-0.017
Head of household	0.181	0.052	0.098	0.071
Women	0.036	-0.107*	-0.077	-0.108*
Seasonal	-0.638*	0.080*	-0.480*	0.018
Tenure	0.012*		0.014*	0.000
Tenure government				
Tenure private business				
Tenure household business				
Union	0.199		0.205	-0.082
Government	0.352*		0.190	-0.032
Private bus.				
Household business				
Pension				
Mining	0.029		-0.104	-0.071
Manufacturing	0.075		0.078	0.147
Service	-0.145		-0.074	-0.005
Construction	-0.181		-0.053	0.136
Second job			0.288*	0.184*
No. obs.	311	311	313	313
R^2	0.276	0.205	0.313	0.251

HWM = log of hourly wage on main job
HRS = log of hours worked on main job
WMS = log of monthly wage on main and secondary job
HRSSM = log of total hours on main and secondary job
* Significantly different from zero at 90 percent confidence level
See table 9.10 for definitions of other dependent variables.

Table 9.15 Nonagricultural Informal Sector

Dependent variable	(1) HWM estimate	(2) HRS estimate	(3) WMS estimate	(4) HRSSM estimate
HWM		0.015		
Experience	0.025*	-0.006	0.026*	0.002
Experience squared	-0.0004*	0.00008	-0.0004*	-0.00004
Primary	-0.015	-0.002	0.018	0.009
Middle	0.013	0.005	-0.007	0.004
Secondary	0.132	-0.033	0.063	-0.002
Teaching technical ed.	-0.266	0.143	- 0.107	0.067
Postsecondary	0.009	0.047	0.065	0.031
Professional vocational ed.	0.265	-0.139	0.114	-0.125
Accra	-0.610*	0.230*	-0.404*	0.081
Urban	0.046	0.019	-0.004	-0.052
Rural-coastal	-0.589*	-0.161	-0.534*	-0.091
Rural-forest	-0.314*	-0.093	-0.354*	0.059
Ghana national	0.316*	0.294*	0.758*	0.286*
Migrant	-0.086	0.048	-0.159	0.029
Head of household	0.224*	0.143*	0.372*	0.137*
Women	-0.163	-0.111*	-0.120	-0.075
Seasonal	0.246*	-0.231*	-0.233	-0.236*
Tenure	-0.006		0.004	0.004
Tenure government				
Tenure private business	0.018		0.010	0.001
Tenure household business				
Union				
Government				
Private business	-0.491*		-0.275*	0.253*
Household business				
Pension				
Mining	1.018*		0.396	-0.014
Manufacturing	0.467*		-0.180	0.009
Service	0.399*		-0.045	0.161
Construction	0.516*		0.163	0.141
Second job			0.356*	0.308*
No. obs.	754	754	756	756
R^2	0.120	0.070	0.159	0.142

HWM = log of hourly wage on main job
HRS = log of hours worked on main job
WMS = log of monthly wage on main and secondary job
HRSSM = log of total hours on main and secondary job
* Significantly different from zero at 90 percent confidence level
See table 9.10 for definitions of other dependent variables.

presents regression results for our extended hourly earnings function, column (2) presents results for the two-stage estimation of labor supply, column (3) presents results for the total monthly earnings equation, and column (4) is the reduced form regression results for total weekly hours.[6]

The results of tables 9.13–9.15 indicate quite different returns to education in the different segments of the labor market. Earnings in informal jobs (excluding household farming) do not indicate any significant returns to education, and earnings on household farms are positively related only to primary education. By contrast, earnings in formal employment relationships are much more closely related to education, especially to middle and secondary school education. Another interesting result is the effect of living in Accra. Table 9.14 indicates that formal sector employment does not provide a premium for individuals living in Accra, however, an informal sector worker earns less in Accra than elsewhere. This result may be due to a Harris-Todaro type of equilibrating mechanism (Harris and Todaro 1970), whereby migration decisions are based on the comparison of a probability weighted sum of earnings in the formal and informal sectors. Since the probability of formal employment is greater in Accra, equilibrating migration flows cause informal sector jobs in Accra to receive less than average earnings. This suggests that informal sector workers in Accra may be among the most disadvantaged workers in urban areas.

The comparative results between sectors also indicate the possibility of different forms of organization or production technologies in these different segments of the labor market. In formal jobs, seasonal workers are paid less and the tenure profile is positive. In informal and in farm jobs there is no tenure profile, and seasonal workers receive higher average hourly earnings. Thus, the presence of job-specific investments appears to be relevant only in the formal sector, consequently, mobility is probably more costly in this sector.

---

6. The regression results of these tables could be biased because of sample selectivity problems; however, preliminary work to correct this type of bias has not produced very different results. Results by Stelcner and others (1987) for Peru, nevertheless, suggest that this bias may be important for assessing public-private wage differentials.

The comparison of the role secondary jobs play in the different segments of the labor market is also quite striking. In both tables 9.14 and 9.15, the effect on monthly earnings of a secondary job is almost totally attributable to an increase in hours worked. This again suggests a labor market without strong frictions, which is not surprising for the informal sector. However, the effect on earnings of having a secondary job in the household farming sector cannot be attributable only to an increase in hours worked. Average hourly earnings for a farmer's second job are therefore probably much higher than on the first job. This result may indicate either the presence of a high fixed cost associated with finding a second job, or simply that the earnings on primary farming jobs are grossly underestimated because of direct consumption. If the latter hypothesis is maintained, secondary jobs provide a good estimate of farmers' returns to work and, in this case, indicate that household farm workers may not be at a great disadvantage relative to workers in other sectors of the economy.

A final observation from the sector-specific estimations is that the labor supply elasticities are all insignificantly different from zero. This suggests, as noted earlier, that the estimate of this elasticity derived from table 9.11 may be biased upward due to the pooling of the different sectors of employment.

In view of the results presented in this and the previous section, the Ghanaian labor market offers some signs of a relatively fluid labor market, for example, the seasonal earning differential and the absence of important earnings differentials for secondary jobs are signs of a well-functioning market. However, the differential patterns of earnings between sectors indicate the possibility of segmentation within the labor market, that is, the rationing of formal sector jobs.

The Role of the Labor Market in the Adjustment Process

We now will try to assess the link between the labor market and the process of adjustment under the ERP. In particular, we will examine how the labor market responded to the adjustment program. Overall, the macroeconomic indicators presented earlier indicate that the stabilization aspects of the ERP have been mostly successful. However, to examine whether any fundamental structural adjustment has really occurred, we must examine the program's impact on the sectoral composition of output. A primary goal of the adjustment program has been to liberalize the price system in the hope of stimulating production in sectors where Ghana possesses a comparative advantage. Table 9.16 presents data on sectoral shares of production between 1978 and 1987 (these shares are evaluated at purchasers' value in current dollars). Since 1983, the sectors of economic activity that have grown fastest are the industrial sector, the government sector, and the cocoa production sector. These changes in the sectoral composition of output accord quite well with the objectives of the ERP. For example, the change in the terms of trade in favor of cocoa production, resulting in part from the depreciation of the cedi, pushed cocoa production from 4 percent of GDP to almost 9 percent of GDP between 1984 and 1987. The improvements in the world price of cocoa between 1982 and 1984 were initially an important factor in this increase, although since 1984 the world price of cocoa has been decreasing (see table 9.1).[7] The large increase in Ghana's main export has contributed greatly to the trade balance surpluses registered in 1986 and 1988. Similarly, the rapid growth of the industrial sector, especially manufacturing, reflects the adjustment program's goal of increasing the capacity utilization rates. These rates are nevertheless still quite low.[8]

Part of the recovery in the industrial sector may be due to the rationalization of the foreign exchange system. Since 1983, the foreign exchange system has gradually changed from a fixed exchange system with controls to an auction system. Within the auction system, firms that value foreign exchange the most are served first (under the constraint of having the required capital). Therefore, the allocation of imported intermediate goods has probably improved in favor of the most productive firms within the industrial sector, thereby encouraging growth. Small firms are nevertheless disadvantaged by the new system. The 100 percent up-front payment requirement for foreign exchange is often prohibitive for small firms

---

7. These figures probably overestimate the real increases in the production of cocoa. Part of the increase is only a redirection of production from smuggling toward official channels.

8. The size of the manufacturing sector in relation to total production was still lower in 1987 than it was in 1970.

Table 9.16 Percentage Distribution of Gross Domestic Product by Kind of Economic Activity, in Producers' Values, 1978–81, 1984–87 *(current cedis millions)*

Sector	1978	1979	1980	1981	1984	1985	1986	1987[*]
Agriculture	47.7	45.6	48.4	43.8	40.8	34.6	34.3	35.7
Cocoa production	7.0	8.1	5.5	1.4	4.1	5.5	8.0	8.9
Forestry	4.8	5.0	4.8	3.7	3.4	3.3	3.7	4.6
Mining	0.6	0.8	1.4	0.5	1.2	1.1	1.7	1.8
Manufacturing	8.6	8.7	7.2	5.9	6.4	11.5	11.2	9.9
Electricity	0.4	0.4	0.6	0.5	0.8	1.2	1.8	1.8
Construction	2.5	2.3	2.3	1.9	2.2	2.9	2.5	2.4
Transportation	2.6	2.7	2.2	2.1	6.4	5.3	4.3	3.7
Trade	13.3	13.8	14.6	30.0	28.3	24.8	19.1	18.5
Finance	3.1	3.6	2.8	2.0	1.7	2.3	3.0	2.6
Government	8.2	7.5	8.5	6.2	3.9	6.2	8.2	8.1

[*] Provisional
Sources: 1978–81: World Bank (1984a); 1984–87: Ghana Statistical Service *Quarterly Digest Statistics* (1988).

(firms are not allowed to borrow from the banking system to buy foreign exchange), which may have greatly limited their expansion.

The growth in the government sector observed in table 9.16 may seem paradoxical given that one of the objectives of the ERP was to cut this sector. The main cause of this observed growth is the increase in public sector pay. Increases were given mainly in an attempt to improve efficiency. The level of wages in the public sector as of 1983 was generally so low that most workers needed other jobs to supplement their income, which often reduced the hours they worked for the government. The results from the estimated earnings functions presented earlier indicate that these increases have probably now brought government sector pay in line with private sector pay. Nevertheless, comparison of the pay structure in Ghana with that in neighboring countries may suggest the need for further increases for educated workers.

Table 9.16 indicates that the major declining sector since 1983 is commerce. This observation must be carefully qualified. Evaluated in constant 1975 dollars, the share of commerce in total production has actually been rising under the ERP. This seemingly contradictory observation is due to a sharp decrease in the relative price of services during the period. The actual quantities of services, including commerce, have been rising quickly rather than declining. Following a period of contraction, such an expansion in the volume of commerce is normally expected. However, a fall in the relative price of trading services is somewhat surprising. This change in relative price is most likely a direct consequence of the ERP's objective of stimulating exports and, as will be shown, it has had a large impact on the remuneration of service sector workers.

The labor market's role in redirecting production observed under the ERP will first be analyzed by examining the wage trends associated with the different sectors of the economy. Table 9.17 presents time series data on real monthly earnings by sector of production. These data come from establishment surveys, and must therefore be considered as indicative as they cover only a small fraction of the economy.

The observed trends in wages have followed the pattern of output quite closely. Real wages were falling rapidly before the ERP and started improving immediately after. However, both the downward and upward trends have been much more accentuated for wages than for outputs. Wages rose some 50 percent between 1983 and 1987, while GNP growth per capita rose by just over 10 percent during the same period.

The sectors where real wages have gained most during the adjustment program are agriculture, mining, and transportation: all sectors favored by the ERP as a means of improving external balance. Real wages in these sectors have reached levels close to or above those prevalent in 1978. In contrast, real wages in the commerce sector were still 25 percent lower in 1987 than in 1978. One possible explanation of the poor wage performance in the commerce sector is that this sector probably served as the main absorbing sector during the crises of the early 1980s. The relative importance of the commerce sector in the total value of production (current prices) went from 13 percent of

Table 9.17 Average Monthly Earnings by Sector, 1978–86
(constant cedis, 1978 = 100)

Sector	1978	1979	1980	1981	1982	1983	1984	1985	1986
Agriculture, forestry, fisheries	100.0	70.3	82.9	58.6	53.2	38.0	70.3	76.3	126.9
Mining, quarrying	100.0	79.8	87.3	56.5	46.8	53.4	58.3	164.1	153.0
Manufacturing	100.0	75.7	78.2	45.1	42.1	31.6	59.2	78.9	100.1
Electricity, water, gas	100.0	85.0	102.2	63.1	54.6	28.4	46.7	70.4	112.2
Construction	100.0	76.2	83.3	54.8	46.0	35.2	44.7	67.0	102.6
Commerce	100.0	85.1	81.3	36.5	44.2	28.6	34.1	56.1	78.5
Transportation, storage, communications	100.0	84.0	93.8	50.6	47.8	33.4	49.5	70.1	163.2
Finance, insurance, real estate	100.0	65.3	67.1	39.9	39.6	25.5	38.4	61.6	103.8
Services	100.0	78.9	86.1	49.1	42.2	30.8	47.2	60.1	113.0
All industries:									
Public sector	100.0	81.3	88.8	53.9	46.2	36.7	51.9	76.7	130.4
Private sector	100.0	82.2	86.2	46.0	48.6	32.8	59.1	76.7	98.9
All sectors	100.0	82.2	88.3	52.5	46.6	36.2	53.2	76.5	124.5
GNP/Capita	100.0	95.0	92.0	87.0	78.0	72.0	78.0	79.0	81.0

Sources: 1978–81: World Bank (1984); 1982–86: Ghana Statistical Service *Quarterly Digest Statistics* (1988).

production in 1978 to 29 percent in 1983. This influx of labor into the commerce sector placed enormous pressure on earnings within the sector, which has not as yet been completely reversed. Another factor that contributed to the decline of earnings in the commerce sector was the reduction in both corruption and the excessive use of market power by traders (*kalabule*). These changes were a direct consequence of Flight Lieutenant J. J. Rawlings' ascent to power.

The real wage flexibility observed in table 9.17 for all sectors of production offers further evidence that the Ghanaian labor market responds to competitive forces, and therefore favors the hypothesis that the functioning of the labor market has probably facilitated the sectoral reallocations sought by the ERP.

For a more detailed assessment of how the returns to labor may have changed since 1982 and thereby created the incentives for workers to relocate, table 9.18 presents information on the changes in earning patterns over the course of adjustment. Column (1) of table 9.18 presents results for the estimated hourly earnings function for workers who began their jobs between 1983 and 1988. Column (2) is the estimated hourly earnings function for workers who began their jobs before 1983. Notice that both equations are estimated using data for the same year (the data come from the GLSS for both regressions). Consequently, the proper interpretation of the difference between these two columns is not obvious. Under the assumption that market forces are much more effective at the margin of new employment, we can interpret the differences between these two columns as indicating changes in patterns of earnings (this is obviously a questionable interpretation).

The results shown in table 9.18 indicate that regional differentials have changed during the adjustment process. While the data indicate that premiums are associated with jobs acquired before 1983 in urban areas other than Accra and in the forest region, these premiums are not apparent for jobs acquired after 1983. The changes in the patterns of regional earnings may be the result of competitive pressures due to migration flows. A second sign of changes in market forces since 1983 is the higher premium associated with being in a union for recently hired workers. The union differential is about 30 percent for workers hired before 1983, but over 60 percent for workers hired after

Table 9.18 Changes in Pattern of Earnings

Dependent variable	(1) HMW tenure < 5 estimate	Standard error	(2) HMW tenure > 5 estimate	Standard error
Experience	0.027*	0.012	0.011	0.011
Experience squared	-0.0003*	0.0002	-0.0001	0.0001
Primary	0.060*	0.032	0.014	0.026
Middle	0.017	0.047	0.010	0.042
Secondary	0.11000*	0.061	0.085	0.063
Teaching technical ed.	-0.071	0.111	0.127	0.097
Postsecondary	0.075	0.096	0.097	0.156
Professional vocational ed.	0.252	0.222	0.166	0.191
Accra	-0.493*	0.207	0.132	0.193
Urban	0.065	0.169	0.495*	0.136
Rural-coastal	-0.268	0.189	-0.147	0.133
Rural-forest	-0.083	0.166	0.326*	0.107
Ghana national	0.187	0.150	0.408*	0.135
Migrant	-0.176*	0.100	-0.042	0.082
Head of household	0.411*	0.119	0.101	0.099
Women	0.272*	0.121	-0.268*	0.095
Seasonal	0.250*	0.134	1.188*	0.231
Tenure	0.013	0.063	0.006	0.005
Tenure government	0.070	0.103	-0.006	0.014
Tenure private business	-0.057	0.097	-0.019	0.015
Tenure household business	0.046	0.077	-0.016*	0.007
Union	0.659*	0.313	0.297	0.317
Government	0.994*	0.404	1.080*	0.292
Private business	0.735*	0.306	0.903*	0.330
Household business	0.963*	0.295	0.748*	0.178
Pension	0.160	0.237	0.027	0.199
Mining	0.665*	0.301	0.434	0.367
Manufacturing	0.178	0.207	0.322*	0.169
Service	0.148	0.182	0.350*	0.146
Construction Second job	0.427	0.275	0.043*	0.227
No. obs.	710		1,090	
R^2	0.281		0.278	

HMW= log of hourly wage on main job
* Significantly different from zero at 90 percent confidence level
See table 9.10 for definitions of other dependent variables.

1983. This suggests that wages for recently hired workers in the unionized sector have adjusted much less rapidly than in the nonunionized sector.

The changes in industry-related earning differentials observed in table 9.18 lend some support to our interpretation of the difference between the columns as indicating changes in the patterns of earnings. As in table 9.17, in table 9.18 the mining differential has increased and the service differential has decreased (both differentials are compared to agriculture). The table also suggests that the returns to education have increased over the course of adjustment (this result is not statistically very significant). In particular, the return associated with a year of primary education has tripled for recently acquired jobs. This increase in the returns to education may reflect in part the government's policy of stretching the wage scale within the public sector as a means of keeping its most educated workers. In 1983, the ratio of relative wages within the public sector was at most 1:1.8. This ratio was much smaller than the equivalent ratio for government employees in neighboring countries, and therefore probably contributed to Ghana's loss of many educated workers. Another explanation for the increased returns to education is the reduction in corruption and *kalabule*, which mainly benefited unskilled labor.

The data on real wage trends indicate that sectoral changes in production were mainly accompanied by changes in wages, however, these data do not provide information on whether adjustments in employment also occurred. Table 9.19 presents information on the intersectoral flow of workers. Among workers who changed jobs since 1983, column (1) of Table 9.19 gives the distribution of the industrial sector of origin, and column (2) gives the sectoral distribution of arrivals. The major flow is observed to be toward the agricultural sector. This coincides with the growth in the agricultural sector, especially the production of cocoa as targeted by the ERP. All our evidence therefore suggests that the ERP's reliance on market signals as a way to achieve structural adjustment has probably been helped by a labor market sensitive to profitable opportunities. Thus, the possibility of exporting the Ghanaian experience probably depends, in part, on both the extent to which the targeted country's labor market has the same degree of flexibility as that observed in Ghana (the

Table 9.19 Employment Flows Between Sectors of Economic Activity, 1983
(percent)

Sector	*(1)* *Origin*	*(2)* *Destination*	*(2) – (1)* *Net*
Farming	23.95	49.81	25.86
Forestry, mining	3.04	2.3	-0.76
Manufacturing	20.15	10.1	-10.01
Construction, transportation	13.18	6.97	-6.21
Services	39.67	30.8	-8.87
Totals	100.00	100.00	0

Source: Authors' calculations from GLSS.

economic crisis in Ghana in the early 1980s may have contributed to the observed flexibility) and on the political regime in power.[9] In the case of Ghana, the reduction in overt corruption is potentially a major factor in the improved allocation of resources.

The Distributional Aspects of the Adjustment Program

The central element of the ERP is the change in relative prices in favor of the tradable goods sector. To assess the distributional impact of such a change, it is helpful to consider a highly stylized model of the Ghanaian economy and to examine whether the theoretical predictions correspond to our observations. In particular, this exercise will permit us to link together many of our previous results and to identify a group likely to be the most adversely affected by the adjustment program.

The simplest model of the Ghanaian economy is a two-sector model with one tradable good sector and one nontradable good sector. The tradable good corresponds to agricultural production and

---

9. Loxley (1988) appropriately emphasizes that a crisis based on supply distortions, as opposed to excess demand, is essential to the understanding, and possible exportation, of the Ghanaian experience.

the nontradable good corresponds to services.[10] The impact on labor earnings of a price change in favor of agricultural products depends on the degree of factor mobility. In the short run, labor is most likely to be immobile, while in the long run our observations suggest that it is probably quite mobile. The other major factor of production is land, which is obviously immobile. Given such a simple model of the economy, the theoretical predictions of the impact of a price change in favor of agriculture, that is, the exportable good, are straightforward. In the short run, the returns to labor in the service sector will fall, in terms of both tradables and nontradables, while labor earnings in the agricultural sector will rise. Workers will react to these changes by moving away from urban areas, where services are concentrated, and toward rural areas, especially export-oriented rural areas. Those hardest hit by the change will therefore be the unprotected workers in urban areas.

The data analyzed in the previous sections are generally consistent with the predictions of this simple model. First, the trends in real wages observed in table 9.17 reflect major gains for agricultural workers relative to service industry workers. Second, the changes in regional earnings differentials derived from table 9.18 indicate that the returns to working in Accra and in other urban areas fell significantly over the course of adjustment. Finally, the returns to unionization, that is, partial protection from market forces, also increased since the introduction of the ERP.

Another implication of the model is that the patterns of migration should have changed during the course of adjustment. Table 9.20 helps assess this possibility. Column (1) indicates that prior to 1970, 46.5 percent of net migration was directed toward Accra. As predicted by theory, columns (2) and (3) indicate that the patterns of migration were completely reversed in the 1980s. Instead of being a region of net inflow, Accra has become the major source of migrants. Between 1982 and 1987, net migration out of Accra accounted for almost 60 percent of net outward migration in Ghana. The main destination of

---

10. The manufacturing sector can be omitted from this discussion given its small size (less than 10 percent of production).

Table 9.20 Net Migration Flows
(percent)

Region	(1) Up to 1970		(2) Up to 1987		(3) 1982–87	
	Destination	Origin	Destination	Origin	Destination	Origin
Western	21.1		74.0		39.0	
Central		22.4		11.0		6.8
Accra	46.5			15.0		57.6
Eastern		17.0		3.0	27.1	
Volta		28.9		31.0		15.3
Ashanti	12.3			40.0		20.3
Brong-Ahafo	20.0		13.0		13.6	
Northern & Upper		31.8	13.0		20.3	
Totals	100.0	100.0	100.0	100.0	100.0	100.0

Sources: (1): Ewusi (1984); (2) and (3): Authors' calculations from the GLSS.

migrants has become the western region, which is the region of expanding cocoa production.

The combination of theoretical predictions and empirical observations clearly suggests that those most adversely affected by the ERP are the young, informal sector workers in urban areas, especially those working in Accra. This group also includes older workers retrenched from the public and private sector over the course of adjustment who have been forced to integrate into the informal sector. Furthermore, since informal sector businesses employ mostly women, female-headed households have probably been hit severely by the ERP. Therefore, any policy aimed at alleviating the costs of adjustment should probably target the informal sector in Accra (this does not imply that this group is the poorest, only that it has probably been hit the hardest).[11] However, the effect of any such policy should

---

11. The Program of Action to Mitigate the Social Costs of Adjustment (PAMSCAD) has already begun to target this group for help.

be considered in a general equilibrium setting given the responsiveness of migration flows.

The ERP's impact on overall poverty is much harder to evaluate. The major changes have been in favor of agricultural workers and against informal sector service workers. Since the relative poverty of each group is difficult to assess, the overall impact is unclear.[12] A valid appraisal of the relative poverty of each group would require a detailed analysis of consumption data, but this is beyond the scope of this chapter. However, casual observation suggests that agricultural workers are poorer than informal sector workers, and therefore that the ERP has most likely reduced the inequality of incomes within the country.

Conclusion

The main aim of this chapter was to assess whether the functioning of the Ghanaian labor market accords well with the ERP's market-oriented export promotion policies. Our assessment is essentially favorable, even though widespread poverty remains an important problem in Ghana. Our main finding is that although most workers in Ghana are either self-employed or employed by household members, labor allocation and remuneration seem to be affected by market forces, and that a market-oriented policy for structural adjustment may therefore be appropriate. In particular, the determination of both hourly and monthly earnings appears to conform somewhat to the theory of compensating wage differentials. Moreover, the evidence indicates that migration may have responded quite promptly to labor earnings differentials between regions, and may therefore be considered as an effective equilibrating force in the long run.

With regard to the specific period covered by the adjustment program, we have found that changes in labor earnings and allocations mainly reflect the objectives sought by the ERP. There have been substantial relative wage gains for agricultural and industrial workers in relation to service sector workers (especially the retail trade sector). Accordingly, the main reallocation of workers has been toward the

---

12. Benjamin and Deaton (1988) conclude for the Côte d'Ivoire that a price change in favor of cocoa production does not significantly affect the distribution of income.

agriculture sector, in particular, the Greater Accra region has been losing workers while the western region (the main cocoa production region) has been gaining them. However, these migration flows have not as yet been large enough to equilibrate earnings across sectors and regions. The young, informal sector workers in urban areas, especially in Accra, are still feeling the adverse effects of the ERP. Helping part of this group to relocate to the faster growing regions of the economy might be warranted.

Finally, even though we believe that a flexible labor market probably helped achieve the macroeconomic improvements observed in Ghana during the 1980s, this factor may be neither the most important factor nor a sufficient condition for further improvements. On the one hand, factors such as the reduction in corruption and the inflows of new capital may have played more important roles than that of the labor market. On the other hand, the probability of maintaining growth based on an export promotion policy depends foremost on the world prices for Ghana's exports, which have been mostly unfavorable lately. Therefore, an overall assessment of the ERP requires taking into account the program's different facets, and not only its link with the labor market, even though the latter provides support for the program.

References

Deaton A., and D. Benjamin, 1988. *The Living Standards Survey and Price Policy Reforms: A Study of Cocoa and Coffee Production in Côte d'Ivoire.* Living Standards Measurement Study Working Paper 44. Washington, D.C.: World Bank.

Ewusi, K. 1978. "The Size of the Labor Force and Structure of Employment in Ghana." Technical Publications Series No. 37. Legon, Ghana: Institute of Statistical, Social, and Economic Research.

_____. 1984. "The Dimensions and Characteristics of Rural Poverty in Ghana." Technical Publication No. 43. Legon, Ghana: Institute of Statistical, Social, and Economic Research.

Glewwe, P., and D. de Tray. 1988. *The Poor During Adjustment: A Case Study of Côte d'Ivoire.* Living Standards Measurement Study Working Paper 47. Washington, D.C.: World Bank.

Government of Ghana. 1983. *Economic Recovery Program, 1984–86*. Vol. 1. Accra.

Green, R. H. 1987. *Stabilization and Adjustment Programmes and Policies: Ghana*. Helsinki: World Institute for Development Economics Research.

Harris, J. R., and M. P. Todaro. 1970. "Migration, Unemployment and Development." *American Economic Review* 60.

Lewis, H. G. 1986. *Union Relative Wage Effects: A Survey*. Chicago: University of Chicago Press.

Loxley, J. 1988. *Ghana: Economic Crisis and the Long Road to Recovery*. Ottawa, Canada: The North-South Institute.

Mincer, J. 1974. *Schooling, Experience, and Earnings*. New York: National Bureau of Economic Research.

Scott, C., and B. Amenuvegbe. 1989. *Sample Designs for the Living Standards Surveys in Ghana and Mauritania*. Living Standards Measurement Study Working Paper 49. Washington, D.C.: World Bank.

Squire, L. 1981. *Employment Policy in Developing Countries: A Survey of Issues and Evidence*. New York: Oxford University Press.

Stelcner, M., J. van der Gaag, and W. Vijverberg. 1987. *Public-Private Sector Wage Differential in Peru: 1985–1986*. Living Standards Measurement Study Working Paper 41. Washington, D.C.: World Bank.

World Bank. 1984a. *Ghana: Policies and Program for Adjustment*. A World Bank Country Study. Washington, D.C.

_____. 1984b. *Toward Sustained Development in Sub-Saharan Africa: A Joint Program of Action*. Washington, D.C.

10

KENYA

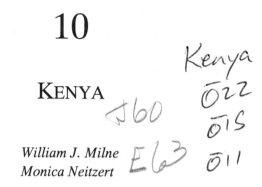

William J. Milne
Monica Neitzert

Kenya, like many other developing countries, suffered through the economic crises of the mid-1970s and early 1980s. International economic events have a strong impact on Kenya's economy. The sources of the economic turmoil included fluctuations in coffee and tea prices; the rapid increase in oil prices in the mid-1970s and 1979–80; the world recession of 1981–82 due, in part, to the rise in world interest rates; the collapse of the East African Community in 1978; and the drought of 1984. While Kenya's real GDP did not fall as it did in many other African countries, changes occurred that signaled the need for structural adjustment. These included a fall in real earnings in all sectors of the monetary economy, a deterioration of the trade balance in 1980–81, and a rapid expansion of external debt.

The labor market has adjusted to these economic events, and apparently this adjustment has, in part, lessened the impact on economic growth. Indeed, while real wage rates have declined, sometimes quite dramatically, unemployment rates in urban areas do not appear to have increased substantially from the late 1970s to the mid-1980s. Of course, with continuing declines in real wages, poverty and basic needs provision are of critical concern. In addition, balance of payments problems and the size of the external debt remain serious constraints for sustained medium- to long-run economic growth.

The authors would like to thank Kenya's Ministry of Planning and National Development for access to some of the data used in this manuscript. Research assistance was provided by D. E. Hyatt.

Table 10.1 Some Macroeconomic Indicators, 1974–89

Year	Real GDP growth (%)	Per capita growth[a] (%)	Trade balance[b] (K£ millions)	Real effective exchange rate[c] (1975=100)	Inflation rate[d] (%)	Growth of wage employment (%)	Growth of real wages[e] (%)	Real per capita consumption growth (%)	External debt (millions of US$ end year)	Government deficit as % of GDP
1974	3.2	-0.6	-199	106	15.3	8.5	-5.1	11.1	999.7	n.a.
1975	2.4	-1.4	-175	100	15.6	-0.9	-0.6	-4.1	1,108.3	n.a.
1976	4.5	0.7	-115	107	10.4	4.7	5.2	-5.8	1,303.6	2.7
1977	8.2	4.4	-89	98	12.8	5.3	-4.2	6.2	1,745.6	1.8
1978	7.9	4.1	-304	84	12.5	1.0	-1.4	12.8	2,321.6	4.6
1979	5.0	1.2	-248	85	8.4	6.7	1.0	-1.2	2,870.3	4.7
1980	4.0	0.2	-513	84	12.9	3.4	0.9	-3.5	3,511.7	6.3
1981	6.0	2.2	-453	101	12.6	1.9	3.6	-7.8	3,389.0	8.4
1982	7.6	3.8	-332	103	22.0	2.1	-13.2	-1.8	3,518.4	8.7
1983	1.5	-2.2	-253	114	14.5	4.5	-6.1	-4.3	3,763.7	4.3
1984	0.7	-3.0	-320	114	9.1	2.4	0.4	2.2	3,725.4	5.8
1985	4.9	1.3	-385	115	10.8	4.9	-2.2	-8.4	4,402.9	4.3
1986	5.5	1.9	-351	106	5.6	3.9	3.0	12.0	4,945.2	7.5
1987	4.8	1.3	-641	120	7.1	3.5	0.1	3.7	5,966.9	3.9
1988	5.2	1.7	-813	126	10.7	3.7	1.9	3.0	5,888.1	4.6
1989	5.0	1.5	-1,219	n.a.	10.5	2.4	1.3	-0.7	n.a.	n.a.

n.a. = not available

Note: The data used throughout this chapter are from revisions to the national accounts provided by the Central Bureau of Statistics, Government of Kenya. They may not, therefore, match the figures in the historical publications.

a. Per capita growth is the percentage change in real GDP per capita. Computed by the authors as the difference between the growth rate of real GDP and the estimated population growth rate.

b. The trade balance is the visible balance (that is, merchandise only) in millions of Kenyan pounds.

c. An increase in the index implies depreciation.

d. The inflation rate is based on an annual average of the consumer price index for the average of three income groups in Nairobi.

e. The real wage rate is defined as the total wage employment annual wage rate for all modern sector employees (both private and public) divided by the average consumer price index for Nairobi.

Sources: Kenya, Republic of, *Economic Survey and Statistical Abstract* (various issues); World Bank (1990).

Origin and Nature of the Adjustment Problem

The period since independence in 1963 through 1973 was characterized by rapid growth, although with substantial fluctuations, in the Kenyan economy. Real GDP growth averaged over 6.5 percent per year and per capita real GDP growth averaged approximately 3.0 percent per year. Much of this growth can be attributed to increases in the land available for cultivation, and a movement from large to small farms and from low- to high-value crops. In addition, land was transferred from foreign to Kenyan hands through a settlement scheme involving one million acres during this period. Within the manufacturing sector, growth was good due to the "easy" phase of import substitution.

By 1973 Kenya had adjusted some of the easiest options for further growth, both in agriculture and in manufacturing. The post-1973 period can be broken into three subperiods, namely, the relatively successful reaction to the first oil crisis (1973–78), the relatively more difficult stabilization and response to the second oil crisis (1979–84), and the beginning of structural adjustment (1985 onward).

Since 1973 economic events in Kenya have been influenced by several international economic events. As table 10.1 shows, per capita real GDP declined in both 1974 and 1975 in response to the rapid rise in world oil prices in 1973–74. In Kenya, the f.o.b. price of crude oil doubled in 1973 and almost tripled between December 1973 and the end of the first quarter of 1974. In addition, international growth was slower and a widespread drought adversely affected agriculture. Besides the decline in real income per capita, these events increased the inflation rate and caused a large decline in the growth rate of wage employment in 1975 and falling real wages in both years.

Beginning in 1976, world coffee and tea prices rose dramatically due to frost in Brazil, which gave a temporary boost to growth. In 1976 and 1977, coffee prices were 130 and 317 percent above their 1975 levels, respectively, while tea prices were 23 and 134 percent above their 1975 levels in the same two years. The result was that between 1975 and 1977 Kenyan coffee exports increased sixfold and tea exports tripled (both in value terms). The result of these increased exports was a significant turnaround in the balance of trade in 1976 and 1977 (table 10.1). During 1976–78, Kenya was able to maintain an average annual growth rate of real GDP of close to 6 percent, which implied relatively strong real GDP per capita growth. However, along with this strong growth came inflation, which persisted even after the adjustment to the oil price shock of 1973–74.

The period 1979 through 1984 presents a different pattern of economic growth. The collapse of the East African Community in 1978 significantly reduced Kenya's exports to Tanzania and Uganda and also led to lower gross fixed capital formation in 1979. There was no net improvement in real per capita income during this period. The second oil price shock more than doubled the world price in 1979. In addition, many developed countries followed restrictive monetary policies in an effort to control inflation in the early 1980s. This resulted in high world interest rates and the worldwide recession of 1981–82, which led to a significant reduction in Kenyan exports, and therefore slowed growth. Also in August 1982, a coup attempt caused temporary political instability, which reduced investment spending and subsequently hurt tourism. In 1983, the world oil price fell, but interest rates remained high, causing Kenya's external debt service requirements to be large. In 1984, due to the worst drought in 40 years, real GDP per capita declined by 3 percent, a reflection of the continuing importance of agriculture in the Kenyan economy.

The year 1985 marked the beginning of a turnaround in Kenya's economic fortunes. Good weather, continued declines in world oil prices, and rising coffee prices led to increases in real GDP per capita. Through 1989, the Kenyan economy grew strongly, although the trade balance continued to deteriorate. Interestingly, in 1988 tourist earnings overtook coffee exports as the main source of foreign exchange.

As table 10.1 indicates, exchange rate policy has also been important. The government announced a small nominal devaluation of about 5 percent against the U.S. dollar in February 1981, and a larger devaluation of over 15 percent in September 1981. The next devaluation took place in December 1982 and there have been no publicly announced devaluations since, rather, the policy is one of continued depreciation of the Kenyan shilling versus a trade-weighted basket of currencies. With the mini coffee boom in 1986, the currency appreciated (in both real and nominal terms) before the downward trend in the rate continued. With the continuing deterioration of the trade balance and inflation rates in Kenya running higher than worldwide inflation, the shilling depreciated by almost 13 percent in nominal terms against the U.S. dollar in 1988 and another 16 percent in 1989. A comparison of exchange rate movements and the trade balance highlights one of the economy's ongoing problems: despite the continuing depreciation of the shilling, the trade balance deficit has increased. While in the first half of the 1980s the government controlled imports as a stabilization measure, there has not been any significant export penetration into new markets and the restructuring of imports does not appear to have occurred. Furthermore, with the sharp drop in coffee prices in 1988 and 1989, the balance of payments problem continues to be serious.

Table 10.1 also indicates another significant problem: the significant erosion in both real consumption per capita and in real wages paid to employees in the modern sector. (The fact that these series move roughly together suggests that although urban employment in the modern sector is only a small part of total employment, the trends in real wages rates are an indication of the aggregate effects.) Consequently, the plight of the working poor remains a serious issue. However, this decline in real wages, which is due, in part, to government policy as discussed later, has allowed wage employment growth in the modern sector to remain strong (at a rate close to the rate of growth of the labor force) throughout the period.

The government deficit, its financing, and the growth of external debt is also of concern. Since 1980, the deficit as a percentage of GDP reached a peak of 7.5 percent in fiscal year 1986–87. It has declined somewhat since, although for fiscal year 1988–89 it still stood at 4.6 percent, which has caused concerns about inflationary pressures. Internal borrowing from nonbank financial sources to finance the deficit has proven difficult. At the margin, the government finances the remaining part of the deficit through bank sources, both the central bank and the commercial banks. This tends to be inflationary and points to the need to develop a functioning capital market so that some financing can be done through the nonbank sector. In this regard, the government has recently set up the Capital Market Authority to explore ways to make trade in treasury bills and bonds more efficient, including the establishment of a secondary market.

In terms of reducing the deficit, the largest source of government revenue remains indirect taxes, since income taxes are hard to assess and collect. These indirect taxation receipts provide more than half of total revenues, with sales taxes being the most important source. Other major sources of indirect taxes are import, excise and export duties. As of January 1990, the sales tax has been replaced with a value added tax, which has the advantages of increasing the base to include some professional and other services as well as removing the bias against the manufacturing sector caused by the sales tax. On the expenditure side, the government faces constraints since the major portion of the budget is in the areas of education and health, both important to the development process.

External debt is also of concern. Between 1972 and 1978, the end of the coffee boom, the external debt (measured in U.S. dollars) grew on average at 36.0 percent per year. During the next six years, the average growth of the debt slowed to 7.9 percent per year, but then accelerated to 17.0 percent per year in 1984–87. Since then, however, external debt has fallen slightly, partly due to debt forgiveness. Recent loans have also been on fairly concessional terms, for example, in 1988, the interest rate on new commitments from public creditors was 1.9 percent with a maturity of 21.8 years. These concessionary loans are an important part of the financing of the deficit. External debt service (foreign loan payments plus foreign interest payments as a percentage of total export earnings) increased from 28 percent in 1981 to almost 38 percent in 1988. Since Kenya's primary exports of coffee and tea and its tourist industry are very sensitive to world economic conditions, this debt service percentage can easily reach unmanageable levels. A slowdown in world economic growth could put Kenya in a very precarious economic situation.

Table 10.2 sets out some information on structural change in the economy from 1972–89. The periods chosen in this table coincide with particular events that affected Kenya's economy. The first period, 1972–76, includes the first oil price shock and its aftermath; the period 1977–78 includes the coffee boom; 1979–81 includes the second oil price shock and the drought of 1979–80; the period 1982–84 encompasses the political turmoil of 1982 and the massive drought of 1984; the final period reflects the beginning of several sectoral structural adjustment programs and the mini coffee boom of 1986.

As development occurs, one expects the secondary sector (including manufacturing and building and construction) and tertiary sector (including the service industries) to increase at the expense of the primary sector (traditional, agriculture, and so on). While table 10.2 clearly demonstrates the declining share of the primary sector, it

Table 10.2 The Industrial Structure of the Kenyan Economy, 1972–89

(percentage of GDP in constant prices)

Category	1972–76	1977–78	1979–81	1982–84	1985–89
Traditional economy	6.20	5.82	5.56	5.51	5.51
Monetary economy					
Agriculture	33.45	33.38	30.88	30.72	29.08
Forestry and fishing	0.84	0.89	0.99	1.15	1.08
Mining and quarrying	0.34	0.29	0.27	0.22	0.26
Manufacturing	9.84	11.98	12.55	12.54	12.99
Electricity and water	0.63	0.74	0.81	0.81	0.87
Building and construction	4.93	4.24	4.56	3.83	3.27
Trade	12.28	11.28	11.30	10.25	11.17
Transport and communication	5.30	5.25	5.28	6.24	6.13
Finance, insurance, and real estate	4.79	5.26	6.68	7.07	7.55
Other	6.92	5.93	5.65	5.76	5.56
Private household services	0.61	0.78	0.99	1.13	1.33
Government	13.87	14.16	14.48	14.77	15.19
Total	100.00	100.00	100.00	100.00	100.00

Note: Other includes the ownership of dwellings, other services, and imputed bank service charges.
Sources: Kenya, Republic of, *Statistical Abstract* (various issues); Central Bureau of Statistics revised data.

is primarily the tertiary sector that has expanded during the period. Although Kenya is the most industrialized country in East Africa, the share of manufacturing, at roughly 13 percent of GDP, is still relatively small, and except for the increased activity during and immediately after the coffee boom of 1977–78, the growth of manufacturing output during 1979–89 was slow. A disturbing feature of the growth of the tertiary sector is the continuing growth in the size of the public sector. Even with the pronouncement in Sessional Paper No. 1 of 1986 on *Economic Management for Renewed Growth* that employment growth in the public sector would be curtailed, there is not much evidence of this to date. However, the government is committed to recommendation 7.6 of the Sessional Paper, which states that "employment in government will no longer be guaranteed for graduates of university and training programs."

In sum, the period since 1974 has been one of fluctuating economic growth. However, real GDP has not suffered a dramatic decline as was the case in many other African countries. The onset of successful structural adjustment is still relatively recent, and continuing short- and medium-term problems include the decline in real wages, persistent balance of payments difficulties, inflation, and external debt. The main long-term issue is attaining a growth rate adequate to keep up with rapid population growth.

The Period of Adjustment: Targets, Instruments, and Results

As already discussed, the period 1979–84 was one of stabilization without proper adjustment (van der Hoeven and Vandemoortele 1987), while the period since 1985 has seen more successful efforts at adjustment. The types of policies in the two periods were not markedly different, but the difference in effect is probably due to the intensity of application and the cumulation of different policy changes.

Fiscal policy was an early priority due to the problems of imported inflation dating back to the first oil crisis. However, as mentioned earlier, Kenya has a fairly narrow tax base and only limited options for cutting government spending. The budget deficit rose in 1980/81 and 1981/82, which led, via the increase in government borrowing, to cancellation of an IMF standby agreement. Through the period 1983–85, the government followed a restrictive stance combined with reasonably tight monetary policy, while continuing price incentives to the agricultural sector. In 1985, the government launched the Budget Rationalization Programme. Through this program the government aimed to control budgetary expenditures more closely. Budget resources, whether recurrent or development, were to be allocated according to well-defined priorities. This resulted in some projects with low potential benefits being cancelled or postponed, and new development projects were only funded if they were "productive investments of high priority." The government's budget deficit increased during 1986–88. However, much of this was a result of education expenditures (reform of the school system, which began in 1985, and increased university intakes), the hosting of the All-Africa Games in 1987, and the general election of 1988. The government has instituted cost sharing in education and health as part of the structural adjustment process. Nevertheless, the deficit remains large, and internal deficit financing from nonbank sources remains a very serious problem that impedes adjustment. Finally, there is still no evidence that the government has curtailed hiring university graduates who are otherwise unable to find a job (see, for example, Mills 1988).

As regards financial policy, by 1980 the government had become aware of the problems created in the financial system due to the continuation of very low and inflexible interest rates, usually negative in real terms. Interest rates rose substantially from 1980 to 1981, increasing by some 400 basis points. Current government policy is to keep real interest rates positive to encourage saving. Over the longer run the government is committed to having interest rates determined by market forces. However, to date there are still interest rate ceilings, which may lead to some investment projects being undertaken that are not as productive as desired, since the capital market may operate inefficiently. These ceilings may also make it more difficult for the small-scale enterprise sector to obtain funds. The government implemented a financial sector reform package in 1989, which aimed at full interest rate liberalization by mid-1991. In addition, the reforms strengthened the central bank's supervision of financial institutions and implemented restructuring for ten troubled financial institutions and two development finance institutions.

As regards exchange rate policy, the currency had a tendency to slide into overvaluation in the late 1970s, particularly during the coffee boom. Beginning in 1981, the currency underwent major devaluations; however, the two 1981 devaluations were undone by increased inflation. In 1982, wage policy changed to reduce inflation compensation, and subsequent nominal devaluations did result in real depreciation of the currency. This has still not led to an increase in manufacturing profits: the increased costs of imported inputs, combined with low substitution possibilities between domestic and imported inputs, caused problems (Vieira da Cunha 1987). However, the measure did address some of the problems of exports.

On trade policy, the government began to shift away from its focus on import substitution and began a gradual move to import liberalization. Beginning with the 1983 budget, the government reduced import duties and import quotas, and by 1985 duties remained on only some 12 percent of imported items. Nevertheless, in 1988 import licenses in two of the four schedules were still very tightly controlled in a manner tantamount to quotas. In 1988 the four schedules were increased to five, automatic licensing was introduced in all but one category, and the licensing system was streamlined. Tariffs were also cut in 1988, and most specific tariffs were replaced with *ad-valorem* ones.

In an attempt to promote exports, the government established export processing zones; set up manufacturing under bond, through which imported inputs are duty free provided the output is for export; and introduced the export compensation scheme, which repays import duties on intermediate imports for goods produced for export. However, implementation had its problems: the export compensation scheme entails long payment delays, and the high initial costs of manufacturing under bond has led to very few applications (according to unpublished World Bank documents, only 38 had been approved by 1990).

Nevertheless, the trade balance continues to deteriorate and limited foreign exchange reserves can constrain economic growth. The disequilibrium in the external sector is of considerable concern, and so far the policies have not achieved better balance.

As for wage policy, the government is heavily involved in wage setting in the modern sector, both public and private. The 1970s and particularly the 1980s marked a watershed in wage policy, from the deliberate high wage policy adopted following independence, to a wage policy more concerned with aiding employment growth. Real wages in production fell 25 percent between 1973 and 1976 after the first oil shock (Vieira da Cunha 1987), but there was more real wage resistance to the second oil shock, due partly to indexed wages catching up with inflation. After 1982 the government reduced sharply the wage indexation allowed by the Industrial Court, and managed to enforce this in wage contracts. The ability to cut real wages in a period of stagnant growth likely helped to prevent further inflation, and also coincided with the government's desire to maintain employment growth. It also probably gave a disincentive to rural-urban migration.

The government intensified its structural adjustment policies in the late 1980s, with an agricultural reform package (1987), industry and trade reforms (1988), and financial reform (1989). The agricultural policies aimed at improving the supply of key inputs, especially fertilizer, and producer incentives, deregulating markets, improving public investment and expenditure in agriculture, and reforming parastatals. The agricultural reforms have had mixed success.

Another aspect of structural adjustment was the removal of price controls. Price controls, where they exist, can lead to shortages and low profits. On the specific list of price-controlled items, only 12 items remain: charcoal, salt, maize and maizemeal, sifted maizemeal, milk, fats and edible oils, bread, wheat flour, tea, rice, sugar, and beer and stouts. Further, at the end of 1989 the price of beer at some establishments was decontrolled and early in 1990, the price of fertilizer was decontrolled. In terms of the consumer price index, price controlled items constitute 22 percent of total expenditures for the middle-income group.

In sum, in the first half of the 1980s, Kenya implemented stabilization programs and the second half of the decade showed some evidence of structural adjustment. Further policy changes are required, however, to permit adjustment on the basis of the "right" prices. The devaluations and recent policy decisions have made for an exchange rate that is more responsive to market conditions, and interest rates are also more responsive to market conditions (despite the interest rate ceilings, which were scheduled to be eliminated by July 1991). It is, however, too early to evaluate the success of the structural adjustment policies.

The Structure of Kenya's Labor Market

This section describes broad patterns in the labor market, namely, employment patterns and participation and unemployment rates, and describes some of the labor market institutions. Kenya remains a predominantly rural country, with some 80 percent of the population living in rural areas. Further, much of the urban population is concentrated in Nairobi, Mombasa, and Kisumu. Data from Fallon (1985) and the sixth *Development Plan* (Kenya, Republic of, 1989), as set out in table 10.3, indicate that the population in rural areas tends to be self-employed, while wage employment predominates in urban areas. Fallon provides some broad groupings of employment in urban and rural areas based on the Presidential Committee on Unemployment (1982/83) and Livingstone (1981), and these definitions are used in the development plan.

As the data in table 10.3 indicate, although small-scale agriculture is the predominant source of jobs in rural areas, modern wage employment is still important. This reflects some large-scale agricultural activities, such as ranching, tea estates, and coffee plantations. In urban areas, the growth of the informal sector is striking, with an annual average growth rate of 12.8 percent during 1980–88 and a projected average annual growth rate of 10.6 percent through 1993.

Given Kenya's rapid population growth, the big question in the long run is whether there will be enough jobs for the rapidly expanding labor force. Labor force growth can be expected to be high through the turn of the century. Indeed, the *Development Plan, 1989–93* (Kenya, Republic of, 1989) predicts an annual average growth rate of 4.3 percent in the labor force. This makes sense, as through 1984 the total fertility rate stood at 7.7 percent or over, and

Table 10.3 Employment in Urban and Rural Sectors of Kenya, Selected Years

	1980		1988		1993	
Type of employment	Number (000's)	Percent	Number (000's)	Percent	Number (000's)	Percent
Rural						
Modern wage employment	544	9.5	443	5.3	499	4.9
Small farm and rural informal	4,458	78.6	6,490	78.2	7,793	76.4
Urban						
Modern wage employment	501	8.8	924	11.1	1,183	11.6
Urban informal	168	3.0	441	5.3	730	7.2
Total	5,671	100.0	8,298	100.0	10,205	100.0

Notes: The estimate for modern wage employment in rural areas seems high for 1980, suggesting a definition change. There is other evidence from the World Bank (1988) that indicates that total wage employment in rural areas comprised 7.9 percent of total employment in 1985. This seems more in line with the development plan's estimate for 1988.
Sources: 1980: Fallon (1985, table 3); 1988 and 1993 projections: Kenya, Republic of (1989).

consequently, potential labor force entrants are already born. Although evidence from the 1989 *Kenya Demographic and Health Survey* (Nairobi: National Council for Population and Development) indicated that rates have declined, this will not affect the rate of labor force growth until well into the first decade of the next century. The other important consequence of this high fertility rate is that young people dominate potential new entrants to the labor force (in 1989, projections indicated that approximately 50 percent of the population was under the age of 15). These young people typically have high unemployment rates due to their lack of experience. With a fast growing supply of labor and with real wages constant or declining, the issue of poverty is a serious one.

Another factor is the increase in the female urban participation rate, which rose from 38.8 percent of the working age population in 1977–78, to 55.8 percent in 1986 (table 10.4). Note, however, that the change in the reference period from one day in 1977–78 to one week in the 1986 survey causes some noncomparability. By contrast, the

Table 10.4 Labor Force Participation Rates, Selected Years
(percent)

Urban

Age	Male 1977–78	Male 1986	Female 1977–78	Female 1986
15–19	23.9	19.6	23.0	31.8
20–24	80.3	73.7	37.9	53.7
25–29	93.4	94.5	47.4	69.4
30–34	97.1	98.8	44.2	64.2
35–39	98.8	96.4	40.1	61.2
40–44	98.6	99.5	39.1	59.9
45–49	97.9	97.4	47.8	60.2
50–54	89.6	95.3	44.1	53.4
55–59	90.8	84.8	34.5	48.1
60–64	87.1	74.0	30.8	47.5
Total	83.9	82.2	38.8	55.8

Rural

Age	Male 1977–78	Male 1988–89	Female 1977–78	Female 1988–89
8–14	55.0	78.1	55.3	82.6
15–24	69.0	84.7	79.4	92.8
25–64	91.3	97.0	92.0	96.8
65+	84.2	86.9	76.5	82.5
Total	83.4	87.2	86.9	91.0

Sources: Kenya, Republic of (1986a, basic report, table 6.1, table 5.1); *Urban Labour Force Survey, 1986* (table 7-1; includes active and passive job search); *Rural Labour Force Survey, 1988–89* (preliminary results).

418

male participation rate in urban areas did not change appreciably between the two surveys, and for prime age males, the participation rate is well over 90 percent. There is a smaller difference between the female participation rates in the two surveys in rural areas. Not surprisingly, the participation rate for both males and females in rural areas is very high; however, the definition for participation is working a minimum of one hour in the past week in the 1988–89 survey.

Table 10.5 sets out unemployment rates from the 1977–78 and 1986 *Urban Labour Force Surveys*. Two alternative definitions are available for 1986, either including or excluding those who engaged in passive job search. As the *African Employment Report 1988* (ILO 1989) indicates, the structure of unemployment has some important features. First, young participants have the highest unemployment rates: those aged 15 to 24 represent two-thirds to three-quarters of the unemployed. Second, women have an unemployment rate nearly twice that of men and their unemployment rates remain remarkably high even beyond 25 years of age, while male unemployment rates fall dramatically. Evidence by educational attainment indicates that unemployment is higher among those with secondary school than those with no formal education. In this survey, nearly half of the unemployed males had completed secondary school. By contrast, university graduates had very low unemployment rates due, in part, to the government's policy of hiring university graduates. This phenomenon of high unemployment among school leavers is also consistent with evidence from Collier and Lal (1986), who find long delays between leaving school and starting work.

Table 10.5 also permits a comparison of unemployment rates in 1977–78 and 1986. Note, however, that the definition of unemployment in this case is quite narrow (although other choices are available in both surveys); it only includes active job search and does not include underemployment. The unemployment patterns by age and sex are quite similar for both surveys: both exhibit a U-shaped curve with age. The overall rate for men declined slightly between the two surveys, while that for females increased significantly (this may be due to the increased female participation rates in urban areas). Thus overall, the unemployment rate has not changed markedly.

Table 10.5 Unemployment Rates by Age and Sex, 1977/78 and 1986 *(percent)*

Age	1977–78	1986
Men		
15–19	32.2	30.5
20–24	22.2	21.3
25–29	5.6	5.1
30–34	1.9	2.9
35–39	1.8	1.1
40–44	0.7	0.4
45–49	1.1	2.0
50–54	1.3	0.5
55–59	0.2	4.9
60–64	3.1	0.0
65+	2.2	n.a.
Average	6.2	5.6
Women		
15–19	21.0	22.4
20–24	11.4	22.6
25–29	2.9	7.6
30–34	1.7	4.1
35–39	1.4	4.0
40–44	0.2	2.1
45–49	0.4	0.0
50–54	0.0	1.8
55–59	1.6	0.0
60–64	0.0	0.0
65+	0.8	n.a.
Average	5.9	9.5
Both sexes		
15–19	24.7	24.6
20–24	17.1	21.8
25–29	4.4	6.1
30–34	1.8	3.3
35–39	1.6	2.0
40–44	0.7	0.7
45–49	1.0	1.5
50–54	1.3	0.8
55–59	1.4	4.1
60–64	3.0	0.0
65+	2.0	n.a.
Average	6.1	6.9

n.a. = not available
Note: Data are based on a one-day reference period.
Source: CBS, *Urban Labour Force Survey, 1986* (table 8.6).

Labor market institutions have important effects on the operation of labor markets. One key feature is the way wages are determined. For small-scale agriculture, rural nonfarm enterprises, and the urban informal sector, wages are market-determined and respond to supply and demand conditions. However, for modern large-scale agriculture, modern industrial enterprises, and the commercial and public sectors, wages are set through Industrial Court's wage guidelines. Hence, collective bargaining forms the basis of the industrial relations system in these sectors. A number of laws cover working hours, vacations, and the minimum wage. While union membership is not compulsory, it accounts for roughly 50 percent of production workers in large-scale manufacturing. All workers working in unionized establishments, whether or not they belong to the union, are covered by the collective agreement. If collective bargaining and voluntary arbitration fail, the Industrial Court can mandate settlements. Thus, the government plays a large role in wage setting behavior, both through the Industrial Court's wage guidelines and because the Central Organization of Trade Unions has government positions on it.

Government policy that sets guidelines for wage negotiations were introduced in 1973. The original guidelines (a) limited wage adjustments to full indexation based on the cost of living index plus a real growth rate that did not exceed the rate of income growth in the economy as a whole; and (b) required wage agreements to cover a minimum period of two years, while allowing only predetermined yearly adjustments.

After the economic turndown in 1974, the guidelines were revised in 1975 with the result that productivity increases could no longer be used to justify wage increases, and full cost of living increases were allowed for only the lowest paid groups. However, given union opposition and the threat of a general strike, the government reversed its actions and also abandoned an attempt to reduce real wages in 1976. With the guidelines of 1979, average productivity increases again could not be passed through, and overall wage increases could be no more than one-half the rise in the cost of living. With the downturn in the early 1980s and the devaluation of the currency in September 1981, another revision of the guidelines limited the overall wage increase for all income groups covered by a contract to three-quarters of the rise in the cost of living. The 1982 revision allowed for separate compensation for housing, which may have reduced the guidelines' effectiveness. The latest development plan (1989–93) reiterates government support for the wage guidelines and the notion of a two-tier wage policy, in which wages paid in rural small-scale agriculture are market-determined, while in the modern sector wages are determined through the Industrial Court's wage guidelines.

Measuring the impact of the wage guidelines is difficult as the average rate of wage increase in contracts settled by the Industrial Court has typically been below the targets contained in the guidelines. This is likely due to the continuing large growth in the supply of labor, which holds the growth of nominal wages in check. However, the fall in real wages since 1982, following the 1982 revision of the guidelines, has been quite marked.

Another component of wage setting behavior is for civil servants. The government reviews and adjusts these salaries roughly every five years. The latest of these reviews was in 1985. The reviews take into account the cost of living and the affordability of the implied wage bill for the government. The net result has been that government employees' wages in real terms have suffered a marked decline since the mid-1970s.

This section has outlined the structure of Kenya's labor market. Fast population growth means that employment creation is an important policy priority. Noteworthy is the increase in the female participation rate in urban areas during 1977–78 to 1986. Rural participation rates have not changed significantly. The structure of unemployment in urban areas indicates that there has been a significant increase in female unemployment, but a compensating decrease in male unemployment, so that overall unemployment rates have not changed. Individuals with some secondary school education tend to have the highest unemployment rates. Institutional arrangements in the labor market affect primarily the urban formal sector and operate through government-implemented wage guidelines.

The Adjustment of Labor Markets

This section examines labor market adjustment during the 1970s and the 1980s, including real wages and employment in aggregate and by sector of GDP, wages and employment in the public and private sectors, wages and employment in the formal and informal sectors, and finally migration.

Sectoral Wages and Employment

One way to examine sectoral adjustment is through the pattern of sectoral real wage and employment growth. Table 10.6 sets out real wage increases in various industries in the private and public sectors during 1974–89, and table 10.7 shows the wage employment share. These data are based on a survey of employment in the modern sector (although some of the informal sector is also included), and include only urban areas. As the table shows, the public sector has suffered a greater real wage loss than the private sector, although some industries in the latter sector (for example, mining and quarrying and construction) have experienced even greater real wage erosion.

Table 10.7 shows the expansion of the service sector, the decline in agriculture, and the stagnation of the manufacturing industry in the private sector. While one expects the share of employment in agriculture to fall during the course of development, structural adjustment requires a resource shift toward tradables that includes a large part of modern agriculture, some of modern manufacturing, and possibly transportation and communication services.

In line with the government's policy on holding wage increases below the rate of inflation, the minimum wage in real terms fell by over 40 percent between 1981 and 1985 as table 10.8 indicates. The minimum wage has fallen quite markedly relative to the average wage, although the latter also fell. The fall in real wages was probably important in helping to prevent a rise in unemployment.

Another way to examine adjustment in the labor market is through data on labor productivity and real wages. Figure 10.1 sets out these data for the modern economy (including both the private and public sectors). As the figure indicates, the real wage index dropped dramatically between 1981 and 1983, while the productivity index did not show such a severe decline. Part of the explanation behind this difference is the deflator used in computing the real wage index. The CPI is used for the real wage, while the GDP deflator for the monetary economy is used to measure productivity. Vieira da Cunha (1987)

Table 10.6 Real Wage Rates by Industry
(index, 1974 = 100)

Sector/year	Agriculture & forestry	Mining & quarrying	Manufacturing	Electricity & water	Construction	Trade, restaurants, & hotels	Transport & communication	Finance, insurance, & real estate	Community, social, and personal services	Total
Private sector										
1974	100.0	100.0	100.0	—	100.0	100.0	100.0	100.0	100.0	100.0
1975	103.3	105.8	98.3	—	100.2	98.4	83.1	95.6	89.3	98.2
1976	111.9	101.1	97.7	—	101.9	95.5	79.0	96.5	96.9	101.6
1977	99.4	68.9	98.7	—	98.5	93.1	78.0	93.0	90.9	98.9
1978	109.2	60.7	94.8	—	104.5	97.1	81.4	85.8	88.3	102.7
1979	108.3	60.1	89.2	—	97.0	98.9	83.2	90.0	94.3	104.1
1980	118.7	56.8	92.3	—	107.2	107.9	81.5	92.0	101.3	114.2
1981	105.7	54.0	83.3	—	98.3	94.9	75.6	87.9	91.5	103.0
1982	93.3	47.2	78.5	—	74.2	82.3	80.1	72.1	79.9	92.9
1983	91.5	44.4	78.3	—	74.4	79.9	68.6	69.8	79.9	90.4
1984	92.1	43.5	76.7	—	72.5	80.0	67.1	69.2	85.3	90.9
1985	89.9	40.6	74.5	—	70.4	76.8	66.5	68.8	84.2	89.1
1986	97.4	41.8	74.4	—	68.1	78.6	67.0	68.8	87.4	90.4
1987	101.5	44.6	77.7	—	76.3	79.7	74.1	72.7	92.4	93.8
1988	105.5	47.1	80.2	—	70.6	85.5	73.7	72.6	89.0	96.3
1989	105.1	60.1	77.7	—	71.3	83.5	64.3	74.0	91.5	97.4

Public sector

1974	100.0	100.0	100.0	100.0	100.0	100.0	100.0	100.0	100.0	100.0
1975	103.1	93.5	96.8	103.0	113.0	97.9	103.2	95.9	93.9	97.7
1976	156.5	90.9	90.3	95.8	112.5	102.2	103.4	103.8	104.9	108.4
1977	145.2	134.2	81.6	81.1	108.5	81.7	95.2	97.8	103.0	103.4
1978	142.6	168.6	83.4	79.6	101.6	95.9	97.7	104.1	103.6	104.1
1979	134.2	167.3	85.0	85.2	102.8	76.6	105.0	92.6	97.6	100.4
1980	100.4	169.6	88.4	83.3	73.6	87.4	103.2	105.6	93.6	94.7
1981	88.5	149.2	75.3	88.7	77.6	87.0	92.4	100.5	91.8	91.3
1982	78.9	142.7	69.4	70.9	75.3	80.9	83.7	90.0	79.3	80.9
1983	79.2	127.4	65.0	68.4	74.0	81.2	84.3	82.7	77.4	79.3
1984	73.7	114.2	66.5	70.0	77.4	75.1	81.5	83.2	73.6	76.9
1985	72.1	106.7	62.9	68.7	72.8	68.9	76.2	84.0	70.8	74.0
1986	76.1	103.5	61.3	74.7	60.7	67.9	79.9	91.9	75.5	78.2
1987	76.6	105.1	62.1	88.9	59.3	71.0	78.8	89.1	71.2	75.8
1988	81.3	95.1	62.5	89.5	57.0	68.6	80.8	90.6	72.7	76.5
1989	75.7	101.7	66.3	91.7	64.2	69.7	79.3	85.3	73.0	77.7

— indicates no employment in the electricity and water industry in the private sector, hence no wage rates

Note: The public sector includes the central government, the Teachers' Service Commission, parastatal bodies, local governments, and firms owned by the public sector through majority control.

Sources: Employment and Earnings (various years); Kenya, Republic of (1990).

Table 10.7 Employment Shares by Industry *(percent)*

Sector/year	Agriculture & forestry	Mining & quarrying	Manufac- turing	Electricity & water	Construction	Trade, restaurants, & hotels	Transport & communi- cation	Finance, insurance, & real estate	Community, social, and personal services	Total
Private sector										
1974	43.1	0.6	16.5	—	5.9	11.2	3.5	3.8	15.5	100.0
1975	41.1	0.6	17.2	—	5.2	10.9	3.5	4.2	17.4	100.0
1976	39.5	0.6	17.6	—	6.0	11.6	3.6	4.2	17.0	100.0
1977	39.2	0.5	18.0	—	5.6	11.5	3.7	4.6	17.0	100.0
1978	36.2	0.4	20.2	—	5.5	11.4	4.0	5.0	17.4	100.0
1979	35.4	0.4	20.5	—	5.9	11.8	4.3	5.1	16.7	100.0
1980	32.3	0.3	20.9	—	5.9	12.4	4.3	6.0	18.0	100.0
1981	32.1	0.3	21.6	—	6.0	12.5	3.5	5.8	18.1	100.0
1982	31.0	0.3	21.5	—	5.9	12.8	3.6	6.4	18.3	100.0
1983	31.4	0.4	20.7	—	5.5	13.2	3.7	6.4	18.7	100.0
1984	31.4	0.4	20.7	—	4.7	13.7	3.5	6.6	19.0	100.0
1985	31.0	0.5	20.6	—	4.3	14.0	3.4	6.7	19.4	100.0
1986	31.1	0.6	20.7	—	4.0	14.2	3.3	6.5	19.6	100.0
1987	30.7	0.6	21.0	—	4.0	14.3	3.0	6.4	19.8	100.0
1988	29.4	0.5	21.1	—	4.5	14.6	3.2	6.6	20.1	100.0
1989	28.6	0.5	21.1	—	4.7	15.0	3.3	6.7	20.0	100.0

Public sector

1974	14.4	0.2	5.9	1.7	4.6	0.5	8.7	1.0	63.0	100.0
1975	13.1	0.2	5.4	2.2	4.6	0.6	8.5	1.1	64.2	100.0
1976	12.7	0.2	5.8	2.4	4.8	0.6	8.3	1.3	63.8	100.0
1977	14.3	0.3	6.2	2.6	5.1	0.6	7.6	1.5	62.0	100.0
1978	13.9	0.2	6.4	2.4	6.8	0.8	7.8	1.6	60.3	100.0
1979	14.3	0.2	6.2	2.3	6.8	1.0	7.4	1.8	60.1	100.0
1980	12.5	0.1	6.3	2.1	6.7	0.9	6.8	1.7	62.8	100.0
1981	12.8	0.1	6.1	2.1	5.9	1.0	7.5	1.7	62.7	100.0
1982	11.1	0.2	6.1	2.7	5.6	1.1	6.5	1.8	64.8	100.0
1983	10.2	0.3	6.0	3.2	5.5	1.1	6.4	1.8	65.5	100.0
1984	10.0	0.3	6.2	3.2	4.1	1.0	6.3	2.2	66.8	100.0
1985	9.6	0.3	6.1	3.1	4.2	1.0	6.1	2.3	67.3	100.0
1986	9.2	0.3	6.0	3.0	5.1	1.1	6.2	2.6	66.5	100.0
1987	9.2	0.1	5.9	3.1	5.1	1.3	6.3	2.6	66.4	100.0
1988	10.1	0.1	5.7	3.1	5.3	1.3	6.1	2.6	65.7	100.0
1989	9.3	0.1	5.8	3.3	5.2	1.3	6.1	2.7	66.2	100.0

— indicates no employment in the electricity and water industry in the private sector, hence no wage rates

Note: The public sector includes the central government, the Teachers' Service Commission, parastatal bodies, local governments, and firms owned by the public sector through majority control.

Sources: Employment and Earnings (various years); Kenya, Republic of (1990).

Table 10.8 Growth Rate of the Real Minimum Wage, 1973–88
(percent)

Year	Growth rate	Year	Growth rate
1973	-8.7	1981	-11.2
1974	19.0	1982	-13.7
1975	8.1	1983	-16.3
1976	-9.4	1984	-4.3
1977	-11.3	1985	8.4
1978	3.7	1986	-5.3
1979	-7.7	1987	3.8
1980	15.4	1988	2.1

Source: Kenya, Republic of (various years).

Figure 10.1 Productivity and Real Wages, 1973-89
(index 1973 = 100))

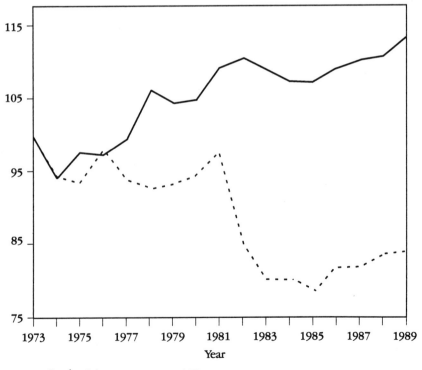

discusses this different behavior in some detail. He argues that the failure of real wages to decline before 1982 led to substantial pressure on manufacturing sector profits. This was relieved somewhat after 1982 when real wages began to fall: however, although real consumer wages (nominal wages deflated by the CPI) fell, real product wages (nominal wages deflated by the manufacturing GDP deflator) continued to rise until 1985. Thus, the wage-productivity gap still did not provide strong relief for manufacturers.

Public Sector Wages and Employment

Public sector wages and employment are another important facet of structural adjustment. As indicated earlier, in *Sessional Paper No. 1 of 1986* (Kenya, Republic of, 1986b) the government announced a policy to reduce the growth rate of public sector employment. Two important issues are relevant here: first, in 1988 employment by the public sector was over 50 percent of modern sector employment, and second, the wage bill as a proportion of total government expenditures is extremely high (approaching 70 percent). This makes it difficult for the government to purchase supplies and equipment (nonwage operating expenses) that can lead to a more productive civil service (Mills 1988).

Through the first half of the 1980s, employment growth in the public sector was very high, averaging an annual growth rate of over 4 percent, but increased to over 4.7 percent per year during 1985–88. Most of this additional growth was through the Teachers' Service Commission, where employment grew at over 7 percent per year because of the implementation of a new education system. Thus, on the employment front, there is little evidence of a government commitment to slowing the growth of public sector jobs. This sector remains the largest source of jobs in the modern sector. The inability to slow employment growth is probably one factor behind the relative decline in public sector wages (table 10.6).

The real wage losses in the public sector have likely led to morale problems in the civil service, including the possibility of some civil servants holding more than one job (O'Connell 1987). Indeed, in the early 1970s, when strict wage guidelines were introduced, a civil service review commission allowed members of the civil service to operate private businesses. The real wage losses are particularly obvious after 1980. Only in 1986 did some turnaround in these real wage rates occur and, in general, rising real wages continued through 1989.

Public sector employees tend to hold on to their jobs despite real wage losses for several reasons. First, the job provides security: being fired from a public sector job is very difficult. Second, a public sector job provides a base for a job search. Finally, employment in the public sector has benefits such as access to loans at subsidized rates.

Another problem is with the wage structure of the public service. On the low end, wage levels tend to be higher than in the private sector and, therefore, an oversupply of workers exists. At the other extreme, for example, engineers and researchers, the pay is substantially lower than what they could obtain in the private sector or at a parastatal. Consequently, the government civil service has difficulty retaining highly skilled workers. Of course, the wage is only part of the compensation package for government workers. They also receive two important fringe benefits: a noncontributory pension scheme and a housing allowance.

The combination of rapid employment growth and fringe benefits has resulted in an increasing proportion of government expenditure going to salaries. This leads to significant inefficiencies in the delivery of services to the public. Furthermore, it creates problems for the government in terms of meeting targets for overall expenditure growth. In this sense, there is little evidence of structural adjustment.

Informal Sector Earnings and Employment

Of course, modern wage employment accounts for a relatively small proportion of aggregate national employment. To consider the overall trends in employment one must also consider the informal sector and small-scale farming activities. The definition of the urban informal sector used in Kenya is that it "consists of semi-organized and unregulated activities undertaken by self employed persons in the open markets, in market stalls, in undeveloped plots or on street pavements within urban centres. They may or may not have licenses from local authorities." (Kenya, Republic of, 1981, p. iii).

The most comprehensive information on informal sector employment comes from the annual Central Bureau of Statistics (CBS) survey, and is summarized in table 10.9. These figures must be treated cautiously, however, for several reasons. First, the coverage of the survey has changed since 1972 in ways that are not completely clear. Initially, the survey covered only four cities: Nairobi, Mombasa, Nakuru, and Kisumu. By 1975, the survey covered 11 municipalities and sampled other towns with populations exceeding 2,000 and rural trading centers with populations less than 2,000 (Ogundo 1977, p. 79). Further, the nature of the sampling technique is unclear. By 1980, some 17 municipalities and all towns exceeding 2,000 population were fully covered while rural trading centers were sampled. Because of the steady broadening of the base on which the informal sector employment has been estimated, the figures for the early 1970s are not comparable with those of the 1980s. (Also there is a discrepancy between the figures published in the *Economic Survey,* as reported here, and the *Development Plan,* as set out in table 10.3.) However, there can be little doubt that employment expanded rapidly in the urban informal sector after 1981. In 1988 alone, the growth was almost 11 percent. This coincides with the period of somewhat slower growth in wage employment. On the basis of the CBS survey and an estimate of the urban labor force in 1986 (based on participation rates from the Urban Labour Force Survey) and a demographic projection model (Milne 1986), the urban informal sector accounts for 21.4 of total urban employment.

An independent estimate of the size of the informal sector can be made from the Urban Labour Force Survey, which showed that in 1986, the informal sector (self-employed nonprofessionals and casual workers) accounted for 21.1 percent of urban employment (excluding the small group of people who reported work in both sectors).[1] This

1. The distinction between the informal and formal sectors is defined by occupation and employment status. An individual is assumed to be in the formal sector if he/she is working in one of the following occupations: engineer, technician, medical, nursing, physical and life science, human relations and other professionals, public administrators, private and personnel management, accountants, post office, radio and television, and was either an employer, was self-employed, or was a public or private sector employee. The other respondents are assumed to be in the informal sector. This definition of the informal sector is quite narrow and this is due to the

estimate of the size of the informal sector seems rather small compared to other countries, but it excludes workers in small-scale establishments.[2] The other 78.9 percent of urban workers had jobs in the formal sector. Examining the data by gender shows that the categories do not represent the population evenly. A larger share of women than men find employment in the informal sector (28.0 versus 17.8 percent), while men are overrepresented among formal sector workers (82.2 versus 72.0 percent).

The government wants to encourage growth in the informal sector as it believes this will be the source of jobs for the expanding labor force, and it has emphasized this sector (along with the rural small farm sector) in policy. Table 10.10 examines the success of this policy, comparing the formal and informal share within occupational categories over time, and shows that the informal sector's share has increased overall. The shift into the informal sector was greatest in agriculture, repair, and transportation, but decreased for sales and professional personnel. This suggests that the incentive structure has changed since 1977 and that rents that had been earned in some informal occupations have diminished.

The pattern of earnings in the informal sector is more difficult to measure. However, some data are available from the report on *Small Scale Enterprises in Rural and Urban Areas of Kenya* (Kenya, Republic of, 1985a) and indicate that informal sector wages, in real terms, increased through the late 1970s before beginning to decline along with the deterioration in the economy. Table 10.11 compares male average wages by occupation. The table shows that real wages fell most dramatically for self-employed sales and agricultural workers and for wage workers in clerical and production occupations. Real wages increased substantially for self-employed service and

---

narrowness of the questions in the survey. That is, there is no way to identify workers in small firms that might be classified in the informal sector. Consequently, the informal sector, as defined here, is substantially underestimated, since it includes only self-employed nonprofessionals, and casual workers.

2. According to a summary of research work on the informal sector by J. Charmes as reported in Turnham and others (1990, p. 21). Employment in the informal sector in Asia and Africa is often in excess of 40 to 50 percent of nonagricultural employment, while the comparable figure for Latin America is above 30 percent.

Table 10.9 Informal Sector Employment, 1972–89
(thousands of people)

Year	Total		Manufacturing		Services		Urban		Rural	
	Old	New	Old	New	Old	New	Old	New	Old	New
1972	33.9	n.a.	2.6	n.a.	31.3	n.a.	n.a.	n.a.	n.a.	n.a.
1973	41.4	n.a.	3.2	n.a.	38.2	n.a.	n.a.	n.a.	n.a.	n.a.
1974	76.2	n.a.	10.9	n.a.	65.3	n.a.	n.a.	n.a.	n.a.	n.a.
1975	74.1	n.a.	9.6	n.a.	64.5	n.a.	n.a.	n.a.	n.a.	n.a.
1976	94.9	n.a.	13.8	n.a.	81.0	n.a.	n.a.	n.a.	n.a.	n.a.
1977	103.9	n.a.	15.3	n.a.	88.6	n.a.	n.a.	n.a.	n.a.	n.a.
1978	113.9	n.a.	17.0	n.a.	96.9	n.a.	80.7	n.a.	33.2	n.a.
1979	121.6	n.a.	17.2	n.a.	104.4	n.a.	88.7	n.a.	32.9	n.a.
1980	123.2	n.a.	18.2	n.a.	105.0	n.a.	91.7	n.a.	31.5	n.a.
1981	157.3	n.a.	25.9	n.a.	131.4	n.a.	105.5	n.a.	51.8	n.a.
1982	175.4	n.a.	28.8	n.a.	146.6	n.a.	n.a.	n.a.	n.a.	n.a.
1983	182.9	n.a.	29.3	n.a.	153.6	n.a.	134.3	n.a.	48.6	n.a.
1984	197.8	n.a.	31.7	n.a.	166.1	n.a.	145.0	n.a.	52.8	n.a.
1985	215.9	254.5	n.a.	43.5	n.a.	211.0	n.a.	166.6	n.a.	87.9
1986	n.a.	281.0	n.a.	49.9	n.a.	231.1	n.a.	182.7	n.a.	98.4
1987	n.a.	312.2	n.a.	58.4	n.a.	253.8	n.a.	202.1	n.a.	110.0
1988	n.a.	346.2	n.a.	66.1	n.a.	280.1	n.a.	223.1	n.a.	123.2
1989	n.a.	390.0	n.a.	74.4	n.a.	315.5	n.a.	251.2	n.a.	138.7

n.a. = not available
Sources: Kenya, Republic of, *Economic Survey* (1989, p. 48; 1986); *Kenya Informal Sector Survey 1985* (tables 1A & 4).

Table 10.10 Occupational Distribution of Urban Employment, 1977 and 1986
(share of total employment)

Employment category	1977		1986	
	Formal	*Informal*	*Formal*	*Informal*
Professional	11.24	0.73	17.85	0.24
Administrative/clerical	22.82	0.45	19.38	0.12
Sales	3.04	9.39	4.52	7.76
Services	17.82	1.01	18.90	2.18
Agriculture	1.18	1.07	2.13	3.96
Production	3.88	2.64	3.07	2.51
Repair	9.61	2.25	8.39	3.22
Transportation	12.55	0.34	5.48	1.11
Total	82.14	17.88	79.92	21.07

Note: Figures do not sum exactly to 100 due to rounding.
Source: Calculations based on Kenya, Republic of, *Urban Labour Force Survey* (1977–78, 1986).

production workers and wage workers in professional, administrative, repair, and transport occupations. Whereas in 1977 average male wages from self-employment were substantially higher than for wage workers in sales, agriculture, production, and repair, by 1986 the situation was reversed. This is consistent with the view that the economy had undergone stabilization, but little structural change and resumption of economic growth. The self-employed sector absorbed excess labor, with a consequent fall in the sector's relative earnings. For occupations likely to be in tradables (agriculture and production), 1986 real average wages were below 1977 levels (with the sole exception of self-employed workers in production). This again is consistent with a lack of successful structural adjustment.

The rural sector, even though it comprises close to 80 percent of employment, is even more difficult to analyze empirically as so few surveys are available. The Integrated Rural Surveys were undertaken in the 1970s and a Rural Household Budget Survey was undertaken in

Table 10.11 Average Wage Rates by Occupation, Urban Males, 1977–78 and 1986
(1977 Kenya shillings per hour)

Occupation	1977–78		1986	
	Wages & casual workers[1]	Non-professional, self-employed	Wage & casual workers[1]	Non-professional, self-employed
Professional	9.36	*	12.91	**
Administrative/clerical	8.14	6.87	4.37	*
Sales	3.17	20.88	2.21	7.37
Service	3.18	1.95	3.29	22.50
Agriculture	3.91	10.52	2.72	6.69
Production	3.77	6.14	2.17	10.75
Repair	3.71	12.42	5.67	9.72
Transportation	4.33	*	5.38	10.02

1. Includes self-employed in professional occupations.
* Very few observations.
** No observations.
Notes: The data are unweighted. The weighting corrects for overenumeration of Nairobi, which was likely a problem in both surveys. The result is that the data are somewhat more representative of Nairobi residents than the average urban dweller. Includes self-employed in professional occupations.
Source: Calculated for Kenya, Republic of, *Urban Labour Force Survey* (1977–78, 1986).

1981–82. One measure of how the rural sector has fared through this period is through an examination of the prices paid to farmers compared to the prices they pay for inputs and consumer goods. Table 10.12 presents data on agriculture output prices, input prices, and the agriculture terms of trade during 1977–89. As these data indicate, the terms of trade have deteriorated since 1980. Noteworthy in these data is the coffee boom of 1977–78, where the index of the output price was above the input price, and the mini coffee boom of 1986, when the trend in the terms of trade was temporarily reversed.

Table 10.12 Prices and Terms of Trade in Agriculture, 1977–89
(1982 = 100)

Year	Output price	Input price	Terms of trade
1977	79.7	72.6	109.8
1978	80.3	78.0	102.9
1979	79.6	85.4	93.2
1980	83.7	77.2	108.4
1981	90.8	87.1	104.2
1982	100.0	100.0	100.0
1983	113.6	111.4	102.0
1984	130.0	131.8	98.6
1985	136.8	146.3	93.5
1986	149.0	150.7	98.9
1987	150.3	158.8	94.7
1988	168.7	170.5	98.9
1989	176.4	181.2	97.4

Note: The input price is a weighted average of purchased inputs and an index of purchased consumer goods in rural areas. The terms of trade is the ratio of the output price to the input price.
Source: Kenya, Republic of, *Economic Survey* (various issues).

Rural-Urban Migration

Migration between rural and urban areas is also a means of adjustment in the labor market. The 1979 census suggested that the rural to urban migration rate (that is, the percentage of the rural population that migrates to urban areas) is around 1 percent a year. Given the large differential between urban and rural wages, it is somewhat surprising that the net migration rate is not higher. Nevertheless, Barber and Milne (1988) indicate the determinants of district to district flows are, at least in part, consistent with the human capital model. They find that distance is an important deterrent to migration and that economic opportunity variables (especially in the destination district) are important.

The 1986 *Urban Labour Force Survey* provides some further information about migration. For those who were employed in 1986 and who had moved between 1977 and 1986, table 10.13 shows the distribution of individuals by the period of move within each occupation. The period 1977–79 was the coffee boom era, 1980–83 were the years of deteriorating income growth, and the years 1984–86 marked the resumption of steady but slow income growth. One would expect that mobility would be highest during the economic shocks of 1980–83 and for mobility to remain fairly high as the incentive structure adjusted during 1984–86.

Of those employed in either the formal or informal sector in 1986, 53 percent had made their last move since 1977 (12 percent had never moved). Apparently, mobility has increased in the 1980s, and has affected formal and informal workers relatively evenly (informal sector workers constitute about 21 percent of the employed in the survey and of the workers that have moved). Professionals and service workers account for almost 50 percent of those who have moved in each period. Since the public sector accounts for the bulk of

Table 10.13 Year of Move by Occupation and Sector, 1977–85 *(percent)*

Occupation	1977–79 Formal sector	1977–79 Informal sector	1980–83 Formal sector	1980–83 Informal sector	1984–85 Formal sector	1984–85 Informal sector
Professional	16.01	0.00	37.15	0.30	45.71	0.84
Administrative/ clerical	20.78	0.00	45.54	0.00	33.69	0.06
Sales	9.76	19.56	16.62	28.46	6.56	18.98
Service	15.08	0.96	31.65	2.87	44.94	4.49
Agriculture	11.38	5.55	8.24	23.59	23.49	27.75
Production	13.63	10.62	22.33	18.22	20.72	14.49
Repair	17.32	4.19	28.84	11.22	25.97	12.45
Transport	16.58	3.28	33.57	5.90	32.40	8.28

Note: Percentages sum across rows to 100 (except for rounding errors).
Source: 1986 Urban Labour Force Data, weighted.

professional and service employment, it is not obvious from this table that individuals are shifting into tradables. Nevertheless, the table does indicate a geographically mobile labor force that responds to changes relatively quickly: for all occupations, except those in formal agriculture, mobility rose dramatically in 1980–83 compared to 1977–79. The movements correspond to wage incentives: table 10.10 showed that agriculture and sales were the only two sectors where informal sector earnings exceeded formal ones, and these account for a large share of informal sector migration.

The government is concerned that the large flows of people to the major urban areas of Nairobi, Mombasa, and Kisumu will create substantial unemployment problems. In *Sessional Paper No. 1 of 1986* (Kenya, Republic of, 1986b), a chapter is devoted to the rural-urban balance that predicts that by the year 2000, almost 30 percent of the population will live in urban areas. The policy that the government has set in place is aimed at encouraging migrants to settle in secondary towns and smaller urban centers. They hope to achieve this by developing urban infrastructure in these towns and by providing more support for rural trading centers.

Table 10.14 shows the distribution of the labor force by current and previous residence. The table shows that only a small portion (13.5 percent) of the surveyed labor force were natives of one of the five largest cities in Kenya in 1986. A larger proportion of town residents, about one-third, were town natives. Further, an equal portion of the labor force residing in towns or cities in 1986 (about 42 percent each) had migrated from rural areas at some time. The table also shows migration between towns and cities is considerable. About one-fifth of those who lived in towns in 1986 had previously resided in large cities, while 39.8 percent of city residents had migrated from smaller towns. The 1977 data indicate that the proportion of town residents who had come from larger cities was almost the same as in the 1986 survey, 19 percent, while the share of large city residents that had emigrated from either towns or rural areas was somewhat higher than in 1986, 91.7 percent compared to 82.6 percent in 1986. This suggests that flows to larger centers still account for a larger, but diminishing, share of migration, and flows to the towns from both rural areas and cities are significant.

Table 10.14 Labor Force by Current and Previous Residence,1986 *(percent)*

Previous residence	Current residence one of the 5 largest cities	Other town
Other country	3.8	2.3
City (1 of 5 largest)	13.5	20.3
Town	39.8	36.0
Rural area	42.9	41.5
Total	100.0	100.0

Source: 1986 *Urban Labour Force Survey*, weighted.

Interestingly, as Fallon (1985) indicates, migration among rural areas is not large even though substantial differences in income exist. For example, in the 1981–82 rural household budget survey, Western and Nyanza provinces had the lowest monthly incomes but the greatest population pressures. This curtailment of migration is likely due to cultural and tribal differences between the regions that make migration difficult.

This section has considered the adjustment of the labor market in Kenya by examining changes in real wage rates and employment by sector, and examined agricultural terms of trade and migration as an adjustment mechanism. On the surface, despite the government's policy direction, the Kenyan labor market has apparently not restructured in a significant way. While the evidence suggests that real wages have dropped significantly and that urban unemployment has not changed significantly, the informal sector, rather than tradables, is absorbing the labor slack. The terms of trade in rural areas worsened, but not dramatically. The data presented on mobility suggest that the Kenyan labor force is indeed highly mobile, and that relative wages are important determinants of mobility. However, the data on wages show that there has not been a clear change in relative wages between tradables and nontradables, thus as of 1986, there had not been any obvious shift into the tradable goods sector. This supports the earlier discussion, which argued that structural adjustment only intensified after 1985, too late to have marked effects on the 1986 labor force survey.

Implications of Labor Market Adjustment

This section considers other economic issues related to labor market adjustment. While Kenya's labor force had not restructured in a significant way, at least by 1986, adjustment policies and other economic factors are significantly altering the returns to the various factors of production. These changes in returns have imposed costs on certain groups of individuals who have also tried to minimize their losses with behavioral changes. This section examines the impact of adjustment on gross fixed capital formation, on women, and on the distribution of income and poverty and analyzes estimated earnings functions.

The Effect on Capital Formation

Investment or gross fixed capital formation measures the addition of new physical assets and the replacement of worn out structures and machines. The need for new capital goes hand-in-hand with necessary increases in labor productivity. Table 10.15 sets out gross investment over the period 1974–89.

These figures clearly show the sharp decline in investment spending following the collapse of the East Africa Community and again following the political instability in 1982. Indeed, even by 1988, the level of investment spending had not reached the levels recorded in the late 1970s and early 1980s. The sharp drop in investment spending during 1982–84 poses problems for long-run growth in the sense that a rising capital to output ratio can imply productivity gains. Further investment spending is necessary to provide infrastructure and machines for efficient production.

On a sectoral basis, the manufacturing sector increased its investment spending in real terms by 16 percent between 1986 and 1988. The government, however, continues to be a major contributor to investment spending, particularly in the area of infrastructure. This public infrastructure is particularly important in ensuring that agriculture output is able to get to the market. Transportation

Table 10.15 Gross Fixed Capital Formation, 1974–89
(millions of Kenyan pounds, constant 1982 prices)

Year	Level	Percentage of GDP	Percentage change
1974	590.5	29.1	–
1975	605.2	29.0	2.5
1976	598.2	27.5	-1.2
1977	723.0	30.7	20.9
1978	852.2	33.6	17.9
1979	787.5	29.6	-7.6
1980	807.3	29.2	2.5
1981	844.0	28.8	4.5
1982	668.2	21.9	-20.8
1983	576.0	18.4	-13.8
1984	593.6	18.8	3.1
1985	597.2	18.0	0.6
1986	668.1	19.1	11.9
1987	708.0	19.3	6.0
1988	769.3	19.9	8.7
1989	781.4	19.3	1.6

Note: GDP is measured at factor cost in 1982 prices.
Source: Kenya, Republic of (1989) and *Economic Survey* (1990).

infrastructure is also crucial in ensuring that Kenya remain self-sufficient in food.

Women in the Labor Market

As noted in the report of the Woman's Bureau to the Conference on Women held in Nairobi in 1985 (Kenya 1985b), women's traditional role has not been to head households. However, as women have become more educated, the evidence indicates that women are marrying later and becoming more independent financially. Further, in rural areas, many women act as heads of households.

The Government of Kenya has significantly aided the education process by eliminating all school fees for the primary grades and introducing a free milk program. However, for women to have more opportunities, further incentives will be required at the secondary school level, but given the state of the Kenyan budget deficit, this may not be possible.

The number of women in formal employment has been small, but steadily increasing. In 1964, women held only 12.2 percent of total formal sector jobs, but this figure increased to 14.8 percent in 1972, 18 percent in 1982, and 21.3 by 1988. Of course, the sectoral distribution of employment is also important. In general, women are employed primarily in the community, social, and personal services sector.

Data for employment of women in the informal sector are difficult to obtain. However, data from Livingstone (1981) based on a 1978 survey of the informal sector in Kenya are set out in table 10.16. As these data indicate, women make up a significant proportion of employment in the retail trade and restaurant part of the informal sector. However, in most cases women do not own the businesses, and while the growth of employment in the informal sector will absorb many female labor force participants in the future, remuneration in the informal sector is significantly lower than in the formal sector. Ng'ethe and Wahome (1989) estimated the percentage of women in the informal sector in 1989, and found that women made up 39.1 percent of employment in four districts of Kenya. This may indicate that women are playing a greater role in the informal sector.

Changes in the returns to labor are apparent from an examination of figures 10.2 and 10.3, which show the age-related hourly wage profiles for men and women, respectively. Figure 10.3 gives the predicted wage, in 1977 Kenyan shillings, for a self-employed, unskilled woman with one year of education working in Nairobi. The figure shows separate profiles for self-employed, nonprofessional ("selfnon") workers and for other employees ("rest") in 1977 and 1986. Figure 10.3 indicates that returns to self-employed, nonprofessional women dropped dramatically between 1977 and 1986. While earnings from self-employment were higher than for other wage employees in 1986, the gap had significantly narrowed since 1977. In 1986, self-employment earnings for women also peaked with age (in the early 1940s) much earlier than for other

Table 10.16 Employment in the Informal Sector by Sex, 1978
(number of people)

Sector	Men	Women	Percentage of women
Retail trade	37,904	26,823	41.4
Restaurants, bars	9,921	5,389	35.2
Manufacturing	15,192	1,824	10.7
Construction and transport	1,181	1	0.1
Other services	15,255	447	2.8
Total	79,453	34,484	30.3

Source: Livingstone (1981, table 6:17).

employees (for whom the peak is in the early 1960s). Consequently, wages of other employees surpass those of the nonprofessional self-employed beyond the age of 59. Thus female workers have all suffered a loss, particularly the self-employed. The picture for men is more or less the same. Figure 10.2 shows that there has certainly been an adjustment in wages between 1977 and 1986, and while all groups have suffered losses, self-employed workers have been particularly affected. The gap between male and female earnings does not appear to have changed much during this period.

Another important aspect of the effect of adjustment on women is through price increases that occur due to decontrol or other upward adjustments in controlled prices to reflect market conditions. As, in large measure, women undertake farming activities in rural areas, these upward price adjustments can result in a significant reduction in purchasing power inasmuch as these increases are for goods and services they must purchase. Further, with user fees established for secondary school and for some health care activities, women must spend a significant portion of their time ensuring they have adequate funds to provide for their children.

Figure 10.2 Male Wage Profiles, 1977 and 1986

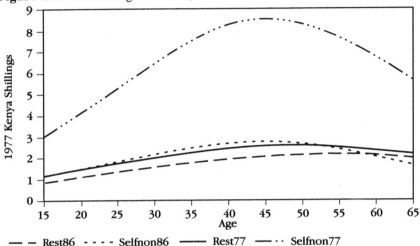

Figure 10.3 Female Wage Profiles, 1977 and 1986

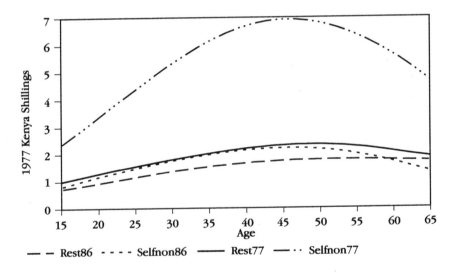

Note: In figures 10.2 and 10.3, the "selfnon" columns show the results of multiplying the parameter estimates from table 10.21 setting education = 1, Nairobi = 1, and female = 1 (figure 10.3). Since unskilled was the omitted category of skills from the regression, these estimates show predicted wages for unskilled workers in Nairobi with one year of education. The "rest" category uses the parameter estimates from regressing the same set of variables for all workers not included in the selfnon group, that is, casual self-employed professionals and regular wage workers.

The *Development Plan, 1989-93* (Kenya, Republic of, 1989), also notes the importance of women in the labor force. With continuing higher levels of education, their participation rate is likely to rise, thereby creating more labor force participants. This is almost sure to require further adjustment in the labor market and the government must put in place programs, such as training programs, so that women may become self-employed to address this expanding role of women in the economy.

Income Distribution and Poverty

An analysis of income distribution is difficult in developing countries. However, as suggested earlier in this chapter, the issue of poverty as a result of the continuing decline in real wages must not be overlooked. Collier and Lal (1986) estimate that in 1974, 29.5 percent of the population was below the poverty line. Smallholders form the largest proportion of the poor, representing 71 percent of persons below the poverty line, followed by those living in rural areas. Further, as indicated in UNICEF (1989), the number of those below the poverty line has probably increased as a result of rapid population growth and poor economic performance during 1980–85.

Morrison (1973) indicates that in 1969, the bottom 10 percent of Kenyans received only 1.8 percent of total income while the top 10 percent received 56.3 percent of income. According to UNICEF (1989), by 1980 the percent of income going to the bottom 10 percent had declined. In Nairobi, the poorest 40 percent of the population received 17.2 percent of income in 1969, 15.1 percent in 1974, and 14.3 percent in 1985. This indicates that over time, the income distribution is shifting toward the rich, an undesirable result. Table 10.17, which displays the shares of total employment income— from all jobs—for 1977 and 1986 by various subcategories, supplies further evidence of this trend. The first notable fact emerging from the table is that in the 1986 survey workers aged 15 to 64 earned almost all income. In the 1977 survey, individuals younger than 15 or over 64 earned 12.6 percent of total employment income for the surveyed population. The table shows clearly that the distribution of employment earnings has changed somewhat between 1977 and 1986. First, while a smaller portion of the working population was engaged in the formal sector in 1986, it commanded a larger portion of total income despite the decline in wages in that sector. This would confirm earlier findings (table 10.11) demonstrating the more dramatic decline in earnings in the informal than the formal sector. Thus, the period saw a substantial transfer of income from the informal sector to the formal sector. The bulk of this transfer has gone to male heads of households. Within the formal sector, employment has shifted from Nairobi and Mombasa to other urban centers, coinciding with a rise in income shares for all urban areas. Within the informal sector employment has expanded in all urban centers, while the greatest income losses have occurred in urban areas other than Nairobi and Mombasa, although almost every group suffered a loss in its share of income. A notable exception to this is households headed by women, which accounted for a smaller share of informal employment in 1986 than in 1977, but a relatively larger share of income (at least in urban areas other than the two largest cities).

The picture that emerges from table 10.17 is not one of a labor force undergoing adjustment. The formal sector accounts for a smaller share of total employment, but nevertheless earned a larger portion of employment income in 1986 than in 1977. Meanwhile the informal sector, which may produce a larger portion of nontradables, provided a larger share of employment and a smaller share of employment income in 1986. An examination of the figures for employment shares in 1986 shows that workers migrated to jobs in the informal sector in Nairobi and Mombasa. The decline in the share of income from informal employment in smaller towns is particularly discouraging.

The information in table 10.18 provides the basis for an analysis of household welfare. This table shows that the share of households with per capita incomes less than the minimum wage fell between 1977 and 1986 (recall from table 10.9, however, that the real minimum wage fell by more than 25 percent between 1977 and 1986). Nevertheless, it is disturbing that more than one-fifth of female headed households in the informal sector had per capita incomes below 25 percent of the minimum wage. Male headed households in the formal sector made the greatest gains: almost two-thirds of them had per capita incomes at least 1.5 times the minimum wage in 1986. This reinforces the view that the income distribution was shifting toward those with more resources, at least up until 1986.

Table 10.17 Share of Total Employment Income Urban Areas, 1977 and 1986
(percent)

Category	1977 share of:		1986 share of:	
	Income	Work force	Income	Work force
Surveyed workers 15–64 years old	87.4	100.0	98.3	100.0
Formal sector	58.0	82.1	76.2	78.9
Residents of Nairobi and Mombasa	43.9	55.2	50.4	41.6
Female household heads	1.3	2.7	1.6	2.5
Male household heads	35.6	40.8	38.6	25.0
Other household members	7.1	11.7	10.2	14.1
Residents of other urban areas	14.0	26.9	25.8	37.2
Female household heads	1.1	2.8	2.9	5.9
Male household heads	11.6	20.5	18.9	23.0
Other household members	1.3	3.7	4.0	8.5
Informal sector	29.4	17.9	14.5	21.1
Residents of Nairobi and Mombasa	18.3	8.8	8.4	8.6
Female household heads	0.1	1.1	0.3	0.8
Male household heads	7.9	5.0	4.1	4.5
Other household members	10.3	2.8	4.0	3.3
Residents of other urban areas	11.1	9.1	6.1	12.5
Female household heads	1.0	2.4	1.2	0.3
Male household heads	9.5	4.4	3.0	5.4
Other household members	0.6	2.2	1.9	4.5
Workers in both sectors*	n.a.	n.a.	7.6	1.8

n.a. = not available
* The 1977 survey did not question respondents about secondary jobs.
Notes: Data for 1986 are weighted, for 1977–78 unweighted. The 1986 data include casual workers in the informal sector. This would tend to increase the share of income relative to employment in the informal sector in 1986 as casual workers represented 5.8 percent of employment and 1.9 percent of employment income in 1986. Thus, the growth of informal sector employment between 1977–78 and 1986 may be overstated in the table.
Sources: 1977–78 and 1986 *Urban Labor Force Surveys.*

Table 10.18 Per Capita Household Income Relative to the Minimum Wage, 1977 and 1986
(percentage of households)

Category	Per Capita Income/Minimum Wage			
	<0.25	*0.25<>0.75*	*0.75<>1.5*	*1.5<*
1977				
Female headed households				
Formal sector	30.93	36.09	18.55	14.43
Informal sector	50.75	29.85	14.93	4.48
Male headed households				
Formal sector	30.32	35.57	19.91	14.21
Informal sector	33.71	33.15	13.48	19.66
1986				
Female headed households				
Formal sector	3.14	21.28	29.95	45.63
Informal sector	28.62	23.03	13.27	35.08
Male headed households				
Formal sector	2.37	12.90	18.18	66.55
Informal sector	11.01	23.81	17.46	47.72

Note: 1986 data are weighted, 1977–78 data are not. The 1986 data include casual workers in the informal sector. This would tend to affect only the lowest income categories and would affect men more than women (more casual workers were men). In addition, it is most likely that many of the casual workers are probably not household heads, so the effect of this revision is probably not great.
Sources: 1977 and 1986 *Urban Labour Forces Surveys.*

An Analysis of Earnings Functions

An alternative method of considering labor market adjustment is through an analysis of earnings functions. Table 10.19 presents some regression results for earnings functions for workers undertaking wage employment in urban areas. Through a comparison of the estimated parameters some insight may be gained into the changes that occurred in the urban labor market between 1977–78 and 1986.

The equations are estimated in a semi-log functional form following Rosen (1977). The dependent variable in the regressions is the logarithm of the hourly wage rate. The results are as expected and are remarkably similar across the two surveys. Education and experience (as proxied by the age of the individual) enter positively. The education variables enter as continuous variables, and one can therefore determine the effect of an additional year of education on earnings. Of course, this effect should depend on the educational attainment of the individual as well as the individual's age. These effects are captured through the introduction of the nonlinear term on education and the interaction between education and age. Table 10.20 sets out the effect on hourly earnings of one more year of education for an individual aged 30. As the figures in this table indicate, the shape of the earnings function has changed somewhat across the surveys, with less benefit accruing to lower levels of education and more benefit to higher educational attainment. This probably follows from the universal primary education program introduced in the mid-1970s beginning to have an effect in the 1980s through the large number of potential labor force entrants with at least a primary school education. However, the costs and entrance requirements associated with secondary school remain high, yet the demand for workers with skills provided by secondary school or the polytechnics is increasing, consequently, the returns to higher education are larger in the 1986 survey than the 1977–78 survey.

In both these surveys a working woman earns less than a working man. In the 1977–78 survey, the difference amounted to approximately 12 percent, but by the 1986 survey this had increased to almost 18 percent. As indicated earlier, this may reflect the increasing number of women in the labor force (as measured by the increase in their participation rate), with the result of a greater differential between male and female earnings. However, since educational and skills differences are controlled for, this implies that women in Kenya are increasingly concentrated in lower paying jobs.

The dummy variables for different skills indicate that professionals or administrative workers consistently earned about 46 percent more than unskilled workers (the omitted group) in 1986. The two skills groups that show the greatest change between the surveys are sales and service workers and professional workers. The drop in premiums paid to professional workers may be due to the increasing number of

Table 10.19 Estimates of Earnings Functions for Wage Workers

Variable	1977–78 survey		1986 survey	
	Mean (Std. deviation)	*Parameter (t-statistic)*	*Mean (Std. deviation)*	*Parameter (t-statistic)*
Intercept	–	-1.0480	–	-0.5487
		(3.16)		(2.59)
Age	33.755	0.0748	32.681	0.0808
	(9.48)	(4.69)	(9.23)	(7.75)
Age^2	1,229.140	-0.0008	1,153.138	-0.0008
	(711.13)	(4.03)	(670.58)	(6.27)
Education	6.433	0.0224	8.518	-0.0130
	(3.91)	(0.79)	(4.28)	(0.79)
Education^2	56.690	0.0024	90.856	0.0052
	(51.57)	(1.96)	(69.31)	(7.82)
Education x age	205.054	0.0008	268.762	0.0005
	(135.93)	(1.39)	(153.82)	(1.50)
Female	0.137	-0.1205	0.248	-0.1799
	(0.34)	(2.00)	(0.43)	(5.52)
Skill classes				
Professional	0.202	0.6291	0.248	0.4649
	(0.40)	(7.84)	(0.43)	(9.00)
Skilled labor	0.077	0.2635	0.071	0.2075
	(0.27)	(2.93)	(0.26)	(3.38)
Semi-skilled	0.116	0.1536	0.155	0.0071
	(0.32)	(1.93)	(0.36)	(0.14)
Clerical	0.178	0.4147	0.117	0.3758
	(0.38)	(5.33)	(0.32)	(6.52)
Sales & service	0.281	-0.0971	0.293	-0.3241
	(0.45)	(1.49)	(0.46)	(7.23)
Location	0.476	0.1414	0.462	0.3221
Nairobi	(0.50)	(3.07)	(0.50)	(11.6)
Mombasa	0.203	0.2969	0.125	0.3184
	(0.40)	(5.08)	(0.33)	(7.57)
Mean of dependent variable	1.275		1.853	
Number of observations	1,106		2,416	
R-squared		0.421		0.533

Sources: 1977–78 and 1986 *Urban Labour Force Surveys*.

Table 10.20 Effect of One More Year of Education on Hourly Earnings, 1977–78 and 1986
(percent)

Educational attainment	1977–78	1986
Primary school graduate	9.11	7.13
Secondary school graduate	11.23	15.73

Note: Calculations assume the individual is aged 30.
Source: Calculated from the parameter estimates in table 10.21.

professionally qualified workers in the labor force, and may also reflect some adjustment in relative wages. Since the majority of professionals work in the public sector, an effective adjustment policy would see their relative wages falling. It is in the sales and service occupations where at least some of the informal sector is located. With the rapid expansion of the informal sector, which typically has lower wages than the modern sector, the narrowing of the wage differentials between the surveys in these sectors is not surprising.

Residence also plays an important role. In both surveys, living in Nairobi or Mombasa (the two largest cities) provides a large wage differential compared to other urban areas. In the case of Nairobi, this may reflect its status as the capital and the consequent demand for goods and services by the government.

Table 10.21 shows the estimates of the earnings equations for self-employed nonprofessionals for 1977–78 and 1986. This is a subcategory of the informal sector, and is likely to be the relatively wealthier portion of informal workers. The equations show the differences in returns to human capital variables for self-employed nonprofessionals between the two surveys. A striking feature of the equations is the lack of explanatory power of the human capital model for the self-employed sector, particularly in 1977. Apparently wages are not determined on the basis of productive characteristics in that sector. The results nevertheless confirm that age-related returns have increased since 1977. The table also shows that the gap between male and female returns remained more or less constant and not significantly different from zero. Disparities in the returns between

Table 10.21 Estimates of Earnings Functions for the Self-Employed Non-Professional, 1977–78 and 1986

Variable	1977–78 survey		1986 survey	
	Mean (Std. deviation)	Parameter (t-statistic)	Mean (Std. deviation)	Parameter (t-statistic)
Intercept	—	-0.2829	—	-0.7390
		(0.25)		(0.96)
Age	37.117	0.0400	34.763	0.1021
	(10.89)	(0.74)	(11.04)	(2.73)
Age^2	1,495.672	-0.0004	1,330.199	-0.0011
	(862.81)	(0.67)	(860.77)	(2.46)
Education	3.564	-0.0025	5.574	0.0233
	(3.60)	(0.02)	(3.95)	(0.34)
$Education^2$	25.601	0.0016	46.647	0.0050
	(33.93)	(0.20)	(47.48)	(1.40)
Education x age	123.453	0.0006	178.533	-0.0003
	(133.82)	(0.27)	(141.72)	(0.26)
Female	0.328	-0.2073	0.490	-0.2091
	(0.47)	(1.08)	(0.50)	(1.71)
Skill classes				
Skilled labor	0.111	0.0191	0.116	-0.2247
	(0.32)	(0.05)	(0.32)	(1.06)
Semi-skilled	0.172	-0.1917	0.066	0.0471
	(0.38)	(0.55)	(0.25)	(0.18)
Sales & service	0.622	0.0575	0.602	-0.1010
	(0.49)	(0.19)	(0.49)	(0.68)
Location				
Nairobi	0.161	-0.2418	0.272	0.5167
	(0.37)	(1.01)	(0.45)	(3.89)
Mombasa	0.311	0.0801	0.147	0.5047
	(0.46)	(0.39)	(0.35)	(2.97)
Mean of dependent variable	1.148		1.665	
Number of observations	180		482	
R-squared		0.053		0.114

skills groups are not significantly different from zero. This implies that factors other than skill variations are more important in determining wages in that sector, and maybe that variations in the technology of production are not wide. It looks as if location and age are much more important in determining wages in the informal sector, and that the importance of these variables has increased since 1977.

The wage premiums earned by workers in Nairobi and Mombasa increased between 1977 and 1986. As long as workers can earn a premium in Nairobi's informal sector, attracting them to jobs in the tradables sector will be difficult. At the same time, with such rapid growth in the labor force, envisaging a policy that would significantly alter relative wages without further impoverishing those already at the bottom end of the income distribution would be difficult.

Table 10.21 thus provides additional evidence that relative wages had not changed all that much up to 1986, but that all returns had fallen. This suggests that the Kenyan labor force had not yet reached the stage of adjustment by 1986, but rather remained in a phase of stabilization where all incomes were declining. Nevertheless, certain groups were bearing a heavier cost than others.

All the estimated wage equations are subject to the criticism of selection bias, as no variable has been introduced that would correct for any unobserved systematic heterogeneity between self-employed, nonprofessional workers and others. There is thus the possibility that some of the parameter estimates are biased, although theory does not provide any guide as to the direction of this bias. On the basis of recent findings for the Côte d'Ivoire, however (Collier and Horsnell 1989), the gender gap may be overstated.

Conclusion

This chapter has attempted to assess the adjustment of the labor market to macroeconomic shocks and the structural adjustment programs of the 1980s. Of particular interest is the period from 1973 to the present. Through this period, there were two significant increases in oil prices, the worldwide recession of 1981–82, a major drought in 1984, and policies aimed at changing the economy's structure. The adjustment of the labor market through wage changes, sectoral changes in employment, increased unemployment, and increased poverty has been the focus of this chapter.

The deterioration of the economy was particularly evident after the second oil price shock in 1979–80. The adjustment to this macro shock took the form of increased interest rates (a tighter monetary policy), adjustments to the value of the Kenyan shilling (with its ensuing depreciation), fiscal restraint (although unsuccessful due to lack of control on the expenditure side), policies to influence the rural-urban balance of the population, and sectoral changes in the labor market. Following stabilization effects during 1979–84, the government instigated policy changes aimed at structural adjustment from 1985 onward.

The public sector continues to be a large source of modern sector employment, accounting for over 50 percent of employment, and while the government is committed to slowing employment growth in the sector, to date this has not materialized. Through the adjustment phase, real wages in all modern sectors fell, although the drop in the public sector was more pronounced. Indeed, real wage rates seem to have provided the major part of the adjustment as there do not appear to have been major changes in the urban unemployment rate between 1977–78 and 1986. This means, however, that poverty has increased, which may cause problems in providing basic needs.

During the period the informal sector seems to have grown substantially, although this is somewhat difficult to assess given the changing coverage of the survey of this sector. Furthermore, relative wages in the informal sector also seem to have fallen since 1979, and the informal sector's share of earnings has fallen. This again points to lack of adjustment and resumed growth.

The rate of capital formation slowed during 1981–84. However, it is difficult to attribute this drop to the economic crises that occurred. Nevertheless, in terms of structural adjustment, investment is critical.

Women in the labor market do not seem to have been any more affected by the economic downturn than men. In terms of the percentage employed in the formal sector, the share of women has increased, although they are more likely to be employed at low paying jobs. For women wage workers, earnings fell relative to men's, but there was no change in women's relative earnings in the self-employed category.

In sum, the labor market has adjusted through the period, but the government still faces serious problems, both with regard to balance of payments considerations and the budget deficit. While some structural policies have been put in place, it is somewhat too early to assess their effects, and significant further changes must be made.

References

Barber, G. M., and W. J. Milne. 1988. "Modelling Interregional Migration in Kenya." *Environment and Planning* A(20): 1185–1196.

Collier, P., and D. Lal. 1986. *Labour and Poverty in Kenya, 1900–1980*. Oxford: Oxford University Press.

Collier, P., and P. Horsnell. 1989. "The Mobility of Women's Labour and Structural Adjustment: Issues and Some Evidence from the Côte d'Ivoire." Processed.

Fallon, P. R. 1985. "The Labour Market in Kenya: Recent Evidence." Processed.

ILO (International Labour Organisation). 1989. *African Employment Report, 1989*. Addis Ababa, Ethiopia: World Employment Program.

Kenya, Republic of, Central Bureau of Statistics. 1981. *Employment and Earnings*. Nairobi: Government Printer.

_____. Various issues, 1990. *Economic 1989 Survey*. Nairobi.

_____. Various issues. *Statistical Abstract*. Nairobi.

Kenya, Republic of. 1985a. *Small Scale Enterprises in Rural and Urban Areas of Kenya*. Nairobi: Central Bureau of Statistics.

_____. 1985b. *Women of Kenya: Review and Evaluation of Progress*. Nairobi: Kenya Literature Bureau.

_____. 1986a. *Labour Force Survey, 1977–78: Basic Report*. Nairobi: Central Bureau of Statistics.

_____. 1986b. *Sessional Paper No. 1 of 1986: Economic Management for Renewed Growth*. Nairobi: Government Printer.

_____. 1988. *Urban Labour Force Survey, 1986*. Nairobi: Long Range Planning Unit and Central Bureau of Statistics.

_____. 1989. *Development Plan, 1989–93*. Nairobi: Government Printer.

Livingstone, I. 1981. *Rural Development, Employment and Incomes in Kenya*. Geneva: International Labour Organisation.

Mills, M. 1988. "Kenya Public Expenditure Review: Government Employment and Personnel Expenditures." Nairobi: World Bank, East Africa Department. Processed.

Milne, W. 1986. *A National and Urban-Rural Population Model for Kenya*. Technical Paper 86-01. Nairobi, Kenya: Ministry of Planning and National Development, Long Range Planning Unit.

Morrison, C. 1973. "Income Distribution in Kenya." Washington, D.C.: World Bank. Processed.

Ng'ethe, N., and J. G. Wahome. 1989. *The Rural Non-Farm Sector in Kenya: A Study of Micro-Enterprises in Nyeri, Meru, Uasin Gishu and Siaya Districts*. IDS Occasional Paper No. 54. Nairobi: University of Nairobi, Institute for Development Studies.

O'Connell, S. A. 1987. "Fiscal Policy in Low-Income Africa." Processed.

Ogundo, O. O. 1977. "Data Collection in the Informal Sector." In F. C. Child, ed., *Employment Technology and Growth and the Role of the Intermediate Sector in Kenya*. Occasional Paper No. 19. Nairobi: University of Nairobi, Institute for Development Studies.

Rosen, S. 1977. "Human Capital: A Survey of Empirical Research." In *Research in Labour Economics*. Greenwich, Connecticut: JAI Press.

Turnham, D., B. Salomé, and A. Schwarz. 1990. *The Informal Sector Revisited.* Paris: OECD.

UNICEF. 1989. *Situation Analysis of Children and Women in Kenya.* Nairobi.

van der Hoeven, R., and J. Vandemoortele. 1987. *Stabilization and Adjustment Policies and Programmes: Kenya.* Helsinki, Finland: World Institute for Development Economics Research of the United Nations University.

Vieira da Cunha, P. 1987. "Trends in Kenyan Manufacturing Wages and Their Impact on Trade Liberalization." Washington, D.C.: World Bank. Processed.

World Bank. 1988. "Employment and Growth in Kenya." Report No. 7393-KE. Washington, D.C.: World Bank.

_____. 1990. *World Tables.* Baltimore, Md.: Johns Hopkins University Press.

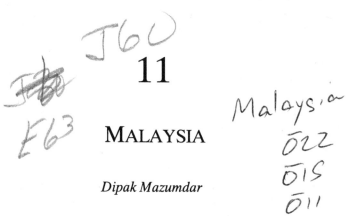

11

MALAYSIA

Dipak Mazumdar

Malaysia has maintained sustained growth for much of the 1970s. As an oil exporter the country received windfall gains during the two oil price hikes, and in the 1970s, a commodity boom also helped growth. Difficulties emerged with the decline of oil prices in the 1980s, which were accompanied by a fall in commodity prices. Malaysia bungled into a rather severe depression in 1985–86, but to the surprise of some observers, the economy recovered very quickly and growth resumed in 1987 and 1988.

The events that led to the recession and its quick turnaround are of interest because Malaysia represents a Southeast Asian prototype. The Republic of Korea and Thailand—although they are not oil exporters—seemed to have experienced much the same type of severe but short depression in the 1980s, followed by a strong recovery. This chapter examines macroeconomic policies that led to the depression and the recovery of the 1980s and analyzes the behavior of labor markets in this context.

The Basic Structure of the Economy

We will discuss in this section the more salient aspects of Malaysia's economic structure, which had a significant effect on its growth and adjustment.

This chapter is a revised version of a document produced for the research project on the Human Resources Development Plan, Module I. Other papers in the module on which this chapter has drawn are those by Gan Wee Beng and L. Krause, R. Richardson and Soon Lee Yin, and to a lesser extent, S. Bhalla. I have also benefited from reading the interim report on the whole project by R. Lucas and D. Verry. I am grateful to Homi Kharas, Sue Horton, and members of the Economic Planning Unit in Malaysia for their helpful comments. Special thanks are due to Homi Kharas for supplying me with clean data tapes of the household surveys.

Openness

Malaysia is a very open economy. Exports as a percentage of GDP hovered just below 50 percent in the 1970s. This share started to increase in 1983, rose more sharply after 1985, and reached a record level of 72 percent in 1988.

Table 11.1 gives the composition of exports by the most important commodity groups for various years. The table shows that Malaysia's economy has been based on natural resources, but that the proportion of manufactures in total exports increased dramatically in the 1980s.

Originally rubber dominated the export scene, but over the years a diversified group of commodities—tin, palm oil, sawlogs, timber—have become more important. Petroleum became important after the oil price increases of the 1970s. The growth rate of the export of manufactured goods has been nothing short of spectacular in the last decade, but unlike some of the newly industrializing countries, exports manufacture has

Table 11.1 Composition of Exports in Malaysia, Selected Years *(percent)*

Export	1970	1975	1980	1984	1987
Food, live animals, beverages, tobacco	5.92	6.72	3.70	3.90	5.56
Crude materials, inedible	53.79	35.00	32.32	21.10	23.46
Mineral fuels	7.08	10.48	24.49	29.59	19.76
Animal and vegetable oils and fats	6.00	16.34	11.11	15.18	9.15
Chemicals, manufactured goods, machinery and transportation equipment, miscellaneous manufactures	26.08	30.40	27.82	29.76	41.58
Other exports	1.12	1.05	0.55	0.55	0.48

Note: Mineral fuels include coke, coal, petroleum, petroleum products, and gas.
Sources: Bank Negara (1986, table VIII.6); Ministry of Finance *Economic Report* 1988–89.

been highly concentrated in Malaysia, with electronics and electrical machinery accounting for over half of total exports in this category.

Instability of exports earnings is a feature of the Malaysian economy, and the high ratio of exports means that this instability is liable to produce large swings in GDP. Although commodity exports are diversified, large fluctuations in earnings from this group of exports are not at all uncommon, for example, the 1985–86 crisis was caused by a simultaneous fall in prices for all five commodity groups. A World Bank study (1988, vol. I, appendix 1) calculated that the standard deviation of the rate of change of export earnings from commodities due to price changes was 15.8 percent. "This implies that one-third of the time, export earnings are likely to deviate from their expected value by more than M\$2 billion (one standard deviation), and one-sixth of the time, there will be a shortfall of this magnitude" (p. 125).

The heavy concentration of manufacturing exports in an industry that is distinguished for its volatile world market adds to the instability. The recession of 1985–86 was in no small measure due to the shakeout in the world semiconductor market.

Importance of the Public Sector

The public sector's role in the economy has increased throughout the period of Malaysia's recent economic growth. The new economic policy initiated in 1973 had as its objective a restructuring of the economy with a view to giving the native Malays (Bhumiputras) a greater share of the economic pie than they had traditionally enjoyed. A major instrument in this transformation was the expansion of employment in the public sector, in which Malays had a favored role.

At the same time, the boom in commodity and oil prices during the 1970s vastly increased the government's resources, which enabled it to sustain its policy of expansion. The expansion took the form of a high rate of growth of the government's wage bill, as well as a massive increase in public investment through nonfinancial public enterprises and other statutory authorities. During 1981–88, public consumption and investment together accounted for an average of 37 percent of GNP, and public investment was 41 percent of gross capital formation in the economy (Malaysia Ministry of Finance 1988, table 2.1, p. x).

The large size of the public sector has meant that it has had an important influence on business cycles in the economy, supplementing the impact of the external sector. As we shall see, public spending has fluctuated sharply in response to external shocks, and not always in a countercyclical way.

The Role of Food

An important variable that determines the impact of external shocks on the economy is whether food is largely a tradable or a nontradable good. The behavior of the consumer price index (of which food is an important component) relative to the index of producer prices depends on the "tradableness" of food.[1] If, for instance, an external shock causes the exchange rate to appreciate, the price of tradables falls relative to the price of nontradables.[2] If food is a tradable commodity, its price also falls relatively, and a downward pressure is exerted on the consumer price index. If real wages are sticky, money wages will still decline relative to producer prices and the pressure on profitability in the traded goods sector will be eased somewhat. However, if food belongs to the nontradable category, product wages are likely to increase, thereby adding to the burden of the producers of tradables unless real wages fall.

Rice is an important component of the basket of goods consumed by Malaysian workers. Ordinarily it would be a commodity traded in the world market, but Malaysia has a system of administered prices for rice for both producers and consumers. The system is administered by the National Paddy and Rice Authority, which is responsible for marketing and pricing rice. The object is to maintain a level of prices for domestic paddy farmers that is higher than the border price of rice. The authority imports rice as necessary to supplement the amount it can procure from domestic producers, and sells the rice to consumers through its retail outlets at predetermined prices that are not very different from prices paid to farmers. In 1974, the cabinet set rice prices at parity with border prices near the peak of the external market, and they have remained virtually unchanged despite a halving of import prices. In nominal terms, the

---

1. The degree of "tradableness" of food varies inversely with the extent to which domestic consumers are insulated from movements in world prices.

2. This is the typical "Dutch disease" case of an oil exporter when the price of oil increases.

constancy of rice prices meant that the price had fallen 39 percent in real terms by 1984.

Thus, one component of the consumption basket is virtually insulated from external events, including exchange rate fluctuations. The consumer price index in Malaysia tends to move with the commodities and services in the basket whose prices are free to vary, which tend to be largely nontradables. Of course, the extent of the variation is less than the price of nontradables because of the constant nominal price of one component of the index.

Thus, Malaysia belongs to the group of countries in which during periods of increase in the ratio of prices of nontradables to tradables, the squeeze on profitability in the tradable sector tends to be accentuated by a rise in the product wage, even if the real (consumer) wage is constant.

Growth and Cycles in the Malaysian Economy

Figure 11.1 plots the yearly rate of growth of GDP in real terms for 1970–88. Because Malaysia is such an open economy, the same figure also shows the index of the terms of trade. The figure shows the high rate of growth of 7 percent or more that Malaysia has been able to sustain for most of the period. In the 1970s, growth was interrupted in a major way only in 1975. More difficulties emerged in the 1980s, culminating in the deep recession of 1985 and 1986. However, the recession did not last long, and by 1988 the economy had bounded back to a growth rate higher than 7 percent.

The figure illustrates the close relationship between the GDP growth rate and the terms of trade. A fall in the terms of trade in 1975 was associated with the sharp downturn in 1975, while the sustained improvement in the terms of trade for the next five years seems to have been reflected in the recovery and maintenance of a generally high GDP growth rate in the second half of the 1970s. In the 1980s, the relationship between terms of trade changes and yearly variations in the growth rate is particularly close, but the deep recession of 1985–86 was much larger than the percentage fall in the terms of trade. Similarly, the recovery in 1987–88 is much stronger than would be warranted by a mere terms of trade improvement. Although led by terms of trade movements, other factors were clearly involved in the rather strong cycle of the 1980s. We shall now discuss the four phases of the cycle in more detail.

Figure 11.1 Terms of Trade and GDP, 1970–88

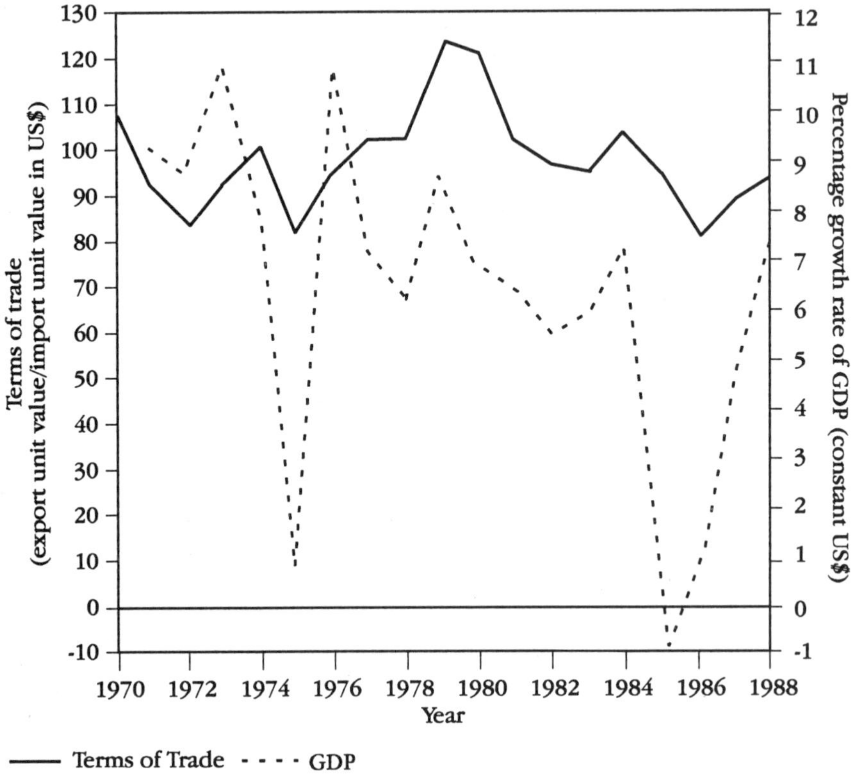

Terms of Trade - - - - GDP

Note: Index for terms of trade: 1978 = 100.
Sources: Krause (1989, table 1); Ministry of Finance (various years).

Phase I: The Upswing (1975–79)

As mentioned earlier, the upswing was fueled by a sharp increase in the terms of trade, which were 51 percent higher in 1979 than in 1975. The prices of crude oil, rubber, tin, and palm oil all rose simultaneously. The volume response was also positive, but was particularly strong for palm oil. The long-term investment in palm oil was now paying off and it emerged as the leading agricultural export in this period, almost catching up with the share of rubber in total exports. In value terms, however, the most dramatic increase in export share was in petroleum, up from 9 to 24 percent during the period.

The large increase in the value of exports increased domestic income through the multiplier process. Insofar as this type of economy depends a great deal for its revenue on taxes on the external sector, the resources for public spending were augmented, but during this phase of the cycle, real incomes in Malaysia rose much more rapidly than expenditures. Savings rose to record heights, averaging 29.6 percent of GNP in 1976–79. Investment, although growing through the period at a substantial rate, averaged less, at 25.3 percent, so that a current account surplus in the balance of payments was maintained throughout this period (figure 11.2).

The respective roles of the private and public sectors in the favorable resource position can also be inferred from figure 11.2. The federal

Figure 11.2 Balance in the Federal Budget and in the Current Account of the Balance of Payments, 1971–88

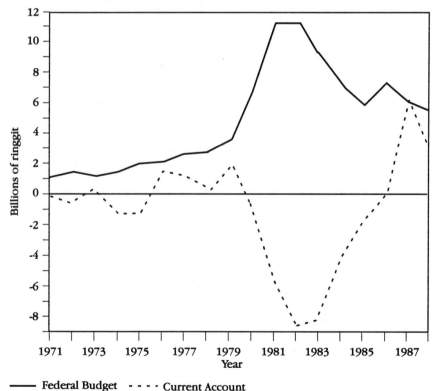

Source: Lucas and Verry (1989).

budget deficit increased in absolute terms during this period, but not in any marked way. As a proportion of GDP it was actually fairly constant. This ratio is plotted in figure 11.3, together with the private sector saving/investment imbalance for the 1970s and 1980s. It shows the contribution of the positive private savings balance in sustaining the external accounts surplus during the upswing of the late 1970s.[3]

Figure 11.3 Consolidated Public Sector Fiscal Deficit and the Private Sector Saving/Investment Imbalance, 1971–88
(percentage of GDP)

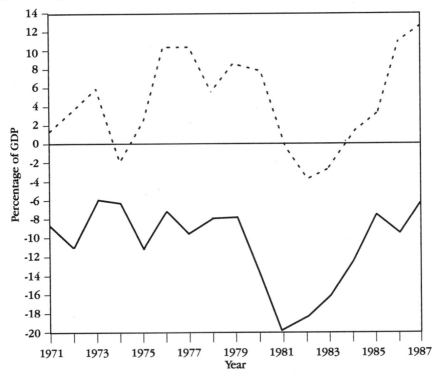

——— Fiscal Deficit   - - - - Private Sector Saving/Investment Imbalance

Source: Lucas and Verry (1989).

---

3. The proportion of consumption goods in total imports fell from 22.2 percent in 1975 to 18.4 percent in 1980, while the proportion of intermediate goods went up from 41.3 to 49.9 percent. Although growth in Malaysia is dependent on imported inputs, the relatively low marginal propensity to import consumer goods helped to prevent deterioration of the balance of payments during this period.

Phase II: The Attempt to Sustain the Upswing (1980–84)

Malaysia's external terms of trade peaked around the mid-1980s. They then turned down until 1986 as commodity prices broke, with a temporary respite in 1984. The decline in the terms of trade during 1980–84 was around 20 percent. At the same time, the slowdown in the economies of the OECD threatened to reduce the growth rate of Malaysian exports.

The government's response to the downswing in the external sector was to adopt a vigorous countercyclical fiscal policy in the expectation that the recession affecting external trade was only temporary. Many people were predicting that petroleum prices would continue to rise and that OECD growth would quickly recover. The expansionary fiscal policy took the form of a very sharp increase in federal government expenditures, which was not compensated by an increase in revenues. The swelling budget deficit, showed in figure 11.2, closely follows the pattern of increase in government expenditures. It peaked in 1982, and although it declined in successive years, the ratio of public deficit to GDP in 1984 was 12.3 percent, nearly double the level of the mid-1970s.

There are only three ways to finance a budget deficit: inflationary finance through an accommodating monetary policy; a reduction in private domestic absorption through a rise in domestic savings and/or a fall in investment; or an increase in foreign borrowing. In Malaysia, the monetary authorities forestalled the first option. The government adopted a policy of monetary restraint explicitly to prevent the budget deficit from spilling over into inflationary pressures and current account deficits in the balance of payments. From 1980 onward, the annual rate of growth of money supply (Ml) declined continuously, registering a negative growth rate of -0.6 percent in 1984.[4] As a consequence, the rate of inflation (measured by the GDP deflator) was at a lower level in phase II, with an average of 4.2 percent compared to phase I, when it averaged 8.9 percent.

As far as private domestic absorption was concerned, unlike in phase I, private savings fell sharply in phase II of the cycle. This is, of course,

4. This policy was in sharp contrast to the general practice of Latin American monetary authorities who seem to follow passively the needs of the fiscal authorities for monetary accommodation. The difference in institutions involved in economic decisionmaking in Malaysia (and other East Asian countries) and Latin American countries is an interesting topic for investigation.

to be expected if consumers behave rationally in attempting to smooth out fluctuations over time. Savings out of transitory income gains increased during an upswing of the terms of trade and decreased when the downswing brought unanticipated losses in income. Private investment did not fall until the recession years (phase III of the cycle), although its composition might have changed. Thus, the saving/ investment balance in the private sector moved in a way opposite to what was required to offset the government budget deficit (figure 11.3).

Thus, only one way remained to finance the deficit: borrowing from external sources. As a result of external debt financing, the debt: GNP ratio increased dramatically from 9.4 in 1980 to 39.0 in 1984. Furthermore, a great deal of the borrowing was done through commercial banks at variable interest rates.[5] Loans of this type increased from 45 percent of total debt in 1980 to 70 percent in 1984, and a high of nearly 80 percent in 1985. The high international interest rates of the early 1980s increased the average interest cost of external debt from 8.1 percent in 1979 to a high of 13.1 percent in 1981 before it fell gradually to 9.7 percent in 1984.

Throughout this period, the Malaysian authorities took a passive attitude to the exchange rate. The capital inflow triggered by the budget deficit was instrumental in causing a significant appreciation of the real exchange rate. This appreciation, together with adverse movements in the labor market, reduced Malaysia's competitiveness in the world market and threatened to create an unsustainable deficit in the current account of the balance of payments.

Phase III: The Period of Adjustment and Recession (1985–86)

The management of economic policy in Malaysia became sensitive to the emerging economic problem soon after the explosive budget deficit of 1981–82. Measures to cut government expenditure were initiated in 1983. The ratio of consolidated public deficit to GDP was drastically reduced from 18 percent in 1982 to 7 percent in 1985. The improvement

---

5. "A substantial proportion of the foreign borrowing (57 percent in 1983–84) was undertaken by public enterprises. This recourse to external funds helped these agencies escape the surveillance and discipline that could have been imposed by the Federal Government had there been a greater reliance on the Treasury as source of funds." (World Bank 1988, vol. I, p. 15).

of the terms of trade in 1984 proved to be temporary, and Malaysia was hit by a further drop in this key variable in 1985–86 (figure 11.1). Without an offsetting rise in public expenditures, Malaysia sustained a severe recession with the rate of growth of GDP actually turning negative for the first time in 1985 and barely positive in 1986.

The recession, short as it was, managed to correct the basic imbalances in the economy fairly quickly. As figure 11.3 shows, the fiscal deficit continued its dramatic improvement in 1985, but failed to sustain it in 1986. Cutting budget deficits in a year of deep recession when revenues are generally falling off is difficult. The private sector surplus of savings over investment, however, continued to increase strongly. Private savings no doubt declined with falling income during the recession, but private investment fell faster. Taking the public and private accounts together, the excess of spending over income finally disappeared in 1986. At the same time, these two years of recession saw for the first time the phenomenon of the current account of the balance of payments improving when the terms of trade were falling. This is because the value of imports fell due to the recession while exports registered a modest increase.

Phase IV: The Recovery (1987–)

Somewhat to the surprise of observers, the Malaysian economy registered a turnaround and a rate of growth of GDP of 5.2 percent in 1987. The performance in 1988 was even better at 7.9 percent, signifying that the recovery was well underway. The upturn was again fueled by the external sector with the terms of trade improving by 18 percent; the prices of the major nonoil commodities once more moving up in unison. At the same time, exports volume, which had already started to grow in 1986, surged forward in 1987–88.

A major development in the behavior of exports was the leading role taken by manufactured goods, whose share in total exports climbed to 48 percent by the end of 1988. However, it remained heavily concentrated in electronics. "The robust expansion in electronics demand in turn follows from the economic growth of the leading industrial countries like Japan and the United States which are currently in their sixth year of growth as well as from the relocation of Japanese investments overseas" (Government of Malaysia 1988, p. 114). At the same time the continued depreciation of the ringgit helped the competitiveness of such exports in the world market. The combined effect of price and volume increase was that the current account of the balance of payments showed a sizeable surplus for the first time since 1979 (figure 11.2).

During this period of recovery, the government restrained the growth of public expenditure. With the public sector deficit holding steady in proportion to GDP and the private savings/investment gap still remaining positive, there was no need for borrowing from abroad. In fact, the accumulation of reserves through the surplus in the current account during these years enabled the government to prepay a substantial amount of its outstanding external debt. The gross debt:GNP ratio fell from a high of 52 percent in 1985 to 37 percent in 1987, and was as low as 30 percent in 1988.

Gan and Krause (1990) underline the point that "the prepayment exercise provides an example of the judicious use of reserves in time of a primary commodity boom. The reserve inflows during the 1987–88 commodity boom would have resulted in the temporary appreciation of the ringgit above its long-run equilibrium value, thereby delaying the adjustment process in transferring resources out of the nontradable to the tradable sector" (p. 23).

Recent information released by the government shows the recovery that started in 1989 has continued despite a softening of commodity prices. At an estimated 7.6 percent, it is only slightly below the strong growth of 1988 (Government of Malaysia *Economic Report* 1990, p. 17). A major factor in the sustained growth is the continued expansion of manufactured exports that grew by more than 30 percent for the third year in a row. Malaysia has been able to sustain its international competitiveness and so achieve a high rate of growth without external imbalance.

The Short-Run Problems of the Macroeconomy

In this section we turn to a detailed analysis of the short-term cyclical problems of the economy.

The Determinants of Exchange Rate Movements

The short-run problems for the Malaysian economy generated by the cycles just described can be understood in terms of the standard three-good model of an open economy. The three goods are commodities whose world prices fluctuate sharply; other tradables with a more stable price determined in the international market; and nontraded goods whose prices are determined in the domestic market. When an upswing occurs in the terms of trade due to a rise in commodity prices, there is a net flow of resources into the economy only a part of which is spent on tradables. Depending on the proportion that is spent on nontradables, in a freely floating exchange rate regime the currency will appreciate.

At this point we must distinguish between three concepts of the exchange rate. The first is the nominal effective exchange rate (NEER), which is the price of the currency in terms of some weighted average of the currencies of the trading partners. The second is the real effective exchange rate (REER), which corrects the nominal rate for differences in inflation rates between the country and its trading partners. This rate is particularly important to the economy's international competitiveness. The third is the real domestic exchange rate (RDER), which is the ratio of the price of nontradables to tradables in the domestic market. This determines the relative profitability in the two sectors, and, therefore, affects the supply function of exports. The REER and RDER will generally move together, but there is no reason (except under very severe assumptions) why the magnitude of the change will be the same.

The "Dutch disease" class of models has stressed the appreciation of the exchange rate because of a terms of trade improvement due to an upswing of the export prices of key commodities. In the Malaysian case the story is somewhat different. Figure 11.4 shows movements in the terms of trade, the REER, and the RDER. Note that while the terms of trade increased in 1975–79, both the REER and RDER declined substantially, with the opposite situation prevailing in 1980–85. The REER reached its highest point in 1984, but the RDER continued to rise until 1986. Then in 1987 and 1988, the RDER declined while the terms of trade improved appreciably. Thus, contrary to the predictions of the standard model, the exchange rate indices and the terms of trade are inversely related in the Malaysian case.

The "spending effect" caused by the terms of trade movements has been dampened by the behavior of private savings, which have moved directly with the terms of trade, and overshadowed by the much stronger countercyclical behavior of public expenditure. The sign and magnitude

Figure 11.4 Terms of Trade and Exchange Rate Variability, 1970–88

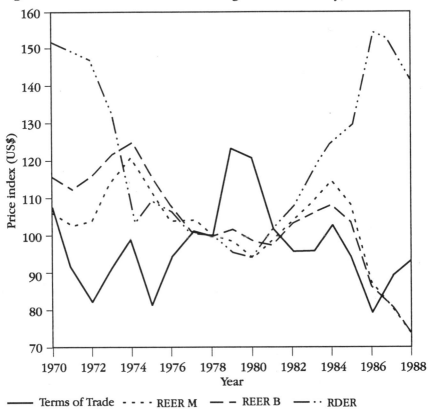

Notes: The terms of trade are the export unit divided by the import unit in U.S. dollars (1980 = 100). REER M is the REER with multilateral trading partner weights. REER B is the REER with bilateral trading partner weights. RDER is the service price index divided by the weighted manufactured export price index (the service price index includes rent, domestic services, transport, and communication).

Sources: Department of Statistics *Monthly Statistics Bulletin* (various issues); IMF *International Financial Statistics* (various issues); *Direction of International Trade* (various issues); Krause (1989, table 1); United Nations *Yearbook of International Statistics* (various years).

of the capital inflow generated by the resultant excess of spending over incomes (whether positive or negative) has been a more dominant effect on the exchange rate than the terms of trade, both in the upswing and the downswing of the latter.

In the upswing of the 1970s, both government and private expenditure increased, but kept pace with the increase in GDP. As already mentioned, the increase in private savings helped to balance the deficit in the government budget, so that the current account of the balance of payments was in surplus during this period. This surplus would have put an upward pressure on the exchange rate if government or private savers or both were not willing to hold foreign assets. As it happened, they did. The net international resources of Bank Negara (valued in U.S. dollars) increased at a substantial rate: the total in 1980 was three times the value in 1975.

As the terms of trade declined in the 1980s, the government attempt to sustain a large countercyclical expenditure through massive foreign borrowing led to a large inflow of capital. It was this inflow that led to an appreciation of the Malaysian ringgit even though the terms of trade were declining.[6] In other words, financial flows in the capital account were the dominant influence in the exchange rate rather than flows generated by the current account of the balance of payments.

Real Exchange Rate Movements and the Short-Run Crisis

As we have seen earlier, the government had to indulge in massive external borrowing to finance its countercyclical budget deficit. This borrowing becomes unsustainable if the attendant appreciation of the REER and RDER dampens the growth of exports so that the current account deficits fuel the soaring debt:GDP ratio.

This section will show that the exchange rate appreciation was indeed a factor in the crisis of the 1980s that led up to the recession, and that the subsequent depreciation was a necessary condition for the recovery.

The performance of the manufacturing sector, especially its export capability, has increasingly become important to Malaysia's growth. As noted earlier, the composition of exports has shifted spectacularly, with manufacturing climbing to nearly half the share of total exports by 1988.

There is *prima facie* evidence about the slowing down of the manufacturing sector during the real exchange rate appreciation of 1980–84.[7] Similarly, the recovery of 1987–88 was accompanied by a strong

---

6. This interpretation differs from that given in Gan and Krause (1990), which tells a standard Dutch disease story. The government expenditure boom of the 1980s is best viewed as a deliberate countercyclical policy rather than a lagged response to the terms of trade increase.

7. The average annual growth in manufacturing output declined from 13 percent in 1973–77 to 7.4 percent in 1980–84. The rate of growth of exports of manufactured goods

revival in the growth of exports from the manufacturing sectors aided by exchange rate depreciation. We need to know, however, if these fluctuations were due to changing economic conditions in the world market rather than movements in the exchange rate. Gan (1988) estimated a reduced form export function as follows:

$$\log X_t = \beta_0 + \sum_{i=0}^{1} \beta_i \log REER_{t-1} + \sum_{i=0}^{1} \log WY_{t-1} + \sum_{i=0} u_i \log Y_{t-1}$$

where WY = real GDP of all OECD countries, Y = domestic real GDP, and X = quantum index of manufactured exports.

The equation was formulated in this way to allow for adjustment lags. It was estimated with quarterly data from 1974:1 to 1985:4. The real income of OECD countries was used because those countries accounted for 70 percent of Malaysian manufactured exports in 1983 (Gan 1988, table 5). OECD real income was clearly significant, along with REER (with different lags), but not domestic real income. However, the long-run elasticity of manufactured exports (the sum of lagged coefficients) was much higher for REER (4.70 percent) than for WY (0.06 percent) (Gan 1988, table 8).

Turning to the supply side of the market, considerable evidence demonstrates the squeezing of profitability in the tradable goods sector due to the appreciation of RDER. The initial expansion of the early 1980s was sustained not only by government spending on services, but also by a construction boom in the private sector that it triggered (World Bank 1989, vol. I, p. 9). Data gathered by Gan and Krause (1990) showed that during the first half of the 1980s, the tradable goods sector in Malaysia (including manufacturing) suffered a steady decline in the pre-tax return on equity and on fixed capital from 1980, while the rates of return in construction and retailing were well above the levels of the 1970s (Gan and Krause 1990, table 16).

---

declined from an annual rate of 56 percent during 1973–79 to 25 percent during 1980–84 (Gan and Krause 1990, tables 17 and 18).

The Cycle and Labor Markets

So far the labor market's responses to the cyclical movements of the economy have not been discussed. It is now necessary to integrate the labor market story into the story of exchange rate movements.

RDER AND THE WAGE RATE. In the simple model of the open economy, the product wage in the tradable sector will rise *pari passu* with the RDER. Under the assumption of full employment, a rise in the price of nontradables is assumed to be fully reflected in an increase in money wages, which rise to the same extent in both sectors. However, with a complex labor market like in Malaysia, we have to examine wage behavior in different segments of the market in a more detailed way.

Unfortunately, wage series on a quarterly and/or annual basis are available only for parts of the formal sector of the market, principally manufacturing and plantations. This is, however, not entirely unhelpful, because a substantial part of the tradable sector coincides with the formal sector of the labor market (in both manufacturing and plantation agriculture). Food, which is produced in the self-employed (or informal) labor market is a nontradable for the purposes of this analysis. Some of the cash crops that are exported, notably rubber, are, however, produced in the informal sector by smallholders.

Thus, we will concentrate here on wage movements in manufacturing and plantations to throw light on the factors that affect changing labor costs in the short run.

MOVEMENTS IN CONSUMPTION (REAL) AND PRODUCT WAGES IN THE FORMAL SECTOR. The series for real wage movements 1968–88 are plotted in figure 11.5 for four subsectors of the formal labor market. The figure shows that in the manufacturing sector, real wages have been increasing steadily since the low points reached in 1973, but the trend rate of growth, which continued to 1985, has not changed very much since the late 1970s. The absence of variations in real wages with the phases of the cycle (and GDP growth) discussed earlier needs explanation and is discussed below, but before discussing this topic an important point about the behavior of the product wage should be noted.

REAL WAGE AND PRODUCT WAGE. From the point of view of producers, the ratio of wages to producer prices, (W/P_p) or the product wage, is the

Figure 11.5 Real Annual Earnings by Industry, 1968–88

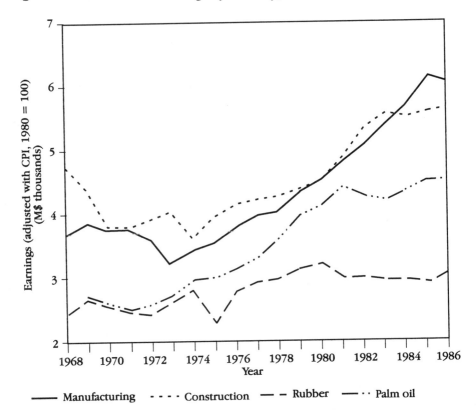

Source: Richardson and Soon (1990, table 5).

critical variable determining costs. The real wage is related to the product wage through the identity

$$\frac{W}{P_p} = \frac{W}{P_c} \cdot \frac{P_c}{P_p}$$

where P_c and P_p are indices of consumer and producer goods respectively.

Now P_c/P_p will be related to the RDER (P_N/P_T) in a way that depends crucially on whether or not food is a tradable good. As mentioned earlier, in Malaysia, because of the policy of maintaining rice prices, food is virtually a nontradable. Thus, when P_N/P_T increased with real exchange rate appreciation, P_c/P_p would have increased with it. It follows that as the real wage W/P_c increased during this period, the producer wage increased even more, putting pressure on costs in the tradable sector.

Figure 11.6 plots the indices of product wages for manufacturing and the two estate sectors, palm oil and rubber. This graph demonstrates

Figure 11.6 Product Wages, 1970–86

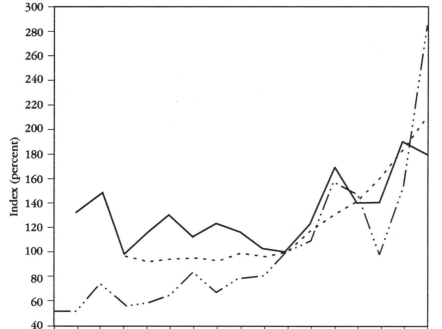

Note: The product wage is the index of the nominal wage rate divided by the index of product price.
a.   Index of rubber estate wage rate divided by index of Malaysian RSS1 rubber price index.
b.   Index of manufacturing wages and salaries per paid employees divided by manufacturing weighted import and export unit value index.
c.   Index of palm oil nominal average earnings per employee divided by index of Malaysian RSS1 palm oil price per metric tonne index. From 1970–74, price used was c.i.f. London $/tonne. From 1974–88, price used was f.o.b. Kuala Lumpur $/tonne.
Sources: Ministry of Finance, *Economic Report* (various issues); Department of Statistics *Industrial Surveys Oil Palm Statistics*; Richardson and Soon (1990).

vividly the remarkable increase in the indices during 1980–86 after comparative stability in the 1970s. This increase was of a magnitude that the trend rate of increase in productivity could not offset. Figure 11.7 illustrates the resulting increase in unit labor costs for manufacturing. The increase in the real (consumption) wage, as well as the relative fall in the price of tradables, contributed to this adverse shock.

DETERMINANTS OF REAL WAGE BEHAVIOR. What determines changes in real wages in the Malaysian economy? The point made above that real wage behavior seemed to bear little relation to the phases of the cycle suggests

Figure 11.7 Real Wage and Labor Productivity, Manufacturing, 1971–87 *(1980 = 100)*

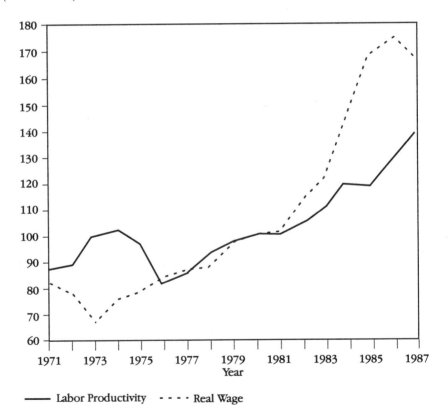

Source: World Bank (1988, vol. I, figure 2).

that wages did not respond significantly or quickly to market forces. Figure 11.8 reinforces this point. Between 1969 and 1973, real wages in manufacturing declined while employment, both in manufacturing and the formal sector as a whole, increased at a significant rate every year. Between 1973 and 1981, the relationship between employment and real wage growth was normal: both increasing. During these years the rate of unemployment was also falling, but during 1981–85, real wages continued to increase almost as fast as in the 1970s, while the rate of unemployment increased every year, and the rate of growth of total employment fell, and was, indeed, stagnant in the manufacturing sector.

Figure 11.8 Manufacturing: Real Wages and Employment, 1968–88 *(1980 = 100)*

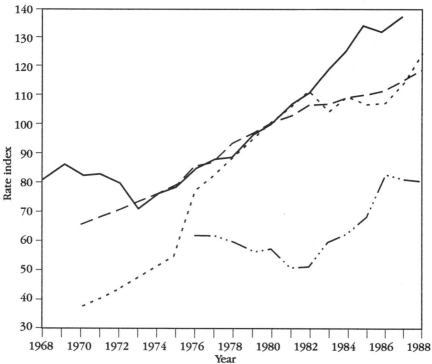

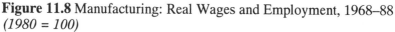

Sources: Real wages: Richardson and Soon (1990); employment and unemployment: Ministry of Finance *Economic Report* (various years).

Richardson and Yin (1989) tried to fit an augmented Phillips curve to nominal wage rate changes in manufacturing, using quarterly data, for 1976–87. The equation is of the form:

$$\Delta W_t = a + b_1 \Delta E_t + \sum a_i I_{t-1}$$

where W is nominal earnings in manufacturing, E is the full-time manufacturing wages, and I is the rate of inflation. All the numbers are in logarithms. The last term is an autoregressive proxy for the (unobservable) rate of inflation expected by actors in the labor market.[8]

The results are given in table 11.2 for the period as a whole and the two subperiods before and after 1980. The employment change variable is negative in both periods, but significant only in the second subperiod. This result underscores the puzzle already noted: even after allowing for the effect of inflation expectations, the relationship between wage increase and employment increase was the opposite of what would be expected from labor market conditions. The puzzle becomes deeper when we look at the divergence in the trend in wages in manufacturing and construction from the trend in the earnings in the plantation sector after 1980. Figure 11.5 shows that during the boom of the late 1970s, wages in both rubber and palm oil estates rose along with manufacturing wages. The absolute gap in earnings in favor of manufacturing was reduced for palm oil and remained the same for rubber, so that the relative gap was squeezed as manufacturing wages were higher. However, after 1980, while wages in the plantation sector were stagnant, manufacturing and construction wages bounded ahead until 1985.

What explains this odd behavior of wages in manufacturing and construction in Malaysia? Part of the explanation could indeed be economic. The wage series available is of average annual earnings. During the downswing, retrenchment of workers will affect those at the

---

8. Note that because of the absence of quarterly data on total formal sector employment, employment in manufacturing is used. The graphs in figure 11.8 show that the correspondence between the two series of annual data is quite close. The wage and employment data are quarterly, run from 1976 to 1987, and are taken from *Monthly Industrial Statistics* published by the Department of Statistics. The change in employment variable, E_t, was instrumented to remove a possible inconsistency being imparted from the joint determination of wages and employment. The instruments used were lagged changes in employment and inflation.

Table 11.2 Nominal Wage Changes in Malaysian Manufacturing, 1976–87

Period (quarter)	Nominal wage changes
1976(3)-1987(4)	$\Delta W_t = 3.385 - 0.134\Delta E_t + \sum a_i 1_{t-i}$ where $\sum a_i = 1.369$
	(4.536) (-2.213) (8.233)
	$R^2 = 0.689$ SEE $= 2.404$
1976(3)-1979(4)	$\Delta W_t = 13.682 - 0.179\Delta E_t + \sum a_i 1_{t-i}$ where $\sum a_i = -0.985$
	(4.789) (-1.242) (-1.877)
	$R^2 = 0.314$ SEE $= 1.732$
1976(3)-1979(4)	$\Delta W_t = 2.920 - 0.233\Delta E_t + \sum a_i 1_{t-1}$ where $\sum a_i = 1.497$
	(3.912) (-3.723) (-9.149)
	$R^2 = 0.799$ SEE $= 2.338$

Note: Figures in parentheses are t-values.
Sources: Richardson and Soon (1990, table 24).

bottom of the wage ladder proportionately more, and this in itself will tend to push up average earnings. Lucas and Verry (1989) examined the characteristics of a sample of workers who were retrenched at some point between 1984 and 1988. Their results confirmed that

> It is the young and the oldest, the less well-educated employees from the private sector and (to a weaker extent statistically) those outside of unionized plants, who are most likely to have been retrenched. . . . However, it was certainly not the only factor, for we know that pay of given individuals continued to rise also (table D.2 and p. 12).

We turn now to institutional factors that might have been important. Unionism is not a very powerful factor in the Malaysian labor market. In manufacturing by 1985, less than a quarter of the workers had been unionized, and in some subsectors, for example, electronics, unionism was forbidden. Paradoxically, the plantation sector, which saw the stagnation of real wages in the 1980s, had the highest proportion of union members. Observers also generally agree that collective bargaining has traditionally been pursued most vigorously in the plantation sector.

We have seen that the public sector has played a dominant role in the Malaysian labor market. Could it be that this sector—in which wages are set administratively—played a wage leadership role in the 1980s? Lucas and Verry (1989) cite evidence to show that for 1980 through 1987, average wages in the public sector increased less rapidly than those for manufacturing.

On these grounds, it would seem difficult to make a case that public service pay has led private pay over the entire period, though in some intervals, such as 1983–84, it may have done so (figure D.14 and p. 21).

The contractual forms of wage agreement—both formal and informal—help explain the rising wages of the 1980s. Two different practices in Malaysian wage setting seem to be particularly relevant here. First, many collective bargaining agreements provide for two- to three-year coverage. Even when the plant is not unionized, formal sector employers are keen to follow the going practice of wage setting. Clearly, with contracts fixed for a long period of time, employers cannot cut the wages of those employees who are not retrenched. Note in this connection that agreements in the plantation sector include provisions for tying workers' wages to the prices of their products through complicated formulas that ensure that, to some extent, wages fluctuate with product prices when severe shocks occur. The stagnation of real wages in the 1980s in the plantations, after a period of rapid increase, may partly reflect this effect of the agreement working itself out after the decline in commodity prices. However, in the manufacturing or construction sectors, where the practice of tying wages to product market conditions does not exist, long contracts mean a substantial lag before wages start to adjust. (This type of delayed adjustment of wages to economic shocks is not uncommon in much of Asia.) In fact, when the rate of inflation is falling, as it did in Malaysia in the 1980s, the length of time that elapses before real rather than money wages begin to fall may be considerable.

The second wage setting practice that is pertinent to the problem of wage flexibility in the Malaysian labor market is that of automatic seniority increments. Malaysian employers, at least in the formal sector, follow the Japanese system of granting pay increases based on years of service in the firm (McCarthy 1988). While the system is expected to increase productivity by securing workers' loyalty, it does not help the rapid adjustment of wages to business conditions, particularly when external shocks tend to be as large as they do for Malaysia. The Japanese wage system provides a safeguard against the seniority system by using bonuses, which are geared to the firm's profitability, as a large component of workers' earnings. In Malaysia, such payments, including fringe benefits, constituted 15 percent of total earnings for male workers in 1984. This, however, was relatively low compared to the Republic of Korea, where the share of bonuses and overtime payments in total compensation in 1982 was as high as 30 percent, split evenly between the two (World Bank 1989, p. 155).

The World Bank (1989) has pointed out that while wages of senior workers are relatively rigid, reduction in entry level salaries is a major element in the downward flexibility of wages, but this particular mechanism could be working strongly only when employment starts to recover and the opportunity to hire a significant number of new workers arises. This is, indeed, what seems to have happened in 1986 and 1987 when the economy started to recover. The wage for new entrants had started to fall in 1985 at the bottom of the depression, but average payments to all employees continued to rise through 1986 (by 7.2 percent that year), reflecting built-in escalators in old contracts, but in 1987 average earnings finally fell, coinciding with the upturn (World Bank 1989, vol. I, p. 26).

LABOR MARKETS AND CHANGES IN COMPETITIVENESS. Malaysia's problem of adjustment in the 1980s stemmed from the same sources as those for other developing countries, a fall in commodity prices, and as an oil exporter, the fall in oil prices. Unlike many other countries, particularly in Latin America, Malaysia had not overborrowed during the upswing of the late 1970s. To the contrary, its strong reserve positions enabled Malaysia to go in for a strong center cyclical policy, with substantial foreign borrowing, when the downturn in the external sector hit.

As an emerging exporter of manufactured goods, the country was heavily dependent on maintaining its international competitiveness, especially when the price of commodities collapsed. One could argue that if wages had shown more flexibility, particularly in the manufacturing sector, when employment growth slowed down in the early 1980s, the recession of the mid-1980s might have been less severe. As it was, the economy needed a sharp, albeit short recession, with a negative growth rate, to avert the increase in wages. Note, however, that it is the dollar cost of labor that is important for competitiveness, not just the domestic unit cost of labor. Thus, an important part of the story is the behavior of the exchange rate.

The World Bank (1989) report commented that other Asian countries (Hong Kong, Korea, Singapore, Taiwan, and Thailand) also suffered from the phenomenon of domestic wages rising faster than productivity. However, because of differences in exchange rate policies in "Korea, Thailand and Taiwan, unit labor costs in manufacturing denominated in US dollars were roughly level with their 1980 values in 1984 and 1985. In Hong Kong they were over 20 percent lower. Only in Singapore and Malaysia is the trend sharply upwards, with a rise of 40–50 percent in just four years" (World Bank 1989, vol. I, p. 11 and table 2.6).[9]

Another point is that labor costs are only part of total costs, with the share of wages in value added in manufacturing being some 31 percent during 1983–86 (Lucas and Verry 1989, p. 57). In the 1980s, tight monetary policy in Malaysia pushed up real borrowing costs: the real prime lending rate rose from 5.9 percent in 1983 to 7.1 percent in 1984 and to 12.3 percent by 1985. At the same time firms in the tradable sector had been severely rationed as concerned credit as progressively more credit was channeled to the construction sector (see Gan and Krause 1990, appendix A, for further details).

Thus, the entire package of fiscal, monetary, and exchange rate policies, acting together with labor market behavior, led to developments that culminated in the deep recession of 1985–86. Similarly, the simultaneous downward movement of interest rates, wage costs, and exchange rates, along with favorable movements in the world market, fueled the recovery.

---

9. The different exchange rate experiences in Korea and Malaysia arise because Korea has a closed capital account and effective central bank control over the nominal parity of the wan. With a floating exchange rate system like Malaysia, and the large inflow of capital, the only way to keep down the dollar costs of labor would be to depress wages.

Compared to the real exchange rate of over 30 percent and the drop in the base lending rate from a peak of 12.25 percent in 1984 to 7.0 percent in 1988, the drop in average earnings per worker was, indeed, marginal. The massive wage costs witnessed in Latin America did not occur, but clearly, unit labor costs fell as productivity increased faster. Second, and more important, the glut in the labor market changed the cost calculations for the employer as far as expanding employment was concerned. As a local economist wrote late in 1987:

> The burden of adjustment has fallen primarily on new entrants into the labor market or otherwise on those who have been unfortunate enough to lose their jobs, either through business failures or retrenchments. This is readily apparent from a comparison of salaries of existing and new employees. In fact, in the case of graduates, the difference in starting salaries now and before can be as much as 50 percent or even more. The difference is somewhat less in the case of non-graduates.

The Long-Run Aspects of Adjustment and Labor Markets

We turn now to a discussion of selected aspects of the longer-run problems of economic adjustment and the labor market problems associated with them.

The Initial Conditions and Objectives of Structural Adjustment

At the time the government initiated the new economic policy (NEP) in 1971, Malaysia's economy was still heavily dependent on agriculture. Over 50 percent of the labor force was engaged in agriculture, and agriculture produced 30 percent of the GDP. The manufacturing sector, though expanding, contributed only 13.4 percent of the GDP and employed just over 10 percent of the labor force.

The incidence of poverty was high—officially 49.3 percent in 1970—but in absolute terms the Malaysian poverty line might have been high by international standards. How could an economy whose relatively high per capita income put it in the middle income category and whose growth rate in the 1960s was a respectable 6 percent per annum have such a high incidence of poverty? Apart from a high population growth rate of 3 percent per annum, observers, including official planners, agreed that the economy contained large pockets of low-income populations. One such pocket could have been in the small-scale tertiary sector activities, which were an important source of employment. Another such pocket existed in agriculture because of its dualistic development. A large proportion of the work force was involved in cultivating smallholdings, either in paddy, in cash crops, or often in both. The estates, principally growing rubber and oil palm, produced a substantial proportion of the cash crops with a high land/labor ratio and employed hired labor. The problem of dualism was exacerbated by the racial concentration in economic activity. Malays dominated the low-income activities, such as paddy, smallholdings, and services. The Chinese were found in the more dynamic industrial and commercial sectors. Thus, the incidence of poverty was much higher among the Malays.

The NEP's objective was to bring about a restructuring of the economy with a view to reducing racial disparities in incomes, and, as a by-product, reduce the incidence of poverty, particularly among the Malays (see Government of Malaysia 1973, 1976). A selective list of the major policy instruments follows:

- price maintenance (at a level higher than world prices) and subsidies on inputs for paddy farmers;

- land development, which took the form of resettling Malay families in newly cleared land at government expense and setting them up as viable smallholders cultivating cash crops, particularly palm oil;

- massive expansion in education, especially at the postprimary level, accompanied by a rapid increase in employment in government services, for which the Malays were given preference;

- application of a racial quota on new employment in industry and commerce.

Clearly the NEP encouraged a massive restructuring of employment, and it was sustained in this effort by the very satisfactory rate of growth of the GDP maintained for the last two decades despite the fluctuations analyzed earlier. We shall now examine the long-term results of this restructuring as it affected the behavior of labor markets and the pattern of earnings.

The Aggregate Supply of and Demand for Labor

Table 11.3 summarizes the trends in the rates of growth of population, the labor force, and employment relative to GDP growth during the last three decades. The rate of growth of the labor force has been higher than the rate of growth of population throughout, partly because of a shift in the age structure toward the working age group, and partly because of an increase in participation rates, especially by women. In the 1960s, employment growth failed to keep up with the growth in the labor force so that unemployment increased in the latter half of the decade, peaking at nearly 10 percent by the end of the decade. The labor market picture was much better in the 1970s, when despite an accelerated growth in the labor force, the employment growth rate stayed ahead, responding to the higher GDP growth stimulated by the NEP in the first half of the decade and by the commodity boom in the second. The unemployment rate fell 5 to 6 percent by the end of the decade. The figures in table 11.3 for the 1980s reflect the short-run crisis and adjustment already discussed. By the second half of the 1980s, the employment rate was back to where it was at the end of the 1960s. As already mentioned, the apparent lack of sensitivity of the unemployment rate to the recovery of 1987–88 has raised the specter of a more long-term structural problem of unemployment in the labor market.

Table 11.3 Growth Rates of Population, the Labor Force, and Employment Relative to GDP in Malaysia, 1961–85
(percent per annum)

Category	1961–70	1971–75	1976–80	1980–85
GDP	5.3	7.3	8.5	4.5
Population	2.8	2.7	2.6	2.6
Labor force	3.1	3.6	3.5	2.8
Employment	2.8	4.6	3.7	2.8

Note: For years prior to 1980, the growth rate of GDP relates to all Malaysia, but the other statistics are for Peninsular Malaysia only.
Source: Until 1980, Wong (1983, table 10); 1980–85: Government of Malaysia data.

Trends in Employment and Earnings in the Formal and Informal Sectors

Real average earnings in manufacturing, after growing rather slowly in the first half of the 1970s, started to accelerate around 1977–78, and went on increasing through the 1980s despite slackening employment growth and rising unemployment. However, these wage data refer entirely to the formal sector. How do these wage movements compare with trends in earnings in the informal sector? We need to know if economic growth in Malaysia has been accompanied by a widening gap in earnings between the formal and the informal sector, thereby accentuating the economic dualism that the NEP was expected to correct. If the evidence suggests that no such disparity exists, this implies that the accelerating wage increase in the formal sector since the late 1970s is symptomatic of Malaysia's transition from a labor surplus to tighter labor market conditions, which the short-run downturn in employment in the 1980s did not affect significantly.

DEFINITIONS OF THE FORMAL AND INFORMAL SECTORS. The informal sector is generally defined to include the self-employed who are outside the wage system, but should exclude those self-employed who work in professions with entry restrictions such as lawyers, doctors, and so on (see Mazumdar 1989, chapter 3, for an extensive discussion of the problems of defining and measuring the informal sector). Generally, a reasonable way to exclude the professionals is to apply an educational cut-off to the self-employed. A further problem is the distinction between self-employed and own-account workers. In the terminology followed in this chapter, the self-employed group includes employers, that is, the owners of small businesses who might also work in their establishments. Their earnings are a mixture of wages, profits, and rents. Own-account workers are paid family or autonomous workers and have no wage earners working for them.

The informal sector should also include small firms employing wage labor that are outside the legal and institutional framework covering larger firms, and that use methods of structuring and deploying labor that are less bureaucratic, and hence more susceptible to the free play of forces of supply and demand. Although arbitrary to some extent, researchers could usefully differentiate between the small and large sectors of a particular economy given sufficient information. Unfortunately, the statistical data collected in Malaysia do not permit this separation for wage employment.

However, a large proportion of the wage earners in Malaysia's small-scale sector are employed in the tertiary sector, which has expanded very fast. Thus, this section will examine the trends in earnings differences between the tertiary and other sectors to establish whether or not there is evidence of pockets of low-income labor developing in the tertiary sector.

TRENDS IN THE DISTRIBUTION OF THE WORK FORCE BY MODE OF EMPLOYMENT. In common with most other developing economies, wage employment in Malaysia has been growing relative to the number of self-employed and own-account workers. However, this growth seems to have taken place only since 1975. Wong's data (Wong 1985, table 12) show that the proportion of employees in total employment in Peninsular Malaysia was about the same in 1975 as in 1957, hovering round 58 percent. Table 11.4 provides data from the labor force survey for more recent years. The table shows that the wage workers' share of employment increased significantly between 1975 and 1984, about 10 percent, but that the recession checked this trend. Between 1984 and 1987, the share of employees in the total actually fell by about 3 percent.

When the information in table 11.4 is broken down by sector (not shown), the resilience of the self-employed in the agricultural sector stands out. Unlike in many developing economies, economic growth has

Table 11.4 Distribution of Employed Labor Force in Peninsular Malaysia by Employment Status, Selected Years
(percent)

Employment status	1975	1980	1984	1987
Employer	2.46	2.74	2.66	2.96
Employee	57.98	64.66	68.57	65.63
Own-account worker	24.50	21.48	19.79	20.72
Unpaid family worker	15.05	11.12	8.98	10.68

Source: Malaysian labor force survey.

not led to a transformation of agriculture from a family-based to a commercial wage economy. Although such a trend is apparent in particular regions, notably the Muda region, the region is not large enough to affect trends in Malaysia's agricultural sector as a whole. Also the major growth in agricultural output has come from the cash crop sector, where the proportion of wage workers in the total employed is much higher than in the food subsector. However, for several reasons, including the land development efforts of agencies like FELDA, this proportion has been declining in the last two decades at a significant rate (see Wong 1985, table 13).

A second point of interest in the Malaysian case is that the proportion of nonwage workers in manufacturing is relatively small compared to many other developing countries. Further, this proportion has been declining over time: when wage workers reached their peak in 1984, the self-employed made up barely 12 percent of the manufacturing work force. Thus, the data imply that the informal manufacturing sector is relatively unimportant.

Outside agriculture, the self-employed are important only in "distribution," but here too they were losing ground between 1975 and 1984. Nevertheless, they continued to account for just under half of the work force in the distributive trades.

TRENDS IN THE DISTRIBUTION OF THE WORK FORCE BY INDUSTRY. Through the 1970s, the share of agriculture in total employment declined fairly continuously. The decline was arrested in the more difficult years of the 1980s as far as the noncash crop sector was concerned, but continued at much the same rate in the rubber, palm oil, and coconut subsectors. Both manufacturing and the tertiary sectors absorbed labor released by industry, but after 1980 the share of manufacturing stabilized, as did employment in government services. The private tertiary sector thus grew at the expense of the declining cash crop sector in the years leading to and during the recession.

Table 11.5 gives a better idea of where the growing labor force went. During the first period of rapid growth, 1970–80, agriculture created very few additional jobs. The manufacturing and the tertiary sectors had to absorb the bulk of the increase in the labor force. The data show that manufacturing played a leading role in providing new jobs to the tune

Table 11.5 Marginal Changes in Employment by Sector in Peninsular
Malaysia, Selected Periods
(percentage of total change)

Sector	1970–80	1980-87	1980–84	1984–87
1. Agriculture, hunting, forestry, fishing	6.2	-0.4	-19.9	32.1
2. Mining, quarrying	-0.9	-1.4	-0.4	-3.1
3. Manufacturing	28.9	16.4	16.0	17.1
4. Electricity, gas, water	1.6	-1.8	-3.4	0.9
5. Construction	10.5	6.2	24.3	-24.1
6. Wholesale/retail trade, restaurants, hotels	} 35.1[a]	30.6	27.4	36.2
7. Financing, insurance, real estate, business services		7.1	5.2	10.2
8. Transport, storage, communication	5.1	3.9	5.7	0.8
9. Community, social, and personal services	13.5	39.4	45.0	29.9
Total	100.0	100.0	100.0	100.0

n.a. = not available
Note: The major discrepancy between 1970 census data and 1980 survey data is the increase in the agricultural labor force. The comparison between 1975 and 1980 gives a slight decrease.
a. Sectors 6 and 7 combined.
Source: 1970 census; Malaysian labor surveys.

of nearly 30 percent of the total increase. Nearly half of the new labor force was absorbed in the private tertiary sector, in which distributive and business services dominated, but construction also played a role. The category "community, social, and personal services" includes both public (government) and private employment. It is sure that its importance in incremental employment is relatively small.

Rather dramatic changes are seen in the second period, 1980–87, which consists of two distinct subperiods in terms of Malaysia's economic cycle. The first, 1980–84, was the period leading to the crisis in which government spending slowed down, but the boom was kept going by the upswing in the private sector, based largely on construction. The second subperiod, 1984–87, was the years of recession. Taking the two subperiods together, the leading role of manufacturing and government in labor absorption falls significantly. Thus, the private tertiary sector was called upon to absorb no less than 72 percent of the increase in new employment during this period as a whole, compared to less than 50 percent in the 1970s. A significant aspect of the changed role of the private tertiary sector was the importance of the private services subsector in the 1980s. We have already drawn attention to the remarkable fact that private services actually lost labor absolutely in the 1970s. However, in both the 1980s subperiods this sector provided more than a quarter of the new jobs.

The recession after 1984 did not help employment in manufacturing to pick up much. The government continued to increase its work force, but at an even lower rate than in the earlier subperiod. At the same time, employment in construction fell precipitously. The lack of employment opportunities in the hitherto booming sectors led to an increase in the rate of unemployment, but table 11.5 reveals another striking aspect of adjustment in the labor market. Employment in agriculture, which had been decreasing at a slow rate in the 1970s and much faster during 1980–84, reversed its trend rather dramatically. New employment in agriculture in the recession years of 1984–87 was nearly a third of the total increase.

DIFFERENCES IN AVERAGE EARNINGS BY INDUSTRY AND MODE OF EMPLOYMENT. Table 11.6 gives the means and first quartile values of the earnings of different groups of workers, with each value expressed relative to the earnings of paddy own-account workers, which are set at 100.

PADDY AND OTHER SECTORS. The first point that stands out from table 11.6 is the substantial increase in the difference between mean incomes of paddy cultivators, on the one hand, and workers in most other sectors on the other. However, while this is true of mean incomes at the different dates, the first quartile value of earnings does not seem to have increased in other sectors relative to paddy, with the exception of own-account workers in smallholdings. What this means is that the earnings distribution in the paddy sector in 1973 was flatter than in the other sectors, so that the difference in first quartile earnings was larger than the difference in means, but in the 1980s, the earnings distribution in paddy became as skewed to the right as in the other sectors.

Table 11.6 Relative Mean and First Quartile Earnings by Usual Employment Status for Males in Peninsular Malaysia for 1973, 1984, and 1987 *(paddy = 100)*

Usual employment status	1973 Mean	1973 First quartile	1984 Mean	1984 First quartile	1987 Mean	1987 First quartile
Rural sector						
Paddy, own-account	100	100	100	100	100	100
Smallholdings, own-account	87	98	168	149	141	155
Estates, employees	119	194	214	191	158	195
Production, employees	132	202	190	224	184	216
Production, own-account	114	141	189	216	227	208
Sales, employees	174	304	208	281	226	271
Services, own-account	196	180	277	255	257	249
Urban sector						
Production, employees	148	247	211	272	215	240
Production, own-account	147	196	226	269	213	245
Production, self-employed	181	206	270	287	258	277
Sales, employees	217	210	230	283	273	233
Sales, own-account	214	271	329	315	273	283
Sales, self-employed	311	314	400	359	320	311
Services, employees	186	239	319	280	241	290
Services, own-account	157	245	335	345	284	280
Services, self-employed	273	275	404	383	370	335

Notes: The self-employed include employers and own-account workers.
Sources: The Malaysian 1987 household income survey and the 1973 household expenditure survey.

The Malaysian paddy sector has traditionally been a pocket of low incomes, and in the 1970s was identified as one of the target groups for poverty reduction. Despite the price support policies mentioned earlier, labor that has remained in this sector has continued to fall behind incomes in other sectors.[10] This has occurred despite the fact that the proportion of the labor force engaged in this sector was halved between 1970 and 1987.

PADDY AND THE CASH CROP SECTOR. Another striking point is the relative improvement in earnings in the cash crop subsector of Malaysian agriculture relative to paddy, both for own-account smallholders and employees on estates. Between 1973 and 1984, mean earnings for both the latter groups increased substantially relative to those of paddy farmers. They fell back somewhat during the downswing of the 1980s, but in 1987 were well above the relative levels of 1973. The point made earlier about the differentials in first quartile earnings holds for estate employees as compared to paddy farmers, but not for smallholders. Evidently, productivity in the cash crop sector responded more positively to the package of policies to help this sector (including land development) than those aimed at paddy farmers.

THE AGRICULTURAL-NONAGRICULTURAL DIFFERENCE. Table 11.6 suggests that the strong economic growth between 1973 and 1984 reduced the differential between mean earnings in nonagriculture and the earnings of both smallholders and estate laborers. However, the impact of the downswing on earnings of the cash crop sector in agriculture was larger than that of the nonagricultural sector, so that in 1987, earnings differentials between the two were back to the same level as in 1973.

THE DIFFERENCE IN EARNINGS BETWEEN THE TERTIARY AND PRODUCTION SECTORS IN NONAGRICULTURE. As we have seen, Malaysia has depended a great deal on the tertiary sector to absorb its growing labor force. In the 1970s, government services played a significant role in providing new jobs, but in the 1980s, the burden shifted more to the private tertiary sector. In 1987, the tertiary sector as a whole—public and private together— accounted for one-half of total employment in Malaysia.

An important question to ask is whether this shift to a service economy in Malaysia has meant that large numbers of people are

---

10. Bhalla's data (Bhalla 1989, table 6.4) suggest that the incomes of paddy farmers have improved in absolute terms, but the incidence of absolute poverty in 1987 was still high at 57 percent, having fallen from 88 percent in 1970.

employed at relatively low incomes in the nonproduction sectors. The figures of earnings for male workers given in table 11.6 do not suggest that this has been the case. There is no evidence of any significant trend in the differential in the 15-year period to 1987. In the service sector earnings seem to have increased relative to production during the upswing of the early 1980s and fallen during the downswing ending in 1987; but even at the end of the period, mean earnings in services, as in sales, were significantly higher than in the corresponding groups in production compared to 1973.

Some economists argue that the earnings distribution in the tertiary sector is markedly skewed to the right, so the high earnings of a minority pull up the mean. Table 11.6 includes the first quartile differentials to take care of this point. We see that generally for all the years the difference in first quartile earnings between tertiary sector workers and production workers is smaller than the difference in means. This supports the hypothesis that the earnings distribution in the tertiary sectors is more skewed to the right than that in production. But, with the possible exception of employees in the sales sector, the value of first quartile earnings in the tertiary groups was higher than in production, and the differentials in first quartile earnings, if anything, increased over time in favor of the tertiary groups.

The skill level of workers will affect their earnings, thus ideally, a comparison of earnings across occupational groups should control for skill differences. One way to deal with this problem is to use the standard human capital model of earnings, which assumes that the major determinants of earnings are education and experience. Anand (1983) estimated a large number of earnings functions for different groups of urban employees in a large data set (Post-Enumeration Survey) for 1970 (table 11.7). We have estimated similar functions from the household income survey data sets of 1984 and 1987. The analysis is confined to male workers.

Table 11.7 presents the results of the estimated equations for the three sectors in which blue collar workers are found, namely, production, sales, and services.[11] The pattern of the coefficients of the equation are

---

11. Note that a large number of workers in government services are excluded as they are likely to be in the clerical or administrative occupational categories.

Table 11.7 Coefficients of the Human Capital Model, Males, 1970, 1984, 1987

Year/occupation	Intercept	S	T	T^2	R^2
1970					
Production	5.74	0.08	0.10	-0.0014	0.40
Services	5.35	0.13	0.11	-0.0014	0.32
Sales	5.21	0.12	0.12	-0.0017	0.47
1984					
Production	7.19	0.07	0.09	-0.001	0.12
Services	6.97	0.09	0.09	-0.001	0.09
Sales	6.36	0.15	0.11	-0.001	0.16
1987					
Production	6.70	0.09	0.10	-0.001	0.20
Services	6.58	0.12	0.10	-0.001	0.07
Sales	6.42	0.13	0.10	-0.001	0.21

S = years of schooling, T = years of experience
Note: All the variables are highly significant.
Sources: 1970: Anand (1983); 1984 and 1987: estimated from HIS data.

strikingly similar in the three years, though the value of R^2 seems to have been reduced drastically in the 1980s. The clear result is that although earnings of raw labor (with no schooling and no experience) are lower in sales and services than in production, the higher coefficients of experience in the tertiary sectors ensure that the differential is reduced, if not eliminated, for some education and experience. This is seen in the figures of predicted earnings given in table 11.8 for two types of labor. Furthermore, the important conclusion emerges that there is no evidence for earnings in the tertiary sectors to fall further below the earnings in production in later years as labor was reallocated more toward the sales and services categories.

Table 11.8 Predicted Relative Earnings for Male Urban Employees in 1970, 1984, 1987
(production workers = 100)

Occupation	Labor with S = 0, T = 0			Labor with S = 6, T = 10		
	1970	*1984*	*1987*	*1970*	*1984*	*1987*
Production	100	100	100	100	100	100
Services	68	80	89	92	91	106
Sales	59	44	76	76	86	117

Source: Calculated from the coefficients in table 11.7.

THE DIFFERENCE IN EARNINGS BETWEEN THE FORMAL AND INFORMAL SECTORS. We now compare labor in the formal sector (defined as employees) with labor in the informal sector (the self-employed who include own-account workers as well as employers).

THE DIFFERENCE IN AGE PROFILES. The literature of the developing countries generally hypothesizes that the informal sector is the depository of low-income workers, partly because it contains a disproportionate number of nonprime age and poorly educated workers. In the Malaysian case we have already noted that this stereotype does not fit the picture very well as far as age is concerned. Blau (1986) produced longitudinal evidence from the Malaysian family life survey carried out in Peninsular Malaysia in 1976–77 to show that for males, both in urban and rural areas, the proportion working as employees fell with age, and the proportion in self-employment increased. The household income surveys do not provide the longitudinal experience of workers, but we can use cross-sectional data to throw some light on this issue. Figure 11.9 gives the age distributions of the three categories of workers, employees, self-employed, and family workers, by sex and rural-urban location. Blau's (1986) point is confirmed for the 1980s. The self-employed are—

Figure 11.9 Distribution of Workers by Age Group in Different Modes of Employment, 1984

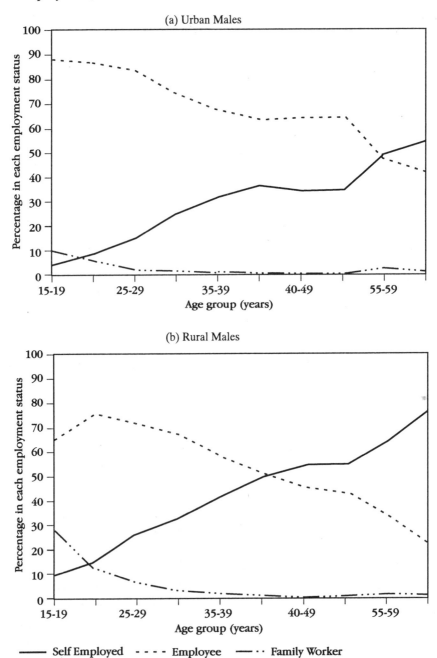

(a) Urban Males

(b) Rural Males

——— Self Employed   - - - - Employee   —— · · Family Worker

Figure 11.9 (continued)

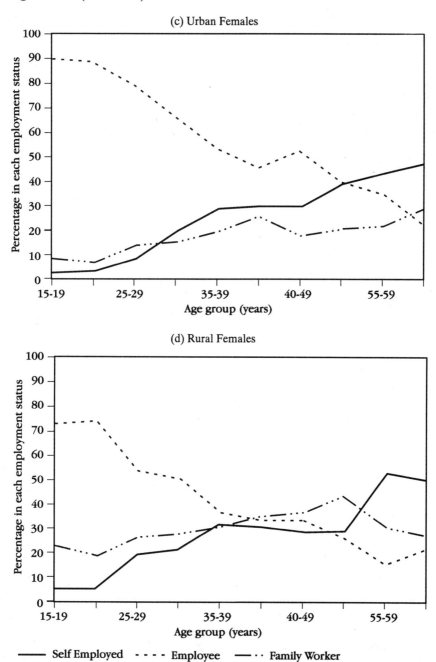

(c) Urban Females

(d) Rural Females

——— Self Employed   - - - - Employee   ——·· Family Worker

contrary to the popular hypothesis—a rising proportion of the work force at successively higher age groups.[12]

DIFFERENCES IN OTHER CHARACTERISTICS. Table 11.9 shows the distribution of employees and the self-employed by various characteristics for 1984 for both sexes. Apart from the marked difference in age profiles already

Table 11.9 Proportions of Employees and Self-Employed in Various Categories, 1984
(total for each category = 1.00)

	Males		Females	
Category	Employees	Self-employed	Employees	Self-Employed
Age				
15–19	0.09	0.02	0.10	0.01
20–24	0.19	0.05	0.27	0.06
25–29	0.20	0.10	0.23	0.10
30–39	0.28	0.30	0.24	0.30
40–49	0.16	0.28	0.12	0.29
50+	0.08	0.25	0.04	0.24
Education				
No schooling	0.05	0.14	0.09	0.37
Completed primary	0.54	0.72	0.41	0.55
LCE or equivalent	0.13	0.07	0.12	0.03
MCE or equivalent	0.20	0.06	0.30	0.04
HSC or equivalent	0.02	0.00	0.02	0.01
College diploma	0.02	0.00	0.04	0.00
University degree	0.04	0.01	0.02	0.00
Race				
Malay	0.44	0.46	0.40	0.66
Chinese	0.39	0.45	0.43	0.37
Indian	0.17	0.09	0.17	0.07
Sector				
Rural	0.30	0.48	0.25	0.49
Urban	0.70	0.52	0.75	0.51

Note: LCE, MCE, and HSC represent the certificates of completion of lower, middle, and high secondary schools, respectively.

12. Note, however, that this cross-sectional picture may be due partly to the shift from employee to self-employed status with age, and partly because the number of employees has been expanding faster than the number of self-employed over time.

noted, very large differences are seen in educational attainment. Only a very small proportion of the self-employed have an education beyond the primary level, and of the females a significant proportion have no schooling—in sharp contrast to the employees. Significant racial difference exists for the females: more of the self-employed are Malays. As expected, while the majority of employees are in the urban sector, the self-employed are equally divided between rural and urban areas.

EARNINGS. We attempt to estimate earnings functions separately for the self-employed and the employees for all three dates. When the whole sample of individual observations is partitioned like this between two groups, the OLS regression estimates of the determinants of earnings will be biased. We examined estimates from a model that permits some selectivity bias. The coefficients of the regressors in the OLS estimates in tables 11.10 and 11.11 are generally very different from those in the models allowing for selectivity bias. But for our present purposes, we want to look at what the pattern of earnings has been for different groups with different modes of employment rather than the expected level of earnings if someone were to relocate from one mode to another. The relevant equations for this are the OLS equations of tables 11.10 and 11.11.

The OLS regressions are used to "predict" the earnings of employees and the self-employed for 1973, 1984, and 1987. Table 11.12 provides three sets of estimates. The first line gives the employee/self-employed earnings difference on the basis of the characteristics actually observed for the two categories of labor at the relevant dates. The next two lines give the hypothetical earnings differences on the assumption that both groups had identical characteristics, first, those shared by employees, and second, those shared by the self-employed. These hypothetical estimates are meant to assess the extent of the earnings difference due to the two groups' different characteristics. The table shows that in most cases the differential is drastically reduced, and sometimes even reversed in favor of the self-employed, when we control for the difference in characteristics.

The differential in favor of the employees is generally much larger for the females. The important point to note for our present purposes is that the trends in the differentials over time are different for the two sexes. As

Table 11.10 Regression Analysis of Male Individual Earnings: Employees and Self-Employed Workers, 1973, 1984, 1987 *(dependent variable: logarithm of total earnings)*

	1973		1984		1987	
Characteristic	Employee	Self-employed	Employee	Self-employed	Employee	Self-employed
Intercept	3.515	2.932	7.175	7.391	7.046	6.945
Age (base = 15–19)						
20–24	0.526	0.668	0.545	0.033	0.578	0.568
25–29	0.876	1.224	0.891	0.362	1.033	0.952
30–39	1.151	1.376	1.180	0.608	1.324	1.139
40–49	1.328	1.531	1.286	0.676	1.445	1.248
50+	1.023	1.233	1.151	0.564	1.368	1.084
Education						
(base = no schooling)						
Completed primary	0.489	0.378	0.277	0.357	0.283	0.249
LCE or equivalent	0.857	0.726	0.483	0.568	0.515	0.451
MCE or equivalent	1.354	0.876	0.791	0.859	0.771	0.602
HSC or equivalent	1.606	0.897	1.095	1.380	0.966	0.710
College diploma	1.857	0.898	1.229	1.145	1.153	0.898
University degree	2.387	2.112	1.728	1.736	1.705	1.409
Race (base = Malay)						
Chinese	0.188	0.807	0.249	0.547	0.183	0.605
Indian	0.065	0.292	0.025	0.158	0.013	0.257
Urban (base = rural)	0.183	0.243	0.164	0.342	0.140	0.137
Number of observations	4,703	2,769	9,616	3,174	9,300	3,535
R^2	0.456	0.307	0.477	0.306	0.472	0.293

Notes: All the coefficients are highly significant.
Sources: Malaysian expenditure survey 1973; Malaysian household survey 1984 and 1987.

far as male workers are concerned, the self-employed increased their earnings relative to employees not only in the boom period ending in 1984, but probably also during the recession of 1984–87. This result is consistent with our earlier finding that male employees in the tertiary sector did not lag behind in earnings relative to earnings in the production sector.

Table 11.11 Regression Analysis of Female Individual Earnings: Employees and Self-Employed Workers, 1973, 1984, 1987 (*dependent variable: logarithm of total earnings*)

Characteristic	1973 Employee	1973 Self-employed	1984 Employee	1984 Self-employed	1987 Employee	1987 Self-employed
Intercept	3.539	2.670	6.828	6.540	6.717	6.835
Age (base = 15–19)						
20–24	0.141	0.332	0.442	0.580	0.443	0.079
25–29	0.383	0.378	0.735	0.665	0.787	0.158
30–39	0.530	0.780	0.854	0.707	0.945	0.346
40–49	0.540	1.086	0.870	0.811	1.005	0.664
50+	0.293	0.900	0.856	0.724	0.967	0.597
Education (base = no schooling)						
Completed primary	0.288	0.278	0.392	0.108	0.422	0.041
LCE or equivalent	0.926	0.854	0.483	0.073	0.769	0.155
MCE or equivalent	1.469	0.813	1.020	0.682	1.056	0.600
HSC or equivalent	1.621	- - -	1.151	1.025	1.202	0.845
College diploma	2.042	1.749	1.586	- - -	1.599	-0.269
University degree	2.576	1.812	1.972	1.032	2.009	1.719
Race (base = Malay)						
Chinese	0.360	0.951	0.151	0.566	0.164	0.641
Indian	0.400	0.226	0.027	0.143	0.012	0.128
Urban (base = rural)	0.070	0.037	0.203	0.238	0.132	0.128
Number of observations	2,275	1,076	4,907	941	5,020	1,042
R^2	0.392	0.225	0.393	0.134	0.373	0.151

Note: All the coefficients are highly significant except those marked with dotted lines.
Sources: Malaysian expenditure survey 1973; Malaysian household survey 1984 and 1987.

The behavior of the female labor market has been quite different. Even though employees earned considerably more than self-employed women in 1973 (even though a substantial part of this difference could be attributed to differences in characteristics), the differential increased significantly during the boom ending in 1984. Thus, the popular expectation that pockets of labor in the informal sector do not share in the upsurge of earnings in the formal sector is borne out for the female labor market. Equally interesting is the phenomenon revealed by the data in table 11.12 that female employees lost relative to the self-employed during the economy's downswing.

This cyclical behavior of the earnings differential may be due to institutional factors operating in the wage labor market, but if it were so, the institutional influences, working to establish a premium for employees, seem to be highly responsive to economic conditions. However, the observed cycle is consistent with a purely economic hypothesis that the supply of female labor to the informal (self-employed) sector is much more elastic than the supply to the formal sector.

Table 11.12 Predicted Incomes for Males and Females, Employees Relative to Self-Employed (=1)

Category	*Males*			*Females*		
	1973	*1984*	*1987*	*1973*	*1984*	*1987*
With own characteristics	1.58	1.03	1.01	2.04	2.37	1.90
With characteristics of employees	1.11	1.00	0.82	1.11	1.63	1.28
With characteristics of self-employed	1.12	0.89	1.07	1.20	1.48	1.08

Source: Calculated from estimated regression coefficients given in tables 11.10 and 11.11 and using the mean values of the explanatory variables in the equations for each year.

Educational Expansion and Change in the Occupational Structure

As indicated earlier, the Malaysian authorities pushed forward with a policy of educational expansion, with one of its objects being to reduce the racial imbalance between Malays and Chinese in educational attainment. By 1984 this had generally been achieved.

The expansion of education in Malaysia has been very rapid. Wong (1985) noted that "the proportion of the labor force with no schooling was reduced by two-thirds (from 43 percent in 1962 to 15 percent in 1979) while the proportion with secondary education and above tripled (from 13 percent to 39 percent)." Note that Wong's figures on the proportion with secondary education are clearly based on the years of schooling recorded, and would thus include drop-outs from the secondary schools.

The structure of demand for labor has changed over time to accommodate the changing skill composition of the work force. As table 11.13 shows, the occupational distribution of the employed has changed significantly over time, with the white collar proportion nearly tripling between 1957 and 1984 until the recession stopped the continuous increase. The question arises whether this upgrading of the labor force proceeded smoothly without creating adjustment problems in the labor market.

Let us first consider the rate of return to education. The gross rates are found from the coefficients of schooling in the basic human capital model reported in table 11.14. As the table shows, despite the expansion in education, the gross rates did not decline in the 1980s compared to 1970. On the contrary, they seem to have increased somewhat, particularly for the Malays, and were higher in 1987 after the downswing than in 1984. Remember, however, that the gross rates do not take account of unemployment or of wages in the length of time taken to find the first job. Nevertheless, the generally higher coefficients of schooling for those who were in wage employment in the 1980s, after more than two decades of expansion in education, is an important point.

The simple human capital earnings function of the type represented in table 11.14 does not take account of another significant issue: differential returns to education at different levels. Earnings functions were estimated for male workers for 1984 and 1987 from the survey data of the

Table 11.13 Employment Trends in Peninsular Malaysia by Occupation *(percent)*

Occupation	1957	1975	1980	1984	1987
Professional	3.10	5.52	6.85	7.58	7.88
Administrative	1.20	1.30	1.90	2.19	2.10
Clerical workers	2.90	7.10	8.46	10.21	9.92
Sales workers	8.60	10.36	10.42	11.38	12.65
Service workers	8.60	8.16	9.42	12.05	12.37
Agricultural workers	56.21	41.86	32.85	26.61	26.94
Production workers	18.90	25.69	30.10	29.99	28.15

Source: Malaysian labor force survey.

Table 11.14 Estimates of the Basic Human Capital Model: Peninsular Malaysia, Urban Males, All Occupations, 1970, 1984, and 1987

Race and year	Constant	Years of schooling	E	E^2	R^2
Malays					
1970	5.42	0.14	0.09	-0.001	0.45
1984	6.20	0.16	0.10	-0.001	0.45
1987	5.93	0.17	0.11	-0.001	0.44
Chinese					
1970	5.32	0.14	0.11	-0.001	0.52
1984	6.66	0.14	0.10	-0.001	0.62
1987	6.34	0.15	0.10	-0.001	0.44
All					
1970	5.42	0.14	0.10	-0.001	0.49
1984	6.51	0.14	0.10	-0.001	0.41
1987	6.21	0.16	0.10	-0.001	0.44

E = years of experience (age minus 6)
Sources: 1970: Anand (1983, table 7.1); 1984, 1987: estimated from the household income surveys data.

household income surveys, which replicated as closely as possible the functions Mazumdar estimated from the PES data for 1970 (Mazumdar 1981, table 8-2). The incremental rates of return for different levels of education are derived from the estimated equations by calculating the differences in the coefficients of the dummies for successive levels of education. They are set out for the years 1970, 1984, and 1987 in table 11.15. Three main points emerge.

1. A major change has occurred at the bottom end of the educational spectrum, with the incremental return to some primary schooling (relative to no schooling) falling drastically in the 1980s, compared to 1970. At the other end of the spectrum, the returns to a high school certificate and tertiary education went up sharply, even though the recession of the mid-1980s reduced the returns somewhat between 1984 and 1987. This finding is consistent with the nature of the upswing, in which public sector job creation played a leading role. Rates of return to completed lower and middle secondary education fell over time, but only slightly.

Table 11.15 Incremental Returns to Education, Urban Male Employees and Self-Employed, 1970, 1984, and 1987

Education Level	1970	1984	1987
Some primary	0.33	0.16	0.16
Completed primary	0.18	0.13	0.18
Forms I to III, no certificate	0.08	0.04	0.11
LCE or equivalent	0.17	0.13	0.10
Forms IV and V, no certificate	0.14	0.00	0.02
MCE or equivalent	0.33	0.30	0.25
Form VI, no certificate	0.18	-0.12	-0.01
HSC or higher	0.44	0.76	0.58

Sources: 1970: calculated from Mazumdar (1981, table 8-2); 1984 and 1987: calculated from estimated equations.

2. Mazumdar (1981) observed that the 1970 data showed evidence of strong increasing returns to education at levels higher than lower secondary. This phenomenon was accentuated in the 1980s.

3. Mazumdar also drew attention to the importance of "credentialism" in the labor market for the educated in Malaysia: at a particular level, the incremental returns to having a certificate are much higher. During 1970–87, this became more pronounced. Note the striking case of those with a form VI education having lower earnings than the completed middle secondary certificate holders, both in 1984 and 1987.

The last two points suggest the existence of significant elements of "administered prices" in the Malaysian labor market. Imbalances between the supply of and the demand for labor would, in this case, result in quantity rather than price adjustments. Thus, the next section examines unemployment.

Unemployment: Trends and Causes

In the 1960s and 1970s, Malaysia suffered from a serious unemployment problem. A study by Mazumdar (1981) indicated that the cause was a supply/demand imbalance in the market for educated labor. Between 1957 and 1967, the rate of growth of unemployment was several times higher than the growth rate of the labor force with post-primary education. The unemployment rate was highest for young first entrants with 7 to 9 years (lower secondary) and 10 to 11 years (middle secondary) of education (Mazumdar 1981, figure 14-1, table 14–8). The imbalance was caused by a growth rate of secondary school leavers well in excess of the growth rate of low-grade white collar occupations to which they aspired, together with sluggish change in their occupational preferences.

Although the Department of Statistics and the Economic Planning Unit (using data from the Treasury) come up with different estimates of the unemployment rate, the broad trends in the rate during the last two decades are clear. Throughout the 1970s, the population grew at about 2.6 percent per annum. The labor force grew at a much higher rate, partly because a higher proportion of the population was in the working age group, and partly because of higher participation rates by women.

Nevertheless, employment grew at an even higher rate, estimated at 3.7 percent per annum. Unemployment fell from some 8 percent to 5 percent through the decade.

As discussed earlier, the boom came to an end with the fall in commodity prices in the early 1980s. Increased government deficit spending and foreign borrowing sustained the GDP growth rate for a while, but employment growth decelerated significantly, falling to at least one-third of its 1970s level. The unemployment rate started to increase after 1982, reaching the 1970 level by 1985. It continued to increase through the depression year of 1986, and fell only slightly, if at all, through the recovery years of 1987, 1988, and 1989.

UNEMPLOYMENT AND AGGREGATE DEMAND. During the upturn of the unemployment rate, Malaysian officials debated the desirability of re-inflating the economy to solve the unemployment problem. However, the consensus among both Malaysian policymakers and the economic staff of international agencies like the World Bank was that a purely Keynesian approach to the unemployment problem was inappropriate. Unemployment could not be related in a simple way to the level of aggregate demand. Substantial evidence pointed to the reemergence of the problem of structural unemployment, which had occurred in the early 1970s.

Figure 11.10 suggested that the link between unemployment and aggregate demand is tenuous. The figure shows no simple relationship between the unemployment rate and the GDP growth rate. In particular, unemployment began to rise well before the downturn in GDP growth in 1985, and increased significantly in 1983 and 1984, when the growth rate of GDP also increased. More recently, the unemployment rate has shown resistance to decline despite the recovery and the strong increase in GDP of 5.2 percent in 1987 and 7.4 percent in 1988 (in real terms).

The slackening of the labor market in several years of the 1980s even though GDP growth was strong suggests that the structure of demand for labor had altered in a way that was less favorable to absorption of labor. The problems would generally arise both on the demand and supply side of the labor market. The need for structural adjustment in a changed external environment alters the composition of demand. Because of rigidities in the labor market, the supply of labor adjusts only slowly to the shifting demand, so that unemployment increases rather more than is warranted by the slowdown in GDP growth.

NATURE OF THE UNEMPLOYED. Malaysia's unemployed are concentrated in the 15 to 19 and 20 to 24 age groups, are mostly first time job seekers, and a disproportionate number of them are secondary school leavers. During the recession, the proportion of the unemployed who were older than 25 increased significantly, from 23 percent in 1982 to 32 percent in 1986 (World Bank 1989, table 33).

Figure 11.10 Actual Unemployment Rates and Real GDP Growth Rates, 1967–87

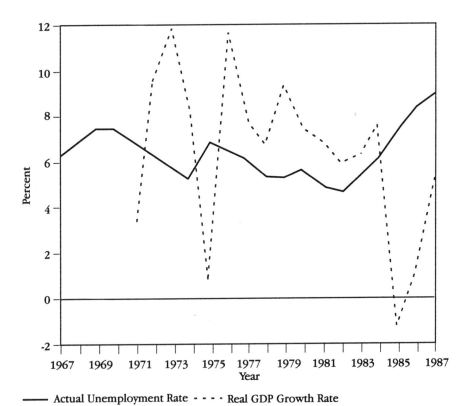

Sources: Reproduced from Salih and Young (1989).

Table 11.16 Total Employment by Age and Education for Males and
Females, Peninsular Malaysia, 1975 and 1987

		Percentage of total employed			
		Males		Females	
Age group	Education (years)	1975	1987	1975	1987
15–19	0				
	1–6	13.9	4.6	13.1	5.4
	7–9	15.6	14.5	14.9	13.9
	10–11	11.8	10.0	15.3	16.4
	12–13	—	—	—	—
	14+	—	—	—	—
20–24	0	—	—	1.8	—
	1–6	8.2	4.6	9.8	3.1
	7–9	9.9	11.2	10.0	7.8
	10–11	9.0	12.5	12.2	20.3
	12–13	2.4	3.1	1.2	7.4
	14+	—	2.2	—	3.2
Total		70.6	62.7	78.3	77.5

Dashes indicate no observation.
Source: Malaysian labor force survey.

Table 11.16 shows the distribution of the unemployed by age and
education for young job seekers for two years—1975 and 1987. Three
important changes are noticeable between the two dates:

1. For both sexes and for both age groups the proportion of the
   unemployed with primary education or less declined substantially.
   This partly reflects the withdrawal of young people from the labor
   force due to the spread of education.
2. The proportion of those with lower secondary education (seven to
   nine years of schooling) declined slightly, particularly for females.
3. The decline in the proportion of those with a lower secondary
   education is offset by a big jump in the percentage of the
   unemployed with middle and higher secondary education and with

post-secondary education. This is true of both sexes in the 20 to 24 age group, but is more marked for females. Females ages 20 to 24 and with more than a lower secondary education now account for nearly a third of the total females unemployed.

THE PROBABILITY OF UNEMPLOYMENT: A MULTIVARIATE ANALYSIS. Table 11.17 shows the results of a profit analysis for the determinants of unemployment for the 1987 sample. The rate of unemployment decreases significantly for both males and females for age groups older than 25. The coefficients are large, confirming the importance of youth unemployment.

The profit analysis brings out clearly the important point that, holding age and other factors constant, education is positively related to the rate of unemployment, but that there is an important difference between males and females. For males the rate of unemployment begins to increase only with the middle secondary certificate, and increases strongly only for upper secondary and college certificates. By contrast, the female unemployment rate increases strongly and monotonically from the level of lower secondary education and all the way to college education. The (positive) coefficients of the successive levels of education are large and increasing, and are all significant. Note also that the coefficients are much larger for females. The important conclusion emerges that the education-unemployment link is stronger and quantitatively much more significant for females.

Another important result is the highly significant negative coefficient of YCAP (the household income per capita). The small value of the coefficient should not mislead, since the variable is used as a continuous one, and only shows the decrease in the rate of unemployment with each ringgit increase in per capita income. The result has implications for the hypothesis of "voluntary unemployment," which has been advanced by some commentators, recently by the World Bank (1989). The clearest test of voluntary unemployment is that it is more important for higher income groups who can afford to wait for the right job to turn up. Our result would seem to negate this hypothesis. While unemployment in Malaysia increased with the level of education (more strongly for females), holding other factors constant, it decreases significantly as the income level of the family goes up.

Table 11.17 Probability of Unemployment, 1987

Variable	Males	Females
Constant	1–0.52	1–1.05
	(-6.25)	(-9.20)
Age (base = 15–24)		
25–34	-0.79	-0.80
	(-15.96)	(-12.06)
35–44	-0.97	-1.08
	(-15.77)	(-10.23)
45–54	-0.89	-1.00
	(-12.20)	(-7.29)
55–64	-0.76	-0.89
	(-7.62)	(-4.91)
Education (base = no certificate)		
Primary	-0.13	0.004
	(-1.89)	(0.04)
Lower secondary	-0.35	0.21
	(-0.50)	(2.03)
Middle secondary	0.08	0.37
	(1.10)	(3.63)
Upper secondary	0.27	0.63
	(2.15)	(4.56)
College	0.33	0.67
	(2.89)	(4.37)
Region (base = region 1)		
Region 2	0.009	0.16
	(0.20)	(2.51)
Region 3	0.041	0.21
	(0.69)	(2.66)
Race (base = Malay)		
Chinese	0.15	-0.17
	(3.13)	(-2.59)
Indian	0.08	-0.005
	(1.26)	(-0.06)
Sector (base = rural)		
Urban	0.22	0.089
	(4.95)	(1.56)
YCAP (household income per capita)	-0.00013	-0.00014
	(-10.30)	(-7.81)

Unfortunately, this result is not as unambiguous a test of voluntary unemployment as one would like it to be. One can always argue that the income per capita of families from which the unemployed come was relatively low because the unemployed were not voluntarily taking a job. However, when we added the potential income of the unemployed to the actual family income (using an earnings function and characteristics of the unemployed), the sign of the income variable in the profit model was reversed. Thus, we can only conclude that the positive association of unemployment with actual household income per capita (which a "strong" version of the voluntary unemployment hypothesis would suggest) is not observed.

As far as location of the unemployed is concerned, for both sexes the rate of unemployment is higher in the urban areas. Another interesting result is that, contrary to the Harris-Todaro type of hypothesis, the incidence of unemployment is not higher in the high income region (Region I). In fact, the unemployment rate for females is significantly higher in the poorer regions.

Apparently, despite the large-scale internal migration of females in recent years, a large proportion of young, educated, female job seekers continue to be "locked in" without employment in low-income labor markets.

Finally, there is an interesting difference between males and females as far as race is concerned. Other things being equal, the incidence of unemployment is higher among Chinese males (relative to Malays) but lower among Chinese females. The locked in female unemployed in poor regions could be expected to be disproportionately Malay.

CAUSES OF UNEMPLOYMENT. The review of the characteristics of the unemployed does not give a precise answer to the question how far is unemployment a structural rather than a demand-related phenomenon? The fact that unemployment increased during 1982–86 among the group that typically has a relatively lower incidence of unemployment, that is, males over 25, suggests that demand deflation had some part to play in the emergence of the problem. But as mentioned earlier, aggregate demand (represented by GDP growth) is not clearly related to the degree of slack in the labor market. A policy of demand expansion would not by itself create a significant dent in the unemployment rate, and may indeed create problems of inflationary pressure.

The fact that secondary school leavers constitute the largest part of the unemployed suggests a structural problem of absorbing the educated in the employed labor force. The problem of jobs for the more educated had clearly become worse in 1987, when we saw a significant increase in the proportion of unemployed who were somewhat older (in the 20 to 24 group) and who had more than lower secondary education compared to the 1970s.

An examination of the occupational distribution of the unemployed throws more light on the causes of unemployment. This information cannot be derived for the entire sample of the unemployed. A large proportion of the unemployed were fresh job seekers. In any event, the labor force survey did not record job seekers' previous occupation or occupational preferences. However, the Treasury's *Annual Economic Report* provides information about the registered unemployed by occupational group (table 11.18).

The changing problem of unemployment is revealed by the marked shift in the occupational structure of those unemployed who were registered. The slackening demand for labor in government services had a major effect on the white collar labor market. The proportion of the unemployed with unsatisfied demand for clerical jobs nearly doubled compared to the mid-1970s, and toward the end of the depression the proportion aspiring to professional and technical jobs also increased significantly.

The resultant unemployment is best viewed as a rationing problem rather than a voluntary job search. Under conditions of an excess supply of labor where job seekers have distinct occupational preferences, people are absorbed into employment more slowly, but the data suggest that the duration or unemployment for the majority has not become excessive (less than six months). In this sense the basic unemployment problem that re-emerged in the 1980s was no different from that observed in the late 1970s, except that the average unemployed person was more educated.

The structural problem in this aspect of the unemployment story is a combination of rigidity in occupational preference and limited wage flexibility. When supply runs ahead of demand, relative wages may fall sufficiently to clear the market, and if this does not happen, employers

Table 11.18 The Unemployed by Occupational Group, Selected Years
(percent)

Year	Production workers	Agriculture	Services	Clerical	Professional/ technical	Other
1975	59.1	4.6	7.5	24.1	4.2	0.6
1983	37.6	1.9	6.2	47.4	5.5	1.3
1986	35.7	1.6	5.2	42.8	12.0	2.7
1987	31.1	1.3	4.8	39.8	14.1	2.9

Source: Treasury *Annual Economic Report* (various years).

would tend to adjust by upgrading the educational requirements of the labor force (bumping). Job seekers of a particular educational skill will lower their expectations and accept jobs requiring lower skill levels. However, the required change in occupational preference comes gradually, and the speed with which the change occurs determines the average period of unemployment that new entrants into the labor market will experience.

Women in the Labor Market and Adjustment

A major feature in the long-term evolution of labor markets in Malaysia has been the increase in participation rates of females. Overall male participation rates have declined by a few percentage points because of the fall in the rates of younger people working due to schooling and of older people due to earlier retirement, but this decline has been more than offset by the increase in female participation. Figures 11.11 and 11.12 show the participation rates by age group for the years 1970, 1980, and 1987 for rural and urban areas. These figures reveal that the increase in female participation rates during 1970–87 is much larger in the urban than in the rural areas. Nevertheless, the basic difference in the rural/urban patterns of female participation rates persists after 20 years of change. In particular, the urban distribution is single-peaked, with the highest participation rate reached at age 20 to 24. By contrast, the rural distribution is currently double-peaked. In 1970, rural females had the highest participation rate in the post-childbearing age group, 35 to 49.

Figure 11.11 Urban Female Participation Rates, 1970, 1980, 1987

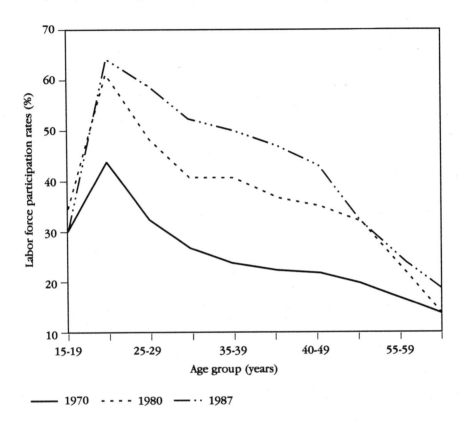

Developments since 1970 have added to the sharpness of this peak, which is now found in the age group 40 to 49, but at the same time there has been a remarkable increase in participation rates in the 20 to 24 age group, resulting in two peaks.

Tables 11.19 and 11.20 show the relative importance of females in total employment by industry and occupation for selected years. The major shift in the employment pattern of females has been away from agriculture.

Figure 11.12 Rural Female Participation Rates, 1970, 1980, 1987

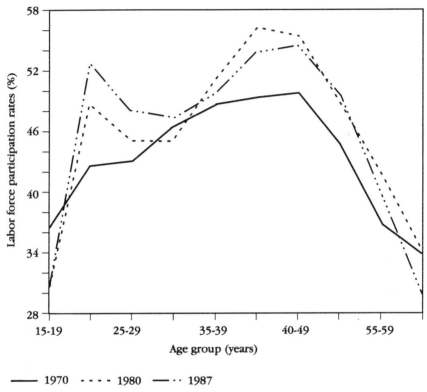

- ——— 1970   - - - - 1980   — ·· 1987

Table 11.19 Percentage Share of Females in Total Employment by Industry, Selected Years

Industry	1975	1980	1984	1987
Agriculture	40.9	39.6	36.6	32.9
Mining	12.3	13.7	11.9	11.1
Manufacturing	39.3	40.7	42.9	46.1
Utilities	3.2	5.7	4.8	2.9
Construction	6.4	5.7	5.5	4.7
Distribution	26.9	31.5	36.5	38.2
Transport	6.3	7.9	9.1	9.9
Services	37.9	34.1	36.0	39.3
Total	34.5	33.5	34.2	35.4

Source: Malaysian labor force surveys.

Table 11.20 Percentage Share of Females in Total Employment by Occupation, Selected Years

Occupation	1975	1980	1984	1987
Professional	35.0	39.3	42.2	46.5
Administrative	3.7	6.5	9.7	10.3
Clerical	35.8	44.2	49.7	51.6
Sales	18.6	28.4	31.2	33.8
Services	45.3	42.3	40.0	43.8
Agriculture	41.2	40.5	38.1	34.0
Production	24.3	24.3	23.8	27.0
Total	34.5	34.1	34.1	35.4

Source: Malaysian labor force surveys.

While the share of agriculture in total employment declined from 38 to 22 percent between 1975 and 1987, the share of females employed in this sector has also declined. Female workers have thus contributed significantly to the growth in employment in the leading tertiary and secondary sectors. By occupation, the professional, administrative, clerical, and sales categories have seen the growth of the female share of employment. Trends in production activities have held their share in the period of fast growth in manufacturing employment. The industrial classification shows that the share of females in this sector is very high and increasing slowly (table 11.19); much higher than in the Republic of Korea, where the female share in manufacturing between 1974 and 1984 hovered around 35 to 37 percent (Grootaert 1987, table 11).

The aggregate figures do not reveal the full story of the role of female labor in Malaysia's industrial growth. The electronics industry has dominated the upsurge in industrialization in Malaysia in the last decade. As in other Southeast Asian countries, transnational cooperations in this industry were lured into Malaysia—particularly into the free trade zones—by the prospect of a plentiful supply of cheap female labor possessing the manual dexterity and pliability needed. Research on the workers in this industry in the late 1970s and early 1980s brought out the importance of female operatives and demonstrated the remarkable uniformity in their characteristics. They were, by and large, unmarried women aged 16 to 24 in their first job, and what might be of some surprise, mostly Malay girls from rural areas (see Young 1987 and the many references cited therein).

We can conclude from this research that creating a newly emergent class of industrial workers in Malaysia was not difficult. Despite the lack of a tradition of industrial work, neither ethnic nor religious barriers prevented young Malay girls from meeting the demands of the leading industry. Note, however, that the state's mediating role was an important one. The objective of the new economic policy was to encourage greater participation by Malays in manufacturing activities. New ventures, particularly transnational ones, cooperated in this process, but did not seem to have faced too many rigidities in tapping the desired source of labor.

Table 11.21 shows the percentage of male and female workers found in different industrial sectors by mode of employment. An interesting point is that female workers in Malaysia are more likely than males to be in wage employment rather than self-employed. This difference has increased over time, and is more pronounced in nonagriculture.

EARNINGS OF MALES AND FEMALES. To examine the relative earnings of males and females over the last 20 years when the employment of women expanded so much in the economy, we again depend on the earnings function analysis. The base estimates are available for 1970 from Anand's (1983) work. We have estimated our own earnings functions from the household income surveys data for 1984 and 1987. These are presented, along with Anand's equations, in table 11.22. The analysis is confined to urban employees.

In 1970 returns to schooling were almost the same for males and females, but returns to experience were higher for males, spectacularly so for Chinese males. Over the years, the returns to both education and experience have increased absolutely for females, and relatively with respect to the males, for both races. At the peak in 1984, returns to schooling were higher for females (relative to the males) for both races, more so for the Malays. Males and females had also reversed their

Table 11.21 Distribution of Employed Labor Force in Peninsular Malaysia by Gender, Industry, and Employment Status *(percent)*

Gender/industry	1975 Employed	1975 Self employed	1980 Employed	1980 Self employed	1984 Employed	1984 Self employed	1987 Employed	1987 Self employed
	Males							
Agriculture	14.86	20.05	12.25	15.20	9.34	13.55	9.61	15.51
Mining	1.44	0.06	1.30	0.08	1.11	0.04	0.81	0.02
Manufacturing	11.78	1.83	14.18	2.05	13.89	1.37	13.55	1.17
Utilities	0.82	0.00	1.71	0.00	0.87	0.00	0.97	0.00
Construction	5.85	1.17	6.95	1.51	10.38	1.36	7.55	1.33
Distribution	7.41	7.22	9.18	7.28	9.77	7.17	10.20	7.69
Transport	4.78	1.59	5.04	1.53	5.23	1.39	4.95	1.44
Commerce	3.44	0.54	3.76	0.54	3.63	0.37	4.01	0.58
Services	15.86	1.25	16.12	1.29	19.20	1.30	19.07	1.51
Total	66.24	33.71	70.49	29.48	73.42	26.55	70.72	29.25
	Females							
Agriculture	25.09	15.40	18.99	12.31	13.85	9.03	10.58	7.77
Mining	0.30	0.19	0.47	0.09	0.35	0.03	0.20	0.04
Manufacturing	16.81	5.06	22.09	3.75	21.63	4.33	22.52	4.77
Utilities	0.06	0.00	0.22	0.00	0.08	0.00	0.02	0.00
Construction	1.32	0.00	1.15	0.02	1.54	0.00	0.94	0.01
Distribution	5.97	4.46	9.05	4.23	11.59	4.99	11.62	5.36
Transport	0.98	0.03	1.23	0.02	1.38	0.03	1.47	0.03
Commerce	3.32	0.08	3.85	0.06	4.87	0.05	5.28	0.11
Services	19.37	1.71	20.81	1.64	24.30	1.91	26.65	2.58
Total	73.22	26.93	77.86	22.12	79.59	20.37	79.28	20.67

Note: Unpaid family workers are excluded from this table.
Source: Malaysian labor force surveys.

relative positions on returns to experience as far as the Malays are concerned. Chinese females had pulled up their returns to experience considerably, but not enough to close the gap with respect to male employees.

Table 11.22 Earnings Functions for Urban Males and Females by Race, All Occupations Together, Selected Years

					1970				
Malay									
log y(males) =	5.42	+	0.142S	+	0.093T	–	$0.0012T^2$	R^2 =	0.451
log y(females) =	5.20	+	0.147S	+	0.071T	–	$0.0011T^2$	R^2 =	0.421
Chinese									
log y(males) =	5.32	+	0.139S	+	0.110T	–	$0.0014T^2$	R^2 =	0.521
log y(females) =	5.46	+	0.133S	+	0.068T	–	$0.0007T^2$	R^2 =	0.437
					1984				
Malay									
log y(males) =	6.20	+	0.157S	+	0.104T	–	$0.0014T^2$	R^2 =	0.452
log y(females) =	5.73	+	0.173S	+	0.124T	–	$0.0022T^2$	R^2 =	0.412
Chinese									
log y(males) =	6.66	+	0.139S	+	0.096T	–	$0.0012T^2$	R^2 =	0.410
log y(females) =	6.36	+	0.148S	+	0.077T	–	$0.0009T^2$	R^2 =	0.351
					1987				
Malay									
log y(males) =	5.94	+	0.171S	+	0.111T	–	$0.0014T^2$	R^2 =	0.439
log y(females) =	5.47	+	0.196S	+	0.110T	–	$0.0016T^2$	R^2 =	0.421
Chinese									
log y(males) =	6.34	+	0.153S	+	0.098T	–	$0.0012T^2$	R^2 =	0.437
log y(females) =	6.25	+	0.152S	+	0.076T	–	$0.0009T^2$	R^2 =	0.326

S = number of years of formal schooling
T = number of years of labor force experience
Note: Years of labor market experience T, are assumed to be measured by age A, minus schooling S, minus 5; that is, T = A – S – 5, where six is assumed to be the age at which schooling starts.
Sources: Malaysian household survey for 1984 and 1987; Anand (1983, tables 7.1 and 7.6).

In 1987, when the data reflect the effects of the recession of the mid-1980s, some interesting differences in the overall trend emerge. Females seemed to have lost ground somewhat with respect to the returns to both education and experience. Returns to experience were now equal for males and females as far as the Malays were concerned, and the higher return to education for females no longer held for the Chinese. The relative decline in returns to human capital factors for females are consistent with labor market behavior in recessions. When the demand for labor slackens, labor with a relatively weak position in the market will be reduced in numbers first. This means that not only workers with low values of experience and education will lose their positions first, but within these groups those with less ability or less attachment to the firms (and therefore with lower earnings) will decline in numbers. Thus, the differential in average earnings between workers with low and high endowments of human capital is reduced. Evidently, this mechanism was more pronounced for females than for males. This aspect could, of course, be reinforced by a more discreet fall in the wages of highly skilled female labor relative to skilled male labor.

What is the evidence on the relative endowments of human capital factors for the two sexes, rather than in the rates of return? Table 11.23 presents the relevant data. Rather surprisingly, females had more years of schooling for both races in 1970 and 1984, but the recession reversed this situation. Thus, the numbers and wages of educated female workers fell relative to those of males in the depression.

The data on experience tells the well-known story that male involvement in the labor force tends to be substantially longer than female participation, but the trend is clear. For both races, the difference in the years of experience between males and females has been substantially reduced over time. In this case, long-run trends in the labor

Table 11.23 Difference in Mean Years of Education and Labor Market Experience for Urban Males and Females by Occupation and Race, Selected Years

Mean years	1970		1984		1987	
	Malay	Chinese	Malay	Chinese	Malay	Chinese
S	(-)0.465	(-)0.234	(-)0.514	(-)0.195	0.561	0.686
T	4.930	3.464	4.024	2.632	3.241	2.166

S = number of years difference between males and females (M–F) of formal schooling
T = number of years difference between males and females (M–F) of labor force experience
Note: Years of labor market experience T, are assumed to be measured by age A, minus schooling S, minus 5; that is T = A – S – 5, where six is assumed to be the age at which schooling starts.
Sources: Malaysian household survey for 1984 and 1987; Anand (1983, tables 7.1 and 7.6).

market and cyclical factors have worked together. During the depression, the relative decline in the numbers of less experienced workers would affect females more. This will reinforce the long-run effects of increasingly stronger attachment of females to the market.

The relative earnings of females are the product of their relative endowments of human capital and the relative returns to these factors. During 1970–84, the trends on both counts would imply an increase in the relative earnings of females. During the recession, the two effects pull in opposite directions, and the outcome is uncertain.

Table 11.24 gives the male-female earnings ratios for the two races, both actual and what is predicted by the human capital equations (given the mean values of education and experience for each sex). As expected, the trend factors during 1970–84 result in an improvement of females' relative earnings, and in a particularly striking way for the Malays. During the recession of 1984–87, the trend improvement was arrested for the Malays. Note also the large difference between the actual and predicted earnings ratio for 1987; a difference that is not nearly so large for the other years. Evidently, factors other than the human capital ones were holding up females' relative earnings during the recession.

Table 11.24 Ratio of Earnings of Urban Females to Those of Males, Employees, by Occupation and Race, Predicted and Actual, Selected Years

Year	Actual		Predicted	
	Malay	*Chinese*	*Malay*	*Chinese*
1970	0.51	0.57	0.52	0.56
1984	0.68	0.60	0.71	0.57
1987	0.65	0.63	0.52	0.54

Note: Predicted values were determined by the equations in table 11.22 and by the mean values of education and experience in table 11.23.
Sources: Malaysian household survey for 1984 and 1987; Anand (1983, tables 7.1 and 7.6).

Regional Effects of Labor Market Adjustment

A very important issue for countries like Malaysia with a rapid growth rate is whether different regions of the country have shared in the benefits of growth. Economic growth, by its nature, is concentrated in particular regions or sectors, but regions lagging in the process could still share in the prosperity if internal migration of labor is sufficiently large and sufficiently responsive to income differentials.

In the economic development literature, the movement of labor from rural to urban areas typically receives prime attention. In the modernization of economies, growth often occurs in the urban sector. Income for workers generated in urban activities is generally much higher than in the rural traditional sector. The nature of urbanization could, however, generate problems of unequal growth if, for example, urban growth is concentrated in one or two very large cities, or if the rural-urban income difference widens significantly during the economy's development .

Malaysia has been no exception to the general experience of developing countries in having its urban population grow fast. Between the census years of 1970 and 1980, the total urban population of Peninsular Malaysia grew by 59 percent, nearly half of which was accounted for by net internal migration. The proportion of the urban population (living in towns of 10,000 people or more) increased from 28.7 to 37.2 percent (Hugo and others 1989 quoting Wee 1985). An important aspect of the rural-urban migration is that the Malays seemed to have participated increasingly in this process. This is in accordance with one of the major objectives of the new economic policy, namely, "the elimination of the identification of race with vocation as well as location" (Hugo and others 1989, p. 45).

Bhalla (1982, p. 25 and table 4.4) reports that trends in urban and rural incomes are consistent with the general trend of improved income distribution in Malaysia since 1970. Urban income per capita in 1973 was twice the level of rural income, but at the peak of the boom in 1984, the differential was no higher. During the recession of 1984–87, urban income per capita (in real terms) fell while rural income remained more or less unchanged, leading to a fall in the differential by about 10 percent.

However, the emergence of a primary city is an important phenomenon in Malaysia as in other Asian countries. The urban concentration based on Kuala Lumpur and the surrounding areas in Selangor during 1970–80 grew at almost twice the rate of the total urban population. The problem of concentration is, of course, not as great as in Thailand, for example, where Bangkok is some 50 times larger than the second city, Chingmai, but a "major change is occurring in the urban system towards a more primate city-size distribution" (Hugo and others 1989, pp. 46–47), as indicated by several indices of concentration in the last two decades.

Related to some extent to the pattern of urbanization is the persistence of interstate differences in income. Internal migration flows in Malaysia have been well documented in official census volumes. A study of these problems summarized by Hugo and others (1989) shows clearly that "the states of Selangor and Patang are the main centers of net immigration— the former largely because of the attraction exerted by the major metropolitan area . . . and the latter which was the focus of expansion of rural settlement" (pp. 45, 55–57). The persistence of these states as recipients of a net inflow of migrants for three decades, with all other states showing net outflow, is striking. The data actually suggest a progressive exacerbation of an established pattern of movement despite the emergence of Penang in the northwest as a new center of industrial growth. Furthermore, the main origins of immigrants to the Selangor-Kuala Lumpur urban complex are the more developed and urbanized states of the west coast. This major migration stream would tend to maintain, if not increase, interregional inequality. It is balanced to some extent by the migration stream to the other major recipient area, the agricultural region of Panang, which attracts migrants mostly from the least developed agricultural areas of the east coast, but also from the agricultural areas of the west coast.

Table 11.25 reproduces Bhalla's (1989) data showing the mean income per capita in 1976 and 1984 by individual states (urban and rural combined), as well as the distribution of population by three regions distinguished by income levels. The correlation in the ranking of the states by income level is very high and is plotted in figure 11.13. The simple regression equation is:

Table 11.25 Per Capita Monthly Income by State and Distribution of Population between Regions, 1976 and 1984

State	Per capita monthly income (ringgits)		Percentage distribution of population	
	1976	1984	1976	1984
Region I (high income)			28.6	29.9
Kuala Lumpur	214	430		
Selangor	129	335		
Pulau Pinang	103	255		
Region II (middle income)			47.2	45.4
Melaka	102	206		
Johore	92	208		
Perak	80	177		
Pahang	96	228		
Negri Sembilan	99	226		
Region III (low income)			24.2	24.7
Perlis	68	129		
Kedah	59	139		
Terenganu	75	153		
Kelantan	58	121		
Mean total	99	227	100	100

Source: Bhalla (1989, tables 4.5a and 4.5b).

$$Y_{1976} = 0.586 + 0.448Y_{1984}$$
$$(0.065) \quad (11.634)$$
$$\text{Adjusted } R^2 : 0.924$$

where Y is per capita income, and t-statistics are in parenthesis.

In 1976, almost all the states had a mean per capita income of 45 percent of that in 1984. We conclude that the high rate of growth during the decade did not alter relative interstate differences in income in any significant way, but clearly absolute differences between per capita income levels have increased markedly along with the increase in overall income levels in the economy. Note finally in table 11.25 that the proportion of population found in the three regions of high, middle, and

Figure 11.13 Per Capita Increase in Income, States of Peninsular Malaysia, 1976 and 1984

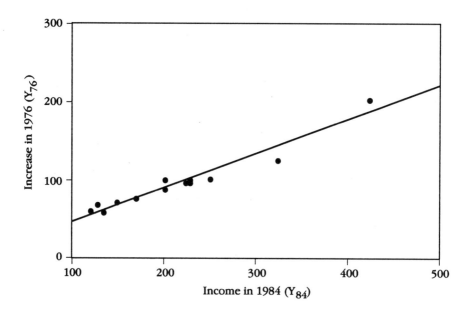

Note: The regression line uses Y_{84} as the independent variable to predict Y_{76} for each state. The data in the scatter diagram show actual values of each state.
Source: Bhalla (1989, table 4.5a).

low per capita income is almost exactly the same at the end of the period as at the beginning.

Conclusion

This chapter has examined both the short-run problems of adjustment as they were affected by changes in labor costs, and the longer-run issues of labor markets during the growth process.

The Short-Run Problems

Malaysia underwent some sharp fluctuations in economic activity in the last two decades associated with the commodity and oil price booms and the subsequent fall in prices in the 1980s. Government expenditure policies—particularly the attempt to pursue a countercyclical fiscal policy to keep the upswing going when commodity prices turned downward in 1980—was not entirely successful. The heavy foreign borrowing needed to finance this policy led to a recession of some severity. The behavior of wages in the tradable sectors—particularly manufacturing—was also of a nature that led to Malaysia's loss of competitiveness in world markets and must have contributed to the sharp recession.

The event in Malaysia differed in some important details from the standard sequence described in the Dutch disease models. In particular, the appreciation of the real exchange rate was not due to greater spending induced by the upswing in commodity prices, but to the inflow of foreign capital to support the government's budget deficit at a later period when the terms of trade were falling. Similarly, the increase in average wages during the period leading up to the recession was not corrected with the rise in the domestic exchange rate (the ratio of the prices of nontradables to tradables) in a fully employed economy. Wage increases in excess of labor productivity increase occurred at a time when employment growth had slowed down, and the rate of unemployment increased significantly. Some labor market institutions common to most East Asian countries, particularly the steep wage-seniority scales and the attachment of workers to firms after a period of service, might have contributed to this perverse behavior of average wages.

However, rising labor costs were only part of the problem of rising costs in Malaysia's tradable sector in the period leading up to the recession. The appreciation of the real exchange rate increased the dollar cost of labor compared to the country's trading partners. A large increase in interest costs contributed to the problem and was a direct consequence of the monetary policies followed. Thus, the entire package of fiscal, monetary, and exchange rate policies, acting together with labor market behavior, led to developments culminating in the recession. However, the recession was short-lived, lasting no more than two years. Factor markets proved to be highly flexible downward, with wages, interest rates, and exchange rates all drifting downward. This "collapse" of factor markets was instrumental in fueling the recovery when favorable trends reasserted themselves in Malaysia's external markets.

Long-Run Aspects

As the short-run problems of labor markets in Malaysia were of limited importance, the longer-run aspects of adjustment in the labor markets in response to rapid economic growth are probably of greater interest.

The chapter showed that real wages in Malaysia's formal sector have increased significantly in the last two decades. Plantations, particularly rubber, lagged somewhat behind manufacturing, but the growth rate of real wages was positive, at least before the slowdown of the 1980s. The question arises whether the nonformal sectors shared in the growth in earnings?

The availability of household surveys for 1973, 1984, and 1987, and the post enumeration survey of 1970 provide some statistical information on this point, since earnings data for the nonformal sector are not collected regularly. In the agricultural sector, paddy farmers and smallholder cash crop growers had significantly lower earnings in 1973 not only than employees in the nonagricultural sector, both rural and urban, but also relative to estate employees. Despite the policy of price maintenance and subsidies the government pursued, paddy farmers have not been able to improve their relative earnings over time, and the differential in earnings of paddy farmers and other workers actually widened significantly during the boom period. It narrowed somewhat in the downswing of the 1980s, but in 1987 the differential was well above that in 1973.

The tertiary sector as a whole increased its share of total employment from 36 percent in 1970 to 49 percent in 1980 and 55 percent in 1987. Employment in government accounted for a growing part of the service sector, at least during the 1970s, but even subtracting the share of government, the private tertiary sector increased its share. The evidence suggests that at least as far as males are concerned, these new workers in the tertiary sector are not a pocket of low-income labor who could not break into the manufacturing sector.

Although Malaysia differs from many other developing countries in that the self-employed in the manufacturing sector do not constitute a very large proportion of the work force (around 15 percent), they constitute rather more than a third of the total in agriculture and the distributive trades. The proportion of the self-employed in the economy as a whole has been declining slowly. The evidence refutes the traditional view of the self-employed, which holds that they enter young, then "graduate" to the formal sector as employees. Both in rural and urban areas and for both males and females, the proportion of the self-employed increases with age.

An analysis of predicted earnings for the years 1973, 1984, and 1987 showed that although employees earned more than the self-employed in all three years, a great deal of the difference could be attributed to differences in characteristics. Holding characteristics constant, the differentials in favor of male employees were within 10 percentage points, and in some cases the differential was actually reversed in favor of the self-employed. Female earnings differences in favor of employees were generally much higher than for males.

There were important differences between the trends in the male and female labor markets. As far as male workers are concerned, the self-employed increased their earnings relative to employees not only in the boom period, but probably also in the recession of 1984–87. The behavior of the female labor market has been quite different. There was a substantial increase in the differential in favor of employees in the boom up to 1984, even though employees started with much higher relative earnings (compared to males) in 1973, but there was a reduction in the differential in the downswing. Female labor fits the prediction of some labor market models that the informal sector does not fully share in the upsurge of earnings in the formal sector in a boom.

Another aspect of structural transformation in the Malaysian labor market is the very large educational upgrading of the labor force. The evidence suggests that although the proportion of nonmanual jobs increased significantly, the rate of increase of educated labor was higher than the rate of growth of white collar jobs. Thus, we see the usual adjustment in the labor market, with a gradual movement of educated labor to blue collar jobs over time. The frictions involved in this process of adjustment leads to a problem of unemployment of the more educated. In Malaysia in the late 1960s, the high rate of unemployment (around 10 percent) was identified as being a problem of secondary school leavers. This problem was alleviated during the boom of the 1970s, but apparently reemerged in the 1980s. This type of unemployment is of the structural kind, not responsive to changes in demand, unless, as in the latter half of the 1970s, the boom is sustained and intense (also perhaps favoring the white collar sector).

Another important feature of Malaysian development has been the increasing participation of women in the labor market, particularly of Malay labor in urban activities. The analysis of the earnings of male and female employees during 1970–87 showed that the trend factors in the acquisition of human capital factors, as well as in the rates of return to these factors, resulted in improved relative earnings by females, and in a particularly striking way for Malays. During the recession of 1984–87, the improvement trend was arrested, but there seems to have been an increase over time in the importance of factors other than education and experience in "explaining" the male-female differential.

Despite substantial internal movements of labor, the income per capita of an individual state in 1976 could be exactly predicted by the per capita income of that state in 1984: it was 44 percent of the 1984 level. The almost bizarre constancy in the relative interstate differences in earnings suggest a serious problem in the sharing of the fruits of economic growth through internal migration of the factors of production. With growth in income over time of the magnitude that Malaysia has experienced, constancy of relative differences produces rather large widening of absolute differences in income per capita. Moreover, the distribution of population among the regions of high, medium, and low income per capita seems to have remained unchanged.

References

Anand, Sudhir. 1983. *Inequality and Poverty in Malaysia: Measurement and Composition.* New York: Oxford University Press.

Bank Negara. 1986. *Quarterly Economic Bulletin* (March/June).

Bhalla, Surjit. 1989. "Restructuring of the Malaysian Economy: An Evaluation." Preliminary draft report prepared for the UNDP/ILO research project on the Malaysian Human Resources Development Plan. Processed.

Blau, David M. 1986. "Self-Employment, Earnings, and Mobility in Peninsular Malaysia." *World Development* 14(7): 839–852.

Gan, Wee Beng. 1988. "Industrialization and Manufacturing Export Performance in Malaysia." Kuala Lumpur. Processed. (Forthcoming in Brian Brogan, ed., *Export Premium as a Bonus to Growth.* Cambridge University Press.)

Gan, Wee Beng, and Lawrence B. Krause. 1990. "Issues of Macro Adjustment Affecting Human Resource Development in Malaysia: Basis for a New Strategy." A report for the Malaysian Human Resource Development Plan, Kuala Lumpur. Processed.

Government of Malaysia. 1973. *Mid-Term Review of the Second Malaysia Plan.* Kuala Lumpur: Government Press.

_____. 1976. *Third Malaysia Plan. 1976–80.* Kuala Lumpur: Government Press.

_____. 1986. *Fifth Malaysia Plan. 1986–90.* Kuala Lumpur: Government Press.

Grootaert, Christiaan. 1987. "The Labor Force Participation of Women in the Republic of Korea: Evolution and Policy Issues." Report No. IDP2. Washington, D.C.: World Bank.

Hugo, Sraeni, Lim Lean, Lean and Suresh Narayan. 1989. *Labor Mobility. Study No. 4, Module II.* Kuala Lumpur: Malaysian Human Resource Development Planning Project. Processed.

Lucas, R., and D. Verry. 1989. "Human Resource Development Project," 2 vols. Kuala Lumpur. Draft, processed.

Malaysia Ministry of Finance. Various years. *Economic Report.* Kuala Lumpur.

Mazumdar, Dipak. 1981. *The Urban Labor Market and Income Distribution: A Study of Malaysia.* New York: Oxford University Press.

_____. 1989. *Micro-Economic Issues of Labor Markets in Developing Countries.* EDI Seminar Paper No. 40. Washington, D.C.: World Bank.

McCarthy, Eugene. 1988. "The Wage and Salary System in Malaysia." Geneva: International Labour Organisation. Processed.

Richardson, R., and Lee Yin Soon. 1990. "Wage Trends and Structures in Malaysia," Kuala Lumpur: Malaysian Human Resources Development Plan Projects. Draft, processed.

Salih, Kamal, and Mei Ling Young. 1989. "Economic Recovery and Employment Growth: Why is Unemployment so Persistent?" Kuala Lumpur: Malaysia Institute of Economic Research. Processed.

Wong, Po Kam. 1985. "Economic Development and Labor Market Changes in Peninsular Malaysia." Working Paper No. 12. Kuala Lumpur Conference: Aseam-Australia Research Project.

World Bank. 1989. *Malaysia: Matching Risks and Rewards in a Mixed Economy*. Washington, D.C.

Young, Mei Ling. 1987. "Women Workers in Malaysia." Discussion paper. Malaysian Institute of Economic Research. Processed.

12

THE REPUBLIC OF KOREA

Dipak Mazumdar

The economy of the Republic of Korea provides a very interesting case study from the point of view of both long-term and short-run adjustments. Since 1965, the economy's growth rate has been very high, and the economy has seen rapid and fundamental restructuring. At the same time, as an open, export-oriented economy that had to depend on the importation of oil and a wide array of intermediate inputs, it has been fully exposed to the external shocks of oil price and interest rate hikes. The economy appears to be more vulnerable than most. In a bid to keep up the rate of investment, Korea borrowed heavily in the world market. It also has a sustained history of walking a tightrope of inflationary pressures and balance of payments deficits. Korea's ability to prevent the economy from going off the rails during difficult periods is as remarkable as its achievement of high, long-run rates of growth.

Cycles in the Korean Economy

Korea's recent economic history can be broken down into four phases. The period 1965–73 was one of sustained growth in the GNP, which although it varied from year to year, was at a generally high level (figure 12.1).[1] Difficulties emerged after the first oil shock. It led to a period when government economic policy leaned toward fostering development in heavy industry so as to make the economy less dependent on the vagaries of the world economy. This policy led to a faster buildup of foreign debt, so that when the second oil price

---

1. The basic time series on which the graphs are based is given in table 12.A2 of the annex.

hike and interest rate hike struck, the economy went into a depression in the early 1980s, the first time the average rate of growth of real GNP fell below zero. However, the depression was extremely shortlived. As in other Southeast Asian countries (with the exception of the Philippines), the economy was able to adjust very quickly to the external shocks (which were aggravated by internal shocks), and since 1982 the recovery has been rapid and sustained.

Phase 1: The Period of Export-Led Growth (1965–73)

As figure 12.2 shows, during the period 1965–73 the barter terms of trade either increased or were constant (except for 1969), while the

Figure 12.1 Real GNP Growth and Current Account/GNP, 1963–88

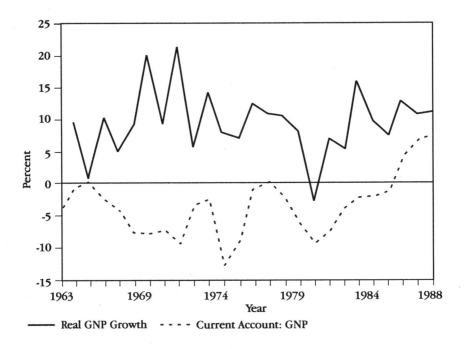

income terms of trade increased at a very high rate from year to year (see annex table 12.A1 for the basic data). Throughout the period, the lowest annual rate of growth of the income terms of trade was 30 percent, and in most years it was well above this. This was the period when Korea's outward-looking strategy was getting established in a spectacular way.

The current account was, however, in deficit throughout this period (figure 12.1), and until 1971 the annual growth rate of the deficit accelerated. It also went up sharply as a percentage of GNP from -3.7 percent in 1966–67 to -8.9 percent in 1971.

Figure 12.2 Growth of the Terms of Trade, 1963–88

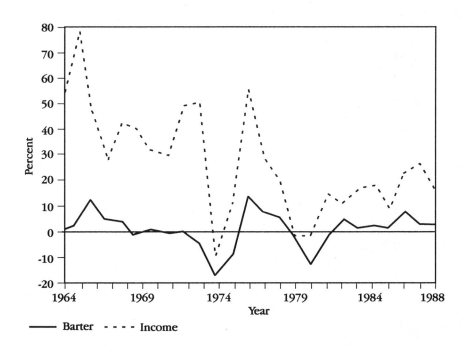

The reason for this deficit was the high rate of investment sustained at a level higher than the domestic rate of savings. Foreign borrowing was used to bridge the gap, as well as to take care of the diminishing role of foreign aid. According to Collins and Park (1987, p. 6): "Firms (especially exporters) were given strong incentives to borrow abroad. A system of loan guarantees substantially reduced the risks and the real cost of borrowing was negative." External debt as a percentage of GNP grew to over 30 percent by the end of the period, but because of the increase in the export: GNP ratio, the ratio of debt to exports—which ultimately determined Korea's ability to finance the debt—fell significantly toward the end of the period (figure 12.3).

Figure 12.3 Korean Debt Ratios, 1970–88

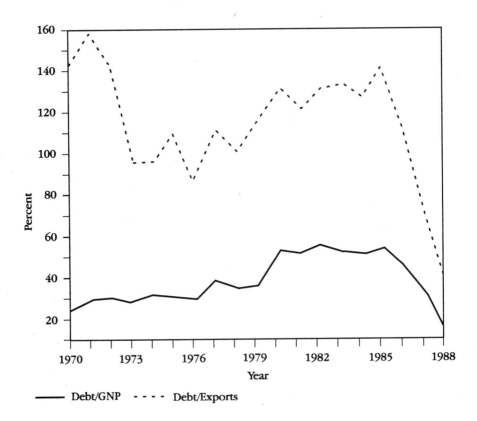

The role of the public sector in maintaining the high rate of investment was limited. This, together with the virtual doubling of tax revenue as a percentage of GNP (Dornbusch and Park 1987, figure 2, p. 408), held the budget deficit at a relatively modest level. Except for 1972 when the deficit was 4.6 percent of GNP, the ratio was generally 2 percent or less.

Phase 2: Period of Directed Heavy Industrialization and the Shadow of Crisis (1973–79)

Korea's difficulties in the 1970s started with the slowdown in the world economy following the increase in the price of oil. As an oil importer, Korea was hurt by the price hike itself. The reduction in the volume of exports aggravated the situation. As figure 12.2 shows, the percentage change in the income terms of trade was negative for the first time in 1974, and even when it recovered to positive levels it was—with the exception of 1975—well below the levels reached in the earlier period.

The government decided to counter the economic slowdown with a big push in the investment program in the heavy and chemical industries. Despite the fall in the domestic savings ratio in the aftermath of the slowdown, Korea elected to borrow through the crisis to keep up its planned investment rate. In 1974 and 1975, the debt/GDP ratio and the budget deficit/GNP ratio reached their highest levels (although neither was excessive by, say, Latin American standards). Government intervention in the form of greater direction of investment decisions increased, as did the chief instruments of control: import restriction and credit rationing. In addition, the exchange rate, which had been allowed to drift downward throughout the previous period, was fixed during 1975–79, and the real exchange rate was allowed to appreciate. While it helped importers of intermediate goods and materials, it clearly eroded Korea's international competitiveness.

This phase of economic policy in Korea has been the subject of controversy. The policy has been justified on the grounds that it laid the basis for long-run diversification of the Korean economy (and its external trade) away from light industry. Although it might have been costly in terms of immediate reallocation, the policy has been commended for wisely anticipating long-run changes in comparative advantage.

In any event, the Korean economy recovered to some extent following the recovery of the world economy in 1975 and 1976. It also benefited from the export of skilled labor to the Middle East and the subsequent flow of remittances. Nevertheless, the shadow of a crisis that the events of this period generated lingered, leading to the major depression at the end of the decade.

Phase 3: The Crisis and Adjustment (1979–82)

The second oil price hike triggered a depression, with the barter terms of trade registering negative percentage changes in 1979, 1980, and 1981. The annual rate of change of the income terms of trade was also negative in 1979 and 1980 (figure 12.1). The GDP growth rate fell and for the first time was negative in 1980. As domestic savings plunged, current account deficits mushroomed. The government resorted to external borrowing on a large scale. This was the period of the most rapid accumulation of foreign debt in Korean history. The debt/GNP ratio climbed from 32 to 53 percent during these years, equaling that of some Latin American borrowers, such as Brazil. Internal balance was also disrupted severely, with inflation rates reaching levels well above those seen in the 1960s and 1970s, with the exception of the years of the previous crisis, 1974–75 (figure 12.4).

Even while Korea stepped up its external borrowing to record levels in response to the crisis following the second oil shock, it had already started to take steps to increase its competitiveness, particularly through wage and exchange rate policies. At the same time, the government took further measures to adjust its fiscal, monetary, and industrial policies. The package of policies immediately started to restore internal and external balance. By the end of 1982, the rate of inflation and the current account deficit had been reduced drastically.

Figure 12.4 Rate of Urban and Rural Inflation, 1968–88

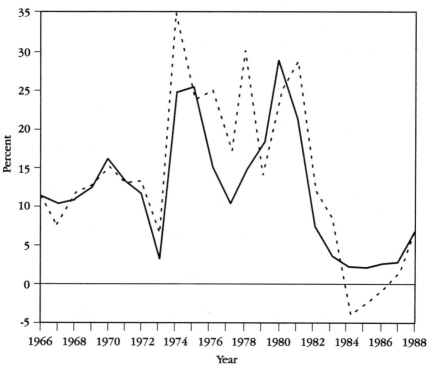

——— Urban Inflation   - - - - Rural Inflation

Phase 4: Recovery and Growth (1982–91)

The rate of growth of GDP was negative only in 1980, but it was
still low by Korean standards in 1981 and 1982. The economic
measures taken in these years, however, prepared Korea for a strong
positive response when world trade rebounded in 1983–84. As figure
12.1 shows, the economy's growth rate increased substantially. This
also produced an increase in domestic savings, which helped to reduce
the deficit in the current account of the balance of payments. When a
slowdown in the world economy threatened to produce another dip in
the growth rate in 1985, Korea countered by substantial real
depreciations of the exchange rate. Note, however, that devaluation did
fuel the inflationary spiral as it apparently did in 1979–80. On the
contrary, the achievement of internal balance sustained the low rate of
inflation attained at the end of 1982.

Since 1986, Korea has been experiencing a remarkable economic boom, with an annual growth rate of 12 percent during 1986–88. As in earlier periods, the boom has been fueled by a remarkable rate of growth of exports, which can, in turn, be traced to a variety of external factors, including the low and stable price of oil, the appreciation of the yen, and the continued strong growth of the OECD economies. The concern about foreign debt that had loomed large in the early 1980s has disappeared as the current account surpluses generated by the export boom have been used to prepay part of the liabilities.

Inflation had been kept under control until 1988, when it showed signs of accelerating. The threat of incipient inflation is the product of new developments, particularly in the foreign exchange and labor markets. The liquidity influx from the trade surplus and capital inflows threaten appreciation of the won beyond levels that are considered "safe" from the point of view of external competitiveness. At the same time, new developments in the labor market threaten to create wage inflation of a kind not yet seen in Korea. Many of these new problems and concerns are outside the scope of this chapter, as it is mainly concerned with Korea's success in adjustment policies after the shocks of 1973–74 and 1979–80. We will, however, refer to the labor market developments of the late 1980s insofar as it helps explain Korean wage movements during the earlier periods of adjustment.

The Characteristics of Korean Stabilization and Adjustment Policies

We now know that the idea that Korea's development was fueled by unregulated free markets is false. The government, both during the regime of Park (who was assassinated in 1979) and subsequently, played a determined regulatory role. The package of policies involved bringing about structural adjustments in the economy and pushing through stabilization measures when the economy threatened to go off the rails due to external and/or internal shocks.

The major strategy in Korea's industrialization has been the promotion of exports. Exports as a percentage of GNP rose from less than 3 percent in the 1950s to 15 percent in 1969 and 35 percent in the early 1980s. This, however, did not mean that the domestic market was ignored, even for industries such as textiles, which were heavily involved in exports. Korea's tariff system was dualistic. Imported intermediate inputs could be duty free, but industries targeted for development were granted tariff protection. When the export growth of textiles threatened to slow down, Korea embarked on its "big push" policy after the first oil crisis with a shift from light to heavy industry.

The major instruments of targeted industrial development were licensing and credit policy. The Economic Planning Board (EPB), which was responsible for targeting, had control over licensing and credit. If a proposal originated from the private sector, the EPB had to approve it, and if it complemented the EPB's overall strategy, the Ministry of Finance would arrange credit. If, however, the government took the initiative, the EPB would typically find a private firm to undertake the project rather than set up a public enterprise. As Amsden (1987, p. 5) points out: "Government control of credit differentiated Korean and Japanese development. The Japanese *zaibatsu* owned their own banks whereas the Korean *chaebol* did not . . . . Direction of the economy was more centralized because power over the purse was more centralized."

The state's central role in credit for industry was possible because of financial repression. Although Korea has a less centrally controlled nonbank financial sector as well as a curb market, the official banking sector has been dominant, at least until the 1980s. Generally, deposit rates were kept low, and sometimes were even negative in real terms. The implicit tax on depositors helped to channel resources into investment in targeted areas, and to finance budget deficits in a noninflationary way (for more details see Dornbusch and Park 1987, pp. 417–19, and the references cited therein).

Nowhere was control over financial flows more important than in the external capital account. The government maintained tight control over foreign borrowing. Both short- and long-term borrowing required government approval, "but the repayments of interest and principal on loans (were) guaranteed by the banks owned or strictly controlled by the government or by the government itself" (Park in Wong and Krause 1981, p. 226). Park also makes the point that for practical purposes "there is no point in distinguishing private borrowing from government indebtedness." The government used foreign borrowing for three purposes. First, it used foreign borrowing to bridge the gap between domestic savings and investment, and thus to maintain a rate of investment higher than would have been possible from domestic savings alone. Second, foreign borrowing was used along with the control over domestic credit to support the priorities of restructuring the economy. Third, it was used to tide over balance of payments difficulties originating from internal or external shocks.

Along with many other economies, especially, in Latin America, Korea had a rising debt/GNP ratio throughout the period 1965–82, which increased strikingly in the years of crisis, 1974–75 and 1979–80. However, Korea managed to avoid having the crises escalate into prolonged difficulties that dampened long-run growth: in each of the two cases of external shock that Korea experienced as an oil importer, for the stabilization measures to succeed, the debt/GNP ratio to fall, and sustained growth to resume took no more than two or three years.

The effective control over the external flow of funds clearly helped. Unlike in many countries of Latin America, capital flight did not deepen the crisis. The major difference with Latin America, however, was Korea's substantially lower debt/export ratio. In 1981 this was 76.6, while the major countries facing difficult problems in the 1980s—Argentina, Brazil, Chile, and Mexico—had debt/export ratios that were three to five times higher. Thus, in Korea during 1980–83, debt servicing was below the level of exports, but in the Latin American countries it exceeded exports by anywhere between 30 and 100 percent (see Sachs 1985, p. 533, table 4, and pp. 532–35 for further discussion of the differences between Asia and Latin America).

Maintaining export growth has thus been as important for Korea's long-term economic development as it has for successful response to the shocks. The factors affecting external competitiveness are therefore of central importance in the analysis of Korea's policies of adjustment and stabilization. The behavior of average wages, particularly in the export-oriented manufacturing sector, together with other factors affecting unit labor costs, are the relevant issues in this connection.

Determinants of Unit Labor Cost and Wage Behavior in Korean Manufacturing

This section focuses on manufacturing firms that employ ten or more workers. This is because detailed data are only available for this sector; but in any case, when it comes to the question of maintaining competitiveness, this is the sector that needs to be singled out for analysis as the exports of manufactured goods have driven Korean growth.

When examining an economy's external competitiveness, the key statistic is the unit labor cost of the exporting country in the international market. The unit labor cost can be expressed as shown in equation 1.

$$U_c = W/V \cdot 1/e \qquad (1)$$

where U_c = unit labor cost in dollars, W = wages per worker, V = value added per worker, and e = the exchange rate (won per dollar). The three elements determining unit labor cost in world prices are (a) wage behavior, (b) changes in labor productivity, and (c) the exchange rate.

Korea has always followed an active exchange rate policy, together with the control over external capital flows described earlier. As table 12.1 shows, the exchange rate depreciated continuously between 1968 and 1975. During the crisis periods of 1971–72 and 1975 the depreciations were particularly large. The won was fixed to the dollar between 1976 and 1979, but active devaluation of the currency resumed following the second oil crisis. Another major devaluation occurred in 1980 like after the first oil shock.

The more or less continuous devaluation of the currency was necessary because of the persistent double-digit inflation rates until after 1982 (figure 12.4). As a result, there has been continuous pressure for the real exchange rate to increase, which had to be countered by devaluation to maintain competitiveness.

Devaluation has, however, not been always a successful way to prevent the real exchange rate from increasing in open economies like Korea, which have to import many materials and intermediate goods, including oil. The higher unit cost of imports adds to the inflationary

Table 12.1 Annual Percentage Change in Unit Labor Costs and Its Components, 1968–86

Year	Wage-productivity gap (1)	Consumer-producer price differential (2)	Nominal average exchange rate (3)	= (1) + (2) – (3) Unit labor costs (US$) (4)
1968	-6.14	3.88	2.27	-4.52
1969	-7.25	3.69	4.16	-7.72
1970	-3.19	3.70	7.77	-7.27
1971	-16.80	8.65	11.78	-19.93
1972	3.63	-2.44	13.18	-11.98
1973	5.17	-8.78	1.38	-4.99
1974	9.47	-1.57	1.54	6.35
1975	-10.45	4.78	19.66	-25.34
1976	10.37	-0.95	0.00	9.42
1977	7.43	-0.65	0.00	6.78
1978	3.59	1.27	0.00	4.86
1979	17.01	-1.00	0.00	16.00
1980	-9.34	1.99	25.50	-32.86
1981	-16.14	7.58	12.12	-20.68
1982	0.30	2.25	7.35	-4.80
1983	-5.65	0.58	6.11	-11.18
1984	-1.59	1.56	3.90	-3.93
1985	2.97	0.05	7.95	-4.92
1986	-2.47	-1.39	1.31	-5.17
Averages				
1967–73	-4.40	1.43	6.66	-9.63
1973–79	6.58	0.29	3.30	3.57
1979–81	-12.60	4.90	18.62	-26.32
1981–86	-1.21	0.60	5.28	-5.89

Sources: CPI and exchange rate: Bank of Korea (various years); deflator: IMF (various years); wage bill and value added: U.N. (various years).

spiral. In the Korean case, devaluation could enhance the rate of inflation through an additional route. Korean food policy has the dual objective of supporting a high price for farmers and enabling consumers to buy at a lower price (although still higher than world prices). The difference between the buying and selling prices creates a deficit for the Grain Management Fund that is used to administer the policy. Apart from domestic procurement, the government has had to import a substantial amount of rice and barley to hold down selling prices. Thus with devaluation, the Grain Management Fund's deficit increases. Although food prices are not directly affected, the inflationary impact of the devaluation through an increase in the fiscal deficit could be significant.

However, as figure 12.4 reveals, although Korea is walking an inflationary tightrope, it has never been faced with the problems of spiraling inflation. Inflation rates jumped to the rather high rates of 25 to 30 percent in both the periods of maxi-devaluation (associated with the oil price shocks), but was brought down to moderate levels very quickly, and rather spectacularly so in the 1980s. The success story on this point involves two main policy and economic responses. First, the budget deficit (and the growth of money supply) was controlled: "The unified budget deficit, although swinging widely, never reached 5 percent of GNP and never stayed very high for more than two years in a row." (Dornbusch and Park 1987, p. 414). Second, a crucial issue was the behavior of wages relative to labor productivity.

Determinants of Unit Labor Cost

We can use equation (1) to derive the following relationship (the dots represent proportionate rates of change):

$$\dot{U}_c = \dot{W} - \dot{V} - \dot{e} = \left(\dot{w} + \dot{P}_c\right) - \left(\dot{v} + \dot{P}_p\right) - \dot{e} = \left(\dot{w} - \dot{v}\right) + \left(\dot{P}_c - \dot{P}_p\right) - \dot{e} \quad (2)$$

The additional variables are defined as follows: w = real wage (in terms of consumer goods), v = index of physical productivity of labor, P_c = index of cost of living, P_p = index of prices of manufactured goods.

Equation (2) decomposes the percentage change in the unit labor cost into three elements: the wage-productivity gap, the shift in the ratio of consumer to producer prices, and the change in the nominal exchange rate. Table 12.1 shows each factor's contribution to the change in unit labor cost (see annex table 12.A3 for the basic data).[2]

The following points in table 12.1 are worth emphasizing:

- The continuous depreciation of the exchange rate did not lead to an increase in the price of tradables relative to the price of nontradables (as approximated by the producers' price index relative to the cost of living index).[3] Thus, the domestic real exchange rate generally moved against manufacturing and increased the unit labor cost in most years. This is because devaluation did not fully compensate for inflation. Nevertheless, it moderated the impact of inflation, and as the table shows, the magnitude of the upward pressure on unit labor cost from this source was small.

- In the years of crisis and stabilization policies, large devaluations and a substantial negative wage-productivity gap helped to reduce unit labor costs. This happened in all three stabilization periods: first, in 1971 when the government moved to counteract a temporary slowdown in exports; second, in 1975 following the first oil price shock; and third, during the "comprehensive" stabilization plan of 1980–81.

- The average figures given for the three periods 1967–73, 1973–79, and 1980–86 show clearly the different trends in unit labor costs associated with varying performances of the economy. They also help us to quantify the relative importance of the wage-productivity gap and the exchange rate movements in accounting for movements in unit labor costs (in dollars).

During the first period of export expansion, unit labor costs declined at a substantial annual rate of 9.6 percent per annum. The depreciation of the nominal exchange rate contributed as much to the decline of unit labor costs as the excess of productivity growth over

---

2. Note that the wage series is really one of average earnings per worker: the annual wage bill divided by the number employed. The wage bill includes basic wages as well as supplementary payments to labor.

3. Cereals, an important part of the CPI, although imported to some extent, are really nontradables in Korea because of the administered price system operated by the Grain Management Fund.

wage growth, despite an adverse movement of the domestic real exchange rate. The problem years after the first oil shock and the big push reversed the trend in unit labor cost. Its sharp increase in the period 1973–79 was largely due to the adverse wage-productivity gap. Although the exchange rate was devalued sharply in 1975, Korea went to a fixed rate for the rest of the 1970s. This policy was abandoned following the second oil shock. The experience of the two years of adjustment—1980 and 1981—shows the large contribution of devaluation, some 50 percent more than the negative wage-productivity gap, to the reduction of unit labor costs. However, the negative wage-productivity gap was substantial, so the unit labor cost decline was massive, offset only slightly by the increase in the domestic real exchange rate. The continued decline of unit labor costs until 1986—which was instrumental in the recovery—was again due more to nominal devaluation than to the negative wage-productivity gap, although the latter contributed significantly to it.

Wage-Productivity Trends

We conclude that the behavior of wages relative to productivity has been of crucial importance both during the periods of Korean growth and the short periods of stabilization. In developing countries with a large farming sector, it is tempting to assume à la Lewis that the negative wage-productivity gap is due to an elastic supply of labor at a constant real wage, while productivity growth in the modern sector is significant due to exogenous technological progress, thereby leading to a fall in unit labor costs over time. But the Korean story is different. As figure 12.5 and annex table 12.A4 show, in most years during the 20-year period under consideration, real wage growth was more than 5 percent per annum. The exceptions were the years of stabilization policies: 1971–72, 1975, and 1980–81. Of these, real wage growth was negative only in 1980–81, but fell by less than 5 percent.

The sustained and substantial rate of increase in labor productivity thus emerges as a critical variable in the achievement of a continued reduction in unit labor costs despite the continuous devaluation of the currency. The productivity growth was sufficient to counter the rising import costs produced by the devaluation and to permit a significant growth of real wages. In the crisis years all or more of the increase in

Figure 12.5 Real Value Added and Wages, 1967–86
(annual figures per worker, 1980 = 100)

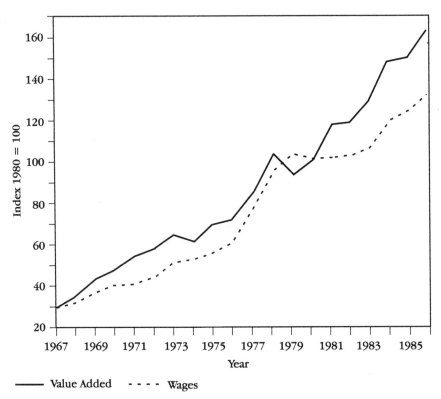

Sources: Bank of Korea (various years); U.N. (various years).

productivity went into reducing unit labor costs while real wage growth was temporarily halted.

The importance of productivity growth for the economy's stability is also relevant for another reason: preventing the emergency of inflationary expectations. We have seen that until after the 1980–81 stabilization, the Korean inflation rate was at double-digit levels and was very high in short bursts. Yet the economy never degenerated into a dangerous spiral of rising wages and prices. Stabilization efforts in most countries generally need a period of stagnation, or even decline, in real wages. Often this wage effect is produced by an abnormal increase in the rate of inflation. Success depends on the subsequent behavior of wages as the inflationary expectations of workers affect them. In many developing countries, particularly in Latin America, inflationary expectations have been explosive. Periods of real wage stability or decline have been followed by spiraling increases in wages and prices, leading to erosion of international competitiveness as workers seek to defend their real wage unsuccessfully through accelerating money wage increases. In an economy like Korea's, productivity growth has sustained a significant rate of real wage growth over many years. Thus, the workers' confidence in the economy's ability to improve their standard of living is continuously reinforced. It is easier for them to accept temporary real wage restraint (or even decline) without demanding money wage increases that feed an explosive inflationary spiral.

While the investment rate in Korea was high, the sustained growth in labor productivity was, to a large extent, due to the growth of total factor productivity. Nishimuzu and Robinson (1984) showed that during the 1960s and 1970s, Korea's total factor productivity growth of 3.7 percent per annum was by far the highest of the countries investigated (1.3 percent per annum for Turkey, 0.5 percent for Yugoslavia, 2 percent for Japan). The increasing efficiency in the use of both capital and labor allowed Korea a safe margin for real wage increases without eating into profitability.

Wage Determination in Korean Manufacturing

The increase in productivity made wage increases possible, but why did this happen at the sustained rate that it did? What was the mechanism of determining wages in industry?

Before the late 1980s, unions' influence on wage levels was minimal: the right to strike was banned by presidential decree in 1971. Unions did exist in large firms, particularly in the textiles, metalworking, and chemical sectors, but they needed prior permission from the government for collective bargaining. Earnings function studies have found no significant effect of unions on relative wages (see, for example, Park 1980, part 3).

From time to time, the Federation of Korean Industries (FKI) and the Federation of Korean Trade Unions specify wage guidelines for both white and blue collar workers. The *chaebol* dominates the former, while the government's influence on the latter has been recognized for some time. The government's own influence was used to support wage restraint, as during the stabilization period of 1980–81, and to ensure that the workers received a share of productivity gains in the years of sustained growth.[4]

With or without government encouragement, Korean industry showed strong predilections toward a profit-sharing system of remuneration. The basic wage constituted no more than 75 percent of total monthly earnings in the early 1970s, and fell to 70 percent in the 1980s (Park and Castaneda 1987, table 17, p. 38). Overtime pay and annual bonuses—both of which are related to business conditions and profitability—constitute the rest.

The industrial firms, particularly the larger ones, seem to have determined the structure of the internal labor market. Starting wages are predominantly determined by a worker's formal schooling and sex, regardless of job content (Park 1980, chapter V). This basic wage rises on an almost regular basis by certain fixed amounts, the so-called "annual base-up." This base-up is directly related to the length of service in the company, and is not necessarily associated with promotion. Promotion takes the form of skipping several base-ups. One econometric study (Amsden 1990, p. 88, quoting Lee 1983) found that "in the case of male workers, one year of 'inside' experience (with the same employer) tended to raise wages on average by about 10 percent, whereas one year of outside experience (with a different employer) raised them by an average of only about 3.8 percent."

With a strong mechanism for rewarding firm-specific skills in place, clearly a major incentive for efficiency would be to share the gains of

---

4. In 1988–89, the Korean government showed a new commitment to a less interventionist policy toward labor markets. The impact on independent wage bargaining was immediate. After two successive years of double-digit nominal wage increases, the Federation of Korean Trade Unions was asking for a 27 percent wage increase in the spring negotiations of 1989. The Federation of Korean Industries countered with an offer of an 8.9 to 12.9 percent increase depending on the sector. The government suggested that nominal wage increases should be no higher than real productivity gains, but as shown by continuing labor unrest, including large-scale strikes, this informal incomes policy is experiencing implementation difficulties.

productivity increases with the workers. An apt question is: what is the exact nature of firm-specific skills that are being rewarded?

Amsden (1987) makes the point that Korea depended heavily on imported technology, and had little experience with such technology with the possible exception of textiles. According to Amsden (1990, p. 89): "Korean managers could never hope to manage in a tight, 'Taylorist' top-down fashion, at least not initially, because no one at the top knew enough about the process (of production) to do so. Under these conditions, it was imperative to rely upon motivated workers, even if they possessed little more than formal schooling, to exercise the most fundamental skill of all—intelligence." This was particularly so because an export-oriented strategy was quite demanding on the maintenance of product quality.

A profit-sharing model of wage determination could explain the observed increase in the real wage at a rate a little below productivity growth in the period before 1974 and again after the adjustment of 1980–81. The successful wage repression of 1971, 1975, and 1980–81, which contributed to the stabilization effort, has the hallmark of state paternalism in wage setting.

However, one might still ask why wages increased significantly faster than productivity during the big push of the second half of the 1970s. Part of the answer is probably the high optimism of the state-driven investments in diversification. Another factor was the tightness of the labor market caused not only by the big push, but also by the rather sudden and substantial emigration of Korean workers to the Middle East to help in the latter's post-oil construction boom.

As annex table 12.A2 shows, the unemployment rate fell to a historic low in 1978 (note that the unemployment rate touched this low again in 1986, and fell even lower in 1987 and 1988). As already pointed out, the events of the last few years have created a new situation in the Korean labor market. The wage explosion, which is still underway, is as much due to the tightness of the labor market as to the government's less paternalistic role in wage determination.

An attempt was made to test these points with an econometric model of wage determination. Our model was the usual augmented Phillips curve, together with an element to capture the profit-sharing aspect. It is hypothesized that workers have a target real wage in any period that is governed by the productivity growth of a previous period. If the percentage increase in real wages falls short of the percentage increase in productivity of the earlier period, then there is additional upward pressure on money wages. Note that the mechanism of the target wage could percolate through the decision of workers, employers, or both. Thus, the model would be:

$$\dot{W}_t = a + b\,P_e + cU_{t-x} + d\left(\dot{v}_{t-y} - \dot{w}_{t-y}\right) \tag{3}$$

where $\dot{W}_t$ = the percentage change in money wage in the current period, P_e = the expected rate of inflation, U_{t-x} = the unemployment rate x periods before, $\dot{v}_{t-y}$ = the percentage increase in productivity y periods before, and $\dot{w}_{t-y}$ = the percentage increase in real wages y periods before. The values of x and y are found by the best fit of the model to the data.

The model was estimated with quarterly data for the period 1970.3–1988.3. The results are given in table 12.2. The expected inflation rate is approximated by the rate of increase in the CPI in the previous period. In the first equation reported in table 12.2, we get a reasonably good fit with all the variables having the right sign and strong significance. The second equation increases the R^2 substantially without reducing the significance of the explanatory variables significantly. The extra term DNOMAW(-4) is the percentage change in money wages since four quarters before the present. The inclusion of the variable increases the R^2 by so much because there is a strong seasonal pattern in the money wage series, in particular, average earnings in the fourth quarter of each year are bumped up as workers are paid their annual bonus.

The variables are defined under the table. The fitted equations strongly support the hypothesis. Both the rate of unemployment and the target real wage based on actual productivity increase enter the process of wage determination.

Table 12.2 Determinants of Percentage Changes in Nominal Wages 1970–88, Quarterly Data Regression Analysis (OLS Estimates)

Constant	DCPI(-1)	UER	Target(-2)	DNOMAW (-4)	Adjusted R-squared	Durbin Watson statistic	F-statistic
0.135	0.869	-0.028	0.214	–	0.519	2.24	25.8
(5.870)	(4.050)	(-5.230)	(4.510)				
0.070	0.478	-0.016	0.097	0.59	0.695	2.24	40.3
(3.300)	(2.620)	(-3.390)	(2.300)	(6.25)			

DCPI(-1)   = inflation rate lagged one quarter.
UER   = unemployment rate.
Target (-2) = difference between growth in productivity and growth in real wages. The variable is lagged two quarters.
DNOMAW(-4) = the dependent variable lagged four quarters.
DNOMAW   = percentage change in nominal monthly earnings per regular employee in manufacturing, averaged for each quarter.

Notes: The variable TARGET (-2) can be broken down into rates of growth of money wages, prices, and productivity, all lagged two periods. When we tried productivity only without the lagged wage and price indices, the estimated equation performed less well, with a smaller R^2 and greatly reduced significance of the TARGET variable. Periods covered by both regressions go from the second quarter of 1971 to the third quarter of 1988 (70 observations). Figures in parentheses are t-statistics.

The Structure of Korean Labor Markets and Wage Differentials

The previous discussion on wages and productivity referred to the formal manufacturing sector. The data was limited to wage employees in firms employing more than ten workers. A great deal of employment in Korea has always been in the informal sector. However, the lack of data means that we cannot provide a comprehensive picture of the whole informal sector. Thus, we focus on specific groups in the sector whose relative earnings appear significant in Korea's process of structural change.

The size of the informal sector employment can be estimated by comparing two sources of employment data: the *Economically Active Population Survey* (Economic Planning Board), which estimates total employment on the basis of a household survey, and the *Actual Labor*

Conditions at Establishment (Ministry of Labor), which estimates employment on the basis of a survey of establishments above a certain size (five or more workers until 1979, then ten or more workers).

Unfortunately, the Ministry of Labor publication excludes public sector employment. Thus, the comparison has to be limited to the economy's production sector: agriculture, mining, manufacturing, and construction. A comparison for 1979 shows that almost all the five million people employed in the agriculture sector and a third of the three million people in manufacturing were in the informal sector. Furthermore, a special census of the commerce sector (wholesale and retail trade, hotels, and restaurants) for 1979 also revealed that 90 percent of the 1.3 million people involved were in establishments employing fewer than ten workers (Lindauer 1984, table 18 and p. 73). The agriculture sector has been declining over time, but the trends in employment in the informal component of the secondary and tertiary sector are not very clear. Likewise, data deficiency does not permit analysis of trends in earnings in all parts of the informal economy. However, examining some specific aspects of the earnings difference between the formal and the informal sectors is possible, including (a) the farm/nonfarm differential, (b) the differentiation in earnings by size of firm within the manufacturing sector, and (c) the male/female differential.

Farm/Nonfarm Differential

Korean data sources allow us to compare average annual farm incomes with annual earnings in manufacturing or with the average income of urban salary and/or wage earners. Alternatively, we can compare real daily farm wages with real daily earnings in manufacturing. Because of the small number of wage earners in agriculture relative to farm operators, the analysis of relative farm earnings is more significant. The series are graphed in figure 12.6. The actual data and discussion of sources are given in annex tables 12.A4 and 12.A5. The figure shows that during the period of expansion, 1966 to the first oil crisis of 1973, farm incomes per earner increased at only a slightly slower rate than average earnings in manufacturing. The differential in favor of manufacturing increased somewhat to about 50 percent at the end of the period. The urban

Figure 12.6 Real Annual Income per Earner, by Earner Type, 1966–85

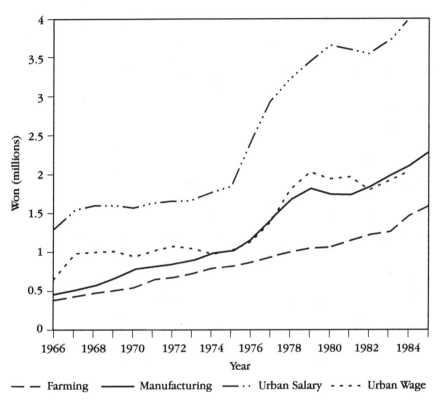

wage earner's household income per earner was significantly higher.[5] However, over the period the rate of growth of household income was substantially lower than that of farm income, so that the differential was squeezed.

After the stabilization efforts following the oil crisis, urban earnings stagnated for a couple of years. Manufacturing earnings had a very low growth only in 1975, but urban wage earners' income fell before this, both in 1973 and 1974. However, the slowdown of the economy had no impact on the growth of income in the farm sector. The rural/urban earnings difference fell during this period of adjustment.

5. This may be due to (a) the exclusion from the sample of single member urban households who would presumably have low earnings, and (b) the inclusion in the family income of supplementary income from other sources.

Earnings in the nonfarm sector took a sharp upward turn during the big push in the second half of the 1970s, when real wages in manufacturing increased at a rapid rate higher than the rate of growth of labor productivity. As figure 12.6 indicates, the incomes of urban households went up even faster. Farm incomes per worker increased by about the same absolute amount per year as in the previous period, so that the rate of growth slowed down. Thus, the period of the big push widened the rural/urban wage differential substantially. In 1979 manufacturing wages were 80 percent higher than farming earnings and urban wage earners' income was 100 percent higher.

As during the first episode of stabilization, urban earnings fell after the second oil shock, while farm earnings continued to grow at much the same rate. The rural/urban differential fell, but not by enough to restore it to the levels of the early 1970s. Since 1982, rural and urban earnings have increased at a somewhat similar rate. The widening of the differential in favor of urban wage earners that occurred in the late 1970s seems to have been a permanent one.

Some economists maintain that the comparison of average incomes, particularly after the stabilization program of the 1980s, may be giving too favorable a picture of the farm sector. The deficit in the Grain Management Fund—which, as we have seen, supported the prices paid to farmers above the prices of cereals sold to consumers— was drastically reduced as part of the post-1981 stabilization package. The slow down in the inflation rate clearly helped the deficit reduction process, but some believe that the terms of trade for the farming population deteriorated. Amsden (1987, p. 36) suggests that such a deterioration prompted the mass exodus out of agriculture between 1982 and 1985 "even larger than the migration associated with the 1980 harvest failure." Moreover, "the last wave of migrants was believed to consist of relatively older people, unequipped to enter the labor force and unaccounted for in the unemployment statistics which, therefore, were lower than otherwise" (Amsden 1987, p. 36).

The outmigration from agriculture might indeed have prevented the rural-urban differential from increasing further in favor of the urban sector in the post-1981 period. Also the earnings distribution within the farm sector might have deteriorated (a point on which no statistical information is available). In any case, taken in conjunction with the earnings differential in favor of urban workers being at a higher level in the 1980s than in the early 1970s, the implication is that the farming sector did suffer a relative deprivation after the boom of the late 1970s and the subsequent adjustment of the economy.

Wage Difference by Size of Firms

The difference in labor earnings between the informal and the formal sectors in the nonfarm economy is of major importance in the history of Korean development. Unfortunately, the absence of comparable household surveys does not permit examination of trends in differentials for too many subsectors. Information does exist, however, on wage difference by size of manufacturing firms. The wage levels in small firms could be expected to approximate levels of earnings in the informal sector.

The government policies that led to Korea's export-oriented industrialization also produced a dualism in the manufacturing sector. "While government policy towards domestic market-oriented small-scale industry has been characterized by benign neglect or active discrimination, export/large scale sector has enjoyed considerable advantages from the government through direct and indirect subsidies" (Park 1980, p. 57).[6]

Credit policy played a central role in this process of differentiations. The preferential interest rate on export credit was reduced to 6 percent in June 1967, while the ordinary bank rate was set at 26 percent in 1965. In addition, exporting firms enjoyed a string of preferences in import licenses, tax concessions, and favorable tariff rates for imported inputs. "These subsidies were disproportionately favorable to large-scale industries. In 1974, only 6 percent of small- or medium-scale industries (less than 200 employees) were designated by government as 'export Industries.' Government export subsidies were also scaled according to export volume and performance" (Park 1980, p. 61).

The government also encouraged Korean industry to adopt state-of-the-art technology developed in the high-income countries to

---

6. See chapter II of this work for an extended discussion of the issues summarized here.

enable it to cater to world markets. This led to the adoption of capital-intensive technology, a trend abetted by the low cost of loanable funds. Further, the recently designed technology of mass production favors large-scale operations to reap the benefits of machine specialization. Thus, successive plants in Korea's export industries have been designed for increasingly large-scale production.

The differences in technology and labor productivity between large and small firms are associated with large differences in wages. To some extent the observed difference in average earnings per worker reflect differences in skill composition, but even for a relatively homogeneous group like semiskilled production workers, very large wage differentials exist. An element of profit sharing clearly enters into the high wages paid by large firms with high labor productivity. As already mentioned, the importance of labor unions in determining wages is relatively small. However, employer paternalism, plus incentives for efficiency and low turnover, is involved in setting wages at high levels in large firms. As noted earlier, basic wages account for only a part of total earnings in Korea. Various allowances and annual special earnings bonuses are a substantial component of earnings, and this proportion increases sharply with firm size.

Table 12.3 shows the evolution of employment, output, and labor productivity by firm size between 1960 and 1982 (note that the definitions of small, medium, and large firms are different in 1960 and 1963 from the definitions for later years). The data show the enormous importance of firms with fewer than 100 employees (small and medium firms) in the early 1960s. Small firms (those employing fewer than 30 workers) employed 45 percent of total workers and produced a third of gross output. Value added per worker in the small firms was half of that in the large firms, and in the medium firms it was two-thirds of that in the large firms.

A major change seems to have taken place between 1969 and 1975. The large firms expanded fast at the expense of the small, with the latter's share dropping from 32 to 17 percent in terms of employment, and from 17 to 8 percent in terms of gross output. At the same time, the difference in value added per worker narrowed markedly, from 14 percent of the level in large firms in 1969 to 40 percent in 1975.

Table 12.3 Technology, Size, and Productivity Differentials in Manufacturing Establishments, Selected Years

Year	Number of employees (% of total)	Gross output (% of total)	Value added per worker index	Fixed assets per worker index
1960				
Small	45.2	36.9	59.4	n.a.
Medium	22.4	20.4	67.8	n.a.
Large	32.3	42.6	100.0	n.a.
1963				
Small	42.0	31.5	46.3	n.a.
Medium	23.0	22.9	66.8	n.a.
Large	34.9	45.5	100.0	n.a.
1969				
Small	31.6	16.6	14.2	16.6
Medium	20.1	15.0	19.8	43.2
Large	48.2	68.3	100.0	100.0
1975				
Small	17.4	8.3	40.5	18.6
Medium	20.2	15.7	69.6	35.4
Large	62.3	75.8	100.0	100.0
1980				
Small	18.3	8.1	42.5	19.8
Medium	22.7	15.6	61.1	42.4
Large	58.9	76.1	100.0	100.0
1982				
Small	21.4	9.1	37.2	22.7
Medium	23.3	17.1	57.1	39.5
Large	55.1	73.6	100.0	100.0

n.a. = not available.
Note: For the years 1960 and 1963, small = 5–29 employees, medium = 30–99 employees, and large = 100+ employees. For the years 1969, 1975, 1980, and 1982, small = 5–49 employees, medium = 50–199 employees, and large = 200+ employees.
Source: Report on Mining and Manufacturing Survey.

The shocks of the mid-1970s and the early 1980s arrested the fast relative expansion of large firms despite the big push of 1975–79. The proportion of employment in large firms fell from 62 to 55 percent. The difference in value added per worker, however, widened somewhat, perhaps reflecting rationalization and weeding out of less efficient firms in the large-scale sector.

Thus, while the Korean experience supports the model of a shrinkage of the large firm sector during the periods of adjustment with the slack taken up by small firms, the changes are not nearly as dramatic in the difficult period of 1975–82 compared to the expansionary phase of 1969–75.

Turning to the differential in earnings by size of firm in manufacturing, Table 12.4 gives the differentials in average earnings. These data show a substantial increase in the differential, particularly with respect to small firms during the 1960s. The trend was reversed in the 1970s, both in the years leading up to the first oil crisis, and subsequently during the big push. By the end of the 1970s the small-large differential was at about the same level as in 1960, but the second oil crisis and the adjustment of the 1980s again saw a widening of the differential, but to a smaller extent than in the 1960s.

Table 12.4 Indices of Differentials in Average Remuneration by Firm Size in Manufacturing, Selected Years

Year	Large/small (small = 100)	Medium/small (small = 100)	Large/medium (medium = 100)
1960	136.5	99.9	136.6
1967	155.7	126.9	122.7
1970	180.9	147.6	122.6
1974	152.4	129.3	117.8
1979	130.1	115.9	112.3
1983	147.6	120.3	122.7
1986	149.0	119.4	124.8

Note: Small firms are defined as having 5–49 workers, medium firms have 50–199 workers, and large firms have 200 or more workers.
Source: Korea—Statistical Yearbooks (1962, 1976, 1981, 1985) and Reports on Mining and Manufacturing Surveys for 1967 and 1970.

The data in table 12.4 do not control for skill, education, and skill differences. When we do control for such differences as is done in table 12.5, a significant decline in the differentials over time is confirmed for the 1970s, except for female university graduates. Taken together with table 12.4, we could conclude that dualism has indeed been accentuated within Korea's manufacturing sector, but that this process has taken the form of selecting workers with better human capital attributes for the large-scale sector rather than widening the standardized wage differential by firm size.

Male-Female Differences

Table 12.6 gives the labor force participation rates of males and females for farm and nonfarm households. The participation rate for females in farm households does not show much of a trend, but the rate in nonfarm households, although well below the rate in farm households, has been slowly increasing since 1970 (except for a small dip in 1981 and 1984).

The process of development is generally accompanied by substantial increases in female participation arising from both the supply and demand sides. On the supply side, important factors helping the process are rising levels of education, reduced fertility, and a general change in attitudes toward market work by women. Korea's educational expansion seems to have benefited women as much as men. The average number of years of schooling of women has risen from 2.92 years in 1960 to 6.63 years in 1980 (as against the overall average of 3.86 and 7.61; Park 1980, p. 6). At the same time fertility levels have declined drastically (by more than half in the last 20 years), reducing the number of small children at home. This would tend to increase market activity for married females. On the demand side, industrialization and the growth of urban services—social and private—create opportunities for female employment. What makes the Korean case unusual is that despite the presence of these factors at levels above those for other developing countries, after two decades of development, the nonfarm participation rate for females is well below that of other countries. Even the neighboring countries of Asia had significantly higher rates: 49.7 percent for Hong Kong, 48.9 percent for Japan, 45.8 percent for Singapore, and a high of 78.4 percent for

Table 12.5 Earnings Differentials by Size of Firm, Sex, and Educational Level of Workers, 1967 and 1980 (base = 100, firms with 10–29 workers in each category)

Firm size (number of workers)	University graduate				Middle or elementary school graduate			
	Male		Female		Male		Female	
	1967	1980	1967	1980	1967	1980	1967	1980
10–29	100.0	100.0	100.0	100.0	100.0	100.0	100.0	100.0
30–99	117.6	103.4	88.5	88.7	113.0	105.1	107.3	98.2
100–299	131.7	111.3	126.5	109.3	124.3	125.2	124.0	103.6
300–499	149.2	112.1	99.9	101.5	157.4	131.7	132.5	104.7
500+	171.0	113.6	96.4	119.0	201.9	133.4	163.3	107.9

Notes: For 1967, firm size ranges from 100 to 199 (instead of the 1980 range of 100 to 299); and from 200 to 499 (instead of the 1980 range of 300 to 499). Therefore, comparisons between these two groups should take this into account. The category for males and females with a middle or elementary school education for 1967 refers to production workers.

Sources: Administration of Labor Affairs (1980, tables III.4 and III.5, pp. 336–461); Bank of Korea (1967, table 2, pp. 50–65).

Table 12.6 Labor Force Participation Rates by Sex, 1970 and 1975–85

Year	Farm households			Nonfarm households		
	Male	*Female*	*All*	*Male*	*Female*	*All*
1970	75.2	48.2	60.9	75.1	29.8	51.5
1975	73.8	51.8	62.7	75.1	31.2	52.5
1976	74.5	55.3	64.8	74.7	33.7	53.3
1977	74.3	52.5	63.3	76.9	33.5	54.0
1978	74.5	54.0	63.9	75.3	35.6	54.6
1979	73.5	54.2	63.6	74.4	35.9	54.4
1980	72.4	53.0	62.5	74.2	36.1	54.4
1981	72.1	53.4	62.6	73.7	35.4	53.8
1982	70.4	53.6	61.9	73.4	37.5	54.7
1983	68.7	51.3	59.8	71.8	37.9	54.2
1984	68.8	50.1	59.3	69.6	36.1	52.2
1985	68.9	50.7	59.7	69.8	37.7	53.1

Source: Grootaert (1987, table 2, p. 5).

Thailand. The United States and Canada have rates of around 52.0 percent (Grootaert 1987, p. 6, quoting the *ILO Yearbook* for 1984).

Institutional changes facilitating greater participation of women in the nonfarm work force have been slow in coming. Grootaert (1987) points out that part-time work is not very common for Korean women; only about 7 to 8 percent work 35 hours or less per week. The distribution of workers by hours worked showed little difference between men and women, except that men do more overtime work (more than 54 hours a week) (Grootaert 1987, table 10, p. 15). Evidently, Korean employers have not taken the initiative in developing the market for jobs in clerical, sales, and assembly line production work that can easily be split into two part-time jobs. Grootaert also points to the government's limited efforts to establish public day care centers and the various restrictions on private sector initiatives.

Turning to the composition of female employment in the nonfarm sector, tables 12.7 and 12.8 show time series for the proportion of female employment by industry and by occupation, respectively. As

Table 12.7 Evolution of Female Employment by Industry, 1963–84 *(female workers as a percentage of the total labor force)*

Year	Agriculture	Mining and manufacturing	Construction	Services
1963	37.98	27.89	8.81	32.26
1964	37.97	29.57	3.83	32.08
1965	38.32	28.03	4.62	34.30
1966	38.84	29.46	3.35	31.79
1967	39.28	30.76	3.86	32.35
1968	40.22	31.75	6.01	34.22
1969	39.01	32.76	8.01	33.59
1970	41.62	31.18	1.76	34.67
1971	41.82	33.40	2.59	34.27
1972	42.95	33.09	2.30	32.90
1973	42.13	37.78	2.96	34.67
1974	41.51	35.31	5.11	35.59
1975	41.53	33.55	4.89	35.91
1976	42.64	37.59	4.91	37.33
1977	41.59	37.99	7.84	35.12
1978	44.10	38.39	7.67	36.56
1979	44.57	38.52	7.66	37.54
1980	43.77	38.05	8.56	38.23
1981	43.66	37.72	7.89	38.43
1982	43.74	37.30	6.98	41.01
1983	43.16	37.10	6.99	42.13
1984	42.72	36.49	7.42	41.43

Source: Economic Planning Board (various years).

Table 12.8 Evolution of Female Employment by Occupation, 1963–
84 *(female workers as a percentage of the total labor force)*

Year	Professional and managerial	Clerical	Sales	Service	Agriculture	Production operations
1963	21.46	11.28	44.81	19.83	38.08	19.83
1964	19.18	10.20	45.52	20.64	38.00	20.64
1965	18.03	10.03	46.21	20.06	38.38	20.06
1966	16.73	9.85	43.97	22.21	38.67	22.21
1967	16.14	11.63	42.77	23.61	39.37	23.61
1968	16.25	17.00	44.25	24.38	40.35	24.38
1969	15.57	13.81	42.95	25.09	39.30	25.09
1970	18.40	13.54	42.70	57.70	42.36	23.35
1971	19.43	16.55	41.25	23.72	41.92	23.72
1972	16.45	16.79	42.10	22.81	42.93	22.81
1973	19.11	17.83	42.08	27.88	41.99	27.88
1974	19.90	19.39	41.67	26.92	41.43	26.92
1975	20.86	20.88	40.72	57.38	41.41	25.84
1976	20.56	23.08	43.03	58.44	42.57	29.96
1977	22.53	24.47	41.60	54.38	41.61	29.92
1978	25.08	27.67	42.21	56.14	44.17	29.16
1979	26.34	30.60	43.41	56.27	44.62	29.02
1980	25.34	32.75	43.72	58.12	43.83	27.73
1981	23.54	33.62	44.21	57.72	43.82	26.68
1982	26.64	34.12	45.96	58.18	44.00	27.10
1983	26.67	34.21	47.35	59.99	43.38	27.89
1984	27.16	33.58	46.82	60.72	42.99	26.99

Note: This survey includes all women age 14+ except those in the armed forces, foreigners, and prisoners.
Source: Economic Planning Board (various years).

far as mining and manufacturing are concerned, the percentage of women workers increased at a modest but steady rate until 1980, and declined somewhat thereafter. There was, however, a decline in the crisis years following the first oil shock in 1974 and 1975. Thus, the evidence suggests that the proportion of women in manufacturing employment responds significantly to cyclical demand factors.

The increase of less than 10 percentage points in the share of female employment in industry must be considered rather marginal compared to the large shifts in the economy's industrial structure in the 20-year period. Much more pronounced growth of female employment is seen in the occupations categories in table 12.8, especially in the clerical and service categories, where the proportion of women in total employment has doubled. However, the increase in female employment in these white collar categories has been confined to narrow low-income groups. "Clearly clerical work has undergone a major and rapid image shift from a male to a female occupation . . . . More than 80 percent of the clerical work force below 25 (in 1984) are women; the clerical work force above age 35 is 95 percent male" (Grootaert 1987, p. 20). In the service categories women appear to be crowded into two subgroups, namely, teachers and medical, dental, and veterinary personnel. In the administrative and managerial category, only 2.9 percent are women, far below the proportion in other East Asian countries (13.1 percent in Hong Kong, 6.1 percent in Japan, 17.4 percent in Singapore, and 19.8 percent in Thailand) (Grootaert 1987, table 14, p. 22).

Another aspect of the differential conditions of employment by sex is revealed by looking at the changes in employment by work status. The employed labor force is classified into self-employed workers, family workers, and employees. The distinction between the first two is important for work status. A self-employed person could be a small entrepreneur, and often earns more than an employee. A family worker, by contrast, is an unpaid working member of the household. One of the most striking developments in Korea is that in 1984, nearly 80 percent of family workers in the mining and manufacturing sector were women. Between 1976 and 1984 the proportion of women among employees remained unchanged, but the proportion of women among family workers rose from 65 to 80 percent, while women's share in the self-employed category was halved to 26 percent (Grootaert 1987, p. 27 and table 18). Evidently, during the big push and the subsequent adjustment, the number of women entrepreneurs dropped sharply.

Employees in Korean labor markets can be categorized as regular, temporary, or daily workers. The security of tenure and access to bonuses and other benefits associated with internal labor markets lead Korean employers to hire a large proportion of their work force on temporary or daily contracts. This allows them to vary the size of the work force with changing business conditions and holds down labor costs. Table 12.9 breaks down the three categories of workers by sex for 1963–85. The table shows that the proportion of regulars among male workers has increased steadily during the period except for the

Table 12.9 Distribution of Total Employment by Sex and Status, 1963–85

(percent, nonfarm households)

Year	Men			Women		
	Regular employees	Temporary employees	Daily workers	Regular employees	Temporary employees	Daily workers
1963	49.6	17.6	32.6	34.6	26.6	38.6
1964	48.6	20.4	30.8	32.0	34.0	33.8
1965	51.4	20.7	27.7	35.2	36.4	28.3
1966	55.3	17.4	27.2	39.3	30.0	30.6
1967	57.5	17.4	25.0	45.7	23.2	30.9
1968	62.9	14.5	22.4	49.0	22.5	28.4
1969	65.7	11.3	22.8	55.3	20.1	24.5
1970	68.8	11.8	19.2	57.9	22.1	19.8
1971	69.2	11.3	19.4	55.2	23.9	20.8
1972	62.4	12.6	24.8	52.0	26.7	21.1
1973	56.5	19.7	23.7	44.7	34.5	20.7
1974	62.3	17.0	20.5	46.7	33.3	19.8
1975	60.9	19.5	19.4	48.3	33.9	17.6
1977	64.9	15.6	19.3	54.9	26.1	18.8
1979	68.3	13.8	17.8	57.7	24.9	17.2
1980	71.5	12.1	16.2	58.5	24.6	16.7
1982	73.7	10.8	15.3	62.3	21.5	16.0
1984	71.9	14.7	13.2	50.6	30.5	18.7
1985	72.3	14.9	12.8	48.8	30.4	20.8

Note: The survey is based on the population aged 14 and over and not in the army, imprisoned, or foreigners.
Source: Economic Planning Board (various years).

period 1972–75, but for women the proportion of regular employees in 1985 was about the same as that in 1968. The percentage of regular female employees fell significantly both after the first oil shock in 1973–75 and following the second period of stabilization in the early 1980s. Evidently, women workers have been used in a more "marginal" way in the last two decades.

Turning to earnings, the trend in the female/male differential for different educational groups is plotted in figure 12.7. This shows that

Figure 12.7 Female/Male Earnings Ratio by Level of Education, 1970–84

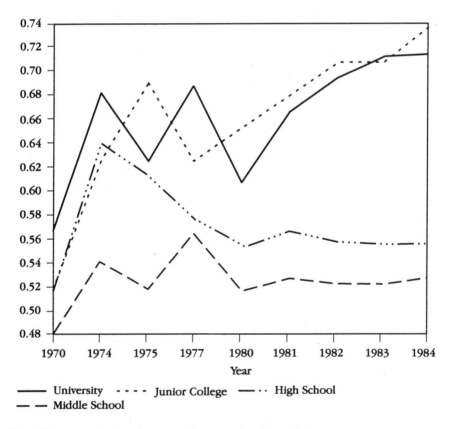

Note: The survey is based on a random sample of establishments employing ten or more regular employees, excluding agriculture, forestry, fishing, government administration, public education, the army, and the police force.
Source: Occupational Wage Survey.

while university and college educated women have improved their relative earnings since 1970 (although still earning a little more than 70 percent of the male average), the bulk of female workers with high school or middle school educations have more or less the same relative earnings as in the early 1970s. A trend toward reducing the gender differential for this group (particularly the high school graduates) was apparent during the big push of the late 1970s, but this gain was lost in the 1980s.

Conclusion

This chapter investigated the successful adjustment to external shocks of an open economy heavily dependent on key imports. In the Korean case, a high investment rate maintained throughout the growth process of the last two decades accentuated the country's macroeconomic problems. The rate of investment continuously outrun the rate of domestic savings, which kept the economy on a tightrope of external deficits on the current account and internal inflationary pressures for much of the period. Maintaining its external competitiveness was of central importance to this export-oriented economy.

The evidence shows that an active exchange rate policy (continuous devaluation of the won except for a few years in the late 1970s and maxi devaluations during shocks) has been central to the mechanism that kept unit labor costs falling throughout the period. However, the devaluation's success in producing the desired result depended on policies affecting both the capital and labor markets. In the capital markets, the maintenance of cheap credit for the large-scale sector cushioned the exporting firms from the rising costs of interest payments and imported inputs that devaluation induced. Equally important was the tight government control of external capital flows that prevented destabilizing speculative movements of capital.

On the labor market front, the evidence shows the importance of state paternalism in wage negotiations in the formal sector in keeping real wage increases in line with productivity growth, but somewhat below it in most periods (again with the exception of the big push period). It was also eminently successful in drastically slowing down, or even halting, real wage growth during the short-run periods of crisis. However, the wage-productivity relationship behaved in the healthy way it did because real wages increased significantly in most years. This experience must have been instrumental both in securing worker acquiescence to the temporary stagnation of wages and in preventing destabilizing inflationary expectations from developing.

The critical factor here was the strongly positive time trend in total factor productivity growth. It is this that kept the rate of real wage growth high at the same time that the unit labor cost in industry was falling.

Real wages in Korea's large-scale manufacturing sector have "risen faster, possibly than in any previous or contemporary industrial revolution" (Amsden 1990, p. 79). Our analysis suggests that the major factor behind this real wage growth was probably profit sharing as an incentive scheme in the process of wage determination. The internal labor market structure of the large manufacturing firms encouraged this process, as did state paternalism. We would expect that in large segments of the labor market outside the large firms, the mechanisms of the internal labor markets would be weak, and wages would be lower in these segments and would rise less fast. This is, indeed, what earlier writers have suggested. For example, Amsden writes: "By world standards, Korea has the highest inter-manufacturing industry wage dispersion and the widest gap in gross wages between the sexes (Krueger and Summers 1986; Lee 1983). Underlying the rapid rise in real wages beginning in 1965 was the preening of a labor aristocracy: male, employed by the *chaebol*, in the new heavy industries. At the opposite end of the spectrum is the economically active population in the informal sector" (1987, p. 4).

The absence of comprehensive household surveys in Korea precluded the investigation of formal-informal earnings differentials in large parts of the labor market, but we were able to examine a limited range of wage differentials. Earnings in the farm sector did not perform all that badly compared to average earnings in the nonfarm or urban sectors. Up to the first oil shock of 1973 annual farm incomes per worker increased at a rate only slightly lower than the average earnings in manufacturing. However, during the big push of the late 1970s, the differential in favor of manufacturing wages increased from 50 to 80 percent, and although it fell somewhat after the adjustment that followed the second oil shock, in the mid-1980s, it was well above earlier levels.

Analysis of wage differentials by firm size within the formal sector (excluding very small firms employing fewer than ten workers) shows very large differences in average earnings that increase significantly over time, but to a large extent these differences are due to differences in skill composition. A comparison of wage differences between more homogeneous categories of labor reveals that the differential, which had stood at about 100 percent in 1967 (for male middle or elementary school graduates), fell to 33 percent in 1980. Taken together, the evidence suggests that the accentuation of labor market dualism in Korea has taken the form of selecting workers with better human capital attributes for the large-scale sector rather than widening the standardized wage differential by firm size. However, the large-scale sector seems to have taken the main brunt of short-run adjustment following the oil shocks. Wages stagnated in this sector for short periods after the adjustment, and the relative expansion of the large firms at the expense of the small, which was occurring rapidly until 1973, halted in the next decade.

Amsden suggested that "not only Korea set world records with its growth rate in wages, it also has outcompeted other countries in its discrimination against women workers" (1990, p. 85). We found evidence of surprisingly small increases in participation rates of women in the nonfarm sectors, severe occupational crowding, a larger proportion of women in lower status jobs like family workers or in temporary positions, and a more or less constant wage differential in favor of male workers over the years. The average earnings of female workers with a high or middle school education were 52 percent of the earnings of men with a similar education. As we expected, women were disproportionately affected during the postshock periods of sharp adjustment.

While Korea's record in solving some of the structural problems in the labor market has not been very good, its astonishing success in managing the economy's short-run macroeconomic balance may also be threatened in the future. A full analysis of contemporary developments in the labor market is beyond the scope of this chapter, but we should, in concluding, draw attention to the explosive increases in wages in manufacturing since 1987. This type of wage push, emanating from a breakdown of the traditional relationship between the Korean Federation of Trade Unions and that of employers, threatens to upset the wage-productivity balance that has been central to the success of Korea's macroeconomic stability. If wages go soaring above productivity growth, Korea's share of the export market relative to its close competitors will undoubtedly be threatened, and in addition, the country might have to deal with an inflationary spiral and the need for much more painful adjustments when external shocks develop in the future. According to the World Bank: "A recent study of manufacturing unit labor costs found that between 1980 and 1986 Taiwan's ULC rose 56 percent relative to Korea's. In 1987 and 1988 the two economies' ULCs increased at the same rate. It was only in the first quarter of 1989 that Korea's ULC began to increase relative to Taiwan" (1989, p. 7). The concern of the coming years is how much and in what way can Korea contain these new developments in the labor market. The other significant question is Korea's ability to sustain—if not to increase—the record rate of total factor productivity growth that it has achieved in the last two decades or more.

APPENDIX

Table 12.A1 Net Barter and Income Terms of Trade, 1963–88
(index, 1980 = 100)

Year	Net barter terms	Income terms of trade	Percent change	
			Barter	Income
1963	111.48	1.21	–	–
1964	112.83	1.88	1.21	55.60
1965	114.87	3.36	1.81	78.39
1966	128.15	4.91	11.57	46.41
1967	132.85	6.23	3.66	26.80
1968	138.06	8.93	3.92	43.31
1969	133.27	12.40	-3.47	38.89
1970	134.19	16.06	0.69	29.45
1971	133.08	20.57	-0.82	28.09
1972	132.35	30.76	-0.55	49.56
1973	125.62	45.82	-5.08	48.97
1974	101.31	40.73	-19.35	-11.12
1975	92.10	45.10	-9.09	10.74
1976	105.10	69.90	14.12	54.99
1977	112.40	89.00	6.95	27.32
1978	117.80	106.70	4.80	19.89
1979	115.30	103.40	-2.12	-3.09
1980	100.00	100.00	-13.27	-3.29
1981	97.90	115.00	-2.10	15.00
1982	102.20	127.90	4.39	11.22
1983	103.10	150.00	0.88	17.28
1984	105.30	177.10	2.13	18.07
1985	105.90	191.70	0.57	8.24
1986	114.70	234.70	8.31	22.43
1987	118.08	296.94	2.95	26.52
1988	121.36	344.87	2.78	16.14

Note: Net barter terms of trade are defined as the ratio of export to import unit value index. Income terms of trade are defined as the product of the net barter terms of trade and the export quantum index.

Table 12.A2 Major Economic Indicators, 1967–88

Year	Real GNP growth (% per annum)	Current account (% GNP)	Exports growth (%)	Budget deficit (% GNP)	Unemployment rate (%)
1967	6.60	-4.12	28.00	–	6.2
1968	11.30	-7.49	42.20	–	5.1
1969	13.80	-7.76	36.90	–	4.8
1970	7.60	-7.35	34.00	1.60	4.5
1971	8.60	-9.38	27.90	2.30	4.5
1972	5.10	-3.56	52.10	4.60	4.5
1973	13.20	-2.28	98.60	1.60	4.0
1973	13.20	-2.28	98.60	1.60	4.0
1974	8.10	-13.05	38.30	4.00	4.1
1975	6.40	-9.05	13.90	4.60	4.1
1976	13.10	-1.09	51.80	2.90	3.9
1977	9.80	0.03	30.20	2.60	3.8
1978	9.80	-2.17	26.50	2.50	3.2
1979	7.20	-6.43	18.40	1.40	3.8
1979	7.20	-6.43	18.40	1.40	3.8
1980	-3.70	-9.56	16.30	3.20	5.2
1981	5.90	-7.21	21.40	4.70	4.5
1982	7.20	-3.91	2.80	4.40	4.3
1982	7.20	-3.91	2.80	4.40	4.3
1983	12.60	-2.07	11.90	1.60	4.1
1984	9.30	-1.62	19.60	1.40	3.8
1985	7.00	-1.01	3.50	1.00	4.0
1986	12.90	4.39	14.60	1.80	3.8
1987	12.80	7.39	36.20	–	3.1
1988	12.20	7.84	28.40	–	2.5

Note: 1988 GNP growth rate is preliminary.
Source: Bank of Korea *Principle Economic Indicators, Economic Statistics Yearbook.*

Table 12.A3 Data Used for Unit Labor Costs in Manufacturing, 1967–86

Year	Annual value added (billion won)	Annual wages (billion won)	Manufacturing deflator (1980 = 100)	CPI (1980 = 100)	Average exchange rate (won/US$)
1967	206.6	53.3	17.1	15.3	270.5
1968	300.1	76.6	18.3	17.0	276.7
1969	424.2	105.7	19.9	19.1	288.2
1970	547.9	137.1	22.3	22.2	310.6
1971	688.6	160.4	23.4	25.2	347.2
1972	899.3	211.5	26.7	28.1	392.9
1973	1,379.6	310.3	29.9	29.0	398.3
1974	1,867.2	451.3	37.7	36.1	404.5
1975	2,828.1	651.6	45.4	45.2	484.0
1976	4,075.1	1,009.1	52.8	52.1	484.0
1977	5,596.9	1,460.4	58.5	57.4	484.0
1978	8,193.0	2,221.8	66.2	65.7	484.0
1979	9,205.0	2,922.1	78.9	77.7	484.0
1980	11,857.0	3,471.7	100.0	100.0	607.4
1981	15,412.0	4,133.5	113.7	121.3	681.0
1982	17,306.0	4,754.1	119.4	130.1	731.1
1983	20,912.0	5,499.6	122.8	134.5	775.8
1984	24,656.0	6,495.1	123.7	137.6	806.0
1985	26,737.0	7,244.5	126.7	141.0	870.0
1986	32,882.0	8,607.3	131.3	144.2	881.5

Source: U.N. *Yearbook of Industrial Statistics*, IMF *International Financial Statistics*, Bank of Korea.

Table 12.A4 Annual Earnings per Worker in the Farming and Manufacturing Sectors, 1966–85

Year	Real annual income per farm worker		Real annual manufacturing earnings	
	Thousands 1980 won	*Percentage change per annum*	*Thousands 1980 won*	*Percentage change per annum*
1966	400	–	467	–
1967	426	6.4	520	11.1
1968	474	11.2	593	14.0
1969	518	9.2	707	19.2
1970	537	3.7	787	11.3
1971	660	22.9	826	5.0
1972	688	4.2	858	3.8
1973	735	6.8	924	7.6
1966–73 average	555	11.9	710	13.9
1974	785	6.7	1,004	8.6
1975	822	4.7	1,018	1.4
1976	876	6.5	1,190	16.8
1977	964	10.1	1,446	21.4
1978	1,004	4.1	1,696	17.3
1974–78 average	890	6.9	1,271	17.2
1979	1,072	6.7	1,845	8.7
1980	1,081	0.8	1,760	-4.6
1981	1,152	6.5	1,742	-0.9
1982	1,232	6.9	1,864	6.9
1983	1,292	4.8	2,023	8.5
1984	1,490	15.3	2,138	5.7
1985	1,579	5.9	2,294	7.2
1979–85 average	1,271	7.8	1,952	4.0

Table 12.A5 Annual Household Income per Earner for Urban Households, 1966–84

Year	Salary earner households		Wage earner households	
	Thousands 1980 won	*Percentage change per annum*	*Thousands 1980 won*	*Percentage change per annum*
1966	1,316	–	681	–
1967	1,569	19.2	981	44.1
1968	1,615	2.9	1,006	2.4
1969	1,609	-0.4	1,038	3.2
1970	1,562	-2.8	975	-6.0
1971	1,652	5.7	1,041	6.7
1972	1,685	1.9	1,073	3.0
1973	1,690	0.2	1,046	-2.5
1966–73 average	1,587	4.0	980	7.6
1974	1,806	6.8	990	-5.3
1975	1,873	3.7	1,052	6.2
1976	2,428	29.6	1,146	8.9
1977	2,932	20.7	1,427	24.5
1978	3,284	12.0	1,851	29.6
1974–78 average	2,465	20.4	1,293	21.7
1979	3,507	6.7	2,058	11.1
1980	3,684	5.0	1,985	-3.5
1981	3,646	-1.0	2,006	1.0
1982	3,568	-2.1	1,787	-10.9
1983	3,760	5.3	1,938	8.4
1984	3,962	5.3	2,074	7.0
1979–84 average	3,688	-16.6	1,975	-16.6

Note on the Data

Data on daily farm wages and incomes were collected from the Korean National Agricultural Cooperative's monthly report. These same figures are reported in the *Statistical Yearbook* published by the Economic Planning Board. Census years were 1970 and 1975; all other years are based on sample surveys. The survey is carried out by the Ministry of Agriculture and Fisheries and is based on a sample of farm households engaged primarily in farming and cultivating a plot of land larger than 0.1 hectare. The survey is conducted monthly and revised after censuses. Income includes agricultural receipts, side-business receipts, nonbusiness receipts (wages, rent, and so on) and property (assets) receipts less farm and side-business expenses. Daily farm wages are also reported in these documents. Here, men's daily wages (cash and in kind) are shown for all workers.

The price index used to deflate farm incomes was the prices paid by farmers index, reported in the same documents. These prices are collected at 85 rural markets covering 201 items.

Farm income was normalized to per worker farm income by dividing total farm income (including income from nonfarm sources) by the number of farm workers.

Data on manufacturing earnings were extracted from the *Statistics Yearbook* published by the Economic Planning Board. These statistics are collected by the Ministry of Labor in a monthly wage survey. The survey covers all manufacturing establishments with ten or more employees. The earnings reported are the average monthly earnings of all (men and women) regular employees. Regular workers are those whose employment contract is for one month or more, and who worked for more than 45 days during the three months prior to the reporting day. Monthly earnings include overtime pay, bonus pay, and base pay.

The deflator used to estimate real earnings for manufacturing and urban household incomes was the all cities consumer price index. This is reported in the Economic Planning Board's *Statistics Yearbook*. Average price data are collected three times a month at nine principal cities, including Seoul, on 394 commodities and services. Until 1965, the city consumer price index survey was carried out only in Seoul.

Urban incomes data was also taken from the *Statistics Yearbook*. This data is based on the Family Income and Expenditure Survey conducted by the Economic Planning Board each month. The survey covers all households residing in one of Korea's 50 cities, excluding farm households, fishing households, single person households, foreign households, and households whose income and expenditure are not easily identified. Income includes earnings, income from subsidiary jobs, and other income.

References

Amsden, Alice. 1987. *Project on Stabilization and Adjustment Policies and Programs.* Country Study No. 14. Helsinki, Finland: World Institute for Development Economic Research.

_____. 1990. "South Korea's Record Wage Rates: Labor in Late Industrialization." *Industrial Relations* 29 (1).

Bank of Korea, Statistics Department. Various years. *Principle Economic Indicators, Economic Statistics Yearbook.* Seoul.

Bank of Korea. 1987. *Report on Wage Survey.* Seoul.

Collins, Susan, and Won Am Park. 1987. *External Debt and Macroeconomic Performance in South Korea.* National Bureau of Economic Research. New York. Processed.

Dornbusch, Rudiger, and Yung Chul Park. 1987. "Korean Growth Policy." *Brookings Papers on Economic Activity* 2: 389–453.

Grootaert, C. 1987. "The Labor Force Participation of Women in the Republic of Korea: Evaluation of Policy Issues." Internal Discussion Paper, Asia Regional Series. Washington, D.C.: World Bank.

IMF. Various years. *International Financial Statistics Yearbook.* Washington, D.C.

Korea. Administration of Labor Affairs. 1980. *Report on Occupational Wage Survey,* vol. I. Seoul.

Korea. Economic Planning Board. Various years. *Report on Mining and Manufacturing Survey.* Seoul.

_____. Various years. *Korean Statistical Yearbook.* Seoul.

_____. Various years. *Year Book of Labor Statistics.* Seoul.

Krueger, A., and L. H. Summers. 1986. *Reflections on the Inter-Industry Wage Structure.* Discussion Paper No. 1252. Cambridge, Massachusetts: Harvard Institute of Economic Research.

Lee, Jong Woo. 1983. "Economic Development and Wage Inequality in Korea." Unpublished Ph.D. dissertation, Harvard University.

Lindauer, David. 1984. *Labor Market Behavior in the Republic of Korea: An Analysis of Wages and Their Impact on the Economy.* Staff Working Paper No. 641. Washington, D.C.: World Bank.

Nishimuzu, M., and S. Robinson. 1984. "Trade Policies and Productivity Change in Semi-Industrialized Countries." *Journal of Development Economics* 16 (1–2): 177–206.

Park, Funkoo, and Torsacio Castaneda. 1987. "Structural Adjustment and the Role of the Labor Market." Working Paper No. 8705. Seoul: Korean Development Institute.

Park, Se-Il. 1980. "Wages in Korea: Determination of the Wage Levels and the Wage Structure in a Dualistic Labor Market." Unpublished Ph.D. dissertation, Cornell University.

Sachs, Jeffrey. 1985. "External Debt and Macroeconomic Performance in Latin America and East Asia." *Brookings Papers on Economic Activity* 2: 523–573.

U.N. Various years. *Industrial Statistics Yearbook.* New York.

Wong, Wontack, and Lawrence B. Krause, ed., 1981. *Trade and Growth of the Advanced Developing Countries in the Pacific Basin.* Seoul: Korean Development Institute.

World Bank. 1989. "Korea: Country Economic Memorandum." Paper No. 7920–KO. Washington, D.C.

13

THAILAND

Chalongphob Sussangkarn

During the last 20 to 30 years, Thailand has been able to achieve a satisfactory pace of economic development despite several major shocks in the world economy, and structural changes in world trade and exchange rate systems. Through out this period, adjustment problems associated with short-term macroeconomic management and external resource gaps have been relatively mild compared to the experiences of many other countries. Although the chronic current account deficit and external debt situation became an important focus of policy concerns during the early to mid-1980s, the on-going boom in manufactured exports, starting around 1986, has diluted this concern substantially. The country is now being talked about as the leader of the next wave of newly industrialized countries.

While overall macroeconomic growth has been good, Thailand faces important structural adjustment problems concerning sectoral and regional balance and income distribution. During the last two decades, the disparities between agriculture and nonagriculture, between regions, and between income groups have been widening noticeably. While industrialization is now proceeding very rapidly and the share of agriculture in GDP is only around 16 percent, more than 60 percent of the labor force is still primarily engaged in agriculture. Most of the dynamic and successful export industries are located in and around the capital city, Bangkok, which is highly developed and about 20 times larger than the next largest city (Chiang Mai). The key question for the future is how to maintain the pace of economic growth while ensuring more balanced development, with the benefits from development spread more evenly among the population.

In addition, with the current rapid growth of industries and services, the composition of demand for labor is changing toward more highly skilled labor. Already shortages of scientific and technical manpower at the higher level are apparent. In the future, the labor market for all types of labor with middle to high levels of education is also likely to get tight. This will create another structural imbalance, one related to labor of different skill types. This may have an adverse impact on the competitiveness of Thailand in foreign trade, as well as implications for the achievement of better distribution of income.

The nature and functioning of the labor markets are clearly related to the problems of structural imbalance. Changes in the structure of production lead to changes in the composition of demand for labor by sector, by location, by skill types. Lags in adjustment in the labor market, or rigidities, will lead to structural imbalance in the structure of employment, which may reinforce other imbalances.

Macroeconomic Growth and External Balance

Table 13.1 shows the rates of growth of real GDP from 1960 to 1989. Between 1960 and 1980, the average rate of real GDP growth was above 7 percent, which is very satisfactory. Breaking down the

Table 13.1 Growth of Real GDP and Real per Capita GNP, 1960–89 *(percent)*

Year	Real GDP	Agriculture	Industry	Service	Real per capita GNP
1960–65	7.2	4.8	11.5	7.2	4.5
1965–70	8.6	6.0	10.4	9.5	5.8
1970–75	5.6	3.8	7.3	5.6	2.9
1975–80	7.9	4.0	10.6	8.2	5.3
1980–85	5.6	4.9	5.0	6.3	3.5
1986	4.5	0.2	7.1	4.6	2.6
1987	8.4	-2.0	12.0	10.1	6.5
1988	11.0	8.6	12.8	10.7	9.1
1989	10.0	–	–	–	–

Note: 1970 figures are based on the New Series of National Accounts.
Source: NESDB (various years).

period from 1960 to 1985 into five-year intervals, the table shows that growth was lowest in the immediate aftermath of the two oil shocks: 1970–75 and 1980–85. However, the 5.6 percent average growth achieved during these periods is very high compared to other countries' experiences. The impact of the first oil shock was cushioned by a boom in commodity prices during the same period. This helped to increase farm income, and improved the poverty situation considerably. In contrast, after the second oil shock, all Thailand's main agricultural commodities suffered a declining price trend. While Thailand still maintained a satisfactory rate of growth, the impact on agricultural incomes was severe, leading to significant increases in poverty incidence. However, after 1986, the economy began a period of very rapid growth. Driven on by fast growth of manufactured exports (currently average 30 to 40 percent per annum) and tourism, economic growth reached 11 percent in 1988 and was about 10 percent in 1989.

As with most developing countries, Thailand has experienced trade and current account deficits during the course of its development. In 1975, the ratio of the stock of debt to GDP was insignificant at 2.3 percent. Since 1975, however, this ratio has risen rapidly. The ratio jumped to 16.1 percent of GDP in 1980, and to 39.0 percent of GDP in 1985 (figure 13.1). After the second oil shock, as a result of the recession in the world economy and declining agricultural commodity prices, the ratio of debt to GDP increased particularly rapidly. In the early to mid-1980s, this issue was of major concern to the government.

After the second oil shock, the Thai government, both at its own initiative and with assistance from the IMF and the World Bank, implemented various structural adjustment policies to control the external imbalance and associated foreign debt problems (see Sahasakul and others 1989). Some taxes were restructured, in particular, the export tax on rice was progressively reduced and finally eliminated. The government tried to control public expenditures, and a major policy in this connection that had important consequences on employment was the ceiling on government employment growth of 2 percent per annum, starting in 1983. This significantly affected the

Figure 13.1 Ratio of Stock of Debt to GDP, 1975–88

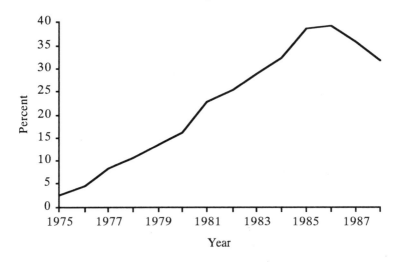

Sources: National Bank of Thailand and NESDB.

employment prospects of the better educated workers, who are predominantly employed by the public sector.

However, the policies that were politically the most difficult to put through were probably the devaluations of 1981 and 1984. In 1981, the baht was devalued from about B20.5 to the dollar to B23.0 to the dollar, and in 1984 a further devaluation took the rate to about B27.0 to the dollar. In both cases the government nearly fell. In contrast, hardly any political problems arose after 1986 when the baht was tied mostly to the U.S. dollar as the dollar depreciated substantially relative to the yen and major European currencies, which meant substantial effective depreciation of the baht with respect to the currencies of Thailand's trading partners. These devaluations and depreciation of the baht were substantial departures from previous exchange rate policies. As figure 13.2 shows, the baht/dollar exchange rate had moved very little between 1950 and 1980.

While the various adjustment policies did not keep the ratio of foreign debt to GDP from rising, they nevertheless kept the problem

Figure 13.2 Baht/Dollar Exchange Rate, 1985–88

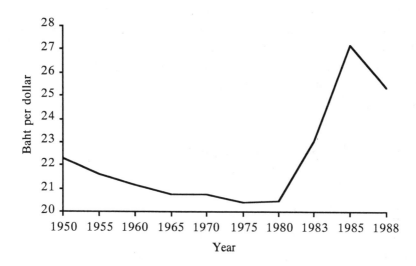

Source: Bank of Thailand.

from getting out of hand. This left Thailand in a good position to take advantage of changes that occurred in the world economic environment starting around 1986. Partly because of the exchange rate adjustments, partly because of the sharp decline in oil prices in 1986, and partly because of the transition of the Asian newly industrializing economies (Hong Kong, the Republic of Korea, Taiwan, and Singapore) to more skilled and technologically intensive exporters, the growth of the Thai economy accelerated significantly after 1986. The growth was mainly driven on by sharp increases in manufactured exports, which started to grow at a rate of about 30 to 40 percent per annum in 1986. These exports are very diverse, and include processed food, textiles, shoes, gems and jewelry, artificial flowers, integrated circuits, toys, and steep pipes. Basically, these products require relatively unsophisticated labor, and are the kinds of items through which the current newly industrializing countries had achieved their success. At the same time, however, Thailand still remains a major player in agricultural exports. Thailand is the largest exporter of rice and cassava in the world, and ranks among the top ten exporters of rubber, sugarcane, maize, and fisheries.

The boom in exports led to a downturn in the ratio of debt to GDP, which declined from about 39 percent in 1986 to about 32 percent in 1988 (figure 13.1). While the external resource gap is starting to widen again in absolute terms, it remains manageable thanks partly to the huge inflow of foreign direct investment. The key macroeconomic issue has shifted more to the question of how to manage the extremely rapid industrial and urban growth.

Structural Imbalance and Adjustment

Although Thailand has been able to achieve a very satisfactory pace of economic growth during the past 20 to 30 years, and short-run adjustment problems have proved to be relatively minor, nevertheless, sectoral and locational imbalance and income distribution problems are significant. Disparities between sectors of production, between regions, and between income groups have been widening.

The importance of agriculture in GDP has continually been on the decline. In 1960, the share of agriculture in GDP was about 40 percent. This declined to 31.5 percent in 1975, and virtually halved to 16.7 percent between 1975 and 1986 (table 13.2). With the declining importance of agriculture in GDP, the decline in the share of employment in agriculture is not surprising. However, the decline in the share of employment in agriculture has been much slower than the share of agriculture in value added. While the share of agriculture in GDP nearly halved between 1975and 1986, the share of employment in agriculture only fell from 73 to 67 percent.[1] This obviously meant a substantial widening of the ratio of value added per head between nonagriculture and agriculture. In 1975, the value added per head in nonagriculture was 5.9 times higher than that in agriculture, and by 1986 it was 10.0 times higher.

---

1. This refers to the share of the work force whose main occupation is in agriculture, and is based on data during the peak agricultural season.

Table 13.2 GDP and Employment by Sector, 1975, 1980, and 1986

Category	1975	1980	1986
GDP (millions of baht)	298,816	684,930	1,098,362
Agriculture	94,063	173,806	183,037
Nonagriculture	204,753	511,124	915,325
Share of GDP (percent)			
Agriculture	31.48	25.38	16.66
Nonagriculture	68.52	74.62	83.34
Employment (millions)	18.182	22.681	26.672
Agriculture	13.270	16.092	17.803
Nonagriculture	4.912	6.589	8.870
Share of employment (percent)			
Agriculture	72.99	70.95	66.75
Nonagriculture	27.01	29.05	33.25
Per capita GDP (baht/month)	1,369.6	2,516.6	3,431.7
Agriculture	590.7	900.1	856.8
Nonagriculture	3,474.0	6,464.7	8,599.9
Ratio of per capita GDP			
Nonagriculture/agriculture	5.88	7.18	10.4

Sources: NESDB (various years); NSO (various years).

The gap between nonagriculture and agriculture widened particularly rapidly between 1980 and 1986, when the prices of most major crops were on a downward trend. The export price of rice declined an average of 7.0 percent per annum, that of rubber by 5.1 percent per annum, and that of sugar by 9.1 percent per annum. The result was that the per capita GDP in agriculture declined in absolute terms (table 13.2).

Because most agricultural households earn a significant part of their income from nonagricultural activities—Sussangkam and others (1988, table 5.6) estimated that agricultural households earn about 46 percent of their income from nonagricultural activities—the disparity in per capita income between agricultural and nonagricultural households is not as large as the disparity in per capita GDP. Nevertheless, agricultural households earn about half as much as

nonagricultural households, and the gap has been widening along with
the trend in per capita GDP. Table 13.3 shows that in 1975/76, the
ratio of per capita income of nonagricultural households to that of
agricultural households was 2.1. This increased to 2.7 in 1986. Also,
during the period from 1981 to 1986, when crop prices were on a
downward trend, nominal per capital income of agricultural
households fell.

Naturally the disparity between agriculture and nonagriculture was
reflected in the disparity between urban and rural areas. However, in
the case of Thailand, extreme differences exist in the economic
conditions in Bangkok compared to the rest of the country. Whereas
the Bangkok region (including the five surrounding provinces)
contain 15.6 percent of the total population in 1985, it accounted for
45.5 percent of total GDP. Of the GDP from industry, 63.7 percent
originates from the Bangkok region. For the most dynamic exporting
industries such as textiles and garments, the proportions originating
from the Bangkok region rise to over 90 percent. Per capita GDP in
Bangkok is more than sevenfold that of the northeast (the poorest
region), and about 2.8 times higher than that of the central region (the
second richest region). Taken by itself, the Bangkok region is already
a "newly industrializing country."

The sectoral and regional disparities are reflected in the distribution
of household income. Table 13.4 shows the shares of incomes
received by various quintiles of households, with the top and bottom
two deciles also separated out. Between 1975 and 1986, the income

Table 13.3 Mean per Capita Income, Agricultural and Nonagricultural
Households, Selected Years, 1975/76–86

Year	*Baht per month*		*Nonagricultural: agricultural*
	Agricultural	*Nonagricultural*	
1975/76	247	513	2.1
1981	503	1,154	2.3
1986	481	1,312	2.7

Source: NSO (1975/76, 1981, 1986).

Table 13.4 Income Share by Quintile of Population, Selected Years, 1975/76–86
(percentage of total)

Quintile	1975/76	1981	1986
First	49.3	51.5	55.6
Top 10 percent	33.4	35.4	39.1
Second 10 percent	15.9	16.1	16.5
Second	21.0	20.6	19.9
Third	14.0	13.4	12.1
Fourth	9.7	9.1	7.9
Fifth	6.0	5.4	4.5
Second bottom 10 percent	3.6	3.3	2.7
Bottom 10 percent	2.4	2.1	1.8

Source: NSO (1975/76, 1981, 1986).

share of the richest 20 percent of households increased from 49.3 percent to 55.6 percent while that of the poorest 20 percent of households declined from 6.0 percent to 4.5 percent. The shares of all quintile below the top quintile continually declined between 1975/76 and 1986. Of the top two deciles, the second decile made only a slight gain. Only the top decile increased its share of income substantially.

Between 1981 and 1986, apart from the worsening in the distribution of income, absolute poverty also increased. Because most of the population depended for their livelihood on agriculture, the decline in crop prices led to a large increase in the share of the population living below the poverty line, from 23 percent in 1981 to 29.5 percent in 1986 (table 13.5). As the table shows, this was a reversal of the excellent progress made in poverty alleviation since the late 1960s.

After 1986, agricultural prices picked up substantially, which helped to reduce poverty. The percentage of the population living below the poverty line declined to 25.2 percent in 1988. This was, however, still higher than the percentage below the poverty line in

Table 13.5 The Incidence of Poverty, Selected Years, 1968/69–1988

Year	Percentage of population below the poverty line
1968/69	39.0
1975/76	30.0
1981	23.0
1986	29.5
1988	25.2

Note: Figures up to 1986 are calculated from various socioeconomic surveys conducted by the NSO. The 1988 figure was based on a Thailand Development Research Institute simulation using the THAM2 model. Sanitary districts are classified as rural.
Sources: Hutaserani and Jitsuchon (1988); Meesook (1979).

1981. The income distribution situation since 1986 still shows a slight worsening trend. Although crop prices increased, the boom in manufactured exports also led to rapid increases in the incomes of those in urban areas, particularly those in the Bangkok area. To some extent, the exchange rate policy and the agricultural taxation policy counteracted the worsening trend of poverty and income distribution between 1981 and 1986.

The devaluations in 1981 and 1984 increased farm incomes more than would have occurred without these devaluations. Although Thailand does have some market power in the major export crops such as paddy, econometric estimates generally find the foreign demand curve to be fairly elastic, and that devaluation would increase domestic farm incomes. Thailand has also had a long history of export taxation on rice.[2] This included export tax, a rice premium, and export quotas on rice exports. The estimated burden on rice farmers is some 30 percent of the foreign price of rice in 1980 (Siamwalla and Setboonsarng 1987). As rice prices fell on the world market, the rate of taxation gradually declined, and in 1986 all taxes on rice exports (explicit and implicit) were removed. This helped to

---

2. There are also smaller taxes on rubber still present today.

keep the domestic farm gate price from falling in line with world prices. Nevertheless, these policies could not reverse the trend of falling farm incomes and worsening inequality.

Labor Markets and Structural Adjustments

The problems of imbalance, poverty, and income distribution described above are clearly related to adjustments occurring in labor markets in response to structural changes on the production side. This section discusses the structure of the labor market in Thailand and the relationship between the labor market and the structural imbalance and disparity issues.

General Employment Situation

As already mentioned and indicated in table 13.2, most of those employed in Thailand work in agriculture. Currently, over 65 percent of all employed individuals have their main occupation in agriculture. Thus, in terms of the employment structure, Thailand is basically an agrarian society. Aggregate indicators do not reveal any serious employment problems. Open unemployment is generally very low, around 1 percent of the work force, although the rate appears to be on the rise (figure 13.3), presumably partly due to the recession in the first part of the 1980s. The low open unemployment rate is not too surprising. Most people in Thailand are either self-employed or unpaid family workers, mainly in agriculture. While the share of self-employed and unpaid family workers in total employment has been gradually falling (table 13.6), in 1988 they still accounted for over 70 percent of all employed people. Also, as in many other developing countries, the informal sector offers many employment opportunities. Here barriers to entry are low, so most of those who really want to work can find something to do.

Underemployment has also been generally low in Thailand. Table 13.7 shows that in 1977, about 4 percent of the employed work force worked less than 20 hours per week. This percentage declined to 1.3 percent in 1984. Despite regional variations, no region had a really serious underemployment problem. The underemployed are almost equally divided between men and women, and over 80 percent of the underemployed are self-employed or unpaid family workers. When

Figure 13.3 Open Unemployment Rates, Selected years, 1977–86

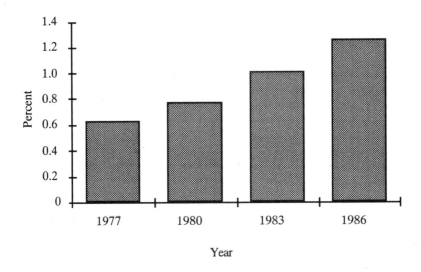

Table 13.6 Employment by Work Status, Selected Years, 1978–88

Status	*1978*	*1983*	*1988*
	Number of people		
Public employees	1,020,528	1,780,834	1,839,900
Private employees	3,291,002	4,470,462	6,176,700
Employers	282,424	253,586	353,500
Self-employed	6,544,122	7,456,259	8,550,600
Unpaid	10,669,761	11,222,386	12,543,300
Total	21,807,837	25,183,527	29,464,000
	Percentage share		
Public employees	4.68	7.07	6.24
Private employees	15.09	17.75	20.96
Employers	1.30	1.01	1.20
Self-employed	30.01	29.61	29.02
Unpaid	48.93	44.56	42.57
Total	100.00	100.00	100.00

Source: NSO (various years).

Table 13.7 Percentage of Employed Working Less than 20 Hours per Week, July–September, 1977 and 1984

Area	1977	1984
North		
Municipal areas	1.69	0.65
Non-municipal areas	1.63	1.55
Northeast		
Municipal areas	2.05	1.57
Non-municipal areas	6.2	0.65
South		
Municipal areas	3.8	0.94
Non-municipal areas	7.49	3.49
Central		
Municipal areas	1.7	0.96
Non-municipal areas	1.95	1.22
Bangkok	1.07	0.76
Whole country	3.97	1.27

Source: NSO (1977, 1984).

asked whether they desired more work, about 64 percent of the underemployed stated that they did not want more work (NSO *Labor Force Survey* 1984).

Labor Market Problems and Structural Adjustment

Three basic types of adjustment problems affect the labor market, namely:

- The seasonal nature of agricultural production results in a short-term problem: in the dry season, there is a lack of agricultural activities in nonirrigated parts of the country, and a very high proportion of the labor force becomes seasonally unemployed.

- Lags in labor movement in line with changes in the production structure result in sectoral and locational disparities.

- Mismatching of supply and demand by educational types is a problem mostly relevant to the middle to upper educational levels.

SEASONAL UNEMPLOYMENT. As most of those employed are dependent on agriculture and work in agriculture has a seasonal nature, seasonal unemployment affects many people. Table 13.8 shows that three to five million people are seasonally unemployed each year. The northeast, the poorest region, is the worst affected, with over 30

Table 13.8 Seasonal Unemployment Numbers and Rates, by Region, 1979–85

Year/category	North	Northeast	South	Central	Total
1977					
Seasonal unemployment	1,065,740	2,306,910	53,660	537,310	3,963,620
Seasonal rate (%)	24.51	30.32	2.34	13.78	21.84
1978					
Seasonal unemployment	863,930	2,673,870	38,850	445,410	4,022,060
Seasonal rate (%)	19.55	35.20	1.54	11.09	21.68
1979					
Seasonal unemployment	985,570	2,823,780	128,080	431,890	4,369,320
Seasonal rate (%)	21.60	36.18	5.38	10.86	23.34
1981					
Seasonal unemployment	1,497,200	3,274,970	48,440	749,980	5,570,590
Seasonal rate (%)	28.98	39.48	3.01	16.48	28.39
1982					
Seasonal unemployment	1,482,030	3,442,910	71,470	460,620	5,457,030
Seasonal rate (%)	27.35	40.13	2.57	9.75	25.38
1983					
Seasonal unemployment	992,420	2,775,220	75,320	573,810	4,416,770
Seasonal rate (%)	20.05	35.90	2.89	13.00	22.42
1984					
Seasonal unemployment	675,410	2,770,270	77,880	244,020	3,767,580
Seasonal rate (%)	12.79	33.26	2.87	5.37	18.05
1985					
Seasonal unemployment	946,680	2,771,820	121,390	348,620	4,188,510
Seasonal rate (%)	17.41	31.47	4.29	7.24	19.14

Source: NSO (various years).

percent of the work force seasonally unemployed. About 40 percent of the seasonally unemployed are self-employed farmers who may not have the opportunity to find off-farm work during the dry season, particularly if this involves seasonal migration. Of the rest, most are unpaid family workers, and consist mainly of the relatively young (14–24 years old) and women.

A study by Bertrand and Squire (1980) suggests that most of the seasonally unemployed are voluntarily unemployed, with the younger workers and females drawn into the labor force only to help in the peak season. However, more recent examinations by Phongpaichit and Baker (1984) and Sussangkarn (1987) contradict this view. The latter analyzed a data set on seasonal migration and showed that most of the seasonally unemployed would like to find work in the dry season, particularly the younger workers and women. Many, however, cannot find jobs or do not know how to look for seasonal migration jobs.

Seasonal unemployment is an important problem for the rural population. It is intrinsically tied to the seasonal nature of agricultural activities. The situation will depend on changes in the cropping pattern in agriculture, as different crops require different amounts of labor at various times of the year. It will also depend on the possibilities for extending irrigation into currently rain-fed areas.

LABOR MOVEMENT AND CHANGING PRODUCTION STRUCTURE. Another important adjustment problem is the imbalance between the sectoral and locational distribution of production and employment. This has led to growing disparities between agriculture and nonagriculture and between different regions. The case of Thailand seems somewhat unusual when compared to other countries. Comparing the ratio of the share of employment in agriculture to the share of agriculture in GDP for a number of countries, Thailand stands out as having one of the highest ratios (table 13.9). This ratio indicates the difference between the value added per head in agriculture and nonagriculture, and is a rough indicator of the disparity between agriculture and nonagriculture.

Part of the explanation for the very large ratio of the share of employment in agriculture to the share of agriculture in GDP may be

Table 13.9 Agricultural Indicators for Selected Asian Countries

Country	(1) Percentage of the labor force in agriculture (1980)	(2) Share of agriculture in GDP (1982)	Ratio (1)/(2)
Bangladesh	75	47	0.63
China	74	37	0.50
India	70	33	0.47
Indonesia	57	26	0.46
Korea, Rep. of	36	16	0.44
Malaysia	23	23	1.00
Myanmar	53	48	0.90
Pakistan	55	31	0.56
Philippines	52	22	0.42
Sri Lanka	53	27	0.51
Thailand	71	22	0.28

Source: World Bank (various years).

because many of those who have their main occupations in agriculture also work in nonagricultural occupations throughout the year, but particularly in the off-season. While this may be true to some extent, it is not the main explanation of the very high ratio in Thailand compared to other countries. First, those engaged in agriculture in other countries are also likely to be engaged in nonagricultural occupations. Second, the nonagricultural opportunities are not abundant everywhere, as evidenced by severe seasonal unemployment problems in many parts of the country. Further, the comparison of incomes of agricultural and nonagricultural households in table 13.3 includes household incomes from all sources, and this shows agricultural households falling behind nonagricultural households in line with widening value added per head between agriculture and nonagriculture.

Two main reasons explain the difference between the ratio of employment in agriculture and the share of agriculture in GDP in

Thailand compared to other Asian countries. The first is the past ready availability of forest areas that could be converted to arable land. These were the main destination for migrants from the rural areas in response to population pressure up until about 1980. Instead of migrating to urban areas, rural migrants would go to the forest areas (often illegally), settle down to cultivate the land, and in effect take ownership. The main migration pattern in the 1960s and 1970s was rural/rural. As a result, until the late 1970s, the rate of expansion of cultivated land in Thailand was 3 to 4 percent per annum (figure 13.4), and was greater than the rate of population growth in the rural areas.

A second reason is the very high proportion of Thai farm households who are owner cultivators. In 1981, the NSO *Socioeconomic Survey* gave this proportion as 83.3 percent of all

Figure 13.4 Total Cultivated Areas of Major Crops, 1972–84

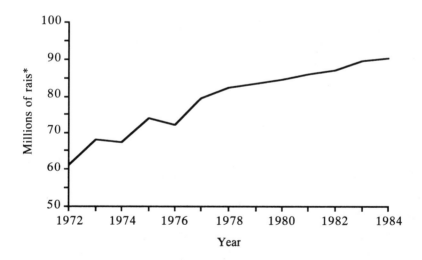

* 1 rai = 1,600 square meters
Note: Rubber and second rice crop not included.
Source: Ministry of Agriculture and Cooperation.

farm households. This is likely to be a factor working against large-scale migration into urban areas. The market for the sale of land in rural areas is thin, and thus owner cultivators who wish to sell their land and migrate to the urban areas may only get a low price for their land. This would increase the opportunity cost of migration. Migration from self-cultivating households would therefore be limited to a few family members such as sons or daughters.

A factor that would reinforce the above reason is that many of the so-called owner cultivators do not have title to their land. The migrants who went into the forest areas to open up new land were taking possession of the land illegally, even though the authorities did not really try to enforce the law. The result is that about 30 percent of private land is not legally documented. This would make it even more costly for a farmer to abandon the land and migrate out of the rural areas (see Chalamwong and Feder 1988).

Until the end of the 1970s, the farmers' migration to open up new agricultural land was logical. Plenty of land was theoretically still available in the forest areas, and crop prices were high and rising. However, once crop prices started to decline in the early 1980s, it was difficult for the farmers to move out of agriculture because of the thin market for land or the lack of legal title to the land.

The high opportunity cost the farmers faced were they to migrate into the urban areas led to long lags in the adjustment of the employment structure to the production structure. However, some adjustments have been occurring, and the pace of adjustment is likely to accelerate, given the rapid industrialization that is currently taking place in Thailand. The benefits of migrating to the urban areas, where the demand for semi-skilled workers is growing rapidly, are getting larger. Data on the rate of growth of the urban population show clearly that rural/urban migration has been increasing since 1980. Between 1960 and 1980, the growth of the urban population was remarkably steady at about 3.5 percent per annum. Between 1980 and 1985, however, the rate jumped to 6.6 percent per annum (figure 13.5). This was the time when crop prices were falling and when the availability of new land for agricultural expansion had become scarce. Thus, there are clearly labor market responses to changes on the production side. However, the responses could not keep pace with

Figure 13.5 Growth per Annum of Urban Population, 1960–85

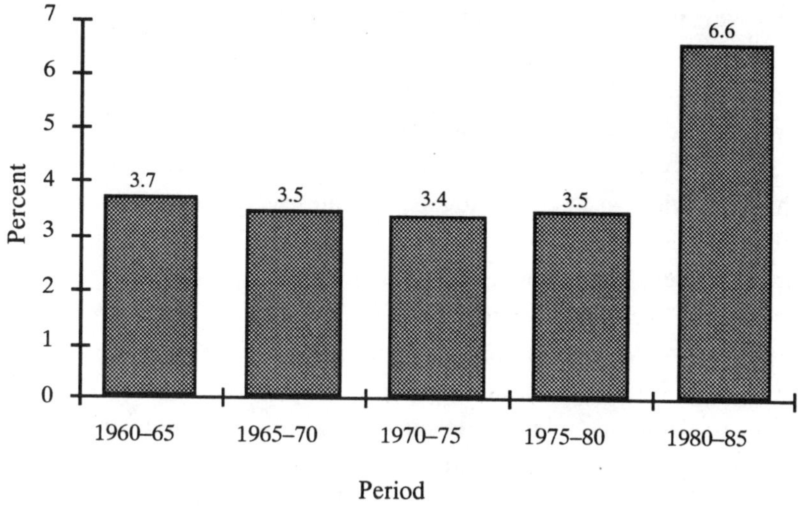

Period

Source: World Bank (various years).

changes that were occurring in the production structure. This led to problems of imbalance and income disparities as discussed earlier.

The current industrial boom will likely lead to even more rapid urban growth. While recent migration data are incomplete (pending results of the 1990 census), migration rates into the Bangkok area have probably accelerated. If Thailand's pace of growth remains similar to past patterns in the newly industrializing Asian countries, population movements out of agriculture and into urban areas are likely to be the key demographic transition over the medium to long term.

THE MISMATCH OF EDUCATED MANPOWER. While the overall open unemployment rate in Thailand is very low, the rates of open unemployment among educated people are quite high, particularly those with a vocational education. This was an important problem around the mid-1980s, and was related to the cutback in government employment growth to 2 percent per annum. Currently, however, due to the economic boom, the problem of educated open unemployment is much less severe, and instead the problem of shortages of engineering and scientific manpower has gained importance. These problems of a mismatch of the demand for and supply of educated manpower relates to structural changes on the demand side, the functioning of the labor market, and the education system.

Table 13.10 shows that the open unemployment rate of those with a primary education or below was about 0.5 percent in 1984 and 1986. At the vocational level, however, the rate was over 10 percent in both years, while at the other levels, the rates were some 3 to 4 percent. Until the economic boom that started after 1986, the number of educated open unemployed had been increasing rapidly. The two groups with the highest growth of open unemployment were those with a university education (averaging 14.3 percent per annum between 1977 and 1986), and a vocational education (averaging 22.7 percent per annum), which was the group with the most serious open unemployment problem. It had the highest open unemployment rate and also the fastest growth in the number of open unemployed. In 1986, the number of unemployed with a vocational education was about equal to the sum of the unemployed with a secondary education, university education, and teacher training combined.

Four basic reasons explain why the educated open unemployment problem was getting worse during the early 1980s. First, the supply of the better educated work force had been rising rapidly: since 1980, workers with a university and vocational education have been increasing at about 15 percent per annum. This was much faster than the overall growth in the labor force.

Table 13.10 Open Unemployment Rates by Education, 1984, 1986, 1988
(percent)

Level of education	1984	1986	1988
Primary or below	0.42	0.56	0.38
Secondary	3.19	3.55	2.47
Vocational	10.22	10.86	5.31
University	4.19	4.58	2.87
Teacher training	3.19	3.96	1.62
Total	0.97	1.26	0.83

Source: NSO (various years).

Second, a fundamental change occurred in the main source of demand for better educated workers. Up until 1983–84, the main absorber of better educated workers was the public sector. Figure 13.6 shows the importance of the government for the employment of the better educated. For those with less than a primary education, the proportion in government employment was only about 0.5 percent. For completed primary education, the proportion was still low at 2.1 percent. As figure 13.6 shows, the importance of the public sector increased rapidly for higher levels of education.

From the mid 1970s to 1984, government employment growth amounted to about 10 percent per annum. This was faster than the growth in the size of private employees, or the numbers of self-employed and unpaid family workers. The high level of growth of government employment created much needed jobs for the rapidly

Figure 13.6 Share of Government Employment by Education, 1984

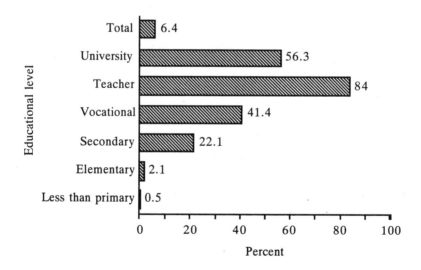

Note: The high number of teachers is because the government is the country's main supplier of education.
Source: NSO (1984).

increasing pool of workers with relatively high levels of education. While this did not slow down the growth in educated open unemployment completely, it helped to contain the problem. However, as part of the structural adjustment policies adopted in the early 1980s, the growth of government employment was cut drastically to only 2 percent per annum. As discussed earlier, in the early to mid-1980s the saving-investment gap and the rapidly rising foreign debt burden were important issues for Thailand. As civil service salaries were taking up more and more of the budget (48 percent of all government revenues by 1984), the government imposed an upper limit on civil service growth to 2 percent per annum, which is still the case for most parts of the civil service today. The consequence was that educated workers could no longer rely on the public sector as the main employer.

The third reason for rising open educated unemployment is that the education system cannot respond quickly to changing needs in the labor market. The skill mix the civil service requires is very different to that for private sector employment needs. Even with the current economic boom, there is an oversupply of graduates in the humanities and social and political sciences, while at the same time there is a severe shortage of graduates in the more technical and scientific disciplines. The education system is mostly public and highly bureaucratic, and reducing the size of any department, despite clear needs to reallocate resources among disciplines to keep up with changing labor market needs, is very difficult.

The fourth reason concerns the structure of the labor market. Previous analyses of the labor market point to the existence of labor market segmentation, with wages not fully responsive to demand and supply (Sussangkarn 1987). Relative wage data by education level (figure 13.7) do not reveal any clear falling trend in the relative wage of the vocational and university groups, even though their open unemployment rates had been rising the most rapidly. Econometric estimations of a segmented labor market model revealed high wage differentials between the formal sector (the public sector and the large private firms) and the informal sector, and the better educated find that being unemployed and waiting for an opening in the formal sector is more worthwhile than going to work in the informal sector.

Figure 13.7 Relative Wage by Educational Level, 1978–84
(index, primary education = 100)

Source: NSO (various years).

The econometric study found that returns to education above the primary level were zero or negligible in the informal sector, while returns to education in the formal sector were large. Thus, the wage differential between the formal and informal sectors increased with the level of education. For a male, nonmigrant, private employee in Bangkok aged 35, the estimates predicted a small formal/informal wage differential at the primary educational level. This differential rose to over 400 percent for those with a university education.

The proportion of those working in the formal sector increases with educational level. In 1988, of those with a primary education and below, only 6.6 percent worked in the formal sector. The ratio quickly rose to 31.6 percent and 35.5 percent for those with a lower and upper secondary education, respectively. For those with a vocational education it was 63.2 percent, and the ratio reached 88.4 percent for those with a university education. Furthermore, most of the educated unemployed came from relatively well-off families who could finance their periods of unemployment.

With the economy experiencing double digit growth, the situation in the labor market is changing rapidly. As table 13.10 shows, by 1988 the open unemployment problem for the better educated had improved tremendously. The problem now is a severe shortage of university educated scientific and technical manpower, especially engineers. The wages of better educated workers have increased rapidly. The larger private firms are bidding workers away from the public sector and the small- and medium-size private firms. The situation is unlikely to improve for some time given the continuous increase in foreign direct investment from Japan, Hong Kong, Taiwan, and elsewhere.

At the vocational level, the technical manpower situation is still one with general excess supply, although shortages are apparent in specific industrial fields. Part of the reason is that many of the booming industries rely more heavily on semi-skilled workers. Another reason is the quality of output at the vocational level. Coordination between the vocational schools, which are mostly public, and the private companies is insufficient. The machinery vocational students learn on is mostly outdated, and the schools do not have enough money to keep pace with the rapid technological advances.

Adjustment Issues for the Future

Thailand's policy focus should be to maintain the pace of economic growth while ensuring more equitable sharing of the benefits of growth among the population. To achieve this goal the government needs to tackle several human resource and labor market problems in line with expected changes in the production structure.

The government must anticipate and plan for the expected rapid growth in rural/urban migration. Bangkok is already very congested and the necessary infrastructure lags far behind actual needs. Currently, the eastern seaboard region between Chonburi and Rayong, some 100–200 kilometers from Bangkok, is developing rapidly. This will help to divert some of the industrial expansion and population movement away from the Bangkok area. However, the eastern seaboard's urban centers need careful management and planning. The social infrastructure is already lagging behind the population movement.

Whereas Thailand has a ready supply of relatively cheap labor available, most of the workers have just a primary education. In Thailand, more than half of those who finish the six years of compulsory education drop out of the formal education system. Currently, 75 percent of the work force have only a primary education. The gross enrollment ratio at the secondary level is only 30 percent. This is very low compared to the newly industrializing Asian countries, and also lower than many countries in the region, who are likely to be Thailand's main competitors in the future (figure 13.8).

For the future, Thailand needs to upgrade the technological and skill base of its industries and services, including agriculture, which is diversifying into higher value added products that require greater levels of skill and knowledge. This will require a more highly educated work force. Current low enrollment at the secondary level

Figure 13.8 Gross Enrollment Ratios, Selected Asian Countries, 1984

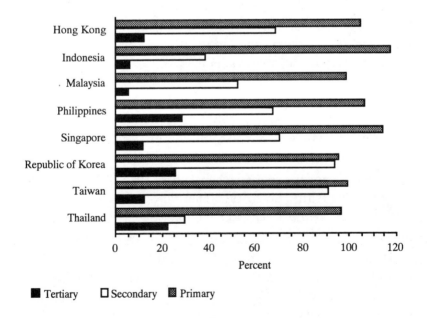

■ Tertiary　□ Secondary　▨ Primary

Source: World Bank (1987).

means that the market for workers with more than a primary education will begin to get tight over the next few years. When this happens, the basic wages of the modern manufacturing sector will begin to rise rapidly, and Thailand's competitiveness will be eroded despite its large pool of low wage workers. Such a development may affect the sustainability of the current growth trend, and also lead to undesirable income distribution consequences, because the majority of workers with just a primary education will continue to fall further and further behind those with a better education. Policies are needed to increase secondary enrollment and to develop effective training programs to upgrade the skills of those who have left the formal education system.

At the higher education level, the education system needs to be made more flexibile so that it can respond better to the labor market's skill requirements. Fields of study that produce an excess supply of workers need to be trimmed, while those where more graduates are needed should be allocated more resources to expand. Private universities and colleges need to be given more flexibility, and more cooperation is needed between the public and private sectors to develop study programs that will meet the labor market's needs. In the future, public education, the dominant source of education, needs to cater to requirements for employment in the private sector rather than to employment in the public sector as in the past.

References

Bertrand, T. J., and L. Squire. 1980. "The Relevance of the Dual Economy Model: A Case Study of Thailand." Oxford Economic Papers.

Chalamwong, Yongyuth, and Gershon Feder. 1988. "The Impact of Landownership Security: Theory and Evidence from Thailand." *World Bank Economic Review* 2(2):187–204.

Hutaserani, S., and S. Jitsuchon. 1988. "Thailand's Income Distribution and Poverty Profile and their Current Situation." Paper presented at the 1988 Thailand Development Research Institute Year-End Conference on Income Distribution and Long-Term Development, December.

Meesook, Oey Astra. 1979. *Income, Consumption and Poverty in Thailand, 1962/63 to 1975/76.* Staff Working Paper 364. Washington, D.C.: World Bank.

NESDB (National Economic and Social Development Board). Various years. *National Income of Thailand.* Bangkok.

NSO (National Statistical Office). Various years, 1977, 1984. *Labor Force Survey.* Bangkok.

_____. 1975/76, 1981, 1986. *Socioeconomic Survey.* Bangkok.

Phongpaichit, P., and C. J. Baker. 1984. "Bertrand's Choice and Seasonal Unemployment Reconsidered." Bangkok, Thailand: Chulalongkorn University, Faculty of Economics. Processed.

Sahasakul, C., N. Thongpakde, and K. Kraisoraphong. 1989. *Lessons from the World Bank's Experience of Structural Adjustment Loans (SALs): A Case Study of Thailand.* Bangkok, Thailand: Thailand Development Research Institute.

Siamwalla, Ammar, and Suthad Setboonsarng. 1987. "Agricultural Pricing Policies in Thailand: 1960–1985." Bangkok, Thailand: Thailand Development Research Institute, Agriculture and Rural Development Program.

Sussangkarn, Chalongphob. 1987. "The Thai Labour Market: A Study of Seasonality and Segmentation." Paper presented at the International Conference of Thai Studies, Australian National University, Canberra.

Sussangkarn, Chalongphob, Pranee Tinakorn, and Tienchai Chongpeerapien. 1988. "The Tax Structure in Thailand and its Distributional Implications." Paper presented at the Thailand Development Research Institute Year-End Conference, Cha-am, December.

World Bank. Various years. *World Development Report.* New York: Oxford University Press.

NA ⟿

INDEX

(Page numbers in italics indicate material in figures or tables)

Added worker effect, 17, 18

Adjustment, 1; fiscal proxies to mimic devaluation in, 266; gradual approach to, 53; labor market flexibility and success of, 143; political sustainability of programs for, 207; public sector employment and, 46; public spending cuts in, 266; results of (for middle income countries), 143; sources of problems with, 483; successful and less successful, 44-45; timing of, 12; varieties of experience with, 8-9, 12, 14; wage flexibility and, 22; *see also individual country entries*

Adjustment policies: quantification and, 12; timing of, *13*; *see also individual country entries*

Agricultural indicators for Asian countries, *600*

Agriculture: in Argentina, 63, 78; in Bolivia, 101, 112, 120; in Costa Rica, 218, 225, 227, 231-32; in Côte d'Ivoire, 268-69, 281-82, 288-89, 291 n.10; debt crises and shift out of, 33; in Egypt, 332, 335, 345, 349; in Ghana, 359, 397, 401; in Kenya, 406, 408, 415, 435, *436*

Argentina: adjustment frustrated in (1987-88), 71-72; aggregate employment in, 84-87, 89; agricultural employment in, 78; balance of payment crisis in, 63; crisis of 1980s

in, 69-71; economic indicators for, *65*; economic policy (late 1970s), 68; employment in manufacturing, 78; employment by sector, *79*; exchange rate policy and wages in, *84*; failure of short-term stabilization program in, 68; immigration to urban centers in, 85; income distribution and poverty in, 91-93; inflation in, 67, 68, 70,84, 93; inward-oriented growth strategy of, 74; labor flows in, 78, 93; labor force participation rates in, 85-86, *87*, *88*; labor market institutions in, 80-81; labor market performance in adjustment in, 82, 84; labor market segmentation and increasing informality in, 79-80; labor scarcity in, 84; lessons for policy makers from, 94; macroeconomic policies in, 62-64; military government's objective in, 67; minimum wages in, 81; overvalued exchange rate policy of, 63; policy favoring nontradables and, 77; political and economic developments (1970s), 64, 67-69; population growth in, 76; public sector employment in, 89-90; real output variability of, 68-69; real wages and foreign terms of trade, *66*; real wages and per capita GDP, *66*; real wage trends in, 74-75; regional and sectoral labor allocation in, 76-78; rural population decline in, 76; sectors in the economy of, 63; suggested la-

lems with data in, 164, 165, 167; public sector and adjustment in, 146; regional differences in distribution of formal sector workers, 153-54; social mobility in, 145; unemployment in, 159; worker eligibility for state benefits in, 152, 153; working class expectations in, 146

Brazilian adjustment (1980s): balance of payments during, 149; consumption during, 151-52; control of imports during, 148 n.2; Cruzado Plan and, 150-51, 162-63; debt moratorium and, 151; failure of, 143, 146; imports and exports during, 149; income distribution and, 162, 164; inflation and, 150, 151, 152, 163; interest on government's internal debt and, 164; internal balance and, 167; investment and, 151, 152; labor movement's voice in policies and, 163; macroeconomic indicators during, *147*; minimum wage decrease and, 161; policies leading to inflation during, 149; political stalemate (1985-89) and, 150; the poor and, 164-66; private sector savings absorbed by public sector deficits, 164; savings and investment changes during, *148*; shock stabilization program and, 150-51; success in trade and external balance and, 166-67

Brazilian labor market in the adjustment process: composition of labor force by sector and, *152*; earnings in formal and informal sectors and, 154; earnings of heads of households and, *155*; flexibility in, 143, 159, 167; government control over labor unions and, 155-56; government credibility and, 167; growth of labor unions and, 157; impact of adjustment measures on informal sector and, 159; labor market outcomes and, *160*; labor unions' targeting

strategy and, 157; minimum wage decrease and, 161; occupations of heads of poor households and, *154*; poor macroeconomic results of labor bargaining system and, 158; rise of labor unions and, 155-59; segmentation of, 152-55; strikes and, 157; wage control and indexation results, 149; wage guidelines flaunting and, 156

Brazilian macroeconomic policy and its outcomes during adjustment, 147

Brazil's adjustment problem, 144-46

Budget deficits: in Côte d'Ivoire, 260; in Ghana, 361-62; in Kenya, 409, 412; in Malaysia, 465-66, 467, 468, 472-73; ways of financing, 467

Buenos Aires, income distribution in, 95

Chile, 169-70; deflation in, 23, 25; empirical definitions of variables in study of, 210-11; implications of case study of, 208-9; model for adjustment policies and labor market response in, 197-207; rigidities in labor market of, 169; unemployment in, 14, *204*

Chilean adjustment program's labor market effects, 197-207; on average real wages, 181; distribution results and, 195-97; on earnings functions, 194-95; on employment, 181, *182-83*, 184-86, 195; private rate of return to schooling and, 195; privatization and, 197; rate of return to experience and, 195; on real wage performance, 187-90; on relative wages, 192-94; social indicators and, *196*; social rate of return to schooling and, 194-95; subsidies to the poor and, 196-97; wage indexation and, 189-92

growth in, 412, 454; public sector job advantages in, 430; real earnings in, 405; real GDP of, 405, 408; school fees in, 441-42, 443; second oil crisis and, 408, 454; stabilization without proper adjustment in, 412; structural adjustment policies of, 415; structural changes in, 410; tourist industry in, 410; trade balances of, 405, 409, 414; trade policy of, 414; unemployment in, 419, *420*; wage bill for public sector in, 429; wage policy in, 415; women in informal sector of, 432

Kenya's labor market: agriculture as source of jobs in, 416; employment in urban and rural sectors and, *417*; rural participation rates in, *418*, 419; population growth, 416 -17; trade unions in, 421; urban female participation rate in, 417, *418*, 419; urban informal sector growth in, 416; wage determination in, 421-22

Kenya's labor market adjustment, 422; capital formation and, 440-41; earnings functions analysis and, 448-49, *450*, 451, *452*, 453; employment by industry and, *426-27*; excess labor absorbed into self-employed sector, 434; female wage profiles, *444*; growth of real minimum wage and, *428*; income distribution and, 445-47, *448*; informal sector earnings and employment, 430-35 , *443*; labor mobility and, 439; male wage profiles and, *444*; public sector wages and employment and, 429-32, *433*, 434; rural sector and, 434-35; sectoral wages and employment and, 423, *424-25*, *426-27*, *428*, 429; rural-urban migration and, 436-40; urban employment and, *434*; wage rates by occupation and, *435*; women in the labor market and, 441-43, *444*, 445, 454

Korea: capital-intensive technology in, 564; currency devaluation in, 545-46, 571; cycles in economy of, 535-42; data in study of, 579-81; earnings per worker in, *578*; economic indicators for, *576*; efficiency incentives in, 552-53; emigration of workers and, 553; exchange rate policy in, 571; export subsidies in, 559; firm size, bonuses, and wages in, 560, 573; firm specific skills in, 552-53; food policy in, 546; government intervention in wage setting in, 45, 551,553; household income per urban worker in, *579*; inflation in, 547, 550-51; investment rate in, 551-55; labor aristocracy in, 572; labor union in, 551, 560, 574; large firm sector shrinkage during adjustment in, 561-62; manufacturing labor cost data, *577*; net barter and income terms of trade in, *575*; overtime pay and bonuses in, 552, 560; profit-sharing in, 552, 553, 572; subsidies for export/large scale sector in, 559; total factor productivity growth in, 551; unemployment in, 14, 17, 553; unit labor cost determinants in, 547-49; unit labor costs and external competitiveness in, 544, 545; value added per worker, 560; wage determination in, 551-55, 571; wage explosion in manufacturing in, 573-74; wage-productivity trends in, 549-51, 572, 574; wages in large scale manufacturing sectors of, 572

Korean labor markets and wage differentials, 555-56; farm/nonfarm differential, 556-59; female participation and, 563, *564*, 564-71, 573; male/female differences and, 563, 565-71; wage differentials by sector, 572-73; wage difference by size of firms and, 559-63, *564*